MW01259854

BAGRATION 1944

OSPREY
PUBLISHING

DEDICATION
For Olivier

BAGRATION 1944

1944

THE GREAT SOVIET OFFENSIVE

PRIT BUTTAR

OSPREY PUBLISHING
Bloomsbury Publishing Plc
Kemp House, Chawley Park, Cumnor Hill, Oxford OX2 9PH, UK
29 Earlsfort Terrace, Dublin 2, Ireland
1385 Broadway, 5th Floor, New York, NY 10018, USA
E-mail: info@ospreypublishing.com

www.ospreypublishing.com

OSPREY is a trademark of Osprey Publishing Ltd

First published in Great Britain in 2025

A catalogue record for this book is available from the British Library.

ISBN: HB 9781472863515; PB 9781472863522; eBook 9781472863539; ePDF 9781472863485; XML 9781472863492; Audio 9781472863508

25 26 27 28 29   10 9 8 7 6 5 4 3 2 1

Plate section image credits are given in full in the List of Illustrations (pp. 7–8).
Maps by Prit Buttar
Index by Alison Worthington

Typeset by Deanta Global Publishing Services, Chennai, India
Printed and bound in Great Britain by CPI (Group) UK Ltd, Croydon CR0 4YY

Editor's note
For ease of comparison please refer to the following conversion table:
1 mile = 1.6km
1 yd = 0.9m
1 ft = 0.3m
1 in. = 2.54cm/25.4mm
1 lb = 0.45kg

Osprey Publishing supports the Woodland Trust, the UK's leading woodland conservation charity.

To find out more about our authors and books visit www.ospreypublishing.com. Here you will find extracts, author interviews, details of forthcoming events and the option to sign up for our newsletter.

CONTENTS

LIST OF ILLUSTRATIONS

An old peasant woman bringing bread to Soviet partisans in Belarus. The partisan movement in Belarus was far stronger than in other regions, and this was exploited to the full during *Bagration*. (Photo by: Sovfoto/Universal Images Group via Getty Images)

A German soldier takes cover behind the blown-off turret of a T-34 during fighting in the area of Army Group Centre during *Bagration*. The strength of the German divisions that faced the Red Army varied greatly. (Sueddeutsche Zeitung Photo / Alamy Stock Photo)

A line of Soviet Yak-9 fighter planes. By 1944, the fighter formations of the Soviet air armies had plenty of aircraft with which to contest and often achieve air superiority along the entire front. (Photo © CORBIS via Getty Images)

A Panther tank of the *Grossdeutschland* division, June 1944. In order to become proficient with the Panther, panzer crewmen had to undergo a prolonged period of training. By the summer of 1944, this process was still incomplete. (Photo by ullstein bild via Getty Images)

Red Army soldiers enter Vitebsk in late June 1944. The impact of the fighting on the city is clearly shown. Nearly 30,000 Germans had been encircled in and near Vitebsk and between 10,000 and 20,000 were captured. (Photo by Backstein/ullstein bild via Getty Images)

As the Soviets reached each of the rivers before Mogilev, the poor infrastructure began to take its toll. The heavy vehicles churned up the approaches to the pontoon bridges, which in turn caused massive traffic jams that led to units falling behind.

For the riflemen, crossing was simpler. (From the fonds of the RGAKFD in Krasnogorsk via Stavka)

The terrain was problematic for both sides. When the Germans began to fall back, their rate of movement was slowed due to so much of the transport being horse powered, the condition of the roads and the numerous streams and rivers to be crossed. (Nik Cornish at www.Stavka.org.uk)

Advancing Red Army troops dancing to the accompaniment of an accordion in Belarus. This interesting photograph was apparently not staged, and may show a glimpse of life between the fighting. (Photo by Vassili Arkashev/Slava Katamidze Collection/Getty Images)

Soviet soldiers clearing mines, west of Minsk, 1944. The advancing Red Army had to deal with numerous minefields that had been laid hastily by the retreating Germans. (Photo by: Universal History Archive/UIG via Getty Images)

Soldiers of 1st Baltic Front in Lithuania, July 1944. The Red Army received a mixed reception from the locals, who had no desire for what they saw as one occupying force to be replaced by another. (From the fonds of the RGAKFD in Krasnogorsk via Stavka)

German equipment left behind in Vilnius, July 1944. The German defence of the 'fortress' did appear to have a significant impact upon the Soviet advance, but the overall balance of resources was still greatly in the Red Army's favour. (Photo by Keystone-France/Gamma-Keystone via Getty Images)

On 17 July, 57,000 German prisoners were paraded through Moscow, led by several of the senior officers who had been captured during the course of *Bagration*. (Photo by: Pictures from History/Universal Images Group via Getty Images)

One of the controversies that arose after *Bagration* was the tragedy of the Warsaw Uprising. Here, a Polish *Armia Krajova* soldier keeps watch over ruined streets. (Photo by Picture Post/Hulton Archive/Getty Images)

Germans east of Warsaw, August 1944. In the space of a few months, the strategic picture in Europe had changed completely for the Germans. (Nik Cornish at www.Stavka.org.uk)

LIST OF MAPS

DRAMATIS PERSONAE

GERMANY

Bach-Zelewski, Erich von dem – Obergruppenführer, *Kampfkommandant* Warsaw

Bamler, Rudolf – Generalleutnant, commander 12th Infantry Division

Beck, Ludwig – Generaloberst, former chief of general staff, anti-Hitler conspirator

Betzel, Clemens – Generalmajor, commander 4th Panzer Division

Blancbois, Gustav-Adolf – Hauptmann, battlegroup commander 12th Panzer Division

Bodenhausen, Erpo Freiherr von – Generalleutnant, commander 12th Panzer Division

Busch, Ernst – Generalfeldmarschall, commander Army Group Centre

Busse, Theodor – Generalleutnant, chief of staff Army Group North Ukraine

Conrady, Alexander – Generalmajor, commander 36th Infantry Division

Decker, Karl – Generalleutnant, commander 5th Panzer Division

Dirlewanger, Oskar – Oberführer, commander of eponymous SS brigade

Drescher, Otto – Generalleutnant, commander 267th Infantry Division

Drewes, Wilhelm – Major, commander 5th Panzer Division battlegroup

Engel, Joachim – Generalmajor, commander 45th Infantry Division

Erdmansdorff, Gottfried von – Generalmajor, commandant of Mogilev

Fischer, Adolf – Generalmajor, commander 367th Infantry Division

Fischer, Ludwig – governor of Warsaw

Flörke, Hermann – Generalleutnant, commander 14th Infantry Division, later commander eponymous battlegroup

Franek, Fritz – Generalleutnant, commander 73rd Infantry Division

Friessner, Johannes – Generaloberst, commander Army Group North

Fromm, Friedrich – Generaloberst, head of *Ersatzheer*

Gehlen, Reinhard – Oberst, head of *Fremde Heere Ost* (*FHO*)

Gersdorff, Rudolf-Christoph Freiherr von – Oberst, chief of staff LXXXII Corps and anti-Hitler conspirator

Gille, Herbert – Obergruppenführer, commander *SS-Wiking*, later commander IV SS-Panzer Corps

Gisevius, Hans – German vice-consul in Zurich and anti-Hitler conspirator

Gollwitzer, Friedrich – General, commander LIII Corps

Gottberg, Curt von – Brigadeführer, commander eponymous SS battlegroup

Guderian, Heinz – Generaloberst, *Generalinspekteur der Panzertruppen*, later chief of the general staff

Haeften, Werner von – Oberleutnant, aide to Stauffenberg and anti-Hitler conspirator

Hähnele, Hermann – Generalleutnant, later commander 367th Infantry Division

Hamann, Adolf – Generalleutnant, commander 383rd Infantry Division and *Festungskommandant* Bobruisk

Harteneck, Gustav – Generalleutnant, commander I Cavalry Corps

Hass, Siegfried – Generalleutnant, commander 170th Infantry Division

Hellsdorff, Wolf-Heinrich Graf von – head of Berlin police, involved in anti-Hitler conspiracy

Herrlein, Friedrich – General, commander LV Corps

Heusinger, Adolf – Generalleutnant, chief of operations staff at *Oberkommando des Heeres* (*OKH*), later chief of the general staff

Hilpert, Carl – General, commander I Corps

Hinnen, Eugen – *Fallschirmjäger* in Vilnius

Hitter, Alfons – Generalleutnant, commander 206th Infantry Division

Hofacker, Caesar von – Oberstleutnant, head of iron and steel procurement in France and anti-Hitler conspirator

Hoffmeister, Edmund – Generalleutnant, commander XLI Panzer Corps, later commander eponymous corps group

Hölz, Johannes – Oberst, chief of staff LV Corps

Jordan, Hans – General, commander Ninth Army

Kaminski, Bronislav – Brigadeführer, commander eponymous SS battlegroup

Keitel, Wilhelm – Generalfeldmarschall, head of *Oberkommando der Wehrmacht* (*OKW*)

Kessel, Mortimer von – Generalleutnant, commander 20th Panzer Division

Kinzel, Eberhard – Generalleutnant, chief of staff Army Group North

Kluge, Günther von – Generalfeldmarschall, former commander Army Group Centre, later *Oberbefehlshaber West*

Kolbe, Fritz – diplomat and anti-Hitler conspirator

Krebs, Hans – Generalleutnant, chief of staff Army Group Centre

Laux, Paul – General, commander Sixteenth Army

Lendle, Hubert – Generalleutnant, commander 212th Security Division and eponymous battlegroup

Lindemann, Georg – Generaloberst, commander Army Group North

Lindig, Maximilian – Generalleutnant, artillery commander Army Group Centre, later commander eponymous battlegroup

Lützow, Kurt-Jürgen Freiherr von – Generalleutnant, commander XXXV Corps

Martinek, Robert – General, commander XXXIX Panzer Corps

Melzer, Walter – Generalleutnant, commander 252nd Infantry Division

Metz, Eduard – Generalleutnant, commander eponymous corps group

Model, Walter – Generalfeldmarschall, commander Army Group North Ukraine, later commander Army Group Centre

Mühlenkamp, Johannes-Rudolf – Standartenführer, commander *SS-Wiking* armoured battlegroup, later division commander

Müller, Gerhard – Oberst, acting commander 12th Panzer Division

Müller, Vincenz – Generalleutnant, commander XII Corps, later commander eponymous corps group

Newiger, Albert – Generalmajor, commander 52nd Security Division and *Festungskommandant* Baranovichi

Olbricht, Friedrich – General, head of *Wehrersatzamt* and anti-Hitler conspirator

Pamberg, Bernhard – Generalmajor, commander *Korps Abteilung D*

Peters, Reinhard – Leutnant, panzer company commander, 4th Panzer Division

Peschel, Rudolf – Generalleutnant, commander 6th Luftwaffe Field Division

Pfeiffer, Georg – General, commander VI Corps

Pflugbeil, Curt – General, commander *Luftflotte 1* and commander eponymous battlegroup

Pössl, Walter – Major, panzer battalion commander, *Grossdeutschland* division

Quirnheim, Albrecht Merz von – Oberst, staff officer and anti-Hitler conspirator

Reinefarth, Heinz – Gruppenführer, commander eponymous SS battlegroup

Reinhardt, Georg-Hans – Generaloberst, commander Third Panzer Army

Remer, Otto – Major, commander of security battalion from *Grossdeutschland* division

Rundstedt, Gerd von – Generalfeldmarschall, *Oberbefehlshaber West*

Saucken, Dietrich von – Generalleutnant, commander eponymous corps, later commander XXXIX Panzer Corps

Scheller, Walter – Generalleutnant, *Kampfkommandant* Brest

Schlabrendorff, Fabian von – Ordonnanzoffizier, anti-Hitler conspirator

Schmalz, Wilhelm – Generalmajor, commander *Fallschirm-Panzer Division Hermann Göring*

Schmidhuber, Gerhard – Generalmajor, commander 7th Panzer Division

Schörner, Ferdinand – Generaloberst, commander Army Group South Ukraine, later commander Army Group North

Schünemann, Otto – Generalmajor, commander 337th Infantry Division, later commander XXXIX Panzer Corps

Schürmann, Paul – Generalleutnant, commander 25th Panzergrenadier Division

Schwerin, Bogislav von – Generalleutnant, commander 221st Security Division

Sensfuss, Franz – Generalleutnant, commander 212th Infantry Division

Stadtke, Helmut – Generalmajor, chief of staff Ninth Army

Stahel, Reiner – Generalleutnant, *Kampfkommandant* Vilnius, later *Kampfkommandant* Warsaw

Stauffenberg, Klaus Schenk Graf von – Oberst, staff officer in the *Ersatzheer* and anti-Hitler conspirator

Stülpnagel, Carl-Heinrich – General, military governor of France and anti-Hitler conspirator

Tippelskirch, Kurt von – General, commander Fourth Army

Tolsdorff, Theodor – Oberst, commander eponymous battlegroup

Traut, Hans – Generalleutnant, commander 78th Sturm Division

Tresckow, Henning von – Generalmajor, chief of staff Second Army and anti-Hitler conspirator

Trowitz, Adolf – Generalmajor, commander 57th Infantry Division

Völckers, Paul – General, commander XXVII Corps

Vormann, Nikolaus von – General, commander Ninth Army

Waldenfels, Rudolf Freiherr von – Generalleutnant, commander 6th Panzer Division

Weidling, Helmuth – General, commander XLI Panzer Corps, later commander eponymous corps group, later commander VI Corps

Weiss, Walter – Generaloberst, commander Second Army

Wiese, Friedrich – Generalleutnant, commander XXXV Corps

Witzleben, Erwin von – Generalfeldmarschall, anti-Hitler conspirator

Wuthmann, Rolf – General, commander IX Corps

Zeitzler, Kurt – Generaloberst, chief of the German general staff

Ziehlberg, Gustav Heistermann von – Generalleutnant, commander 28th Jäger Division

SOVIET UNION

Antonov, Aleksei Innokentovich – General, deputy chief of the Soviet general staff

Bagramian, Ivan Christoforovich – General, commander 1st Baltic Front

Batov, Pavel Ivanovich – Lieutenant General, commander Sixty-Fifth Army

Beloborodov, Afanasy Pavlantevich – Lieutenant General, commander Forty-Second Army

Beriya, Lavrenty Pavlovich – head of the NKVD

Bogdanov, Semen Ilyich – Colonel General, commander Second Tank Army

Boiko, Vasily Romanovich – Major General, member of Thirty-Ninth Army military council

Burdeiny, Aleksei Semenovich – Major General, commander II Guards Tank Corps

Butkov, Vasily Vasilyevich – Lieutenant General, commander I Tank Corps

Cherniakhovsky, Ivan Danilovich – Colonel General, commander 3rd Belarusian Front

Chistiakov, Ivan Mikhailovich – Lieutenant General, commander Sixth Guards Army

Degen, Ion Lazarevich – tank commander, 2nd Guards Tank Brigade

Galitsky, Kuzma Nikitovich – Lieutenant General, commander Eleventh Guards Army

Gorbatov, Aleksandr Vasilyevich – Lieutenant General, commander Third Army

Gurevich, Arkady Grigoryevich – gunner, Eleventh Guards Army

Kharin, Vasily Georgiyevich – Red Army anti-tank gunner

Kreizer, Iakov Grigoryevich – Lieutenant General, commander Fifty-First Army

Krylov, Nikolai Ivanovich – Lieutenant General, commander Fifth Army

Krylov, Vasily Vasilyevich – Lieutenant General, commander Thirty-First Army

Kryuchenkin, Vasily Dmitriyevich – Lieutenant General, commander Thirty-Third Army

Luchinsky, Aleksandr Aleksandrovich – Lieutenant General, commander Twenty-Eighth Army

Lyudnikov, Ivan Ilyich – Lieutenant General, commander Thirty-Ninth Army

Malinin, Mikhail Sergeyevich – Colonel General, chief of staff 1st Belarusian Front

Mazanik, Yelena Grigoryevna – partisan

Mekhlis, Lev Zakharovich – deputy defence minister

Molotov, Vyacheslav Mikhailovich – Soviet foreign minister

Obukhov, Viktor Timofeyevich – Lieutenant General, commander III Guards Mechanised Corps

Oslikovsky, Nikolai Sergeyevich – Lieutenant General, commander cavalry-mechanised group 3rd Belarusian Front

Pankin, Aleksandr Fedorovich – ISU-152 crewman

Panov, Mikhail Fedorovich – Major General, commander I Guards Tank Corps

Pliev, Issa Alexsandrovich – Lieutenant General, commander IV Guards Cavalry Corps

Radzievsky, Aleksei Ivanovich – Major General, later commander Second Tank Army

Repin, Vasily Ivanovich – Red Army sapper

Rokossovsky, Konstantin Konstantinovich – General, commander 1st Belarusian Front

Rotmistrov, Pavel Alekseyevich – Marshal, commander Fifth Guards Tank Army

Shtemenko, Sergei Matveyevich – Colonel General, head of Operations Directorate

Smirnov, Dmitry Ivanovich – Major General, commander CXXI Rifle Corps

Telegin, Konstantin Fedorovich – Lieutenant General, member of military council 1st Belarusian Front

Vasilevsky, Aleksandr Mikhailovich – Marshal, chief of the Soviet general staff

Vedeneyev, Nikolai Denisovich – Major General, commander III Tank Corps

Voroshilov, Kliment Yefremovich – member of *Stavka*

Zakharov, Georgy Fedorovich – Colonel General, commander 2nd Belarusian Front

Zhukov, Georgy Konstantinovich – Marshal, deputy supreme commander of the Red Army

POLAND

Berling, Zygmunt – Lieutenant General, commander First Polish Army

Bór-Komorowski, Tadeusz – General, commander of the *Armia Krajova* (*AK*)

Kalenkiewicz, Maciej – Lieutenant Colonel, *AK* officer in Vilnius

Krzeszowski, Lubosław – Colonel, *AK* officer in Vilnius

Krzyżanowski, Aleksander – General, commander of *AK* forces in Vilnius region

Liniarski, Władysław – Colonel, commander *AK* forces in Białystok

Mikołajczyk, Stanisław – prime minister of government-in-exile in London

Tatar, Stanisław – Brigadier General, senior Polish Army officer with government-in-exile in London

INTRODUCTION: TEHRAN

The city of Tehran, situated about 66 miles south of the Caspian Sea, has been a place for human settlement for several thousand years. It is in an area of considerable climatic extremes. In the summer, daily temperatures usually exceed 30°C, unremarkable for such a southerly latitude, but built on a plateau about 3,000 feet above sea level, it experiences cold winters with frequent sharp frosts. In late 1943, it was chosen as a venue for an important meeting because of its convenient location where the leaders of the somewhat odd alliance arrayed against Germany could have their first full face-to-face meeting. The fruits of this meeting were to have a profound effect on the events of 1944. As temperatures fell closer to freezing point, delegations from the Soviet Union, Britain, and the USA met to discuss how best to ensure the defeat of Hitler. In many ways, the falling temperatures that were interspersed with warmer spells were an appropriate backdrop to the discussions, overshadowed by suspicions on all sides and a charm offensive by the Soviet leader in an attempt to exploit differences between the British and Americans.

Prior to the Second World War, relations between the Soviet Union and the Western Powers had been cool and distant at best. The Molotov–Ribbentrop Pact, which resulted in the division of Poland between the Germans and the Soviets, led to a further deterioration, but after the Wehrmacht invaded the Soviet Union on 22 June 1941 there was a change. That evening, Churchill outlined the new situation in a radio broadcast, highlighting that this development had been expected for some time and also stressing that regardless of the repugnance felt by many people in the west towards Communism, the war created its own priorities:

> [The German invasion of the Soviet Union] was no surprise to me. In fact I gave clear and precise warnings to Stalin of what was coming. I gave him warnings as I have given warnings to others before. I can only hope that these warnings did not fall unheeded …

The Nazi regime is indistinguishable from the worst features of Communism … It excels in all forms of human wickedness, in the efficiency of its cruelty and ferocious aggression. No one has been a more consistent opponent of Communism than I have for the last 25 years. I will unsay no words that I've spoken about it. But all this fades away before the spectacle which is now unfolding …

We have but one aim and one single irrevocable purpose. We are resolved to destroy Hitler and every vestige of the Nazi regime. From this nothing will turn us …

Any man or state who fights against Nazism will have our aid. Any man or state who marches with Hitler is our foe …

It follows therefore, that we shall give whatever help we can to Russia and to the Russian people. We shall appeal to our friends and Allies in every part of the world to take the same course and pursue it as we shall, faithfully and steadfastly to the end.

We have offered to the government of Soviet Russia any technical or economic assistance which is in our power and which is likely to be of service to them …

If Hitler imagines that his attack on Soviet Russia will cause the slightest division of aims or slackening of effort in the great democracies, who are resolved upon his doom, he is woefully mistaken. On the contrary, we shall be fortified and encouraged in our efforts to rescue mankind from his tyranny.[1]

For Stalin, the offer of help in Churchill's speech – which, not for the last time, showed a dangerous tendency on the part of western politicians to regard 'Soviet' and 'Russian' as effectively synonymous – was perhaps the only positive item of news that day, with catastrophes developing all along the front line. Despite numerous warnings of an imminent German attack from a variety of sources, Stalin repeatedly failed to take appropriate steps. Although many front-line divisions were brought up to strength by partial mobilisation of reservists, the Soviet ruler continued to believe that the pact agreed in 1939 would hold and the Germans would not attack. Even once hostilities had started, Soviet units were ordered not to attack any targets west of the old frontier.

The background to this change of attitude in London, which was endorsed and supported by Roosevelt in August 1941, was one of years of suspicion and outright hostility. Even as the Bolsheviks seized and consolidated power in 1917, there were attempts to intervene against them. An expeditionary force that included soldiers from Britain, Canada, Australia, France, Italy, and the USA was dispatched to seize Archangelsk in the north of Russia; the force continued to operate in the area for nearly a year in the hope that the anti-Bolshevik White Russian forces would be able to reverse the October Revolution. British warships operated in the Baltic Sea and the Gulf of Finland, providing fire support for Estonian nationalists fighting against an attempt by the Bolsheviks to seize the country and sinking several vessels in two raids on the naval base in Kronstadt, and the British and French provided considerable support to the attempt by White Russian forces to march from Estonia to Petrograd – the White Russian force even included a small group of British tanks manned by British volunteers.[2] With this history of hostility from the Western Powers to the Bolsheviks, it was unsurprising that Stalin harboured longstanding suspicions about the ultimate intentions of the governments of France, Britain, and the USA. During the 1930s, as his paranoia developed further and resulted in widespread purges of much of Soviet society, these suspicions hardened. It was therefore unsurprising that he paid little attention to Churchill's warnings of an imminent German attack.

As reports of disasters on the front line began to flood into Moscow, Stalin continued to doubt that Hitler had actually attacked; at various stages on the first day of the war, he speculated whether the fighting had been due to unauthorised action by senior German military figures, or that the outbreak of war was in some way due to trickery on the part of Ribbentrop, the German foreign minister. It was only when Schulenburg, the German ambassador in Moscow, presented the Soviet government with a telegram from Berlin confirming the commencement of war that Stalin accepted that the warnings he had received from Churchill and others had been correct, but orders sent to the Red Army still reiterated earlier instructions not to cross the old frontier.

The first public pronouncement from the Kremlin about the war was made by Molotov, Stalin's foreign minister, whose broadcast had been drafted during the morning by several people in addition to Stalin. Molotov's emotionless, quavering voice was heard by millions across the nation as he laid the foundations for what would become known as the Great Patriotic War, deliberately recalling the memory of the previous Patriotic War of 1812:

> Today, at 4am, German troops entered our country … without a declaration of war …
>
> This attack is unheard of and is a treacherous act that has no equal in the history of civilised peoples. The attack on our country was launched despite the fact that a non-aggression treaty between the USSR and Germany has been signed and that the Soviet Union has observed all conditions of this treaty …

It is not the first time that our people face an arrogant aggressor. During Napoleon's Russian campaign, our people responded with the Patriotic War ... The Red Army and our population shall once more wage a triumphant Patriotic War for our homeland, for honour, and for freedom ...

Our cause is just. The enemy shall be defeated. Victory will be ours.[3]

Stalin didn't speak to the Soviet public until 3 July, by which time the German armies were deep inside Soviet territory and the Red Army seemed to be falling apart. Every expectation, all the strategies that had been planned to defend against an attack – all were in complete disarray. Nonetheless, Stalin projected a confident message. Towards the end of the speech, he portrayed the war as involving all who opposed Germany:

The goal of this Patriotic War ... is not only to remove the danger that hangs over our country but also to help all European peoples that suffer under the rule of German Fascism. In this war of liberation, we will not stand alone. In this great war we will have at our disposal loyal allies in the form of European and American people, also including the German people that have been enslaved by the Hitlerian renegades. Our war for the freedom of our fatherland will blend in with the struggle of the European and American population for their independence, for democratic freedom. This will be a united front of people who promote freedom ... In this connection, the historical statement of the British Prime Minister Mr Churchill about aid to the Soviet Union and the declaration of the American government about its willingness to come to the aid of our nation are completely understandable and characteristic, and cannot evoke anything other than feelings of gratitude from the hearts of the Soviet people.[4]

But almost from the outset, there were discrepancies between what Stalin expected in terms of aid and what the British were prepared to offer. Desperate to reduce the devastating pressure upon the Red Army, Stalin sent a telegram to Churchill on 18 July. He suggested that the British should open new land fronts against Germany – one in northern France and one in the north in Norway. Churchill's response was disheartening: any such proposal was beyond the resources of Britain. Until sufficient forces were available, aid would be in the form of material help. The first convoy to Archangelsk, making the dangerous journey past German-held Norway, would set sail in August and would be repeated as regularly as conditions permitted.

A day after this exchange, Stalin had more bad news. A radio broadcast from Berlin announced gleefully that Yakov Iosifovich Dzugashvili, Stalin's son, had been taken prisoner when a Red Army artillery position near Smolensk was overrun. Stalin's reaction was blunt: 'The fool,' he muttered when he received written confirmation, 'he couldn't even shoot himself!'[5] With no end in sight to the constant German advances, Stalin asked once more for substantial aid from the British. On 13 September, with Leningrad cut off and a Soviet counteroffensive near Bryansk unravelling with further heavy losses, Stalin suggested that the British should send troops to help fight against the German invasion: 'England could without risk land 25–30 divisions at Archangelsk or transport them across Persia to the southern regions of the Soviet Union for military cooperation with Soviet troops on the territory of the Soviet Union.'[6]

The logistic difficulties in supporting such an expeditionary force would have been immense, and in any event Churchill had no intention of dispatching what would amount to a very large portion of the British Army to fight – and quite possibly be destroyed – on the Eastern Front. Instead, he repeated his earlier promises of delivery of arms and supplies to the Soviet Union. The first aid convoy had reached Archangelsk at the end of August 1941. It consisted of just six ships and Soviet officials were dismayed by the modest quantity of supplies that were delivered. In the rest of 1941, a further six convoys reached either Archangelsk or Murmansk, usually sailing from Iceland. In time, the quantity of materiel delivered would increase significantly, particularly after the US entry into the war, which resulted in major shipments across the Pacific Ocean, but Soviet disappointment at the level of support continued to grow.

At the end of 1941, Churchill travelled to Washington for direct talks with Roosevelt. The conference, codenamed *Arcadia*, lasted until mid-January 1942 and concluded with the two nations agreeing a 'Europe first' strategy – the defeat of Germany was to take precedence over the defeat of Japan. To that end, it was agreed that American bombers would be deployed in Britain to aid the strategic bombing campaign against Germany and to plan for an invasion of North Africa before the end of 1942. Although there were discussions about a possible landing on mainland Europe in the coming year, the British remained highly sceptical, suggesting that 1943 was the earliest that such an operation could be attempted. The only public outcome of the meeting was the Declaration by United Nations, which committed all signatories to defeat Germany, Italy, and Japan and not to make any separate peace.

For Stalin, whose continuing paranoia had resulted in several senior officers being arrested, imprisoned, or even executed after the German invasion had commenced, this amounted to little of any significance. His armies continued to suffer huge losses and there was a widely held view both in the Kremlin and the Red Army that the Western Powers were happy to stand on the sidelines while Germany and the Soviet Union exhausted themselves on the Eastern Front. This viewpoint was strengthened by the outcome of a meeting between an American delegation and the British in London in April 1942. The Americans suggested that if the situation on the Eastern Front deteriorated badly for the Red Army, a limited operation should be launched against the European mainland. The British repeated their doubts about the practicality of such an operation and told their American counterparts that, at best, a force of only seven infantry and two armoured divisions could be made available. Given what was known about the substantial German forces currently deployed in France, this force would rapidly be crushed. Nonetheless, it was agreed to conduct planning for this limited operation, which became known as *Sledgehammer*.

A month later, Molotov flew to London for discussions with the Western Powers. From the outset, there were significant disagreements. Molotov wanted the allies of the Soviet Union to recognise the western frontier of the Soviet Union as it had existed at the outset of the German invasion in the summer of 1941. This would mean the acceptance of the Soviet occupation of eastern Poland, the Baltic States, and Bessarabia, and was immediately rejected. For Molotov, this was a major setback and he was minded to break off further discussions, but Stalin sent him a message telling him not to contest the issue – ultimately, Stalin advised his foreign minister, frontiers would be decided by the reality on the ground and there was no possibility of the armies of the Western Allies being in a position to contest Soviet claims in Eastern Europe at the end of a successful war.[7] Consequently, the objections raised by the British could be ignored without further comment.

Molotov then raised the continuing issue of a Second Front. He told the British that a German summer offensive was anticipated at any moment – at the time, the Soviet Union expected a renewed attack against Moscow, despite growing evidence that the Germans intended to attack further south towards the lower Volga and into the Caucasus region. In order to alleviate pressure, Molotov delivered a demand from Stalin that the Western Powers should make preparations for the creation of a new Second Front as soon as possible in order to tie down at least 40 German divisions. Once more, the British delegates pointed out the practical difficulties. The US and British Armies were still building up their strength and lacked the resources for such an undertaking. There weren't sufficient landing craft available to deliver even the forces that were currently available, and it was best to wait until 1943. By then, the British informed Molotov, it would be possible to attack with 48 divisions. In the meantime, Churchill offered a small crumb of comfort: it might be possible to mount a limited operation to capture the northern parts of Norway in order to reduce the aerial threat to the convoys carrying supplies to the Soviet Union.

Unimpressed by the British, Molotov travelled on to Washington. At first, he was gratified that Roosevelt seemed in favour of an invasion of the European mainland before the end of 1942, but such hopes were rapidly dashed when US military figures became involved in the discussions. Like the British, they rejected any such suggestion as premature and unlike several of the nations in the Second World War, the United States was fortunate to have a president who made little attempt to impose his personal beliefs upon his professional soldiers. Molotov returned to Moscow via London and gave Stalin a blunt assessment of the intentions of the Western Powers; the British in particular seemed to offer little hope of a Second Front at any time in the near future. The Soviet Union would have to continue bearing the burden of land warfare against Germany for the foreseeable future.

Roosevelt's initial optimism about land operations in the west was now fading rapidly. Churchill travelled to Washington a few weeks after Molotov's visit and in discussions involving senior military figures of both nations, the two leaders reviewed the plans that had been drawn up for *Sledgehammer*. Given the limited resources available, planners proposed an operation to seize Cherbourg and the Cotentin Peninsula in Normandy. The narrow neck of the peninsula – just 21 miles – would limit German options for counterattacks and it would be possible for the Allies to hold their positions while building up their strength. But this required the port to be captured intact and just as German counterattacks would have to take place on a limited frontage, any Allied breakout faced precisely the same problem. Roosevelt and Churchill concluded that *Sledgehammer* would be pointless and was doomed to fail; the plan was formally abandoned and instead priority was given to landings in North Africa, initially under the codename *Gymnast*, later changed to *Torch*.

As the summer days grew longer, the convoys passing the northern tip of Norway lost the protection of darkness and began to suffer increasingly heavy losses. In July, it was necessary to suspend sailings until September. News of this reached Stalin at the same time as the decision of the Western Allies to abandon plans for any assault on Western Europe and to concentrate on North Africa. The reaction was entirely predictable: Stalin accused the Western Allies, the British in particular, of reneging on agreements to open a Second Front.

Delaying an invasion of mainland Europe until 1943 at the earliest was unacceptable. By this time, the Wehrmacht had launched Operation *Blau*, its major summer offensive aimed at reaching the lower Volga and pressing on to the Caucasus. Once again, the Red Army had been unable to halt the German thrusts, and Stalin was aware that there was a real possibility that the Soviet Union would be forced out of the war before the Western Allies were prepared to launch an invasion.

Stalin wasn't the only person to feel that the delays in instigating a Second Front were too great. When the decision of Roosevelt and Churchill was passed to senior commanders, several Americans – in particular, General George Marshall and Admiral Ernest King – opposed the proposed landings in North Africa, raising once again the suggestion of an invasion of France before the end of 1942. When the British refused to accept this, Marshall contacted the US president directly and suggested that this made a nonsense of the agreed policy of defeating Germany before turning against Japan. If the British were determined to block any invasion of mainland Europe, perhaps US forces should simply concentrate their energies in the Pacific theatre. Roosevelt knew that *Torch* would have only a modest effect on the ability of the Germans to concentrate their resources against the Soviet Union, but Admiral William Leahy, the newly appointed chief of staff of the army and navy, advised him that even this limited impact was far greater than any effect a major offensive in the Pacific might have on Germany – at best, it would bring the eventual defeat of Japan closer, but in the meantime the Soviet Union would continue to bear the brunt of the land war against Germany. Roosevelt therefore overruled Marshall and King, insisting that *Torch* was to go ahead.

Aware of Stalin's bitter disappointment and the effect that it would have on trust and cooperation, Churchill accepted an invitation to travel to Moscow for further talks. These proved to be every bit as difficult as the British had anticipated. Stalin was dismissive of British concerns that an early invasion of France carried too many risks; his armies were fighting and dying in huge numbers, and from his perspective the British seemed to be too risk-averse, further reinforcing Soviet suspicions that the British in particular were perfectly happy for Germany and the Soviet Union to fight a brutal and costly war against each other. On the other hand, Stalin appeared to be impressed by the potential benefits of *Torch*, recognising how it might expose the 'underbelly' of Western Europe to future operations, but the same strategic acumen that he showed in this analysis would have alerted him to another underlying truth: British plans for the Mediterranean theatre were at least partly influenced by concerns about the safety of the Suez Canal and therefore access to British colonial possessions in Asia. Ill-tempered exchanges continued, with Churchill increasingly irritated by Stalin's thinly veiled distrust and contempt. In a final meeting, the two men were able to put their differences to one side with the help of copious quantities of alcohol and a degree of concordance was achieved.

Nevertheless, the issue of the Second Front and the huge burden being carried by the Red Army continued to have repercussions. The 1942 campaign on the Eastern Front reached its climax in the ruins of Stalingrad and the Red Army launched Operation *Uranus*, the encirclement of the German Sixth Army. The winter fighting that followed saw great movements of troops across the frozen landscape as the Germans were forced out of the Caucasus region. Briefly, it seemed as if the entire German position in the southern sector of the Eastern Front was about to collapse, but the fluid nature of operations, lengthening Soviet supply lines, and Red Army casualties – even if the destruction of the German Sixth Army is included, Soviet losses exceeded those of the Germans – allowed the Wehrmacht to restore its front line.[8] The fact that this was achieved partly through the transfer of substantial forces from Western Europe was not lost on Stalin. The failure of the Western Allies to create the long-demanded Second Front once more became a thorny issue.

As the snows of winter began to thaw in March and April 1943, the annual spring *rasputitsa* or 'muddy season' forced a halt to major operations. While the Red Army rebuilt its depleted armies and began planning for the summer campaign – details of German plans to attack the Kursk salient arrived in a constant stream in Moscow from a variety of sources – Stalin attempted to put pressure on the British and Americans. The Swedish government had offered to act as an intermediary between Germany and the Soviet Union, and although the Soviet ambassador in Stockholm, Aleksandra Mikhailovna Kollontai, was a devout Germanphobe, Stalin authorised two junior diplomats, Vladimir Semenovich Semyonov and Boris Yartsev, to hold informal discussions. Stalin offered Hitler a peace treaty with the restoration of the 1941 frontier; on Hitler's orders, the Germans involved in the discussions offered the line of the Dnepr River with the creation of a Ukrainian puppet state under German control to the west of the river. Any such discussions were contrary to the declarations of the previous year in which the nations arrayed against Germany had agreed not to make a separate peace, and it is difficult to know how serious Stalin was in his offer. Given the failure of the Germans to respect their previous non-aggression pact with the Soviet Union, the Soviet leader must have had doubts about the credibility of any new agreement with Hitler, and it seems far more likely that the discussions were an attempt to put pressure upon London and Washington: unless the Western Powers fulfilled their promises to establish a Second Front, the Soviet Union might be forced to take matters into its own hands.[9] In a message to Churchill, Stalin made the matter clear: 'The vagueness of your statements regarding the planned Anglo-American offensive on the other side of the Channel arouses in me an anxiety, about which I cannot be silent.'[10]

Despite the alarming reports about the tentative discussions in Stockholm, the British continued to oppose any early invasion of France. In May 1943, Churchill and Roosevelt met once more in Washington in a conference codenamed *Trident*. The invasion of North Africa had been a resounding success and Churchill proposed an early attack on Sicily. This could be followed by further attacks on Italy itself, with the prospect of Germany's ally being knocked out of the war. It would also go a small distance towards satisfying Stalin's demands for the Western Powers to tie down German forces in land warfare in the west. The plans for an Allied attack against France – at this stage, codenamed *Round-up* – were reviewed and it was concluded that despite the delays, there was no prospect of success in 1943. Instead, the invasion, now renamed *Overlord*, would have to wait until May 1944 at the earliest. Given Stalin's hostility during the Moscow meeting the previous summer, Churchill can have had no doubt that this news would be received badly by Stalin and the reaction from Moscow was unsurprising. After receiving the news from the American ambassador, Stalin wrote to Churchill:

> This decision [to postpone the invasion until 1944] creates quite exceptional difficulties for the Soviet Union, which has been waging war for already two years under the greatest strain against the main forces of Germany and her satellites. This decision leaves also the Soviet Army, which is fighting not only for its own country, but for the Allies as well, to combat nearly single-handed a still very strong and dangerous enemy.[11]

Churchill's response was equally acerbic:

> It would be no help to Russia if we threw away a hundred thousand men in a disastrous cross-Channel attack such as would, in my opinion, certainly occur if we tried under present conditions and with forces too weak to exploit any success at very heavy cost.[12]

From the perspective of Stalin, who had thrown the Red Army repeatedly at the Wehrmacht with casualties for each operation that ran into six figures, this seemed like a paltry excuse. He rejected Churchill's response as showing disregard for vital Soviet interests and ignoring the millions of future casualties that could be prevented by an early invasion of France. Compared to the huge losses suffered by the Red Army, the casualties that Churchill feared seemed modest at best.

It was against this background of mistrust that plans were drawn up for the first face-to-face meeting of Roosevelt, Churchill, and Stalin. The American president's health was steadily deteriorating and Stalin had a longstanding aversion to flying. The first proposed location for the conference was Cairo, but Stalin rejected this, suggesting Baghdad or Basra as alternatives before Tehran was agreed. The foreign ministers of the three nations met in Moscow to lay the foundations for the conference and the Soviet leader began his journey on 26 November, travelling by train to Baku before boarding one of four transport planes. Escorted by nearly 30 fighters, the transports flew to Tehran without incident, though a moment of turbulence led to near-panic on Stalin's part; it was his first flight.

Stalin was the first of the 'Big Three' to arrive in Tehran. Immediately, the Soviet delegation revealed to the British and Americans that they had uncovered a plot by the Germans to conduct a suicide mission led by Obersturmbannführer Otto Skorzeny against those attending. In order to improve security, they suggested that the Americans move to the Soviet embassy compound. It is highly unlikely that any plot existed – delivering a group of parachutists to the area would have been at the extreme range of any German aircraft, and after the war Skorzeny denied any such plans had been made – and the Americans were doubtful of the Soviet claims, but Roosevelt agreed to move to the Soviet buildings.[13] Roosevelt and the American delegation were aware that their conversations were being monitored, but the American president hoped that this would help alleviate Stalin's mistrust and therefore raised no objection. In addition to putting the Americans in buildings where their conversations could be monitored, Stalin calculated – correctly – that Roosevelt would oppose any plans Churchill might have to preserve the British Empire, and wished to discuss matters in private before the full conference.

On 28 November, as the sun began to set in a cold, cloudless autumnal sky, the three men finally met. For Stalin, the foremost priority was to pin down the Western Powers to a date for the invasion of France, followed very closely by securing acceptance of his plans for the western frontiers of the Soviet Union. At an early stage, when he learned that the British and Americans had yet to appoint an overall commander for their planned landings in France, Stalin threatened to walk out of the conference. Roosevelt hastened to reassure him; plans were progressing, and an invasion would definitely take place in May 1944 regardless of who took overall command. Churchill expressed doubts and stated his preference for an operation in the Mediterranean, but was outvoted. The British prime minister accepted the decision with ill-disguised irritation, while Stalin and Roosevelt exchanged conspiratorial smiles. It was the first significant wedge that Stalin inserted between the British and Americans.

For the moment, Stalin was content to welcome what he treated as a firm commitment to a Second Front; his monitoring of conversations between members of the American delegation left him satisfied that, unlike the British, he could trust the Americans. He expressed gratitude that the long-awaited invasion would take place within months and added that he would ensure a simultaneous attack in the east. Such coordination of offensives against Germany had taken place in the First World War, when the Entente Powers – France, Britain, and Russia – agreed to mount constant offensives on all fronts in the expectation that by doing so, they would prevent the Germans from being able to switch reserves from one front to another. Sooner or later, such pressure would exceed the ability of the Germans to respond and a major breakthrough would result. As the First World War progressed, the Western Powers put pressure upon Russia to attack when the Germans were mounting a major offensive against Verdun; the result was the bloody battles near Lake Naroch, resulting in tens of thousands of Russian dead for no tangible gain, either in terms of territory or diversion of German resources.[14] On this occasion, all sides hoped for a better outcome.

When the Tehran Conference took place, the Wehrmacht had been driven out of central Ukraine and most of the line of the Dnepr River was in Soviet hands. Kiev fell to the Red Army in early November and although a counteroffensive by German forces shored up the front line to the west of the city, German hopes of establishing a lasting position along the Dnepr had been dashed. After its triumphant though costly advance to and over the Dnepr, the Red Army was forced to pause for breath while railway lines were restored and supplies and reinforcements were brought forward, but offensive operations would continue on a lesser scale through the winter. When he met Churchill and Roosevelt, Stalin was aware that further plans were being drawn up for these attacks all along the Eastern Front and it was far too soon to consider where exactly the offensive timed to coincide with a western invasion of France would take place. Nonetheless, the strategic initiative was firmly with the Red Army. Regardless of how the front line moved in the intervening months, there would be sufficient resources for an offensive in the summer of 1944. Coordination with the British and Americans was valuable, but not essential.

Despite this apparent agreement, many in the Soviet delegation continued to doubt the commitment of the Western Powers. Marshal Kliment Yefremovich Voroshilov had been given various posts during the war but had shown little aptitude for modern warfare and despite his loyalty to an old comrade from the days of the Civil War, Stalin ensured that Voroshilov was restricted to roles in which he could do little harm. The marshal was part of the Soviet delegation in Tehran and his British and American counterparts were unimpressed by his military acumen. Even though the 'Big Three' had agreed on an invasion of France in May 1944, Voroshilov expressed lack of understanding in the delay when he met British and American military figures in separate discussions. The western officers were alarmed and quietly astonished that the Soviet marshal seemed to regard an assault across the English Channel as little more than a large-scale river crossing. The Red Army had repeatedly improvised in forcing such crossings, he lectured the British and Americans. What was needed was greater commitment.

In the main conference, discussions also addressed the shape of Europe after the war, and the arguments between Molotov and Churchill the previous year were aired once more. For the Soviet Union, the war commenced in June 1941 and all talk of restoration of pre-war frontiers was assumed to refer to the shape of Eastern Europe on the day that German troops invaded the Soviet Union. For the British, who had entered the war in support of Poland, there was considerable unease at any settlement that was seen as detrimental to their ally, But on this matter too, Churchill rapidly realised that support from Roosevelt would be limited. Although the forthcoming US elections – and awareness of the sensitivities of the large Polish American community – made Roosevelt reluctant to make any controversial commitments, the American president was prepared to look sympathetically on the Soviet point of view; for the United States, too, the war had commenced in 1941, weakening the British argument that 'pre-war frontiers' should refer to the situation in September 1939. Stalin continued to be inflexible on the subject of the eastern border of Poland, and in exchanges in the preceding weeks he had reminded the British in particular that Lord George Curzon, the British foreign secretary after the First World War, had suggested a frontier along a line that bore his name but the Poles had seized territory further east during their war with the Bolsheviks. This area contained large numbers of ethnic Russians, Ukrainians, and Belarusians and had become part of the Soviet occupied zone as a result of the Molotov–Ribbentrop Pact. Aware that the British position was weak, Churchill now proposed a new eastern frontier for Poland along the Curzon Line. Poland would receive territory from Germany in the west – this would serve as compensation for the lost territory in the east and would also weaken Germany as part of measures to prevent any future wars. He was able to justify this – at least to himself – by describing the Polish territories in the east that would be assigned to the Soviet Union as being largely swamps and forests, whereas the German territories in East and West Prussia, Pomerania, and Silesia that would be assigned to Poland were rich in industrial, mineral, and agricultural resources. Final ratification would have to await a further conference to be held after the war, but the potential to alter the map of Europe was unequivocally recognised and accepted by the Western Powers.

Such agreements were all well and good, but Stalin remained doubtful that the British would actually stick to them. It was therefore important to ensure that by the time any post-war conference took place, the reality on the ground was such that the Soviet Union would have little difficulty in imposing its will. Stalin saw a danger to Soviet interests in Churchill's preference for landings in the Mediterranean; he rightly assessed Churchill's intention to try to occupy much of the central and eastern parts of Europe before the arrival of the Red Army. He also showed greater strategic and operational understanding than his British counterpart. Any invasion of the northern coastline of the Mediterranean – apart from in southern France – would inevitably result in protracted fighting in difficult, mountainous country. From a purely military point of view, an attack on France from the northwest had far greater likelihood of success.

It is worth noting that despite all their protestations that they were fighting for democracy and freedom, the 'Big Three' made decisions about the future of Poland without any consultation with the Poles themselves. Whilst such behaviour was unsurprising from the Soviet side, there were already tensions between Churchill and Roosevelt on this matter. As early as their meeting in Newfoundland in August 1941, the American president had commented that he had difficulty believing that the two nations were fighting a war against Fascism (at this stage, the USA was not actually at war, but was providing substantial aid to the British) but were making no attempt to rid the world of colonialism.[15] After returning to London, Churchill felt it necessary to reassure the British parliament that the agreements reached with the Americans, known as the Atlantic Charter, referred only to the countries conquered by Germany and its allies – the British Empire was not included. The following year, Roosevelt angered Churchill once more on the subject of Britain's imperial possessions, comparing the status of India with the

American colonies on the eve of the War of Independence. The American position was not without problems of its own – at this time, the US Army remained racially segregated and there was widespread discrimination against non-white people across the USA – but it is unsurprising that Stalin correctly calculated that colonialism in general and the British Empire in particular represented a fault line between Roosevelt and Churchill that was ripe for exploitation.

Roosevelt may have been charmed by Stalin and may have thought that he had won the Soviet leader's trust, but Churchill remained doubtful of Soviet intentions. His fears seemed to be confirmed at a dinner in which Stalin appeared to go to considerable lengths to irritate the British prime minister while the American president looked on with a smile. Speculating on the final outcome of the war, Stalin mused that it might be necessary to execute 50,000 German officers after the war, or even larger numbers. Already unhappy that he had been forced to concede on *Overlord*, Churchill snapped back that such an attitude would be unacceptable to Britain. He wasn't mollified by Roosevelt's attempt at humour – the president suggested that in the spirit of compromise, perhaps a number of 49,000 might be sufficient – and matters were worsened by Elliot Roosevelt, the president's son, who quipped that 50,000 were likely to be killed in combat in any case. Churchill stormed from the room only to be stopped by Stalin and Molotov who clapped him on his shoulder and protested that the comments had been made in jest. Aware of intelligence that suggested the Soviet Union had already massacred thousands of Polish officers at Katyn, Churchill knew that jest or otherwise, there was every likelihood of mass executions.

In the weeks and months that followed the Tehran Conference, the configuration of the Eastern Front changed significantly, but the agenda for the following year had been set. The Western Powers would launch the long-demanded Second Front in France, while the Red Army continued to drive back the Germans in the east. To increase the likelihood of success, the two assaults would be timed to coincide. This, it was expected, would create the conditions for the collapse of Germany, but Stalin intended to ensure that he would end the war in a position to redraw the map of Europe in a manner that favoured the Soviet Union. Despite all that had been agreed in Tehran, this could only be guaranteed if the Red Army was physically in possession of most of Eastern Europe; whilst there now seemed little doubt that the nations arrayed against Germany were heading for victory, there remained the possibility in the mind of the Soviet leader that a sudden change of circumstances in Germany – the death of Hitler, for example, and the rise of a new government – might result in unfavourable developments. It seemed possible that the Western Powers might seek a separate peace, leaving the Soviet Union to fight on alone, and it was therefore essential to deliver a killing blow as soon as possible.

Even as the Allies to the east and west of Germany drew up their plans for their operations in 1944, a group of German conspirators made preparations of their own. Before the horror of land fighting reached German soil, they intended to kill Hitler and then seek precisely the separate peace with the Western Powers that Stalin feared. The development of this plot would coincide with momentous events on the front line, creating a situation in which – for the briefest of moments – the most unlikely outcomes seemed possible.

CHAPTER 1

FRITZ AND IVAN: THE STATE OF THE ARMIES OF THE EASTERN FRONT

The original plan for the invasion of France by the Western Powers, drawn up within a month of the Tehran Conference, called for amphibious assaults by three divisions, but at an early stage this was expanded to include airborne assaults and a larger amphibious component; as a consequence, the original start date of 1 May had to be put back by a month. Whilst Stalin had been deeply critical of repeated delays in the past, he accepted this without much protest, as it would give the Red Army more time to complete its preparations for its summer offensive. Weather concerns forced a further short postponement of the invasion and finally, early on 6 June 1944, the first soldiers of the great invasion force assembled by the Americans, British, Canadians, and others – contingents from at least 13 nations were involved – splashed ashore in Normandy.[1] Paratroopers had already landed overnight. Operation *Overlord* had commenced.

In the east, the Red Army was also preparing to launch its summer offensive. Although 1942 and 1943 had seen major movements in the southern sector of the Eastern Front, the central sector and particularly the northern sector had altered far less dramatically. Nonetheless, these sectors saw heavy fighting as the Red Army made repeated attempts to break the German defences, and although the Germans were driven back from cities like Smolensk, the cost to the Soviet Union was appallingly high. Sustaining such operations was almost impossible. But the series of operations that ran through the winter of 1943–44 resulted in the overall map of the Eastern Front changing significantly, greatly to the detriment of Germany. However, even though these changes were operationally and strategically significant, they were dwarfed by the implications of the news from Normandy. The two-front war, long feared by Germany, was now a reality.

Faced with the inevitability of an attack by the Western Allies and the resurgence of the Soviet Union from the dark days of late 1941, Hitler formulated a new strategy for Germany to continue the war. Sustaining a two-front war in anything other than the short term was clearly impossible, and it was therefore vital to achieve victory on one front. Given the weakness of German forces in the east, defeating the Soviet Union quickly was unachievable. Therefore, in his Führer Directive 51 of 3 November 1943, Hitler declared that whilst the struggle in the east remained of great importance, the threat from the west was greater. The task of the armies facing the Soviet Union was to conduct the most stubborn defence possible, conceding ground only when necessary, while forces in France were strengthened in anticipation of the coming invasion. They would then be used to deal a decisive blow to destroy the invasion force of the Western Powers. Thereafter, the delivery of new U-boats to the navy would permit the resumption of the Battle of the Atlantic with the aim of hindering any further American reinforcements for a renewed invasion attempt, and land and air forces would be transferred from France to the Eastern Front to permit major operations against the Soviet Union.[2] It was in many respects a strategy of desperation – a 'least worst' option for Germany in a situation that was hugely unfavourable and worsened almost with each passing month.

Within a few weeks, the weaknesses of this policy were being exposed. The options for where the Western Powers might attempt an invasion seemed to be numerous and this required substantial forces to be held in almost every area, or at least sufficient to halt an initial landing until reinforcements arrived. This in turn meant that too few forces were available to deal with the rolling series of catastrophes in the east and, in an attempt to provide a more manageable solution, Oberkommando der Wehrmacht ('Armed Forces High Command' or OKW), effectively in charge of all German forces not on the Eastern Front, suggested that units in the west should be concentrated in regions where the likelihood of invasion was highest. Even while this proposal was being discussed, British and American troops came ashore at Anzio in Italy on 22 January 1944, giving the Germans the impression that their enemies had sufficient resources to attempt landings at more than one location. Thereafter, even those who doubted Hitler's strategy had to conclude that it was the only means of continuing the war. A definitive resolution of the problems on the Eastern Front would have to wait until the Western Powers had been defeated.

In the meantime, Hitler produced a further decree that was to have a profoundly limiting effect on the ability of the Wehrmacht to use its traditional strengths of flexibility and tactical skill. After Rovno and Nevel were abandoned despite orders from Hitler that they were to be defended stubbornly, *Führer-Befehl 11* ('Führer Order 11') was issued on 8 March 1944 in an attempt to prevent any repetition:

In view of recent incidents, I issue the following orders:

1. A distinction will be made between *feste Plätze* ['fortified locations'], each under a *Festungskommandant* ['fortress commander'] and *Ortsstützpunkte* ['local strongpoints'], each under a *Kampfkommandant* ['battle commander']. The *feste Plätze* will fulfil the functions of fortresses in former historical times. They will ensure that the enemy does not occupy these areas of decisive operational importance. They will permit themselves to be surrounded, thereby holding down the largest possible number of enemy forces, and establishing conditions for successful counterattacks. *Ortsstützpunkte* deep in the battle area will be defended tenaciously in the event of an enemy penetration. By being part of the main line of battle they will act as a bolster to the defences and should the enemy break through, as hinges and cornerstones for the front, forming positions from which counterattacks can be launched.

2. Each *Festungskommandant* should be a carefully selected, experienced soldier, preferably of the rank of general. He will be appointed by the relevant army group. The *Festungskommandant* will be personally responsible to the army group commander. The *Festungskommandant* will pledge his honour as a soldier to carry out his duties to the last. Only the army group commander can, with my approval, relieve the *Festungskommandant* of his duties and perhaps order the surrender of the *fester Platz* … In addition to the garrison and its security personnel, all persons within a *fester Platz* or who have gathered there are under the orders of the *Festungskommandant* regardless of whether they are soldiers or civilians and without regard to their rank or appointment …

3. The garrison of a *fester Platz* consists of the security garrison and the general garrison … The general garrison must be made available to the *Kommandant* of the *fester Platz* in sufficient time for the men to have taken up defensive positions and to be in position when a full-scale enemy attack threatens.[3]

The flaws in this policy were easy for almost everyone to see. There were no significant examples from the previous century of fortresses enduring a siege successfully in the manner that Hitler described. Much of the strategy of the Great Powers in preparation for the First World War in Eastern Europe had relied on systems of fortresses but only in one case – the Austro-Hungarian fortress of Przemyśl in modern southeast Poland – was there a prolonged siege. It ended with the surrender of the entire garrison and the deaths of tens of thousands of men in failed attempts to lift the siege. In many cases, Hitler would declare locations to be fortresses far too late for any meaningful preparations to be made for their defence, and even if such forces had been allocated, their passive defence of the fortress was meaningless without sufficient German forces being available to rescue them. Moreover, after the experience of Stalingrad, the Red Army was determined not to allow any encircled German units to tie down large numbers of Soviet troops. Such encirclements were to be reduced as rapidly as possible so that the momentum of the advance could be maintained and if this was impossible, sufficient forces would be provided in the second echelon to destroy the fortress while the first echelon continued its advance. Almost immediately after issuing this order, Hitler declared 26 locations on the Eastern Front as fortresses. The hard-pressed commanders of the German armies along the front had no choice but to designate troops that were to serve as garrisons in the knowledge that these units were almost certain to be destroyed.

Even without the appearance of the forces of the Western Allies in France, the changes of positions on the Eastern Front in the preceding months had created a deeply threatening situation. In the north, the Siege of Leningrad came to an end with the Wehrmacht being driven back to Estonia, though Soviet attempts to exploit their success by penetrating further west or by trapping large parts of the German Army Group North all failed. In the south, winter fighting drove the Germans back from Kirovograd in early 1944; combined with Soviet gains in the last weeks of 1943, this created a large salient that contained most of the German Eighth Army, and the Red Army succeeded in cutting off this grouping in what became known as the Battle of Cherkassy. Although most of the encircled troops managed to break out to the west, they were forced to abandon their heavy equipment and the attempts to rescue them resulted in the commitment of more than half the panzer divisions on the Eastern Front.[4] When a new Soviet offensive commenced in the southern sector shortly after, the exhausted Germans were in no state to put up prolonged resistance and were driven in disarray from Ukraine. The relatively successful German withdrawal from central Ukraine to and over the Dnepr River was accomplished largely due to the efficacy of the panzer divisions of Army Group South, which fought constant rearguard actions and repeatedly blunted attempts by the Red Army to outflank the retreating German formations, but the result was that the panzer divisions were badly depleted by the end of 1943.

Their heavy use in the Battle of Cherkassy weakened them still further, and the result was a near-rout as the Red Army relentlessly pressed forward. Finally, operating at the end of lengthy supply lines and badly degraded by the constant fighting, the Soviet forces came to a halt along the Dniester River.

Briefly, the German First Panzer Army was cut off around the city of Kamanyets-Podolskyi, but was able to break out to the west. At no stage did the Red Army achieve a proper, closely sealed encirclement of the sort established at Stalingrad or during the Battle of Cherkassy, but the escape of First Panzer Army was due at least partly to the transfer of two SS panzer divisions from France to the Eastern Front. As fighting came to a close in the spring thaw of 1944, these divisions were extracted and sent back to the west in anticipation of an invasion by the Western Allies. The episode highlighted the importance of coordinated action: in order to maximise success in both the east and the west, it was necessary for Germany's enemies to mount simultaneous offensives to prevent the Germans from switching resources from one front to another.

In the central sector, there had also been significant changes. In early 1942, the aftermath of the Battle of Moscow left the Wehrmacht occupying a large north-projecting salient with the city of Rzhev at its tip, and the rest of 1942 saw repeated, bloody attempts by the Red Army to destroy this salient. All of the Soviet attacks failed with losses that were appallingly high even by the standards of the Eastern Front, and the Germans finally evacuated the salient in early 1943 as part of their preparations for the Battle of Kursk. The Red Army chose to deal with the German attack on the Kursk salient by adopting a defensive posture, but significant forces were positioned in anticipation of an early switch to offensive operations on either side of the salient. On the northern side, this was anticipated by the Germans and the commander of Ninth Army, Generaloberst Walter Model – who was promoted to Generalfeldmarschall in March 1944 – deliberately held back his panzer divisions so that they would be available to intercept any Soviet offensive operation. Partly as a result of this and partly due to the strength of the German defences, the Soviet attack, codenamed Operation *Kutuzov*, was hugely costly. The Germans were forced out of the city of Orel, falling back to the Hagen defensive line near Bryansk; the Wehrmacht suffered the loss of about 86,000 men, but Red Army losses were far greater at nearly 430,000 killed, wounded, or missing.[5]

The losses suffered by the Wehrmacht might have been a fraction of those inflicted upon the Red Army, but the casualties included large numbers of experienced soldiers, non-commissioned officers (NCOs), and officers who were almost irreplaceable. By contrast, the huge resources of the Soviet Union meant that almost immediately the Red Army was able to launch the Smolensk Operation. As is often the case in battles involving troops of different levels of experience, the bulk of Red Army losses were in the newer drafts – men who survived their first few battles learned how to reduce the risks they faced in future actions. As a result, replenishing the depleted ranks with new drafts of 'green' troops allowed the Soviet units to function at broadly the same level of capability as before – far short of the standards achieved by Germany or the Western Powers, but sufficient if deployed in large numbers to apply constant pressure on the Germans. With replacement drafts falling far short of their losses, the Germans were unable to match this replenishment.

The Smolensk Operation continued until October 1943 with similar losses suffered by both sides as had occurred during *Kutuzov*, but the consequence was that as a result of the two Soviet operations, the German Army Group Centre was forced back up to 200 miles. If German losses during *Kutuzov* represented a major setback, doubling these losses during the Smolensk Operation left the front line manned by units that were dangerously weak in terms of numbers, and importantly also in terms of quality. In an attempt to address the deleterious effects of the loss of so many experienced leaders and to improve upon the inadequate training of new drafts sent to the front line, most German armies on the Eastern Front established leadership schools and heavy weapons schools to try to train new NCOs and to improve upon the basic training of the new drafts, but despite this the performance of German units continued to decline steadily. Writing after the war, several German officers described how the exhausted and demoralised survivors of Army Group Centre, with few reserves supporting them, were forced to hold dangerously long sectors of front line – this might have been possible with the experienced soldiers of earlier years, but to attempt the same with the current troops was a risky undertaking.[6] If there was a further Soviet onslaught in the central sector, the ability of the Wehrmacht to halt the Soviet forces was highly questionable – even the initial stiff resistance that German units had consistently been able to put up might not be possible. The priority given by Hitler to reinforcing the defences in the west in anticipation of an invasion by the Western Powers would greatly reduce the resources available to replenish the battered German divisions of Army Group Centre. This, combined with the longer-term trends of the war, would create a situation that was potentially catastrophic.

Nevertheless, as the armies paused for breath during the spring thaw of 1944, there were grounds for hope. After becoming armaments minister in February 1942, Albert Speer took several measures to improve the efficiency of German armaments production and as a consequence German factories turned out huge numbers of tanks, guns, and planes despite constant bombing attacks. In January 1944, the Luftwaffe possessed a little over 5,500 aircraft; a year before, the figure had been about 3,900. Fighter production continued to increase through the year before peaking in September, replacing aircraft that had been destroyed, but the casualties amongst experienced aircrew were of course far harder to remedy. Tank production also peaked in September, and the consequence was that the large numbers of soldiers who had retreated from the near-rout of German forces in the southern sector were rapidly re-equipped, restoring the fighting strength of the divisions.[7] One of the longstanding weaknesses of the Wehrmacht – the poor provision of anti-tank weaponry for infantry units – had also been addressed, at least partially. The advent of the *Panzerschreck* and *Panzerfaust* man-portable anti-tank weapons provided infantrymen with the ability to destroy almost any tank they might encounter, albeit often at terrifyingly close range.

In 1941 and for much of 1942, the Red Army had been comprehensively outclassed and outfought by the Wehrmacht, suffering huge casualties and losing a vast amount of territory. In late 1942, the Soviet forces showed just how much they had improved – in terms of their equipment, their efficacy on the battlefield, and their ability to plan and mount sustained operations – in the battles around Stalingrad, though the cost of the eventual Soviet victory demonstrated that there was still much to be learned and that the Wehrmacht remained a formidable opponent. Much of 1943 was spent preparing for the Battle of Kursk, and here the Red Army was able to prevent the concentrated power of the Wehrmacht's panzer divisions from achieving a breakthrough; it also rapidly transitioned to an offensive posture and drove the Germans back, but again at a terrible cost in terms of dead and wounded. As 1944 began, there were further signs of Soviet improvements. Although the winter fighting around Leningrad in the north and across the western parts of Ukraine in the south proved once more to be costly, the losses were far closer to those inflicted upon the exhausted divisions of the Wehrmacht. Equipment had also improved considerably. The T-34, which outclassed all German tanks at the beginning of the German invasion, had now been upgraded with better armour and a more powerful 85mm gun in place of the old 76mm gun; the old weapon proved to be unable to penetrate the armour of Tiger tanks even at close range. Large numbers of assault guns had also been produced, providing better support for infantry in formal assaults on prepared positions, and the need to switch German fighters from the Eastern Front to the German homeland to counter the constant bombing attacks on German cities permitted Soviet aviation, particularly the Ilyushin Il-2 *Sturmovik*, to be used in greater numbers.

As was the case with the Wehrmacht, older items of equipment that were becoming obsolescent remained in service in the Red Army largely because replacing them with more effective weapons was impossible. One such weapon was the 45mm anti-tank gun, known to its crews as the *Soropyatka* (a diminutive term for 'forty-five'). Vasily Georgiyevich Kharin was the commander of one such gun crew:

> We were called anti-tank gunners, more often just gunners, and sometimes *Proshchai Rodina* ['farewell motherland']. This last nickname had a certain truth to it. Our *Sorokopyatka* were almost always deployed forward of other guns directly in the front line, so their firing positions were subjected to the most intense enemy fire. But this nickname – *Proshchai Rodina* – offended and angered us within our arm. We told others that our commander, Senior Sergeant Fomin, who had been with the battery since 1942, was still alive and well. We refused to accept the validity of this nickname.
>
> During the three years of the war, the equipment of our side and that of the enemy changed significantly. They had Tigers, Panthers, and Ferdinands, but our 45mm gun remained the same and it was harder and harder for us to engage German tanks.[8]

Despite this sense of being opposed by superior tanks, the crews of the 45mm guns were aware that they could still provide useful service. Regardless of the strength of the armour of a tank, a hit on its tracks was likely to leave it immobilised, and an easy target for heavier weapons, though this required the gun crews to engage their opponents at close range while deliberately aiming at the tracks. Moreover, there were plenty of easier targets for the 45mm guns, such as half-tracks and infantry positions, and the gunners had to hope that their comrades who manned the more effective 76mm guns would protect them from German tanks.

Like many nations, the Soviet Union entered the Second World War with military leadership of highly variable quality. Weakened almost fatally by Stalin's paranoia and the resultant purges, the Red Army was further handicapped by faulty doctrine. At first, Stalin's response to setbacks was to continue the policies of the pre-war purges: several senior officers were arrested and executed for failing to stop the German advances. But by the first winter of the conflict, it was clear that the Soviet Union was going to have to fight with what it had available. Some officers, many of whom would play major roles in the huge battles of the summer of 1944, had demonstrated that they were flexible and highly skilled in modern warfare; others remained in post largely because there were no alternative figures to replace them.

Whilst all of the signs of improvement in the Soviet armed forces were gratifying, they could not disguise some fundamental realities. In most respects, the Red Army – like its predecessor, the Russian Army of the tsars, and its successors, the Soviet Army of the Cold War era and the modern Russian Army – remained a blunt instrument, a cudgel or a mace rather than a sword. Close cooperation between infantry, artillery, and armour continued to be patchy at best and was often non-existent; all three arms frequently adhered rigidly to the original battle plan and if one was forced to adapt to unexpected circumstances, the others then struggled to alter their plans. Consequently, infantry often became separated from accompanying tanks and assault guns and had difficulty calling in artillery strikes to crush stubborn defences. Similarly, cooperation between ground and air forces fell far short of the standards of German forces and those of the Western Powers. The Red Army had improved hugely during the war, learning the realities of mechanised warfare in the most testing environment imaginable, and its leadership was now far more effective; but however well it was wielded it remained fundamentally a means of bludgeoning its opponent into submission. Although some of the high-ranking figures in the Red Army became almost synonymous with heavy casualties, this was often a reflection of the limited abilities of the forces that they led. But although much of the growing success of the Red Army reflected its undoubted improvements, its growing superiority was also due to the declining capabilities and resources of the Wehrmacht.

A great deal has been written about the early successes of the German armed forces in the Second World War. In particular, the speed of the advances across Poland in 1939, France and Belgium in 1940, and the western parts of the Soviet Union in 1941 seemed to show a huge gulf between German capabilities and those of Germany's enemies. Undoubtedly, many elements of the German military machine were innovative and changed the nature of warfare. Panzer divisions functioned with greater flexibility and independence than any equivalent formation, and close cooperation between ground forces and air support played a major part in the early German victories. But the early triumphs also hid many underlying weaknesses, which became far more important as the war progressed. At an individual level, German tanks were frequently inferior in terms of firepower and armour to the enemy tanks that they encountered, and their success was often due to better organisation and tactical use, greatly benefiting from the universal presence of radios that allowed commanders to coordinate their tanks with great effect. Although the Luftwaffe provided highly effective air support, many of its bombers were outdated even at the time of the western campaign of 1940. They could function effectively if air superiority had been achieved, but were often highly vulnerable to enemy fighters in other circumstances. Despite the manner in which Goebbels and his propaganda ministry highlighted the efficacy of German forces in 'Blitzkrieg' warfare, the great mobility and striking power of the panzer divisions exposed the relative lack of motorisation of other parts of the German Army. Infantry divisions marched on foot, and even in the relatively short campaigns in Poland, Belgium, and northern France they struggled to keep up with the armoured columns that were streaking ahead; in the vast landscape of the Soviet Union, this became an even greater issue. The infantry units were highly dependent upon horses to tow much of their artillery and other heavy equipment, and these draught animals perished in large numbers in the first months of the war with the Soviet Union. Throughout 1942, this was of little significance with most of the northern and central sectors relatively immobile, but as the war progressed the lack of mobility of German infantry units became far more problematic. Lacking sufficient horses to tow their equipment, the infantry divisions were able to put up tough resistance in the face of Soviet attacks, but if they were driven from their positions they had little option but to abandon their artillery. Artillery was a critical part of the tactics used by the Germans in defensive fighting; consequently, although breaking German defensive lines remained costly and problematic, there was high likelihood of success if the lines were breached. Red Army soldiers and junior officers were repeatedly told that the first kilometre of any advance was the hardest. If the Germans could be driven back from their prepared positions, further advances would become far easier.

German armour had improved qualitatively during the war, as had the tanks of all nations. At an individual level, the German tanks – the later versions of the Pz.IV, and the Panther and Tiger tanks that appeared in 1942 and 1943 – were at least equal and often superior to anything they might encounter on the battlefield. But here too, there were weaknesses. The German tanks were often technically complex and some – in particular, early versions of the Panther tank – were prone to breakdowns. Maintaining such complex vehicles was also problematic. Although only one model of the Tiger tank was deployed in the east at this time, there were many variations and modifications that had been introduced as incremental improvements. In some cases, these were relatively minor, but in other cases the result was incompatibility of engine parts and other components, greatly exacerbating problems of maintenance. The sheer weight of the newer tanks also caused problems, particularly in the occupied parts of the Soviet Union, where roads and bridges were often unable to cope with such heavy vehicles.

Whilst the infantry units of the Wehrmacht were handicapped by their lack of motorisation and reliance on horses, the panzer divisions faced mobility problems for another reason: Germany's longstanding shortage of fuel. The only substantial oilfields accessible by the Germans were in Romania, accounting for over 30 per cent of all Axis oil production, and the Western Powers attempted to deal a crippling blow by striking at this supply of fuel. In August 1943 bombers of the US Army Air Forces (USAAF) flew from Libya to strike at nine oil refineries around the city of Ploieşti in Operation *Tidal Wave*. Some 177 B-24 bombers set off from their airfields near Benghazi, and 162 reached their targets where they encountered strong air defences. A total of 53 US bombers were destroyed, but fuel production in the refineries was substantially reduced. Almost all of the damage inflicted was repaired within weeks, but the vulnerability of Germany's oil supply was amply demonstrated and the refineries would continue to be the targets of further air operations.[9] Synthetic production of fuel from a variety of sources – either coal or oil shale – provided only modest amounts, and the overall consequence was that even as early as 1942, German operations were frequently hindered by fuel shortages. Every major German offensive operation of the war, from the invasion of Poland to the Battle of the Bulge in late 1944, was preceded by a period of careful stockpiling of fuel. Few such stockpiles were present on the Eastern Front in the early summer of 1944, and this would greatly reduce the ability of panzer divisions to function in either a defensive or offensive role.

But as was the case with equipment levels, there were reasons for cautious confidence. The British and American bombing campaigns continued to strike at oil production facilities across the Reich but their overall efficacy was controversial. The RAF later claimed that bombing by the two air forces reduced oil production from wells in Ploieşti and elsewhere by 40 per cent and synthetic oil production by 90 per cent, but these figures are not consistent with the ability of German formations to continue operations – indeed, the Luftwaffe's reported fuel stocks at the beginning of 1944 were greater than they had been 12 months previously.[10] Whilst air attacks caused considerable disruption and might have achieved the reported reductions, these would have been for short periods and the Germans were swiftly able to restore much of their damaged capacity.

German defensive doctrine placed great importance upon counterattacks; this pre-dated the Second World War and relied both on local reserves held by infantry units in the immediate front line and on motorised formations operating to their rear. Soviet attacks were to be resisted strongly, making maximum use of heavy defensive fire from infantry weapons and artillery fire to create barriers that would hinder enemy reinforcements from moving forward in support of the initial assault wave. This was further refined by the deliberate positioning of the leading edge of the defensive line a short distance ahead of the main line of resistance in the expectation that Soviet artillery bombardments would fall largely on these advanced positions, which would then be abandoned early in the battle. The local reserves were expected to deal with Soviet penetrations that broke into the defensive belt, but if the Red Army succeeded in breaking through into the rear zone, panzer divisions and other mobile troops were then expected to restore the situation rapidly. Major counterattacks would then be staged to restore the original front line.

For such doctrine to succeed, several factors had to be in place. Firstly, the defending infantry had to have sufficient firepower and ammunition to be able to mount a sustained defence of the main line of resistance. Secondly, they needed local reserves both to reinforce weakened sectors and for local counterattacks. Thirdly, they needed sufficient artillery (which in turn needed sufficient ammunition) to be able to disrupt Soviet attacks and to block second echelons from moving forward. And fourthly, they required well-supplied motorised forces operating to their rear to eliminate any Soviet forces that broke through the main line of resistance. Such measures had been available, for example, in the prolonged German defence of the Rzhev salient in 1942, but the situation in 1944 was markedly different. Instead of the nine infantry battalions fielded by German infantry divisions in earlier years, most infantry divisions now had only two battalions in each of their three regiments; an additional 'fusilier battalion' was meant to be available as a reserve force. Despite being numerically weaker than the old divisions, these units were expected to hold roughly the same length of front line as before on the basis that they possessed significantly more firepower in terms of machine-guns and infantry support weapons. But this greater firepower was needed purely to offset the improvements in the strength of the enemy, and many divisions had little choice but to place all of their combat elements, including their fusilier battalions, in the front line. Ad hoc reserves were then improvised by extracting a couple of rifle companies from these battalions, but they were no substitute for a cohesive group that had trained together and was able to function as a coherent whole.

At almost every level, the Germans continued to enjoy one significant advantage over their Soviet opponents. The quality of the officers of the Wehrmacht remained high, despite the loss of so many men at every level. In most – though crucially, not all – cases, the men who commanded German army groups, armies, corps, divisions, and lower formations were well-trained and experienced soldiers, and they were supported by a staff officer system that was of the highest quality. The ability of these men to improvise in the face of difficulty and to delegate decision-making effectively to their very able subordinates played a major part in the manner in which German units put up effective resistance even when greatly outnumbered. By contrast, the Red Army in 1941 was greatly handicapped by an almost comprehensive lack of initiative at every level. Fearful of the continuing purges and aware that the political commissars in the Red Army were monitoring and often reporting their every move, Soviet officers played safe by adhering to their orders even when implementation of those orders was clearly impossible –

any deviation from these orders might be interpreted as sabotage, with fatal consequences. As the war progressed, the restrictive role of commissars was greatly reduced and a new wartime generation of Soviet officers came to the fore, men who had learned through bitter experience the need to improvise on rapidly evolving battlefields, and their superiors learned – in some cases rather more than in others – to permit these men to use their initiative as required. By contrast, the Wehrmacht seemed to be developing in the opposite direction. After the defeat of the German Army Group Centre outside Moscow in late 1941 and particularly during the Soviet counteroffensive that followed, Hitler increasingly interfered in the decision-making of German units. It was impossible for senior commanders to move units without securing permission from *Oberkommando des Heeres* ('Army High Command' or *OKH*), effectively from Hitler personally. This meant that these field commanders had to impose increasing rigidity on those below them, greatly reducing the flexibility that had been such a feature of Wehrmacht operations in the earlier campaigns of the war. During the retreat of Army Group North from the outskirts of Leningrad in the first weeks of 1944, there were occasions when Hitler's attention was focused upon the operations of the Western Powers at Anzio in Italy, resulting in critical delays in giving approval for withdrawals by Army Group North; in the summer of 1944, with Germany's opponents planning major operations in the east and west that would coincide, there was potential for both German military resources and Hitler's decision-making to be overwhelmed by too many simultaneous pressures.

It is arguable – indeed, highly likely – that Germany was doomed to defeat even before the first soldiers came ashore in Normandy, and certainly before the onset of the Soviet summer offensive in the east. The huge mismatch between the resources of Germany and those available to Germany's enemies effectively ensured the outcome of the war, even before taking into account the world-changing nature of the Manhattan Project and the development of the atomic bomb. The degree to which senior German military figures were aware of this is in some respects difficult to assess. In 1942, there occurred an incident that had long-lasting consequences on how information was shared within the German Army. A small plane carrying a staff officer from one of Army Group South's panzer divisions was shot down and crashed in Soviet-held territory; detailed plans for the forthcoming offensive to Stalingrad and the Caucasus region were recovered by the Soviets, but Stalin interpreted them as a deliberate attempt to mislead the Red Army – like many others in the upper echelons of the Soviet leadership, he remained convinced that the Germans would attack once more in the central sector in an attempt to reach Moscow. But if Stalin dismissed this intelligence windfall, Hitler had far stronger views. Such potentially disastrous leaks of information were to be avoided at all costs, and he ordered that units were to avoid sharing information with their neighbouring formations – both command structures and information distribution became increasingly vertical, with few official lateral channels. Inevitably, many field commanders made informal arrangements with their neighbours, but nonetheless it is likely that division commanders had limited knowledge of the overall situation beyond their immediate neighbourhood; other divisions within the same corps might be taking advantage of these informal links, but there was little opportunity for wider information sharing. Corps commanders might have had a broad idea of the situation of their parent army, but would have had little information – at least through official channels – of what was happening across the entire army group and even less idea of developments in other army groups. Only army and army group commanders would have attended occasional conferences where such information might be shared. Nonetheless, the unending series of defeats suffered by the Wehrmacht across Ukraine and the slow, bloody retreats in the central and northern sectors, together with clearly inadequate replacements and supplies, must have shown the highly professional officers of the Wehrmacht that Germany was approaching the end of its strength, even before the Western Powers launched their invasion of France. Many officers who wrote their memoirs after the war, such as Erich von Manstein, dismissed as commander of Army Group South immediately before the spring thaw of 1944, described how they repeatedly demanded substantial reinforcements as the price for fulfilling Hitler's instructions to hold firm against Soviet attacks; most of those at high levels must have been aware that such reinforcements were simply not available.

In such circumstances, many must have concluded that Hitler's Führer Directive 51 was unachievable. Their response to this realisation varied. For the great majority of German officers, the stumbling block was the oath of loyalty that they had given to Hitler. In 1935, this replaced the oath given by the old German Army first to the Kaiser and then to the constitution of the Weimar Republic or to the German people:

> I swear to God this holy oath that I shall render unconditional obedience to the leadership of the Führer of the German Reich and people, Adolf Hitler, supreme commander of the Wehrmacht, and that as a brave soldier I shall at all times be prepared to give my life for this oath.[11]

It is difficult to be certain how many officers truly felt that they couldn't break this oath, and how many used the oath in later years to justify their unwillingness to take the hugely risky step of attempting to resist the regime. Even officers in the SS expressed doubts about the limitless nature of loyalty to higher commands. Paul Hausser, who rose to the rank of Oberstgruppenführer, wrote after the war to justify his direct refusal to obey Hitler's order not to retreat from Kharkov in February 1943:

> There will always be different opinions when assessing a situation. In such cases, orders are decisive. Without obedience there can be no armed forces.
>
> If a subordinate thinks an order is wrong, he must report his opinion, justifying it and requesting an alteration. If the higher authority adheres to its decision, the subordinate must obey. If he believes that he cannot do so, he takes personal responsibility and must be prepared to answer for it. Whilst disobedience may be reported as an act of wilfulness, this overlooks the duty of a commander of men: 'responsibility for subordinate troops'!
>
> The threatened destruction of the troops must awaken the conscience of the commander! Thus it was at Kharkov!
>
> A decision to disobey is not taken lightly by a responsible man, particularly against a thrice-reiterated order of the highest command. It helped that all intermediate superiors agreed inwardly. Besides, there was the menacing example of Stalingrad, which had concluded catastrophically two weeks earlier.
>
> But the intermediate superiors cannot be assessed by the same measure; the decision to disobey was *not* required of them. Only the immediate commander, who experienced the combat of the troops every day and also heard from them, was in that situation.
>
> Correct assessment requires training, personal experience, and also probably a degree of courage.[12]

If such disobedience could be justified in the case of a battle for a single city, the same logic applied at higher levels. Senior officers who knew that there was no longer any prospect of victory had responsibility to their 'subordinate troops' to avoid futile bloodshed, and given the refusal of the enemies of Germany to consider a negotiated peace with Hitler, the only logical conclusion was that he had to be removed from power. Even if the majority of officers were unwilling to take any action, some at least were beginning to move against Hitler. Their plans would come to fruition in the midst of the huge battles that were about to commence both in the east and in the west.

*   *   *

As the landscape of the Eastern Front turned to mud in the spring of 1944, Stalin and other senior figures in *Stavka* (the Soviet military high command) began to consider the best place to launch their summer offensive. Numerous options were available, with varying degrees of risk and reward. The key was to select the option that stood the greatest chance of inflicting a potentially war-ending defeat upon the Wehrmacht, and that would leave the Red Army closer to controlling the regions where Stalin intended to rewrite the map of Europe.

In 1943, the most spectacular gains of the Red Army had been in the south. After the Germans abandoned the Battle of Kursk, Operation *Polkovodets Rumyantsev* saw Soviet troops attack towards Belgorod, Akhtyrka, and Kharkov, and in heavy fighting – the Red Army suffered some of its highest daily casualty rates during the attack – the Germans were driven back from all three cities. Thereafter, fighting continued across central Ukraine and over the Dnepr River, and in the first weeks of 1944 the entire German position in the south came close to collapse. Much of the German Eighth Army was encircled in the Battle of Cherkassy, and although most of the trapped troops managed to escape, they lost all their heavy equipment; Sixth Army, reformed after the destruction of the original Sixth Army in Stalingrad, was effectively routed as it attempted to pull back to the Southern Bug and Dniester, and its troops escaped once more only at the cost of losing most of their heavy weapons; and First Panzer Army was briefly cut off before pulling back to the west. The final attempts to inflict further losses on the Germans before they could catch their breath failed in the fighting around Iaşi in April 1944, leaving the Wehrmacht defending a line that ran along much of the lower Dniester before turning west past Iaşi. A resumption of offensives in this sector was a clear option for a summer campaign, with the prospect of a drive south through Iaşi through the 'Focşani Gap' – the relatively open ground between the eastern edge of the Carpathian Mountains and the Black Sea – into Romania. Such an attack would almost certainly knock Romania out of the war and would end German access to the oilfields around Ploieşti.

Whilst this option had attractions, it also suffered from several disadvantages. The terrain of the Focşani Gap looked temptingly flat and open, but was crossed by numerous irrigation channels. A defending force could exploit these to create large swampy areas, channelling a Soviet attack into areas where it could be defeated. But perhaps the most significant drawback was the presence of a major supply route from the west that ran through the Iaşi region. The Germans regarded this as essential for supplying their forces along the lower Dniester, and if the Red Army were to launch a strike towards the Focşani Gap, this supply route would provide the Germans with an excellent means of concentrating forces on the western flank of the Soviet advance. There was therefore a danger that the Germans would once more use their prowess at mobile operations to overturn any Soviet gains; it was therefore better to use this axis as one for an offensive later in the year after German resources had been further depleted, making such a counterattack almost impossible.

A second option was to mount a major operation from the most westerly point reached by the Red Army, the region immediately to the east of the city now known as Lviv; at the time, the Germans had restored its old Austro-Hungarian name of Lemberg, whilst it was known to the Soviet Union as Lvov. From here, an attack could be launched towards the northwest, aimed first at Warsaw and then to the Baltic coast beyond. In many respects, this offered the highest potential reward. The German Army Group Centre and Army Group North would be cut off from Germany and the potentially contentious parts of Poland would fall under Soviet control long before the war was over. But just as it offered the greatest rewards, this proposal also carried the greatest risks. The initial advance would be through hilly country until it reached the relatively open area to the south of Lublin, and it was likely that the Germans would be able to conduct prolonged defensive actions in this area. As a result, the Soviet armies in the assault were likely to be significantly degraded by the time they reached open ground. Just as the major road and rail links to the west of Iaşi could be used by the Wehrmacht to concentrate forces against a thrust towards the Focşani Gap, the orientation of railways across Silesia and southern Poland would facilitate any German attempts to prepare and conduct a counteroffensive into the western flank of the Soviet advance. Moreover, the sheer number of German units that would be threatened with isolation meant that it would be highly likely that any such German counteroffensive would be supported by an attack from the east using the forces that faced encirclement.

In the north, the German retreat from Leningrad ended along the line of the Narva River and the city of Narva. Further south of Lakes Peipus and Pskov, the Wehrmacht continued to hold a small area of Russian territory to the east of the old Estonian–Latvian frontier. A new offensive here would have to be divided onto two axes – one to the north of the lakes, through the tough German positions between Narva and the coast of the Gulf of Finland, and one to the south of the lakes. The terrain was unfavourable for such a major attack. The land corridor to the north of the lakes is about 34 miles wide, but in 1944 at least half of this consisted of swamps and woodland. Any offensive would therefore be forced into a far narrower channel, largely between Narva and the coast – a frontage of just seven miles at its narrowest point. At the time when such considerations were being discussed, the Germans were constructing new fortified positions in the Sinimäed Hills, immediately to the west of the Narva line;

although the Red Army was unaware of these preparations, the usefulness of these hills as defensive positions was clearly recognised. An attack from the south of Lake Pskov roughly along the old Estonian–Latvian frontier towards the west offered the potential to cut off the German Eighteenth Army to the north if the attacking forces could reach the Baltic coast. This would require an advance of about 140 miles through a region with multiple rivers, swamps, and forests. The southern flank of any such advance would be badly exposed to German counterattacks, and the relatively modest potential gain seemed to be significantly outweighed by the risks.

These preliminary assessments of potential summer operations then considered the central sector. The battles that followed the fighting around the Kursk salient had left the Germans occupying a position that projected to the east. At the northern end of this substantial bulge was the city of Vitebsk; from here, the front line ran south immediately to the east of Orsha and Mogilev. All three cities were part of the series of fortresses recently announced by Hitler. From Mogilev, the front line turned to the west, running through the expanse of the Polesie or Pripet Marshes. This entire sector represented a tempting target for the Red Army, not least because from their positions within this bulge, German forces could conceivably threaten the flanks of any Soviet attacks to the north or south. The costly fighting of *Kutuzov* and the subsequent advance to and beyond Smolensk had demonstrated the continuing ability of the Wehrmacht to fight very effectively in defence in this region, inflicting major losses on the Red Army, but as was the case with every major Soviet operation there were extensive attempts to analyse the manner in which those operations had unfolded. Colonel General Sergei Matveyevich Shtemenko was head of the Operations Directorate of the Soviet general staff and therefore heavily involved both in these retrospective analyses and planning for the operation of summer 1944. He later described the conclusions of discussions in his directorate:

> The general staff believed that the main cause of our failures north of the Polesie was not so much the strength of the enemy positions as the bad mistakes committed by certain commanders and staffs in organising, supplying and conducting the offensive. This could and should be avoided ...
>
> Analysis and re-analysis of the strategic situation gave us the growing conviction that success in the summer campaign of 1944 was to be sought in Belarus and western Ukraine. A major victory in this area would bring Soviet troops out on the vital frontiers of the Third Reich by the shortest route possible. At the same time more favourable conditions would be created for hitting the enemy hard on all other sectors.[13]

The attractions of an assault in the centre were numerous. Bounded on the north by the Dvina River and the south by the Dnepr, the region often known as the 'Smolensk Gate' – a corridor of land about 45 miles wide to the west of Smolensk – has historically been regarded as the optimum route for military operations in both easterly and westerly directions. Although much of the land is low-lying with numerous rivers, widespread swamps, and huge forests, it also has several areas of higher ground and crucially the main road and rail corridor running from Moscow through Smolensk and on towards Minsk and Warsaw. If the Red Army attacked in this area, the southern flank of any advance would be relatively well protected by the swamps of the Polesie region. Moreover, with the German line forming an east-facing bulge, the natural course of any offensive would result in Soviet forces operating on converging axes of advance. The relatively good road and rail link to the west could of course be used by the Germans to bring forward reinforcements, but unlike the other options that were considered for a summer offensive, any such reinforcements would find themselves meeting the advancing Red Army head-on rather than appearing on an exposed flank.

Other factors also influenced the decision to attack in the central region. Success here would facilitate follow-on operations to the north and south, and as a consequence there was every likelihood of the western frontiers of the Soviet Union being firmly in Stalin's hands even if an invasion of France by the Western Powers resulted in a precipitate collapse of Germany. But Stalin's thoughts were moving beyond the frontier and he was increasingly considering the future of all of Eastern Europe. In particular, four countries took a high priority in his thinking: the Baltic States and Poland.

Of the three Baltic States, only Lithuania had a history of independence prior to the First World War. All three had been incorporated into the Russian Empire but repeated and often heavy-handed attempts at 'Russification' failed to suppress growing nationalist movements in the 19th century. The Treaty of Brest-Litovsk in 1918 saw Bolshevik Russia cede control of the Baltic region, which was meant to come under German hegemony, but the subsequent collapse of Germany resulted in all three states declaring independence. With help from the Western Powers and from elements of the German *Freikorps* – units of the German Army that were retained as 'volunteers' to fight Bolshevism and other perceived enemies both within and outside Germany – all three states were able to beat off attempts by Soviet Russia to restore the old eastern frontiers of the Russian Empire. In the years that followed, the three states trod an often difficult path between their powerful neighbours, and the Molotov–Ribbentrop Pact ultimately resulted in all three becoming part of the Soviet sphere of influence. They were forced to accept Soviet troops on their soil in 1939 and under constant pressure their governments were dismissed and new elections held. Some pro-Soviet groups triumphantly reported that turnout in some areas exceeded 100 per cent; with widespread electoral fraud and intimidation, Communist candidates were elected in every constituency and all three new governments immediately applied for membership of the Soviet Union. Many in the west refused to recognise the annexation of the three states, but were in no position to do anything more than register their protests.

The issue of Poland was somewhat different. Poland had a long history as an independent nation, often as a Commonwealth that included Lithuania, but this independence came to an end with the First Partition of Poland in 1772, followed by a Second Partition in 1790 and a Third Partition in 1795. The southern parts of modern Poland (and parts of what is now western Ukraine) became the Austro-Hungarian territory of Galicia; the Prussians gained control of much of western Poland; and Russia secured the eastern parts of the country, including Warsaw. Attempts to suppress nationalist movements in Poland proved to be even less successful than in the Baltic States. As the First World War raged across Europe, pressure for the restoration of an independent Poland grew steadily, not least because of the large Polish émigré community in France – the French government saw a major advantage in the restoration of a strong, independent Poland to the east of Germany to act as a counterweight and to inhibit any future German attempts to attack France, and when the United States entered the war, Polish independence was one of the Fourteen Points listed by President Woodrow Wilson in early 1918 as conditions for peace.

For Bolshevik Russia, the humiliating terms of the Treaty of Brest-Litovsk were accepted purely because the Russian Army was in no state to continue hostilities at a time when there was a growing threat of counter-revolution and civil war. Once these dangers had diminished, the new Soviet state attempted to reverse the losses of the treaty. Ukraine, which had also been ceded, was rapidly reabsorbed; although there were several nationalist movements, there was little unity of purpose and much of the region saw heavy fighting between pro-Bolshevik forces and the White Russian armies attempting to overthrow Bolshevik rule. Kiev (now Kyiv) changed hands no fewer than five times in 1919 and all that was left of the dreams of independence were a few suppressed nationalist movements, often at loggerheads with each other as much as with Soviet rule.

Poland escaped such a fate, not least because of the dynamic and powerful leadership of Jósef Piłsudski and the backing of Poland by the Entente Powers.

The newly established Polish Army included large numbers of men who had served in the armies of the three powers that had occupied Poland before the war – Germany, Russia, and Austria-Hungary – and were well armed with a mixture of weapons obtained from retreating German units and supplied by the west, predominantly the French. Piłsudski's vision of a future state included the incorporation of Lithuania and he took several steps to try to achieve this, whilst also having to fend off attacks from the Red Army in the east. The crushing defeat inflicted upon the Red Army at the Battle of Warsaw in 1920 was followed by a triumphant advance towards the east, resulting in the incorporation of considerable territory into Poland. The region had a mixed population of Poles, Belarusians, Russians, Ukrainians, and Jews – no single group formed a majority, making it possible for different states to claim ownership. The Red Army entered this area in late 1939 when the bulk of the Polish Army was fighting desperately against the German invasion from the west and north, announcing that Moscow was sending troops to the region in order to protect civilians from the disorder caused by the war and the flight of the Polish government from Warsaw; at the time, the Polish government was still in the country, and the reality was that this occupation was part of the secret protocol agreed with Germany under the terms of the Molotov–Ribbentrop Pact.

As was the case with the Baltic States, many in the west were unwilling to accept Soviet control of what had been eastern Poland and much of the ongoing differences of opinion between Stalin and the British in particular hinged on the meaning of restoring the pre-war frontiers. For Moscow, this meant the frontier as it had existed in 1941, with all three Baltic States incorporated into the Soviet Union together with the eastern parts of Poland and Bessarabia to the south. The Polish government-in-exile in London in particular strongly objected to this, demanding the restoration of the 1939 frontiers of Poland. Bowing to the need to appease Stalin, Churchill had already conceded this point in Tehran at the end of 1943, but Stalin remained concerned that the Western Powers might attempt to raise the issue once more. To complicate matters still further, remnants of the Polish Army and resistance groups had merged in 1942 to create the *Armia Krajowa* ('Home Army'), a highly effective resistance group that extended across almost all of Poland. Stalin knew that this group was loyal to the Polish government-in-exile and wanted to create an independent Polish state closely tied to the west. Stalin had no intention of permitting such a situation to arise: he wanted to ensure that Poland, like all the other nations on the western borders of the Soviet Union, was ruled by a government that was effectively under Soviet control. In order to eliminate any possibility of his intentions being blocked, Stalin was determined to place the region under Soviet control as quickly as possible.

There was also the question of Belarus, which would effectively be the battlefield in the coming offensive. As was the case in many parts of the Russian Empire, Belarusian nationalism began to rise towards the end of the 19th century, but was largely confined to the urban intelligentsia who formed only a small fraction of the population. As hostilities with Germany came to an end in 1918 many within Belarus wanted to create an independent republic while others proposed continuing union with Russia as a more pragmatic option. A heavy-handed attempt by Bolshevik supporters to force the issue in a congress to decide the future of Belarus backfired with the declaration of the Belarusian Democratic Republic, but the new state failed to secure any international recognition and was too weak to defend itself; it was rapidly reincorporated into the new Soviet state, though the consequences of the Polish–Soviet War left significant parts of Belarus – and large numbers of Belarusians – under Polish control. In the years between the wars, Belarusian nationalists on either side of the Polish–Soviet frontier faced suspicion and repression, but there was little serious consideration of creating an independent Belarusian state. Nonetheless, it was clearly in the interests of the Soviet Union to ensure that its forces were in position as rapidly as possible to prevent any resurgence of nationalism.

From the very outset, the invasion of the Soviet Union had been explicitly about seizing land for German settlement. The future of the conquered people was as servants to the *Herrenvolk* who would move into the area, and in order to create an agricultural surplus that could be exported to Germany and other parts of Europe, it was expected and required from the outset that millions of Soviet citizens – mainly but not exclusively the urban populations – would perish.[14] Whilst a few within German circles saw benefits in creating a series of client states from the conquered areas of the Soviet Union, this was anathema to Hitler. In many respects, the failure of Hitler to recognise the potential of harnessing anti-Soviet resentment in the western parts of the Soviet Union represents the greatest missed opportunity for Germany to have won the war.

Stalin and his associates therefore made a decision to attack the German Army Group Centre. Whilst the operation had risks, these were perceived to be fewer than the risks of the other options available to the Red Army, and success in an offensive across Belarus would permit secondary operations to the north and south that would achieve almost all of the potential benefits of those other options. And the political benefits of an attack that brought the Red Army into

Poland and the Baltic region were not to be underestimated. For the commanders in the field, the decision would result in mixed feelings. The Soviet forces in the central sector had few major victories to match those achieved by their comrades to the south at Stalingrad and Kursk and with the sweeping advance into western Ukraine, or in the north where after several bloody failures the German siege ring around Leningrad was first pierced and then thrown back in disarray into Estonia. By making the central sector the focus of the summer campaign of 1944, *Stavka* offered the field armies of the region a chance to wipe away the memories of the disastrous failures around the Rzhev salient and the costly, grinding advance of *Kutuzov* and the fighting around Smolensk. But this also raised doubts in the minds of many. There was a risk in assigning such an important operation to a sector that had performed poorly in the past.

The German forces in Belarus were under the overall control of Army Group Centre. Its commander was the 58-year-old Generalfeldmarschall Ernst Busch, who had led Sixteenth Army in its advance into the Soviet Union as part of Army Group North. He inherited command of the army group when the previous commander, Generalfeldmarschall Günther von Kluge, was injured in a car crash in late October 1943. In his earlier commands Busch had performed competently but without demonstrating any spectacular flair. Like many senior officers, he was initially sceptical about the use of panzer divisions, preferring to deploy tanks within infantry divisions, but he was a rapid convert when he experienced their efficacy on the battlefield. A factor that was probably important in his selection as Kluge's replacement was that he showed no inclination to disobey Hitler's orders, including the infamous instructions regarding the conduct of the war against the Soviet Union. Oberst Peter von der Groeben, one of his staff officers, later wrote:

> I was present at some of the discussions in which he attempted to dissuade Hitler from a particular course of action. If he failed, he considered himself committed to carrying out the decision. He often said to me, 'Groeben, I have learnt to obey.' Then against his better judgement he would carry out the order.[15]

Despite his stolid performance, Busch was in many respects a reasonable choice for the post. Hitler expected him to conduct a tough and determined defence against any Soviet attacks, much as he had done with Sixteenth Army in the north along the long front line on either side of Lake Ilmen. Spectacular manoeuvres were no longer in favour and rigid obedience was at a priority.

Busch controlled four German armies. In the north was Third Panzer Army in and on either side of Vitebsk, commanded by Generaloberst Georg-Hans

Reinhardt, an experienced and capable panzer commander who had led 4th Panzer Division in the invasion of Poland in 1939 and XLI Panzer Corps in the invasion of the Soviet Union in 1941. He was highly regarded by his contemporaries, but despite his undoubted operational talents he showed little inclination to challenge Hitler's decision-making, perhaps a factor in his continuing prominence. Third Panzer Army consisted of three corps with nine infantry divisions in the front line and two in reserve (one was a security division with limited combat power), but although it had started the war with the Soviet Union as Third Panzer Group with a large complement of panzer divisions, those had departed long ago and its armour consisted of fewer than 100 assault guns.

To the south of Third Panzer Army, holding the front line from Orsha to a point south of Mogilev, was Fourth Army. It had been under the command of Generaloberst Gotthard Heinrici since the beginning of 1944, but in early June he had to return to Germany for medical treatment. His replacement was General Kurt von Tippelskirch, the latest in a series of senior Prussian and

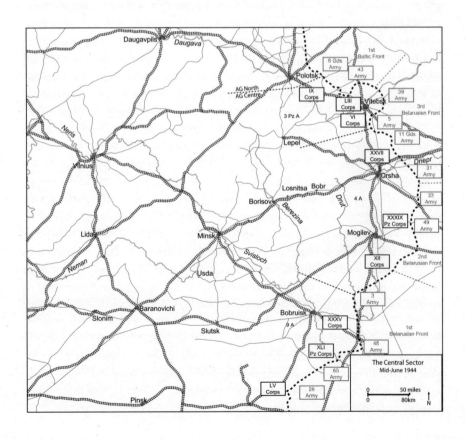

German officers from the same family. After serving in the Reichswehr between the wars he was appointed to senior staff posts in Berlin before returning to the front line as commander of 30th Infantry Division in the invasion of the Soviet Union. Subsequently he commanded XII Corps and was recognised for his determined defence in the fighting of late 1943. In his new post as commander of Fourth Army he had control of XXXIX Panzer Corps and two other corps, comprising between them nine divisions in the front line including 18th Panzergrenadier Division. In addition, Tippelskirch had a security division in reserve.

Continuing the front line into the region of the marshland of the Polesie region was Ninth Army. Its commander was General Hans Jordan who had led his troops – first 49th Infantry Regiment, then 7th Infantry Division – to the outskirts of Moscow in late 1941. He then commanded VI Corps before taking control of Ninth Army in May 1944. His forces on paper at least were powerful formations. XXXV Corps had five infantry divisions in the front line. In addition, it had 707th Infantry Division deployed in the city of Bobruisk; raised in 1941, this formation originally had only two regiments and numbered fewer than 5,000 men. Lacking its full artillery complement and with no anti-tank weaponry, it was of little use in the front line and after receiving further drafts of soldiers mainly raised in Belgium it was deployed in rear area roles under the command of Gustav Freiherr von Mauchenheim, who used his old family name of Bechtolsheim. A hard-line anti-Semite, Bechtolsheim issued unequivocal orders to his men: 'Wherever Jewish groups, either large or small, are encountered in the countryside they should either be killed or gathered together in the ghettos of a few large cities.'[16]

By the end of 1941, the division's personnel had been involved in the killing of over 10,000 Jews. The following year it took part in major anti-partisan operations in 1942, earning a reputation for brutality; in one operation, it killed almost 4,400 people but in the process recovered only 47 weapons, indicating that almost all of those slaughtered were merely civilians who happened to be in its path. After receiving further reinforcements it saw limited front-line service before being assigned to the garrison of Bobruisk. By this stage Bechtolsheim had moved on, taking up an administrative role in the Rhineland. He escaped attention after the war until 1961 when he was implicated by a statement given by the commander of a police battalion that had served alongside 707th Infantry Division and had been involved in the mass murder of Jews. Bechtolsheim denied that he and his division had been involved in the killings and despite plentiful evidence to the contrary, the examining magistrate chose to believe him and no charges were ever brought against him.

In addition to these units, XXXV Corps was bolstered by a brigade of assault guns. Its southern neighbour was XLI Panzer Corps with three further infantry divisions; finally on the southern flank was LV Corps and another two infantry divisions. Ninth Army would need these units: the positions it held were exposed and vulnerable. The last army of Busch's army group, Second Army, continued the front line beyond the Polesie region; it would play little part in the first phase of the coming Soviet assault.

On the Soviet side of the front line, the troops facing Army Group Centre were organised into a series of Fronts. In the north was 1st Baltic Front, opposite the German defences in and around Vitebsk. The commander was General Ivan Christoforovich Bagramian, of Armenian origin. 'Vanya' Bagramian was popular with his contemporaries, and was a senior instructor in the Soviet general staff academy in the late 1930s; but he seemed to be sidelined, partly because he flirted with involvement with Armenian nationalist groups in the early 1930s, until he wrote a paper on offensive military operations using modern technology. This caught the eye of senior figures and he became a rapidly rising staff officer. He was caught up in the Red Army's defeat in western Ukraine in 1941 and was fortunate to escape encirclement in the disaster that befell Soviet forces around Kiev. He was under a considerable cloud following this defeat but acquitted himself well in the fighting near Rostov and then outside Moscow. As a consequence he was appointed as chief of staff of Southwest Front where he was involved in the failed Soviet offensive towards Kharkov.

Bagramian's involvement in the disasters at Kiev in 1941 and Kharkov in 1942 was unfortunate in that both were caused by close associates of Stalin. Marshal Semen Mikhailovich Budennyi had commanded Bolshevik cavalry formations during the Russian Civil War and the conflict with Poland immediately after, and his reputation was built largely on fighting against White Russian Cossacks in the Don valley in late 1919. He was one of many military figures of the era who struggled to adapt to the advent of mechanisation. He repeatedly argued against the expansion of the Soviet Union's armoured forces on the grounds that the money could be better spent on training soldiers as cavalrymen, particularly as more recruits knew how to ride than to drive. He played a leading part in the purges of the Red Army, being one of the officers who presided over the trial of Marshal Mikhail Nikolayevich Tukhashevsky, but it seems that there were attempts by Lavrenty Beriya – head of the *NKVD** – to have Budennyi arrested for involvement in conspiracies, real or imagined, against the government.

---

* *Narodny Komissariat Vnutrennikh Del* or 'People's Commissariat for Internal Affairs', the Soviet Union's internal security force and forerunner of the KGB.

But Stalin was a close personal friend of Budennyi and his intervention ensured that Budennyi was not detained. Budennyi found himself in command of two Soviet Fronts that faced encirclement in Kiev in 1941 and the combination of Stalin's reluctance to authorise a timely retreat and constant interference and micro-management and Budennyi's own errors resulted in the loss of perhaps 1.5 million Red Army personnel. In 1942, Marshal Semen Konstantinovich Timoshenko, another cavalryman of the Civil War era, had inherited the remnants of Budennyi's forces and after receiving substantial reinforcements launched an offensive with the intention of recapturing Kharkov. Unfortunately for the Red Army, this coincided with German preparations for the summer offensive towards the Don and Volga and the Wehrmacht was well positioned to launch flanking attacks that led to the destruction of most of Timoshenko's forces. In both cases, Stalin was heavily critical of his two old cronies, but nonetheless Bagramian was caught up in the general fallout.

After the Soviet defeat outside Kharkov in 1942, Bagramian was given a last chance as chief of staff of Twenty-Eighth Army and once more he faced criticism as the weak army was rapidly overwhelmed by the Germans in their offensive towards the Don River. On this occasion, he was saved by the intervention of Georgy Konstantinovich Zhukov, deputy commander of the Red Army, who had taken a personal interest in Bagramian's career; he requested the transfer of Bagramian to Western Front. At the end of the year he took command of Sixteenth Army and its success in the winter fighting resulted in it being renamed Eleventh Guards Army. In November 1943, Bagramian became commander of 1st Baltic Front, leading it in several assaults that slowly edged closer to Vitebsk; although the city remained in German hands, the result of the fighting was that the Germans in the city were in an exposed salient. For the summer offensive, Bagramian would have several armies at his disposal. Sixth Guards Army had 11 rifle divisions; Forty-Third Army had eight rifle divisions; and Fourth Shock Army had four rifle divisions. In addition, 1st Baltic Front had an exploitation force consisting of I Tank Corps.

To Bagramian's south was 3rd Belarusian Front under the command of Colonel General Ivan Danilovich Cherniakhovsky. He started the war as commander of a tank division and rapidly rose to command of Sixtieth Army, which he led in a rapid advance from Voronezh to Kursk in early 1943. An aggressive and energetic officer, he became commander of Western Front – renamed 3rd Belarusian Front a few days later – in April 1944 at the age of just 37. He seems to have been genuinely popular with both his contemporaries and his subordinates, despite consistently demanding the highest possible performance from his men. Many soldiers who served under his command later recalled with fondness his unexpected visits to the front line; the first inkling they had of his arrival was his surprisingly deep, sonorous voice as he chatted and joked with the men before questioning them closely on their positions and the local situation. Aleksandr Petrovich Pokrovsky, who was his chief of staff at 3rd Belarusian Front, later said:

> He spent a lot of time in the front line with the troops, he was constantly with them. He was a self-possessed man and despite his strong-willed character he didn't show this in rudeness or harshness. He knew how to make demands, how to be firm, but he didn't swear, he didn't rage at people, and he didn't humiliate them.[17]

In the coming offensive his troops consisted of Thirty-Ninth Army with five rifle divisions, Fifth Army with eight rifle divisions, Eleventh Guards Army with nine rifle divisions, and Thirty-First Army with five rifle divisions. The exploitation forces of the Front were made up of the powerful Fifth Guards Tank Army, with a tank corps, a mechanised corps, and a cavalry corps.

The next Red Army command was 2nd Belarusian Front, led by the imposing figure of Colonel General Georgy Fedorovich Zakharov. As chief of staff of first Southeast Front and then Stalingrad Front and then as deputy commander of Stalingrad Front, the bullet-headed, thickset Zakharov was heavily involved in the defence of the city of Stalingrad, followed by the great Soviet counteroffensive of late 1942. The following year he led Second Guards Army in its successful attacks on German defensive positions in eastern Ukraine and into Crimea before taking up command of 2nd Belarusian Front. He was recognised by his contemporaries as an effective commander, but was also known for his fiery temper. His Front consisted of Thirty-Third Army with three rifle divisions, Forty-Ninth Army with 11 rifle divisions, and Fiftieth Army with eight rifle divisions. In addition, an exploitation force of a rifle division, two tank brigades, and an anti-tank brigade was available for exploitation.

The final major formation facing Army Group Centre was 1st Belarusian Front. Its commander was General Konstantin Konstantinovich Rokossovsky, a Polish Russian who had held several commands as a cavalryman before he was arrested in August 1937 during Stalin's purges of the Red Army. His arrest was on the basis of an incriminating statement given by another officer who had been arrested and interrogated under severe physical duress; such a development was a frequent occurrence, with people enduring appalling mistreatment simply giving their persecutors a name in the hope that it would bring an end to their torment. In many – perhaps most – cases, the named individual was completely innocent, but Stalin and those around him seized upon the proliferation of denunciations as evidence of just how widespread conspiracies were, and the result was that the purges spread ever wider through the army and Soviet society. Despite several beatings which cost him his teeth, Rokossovsky refused to admit involvement in any of the imagined conspiracies or to implicate anyone else. He remained imprisoned until March 1940 when he was suddenly released, though without being exonerated. It is striking that his memoirs commence shortly after his release, with a summons to a meeting with Timoshenko 'after a holiday with my family in Sochi on the Black Sea coast'.[18] The holiday was in reality an opportunity for him to recover from the ordeal of his imprisonment.

At the start of the war with Germany Rokossovsky was commander of IX Mechanised Corps and then of Sixteenth Army; he inflicted a critical counterattack on the Germans near Smolensk in the late summer of 1941 and although the outcome was another defeat for the Red Army, resulting in the destruction of much of his command, the losses inflicted upon the Germans and the ensuing delay in further German operations were to prove critical factors in the outcome of the Battle of Moscow. After leading his army during the winter fighting he took command of several Fronts, and was involved in the encirclement of the German Sixth Army in Stalingrad and later in the Battle of Kursk. Stalin continued to tell him, allegedly in jest, that the charges brought against him that had led to his arrest in 1937 had not formally been dismissed; Rokossovsky, who wore a set of stainless steel dentures as a deliberately visible mark of his beating during his period of detention, needed little reminding.

For the summer offensive of 1944, Rokossovsky's Front had substantial forces available. Third Army had 13 rifle divisions and a tank corps, and substantial numbers of independent assault gun brigades and motorised infantry units. Forty-Eighth Army fielded nine rifle divisions, Sixty-Fifth Army had a further eight rifle divisions and a tank corps, and Twenty-Eighth Army had nine rifle divisions.

The stark numbers of divisions are not the full story of the resources available to the Red Army. For much of the war, German units had been equivalent in fighting power to Soviet units of a higher level: a German field army was roughly as powerful as a Red Army Front; a German corps could deal with a Soviet field army; a German division was as powerful as a Soviet corps; and a German regiment was as strong as a Soviet division. By the summer of 1944, despite the increased firepower of German divisions this was no longer the case. A German division could still face a Soviet division with every confidence of success, but the mismatch was far less than had been the case in the past. Additionally, Soviet rifle divisions now had integral tank formations; by contrast, German infantry divisions relied largely on armoured units being assigned to them from assault gun brigades or independent panzer regiments. The commanders of these armoured formations often resented the manner in which their subunits were parcelled out to different divisions; from the point of view of the infantry, this support was felt to be essential if they were to stand firm in the face of enemy forces that increasingly contained tanks, but the German armoured unit commanders felt that their training and doctrine required their vehicles to be used in a concentrated manner. Given the huge demands placed upon German resources, it was impossible to satisfy both infantry units and armoured units, and as has been described, the armoured assets available to Army Group Centre were very limited.

For the Red Army, there was an additional asset that could be used in the coming summer offensive. This gave Soviet commanders further reason to believe that an offensive in this sector would have better prospects than elsewhere along the Eastern Front: the partisan movement in Belarus was far stronger than in other regions, and this would be exploited to the full.

CHAPTER 2

THE FRONT BEHIND THE FRONT: PARTISANS IN BELARUS

Few things could demonstrate the solidarity of the Soviet people in their struggle against the Fascist invaders more clearly than their determination to oppose the Germans even after their cities, towns, and villages had been overrun, and the partisan movement in the occupied regions of the Soviet Union became a major theme in orthodox post-war Soviet historiography. Whilst the partisan movement played a major role in the war, its efficacy became the stuff of propaganda and often outright distortion. Nonetheless, it was a major factor in the final defeat of the Wehrmacht.

Before the German invasion began in 1941, Soviet planners had considered the potential use of partisans in a future war in great detail. Field exercises took place in 1932 to assess the potential ability of partisans to disrupt road and rail traffic by sabotaging bridges, embankments, and railway infrastructure, and the results were sufficiently encouraging for plans to be developed further. Small stockpiles of personal weapons, ammunition, and explosives were buried or hidden at numerous locations in the western parts of the Soviet Union, particularly along the main axes of any anticipated invasion across Belarus close to the main road and rail links running from Warsaw to Minsk and onwards to Smolensk and Moscow. The work in this region was coordinated by the commander of the Belarusian Military District, Colonel General Ieronim Petrovich Uborevich.[1] However, these early preparations fell foul of the growing paranoia of the 1930s; preparations for partisan warfare against an invading enemy might be used by enemies of the state – or at least enemies of Stalin – in an uprising against his rule. The weapons and explosives were recovered and all steps that had been taken to organise stay-behind resistance cells were cancelled.[2]

Despite a near-impeccable record – after serving in the Russian Army as an artillery officer, he had been an early organiser of the pro-Bolshevik Red Guards and had commanded armies in the Russian Civil War with considerable success – Uborevich was arrested in May 1937 while travelling by train to Moscow. Less than two weeks later, he was found guilty of participating in a military conspiracy in the Red Army to overthrow the Soviet government and was immediately executed.

When German troops crossed the western frontier of the Soviet Union in June 1941, the initial steps to prepare for partisan warfare were fading memories. Almost immediately, the subject was raised once more and a week after the commencement of the war with Germany the Central Committee of the Communist Party ordered all local party and government bodies in the threatened regions to commence preparations. All railway rolling stock was to be either evacuated or destroyed together with fuel and food stocks; farm livestock was to be evacuated east before the Germans arrived; and active resistance was to be organised if areas fell under German control. Local Communist Party leaders were to ensure that sufficient numbers of trusted Party officials remained in areas under occupation in order to organise resistance.[3]

Given the manner in which all previous preparations had been reversed, this was a considerable challenge, made worse by the decision of Lavrenty Pavlovich Beriya, head of the NKVD, to issue instructions that his agency was to have a degree of control of the partisan groups. In practice, this resulted in unnecessary complexity and confusion, worsened when the Red Army also decided to get involved. Further instructions were sent out in the days that followed, specifying that partisan groups should be organised into formations of no more than 150 people grouped into two or three companies. They were to operate in areas known to them in order to maximise their ability to merge in with the general population and to take advantage of their local knowledge. A central headquarters was established to coordinate partisan activity but almost immediately it ran into problems when Beriya ordered the arrests of several key figures on spurious grounds; the true purpose of the arrests was a heavy-handed attempt to ensure that the new partisan organisations were firmly under Beriya's supervision.

In Belarus, which saw some of the fastest German advances of the opening weeks of the war, orders were issued by the local Soviet authorities for the creation of 14 partisan units, which totalled a little over 1,100 combatants. Of these, most were either NKVD personnel or members of other security services. Similar steps were taken all along the front line, but groups with large numbers of NKVD personnel suffered disproportionately high casualties. The popularity of Soviet rule was lowest in the western parts of the nation, particularly in western Ukraine and the Baltic States where NKVD personnel had been extensively involved in mass arrests and deportations, and in many areas local people were swift to take their revenge, denouncing NKVD partisans to the Germans. Many of these groups struggled on for many months, but by the summer of 1942 over 90 per cent of the first wave of partisan formations had been destroyed.[4] Of the 14 Belarusian groups, most were eliminated by the Germans within the first weeks of occupation. Fighting the German occupiers in any meaningful way was beyond the abilities of these early groups: their priority was survival.

The partisans faced a difficult learning curve. Initially, they operated under flawed pre-war plans about warfare and their use to engage German military units in the rear areas proved to be a mistake as they lacked the firepower to overcome any but the most lightly armed German groups they encountered. These early partisan actions proved to be disastrous for the local population: when the creation of partisan groups became known to the Germans, Hitler informed his associates that this would serve as an excellent pretext to take brutal repressive measures against any form of resistance. Anyone suspected of aiding partisans or being a partisan was to be arrested, and all those likely to oppose German occupation – particularly suspected Communists and Jews – were automatically regarded as supporting the partisans. The scale of repression was so great that at the end of July 1941, orders were issued to German occupation forces stating that the number of security personnel available was insufficient for proper legal process to be followed in all cases and consequently the occupation forces were to take whatever severe measures were needed to intimidate local people from supporting the partisans. In effect, this gave the commanders of security units *carte blanche* to massacre civilians almost indiscriminately.

Towards the end of the summer of 1941, partisan tactics changed. Instead of attempting to engage German military units, the groups began to attack communications – bridges, railway lines, telegraph cables, etc. With the destruction of so many of the first wave of groups, new groups were hastily organised and these had far fewer NKVD or security personnel in their ranks, not least because most such personnel were already dead or in captivity. By the end of 1941, a further 78 groups had been created in Belarus, incorporating a mixture of local Communist Party officials, civilian volunteers, and Red Army soldiers who had either been left behind deliberately to assist partisan groups or more often were stragglers and survivors of destroyed units. The efficacy of the partisans improved markedly as soldiers took a more prominent role, leaving Communist Party officials to address administrative and organisational matters, but German repression was widespread and brutal. The cold language of a report by the commander of a company from a battalion of *Ordnungspolizei* shows the typical fate that entire villages faced as the Germans carried out collective punishments:

> At dawn, the headman in Borisovka gathered the entire population together. After they had been checked five families were relocated to Divin with the help of local police. The rest were shot by a specially selected team and buried 500m northeast of Borisovka. A total of 169 people were shot, comprising 49 men, 97 women and 23 children. The village itself was destroyed … The executions only commenced at noon because it was necessary to dig graves beforehand …
>
> [When the buildings were set ablaze] there were explosions caused by ammunition hidden in some buildings.[5]

Another company from the same battalion was active in the village of Zabolotye. The officer in command had a particularly arbitrary method of deciding guilt: anyone who failed to break down and beg for mercy when threatened with a gun was presumed to be hiding something. He concluded his report by stating that with one exception – a villager who attempted in vain to flee – the victims showed a stoic calmness: 'Most of the villagers maintained their composure as they went to their well-deserved fate which, due to their bad conscience, clearly did not come as a surprise to them.'[6]

By the beginning of 1942 barely half of the second wave of partisan groups in Belarus were still functioning.[7] Dozens of villages had been destroyed and the number of those killed ran into tens of thousands.

Anticipating that there might be considerable unrest in the conquered territories, the German armies that invaded the Soviet Union were accompanied by security divisions. These were made up of a mixture of older soldiers deemed to be unfit for service in combat formations and battalions of *Ordnungspolizei* ('Order Police', the uniformed police force of Germany). Many of the subunits of these security divisions were used as guards on railway lines, bridges etc., but from the outset the divisions were also involved in mass killings of Jews, suspected Communists, and other parts of the population that were regarded as 'undesirable'. Inevitably, these killings drove large numbers of people, particularly Jews, into the ranks of the partisans. As the first winter of the war began, Army Group Centre was operating four security divisions, two SS brigades, and dozens of smaller formations in anti-partisan and security roles. An indication of the overlap between anti-partisan activities and the mass killings of Jews and others can be seen by the record of one of these units, the SS Cavalry Brigade commanded by Oberführer Hermann Fegelein. The brigade was sent into the Polesie region to root out partisan groups in the second half of 1941 and its initial report stated that nearly 14,000 people had been killed; over 90 per cent were identified as Jews. Despite this appalling death toll, Heinrich Himmler criticised the brigade for not killing sufficient people to suppress the partisan movement, and the death rate rose significantly. By the end of 1941, Fegelein boasted that his men had slaughtered about 40,000 people, again stressing that they were predominantly Jews. The number included a large proportion of women and children and the number of weapons recovered suggests that the majority were unarmed and were probably just local people who were rounded up and summarily executed.[8]

At first, the German response to any act of sabotage was to seize large numbers of hostages and to execute them if the perpetrators of sabotage were not handed over. Villages regarded by the Germans as being sympathetic to partisans were often simply razed and their occupants massacred, and on occasions the partisans behaved in a similar manner if they suspected local people of cooperating with the Germans. Attempts were made by the Germans – with varying degrees of success – to infiltrate partisan groups, but the steady increase in resistance activity forced a rethink. The sheer scale of the conquered regions was such that it was impossible for the Germans to enforce their policies without help, and many units of *Hilfspolizei* ('Assistance Police') were raised from local populations. Inevitably, these included infiltrators from the partisans, and significant numbers of *Hilfspolizei* deserted, taking their weapons with them.

Even by the autumn of 1941, the initial German measures were proving ineffective in large swathes of territory and fresh instructions were issued by *OKW*:

In every case of resistance to the German occupation forces, it should be inferred that this is of Communist origin, regardless of the individual circumstances.

In order to nip these acts in the bud, the most drastic measures should be taken immediately at the first indication [of trouble] so that the authority of the occupation forces can be maintained and further unrest can be prevented. In this connection it is to be remembered that a human life in unsettled countries often counts for nothing and deterrence can only be achieved by unusual severity. The death penalty for 50–100 Communists in atonement for one German soldier's life should generally be considered in these cases. The manner in which sentence is carried out should further increase the deterrent value. The reverse policy of imposing relatively lenient penalties and of being content with the use of the threat of more severe measures as deterrence does not accord with these principles and is therefore not to be followed.[9]

As the German summer offensive of 1942 towards Stalingrad commenced, there was a reiteration of the need for harsh measures against suspected partisans but with growing evidence that this policy at best was ineffective and at worst was driving civilians into the ranks of the partisans, there was a change of heart. On 18 August, new instructions were issued. These stressed that the suppression of resistance had to involve both carrots and sticks: civilians should be encouraged to cooperate with the Germans in return for extra food supplies and other privileges at the same time that any collaboration with partisans was punished. There was to be a more nuanced approach, with units instructed to determine whether civilians had been coerced into cooperation with the partisans – in such cases, reprisals were to be strictly limited. In many respects, this change of heart came too late. Many civilians were implacably opposed to the Germans, but some chose to cooperate with whichever side was the most threatening at any time.

In the first parts of Belarus to come under German control, there were additional complications. This area had been part of Poland until it was seized by the Red Army in 1939 and there was a substantial Polish population. There were also the remnants of the Polish Army, and these groups would join with other anti-German Polish partisans to create the *Armia Krajova* ('Home Army' or *AK*) in 1942. These Polish forces were as hostile to the Soviet authorities as they were to the Germans. From September 1939 to June 1941, the new Soviet authorities in the region were responsible for severe repression and between 330,000 and 400,000 people were deported to Siberia; many thousands died in captivity, both within the region and in prison camps across the Soviet Union.[10] The first victims were Polish government officials and the sudden transformation of the Polish community – many of whom had settled in the area in the 1920s and 1930s – from a privileged status compared to the Belarusian population was greeted with satisfaction by many Belarusians. But within months, the implementation of Soviet agricultural collectivisation resulted in a change of mood. Many Jews in the region welcomed the arrival of the Soviet troops not least because they were seen as a lesser evil compared to German rule, but the Jews were also targeted by the new authorities. Jewish refugees who had succeeded in reaching the region from the western parts of Poland were regarded as suspect and were deported in large numbers, and other Jews had their businesses forcibly confiscated as part of Sovietisation. By the summer of 1941, relations between the different ethnic groups were dominated by suspicion and fear. It was far from an ideal starting point for organising a resistance movement against the Germans.

Inevitably, the Jewish population of the area suffered severely following the arrival of German forces. Many were executed in mass killings within days of the area coming under German control – in the city of Białystok, the Germans carried out a mass round-up of Jews on 2 June 1941, just five days after the war had commenced. During that day, over 1,000 Jews were killed, including 700 who were incarcerated in the city's main synagogue before the building was set alight.[11] By the end of the German occupation of the region, about one million Jews had been killed, either in local executions or in the extermination camps that started to function in 1942. Inevitably, the persecution of the Jews resulted in Jewish partisan groups appearing, and the widespread anti-Semitism of pre-war Poland meant that these groups were in turn often in conflict with other partisans. But despite these complications and despite (or even because of) brutal German repression, the number of people involved in the partisan struggle grew steadily as the war progressed. By late 1942, there were an estimated 47,000 people involved in Belarus, rising to over 55,000 in the first months of 1943.

The daily experience of civilians under occupation could almost have been designed to alienate them and encourage resistance. Food and other resources were routinely seized with little regard for the needs of the local population and brutal punishments were inflicted for insignificant or imagined wrongdoing. There was widespread rape and many women were taken away and forced to work in brothels for the occupation forces, and many civilians witnessed the manner in which the Germans treated captured Red Army personnel. Aleksandr Mikhailovich Adamovich was a teenager in 1941 living in a small village near Bobruisk and a prisoner-of-war camp was set up nearby. He saw prisoners being used as forced labour on roads, chopping down trees to create open ground on either side to reduce the risk of ambush. Prisoners were beaten all the time and died in large numbers. Many were already showing signs of malnutrition when they arrived and local people shared what little they could whenever the opportunity arose, risking the wrath of German guards.[12]

At first, overall control of the partisan movement was severely limited, largely because few partisan groups had radios or indeed any other supplies. The first winter of the war, particularly severe in European Russia, saw many groups reduced to just a handful of fighters with few weapons or other equipment. As the winter came to an end, the partisan groups began to reorganise with brigades taking control of several subordinate groups and radios and other equipment began to arrive by parachute drops, small aircraft landing in remote locations, and even by land routes – contact between the German Army Groups North and South was poor and substantial bodies of Soviet partisans were able to move relatively freely through this region, either withdrawing to Soviet-held areas for rest and replenishment or entering German-held areas once they were back up to strength. With their original mixture of local resistance fighters and Red Army stragglers now augmented by specialists sent as reinforcements, the partisans became increasingly active and effective. Not all the partisans were active at any one time, but the movement was steadily gaining strength and becoming more effective.

Although the various Jewish, Soviet, and Polish partisan groups clashed from time to time, there was generally a degree of uneasy coexistence, but tensions between pro-Polish resistance groups and those supporting Moscow came to a climax in April 1943. After the Soviet seizure of the eastern parts of Poland in 1939, tens of thousands of Polish soldiers and police personnel were taken prisoner. Many were then released but large numbers continued to be held in camps run by the NKVD. In March 1940, the Soviet Politburo signed orders authorising the execution of large numbers of Polish prisoners who were classified as Polish nationalists or 'counter-revolutionaries'. In the weeks that followed, about 22,000 Poles were shot in the forests near the town of Katyn and two other locations.[13] The killings in Katyn were carried out under the leadership of Major General Vasily Mikhailovich Blokhin of the NKVD. He organised the construction of a hut with soundproofed walls specifically for the killings. The scale of the massacres was far greater than previous executions carried out by the NKVD; wearing a leather butcher's apron that he had purchased specially for the task, Blokhin took part in the shooting of 7,000 men over four weeks, using a German pistol in an attempt to avoid exposure at a later date if the bodies were discovered.[14]

Unaware of this massacre, the Polish government-in-exile signed an agreement with the Soviet Union shortly after the German invasion commenced, pledging cooperation in the fight against Nazi Germany; this included agreement to create a Polish army on Soviet territory under the command of the Polish general Władysław Anders. He and his staff were of course aware that large numbers of Polish officers had been detained by the Soviet Union during 1939 and requested details from the Soviet authorities with the intention of using these men as part of the new Polish force that was being created. Stalin met Anders and informed him that most of the prisoners had been freed, while small numbers were thought to be somewhere in prison camps somewhere in the Soviet interior and it was proving difficult to locate them; some of the prisoners had escaped, he told Anders, but attempts would be made to locate them.[15]

In early 1943, a German intelligence officer in Army Group Centre became aware of reports of mass graves near Katyn. He investigated the graves, uncovering considerable material that identified the victims as Polish military personnel, and submitted a report to Berlin. The first details were sent using the *Enigma* cipher system and were picked up by British intelligence officers in Bletchley Park, where they were decoded. When Goebbels learned of the discovery, he saw it as an opportunity to create divisions between the Poles and the Soviet Union and on 13 April there was a radio broadcast from Berlin announcing to the world that German forces had discovered a mass grave containing the remains of thousands of Polish officers. A Red Cross committee with members from several European countries was invited to visit the site and the Polish government-in-exile in London immediately demanded an enquiry. Stalin rejected the demand and the Moscow government announced that whilst the Poles had indeed been Soviet prisoners, they were part of a labour gang working in the area that was captured and killed by the Germans in 1941. This was unsatisfactory for the Polish government-in-exile and the uneasy relationship that had developed with the Soviet Union came to an abrupt end. Almost immediately, Stalin set up a pro-Soviet Polish government-in-exile under the leadership of Wanda Wasilewska.

The creation of a Polish military force under Anders' leadership had been difficult with the Soviet authorities unwilling or unable to provide adequate logistic support, and in March 1942 Stalin agreed to transfer the Poles to British control via Iran. In the occupied parts of Belarus, the rudimentary coexistence of the *AK* and pro-Soviet partisans ceased entirely after the German announcement of the discovery of the Katyn massacre. The Soviet groups declared that the *AK* units were 'white Poles' or German collaborators, and thenceforth most of the coordinated partisan activity against the Germans was by groups entirely under the control of Moscow.[16] There were repeated clashes between pro-Polish and pro-Soviet partisans – at least 230 such incidents were reported in the months that followed the German announcement of the discovery of the Katyn graves and the arrival of the Red Army in the region during the summer of 1944.[17] It is difficult to know for certain the overall ethnic makeup of the partisan groups, but one estimate from October 1943 suggests that about 59 per cent were Belarusians, 27 per cent were Russians, 8 per cent were Jews, and 4 per cent were Ukrainians; Poles made up less than 1 per cent of the total. About 14 per cent of the partisans were Red Army stragglers and men who had been parachuted into the region, 16 per cent were escaped prisoners of war, and 4 per cent were escapees from concentration camps. Women made up about 8 per cent of the total.[18] These figures almost certainly understate the number of Poles involved in resistance work for several reasons. Firstly, as was the case in so many Soviet-era reports, the author of the document was probably mindful of the views of his superiors; at a time when the Poles were being reclassified as enemies and as Fascist collaborators, any suggestion that they were playing a major role in fighting the Germans was unwelcome. Secondly, the Polish groups had never been formally integrated into the Soviet-controlled partisan movement and therefore knowledge of the strength and capability of the Poles was very limited. Finally, the level of activity that occurred amongst Polish groups as the Red Army approached the old territory of eastern Poland escalated, as is described below; this scale of operations would have been impossible if fewer than 1 per cent of partisans were Poles.

After the evidence about Katyn began to emerge and instructions were issued to pro-Soviet groups to treat Polish partisans as enemies, there were increasingly frequent clashes between the two sides. The first such fights were not actually triggered by the changing political atmosphere: in May, a Polish group near Novogrodek attacked a pro-Soviet group that had been terrorising the local population and indulging in arbitrary looting. Attempts by local Polish commanders for resumed cooperation in the struggle against the Germans were rebuffed on orders from Moscow. Panteleimon Kondratyevich Ponomarenko, First Secretary of the Belarusian Communist Party and a senior figure in the partisan movement, issued clear instructions to his groups in the western parts of Belarus in June 1943 about the Polish *AK*-affiliated partisans:

> Our partisan detachments and Party organisations must work to identify all Polish underground organisations and then expose them to attacks by the German occupiers by any means possible. The Germans will not hesitate to shoot people if they discover that they are leaders of the Polish underground or other Polish military bodies. No cooperation is required. How is it to be done? You must have no scruples when choosing the means. These must be broad-based so that all progresses smoothly.[19]

In August 1943, Soviet partisans moved against a Polish group of about 300 fighters not far from Vilnius after inviting the Polish leaders to a meeting where they were taken prisoner. The rest of the Polish group was then disarmed and about 80 Poles were killed. Further east, there were similar actions and the captured Polish leaders were in many cases flown out and sent to Moscow. Inevitably, this resulted in attacks by Poles on pro-Soviet groups and in one such attack the Polish fighters captured documents from Moscow ordering the partisans to betray and attack the Polish groups; these documents were then passed back through the Polish chain of command to London. Fighting between the Germans, Poles, and pro-Soviet partisans became increasingly confused; the Polish groups recorded nearly as many actions against pro-Soviet partisans as against the German occupation forces.[20] However, copies of the orders from Moscow also fell into the hands of the Germans who were quick to realise their potential value in increasing mistrust between the two partisan groupings. As the Red Army approached the area, the Germans would attempt to exploit anti-Soviet sentiments amongst Polish fighters in more concrete ways.

The story of Ihor Rudko is typical of many men who ended up in the ranks of the partisans. He was in command of the supply services of a Red Army tank division at the beginning of the war and became a prisoner of war in mid-September 1941. He escaped from captivity the following March, living in the forests with help from local people and after a few weeks he encountered a partisan group of nine men. Only seven were armed, and Rudko took on the task of building up the strength of the group. By combining with other bands, his small group became part of a body of about 250 fighters by midsummer 1942. In his opinion, the leadership of the group was poor – neither the commander nor his deputy showed much tactical acumen and the only effective leader, a commissar, was killed in a clash with the Germans. The equipment and leadership of the group improved in fits and starts, but securing sufficient supplies remained difficult. Seizure of food from local villagers resulted in resentment, and Rudko later described an encounter with a local farmer:

> Without any prevarication, the farmer said, 'To hell with partisans like these who take away my last possessions and aren't able to protect me from the Germans. If it wasn't for them, the Germans wouldn't beat me or set my house ablaze.'[21]

Attempts to improve matters by parachuting officers and supplies to the partisans had mixed results, highlighting the poor command and control of the various elements operating behind German lines. In the summer of 1943, the commander of the *Pervomayiskaya* partisan brigade wrote a report for his superiors:

> Whilst visiting detachments to check on their activities, I encountered a detachment that said it was made up of 'airborne soldiers' of Lieutenant Colonel Znamensky's detachment. After meeting the unit commander and his commissar, I suggested that they should contact you. The detachment commander, M L Bockin, replied 'I don't know who that person is. How did he come here, where was he when we were fighting our way through here? Perhaps he's a spy.' I had to reprimand him and his commissar, who was supporting him, and gave them an ultimatum to contact you within ten days.
>
> Examination [of documents] showed that only three were paratroopers. The rest came from nearby villages and from eastern Belarus. They merely interfered with our operations. For example, we armed cooperative local residents and issued them special identity documents. When the paratroopers discovered this, they seized these weapons and, if the opportunity arose, horses or food too. They have not been involved in combat recently … They state they are on a special mission and will not place themselves under anyone's control.[22]

In addition to such friction and the greater tension between the Poles and pro-Soviet groups, Jewish partisan groups also sometimes had difficulties with groups consisting of Red Army soldiers. Meir Hadash was a Jewish partisan operating near Naroch, north of Minsk:

> Once [in 1943] we encountered a group of partisans from Major Cherkasov's unit, which was made up entirely of former prisoners of war. They attacked us and took our weapons and clothes. We tried to defend ourselves but we were unsuccessful. There were too many of them, and they were well armed and threatened to kill us all.[23]

Despite these problems, the partisan movement was gathering strength throughout this time and as command and control improved, Jewish groups were better integrated into the overall organisation of partisan groups, greatly reducing (but not entirely eliminating) clashes with non-Jewish groups, and the picture remained mixed. In late 1943, for example, a group of about 70 Jewish fighters who had escaped from the Vilnius ghetto was operating in forests in the western parts of Belarus in close proximity to a partisan group formed by a group of Red Army paratroopers. The Jews suggested that the two groups combine, something that the paratroopers rejected. But elsewhere, there was close cooperation. Near Minsk, discussions between Jews who had escaped from the city ghetto and a partisan leader resulted in a special group being created composed of the Jews with additional non-Jewish personnel from existing partisan groups. In addition to attacking German targets, the group specifically attempted to rescue Jews from the nearby city and as the number of Jews hiding in the forest increased, the leader of the group, Sholom Zorin, selected medically trained refugees to create a hospital, while other refugees set up a tailoring workshop, a shoemaking workshop, an armoury, and a mill, providing services to both Jewish and non-Jewish partisan groups.[24] Sometimes, there were complex three-way tensions between all of the various partisan factions. A group of Polish fighters under the command of Kaspar Milashevsky, a lieutenant in the Polish Army, was functioning near Minsk and joined a Soviet group. For a while, the Poles were able to hide their identities but they eventually were recognised as Polish and in the summer of 1943 orders were received from higher commands for partisans to include steps against 'bourgeois-nationalist Polish units' in their activities. The Soviet commander of the region declined to follow the instructions, and a few months later the Poles were operating in the Ivanets region where they encountered a Jewish group attempting to appropriate food supplies. Local people asked the Poles to help them, accusing the Jews of robbing them. Such appropriation was normal for all partisan groups, but the Poles used this as a pretext to open fire on the Jewish group. Several Jews were taken prisoner and 11 were shot; one survived and when he reported the incident, Milashevsky and the other Polish leaders were arrested by Soviet partisans. Several were executed for 'creating a Polish nationalist counter-revolutionary organisation and anti-Soviet activities'. Many of the surviving Poles then fled, and there were suggestions that they fought alongside the Germans against the Soviet partisans and the Red Army.[25]

As the German armies pressed ever deeper into the Soviet Union, large numbers of bypassed Red Army soldiers continued to move relatively freely in the conquered areas. Many were trying to escape to the east and others who had been recruited from the local area attempted to return to their homes, but others joined the partisans. In mid-August 1944, the German Army Group Centre issued a proclamation to the population stating that any Soviet soldiers found to the west of the Berezina River would be regarded as guerrillas and treated accordingly – until this time, men in uniform were treated as legitimate combatants and therefore could expect to be treated as prisoners of war. Although the German handling of Soviet prisoners in the opening months of the conflict amounted to mass murder through starvation, the proclamation of 1944 resulted in thousands of Red Army soldiers handing themselves in.[26]

The tactics used by the Germans in field operations against partisans evolved as the war dragged on. The initial plan to use armed police battalions and the security divisions, with support from units like the SS Cavalry Brigade, proved to be inadequate even after *Hilfspolizei* battalions were raised. Increasingly, front-line formations were required to release subunits for use in anti-partisan operations, sometimes resulting in entire divisions being pulled out of the front line. During 1942, large numbers of Red Army personnel were operating behind the German front line to the west of Moscow – a mixture of paratroopers, a cavalry corps, and stragglers left in the region from the initial German advance – and a major operation was organised to secure the area. Several infantry divisions formed a 'catch line' while 5th Panzer Division provided mobile firepower in a sweep through the area, an operation codenamed *Hannover*.[27] Such sweeps were effective in suppressing partisan activity, but usually only on a temporary basis. The most effective examples of anti-partisan warfare involved the use of small units that were able to operate in the same swamps and forests that the partisans used for cover, and the physical demands of such activity were often greater than what could be expected from the older personnel of security divisions and *Ordnungspolizei* battalions.

Despite the anti-partisan sweeps, the frequency of attacks on German rear area units and supply and communications lines slowly increased as the war progressed, not least because of more effective support by the Red Army. Supplies and specialist personnel were delivered in increasing quantities, and the manpower pressures upon the Wehrmacht necessitated the use of security divisions in the front line, leaving fewer formations to protect roads, bridges, and other important locations. The growing strength of the partisans meant that by early 1944, they were able to take on regular German units with increasing confidence and large areas behind the front line were effectively under partisan control. In the area behind the northern flank of Army Group Centre for example, Colonel Vladimir Eliseyevich Lobanok, a Communist Party official with little formal military training, had been involved in setting up partisan units since the beginning of the war. As preparations began for the summer offensive of 1944, Lobanok had about 18,000 partisans under his command, controlling a region between the cities of Lepel and Polotsk that was about 40 miles across. The region was relatively close to the front line and a steady stream of supplies from the Red Army ensured that the partisans in what was known as the *Ushachskaya Partizanskaya Respublika* ('Ushachi Partisan Republic') posed a constant threat to the Germans. They sat astride the roads running directly between Vitebsk and Vilnius and were able to mount raids towards the south against the main supply axes near Minsk.

It was impossible for Army Group Centre to ignore the presence of such a potent threat in the immediate rear area, particularly as there were smaller but equally active partisan groups operating across the entire region. Taking advantage of a lull in front-line fighting, several anti-partisan operations were launched in the Bobruisk area in early 1944 – *Wolfsjagd* ('Wolf Hunt') and *Sumpfhahn* ('Swamp Fowl') in the first two weeks of February, followed by *Auerhahn* ('Grouse') in April. The fact that so many operations had to be mounted in a short space of time indicates that while they may have had an immediate impact in suppressing partisan activity, the benefit was short-lived. Operations were also mounted against the Ushachi partisans, with about 20,000 German troops being pulled out of the front line and deployed in an operation codenamed *Regenschauer* ('Rain Shower') in April. Soviet aircraft provided considerable support for the partisans in terms of both dropping supplies and attacking the Germans, and extensive minefields and fortifications had been prepared by the partisans to defend their territory, but the German forces made short work of most of the partisans they encountered. Many of the partisan units had little experience of combat, having been restricted to intelligence gathering or sabotage, and in many cases their leadership proved to be inadequate in such conditions. The German attack moved forward in a careful sweep along the left bank of the Daugava River in a westward direction into the lake region south of Polotsk. Having secured this area, the Germans halted and a second operation codenamed *Frühlingsfest* ('Spring Festival') commenced – the German forces used in the advance during *Frühlingsfest* now formed a blocking line while other units moved forward from the north, west, and south.

Partisan resistance to *Regenschauer* might have been limited with many groups choosing to evade the Germans rather than fight them, but the response to *Frühlingsfest* was different. Fighting intensified, but the Germans continued to advance. By the end of their operations, the Germans had killed an estimated 7,000 partisans and taken a similar number prisoner.[28] The Ushachi Partisan Republic effectively ceased to exist with about 3,500 of Lobanok's surviving fighters slipping away further to the west.[29] But there was still a substantial partisan presence further south and the Germans decided that further operations were necessary if only to prevent these partisans from re-infiltrating the region that had just been cleared. On 22 May, they commenced Operation *Kormoran* ('Cormorant') to clear the area north of Minsk and Borisov. A blocking line was established around the perimeter of the region while the main attack was made from the Moledochno area. Partisan command and control in this sector was poor and fragmentary; about 7,700 partisans were claimed as killed and over 5,000 captured. How many of these were real partisans and how many were unfortunate civilians who were caught up in the fighting is impossible to determine.

The efficacy of the partisan movement was lauded by Soviet writers after the war, with claims of the destruction of improbably large numbers of bridges and trains and the killing of thousands of German soldiers. Without question, many such attacks occurred, but there was a tendency – seen in other armed forces almost since the start of recorded history – for each level of command to inflate its reports. As these reports progressed up the chain of command, each tier added its distortions. A report from the Baranovichi region in May 1944, for example, claimed that the partisans had to date derailed 1,058 trains, killed or wounded over 70,000 German soldiers, and destroyed 200 supply dumps since becoming active.[30] It seems highly improbable that this partisan group had effectively accounted for sufficient German soldiers to form five infantry divisions. One of the anti-partisan groups operating in this area was the infamous SS brigade commanded by Oberführer Oskar Dirlewanger, a man who was described in the early 1920s in a police report as 'a mentally unstable, violent fanatic and alcoholic, who has the habit of erupting into violence under the influence of drugs.'[31] Dirlewanger's brigade was involved in repeated clashes with partisans in Belarus in the summer of 1943 and the disparities between the accounts of the two sides are striking. The partisans described how they killed or wounded 3,000 Germans and pro-German paramilitaries, took 29 men prisoner, and destroyed 60 wheeled vehicles, three tanks, and four other armoured vehicles for the loss of 129 dead, 50 wounded, and 24 missing.[32] By contrast, the reports from Dirlewanger's brigade record the loss of 52 men with 155 wounded and four missing, and partisan losses as 4,280 dead and 654 prisoners.[33] It seems likely that both sides were inflating their efficacy, but the claim by the partisans that they had destroyed Dirlewanger's headquarters and killed all its personnel was clearly incorrect. Dirlewanger survived the war, carving a path of death and atrocities in the process.

Other reports were in many respects more modest but nonetheless were probably inflated. One partisan commander wrote that his men repeatedly attacked the railway line between Minsk and Baranovichi in September 1942, destroying or derailing four trains carrying ammunition, one carrying personnel, one carrying civilian passengers, one mixed train, and four of unknown composition – a total of 11 trains.[34] Even this seems improbable, as it would require an average of one train attack every three days and such activity would be certain to result in greater German security arrangements. The report concluded with an 'urgent' request for guns, ammunition, explosives, portable radios, and other equipment. If such supplies were urgently needed, it seems questionable that so many attacks could have been carried out on the railway line. However, German memoirs frequently describe railway disruption with trains having to undertake long diversions and personnel in transit being pressed into use in local anti-partisan sweeps.

Despite the questionable nature of so many claims, the repeated attempts of the Germans to suppress the partisans are testament to their efficacy. After surviving the first winter of the conflict, the partisan movement increased its activities beyond simple survival and concentrated on several areas. Firstly, intelligence was gathered on German troop movements. This was of great value to the Red Army as it often identified the location of German reserves or units recovering in rear areas. Secondly, disruption of supply lines and communications steadily increased as supplies of explosives and the arrival of special teams of personnel trained in demolition and sabotage strengthened the capabilities of the partisan groups. Thirdly, isolated German occupation personnel and their local auxiliaries were targeted and attacked. Matters were complicated by the manner in which some partisan groups avoided combat and restricted themselves to seizing food and other items, behaving more as criminal gangs than as forces engaged in the war against the occupation forces.

Intelligence gathering was not restricted to monitoring the movements and locations of occupation forces. Stalin and particularly Beriya were keen to obtain information about the state of mind of civilians in the area – Red Army soldiers who had been held captive even for short periods were regarded as potentially 'contaminated' by exposure to anti-Bolshevik views, and similar suspicions were directed at the populations of the occupied territories. Consequently, reports from partisan groups often commented on the state of mind of civilians, and the report from 125th 'Stalin' Partisan Group at the end of 1942 sheds interesting light upon the interaction of the civilians with both the German occupiers and the partisans:

> The majority of the civilian population in the Baranovichi and Minsk oblasts impatiently awaits the arrival of the Red Army to liberate them from Fascism. A great many people wish to join the partisan groups but to date they have not been recruited as they are unarmed. The occupation authorities take advantage of this, forcibly mobilising the population for their own purposes with the consequence that people who support the Soviet state are forced to aid their enemies against their will. In addition, the lack of consistent leadership in partisan groups results in several small partisan groups (and on occasion also larger groups) adopting a wait-and-see policy; they remain inactive in the forests and instead of fighting the occupiers they rob the civilian population, bringing the entire partisan movement into disrepute. Consequently, this gives the Germans the opportunity to establish 'self-defence groups' in villages, which are then used exclusively in anti-partisan warfare. The lack of activity of [many] partisans is largely due to shortages of ammunition and explosives.[35]

The statement that the majority of the population were impatiently awaiting the arrival of the Red Army is questionable – liberation from German occupation was certainly seen as very desirable, but the restoration of Soviet rule, particularly in the former Polish parts of Belarus, was, for many, barely any better. The report hinted at this:

> At present, the personnel of [local] police units are exclusively recruited by force. Refusal to serve in the police or desertion from its ranks results in the families of the police officers concerned being shot and their homes set ablaze. Only Belarusians are recruited into the police and other nationalities are now no longer used. Poles are completely barred from joining the police force and state administrative agencies and are monitored almost as much as the Jews. Consequently the entire Polish population awaits the Red Army but for many Poles this does not mean Soviet power, but rather the ability to re-establish the Polish state.[36]

Post-war Soviet historiography consistently portrayed the relationship between partisans and local civilians as friendly – only the Poles were described as showing any hostility to pro-Soviet partisan groups, and the partisans were always described as behaving with exemplary correctness. Almost inevitably, Polish partisan groups described things differently. A report from the summer of 1942 written by the commander of a group from the *AK* recorded growing Soviet partisan activity:

> The fact is that in these districts Soviet partisans are running rampant, forming ad hoc bands that have become the worst sort of nuisance in this area. Well-armed hotheads raid mainly municipal stores and estates and occasionally wealthy peasants.[37]

Such acts against municipal assets and wealthy peasants – who could perhaps be accused of being anti-Soviet by the very fact that they were wealthy – were arguably justifiable, and it is worth noting that the Polish *AK* was hostile to the Soviet Union and would therefore be expected to portray the activities of pro-Soviet groups in a negative manner. But reports from pro-Soviet groups confirm that many partisans were a burden on the local population and showed little energy in taking on the occupying forces. A report from 1942 was highly critical of these reluctant fighters:

> Since they don't fight, inevitably they become an additional burden on the peasantry and this makes the peasantry hostile to the partisan movement in general. Consequently, this harms both the Party and the government … When the Germans are absent [from an area], the partisans go to and from the village without hindrance, offer no assistance to the peasants, take their cattle, sheep, bread and other food. But as soon as a [German] punitive force appears, the partisans flee without offering any resistance, and the peasants are then beaten and their houses burned down for supporting and feeding the partisans.[38]

Theft wasn't the only reason why many civilians came to resent the partisans. Near Naliboki, 44 miles west of Minsk, a pro-Soviet partisan group attacked what it identified as a 'fortified position'. They stole about 100 cattle and 70 horses and left 127 dead civilians amidst the burned buildings. Two months later, the Germans mounted a punitive anti-partisan sweep through the same area and razed the few remaining buildings, killing another ten civilians and rounding up a further 3,000 as forced labourers.[39] In an attempt to improve the standing of partisans and to restore discipline, some partisan leaders took forceful measures against groups that seemed to be more interested in looting than in fighting the Germans. Some of these measures were local initiatives, but as the war continued the improvements in command, control, and discipline of the partisans were matched – and to an extent strongly influenced – by far greater political education of the rank and file of the groups. Formal instructions were sent out to all groups in Belarus to refrain from the measures that had brought many partisans into disrepute and strict controls were applied to which groups could visit which villages to obtain food, and how much they were permitted to take. Alcoholism was to be curbed, though this proved difficult. In May 1943, the chief of staff of the Belarusian partisan command wrote:

> During my time with the *Aleksandr Nevsky* detachment, it was clear that some commanders repeatedly organised drinking bouts with their subordinates, during which they frequently fired their personal weapons. This behaviour results in reduced vigilance, deterioration of discipline, impaired unit combat capability, and the undermining of its standing with the populace ...
>
> Bogtyarev [chief of staff of the *Aleksandr Nevsky* partisans] disregarded my reprimand and that of the detachment commander, Boykov, and our orders to cease drinking and to make no contact with those placed under arrest [for being drunk]. Still intoxicated, he abused his authority as chief of staff, ignoring the guards' warning that it was forbidden to visit the arrested individuals and drink more alcohol with them.
>
> On 3 May, Bogtyarev with his subordinate Filipovich commenced a long burst of shooting with a rifle and a machine-pistol near the village of Potasnya while drunk. Despite being warned twice by me personally and despite his promises to desist, Bogtyarev was again drunk on 17 May in Potasnya, made his subordinate Visoulov drink to excess, and opened fire again in the building before firing elsewhere in the village and the meadow and didn't return to the camp until the evening of 18 May.
>
> For repeated alcohol abuse and for encouraging his subordinates to drunkenness and for aimless gunfire whilst under the influence of alcohol I issued a further reprimand and a warning to Bogtyarev. Should there be any similar incidents in future, these will be considered intentional disobedience and will be punished more severely.[40]

A few weeks later, in July 1943, another senior officer wrote a report attempting to pass the blame for misconduct onto the Germans:

> When I visited villages in the area of operations of the brigade, I heard several complaints from the population about the erroneous behaviour of partisans

towards the populace. In several cases, I was able to confirm these complaints as accurate. A few commanders and partisans do not understand that disaffection between the populace and the partisans must be most strictly forbidden. Marauding, coercion, rape, and insulting behaviour are extraordinarily serious crimes. This can only be the work of German agents who have infiltrated and pass themselves off as partisans, inflicting suffering on the population and thus turning them away from the partisans.[41]

Whilst this may have been true in some cases, in others it was unquestionable that partisans – not always under the influence of alcohol – were taking advantage of the general lawlessness in the occupied territories to behave as they pleased, as other reports clearly stated. Increasingly strict orders were issued to the commanders of partisan groups to eradicate all such behaviour, authorising severe punishments if required. Mikhail Denisovich Minin, a lieutenant in a partisan group, was found guilty in early 1944 of drunkenness, theft, assault, rape, and murder over a period of many months; during this time, he had repeatedly been reprimanded and warned about his behaviour. He was executed by firing squad.[42]

In addition to giving information about German troop movements, reports from the partisan groups also provided plentiful evidence of German atrocities and war crimes. A report from a partisan brigade at the end of the summer of 1943 recorded that during a recent German operation in the area, nearly 4,700 civilians had been rounded up in a number of villages and sent to Germany as forced labourers. In addition, it added that a teacher in one village was raped and then burned alive; her 15-year-old son was beaten and also thrown into the flames. Six other villagers who were found to be in possession of ammunition were beaten to death. In a neighbouring village, two women were raped and a war veteran from the First World War and his wife were killed merely because they asked the Germans to return stolen property to them:

> The bestiality of the German Fascists against the civilian population shows no sign of abating. In almost every village in which troops found themselves during the operation, the Germans left a bloodstained trail behind them. These incidents are so numerous that it is almost impossible to record them all.[43]

The Soviet leadership had already realised the propaganda value of evidence of German atrocities in areas that had been recaptured by the Red Army and used such evidence to bolster the will of soldiers to fight against the hated Fascists; the reports from the partisan groups were added to this growing body of information.

The German occupation authorities had overlapping roles, resulting in frequent disputes between the different agencies. Wilhelm Kube was *Generalkommissar* of the region known to the Germans as *Generalbezierk Weissruthenien* ('General District White Ruthenia'), covering western Belarus. When SS personnel and Lithuanian auxiliaries slaughtered thousands of civilians in the city of Slutsk in October 1941, he protested to Himmler about the killings. Most of the victims were Jews, but Kube's concerns were restricted to the fact that many non-Jewish Belarusians were also killed, and he complained about the effect this had upon the local population. He showed little concern about the killing of Jews, even children; on one occasion in March 1942, he witnessed the killing of children who were buried alive in deep sand and even threw sweets to them as they struggled.[44] On the other hand, he objected strongly to the killing of Jews deported from Germany, particularly those who had served in the German Army in the First World War. Like all figures in the occupation forces, he was widely hated by the civilian population and in September 1943, the partisans achieved a spectacular success.

For several weeks, local partisans had been planning to assassinate the *Generalkommissar*, having received clearance from Moscow for such an attempt – it was widely recognised, particularly after the killing of Reinhard Heydrich in Prague by Czech freedom fighters in 1942, that the death of senior Nazi figures would result in widespread reprisals against civilians. The first attempt was on 22 July, when the partisans detonated a bomb in a theatre and killed or injured 70 Germans; however, they missed their main target, as Kube had left just before the explosion. A second bomb blast on 6 September in a military dining hall also killed or wounded several Germans, but once more Kube was not present. A new approach was required that specifically targeted Kube.

Yelena Grigoryevna Mazanik was the wife of a member of the NKVD but managed to hide this information from the Germans and worked as a waitress in a dining hall used by German officers. In June 1943 she joined the domestic staff of Kube's residence as a cleaner and was approached by partisans who asked for her help; she agreed to cooperate on condition that her family was evacuated from Minsk to avoid them being caught up in any German reprisals. Despite the partisans agreeing to help her, she remained reluctant to get involved until she had a face-to-face meeting with a senior partisan officer. On the night of 21 September, she activated the timer of a bomb and placed it under Kube's mattress. The device exploded early on 22 September, killing Kube.

The Germans inevitably exacted a brutal revenge. Over 1,000 civilians in Minsk were forced to dig their own graves and were then shot. Mazanik fled from Minsk and was later evacuated by air to Soviet-controlled territory; her family had already left the city a day before the attack. Together with three other partisans involved in the operation, she found herself taken to Moscow where she might have expected a warm welcome, but instead she was placed under arrest and repeatedly interrogated by the NKVD. She was later told that the NKVD wished to name another agent as the assassin and considered eliminating her.[45]

The situation on the ground in Belarus was therefore rather different from the picture painted by Soviet historiography after the war. Whilst many partisan groups were involved in repeated and often successful attacks on German rear area units, supply dumps, and lines of communication, others showed little fighting ability and a few indulged in lawlessness either as individuals or as entire groups. Nonetheless, the disruption that they caused was considerable. As the days lengthened in 1944, several German commanders wrote that they were unable to ensure complete control of the hinterland. They might be able to stamp out partisan activity by conducting major sweeps, but within weeks they found that partisan attacks were rapidly rising once more. Such sweeps were only possible when the front line was quiet, and the steadily worsening manpower shortages ensured that there were insufficient personnel available to garrison the rear areas in sufficient strength to ensure a permanent reduction in partisan attacks. To make matters worse, the deteriorating war situation meant that the desertion rate of locally recruited security personnel increased steadily. In early 1944, as part of the overall preparations for the coming summer offensive, several thousand partisans moved out of the eastern parts of Belarus and commenced activity further west, and this created a further problem for the Germans. Releasing units from the front line for anti-partisan operations was difficult enough when the operations were in the east; attempting to mount operations at a greater distance from the front line posed difficulties of transport and supplies, and meant that the troops were further from their units if the Red Army was to launch a sudden attack.

It wasn't just the pro-Soviet partisans who were making preparations for the expected summer advance of the Red Army. The Polish *AK* was determined not to allow the Soviet authorities a free hand in establishing pro-Soviet rule in Polish territories and General Tadeusz Bór-Komorowski, commander-in-chief of the *AK*, drew up plans for his units to attempt to seize control of major cities. These operations were to commence as the front line approached, in the hope that the Germans would be impaired from taking countermeasures as they would have their hands full fighting off the Red Army. In many cases, particularly in the cities to the east, there was little expectation that the *AK* would be able to establish permanent control; the Red Army would rapidly disarm the *AK* units and attempt to assert its authority, but the intention was to make clear to the world in general and the Soviet Union in particular that these areas had already been liberated from German control before the arrival of the Red Army. But the planned uprising in Warsaw was a different matter. Here, the *AK* could concentrate far greater forces and it was hoped that the Polish capital was sufficiently far to the west for the Poles to be supported by the Western Powers. All would depend upon timing: too soon and the Germans would have the opportunity to crush the Poles before the Red Army arrived, too late and the Soviet Union would claim credit for 'liberating' the various cities. As the days lengthened in the early summer of 1944, both the Poles and the Germans watched and waited for signs that the Soviet forces were about to attack.

CHAPTER 3

PREPARING THE BLOW

Prince Petr Ivanovich Bagration was a general of Georgian origins. He was born in 1765 and became a soldier at the age of just 18, rising steadily until holding major commands during the Napoleonic Wars. He was in charge of the right wing of the Russian forces at the Battle of Austerlitz in 1805 and in 1812, during what later became known in Russia and the Soviet Union as the First Patriotic War, he commanded half of the Russian Army. He was an aggressive general, wanting to fight a major battle to stop the French invasion, whereas Mikhail Illarionovich Kutuzov and Michael Barclay de Tolly, the other senior Russian commanders, favoured a scorched earth policy, drawing the French deeper into Russia. Bagration finally got his way at Borodino in September 1812, where he was mortally wounded. When *Stavka* drew up plans for its new summer offensive of 1944, it chose *Bagration* as the codename.

By the spring of 1944, the Red Army had considerable experience of attacking German defensive positions. The outcome of those attacks had been mixed, and a large part of planning for the summer offensive was to consider why attacks had often failed. Everything possible would be done to ensure that the new assault succeeded. Such steps had of course been taken before, with only limited success, and major attempts were made to achieve a greater degree of success on this occasion.

The first Soviet attempts to break German defensive positions occurred in the late summer of 1941 when the Red Army launched numerous local counterattacks against the advancing Wehrmacht. In many cases, these enjoyed initial success but this was largely because the Germans were advancing swiftly into the Soviet interior and infantry formations were unable to keep up with the panzer divisions that were racing ahead. In addition, the Germans were in an offensive posture, far from ideal for defensive fighting. Despite these disadvantages, the Wehrmacht swiftly crushed these early attacks, not least because of the well-established German doctrine of rapid counterattacks, but even at this stage there were a few pointers to what lay ahead. Soviet armoured units sometimes burst through the German lines because their tanks were far more heavily armoured than the Germans had anticipated; as a result, the limited anti-tank firepower even of panzer divisions was inadequate to deal with the threat. Had these tanks been used in a more coordinated and efficient manner, the damage they might have inflicted on the Wehrmacht would have been far greater, but in any event they delivered a number of checks to the German advance.

In the winter of 1941–42, there were several large-scale Soviet attacks in numerous sectors of the Eastern Front. The first wave of such operations came before the final German attempts to reach Moscow and made almost no impression, but after the Wehrmacht's attack finally ground to a halt in the bitter cold of early December, a large-scale Soviet counteroffensive tore apart the German lines. For a brief time, it seemed as if the tide had turned against the Germans and the badly exposed panzer spearheads were threatened with envelopment, but within a few short weeks the crisis had passed.

A consistent pattern of Red Army procedure was an analysis of operations soon after they came to an end. These analyses almost inevitably suffered from several flaws. Sometimes, they failed to identify the issues that lay behind setbacks, or attributed these setbacks entirely to one or two identified issues without looking in detail for all possible causes. Secondly, the ability of the Soviet system to remedy the identified issues proved to be very limited. Repeatedly, the same problems were identified but it seemed as if little changed. Reconnaissance of German positions was often inadequate, hampered considerably by the lack of specialist reconnaissance aircraft. When attacks began, coordination between artillery, infantry, and armour rapidly deteriorated (and on occasion was lacking from the very outset). Tanks became separated from infantrymen and neither was able to make any progress in the absence of the other. The ability to call in fresh artillery fire against stubborn positions was limited and often impossible, because of either poor communications or inadequate stocks of artillery ammunition. From the beginning of the war, the Germans enjoyed close cooperation between ground and air forces, but in 1941 this was almost non-existent in the Soviet forces. The first counteroffensive in the Battle of Moscow succeeded largely because it caught the Wehrmacht in the open in exposed positions. Once the Germans had fallen back and had established defensive lines, they were able to put up much stronger resistance. The years of Stalin's purges and the ever-present fear of arrest for failing to carry out orders stifled any sense of initiative in the Red

Army and the German defenders watched with amazement as Soviet commanders repeatedly threw men in futile, costly assaults against their positions. A German infantry officer's memory of the battles was shared by most of his contemporaries in the Wehrmacht:

> We keep asking ourselves why the Russians make these pointless attacks repeatedly at the same positions around which we have now closed up, where nothing can slip past us any more. What are they trying to achieve? They may well capture a few villages – so what?'[1]

The lessons of the winter fighting were simple: despite their modest anti-tank firepower, the German forces were able to defeat most Soviet attacks on their positions if they were in even the most rudimentary fortified positions. At this stage, although the Red Army's cavalry and other mobile units might slip through gaps in the German lines, they lacked the skill to exploit any such advances and to crush the isolated German defences.

Within weeks, the Red Army tried again. As already mentioned, Timoshenko's counteroffensive near Kharkov ended with heavy losses, but importantly the initial attack on the German positions succeeded in breaking through. Similarly, an attempt was made to lift the Siege of Leningrad with a powerful attack to clear the Volkhov River before advancing through Lyuban and Tosno to the beleaguered city. This too ended in disaster with the almost complete destruction of the Soviet Second Shock Army, but the initial attacks on German defences succeeded, albeit at huge cost. Much of 1942 also saw repeated attempts by the Red Army to eliminate the German-held salient around Rzhev. In a few locations, German defences were penetrated, but exploitation of these modest gains proved to be almost impossible and the Wehrmacht recaptured almost all of their original positions.

The fairly careful analysis of these setbacks by Red Army staff officers continued to identify the same problems. German defences hadn't been identified properly by reconnaissance, and artillery preparation – whilst visually impressive – often failed in its task of suppressing German defensive firepower. Once the ground forces moved forward, they suffered excessively heavy losses storming the German positions with the result that any penetration was often too narrow, giving the Germans every opportunity for counterattacks to restore their positions. Although exploitation forces were often identified and held in readiness, these were frequently committed to help the first echelon achieve the initial penetration with the result that subsequent exploitation was usually too weak to achieve its purposes. Once the Germans were in position to mount major counterattacks, their tactical superiority usually resulted in rapid defeat of the Soviet operations.

If matters were to improve, several problems had to be rectified. Reconnaissance had to be improved. Artillery preparation had to be more precise and there had to be a capability to give additional support to the attacking forces if they ran into difficulties, and this necessitated better communications and larger stocks of ammunition. Coordination between tanks and accompanying infantry was very poor and had to be remedied. But although *Uranus* – the great counteroffensive of late 1942 that resulted in the encirclement of the German Sixth Army in Stalingrad – succeeded, it is worth noting that both pincers of the Soviet attack encountered considerable difficulties. They deliberately fell upon positions held by Romanian troops, regarded by both the Red Army and the Wehrmacht as inferior to German units, but particularly in the case of the northern pincer overcoming these defences proved to be far from straightforward, with several Romanian units delaying the initial Soviet assault with their dogged resistance. But there were also signs that the ability of German forces to resist every Red Army attack was not guaranteed. As the Red Army smashed the enemy lines along the Don valley in a series of successive operations, it crushed first the Italian forces and then the Hungarians before turning its attention to the German Second Army, which proved to be every bit as fragile as the weaker divisions of the other Axis nations.

In the battles of 1943, the Red Army was able to overcome German defences in both the central and the southern regions, but at huge cost. The same issues with inadequate reconnaissance and poor inter-arms cooperation seemed to be almost insoluble – new training manuals had been drawn up, but the manner in which the Red Army conducted training proved to be a major handicap. Recruits received basic training, often truncated in attempts to get men to the front line as fast as possible, and were then sent to their front-line units in the expectation that these formations would complete their training, ranging from the use of heavy weapons to inter-arms cooperation. In many cases, the recruits formed new regiments and divisions and these had an opportunity – again, often truncated as the units were rushed into action – to work up to an adequate level of effectiveness, but their preparation was weakened by there being relatively few experienced personnel in their ranks. On many occasions, the poorly trained new drafts were used to bring depleted units up to strength and if the reconstituted units had been given sufficient time to absorb these replacements, the survivors of earlier operations might have had an opportunity to pass on their skills to the new arrivals, but as soon as their strength had been restored these formations were often sent straight into action. Even if there was time and opportunity for training to be completed, the Red Army lacked the core of experienced career NCOs that have repeatedly been shown to be an invaluable resource in so many armies – the men with the knowledge to ensure that recruits were prepared properly for combat in every respect, ranging from proper training to looking after themselves and their equipment.

Herein lay the biggest handicap of the Red Army. Caught up in a war of survival, it had no opportunity to change its underlying nature. It was impossible to implement the sorts of changes that might have led to the creation of proper NCO cadres – that would have required reforms over perhaps a decade. The environment of fear created by the purges of the 1930s continued to have a deadening effect upon local initiative, but to an extent this was improving by 1944 – interestingly, as Stalin and the Red Army learned that they needed to reduce central interference and micro-management if the Soviet Union was to prevail, the Germans were moving in the opposite direction, with an increasingly distrustful Hitler applying ever-greater limitations to the flexibility and resourcefulness that had been such a strong feature of German operations in earlier years. As they prepared for the summer offensive, the senior officers of the Red Army were confident of success in the coming operations, but they knew that if they were to maximise their results, they would need to ensure that as many of the problems of the past had been eliminated or at least mitigated. Even the Soviet Union didn't have endless resources of manpower, and whilst casualties at levels that would have been unimaginable in the Western Powers were acceptable to Moscow, the benefits had to be commensurate.

Within these limitations, changes were made to try to improve the performance of the Red Army. Semen Moiseyevich Vinopol was a junior officer in a mortar platoon in 1st Baltic Front, preparing to attack from positions to the northwest of Vitebsk:

> We prepared intensively for the offensive. In front of us were German positions covering the approaches to the Shumilino station. Our rifle battalions were replenished to full strength with recruits being brought in, all born in 1926. In each battalion, there was one 'armoured company' of submachine-gunners, with the soldiers being issued steel 'shells' – breastplates such as had previously only been used by assault sapper brigades. In the rear area of the army, a 10km section of the German defences was specially constructed with three defensive lines, identical to the real German positions, and there the infantry prepared for the assault. The approach to the offensive operation was very different from the past. In 1943, soldiers were told, 'Take the German position, gain a foothold and cling to it with all your strength, to the last bullet.' Now the instructions were different:

'Rush into the first line, shoot, throw grenades, and then run forward immediately. Don't linger, don't get involved in a fight in the trench. Behind you is a second wave of advancing infantry and it will clear the German trenches. Just press on!'[2]

Others had less favourable memories of their training. Nikolai Ivanovich Safonov was a teenager in the city of Kaluga when the area was occupied by the advancing Wehrmacht and survived until the arrival of the Red Army in early 1942. He was then conscripted in time for the fighting in 1944:

Almost nothing of what they taught us [in basic training] was any use in the front line. We were taught how everything should be done according to the rules and the regulations, but when was it ever like that at the front? When I was sent to the front line, we didn't even have enough rifles for everyone. I was indignant and asked our commander, 'How can we go on the attack without weapons?' He replied, 'What are you worried about? After five minutes of battle, half the men will be dead, and there will be plenty of spare rifles.'[3]

Such shortages had been eliminated by 1944, but the inadequacy of basic training remained problematic.

The first step in planning the summer offensive – the selection of the sector in which to make the main effort for 1944, in order to maximise the chances of success whilst keeping the risks as low as possible – was completed in the first few weeks of the year. The second was to ensure that sufficient resources were available for the offensive. Despite the disruption to Soviet armoured vehicle production from the relocation of factories from cities in the west to the Urals and beyond, the output of armoured vehicles climbed steadily. The SU-76 assault gun, the first examples of which were manufactured in 1942, saw production climb to nearly 2,000 vehicles in 1943 and over 7,000 throughout 1944.[4] The older version of the T-34 with a 76mm gun peaked in production in 1943 with nearly 16,000 rolling out of factories, and nearly 4,000 more were manufactured in 1944. This lower figure was due to switching production to the new version of the tank with a larger turret, better armour and the more powerful 85mm gun. This T-34/85 was produced in rapidly increasing quantities as 1944 progressed, with over 10,600 being handed over to the Red Army by the end of the year. The heavy IS-2 was built in only small numbers in 1943 but during 1944 more than 2,200 were produced.[5] These heavy tanks had limited mobility and carried only a small supply of ammunition, but they were grouped in dedicated heavy tank regiments that could be used to achieve breakthroughs. In addition, nearly 3,000 other assault guns – SU-85s, SU-100s, ISU-122s, and ISU-152s – entered service during the year, meaning that the Red Army took delivery of nearly 20,000 new tanks and assault guns during 1944. These vehicles were badly needed. Tank losses are difficult to ascertain with any degree of accuracy, as reports of friendly and enemy losses are both subject to distortion, but the overall size of the Red Army's tank fleet gives a reasonable estimate: during the period that these tanks were manufactured, losses amounted to nearly 17,000 tanks and assault guns.[6] The T-34 would end the war with the dubious distinction of being the tank that was destroyed in greater numbers than any other in history.

The figures for indigenous Soviet tank production were impressive enough, but the Red Army also received a further boost in equipment. Although Stalin had repeatedly urged the Western Powers to show more alacrity with respect to creating a Second Front, he had few reasons to criticise the flow of equipment arriving from Britain and the USA. In the 12 months prior to the summer offensive, over 3.1 million tons of tanks, trucks, ammunition, aircraft, food, and other supplies were delivered to the Soviet Union.[7] Some Red Army veterans were disparaging about the tanks they received from the Western Powers, but they added considerably to the firepower of the Red Army and the supply of trucks – over 400,000 during the entire war – gave the Soviet forces a steadily increasing advantage in terms of mobility over the Wehrmacht.

German armaments manufacture was also approaching its peak in 1944, and during the year an impressive total of nearly 19,000 tanks and assault guns reached the front line. As was the case with Soviet tank production, these numbers had to be offset against losses and the result was only a modest overall increase in the number of tanks and assault guns. Moreover, about 1,500 German tanks were deployed in the west (and a smaller number in Italy), reducing still further the number available for use on the Eastern Front. And the Red Army had a further advantage: as the attacker, it could choose where to concentrate its resources for maximum effect, creating local force ratios that were greatly advantageous.

After the disaster at Stalingrad, German officers repeatedly wrote about how they expected the Red Army to start running out of manpower. The losses inflicted by the Wehrmacht continued to be huge and the figures defy imagination. By the end of 1941, casualties in terms of dead, wounded, and missing amounted to a staggering 4.4 million men; a further 7.4 million were lost in 1942, 7.8 million in 1943, and over 2.1 million in the first three months of 1944.[8] Surely even the Soviet Union couldn't continue taking casualties on such a scale. Every report of younger Red Army prisoners or increasing numbers of Soviet soldiers from the eastern territories – almost always described as 'Asiatic' or 'Mongolian' in German accounts – was seized upon as evidence. This was part of Hitler's strategy: if the casualty rates could be kept sufficiently high, the Soviet forces would be bled white and would be unable to continue the war. There can be no question that the casualties suffered by the Red Army were almost unimaginably high – the figures above give a total of 21.7 million, of which 8.8 million were 'irrecoverable', i.e. dead, missing (many of whom were prisoners who suffered high death rates in German captivity), or too badly wounded to return to service. But despite this, the Soviet Union continued to supply men to the front line. However, strains were beginning to show. Throughout the second half of 1943 and the early months of 1944, men in newly recovered territories were rounded up and conscripted into service, often with only the most rudimentary training, in order to try to keep combat units at an effective strength. Inevitably, the casualty rates of such poorly trained recruits were even higher than those of fresh recruits from the Soviet interior.

Despite these issues of manpower, the Red Army was in a strong numerical position by the summer of 1944, particularly given the advantage of being able to concentrate forces in a selected area for an offensive. To increase the advantage still further, the Red Army implemented a novel type of formation. From the beginning of 1942, the *Ukrepleyonny Raion* ('Fortified Region') began to appear, consisting of about 4,500 men with large numbers of machine-guns and heavy weapons. Each of these relatively immobile formations could take up defensive positions that would otherwise require one or even two rifle divisions, thus freeing the rifle divisions for offensive operations.

As the war progressed, a large number of Soviet formations were given the honorific title of 'Guards', usually after performing well in a major battle or being involved in the liberation of a large town or city. One such formation was Eleventh Guards Army, commanded by Lieutenant General Kuzma Nikitovich Galitsky. Prior to its promotion to 'Guards' status, it had been Sixteenth Army, heavily involved in the battles in the central sector throughout 1942 and 1943, and it continued to be used in heavy fighting as the German Army Group Centre was slowly driven back in the second half of 1943 and early 1944, as a result of which it was left badly weakened. In preparation for *Bagration*, it received a steady stream of fresh troops to bring it back to full strength, as Galitsky described:

Replenishment drafts began to arrive – up to 3,000 men per day. These were soldiers who had undergone three or four months of training in reserve regiments and brigades. They were well-dressed, smart, and in good spirits. In just a few days, my army received 20,000 personnel. Thanks to this, we were able to increase the strength of each division to about 7,300 officers and men.[9]

It is a measure of how weak Eleventh Guards Army was, that even with 20,000 replacement drafts its divisions remained below their establishment strength of 10,700 men. Further fresh conscripts arrived in the weeks that followed, together with new equipment in quantities that were far more lavish than ever before:

> Our fleet of motor vehicles and caterpillar tractors for artillery as well as horse-drawn wagons increased significantly. The arrival of 120 SU-76 assault guns, which began to be delivered to the front line in large numbers, was especially pleasing. In addition the army received about 9,000 machine-guns, 6,500 rifles, 42 regimental guns [used for close infantry support], and 167 anti-tank guns of the 1943 specification.
>
> The armament of each division now looked very impressive. Each had a detachment of self-propelled guns consisting of 13 SU-76s, with 48 76mm and 122mm guns, 30 anti-tank guns, 75 medium and heavy mortars, about 2,300 machine-guns and submachine-guns, 18 large calibre anti-aircraft machine-guns, 4,000 rifles, and 80–90 motor vehicles.[10]

These new weapons created new problems. Whilst the appearance of the SU-76 in larger numbers than before was very welcome, few of the relatively small number of veterans in Galitsky's divisions – and almost none of the replacement drafts – had experience of working with them. Training was therefore urgently needed, and Galitsky and his staff immediately set to work. If Eleventh Guards Army was to perform successfully in the coming offensive, Galitsky knew from the experiences of preceding months that it would have to fight far more effectively to overcome tough defensive positions without suffering crippling losses.

> In preparing the rifle formations, the main area of attention was tactical exercises. These took up 60 per cent of training. Sappers, scouts, artillery spotters, anti-tank teams, snipers, medics, and others were given their own training programmes.
>
> We assigned the NCOs of rifle companies and gun batteries to special groups. They took part in a special programme that concentrated on the peculiarities of the role of NCOs both during the preparation of the operation and in the subsequent battle. The timely delivery of ammunition and the repair and maintenance of weapons, food, and uniforms of the soldiers depended largely on these NCOs. An experienced and courageous NCO is a reliable asset for his company commander. Therefore, we not only trained them separately, but also organised a ten-day training camp especially for them. The best company and

battalion commanders as well as instructors who had worked with junior officers were used in this. The outcome was very favourable and undoubtedly increased their efficacy ...

By 10 May, that is in less than a month, each battalion had conducted up to 15 field exercises lasting at least six hours. In addition to attacking enemy positions, the battalions practised fighting in forests and villages, and in conducting river crossings ...

Two options were considered for forcing rivers. The first was for when the enemy had prepared to defend the water line in advance and had put up a system of various obstacles in front of his positions, supported by artillery fire from the depths of the position, and the second was in the absence of enemy defences. The exercises were carried out on the Usha and Obol Rivers and on Lake Ordovo. Battalion, regiment, and division commanders were required to choose the most advantageous line of approach to the water obstacle, consider carefully its depth, the speed of the current, and the nature of defences, and determine the enemy's capabilities, taking into account artillery and air support, the use of sappers, and the availability of bridging resources.

Six-day exercises for rifle battalion commanders were held, in which the conduct of offensive operations was rehearsed. The deputy commander of the army led these classes and the most experienced rifle division deputy commanders and their deputies as well as the chiefs of artillery and armoured and mechanised troops from the Army headquarters and the signals chief took part as teachers. Much time was assigned to the exchange of experience by battalion commanders.

At the same time, corps and division commanders joined me in a training exercise. Regimental commanders attended a three-day course and company commanders a five-day course ...

Coming to terms with new technology and its use in combat took place on training areas that we constructed, simulating the conditions of combat. Joint exercises of rifle units and tanks, assault guns, and engineers were held including live artillery fire. On the same training grounds, soldiers and officers of the replacement drafts, who had no experience of battle, were 'baptised' with artillery fire and encounters with tanks.[11]

The emphasis on longer courses for battalion commanders than others is interesting. This reflected high casualty rates amongst such officers with the result that many were as inexperienced as their soldiers. But it also highlights the belief in the Red Army that the battalion was the primary unit in combat. This practice continued in the Soviet Army after the war and persists in the post-Soviet era, with emphasis on what are now known as 'battalion tactical groups'.

Another unit that would take part in the summer offensive was Thirty-Ninth Army; its commander, Lieutenant General Nikolai Erastovich Berzarin, would be replaced by Lieutenant General Ivan Ilyich Lyudnikov in the last days of May. Major General Vasily Romanovich Boiko was a member of the army's military council and he was heavily involved in the absorption of new recruits. As his duties were of a more political nature, he concentrated on other aspects of their induction:

> From 10 May to 15 June 1944, about 25,000 soldiers and NCOs were sent to us. These new drafts had many features in common.
>
> The great majority were aged between 18 and 20, though most had already completed four months of basic training. The new arrivals knew how to use weapons and had rudimentary training in small unit tactics. But it was necessary to teach them as quickly as possible how to operate not just in training but in real combat situations. The military council recommended that commanders and commissars make extensive use of seasoned soldiers for these purposes, ensuring even distribution through all units and thus organising the passing on of combat experience and practices from the veterans to the youngsters ...
>
> For the first time we also had to deal with the fact that most of these replenishment drafts came from the recently liberated regions of the country, which had been under occupation for a long time. These young people, having experienced the cruelty of the Nazi invaders, were keen to fight but didn't have the necessary moral and political preparation to withstand the harsh and lengthy trials of military life. Only an insignificant proportion of those amongst the replenishments were Komsomols [junior Communist Party members].[12]

Whilst many of the men conscripted from recently liberated areas might have been highly motivated to fight, the paranoia that underlay so much of Stalin's era was never far away and throughout their basic training, these recruits would have been carefully monitored to ensure that they had not become corrupted by their exposure to the Germans.

Previous operations had been handicapped by poor road and rail access and sapper units were deployed to try to improve the situation. Vasily Ivanovich Repin was a soldier in one such battalion:

> In the first half of May, our battalion was ordered to lay a corduroy road through the forest parallel to the front line. Several side-roads were supposed to stretch from it towards the front line, constructed in the same manner with logs laid next to each other.

The kilometres through the forest were hard work for us. It was physically difficult: construction had to be carried out at a high tempo, day and night. More than once we had to plunge almost to our necks into the cold slurry when laying the roadway through swamps. And we had no time to dry our clothing – everything dried on us if we were warm enough. Tunics, greatcoats tucked under our belt, the steam rose from us as we laboured. But we worked with huge enthusiasm knowing why these roads were being built. As soon as the hour for a new offensive arrived, our tanks, guns, and vehicles carrying infantry and ammunition were supposed to pass over them. But sometimes we felt a deep bitterness at the sight of hundreds of beautiful fir trees, first-rate silver birch trunks, and resinous pines falling to the ground as we wielded our axes and saws. The war disfigured the forest and all our land. How useful would these logs that fell into the mud be for the reconstruction of the villages burned down by the Fascist invaders! But immediately it occurred to me that it was precisely in order that villages wouldn't be burned down in future and people wouldn't have to huddle in dugouts, that we must now do our job with tripled, tenfold energy, building this difficult road that brought us closer to victory.

The main road and the side branches were completed four days ahead of schedule. And immediately after, we started manufacturing components for the construction of prefabricated bridges with frame supports. It was clear to us sappers that this could only mean that there would be a major operation that involved forcing a large river. Such a waterway lay ahead of us to the west, the Western Dvina [Daugava] with its numerous tributaries.[13]

As is described below, the Germans were confidently predicting that the Red Army's attacks would not be against Army Group Centre. They monitored the apparent build-up of Soviet forces opposite Army Group North Ukraine, where they expected the blow to fall; but this was in fact part of a large-scale deception plan. Such deception came under the overall term *Maskirovka*, with deception intended to take place at strategic, operational, and tactical levels:

[*Maskirovka* is] the means of securing combat operations and the daily activity of forces; a complexity of measures, directed to mislead the enemy regarding the presence and disposition of forces, various military objectives, their condition, combat readiness and also the plans of the command ... *Maskirovka* contributes to the achievement of surprise for the actions of forces, the preservation of combat readiness, and the increased attainment of objectives.[14]

At the level of Front and army headquarters, small teams of staff officers were given responsibility to oversee all *Maskirovka* measures, which largely fell into two headings: preventing the Germans from learning about Red Army intentions; and deliberately misleading the Germans. Experience of the successful encirclement of Stalingrad and less successful operations elsewhere provided the broad outline of how the first part should be achieved. Documents relating to the overall aim of the coming offensive were tightly restricted to a small number of senior officers. Wherever possible, instructions were passed verbally in person – radio transmission was avoided, as was the creation of documents that might fall into enemy hands. Units were moved at night unless daytime movement was unavoidable, and there was careful attention to camouflaging them on arrival at their new locations, and as many civilians as possible were removed from concentration areas; this was also extended to non-essential military personnel. In order to maintain the illusion that the area was not being reinforced, only units that had been in the sector in the past were permitted to conduct reconnaissance patrols so that any men who fell into German hands wouldn't reveal the appearance of new formations.

Factors that had repeatedly alerted the Germans to impending Soviet attacks included the use of registration fire by newly arrived artillery batteries; this was kept to a minimum wherever possible. Instead, there would be occasional shelling of almost any sector, and under cover of this bombardment the new gun batteries would have the opportunity to try to 'range in' their guns. Another failing in earlier operations was the habit of many units, particularly armoured formations, of making brief radio transmissions when they reached their destination in order to ensure that their radio links were working – this was now expressly forbidden. In order to counter the past success of Luftwaffe aerial reconnaissance, greater attention was made to preventing such flights by the deployment of Soviet fighter formations, but again it was important not to draw attention to any one sector by intensifying fighter patrols in a limited region; instead, fighter units were to be more aggressive along the entire front line against Luftwaffe reconnaissance aircraft. In the first two years of the war, the huge losses suffered by Soviet air armies in the opening days of the fighting – which saw hundreds of Soviet fighters and bombers destroyed on the ground – had left the Luftwaffe with almost complete air superiority, but the increased resources available to Soviet aviation were now tipping the balance against the Germans, particularly as so many German fighter formations had been transferred to the west in order to try to counter the bombing attacks on German cities by the Western Powers. Again, lend-lease played a part. By the end of the war, over 10,000 fighter planes had been delivered by the USA to the Soviet Union.[15] The great majority of these would have been regarded as obsolescent in the aerial battles over Western Europe but both sides in the east operated large numbers of outdated aircraft with considerable success. In addition, indigenous production of fighter aircraft – the Lavochkin La-5 and La-7, the Lavochkin-Gorbunov-Gudkov LaGG-3, and the Yakovlev Yak-1, Yak-3, Yak-7, and Yak-9 – rose steadily after factories were relocated to the Urals in the first months of the war. By 1944, therefore, the fighter formations of the Soviet air armies had plenty of aircraft with which to contest and often achieve air superiority along the entire front. By contrast, the Germans could achieve local dominance by concentrating resources, but only for short spells.

The use of *Maskirovka* both to disguise the deployment of forces for an offensive and to mislead the enemy about where such an offensive would take place took many forms. Information about German assessments of Red Army intentions arrived from a number of sources, and *Stavka* was therefore well aware that the Germans believed a further Soviet effort in the southern sector would take place. To reinforce this, 3rd Ukrainian Front was ordered to undertake several steps to create the impression of a substantial build-up of forces. Whilst increases in air activity and anti-aircraft defences were to be avoided in the areas where armies were preparing for the new offensive, 3rd Ukrainian Front deployed such assets relatively openly, particularly around areas where the concentration of several rifle divisions was being simulated. The Germans repeatedly observed empty troop trains heading east from the front line during daytime, and aware that the Red Army preferred to move its units at night, concluded that these trains must have delivered troops during the preceding hours of darkness; in reality, the trains had indeed travelled to the front line at night but without any passengers. Several infantry divisions were ordered to carry out repetitive marches in the area behind 3rd Ukrainian Front so that they might be observed by the Germans marching towards concentration areas either at first light or at dusk, as a Red Army battalion commander described:

> The troops would be moved out [i.e. withdrawn to the east] during the night, and then to give the impression that ten divisions had built up, our division would actually have moved backwards and forwards for ten nights. We'd move out at night, come back in the morning, sleep the whole day, and then repeat it all over again.[16]

It wasn't just 3rd Ukrainian Front that took part in this deception. Although General Ivan Stepanovich Konev's 1st Ukrainian Front was receiving substantial reinforcements to make up for its losses in the preceding months, the scale of this reinforcement was deliberately exaggerated to confirm the mistaken assumption by the Germans that this area would see the Red Army's main effort. Extensive use of dummy wooden tanks and aircraft, modestly camouflaged, also added to the impression of growing strength in the southern region. Similarly, 3rd Baltic Front in the north undertook steps to simulate the arrival and preparation of fresh rifle divisions.

German prisoners who were captured during the preparation phase were carefully interrogated to try to discover how much the Germans knew of what was happening. In early June, partisans reported that they had seized a soldier from the *Feldherrnhalle* panzergrenadier division. He told his captors that the division had been transferred to the region from the Narva sector in Estonia and was in poor shape; it was currently in villages and towns between Mogilev and Minsk, where it was awaiting replenishment. There was considerable consternation in *Stavka*. Was the division genuinely recuperating in what the Germans had decided was a 'quiet' sector, or had it been positioned in anticipation of a Soviet attack? Further intelligence was gathered and it became clear that the division was indeed badly depleted. This was most welcome news for two reasons: firstly, the division was too weak to play a major role in the coming battles; and secondly, its dispatch to this sector suggested that the Germans were not expecting any major fighting in the area.

As was the case with the partisan movement, the use of *Maskirovka* became part of the mythology that grew up in Soviet accounts of the war. Undoubtedly, the use of camouflage and deception was often effective, especially on occasions like the summer of 1944 where everything seemed to fit with preconceived German expectations. However, the Germans could not fail to detect the presence of so many formations in the central area as the days grew longer and warmer. It became clear that the Soviet forces facing Army Group Centre certainly had the capability to mount a major attack, but the scale of any such attack continued to be underestimated. Crucially, the Germans failed to detect the arrival of Fifth Guards Tank Army in the central region. Its commander, Marshal Pavel Alekseyevich Rotmistrov, was actually identified by a captured Red Army soldier, but the significance of his presence was discounted – no major armoured units had been spotted, and it was easy to assume that his presence had nothing to do with any plans for imminent attacks in the region.

A recurring feature of Red Army operations throughout the war was the use of reconnaissance in force. In many cases, particularly in 1942, the intention was to try to simulate a full-scale attack by deploying just one or two battalions in the hope that this would result in the Germans opening fire with all of their defensive weapons; these weapons could then be identified and artillery could be tasked with their destruction when the main assault took place. The efficacy of this form of reconnaissance in force was highly questionable. Many senior officers regarded it as an essential exercise, but most of the soldiers involved had a different opinion. Although the memoirs of some senior Red Army figures describe the use of specially trained battalions, in most cases it seems that units received orders to carry out reconnaissance in force at short notice and had little time or opportunity for specialist training or preparation. As a consequence, casualties were often very heavy. Moreover, if the reconnaissance in force took place several days before the planned major attack, its value was lost – the Germans would have ample time to redeploy their support weapons. If the reconnaissance in force was very close to the day of the main effort, passing the intelligence that had been acquired to artillery units in a timely manner often caused difficulties, and in any case the very act of reconnaissance in force might alert the Germans that a major attack was imminent.

In 1944, this form of reconnaissance in force continued, but further nuances had developed. Raids to provoke defensive fire continued to take place, but additionally there would be aggressive probes on the eve of the main attack to identify hitherto-undetected weaknesses, or to secure better starting points for the assault forces. In order to avoid the Germans using these attacks to identify the location of the main attack, it became commonplace for reconnaissance in force to take place at as many locations as possible over several days or even weeks prior to an attack. The cost in dead and wounded was high, but despite its terrible losses the Red Army had men to spare. And in any case, if the reconnaissance in force was effective, it would potentially reduce losses in the main assault. As the start date of *Bagration* approached, Soviet armies along the entire Eastern Front carried out local reconnaissance probes as part of the *Maskirovka* operation. These were particularly pronounced in the southern sectors.

The scale of the forthcoming operation would be huge, and in order to prepare as effectively as possible many senior officers urged Stalin to discontinue offensive operations for several months prior to the assault, particularly in the central sector. At first, Stalin was disinclined to agree, preferring to continue attacks, but the poor efficacy of such attacks in the central region – particularly the very high cost compared to the modest gains – persuaded him to change his mind. An additional small delay in the onset of *Bagration* actually worked in favour of the Red Army; attacks wound down over several days, giving the impression of exhaustion as the cause. This added to German complacency that the Soviet forces in the central sector were unlikely to mount major operations in the summer.

The issue of poor cooperation between different arms was a repeated criticism of Soviet operations and attempts were made to improve this. As the

Soviet armies prepared for the summer offensive, units were subjected to intensive training with infantry and tanks working together. The quality of this training in offensives prior to *Bagration* was variable. According to some veterans, it amounted to little more than walk-through exercises with little attempt to simulate the confusion of battle; consequently, junior leaders had little opportunity to learn how to improvise and adapt in the face of unexpected circumstances. Infantrymen were also put through exercises involving artillery fire in an attempt to acclimatise them to the shock and noise of shelling – when they attacked, the infantry was expected to move forward with a rolling barrage of shellfire preceding them, and attacks in earlier battles often failed because new recruits were too scared to keep up with the barrage. Although some soldiers later described these exercises as too artificial to be of any use, it seems that the preparatory training of the assault forces was more effective than had been the case in earlier offensives. Officers at every level rehearsed the coming attack and the senior staff officers overseeing their preparations attempted to introduce the uncertainty and confusion of war into the exercises. Riflemen and tank crews repeatedly took part in movements through difficult terrain and replicas of German defences were constructed, making use of what had been learned from the capture of German defensive lines in the past. In particular, after the Wehrmacht withdrew from the Rzhev salient in early 1943, the depth of the German defensive positions was found to be far greater than had been suspected; this knowledge was now used to help shape preparations for *Bagration*.

The Red Army's artillery also underwent extensive training and preparation. The weight of Soviet artillery barrages steadily increased as the war continued, but their efficacy was often disappointing and in preparation for the summer offensive there was considerable effort to improve the quality of reconnaissance and the appropriate allocation of artillery units for specific targets. It had been almost standard practice for the preliminary artillery preparation to conclude with salvoes of *Katyusha* rockets, but this was proving to be problematic. Knowing that they might face heavy bombardment, the Germans had become adept at digging deep bunkers in which they stood a good chance of survival. When they heard the distinctive screech of the *Katyusha* volleys, they knew the infantry and tank assault was imminent and returned to their firing positions, and in combination with the reluctance of inexperienced Soviet infantry to keep up with the artillery barrage as it moved into the depths of the German position, this greatly reduced the efficacy of the initial bombardment. The remedy was obvious. After the *Katyusha* salvoes, there would be a further spell of shelling of German front-line positions, either to catch any Germans who had emerged from their bunkers or to discourage them from making any attempt to do so.

Another recurrent failing of earlier Soviet operations was the inability of artillery and support service to keep up with the advance. The huge numbers of trucks supplied by the Western Powers went a considerable way towards remedying this, as did the terrain on which the operation would take place. Although a large proportion of the Belarusian landscape was covered with swamps and woodland, the modest areas of high ground provided firmer routes for motorised movement, particularly during the dry summer months. The roads of the area, whilst poor by the standards of Western Europe, were considerably better than those over which both sides had conducted operations further east, and the Red Army now had better bridging capabilities to construct crossings over the rivers in its path. There were three types of bridging unit depending on the size and weight of bridge, and the attacking armies would be accompanied by these units to ensure that they were able to sustain a high tempo of advance. The advance across Ukraine in 1943 and early 1944 had been repeatedly held up by having to secure crossings over the great waterways of the region, but although there were several rivers in Belarus that would play a major part in the coming fighting, they were far smaller than the Dnepr, Southern Bug, and Dniester further to the south.

Plans for all major Soviet operations involved objectives at a variety of levels. The initial task was of course to overcome the enemy defences. Once this was achieved, there were local objectives to be secured, and operational orders then outlined deeper objectives that were often far to the rear of the German positions. In most cases prior to *Bagration*, these deeper objectives were not achieved and with hindsight it was easy to see why – simply breaking the German defences took up a great deal of Soviet resources, leaving too little for deep exploitation. As the staff officers of the Red Army began to draw up their plans for the summer of 1944, there was a great deal of attention paid to ensuring that exploitation formations were strong enough to sustain the operation into the full depths of Belarus. This meant more than simply ensuring these units were sufficiently strong; they also required substantial stocks of ammunition, fuel, and food, and the means to move this forward quickly.

The scale of the planned operation created substantial difficulties in terms of building up sufficient resources. Most artillery formations would start the battle with a nominal stock of between two and four 'combat loads', i.e. sufficient ammunition for two to four days, but there was considerable variation. Bagramian's armies, for example, complained throughout the preparatory phase that there was insufficient ammunition for 45mm guns, which were used in close support of the rifle units. Food supplies also proved problematic. By mid-June, stockpiles close to the front line were sufficient for about two or three weeks, but the widespread use of cavalry added to supply demands. Horses consume a great deal of fodder; in the First World War, for example, the Russian Army devoted more railway capacity to moving feed for horses than for soldiers. As the day of the offensive drew closer, many cavalry formations reported that they had only a week's supply of oats. All they could do was hope that they would be able to find sufficient fodder as they advanced.[17]

Shtemenko spent much of the preparation phase working with the various Fronts to try to sort out the myriad problems of assembling such large forces and their essential supplies. Even in the week before the offensive began, he remained worried about the repeated failure of the railway system to provide

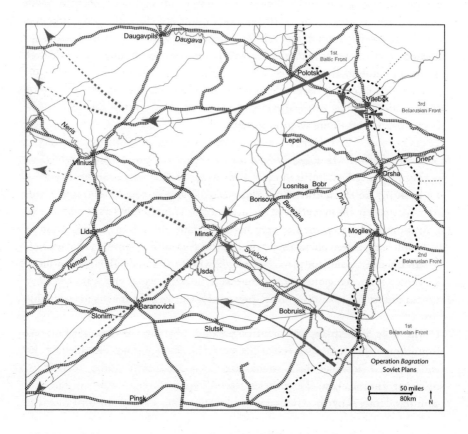

sufficient trains to move everything into position. Even when railway capacity was available, other problems arose. Rotmistrov's Fifth Guards Tank Army was to be transferred from 2nd Ukrainian Front to 3rd Belarusian Front and there was considerable alarm when staff officers realised that Marshal Rodion Yakovlevich Malinovsky, who had just taken command of 2nd Ukrainian Front, intended to transfer only some of Rotmistrov's tanks – he wanted to keep the majority in order to bring his other units up to strength. It took forcible representations by several senior figures before Malinovsky agreed to release all of Fifth Guards Tank Army's vehicles.

Planning progressed steadily, with each Front considering how best to achieve its designated objectives.[18] Bagramian was summoned to Moscow from the headquarters of 1st Baltic Front in early May, where he had a meeting with General Aleksei Innokentovich Antonov, the deputy chief of the Soviet general staff – Marshal Aleksandr Mikhailovich Vasilevsky was his superior, but was often used by Stalin to coordinate the operations of multiple Fronts and in his absence the capable Antonov took over almost all of his duties. Bagramian had already received instructions to commence the evacuation of non-essential civilians from his Front's area and had guessed that this was a precursor to a major operation; he now received a broad outline and was asked to commence detailed planning. Further meetings in Moscow followed, often involving the commanders of one or more other Fronts and also involving Zhukov, the deputy commander-in-chief of the Red Army. At one such meeting, Zhukov asked Bagramian for his thoughts on the plan:

> I replied that I was delighted with the concept of the plan with its bold and decisive objectives. But at the same time, I expressed concerns about our right flank [i.e. to the north] as our right neighbour, 2nd Baltic Front, was not taking part in the first phase of the attack. After all, our Front was to assist not just in breaking up the northern flank of Army Group Centre, but also in conducting a deep encirclement of the central grouping from the northwest. 'In this case,' I said, 'the powerful Army Group North could mount a powerful thrust from the north against our overstretched flank into the rear of our Front.'[19]

It was to be a recurring worry for Bagramian, that the Germans might attack from the north. His assessment of the 'powerful' Army Group North was rather wide of the mark – of the German army groups on the Eastern Front, it was probably the weakest. Nonetheless, the skilful use of armoured forces in counteroffensives by the Germans had left men like Bagramian with a healthy respect for their enemy's capabilities. Zhukov reassured him that 2nd Baltic Front would attack shortly after Bagramian's Front; after further discussions, it was agreed that Bagramian was to move the axis of his Front's operation from an overall southwesterly direction to a more westerly axis in order to ensure better protection of the northern flank. But an important factor in Soviet calculations about the possibility of German counterattacks and in how the operation eventually unfolded was the crucial difference between the summer of 1944 and earlier years: Germany would be unable to draw upon forces in Western Europe as reinforcements as had been the case in almost every crisis that had erupted along the Eastern Front. Any German counterstrokes against *Bagration* would have to be made with the forces available, and *Stavka* intended to launch attacks to both the north and the south in order to tie down German formations. By the end of May, several initial iterations had been considered and detailed instructions were passed to Front commanders. Bagramian's orders became clearer. He was to attack and destroy German units in and to the west of Vitebsk with a major attack from the area to the northwest of the German-held salient around Vitebsk. The overall operation was expected to unfold in three phases; the timing of the first parts was clearly stipulated, but the ultimate end-point of *Bagration* would depend upon how events unfolded.

The first phase was to penetrate the German defences to the west of Vitebsk. Reconnaissance of the region, supplemented by intelligence reports from partisan units and prisoner interrogations, gave an estimated maximum depth of the German positions of six miles and complete penetration was expected on the first day. The second phase anticipated an advance to the Western Dvina or Daugava River with the intention of securing crossings in the area of the town of Beshenkovichi, 30 miles west of Vitebsk; the Daugava River flowed west from Vitebsk to this town before angling to the northwest and it was important to secure crossings as quickly as possible. The plans expected this to be achieved by the end of the fourth day of the operation. Thereafter, Bagramian was to press on with the third phase, the forcing of the Ulla River and an advance towards Lepel, a further 32 miles to the west, while ensuring strong units faced north to protect the flank of the entire operation. If these phases of the operation went as anticipated, 1st Baltic Front would have covered half the distance to Minsk, and it was anticipated that subsequent attacks towards the Belarusian capital would follow in conjunction with the other Fronts involved.

The attack to capture Vitebsk by 1st Baltic Front from the north would be complemented by the initial attack of Cherniakhovsky's 3rd Belarusian Front. There would be two main axes of attack. The first, from a start line to the southeast and east of Vitebsk, involved Thirty-Ninth and Fifth Armies; the latter was to sweep past the southern flank of the city and then angle to the northwest to link up with Bagramian's advancing forces, while the former overwhelmed the German forces trapped within Vitebsk itself. At the same time, Eleventh Guards Army and Thirty-First Army were to advance along the main Moscow–Smolensk–Minsk highway towards Borisov, outflanking German positions in Orsha immediately to the south and then overwhelming them. This thrust was to reach and cross the Berezina River by the tenth day of the attack. Cherniakhovsky's exploitation force was another example of continuing Soviet experimentation. The issue of infantry being unable to keep up with armoured units had hindered both the Red Army and the Wehrmacht, and in addition the Red Army had often struggled to find an effective use for its numerous cavalry formations – whilst they had good mobility, they were too lightly armed to be able to engage major enemy formations. The solution that enjoyed considerable success in the southern sector in late 1943 and early 1944 was the creation of a cavalry-mechanised group with a mixture of tanks, assault guns, and horsemen; the cavalry could keep up with the tanks and would dismount and function as infantry when opposition was encountered. Cherniakhovsky designated III Guards Mechanised Corps and III Guards Cavalry Corps to form such a group; it would enter battle after Fifth Army had broken through the German defences to the south of Vitebsk.

The thrust along the Minsk highway would be led by Eleventh Guards Army, and it was reinforced by II Guards Tank Corps which would act as its exploitation force. After sweeping past the German 'fortress' of Orsha, the tank corps was to press on towards the southwest with the intention of reaching the Berezina and capturing crossings on the sixth day of the operation. Whilst the cavalry-mechanised group and II Guards Tank Corps were strong exploitation forces, the real striking power of 3rd Belarusian Front was Rotmistrov's Fifth Guards Tank Army. The bespectacled and balding Rotmistrov was at first glance an unlikely commander of armoured forces, but he had led such units from the outset of the war. He caught Stalin's eye at an early stage of the conflict and impressed the Soviet leader with his clear and logical analysis of the deficiencies of Soviet armoured forces and particularly with his practical suggestions for improvements such as the addition of handles to the outer hull of tanks so that 'tank riders' could accompany the tanks as they advanced. He took command of Fifth Guards Tank Army when it was created in early 1943, but his subsequent operational performance was perhaps less impressive than his earlier achievements. In what was admittedly some of the heaviest fighting of the war, Fifth Guards Tank Army repeatedly suffered heavy casualties and there was concern that Rotmistrov showed little inclination to manoeuvre around strong positions, relying instead on the sheer weight and power of his formations to overcome all resistance.

It was a sign of the growing competence and flexibility of the Red Army that the deployment of Fifth Guards Tank Army would depend upon how the operation unfolded. It would either move through the ranks of Eleventh Guards Army in order to thrust down the Minsk highway towards Borisov; or, if there were delays in this part of the operation, be deployed in Fifth Army's sector immediately to the south of Vitebsk, from where it would make its way to the Minsk highway from the northeast, thus outflanking any forces holding up Eleventh Guards Army. Rotmistrov and his staff were to reconnoitre approach routes for both axes from their holding area over 20 miles behind the front line. As part of these preparations, they identified all other units that either would be in their path or might wish to use the same roads and negotiated appropriate access.

To the south of Cherniakhovsky's armies was Zakharov's 2nd Belarusian Front. He had only recently taken up his post after the dismissal of Colonel General Ivan Yefimovich Petrov, who seemed to be dogged by the misfortune of Stalin's distrust. He led a rifle division with distinction in the battles for Odessa in 1941 and oversaw the evacuation of the city by sea to Crimea, where he played a major role in the defence of Sevastopol. When the city fell to the Germans in 1942, he was one of a handful of senior officers who were evacuated by submarine; disheartened by his defeat, Petrov attempted to commit suicide and had to be forcibly restrained by his colleagues. He commanded Forty-Fourth Army in the Caucasus where once more he fought with distinction, and was in charge of Soviet forces attempting to cross the Kerch Strait into Crimea in the winter of 1943–44. Petrov's attempts were largely defeated, mainly because he had inadequate resources for such an operation, but he was dismissed from his command. Within a short time, he was appointed first to command of Thirty-Third Army and then 2nd Belarusian Front, but he then fell foul of the malign influence of Lev Zakharovich Mekhlis, one of several deputy defence ministers. Mekhlis had no military experience but was unswervingly loyal to Stalin, who repeatedly sent him to different sectors to advise Stalin on the fitness of field commanders to retain their posts. It seems that Stalin had a low opinion of Mekhlis, but nonetheless found his loyalty useful and regarded his assessments as accurate and reliable. In the early summer of 1944, Mekhlis – now acting as a member of the Military Council of 2nd Belarusian Front – wrote to the Soviet leader about Petrov's 'flabbiness and inability' and suggested that his health was too poor for him to hold such a post.[20] The result was Petrov's dismissal, though he was then appointed commander of 4th Ukrainian Front just a few weeks later.

Shtemenko had a low opinion of Zakharov, the new commander of 2nd Belarusian Front, regarding him as 'extremely headstrong' and 'over-impetuous'.[21] The initial planning for 2nd Belarusian Front's role in *Bagration* had been carried out by Petrov, and Shtemenko was anxious to prevent Zakharov from imposing a completely new interpretation of the operation. As soon as he took up his post, Zakharov visited his armies with Shtemenko:

> Zakharov, as we had expected, promptly declared everything unsatisfactory and said he would have a great deal to do, putting right other people's mistakes. He immediately produced arguments against launching the main attack in the prepared direction ... [Only after his alternative proposals were rejected by *Stavka*] did Zakharov grudgingly give way.[22]

An attack in this sector faced formidable defences: Red Army reconnaissance and information from prisoner interrogations and from partisans suggested that the main defensive line extended to a depth of up to three miles with two further defensive lines to the rear. In addition, there were several rivers in the path of the attack, which necessitated either the capture of bridges or the rapid deployment of bridging formations if the pace of the advance was to be sustained. Zakharov was given the task of destroying German forces around Mogilev and he submitted his final proposals to *Stavka* on 10 June. The main assault would be made immediately north of Mogilev with the intention of securing crossings over the Dnepr River, which ran south from Orsha to Mogilev and onwards towards Ukraine. Forty-Ninth Army would attack from its start line to the east of Mogilev with the intention of forcing the line of the Basia River before turning the northern flank of the city's defences and making converging attacks to capture Mogilev itself. With fewer resources at his disposal than Cherniakhovsky, Zakharov formed an exploitation group of a single rifle division with two tank brigades and an anti-tank brigade. This would enter the battle once crossings over the Basia had been secured and would lead the way to the rather larger obstacle of the Dnepr – even this far from where it flows into the Black Sea, the river is 130 feet wide. Four brigades of engineers were assigned to support 2nd Belarusian Front and these included substantial bridging resources.

While Forty-Ninth Army and the exploitation group surged past the northern edge of Mogilev, the Front's southern flank, Fiftieth Army, would take a more passive role. It was to mount aggressive probes with the intention of keeping the Germans pinned in their positions while they were outflanked, and was to be ready to conduct offensive operations as the battle unfolded.

The final formation involved in *Bagration* was Rokossovsky's 1st Belarusian Front in the south. As was the case elsewhere, the Soviet forces in this sector were heavily involved in the *Maskirovka* phase of preparation; Rokossovsky later wrote that Colonel General Mikhail Sergeyevich Malinin, his chief of staff, was 'inexhaustibly inventive', organising train movements to give the impression that large numbers of men were being withdrawn from the sector.[23] For *Bagration*, the main task would be the capture of Bobruisk using the armies on the right wing of 1st Belarusian Front. Anticipating an attack on the city, the German divisions in the sector had constructed up to five defensive lines to the east of Bobruisk, though only the first two lines were heavily fortified.

During the planning of the contribution of Rokossovsky's armies to *Bagration*, there was – according to some sources – a difference of opinion about how precisely Rokossovsky was to deploy his forces for the assault on Bobruisk. Writing in a military journal in 1954, Rokossovsky recalled:

> Our plan to deliver two equal blows on the right wing of the Front [at Bobruisk] was strongly criticised. The supreme commander [Stalin] and some members of *Stavka* did not agree with this plan. They insisted on delivering one main blow from the bridgehead on the Dnepr in Third Army's sector. My arguments that the operational capacity along this axis was very limited, the terrain was difficult, and there were strong enemy forces to the north, were not taken into account. Stalin's stubborn insistence on striking a single powerful blow was apparently based upon his concept of a primary assault. But in this case, the local situation required a departure from the established pattern.
>
> Stalin twice suggested that I go into the next room to consider the proposal of *Stavka* [i.e. for a single attack] and then to report my decision. During the second 'pause for thought' Molotov and [Georgy Maksimilyanovich] Malenkov [longstanding associates of Stalin and amongst other posts members of the State Defence Committee] entered the room. They expressed disapproval of me arguing with the supreme commander and insisted that I accept *Stavka*'s proposals. I replied that I was convinced I was right and that if *Stavka* ordered to strike just one blow, I would ask for permission to relinquish command of the Front.[24]

When the main conference reconvened, Rokossovsky doggedly insisted that two attacks would be better, and Stalin conceded.[25] However, there is some dispute as to whether this incident took place as described; in his memoirs, Zhukov explicitly denied it happened, but other sources suggest that Stalin and particularly his acolytes Molotov and Malenkov attempted to browbeat Rokossovsky into accepting Stalin's original plan.[26] More recently, a Russian author's analysis of the various iterations of plans and orders attempted to cast doubt on Rokossovsky's version of events and there is certainly some indication that from an early stage, attacks either side of Bobruisk were explicitly written into the plan.[27] However, in many documents these two attacks are described as the 'main' attack and the 'auxiliary' attack. Lieutenant General Konstantin Fedorovich Telegin, a member of the military council of Rokossovsky's 1st Belarusian Front, described in his memoirs how Rokossovsky told him about the incident on his return from *Stavka* and also about a later meeting with Zhukov:

> Before we left, Zhukov spoke firmly in his characteristic manner in defence of delivering the main blow from the Rogachev sector [i.e. a single thrust] but after Rokossovsky's equally firm words about his conviction that the chosen plan was the correct one, he said half-jokingly,
>
> 'Fine, as you wish! I will go to [Lieutenant General Aleksandr Vasilyevich] Gorbatov's headquarters [commander of Third Army, which was delivering the eastern thrust towards Bobruisk]. We will give you a helping hand across the Berezina, we'll be there to pull you out of the swamps and get you to Bobruisk!'
>
> With that, he left for Rogachev. One can imagine the general atmosphere, the mood of like-minded people whose decision was about to be put to a severe test in the presence of an arbitrator who was far from impartial and in possession of high authority and great power.[28]

It seems therefore that there was a disagreement between Rokossovsky on one hand and Stalin and Zhukov on the other about how best to attack Bobruisk, but the detailed accounts are largely based on Rokossovsky's memoirs and may therefore contain an element of bias. The stage at which he was given permission to treat them as equally important is not clear, but his assessment – that the single 'main' attack would have faced considerable terrain difficulties and that it would have been difficult to assemble sufficient forces in the small Dnepr bridgehead from which this attack was to be launched – was correct.

Regardless of when the decision was made, Rokossovsky was able to add further details to the assaults that were to sweep past both flanks of the German units in and around Bobruisk. Third Army would attempt to turn the northern flank of the German line by attacking from the Dnepr bridgehead near Rogachev, while Twenty-Eighth Army attacked from the south with the intention of cutting the roads running west from Bobruisk. Between these two attacks, Forty-Eighth and Sixty-Fifth Armies would advance towards the city and were to assist in its capture.

Like Cherniakhovsky, Rokossovsky had a cavalry-mechanised group at his disposal, consisting of IV Guards Cavalry Corps and I Mechanised Corps; these were under the command of the excellent Lieutenant General Issa Aleksandrovich Pliev. Unlike so many other senior officers on both sides, Pliev was too young to have served in the First World War. He rose steadily through the ranks of the Red Army's cavalry and at the beginning of the war with Germany he was commander of 50th Cavalry Division. His formation was heavily involved in the Soviet counterattack near Smolensk and then formed part of Rokossovsky's Sixteenth Army in the Battle of Moscow; in recognition of its performance, the division was renamed 3rd Guards Cavalry Division. He took command of IV Guards Cavalry Corps in late 1943 and shortly after he was also appointed commander of a cavalry-mechanised group when tank units were added; he led this group with great energy in the Soviet advance into southwest Ukraine, playing a leading role in outflanking German positions near Odessa and capturing vital infrastructure before it could be destroyed by the retreating Wehrmacht. He was an energetic commander, rare in the Red Army in having both the ability and the inclination to improvise in fluid situations, particularly when conducting a pursuit.

Rokossovsky and Pliev clearly had a warm relationship founded upon their shared experiences in the Battle of Moscow. Pliev later described how Rokossovsky enthusiastically hugged him when he arrived at 1st Belarusian Front headquarters with the words 'Thank God you've arrived.'[29] Pliev brought with him the veteran formations of his cavalry corps – 9th and 10th Guards Cavalry Divisions and 30th Cavalry Division, all restored to full strength after the fighting near Odessa; in addition, he would have I Mechanised Corps with 19th, 35th, and 37th Mechanised Brigades and 129th Tank Brigade. The mechanised corps was led by Lieutenant General Semen Moiseyevich Krivoshein, a highly experienced commander of mechanised and armoured formations. The combination of veteran personnel – although Pliev's divisions had suffered losses in the fighting near Odessa, these were not as heavy as in other units and the number of experienced soldiers was therefore relatively high – and some of the best senior officers in the Red Army made the cavalry-mechanised group a formidable force.

As was the case in other sectors, there were irritating delays for 1st Belarusian Front as its forces assembled for the coming assault. On the southern flank of the huge theatre of battle, Rokossovsky fretted throughout June as the arrival of IX Tank Corps was repeatedly delayed. Its vehicles finally moved into position in the second week of June, but ammunition deliveries to 1st Belarusian Front continued to lag behind schedule. In particular, there were concerns that Third Army lacked the ammunition required to penetrate German defences and the final trainloads were still arriving as the countdown to the commencement of *Bagration* moved into its last day.

When several Red Army Fronts were operating together in a large-scale operation, it was increasingly common for *Stavka* to appoint a senior representative to coordinate planning and the conduct of the campaign. For *Bagration*, the representatives were Zhukov and Vasilevsky. Zhukov would end the war as the best-known Soviet commander. His military reputation was first established when he secured a decisive victory over the Japanese at Khalkin Gol in Manchuria in 1939, and in 1941 he was dispatched by Stalin to Leningrad when it seemed as if the city's defences were about to collapse. Zhukov was credited with reorganising the armies attempting to hold back Army Group North, but it is difficult to identify with any certainty if his personal intervention actually mattered – most of the steps taken to halt the Germans were already underway and others were instigated by commanders who were already in post before Zhukov arrived. It is perhaps characteristic that he was quite willing to take full credit regardless of his contribution, and he was then summoned back to Moscow where he oversaw the defence of the city. Here, his role was far clearer; he tried to dissuade Stalin from a premature counteroffensive and then oversaw the successful attacks that drove Army Group Centre's panzer groups away from the Soviet capital. But after this triumph, the battle degenerated into increasingly costly and futile frontal assaults on German positions as Zhukov ruthlessly ordered his armies to continue applying pressure.

In defence of Zhukov, it must be recognised that Stalin, who seems to have been convinced that the Battle of Moscow represented the great turning point of the war and that the strength of the Wehrmacht was irretrievably broken, was responsible for the wasteful continuance of attacks even after the Germans had successfully transitioned to a defensive posture. But Zhukov's brutal determination to pursue plans even in the face of adverse events was repeatedly shown through 1942. He sent his deputy, Major General Zakharov (who as Colonel General would command 2nd Belarusian Front), to demand that a cavalry corps break through into the rear of the German positions regardless of its losses, and almost certainly on Zhukov's direct instructions, Zakharov was blunt and uncompromising:

> The task assigned by the Front is clear to you: you must break through the
> Varshavskoe highway into the rear of the enemy or die. And let me make it clear:
> either a brave death on the highway, as heroes behind enemy lines, or a shameful
> death here. I repeat, this is a task set by Zhukov, the Front, *Stavka*, and Stalin

himself. I was sent here to force you to complete the task by any means possible and I swear I will make you complete it, I will drive you into the rear of the German lines even if I have to shoot half your corps to do this. You must break through to the rear of the enemy with the means that you now have. That is why here, in our discussions, we can only talk about how to complete the task, not about what is required to complete it.[30]

Although Zhukov played a part in the planning of the great encirclement of the German Sixth Army in Stalingrad, his role was far smaller than that of other senior officers, particularly Vasilevsky, but once again Zhukov assumed a greater share of credit than was justified. At the same time, he oversaw the disastrous operation codenamed *Mars*, which saw the Red Army launch further futile and hugely costly assaults against the Rzhev salient. But despite his propensity for fighting battles that resulted in terrible Soviet losses, he remained in favour with Stalin. The Soviet leader had perhaps realised that given the nature of the Red Army as a blunt instrument, it needed to be wielded by a brutal figure like Zhukov. Prior to *Bagration*, Zhukov had overseen operations in north Ukraine, taking command of 1st Ukrainian Front when General Nikolai Fedorovich Vatutin was fatally wounded by Ukrainian nationalists.

One of the armies preparing to go into action in Rokossovsky's Front was Sixty-Fifth Army, commanded by Lieutenant General Pavel Ivanovich Batov. Reading between the lines of his memoirs, it seems that he and Zhukov did not enjoy a warm relationship. During a visit to the front line, Zhukov was irritated that Major General Ivan Ivanovich Ivanov, the commander of one of Batov's rifle corps, wasn't present when the group reached the command post of one of Ivanov's rifle divisions. When Ivanov belatedly appeared, Zhukov dismissed him brusquely.

The visit continued to go badly. The commander of the next division was Colonel Pavel Gavrilovich Petrov who had endured several misfortunes during the war. He was a regimental commander at the beginning of hostilities and found himself trapped in the encirclement of Soviet troops near Smolensk. Although he managed to fight his way to safety, he was relieved of his command and sent on a series of training courses before returning to the front line in the Caucasus region in late 1942. His performance was regarded as satisfactory – he was awarded the Order of the Red Banner – and after a further training course he took command of 44th Guards Rifle Division. When Zhukov, Rokossovsky, and Batov visited his command post, he appeared to be flustered and gave a muddled report; matters were worsened by sporadic German mortar fire.

The senior officers then drove away from the front line and Batov was given an unexpected order:

> The car bounced over tree roots through the forest. Without turning to look at me, Zhukov – who was sitting next to the driver – said, 'The corps commander [Ivanov] is to be relieved of his post. Transfer the commander of 44th [Guards Rifle] Division to a penal company.'
>
> The order struck me like a bolt from the blue. In our army it was an established rule not to remove anyone from their command without a proper investigation and without attempting to retrain those who had made mistakes. All of my staff and the military council agreed with this. The same procedure was followed in my corps. But how should I defend my subordinate?
>
> 'Why don't you answer?' Zhukov asked me.
>
> 'I'm listening, Comrade Marshal, and I'll make a note of both points. It isn't my habit to interrupt anyone.'
>
> 'There's nothing more to discuss. The army is ramshackle.'
>
> 'Perhaps, but in that case you should first and foremost punish the army commander. Please allow me to give you my opinion of these two officers.' I then told the marshal everything I knew about the careers of Petrov and Ivanov. 'They are dedicated, capable men. I have a long acquaintance with Petrov and had helped him recover his self-confidence. He has turned out well. General Ivanov is one of the heroes of the Dnepr battles.'
>
> 'So what exactly are your suggestions?'
>
> 'A warning. I know these two comrades personally from their service in my army and many years of service before the war and I trust them.'
>
> 'A typical case of family loyalty! Let me have your draft order.' ...
>
> My draft order was rejected. Nevertheless, at Rokossovsky's insistence, Zhukov finally agreed to a reduced sentence. Ivanov was reprimanded and the division commander was relieved of his post [but escaped being sent to a penal unit].[31]

While Zhukov coordinated the two Fronts in the southern half of the forthcoming operation, Vasilevsky would perform the same task with the two Fronts to the north. He was a completely different character from Zhukov – he rarely attempted to claim credit, even when it would have been justified, and his memoirs are striking in that they make little attempt to inflate his achievements. Indeed, many in the Red Army regarded him as too much of a yes-man, someone who was not inclined to argue with Stalin, but it seems that he rarely had to resort to disagreement and argument. The two men had an excellent personal relationship, perhaps because Stalin recognised that despite his unquestioned expertise, Vasilevsky was not as ambitious as other senior Soviet figures and therefore posed no threat to him personally.

Vasilevsky had been in Crimea overseeing the Soviet reconquest of the peninsula, and was driving towards Sevastopol on 12 May when the city fell to the Red Army. His vehicle passed over a landmine and he was injured in the explosion; while he recovered in hospital, he started to assist in preparations for *Bagration*.[32] He played an important role in the appointment of Cherniakhovsky as commander of 3rd Belarusian Front, and the assignment of Vasilevsky to the northern half of the offensive was deliberate. He was recognised as a better teacher and mentor than Zhukov, and this battle would be the first in which the young Cherniakhovsky controlled such a large-scale group of forces.

The overall plans for *Bagration* were firmly established by the end of May or early June. It is worth noting that the plans were drawn up in awareness of earlier shortcomings, as Shtemenko later described:

> We had no doubts about the Vitebsk area. Soviet troops had powerful pincers on this fortified centre and the logical thing was to encircle and immediately go on to break up and destroy the enemy grouping piecemeal. The term 'encirclement' was not used, however, with regard to the other lines of advance. As in Operation *Rumyantsev* [the Soviet advance across central Ukraine after the end of the Battle of Kursk in the second half of 1943], great care was taken over method. The experience gained in the Battle of Stalingrad and other major battles had shown that encirclement and destruction of the enemy entailed great expenditure of men and materiel and loss of time. Any delay on so broad an offensive front as Belarus would give the enemy a chance to bring up reserves and parry our blows ...
>
> We decided that previous methods of destroying the enemy were not suited to the present concrete situation. The new idea that took shape was as follows. Having shattered the bulk of the enemy's forces in the tactical zone of his defence with a powerful artillery and air onslaught, we should knock the remnants out of their fortified positions into the woods and marshes. There they would be at a disadvantage and we should harass them from the flanks and the air, while the partisans helped us in the rear.[33]

The intention therefore was that with the exception of Vitebsk, German forces were to be dispersed and scattered so that they could be finished off at a later stage by units following on from the main assault. The importance of maintaining the pace of the operation was repeatedly stressed. Although Stalingrad had been a stunning victory, the Germans had been able to restore their front line because so much of the Red Army's strength was tied down in the siege perimeter around the isolated city. Such a situation was to be avoided if at all possible.

Just as *Overlord* had been delayed in the west, *Bagration* was beset with problems and the start date slipped from the original intention to attack on 19 June and was now set for 22 June. As the Western Powers fought their way out of the beachheads and struggled towards Caen and Saint-Lô, Soviet railway engineers pushed the capacity of their rail net to the limit to deliver troops, equipment, and supplies to the waiting armies. Finally, all that could be achieved had been achieved, and the staff officers at every level from *Stavka* to individual regiments could do no more. A huge force had been assembled: nearly 1.7 million men; over 3,800 tanks; nearly 2,000 assault guns; over 32,700 guns, rocket launchers, and mortars; and 7,800 aircraft, together with as much in the way of supplies as could be gathered.[34] Now the planners waited with tense expectation to see how their plans unfolded.

CHAPTER 4

WAITING FOR THE HAMMER TO FALL

The strategy described by Hitler in his Führer Directive 51 was founded upon the intention to crush the Western Allies when they attempted their invasion before diverting land forces to the east; as the new Type XXI U-boats became available, they would permit the Battle of the Atlantic to be resumed, preventing the Americans from rebuilding their forces in Britain. As the first weeks of June progressed, this strategy was already unravelling as events on almost every front combined to the detriment of Germany.

Counterattacks at every level, from tactical to operational, were a hallmark of German military thinking. For this approach to succeed, local commanders needed sufficient forces to conduct such counterattacks and, critically, the freedom of action to implement them. From the very outset of *Overlord*, obstacles to both factors were beginning to have a detrimental impact. Substantial forces had indeed been held in readiness for the expected invasion, but just as German intelligence identified the wrong sector for an attack on the Eastern Front, the German forces in the west and the German high command made errors in France. Much like the planners of the Western Powers, the Germans had correctly identified the two most likely areas for landings, Normandy and Calais. The attraction of the latter was obvious – it was the shortest crossing point, and would allow Allied aircraft to operate further into the hinterland than was the case in Normandy. But the large number of waterways in the Calais region would have made exploitation of any landing much more difficult than was the case in Normandy. Although the sea crossing was much longer for Normandy, a breakout from the beachheads would rapidly threaten Cherbourg, the ports of Brittany, and Paris and the French heartland.

Just as the Soviet Union went to great lengths to mislead the Germans about their intentions for the summer of 1944, the Western Powers did all they could to persuade their enemies that they would be landing their forces elsewhere than Normandy. The overall deception plan was codenamed *Bodyguard*, which built on the experiences of earlier attempts to mislead the Germans. Its main components were given further codenames. *Fortitude* was based upon the suggestion that the Western Allies would attempt two landings, one in Norway and one near Calais; the details of these were entitled *Fortitude North* and *Fortitude South* respectively. Illusory armies were created and extensive measures were taken to simulate radio traffic. Information was deliberately leaked to reinforce the deception, and extensive air operations were mounted over the Pas-de-Calais.[1]

The overall impact of *Bodyguard* and *Fortitude* was largely successful, partly because just as was the case with Soviet *Maskirovka* plans, it reinforced pre-existing beliefs on the German side. The limited invasion plans drawn up in 1940 for an attack on southern England had left the Germans with a healthy respect for the difficulties of mounting such an operation and they naturally regarded the shortest possible crossing as the best way of reducing risks. Moreover, the Pas-de-Calais was the location for the V-weapons that were being constructed for a devastating bombardment of London. Given that the presence of launching sites for V-1 and V-2 rockets required the presence of substantial defences, there were already extensive preparations to beat off any attack in this area.

As a consequence, substantial German forces that had been allocated to defending against an invasion were in the control of Fifteenth Army in the Pas-de-Calais. Even after Allied forces went ashore in Normandy, there was great reluctance to release these forces – another aspect of *Bodyguard* was the portrayal of landings on the Normandy beaches as a deception to lure away German mobile forces. The counterattacking resources available in the Normandy sector were therefore very limited. The only major armoured formation was Generalmajor Edgar Feuchtinger's 21st Panzer Division to the south of Caen. This was still a powerful unit with about 200 tanks and assault guns and its proximity to the British and Canadian sectors offered the possibility of a decisive and destructive counterattack.

At this point, the second factor required for successful counterattacks – the freedom of action to implement such plans – became an important factor. Hitler had explicitly forbidden the use of panzer divisions in counterattacks without his express permission. Delays in granting such permission proved critical and when the division finally moved forward in the afternoon of D-Day, its attack achieved only limited success; losses accumulated at an alarming rate and as more German armoured units were released for deployment, they too failed to have the decisive impact that had been expected. In the days that followed the first landings on 6 June, the Western Allies gradually fought their way inland. The likelihood of a successful counterattack to throw them back into the sea faded with each day, and consequently the overall strategy of Führer Directive 51 became increasingly unachievable.

There were further developments in early June that added to the dismay and gloom in German circles. At the beginning of the year, the Western Allies had attempted to outflank German defences in southern Italy by carrying out an amphibious landing at Anzio. The campaign proved to be difficult and protracted but the German Caesar Line was finally overcome on 2 June. Rather than risk the encirclement and destruction of the German Fourteenth Army in Rome, Hitler ordered it to pull back to the north. Two days later, American troops entered the Italian capital. The military significance was limited, but the propaganda value to the Western Allies of the German setback was far greater. General Mark Clark, commander of the US Fifth Army, held a press conference on the Capitoline Hill on the day that his troops entered the city to stress the point, though the momentous news of the Normandy Landings two days later relegated the liberation of Rome from the front pages of most newspapers.

The German commanders on the Eastern Front had limited information on what was happening in Normandy, but would have known from their past experiences that the anticipated counterattacks against the Western Allies had not taken place or at least had not been successful. In 1914, the Russian invasion of East Prussia had resulted in a precipitate transfer of troops from the Western Front; similarly, the isolation of First Panzer Army earlier in 1944 in western Ukraine had required the temporary transfer of two SS panzer divisions from France to the east. The ongoing fighting in Normandy meant that it was highly unlikely any such transfer would be possible in the foreseeable future. Consequently, the units of the *Ostheer* (i.e. the German forces on the Eastern Front) would have to face the full weight of the coming onslaught with the forces they had available.

If the Soviet plans for *Bagration* were to succeed, it was essential to mislead the Germans as much as possible about both the scale of Red Army preparations and the details of the plan. Conversely, the Germans were anxious to get as clear a picture as possible of Soviet intentions so that they could position their limited assets – particularly the precious panzer divisions – in anticipation. German military intelligence was in the hands of Reinhard Gehlen, who at that time held the rank of Oberst. He had taken command of *Fremde Heere Ost* ('Foreign Armies East' or *FHO*) in May 1942, and despite his very limited experience of intelligence matters had reorganised the department with some success, making more effective use of linguists and geographers. However, like so many senior figures in Nazi Germany he continued to be handicapped by the pervasive racial theories of the regime, and his staff included anthropologists who were meant to provide information about the capabilities of the inferior Slavs.[2]

The sources of information for Gehlen's *FHO* were limited. At the start of the war with the Soviet Union, the Germans learned a great deal from monitoring Red Army radio transmissions but improvements in signals discipline were gradually implemented; moreover, the Red Army began to exploit German radio monitoring, attempting to mislead the listeners by transmitting false information. Both sides used networks of spies, but many German spies were either double agents working for both sides or were entirely under the control of the Soviet Union. The one area in which the Germans consistently had an advantage over their Soviet opponents for most of the war was aerial reconnaissance; the Luftwaffe operated several specialist reconnaissance aircraft equipped with high quality cameras and also often used to direct artillery fire, and if the Soviet plans to mislead the Germans about the summer offensive were to succeed, this advantage would have to be neutralised.

Perhaps to compensate for the relatively limited resources at his disposal and to avoid censure, Gehlen became an expert in writing reports of masterful ambiguity as the war progressed. His assessments of Red Army intentions from late 1943 onwards were typical in this respect. In November 1943, he wrote that the enemy's main effort would continue to be in the southern sectors with the intention of driving the Germans back to the Balkans and to penetrate into the southeast parts of Poland. Given the sheer weight of Red Army units attacking the German Army Group South at the time, this was hardly a revelation to anyone, but the scale of the German retreat across Ukraine and what seemed like confirmatory information from *FHO* left *OKH* and the entire German high command with the firm impression that this theatre would continue to be where the Red Army would make its main effort in 1944. In the spring of 1944, Gehlen repeated this opinion, adding that in addition, the Soviet forces facing Army Group North might attempt to break through to the Baltic coast in an attempt to isolate the northern wing of the army group in Estonia. With regard to the central region, Gehlen concluded that there was little likelihood of a major Soviet operation to the north of the Polesie region. A staff officer in Army Group Centre later described the German view of the overall situation:

The outcome of the winter fighting resulted in a strong concentration of Russian forces in western Ukraine. It was here in eastern Galicia, where the advance of the enemy east of Lemberg [Lviv] was only halted with considerable difficulty, that

Hitler was of the opinion – strengthened by the advice he received from *OKW* and *OKH* – the great Russian summer offensive could be expected … This disposition of the enemy was in fact very threatening to the overall German military situation. Was this opinion so convincing that later, even when the evidence for it was no longer so strong, it could still not be discarded? In any event the German high command chose to concentrate all available reserves, in the first case the majority of the panzer divisions, in Galicia. The first, decisive blow would fall on Army Group North Ukraine.[3]

This statement highlights a common failing: once opinions are formed, it becomes increasingly difficult to alter them. Confirmation bias ensures that further incoming information that corroborates the pre-existing opinion is frequently overvalued while contrary evidence is discounted. The thinking of Hitler and other senior figures on this occasion followed this pattern, but similar mistakes had been made by others. In 1942, Stalin continued to believe that the main German effort in the summer would be to launch a fresh attack on Moscow, persisting in this belief even when complete plans for the German offensive towards Stalingrad and the Caucasus fell into Soviet hands. In 1944, Hitler continued to believe that the main Soviet effort would be in the south; he was encouraged in this belief by his favourite general, Model, who had no desire to relinquish control of the panzer divisions he was holding in preparation.

In May 1944, *FHO* wrote once more about the main Soviet effort falling in the south, but with a slight variation. Gehlen warned that the Red Army might attempt to break through the northern flank of Army Group North Ukraine – the new command created from the northern half of the old Army Group South – with the intention of first advancing towards the west, and then angling north towards Warsaw and onwards to the Baltic coast. This was indeed one of the options that the Red Army had considered, but it had been rejected as being too risky and probably beyond the resources and capabilities of the forces available. Gehlen added comments that mirrored the Soviet view almost exactly: such an ambitious operation was currently unachievable for the Red Army. Therefore, he predicted the main Soviet effort would be a further attack across the Dniester into Romania with the intention of then turning the southern flank of the Carpathian mountain range. However, he added that aerial reconnaissance had also detected substantial Soviet forces massing at the junction of Army Group Centre and Army Group North Ukraine, and therefore a secondary Soviet attack towards southeast Poland was also likely to develop.[4]

For the Germans, this latter report was not entirely unwelcome. The configuration of the railway network meant that it would be comparatively easy for the Wehrmacht to concentrate considerable forces against any Soviet attack immediately south of the Polesie region, assuming that other major sectors of the Eastern Front remained quiet. The southern formation of Army Group Centre was LVI Panzer Corps, part of Second Army, and this was reinforced in anticipation of a Soviet attack; ultimately, *OKH* hoped to add to the forces in this area to create a complete army that could be used in a decisive counterattack to smash any Soviet advance. Many staff officers in both Army Group Centre and Army Group North Ukraine preferred to remain in a defensive posture, but rivalries and ambition now played a part in developments. The commander of Army Group North Ukraine was Generalfeldmarschall Walter Model, Hitler's favourite senior officer, who had earned a reputation for successful defensive fighting where others had failed. Whilst his defence of the Rzhev salient in 1942 (as commander of Ninth Army) was exemplary, his successes thereafter owed as much to fortuitous timing as to his inherent abilities. He arrived in the north to take command of the shattered German forces reeling back from the Leningrad perimeter when the Soviet offensive was beginning to run out of steam due to escalating casualties and supply difficulties, and something similar occurred when he took control of Army Group North Ukraine, where the Red Army's logistic leash ran across the devastated territory of central and western Ukraine. When he was commander of Army Group North, Model had attempted without success to implement what he and Hitler described as *Schild und Schwert* ('shield and sword'): he would build a strong defensive line to halt the Red Army's attack while creating a mobile force with which to mount a powerful counterattack. There was little that was revolutionary about this concept, and in many respects it was little more than a restatement of standard German doctrine, but Model's new wording caught Hitler's imagination.

Regardless of his defensive skills, Model sometimes showed complete unwillingness to consider the importance of sectors other than his own. When he was commander of Army Group North in the first months of 1944, he received a request from Generaloberst Kurt Zeitzler, chief of the German general staff, for information on how many divisions he might be able to release for use elsewhere. Model's response was that he could perhaps spare a single infantry division. Just a few days later, he was summoned to Hitler's headquarters and informed that he was being sent to take over Army Group North Ukraine, and immediately declared that first five, then six infantry divisions could be released from Army Group North – he was aware that most of these forces would be sent to shore up the battered line in the southern half of the Eastern Front and he clearly wanted to make sure that his new command was as strong as possible, regardless of any consequences for Army Group North. He even sent orders by radio to Army

Group North instructing his staff to commence the transfer of these forces; an increasingly alarmed Zeitzler had to countermand these orders to prevent a potentially fatal weakening of Army Group North.[5]

Given this cynical behaviour in the past, it was unsurprising to Zeitzler that in the late spring of 1944, Model took advantage of his high standing with Hitler to suggest that LVI Panzer Corps be reassigned to his army group's northern formation. Model argued that these armoured assets would at the very least give him the firepower that would be needed to defeat the Soviet summer offensive, and, aware of Hitler's frustration that the Red Army controlled the initiative in the east, he also held out the possibility of using them in a pre-emptive attack. Given Gehlen's reports that the Red Army's main efforts would both be made to the south of the Polesie, Hitler agreed. At a stroke, Busch's Army Group Centre was deprived of its main armoured forces. The commander of Second Army, Generaloberst Walter Weiss, protested strongly to Busch that the transfer of LVI Panzer Corps might benefit Model's Army Group North Ukraine but was a potentially fatal overall weakening of Army Group Centre; Busch informed him that Hitler's orders were to be obeyed in full.

As described above, a mixture of preconceived opinion and the reluctance of Model to part with any of the panzer formations under his command – indeed, his desire to have even more forces transferred to Army Group North Ukraine – was fed by Soviet *Maskirovka* with the result that it was the almost universal view amongst German senior figures that the Soviet summer offensive would fall on Army Group North Ukraine. On 5 May, Busch's Army Group Centre headquarters issued a 'brief assessment of the enemy's situation' which expressed concern about possible developments to the south, at the seam between Army Group Centre and Army Group North Ukraine:

> The fundamental point is that the enemy situation in front of the extreme southern wing of the army group is unclear. On the basis of transports observed or assumed to have arrived it is estimated that 15–25 as yet unidentified units are in the depths [of the enemy position] around Lutsk, Kovel, and Sarny …
>
> Apart from fighting as a result of their local attacks in the Turya sector, the enemy has been strikingly quiet in the recent period. Limited raiding activity in the area of Kamen Kachirsk (Second Army), in Ninth Army's sector, and along the front of Fourth Army has been reported …
>
> On the basis of the overall assessment, the point of main effort of the Soviet summer offensive is expected in the Balkan region. At the same time an attack with a powerful army group in Army Group North Ukraine's sector and against

the southern flank of Army Group Centre towards the *Generalgouvernement* [the German name for the administration of what remained of Poland] is expected …

At the same time as the expected major offensive against our southern flank, the enemy will conduct pinning attacks against the front of Army Group Centre with the expectation of capturing local objectives in view of our overstretched resources. These include Bobruisk, Mogilev, Orsha, and possibly Vitebsk.[6]

In summary: about six weeks before the storm broke, Army Group Centre was more concerned about the threat to the south and expected only limited attacks along its front line to try to pin down its forces, though with the caveat that even these might result in the loss of the cities that Hitler had designated as fortresses. Indeed, the German view of the entire Eastern Front was astonishingly complacent. A few days after Busch's optimistic report, Generalfeldmarschall Wilhelm Keitel, head of *OKW*, addressed a conference of senior commanders from the Eastern Front, assuring them that they faced few serious dangers: 'The situation on the Eastern Front has stabilised. You can rest assured that the Russians will not be able to mount a serious offensive soon.'[7]

Even if an attack fell on Army Group Centre, Hitler remained confident that his new fortress policy would limit its effect. But the likelihood of the 'fortresses' holding firm was highly doubtful. In the sector of Third Panzer Army, Vitebsk was one such fortress and it led to repeated arguments between Busch and Reinhardt, commander of Third Panzer Army. In mid-March, Reinhardt warned Busch that if Vitebsk were to be encircled, it was highly likely that this would result in perhaps five divisions being trapped; without these divisions, he doubted his army would be able to maintain a continuous front line. The plans for Vitebsk specified that up to 18,000 tons of supplies were to be stockpiled in the city, which created several problems. Firstly, there were few locations where such large stores could be held; secondly, creating such a huge stockpile would be at the detriment of supplying the rest of Third Panzer Army.

This was followed by a meeting between Busch and Reinhardt on 21 April. The exchange that followed showed the gulf between officers like Reinhardt who were attempting to apply their professional skills to the tasks assigned to them and those like Busch for whom rigid obedience to Hitler was the most important thing. Reinhardt asked for the fortress designation to be removed as it would be of no tactical or operational value:

Busch: Vitebsk shall retain its status as a fortress and under no circumstances will the Führer relinquish it. He is adamant that the city will tie down thirty to forty enemy divisions that would otherwise be free to drive towards the west and southwest.

Reinhardt: This fortress only makes sense if it can be relieved by the panzer army at a later stage, but there is no guarantee that this will be the case.

Busch: It is also about prestige. Vitebsk is the only place on the Eastern Front whose loss will be noticed the world over.

Reinhardt: Vitebsk on its own will not tie down considerable enemy forces. The threat posed by the enemy can only be dealt with by the panzer army in its entirety. It would therefore be much better to pull everything out of the city and to hold the flanks that extend south and west. The fortress is of secondary importance.[8]

General Friedrich Gollwitzer, commander of LIII Corps in Vitebsk, later recalled a bad-tempered conversation involving Busch, the corps quartermaster, and himself, which revealed the unreality of what was being ordered:

Quartermaster: Where does the [fortress] commandant get his staff?

Busch: That's your business. Apply to your army [i.e. to Reinhardt].

Quartermaster: The strength of the garrison is not sufficient for all-round defence.

Busch: More troops are not available. Take them from units withdrawing from the front.

Gollwitzer: Who can build the Vitebsk defences as there are no civilians who can do the work, and combat troops cannot be used?

Busch: Staff personnel, administrative troops and *Hilfswillige* [prisoners of war who volunteered, with varying degrees of willingness, to work as auxiliaries for the Wehrmacht; often abbreviated to *Hiwi*].

Gollwitzer: If there is an attack threatened, can the corps expect any reserves to prevent the encirclement of its flanks?

Busch: No! Put the strongest part of your defences at the junction with your neighbours!

Gollwitzer: The junctions of my LIII Corps are with my neighbouring corps, VI [to the south] and IX [to the north]. Presumably they will halt the first attacks and must build up strong defences at these points.

Busch: Everything will be as I have said! The Führer has ordered it![9]

In mid-May, a further German assessment of Red Army strength and intentions drew similar conclusions. Soviet troop movements in front of Army Group Centre had now been detected, but the report – identifying V Guards Rifle Corps and Eleventh Guards Army – interpreted these either as withdrawals or as regrouping prior to local attacks. The suggestion that these local attacks might result in the loss of Hitler's fortresses began to cause increasing concern, and Hitler was particularly anxious about the relatively weak defensive line to the east of Mogilev. There were discussions about sending reinforcements; but although almost everyone in *OKH* agreed that the sector was too weak to hold back a determined attack, no reinforcements were available.

Somewhat tardily, Busch began to express concern about the lack of mechanised forces that could act as reserves for his army group. Without such reserves, even local Red Army attacks would result in irrecoverable loss of territory, particularly given the overstretched units deployed in the front line. In the absence of mobile reserves, Busch suggested two possibilities to improve the situation. The first was to shorten the front line by a voluntary withdrawal from the east-facing bulge that ran from Vitebsk in the north to Bobruisk in the south. Such a withdrawal would release at least local reserves. The second option was to abandon the current policy of rigid, tenacious defence; when the Red Army attacked, Army Group Centre would fall back and concede ground with the intention of stopping the attack further to the west. However, in the absence of mobile reserves, there would be little chance of recovering the lost ground.

Of these two options, a withdrawal to a shorter line seemed the most attractive to the professional soldiers, particularly given the lack of mobile forces with which an elastic defence could be conducted. There were two options available: the 'small' option would involve a retreat of about 33 miles; and the 'large' option would pull German forces back 84 miles. These would shorten the frontage of Army Group Centre by 48 miles and 92 miles respectively and would therefore release substantial reserves. By contrast, a fighting withdrawal to either line after the commencement of Soviet attacks would be a far more difficult undertaking with the likelihood that the retreating German units would lose much of their strength in the process. The successful conduct of Operation *Büffel* ('Buffalo'), the withdrawal from the Rzhev salient in March 1943, offered a good model for what was proposed and also provided plenty of experience. On the basis of this, Busch's staff officers anticipated that preparations for either the 'small' or 'large' options would take at least two months while roads were improved and intermediate holding positions were constructed. Nor was such a withdrawal a risk-free option – the Red Army hadn't pursued the Germans aggressively during *Büffel*, and it was likely that a new withdrawal would see far more energetic attempts to pin down the retreating units, particularly as the overall balance of strength had tilted much further against the Wehrmacht. Moreover, there was the continuing irritation of the partisans. During the retreat from the Leningrad perimeter and the Volkhov River in early

1944, Army Group North had had to deal with constant partisan attacks on its columns and the greater density of partisan groups in Belarus could be expected to result in more energetic activity.

In any event, the men who started considering such plans must have known that there was almost no chance of securing approval, as they were completely contrary to Hitler's stated intention to conduct a determined defence of every metre of ground in the east, to hold the Red Army as far from German territory as possible until the threat from the west had been eliminated. Recognising this, Busch ordered alternative plans to be drawn up – instead of a timely and orderly withdrawal to a shorter line, his army group would have to pull back if it came under pressure from the Red Army. Orders were issued to commence construction of a defensive line along the Berezina River as early as January 1944 but the work was given a low priority and progress was limited.

On 20 May, Busch travelled to Hitler's headquarters to try to persuade the Führer that a timely withdrawal to a shorter line was the best way to ensure a successful defence against Soviet attacks in the summer. He outlined the 'small' and 'large' options, explaining in some detail how many divisions could be freed by either choice. Hitler bluntly rejected the proposals, adding disparagingly that until now he had not considered Busch to be one of those generals who was constantly looking behind him for positions to which he could retreat. It was a rebuke that was directed at those who Hitler felt had failed to show the requisite determination to conduct a determined or 'fanatical' defence against the Red Army; perhaps foremost amongst such figures was Generalfeldmarschall Erich von Manstein, who had overseen Army Group South's retreat across Ukraine in 1943 and the first part of 1944. Manstein's desire to conduct an elastic defence might have been the only practical solution to the problems that his forces faced, but brought him into direct conflict with Hitler. The Führer's immediate circle constantly criticised Manstein as being more interested in personal glory and fancy mobile operations than in obeying Hitler's orders; there was no insight whatever into the unreality of those orders.

A repeated justification used by Hitler to overrule requests for withdrawals was that Wehrmacht generals didn't understand economic issues. For example, Manstein's troops found themselves defending a small bridgehead to the east of the lower Dnepr River in late 1943 and Hitler insisted that this bridgehead was to be held at all costs, as the region was a valuable source of manganese. Without this, he insisted, Germany would be unable to produce steel alloys that were essential for the war effort. Albert Speer, Germany's armaments minister, took it upon himself to investigate and sent a memorandum to both Hitler and Zeitzler that by using alternatives, it would be possible to continue steel production for at least 18 months even if Nikopol was abandoned. Whilst Speer might have regarded this as good news, Hitler was furious, as Speer later described:

> When I arrived at the Führer's headquarters two days later, Hitler snarled at me in a tone he had never used toward me before: 'What was the idea of your giving the chief of staff your memorandum on the manganese situation?'
>
> I had expected to find him well pleased with me, and managed only to reply, stunned: 'But, *mein Führer*, it's good news after all!'
>
> Hitler did not accept that. 'You are not to give the chief of staff any memoranda at all! If you have some information, kindly send it to me. You've put me in an intolerable situation. I have just given orders for all available forces to be concentrated for the defence of Nikopol. At last I have a reason to force the army group to fight! And then Zeitzler comes along with your memo. It makes me out a liar! If Nikopol is lost now, it's your fault! I forbid you once and for all' – his voice rose to a scream at the end – 'to pass memoranda to anybody but myself. Do you understand that? I forbid it!'[10]

It was a moment of insight into Hitler's mindset. Always distrustful of the ultimate loyalty of senior army officers, many of whom made little attempt to hide their contempt for the Nazi Party, the Führer's attitude towards those officers deteriorated in the aftermath of the Battle of Moscow. The events of the years that followed did little to improve matters and the constant friction between commanders who demanded freedom of manoeuvre and Hitler who insisted on 'fanatical' defence of every square metre of ground created a downward spiral. Under huge pressure, officers like Manstein requested a withdrawal to a shorter line in order to free up sufficient men to mount an effective defence. Hitler refused until such a retreat became inevitable, by which time the situation had deteriorated so much that the expected benefits were now inadequate, triggering a further round of arguments about the next withdrawal. Consequently, Hitler was increasingly minded to use economic arguments in an attempt to overcome what he saw as reluctance on the part of men like Manstein to stand and fight. In many respects, Hitler's thinking was strongly influenced by his personal memories of the First World War. He had endured the endless trench warfare of the Western Front and saw this as the perfect model for the conduct of war against the Red Army. The sheer scale of the Eastern Front made such a policy almost impossible. But the elastic defence that Manstein and others wished to conduct also posed difficulties. Without the large numbers of panzer formations deployed in the west, such a policy was unlikely to succeed, especially given the ever-increasing strength of the Red Army's armoured formations. The truth was that the war was unwinnable for Germany, but a great deal of blood would have to be spilled before the conflict came to its inevitable conclusion.

Busch was a very different figure from Manstein, who would have argued strongly with the Führer and might have threatened to resign. Having presented his proposals, the commander of Army Group Centre quietly accepted their rejection and returned to his headquarters in Minsk. On 24 May, he held a conference where he addressed his army commanders and senior Luftwaffe officers. He informed them of Hitler's instructions for the current line to be defended 'at all costs'. All he could suggest that might facilitate this was increased construction of defences. For the Luftwaffe officers, this was of little comfort. In earlier offensive operations, Soviet air power had rarely achieved very much impact, but the balance of air power was swinging steadily away from Germany. In the first phase of *Bagration*, Soviet air units would field a total of over 2,300 fighters, 1,700 ground attack aircraft, and 1,800 bombers, with a further 1,000 longer-range bombers available from airfields further to the rear or from neighbouring sectors.[11] The intention was to prevent any intervention by the Luftwaffe and to strike at targets deep in the rear of the German front line, targeting headquarters, supply dumps, local reserve forces, and likely lines of march both for reserves approaching the front line and for German units in the front line that were attempting to pull back. Opposing this aerial armada were the depleted resources of local Luftwaffe formations, which between them could put up modest resources. At the beginning of June, Army Group Centre was supported by 66 single-engined fighters (mainly Messerschmitt BF-109Gs), 19 night fighters (Messerschmitt Me-110s), 312 bombers (mainly Heinkel He-IIIs and Ju-88s), 106 ground attack aircraft (Stuka dive-bombers, Henschel Hs-129s, and Focke-Wulf FW-190s), and 48 older bombers capable of conducting operations only at night as they were too vulnerable to interception for daytime use.[12] To make matters worse, half of the single-engined fighters were transferred to the Mediterranean theatre immediately before the onset of *Bagration*.

The transfer of LVI Panzer Corps from Army Group Centre to Army Group South took place a week later, reducing still further the mechanised forces available to Busch. Whilst this was unwelcome, the Germans continued to regard the main axis of the forthcoming Soviet attack as being in the south. On 2 June, Army Group Centre reported that it still expected the main Red Army effort to fall on its southern neighbour, and Busch's main concern was about the potential impact on the seam between his army group and that of Model. Local attacks were expected to the southeast of Vitebsk and elsewhere, with the caveat that the Red Army could be expected to deploy its plentiful reserves to exploit any local gains as rapidly as possible.[13]

The complacency in the German high command was not shared by soldiers in the front line. To the east of Mogilev was Fourth Army's XXXIX Panzer Corps, part of which was 12th Infantry Division. One of its battalion commanders later described how Red Army activity changed in the second week of June:

> In the forest, wood was being cut to make access tracks for tanks. Occasionally we heard guns registering from previously unknown positions. Also Russian patrols were trying to reconnoitre fords and possible bridging sites across the [Pronja] river. We were also able to establish that there was a distinct increase in the level of Russian telephone traffic. When we reported this, we were told at both corps and division [headquarters] that this was merely decoy action and that the main Soviet attack was expected in the south.[14]

It was a further example of the all-pervasive confirmation bias in Wehrmacht commands. With such limited resources available, the German forces facing the Red Army had sufficient strength to mount perhaps one effective defensive campaign, and this required them to guess correctly where the Soviet blow would fall. With so much opinion and so many reputations now invested in the expectation that this would take place in the southern sector, few men outside the immediate front line were willing to question the prevailing view.

One of the few senior German officers who was prepared to raise such awkward questions was Hans Jordan, the commander of Ninth Army. At several conferences held by Army Group Centre he raised doubts, pointing out that all evidence to the contrary was being systematically disregarded or downgraded. But his pleas for his fellow officers to keep an open mind were ignored. The Soviet summer offensive would strike against Army Group North Ukraine with subsidiary attacks on either flank. Army Group Centre was to prepare for these, and would have to fight the coming battle in its current positions with the forces available, which Busch insisted would be sufficient to fend off local Soviet probes and holding attacks.

The German soldiers in the front line dug their trenches and bunkers, and sappers added to the arrays of obstacles and minefields. In the absence of mobile reserves or freedom to conduct an elastic defence, it was all that could be done. The result might be a somewhat stronger front line, but the simple truth was that if this line gave way, the relative immobility of German forces and the shortage of mobile reserves was likely to result in catastrophe, particularly as any preparations for mobile warfare were expressly forbidden. Construction of positions to the rear that might be used if a retreat became necessary was also not permitted; the experiences of the summer of 1943, when German soldiers struggled back across central Ukraine towards the Dnepr valley where they hoped in vain to find prepared defensive positions awaiting them, had left a strong impression on Hitler. The construction of positions to the rear of the front line, he now argued, gave soldiers and officers a false sense of security and if faced with a choice between resolute defence of their current positions or falling back to what was perceived to be a stronger position to the rear, they would choose the latter; and Hitler was determined to make the Wehrmacht contest every inch of ground regardless of the cost. By the second week of June, there could no longer be any doubt that an attack on Army Group Centre was coming, but its scale continued to be underestimated. The preparations reported in 12th Infantry Division's sector were mirrored by similar observations all along the front line of Army Group Centre. Gehlen had anticipated the possibility of moderate attacks intended to probe German defences and to pin down formations in order to prevent their transfer to other sectors, and Jordan and the other army commanders of Army Group Centre fervently hoped that this would prove to be the case. It was unthinkable that the central sector might be the region in which the Red Army launched its main summer effort.

As the war dragged on, every unit in the German military was permitted to send small numbers of men home on leave for short spells. After making their way from the front line to the nearest railhead, they were given an opportunity to clean their uniforms and were subjected to delousing treatment before boarding trains that took them to Germany. At first, soldiers looked forward with great anticipation to such opportunities to escape the front line and to see their families, and many took the opportunity to marry their sweethearts, but by 1944 the mood was changing. Some soldiers chose not to return to cities like Hamburg and Berlin – the sight of so much devastation as a consequence of British and American air raids was too disheartening. On 12 June 1944, all leave was cancelled until further notice in expectation of the Soviet summer offensive. Whilst this prevented any further depletion of the front line, an additional order was less welcome. Men who were already on leave would not return to their divisions; instead, they would be used to create up to eight new divisions. This was of course at the expense of weakening their previous formations, but Hitler remained obsessed throughout the war with the creation of new divisions rather than ensuring that existing formations were kept up to strength. This new arrangement was unpopular with senior commanders on the Eastern Front and after several protests were registered, about 10,000 men from Army Group Centre were permitted to return to their units rather than being used to create a new division.[15] There was further welcome news for Busch. Although his army group had been deprived of LVI Panzer Corps, he was informed that 20th Panzer

Division was being transferred from Army Group North Ukraine to Army Group Centre, and would begin arriving in Bobruisk in the middle of the month. The division was far from being at full strength, with fewer than 80 Pz.IV tanks; it is an indication of the weakness of Army Group Centre that this force more than doubled the tanks available.

The return of men who had been on leave and the transfer of 20th Panzer Division were the only positive developments for Army Group Centre in June. It was now clear that the Red Army was preparing for operations all along the east-facing bulge held by Busch's armies. Third Panzer Army reported that it expected Soviet attacks against its lines to the southeast of Vitebsk; crucially, the preparations of Bagramian's 1st Baltic Front to the northwest of Vitebsk either were not detected or were not interpreted as being part of a planned attack to cut off the city. Fourth Army anticipated that the Red Army would attack south of the main Smolensk–Minsk highway towards Orsha, and Ninth Army detected preparations for attacks towards Rogachev and Gomel. On 14 June, Zeitzler convened a conference of army group commanders and their chiefs of staff at *OKH*. Generalleutnant Hans Krebs, Busch's chief of staff, had a lengthy conversation with Zeitzler. Although he discussed the clear Red Army preparations for attacks against Army Group Centre, Zeitzler concentrated mainly on the reports from Ninth Army on the southern end of the east-facing bulge. These expected attacks would, it was assumed, form the northern element of the main Soviet effort that would be falling on Army Group North Ukraine. Zeitzler replied:

> The section chief of *Fremde Heere Ost* [Gehlen] has given the following opinion on the likely conduct of the forthcoming offensive: phase one will see simultaneous attacks on Army Groups South Ukraine and Centre, which will be followed a short time later by the main assault on Army Group North Ukraine.[16]

During the conference, Zeitzler reiterated this point. He assured all attendees that there was nothing to indicate that German assumptions about an impending attack in the southern sector were incorrect. The daily report from Army Group Centre stated that it was increasingly difficult to determine with any accuracy what was happening on the other side of the front line due to Soviet radio silence and increasing Soviet fighter patrols that prevented aerial reconnaissance, but this was dismissed as not relevant. At most, such measures were attempts by the Soviets to mislead the Germans.[17]

Busch and Krebs returned to Minsk where evidence of Soviet preparations continued to accumulate. Units all along the front reported the identification of hitherto-undetected Red Army units and there were worrying reports from the interrogation of prisoners. A downed Soviet pilot informed the Germans that Zhukov was overseeing Red Army preparations in the area, and several Soviet soldiers who were captured by patrols stated that the nature of political preparation had changed in recent weeks. Throughout April and May, all such lectures by Red Army commissars had deliberately concentrated on the importance of defence against the Germans; now, the emphasis had changed completely and soldiers were being told of the paramount importance of driving the Germans from all Soviet territory.[18]

Reports from Busch's armies confirmed the growing disquiet amongst German officers near the front line. Reinhardt's Third Panzer Army reported the appearance of Soviet tank units and continued to expect a Red Army assault to the southeast of Vitebsk, and on 18 June a wireless intercept reported the presence of Fifth Guards Tank Army – this was the first indication that the Germans received that this powerful formation was now facing Army Group Centre rather than preparing for an offensive operation to the south. Tippelskirch's Fourth Army also reported growing signs of Red Army preparations but added that any major attack was unlikely before 26 June. On the southern flank of Fourth Army, Jordan reported from Ninth Army headquarters that there was growing Soviet artillery activity. The partisans in the area were also carrying out more frequent attacks and signals intelligence confirmed the presence of I Guards Tank Corps. Even more alarming was a prisoner interrogation report that Zhukov had visited the front-line trenches. Given that the Red Army's attack in the southern sector was regarded as imminent, Zhukov's presence in any other sector was a surprise and his visit to units in the front line even more remarkable.

Despite these reports, Busch remained almost completely inactive. It was a feature of staff officer training that senior officers were strongly advised to keep an open mind on possible options, yet as the days grew longer in 1944, the willingness or ability of most senior figures in the Wehrmacht to question the assumption of where the Red Army would attack was almost non-existent. In some respects, this was a reflection of the men that were now in senior positions in the German military machine. Hitler's top criteria for judging his generals were their loyalty and even more importantly their obedience.

In its preparations for *Bagration*, *Stavka* made full use of the extensive partisan groups operating behind German lines. Despite the recent anti-partisan sweeps, several thousand fighters remained active across Belarus, even if their efficacy varied greatly.[19] Just as the operations of the Red Army were repeatedly analysed, the performance of the partisans in the recent Soviet advances in the central sector was also discussed. The conclusions were that too many targets had been attacked, many of them of limited value. Better command and control was needed and this was organised by sending combat-experienced regular officers to act both as commanders and as advisers to the partisans. The result was that many partisan groups were placed under combined command and were now able to dominate large parts of the region, concentrating their resources to attack key targets. The participation of the partisans in *Bagration* was expected to be in two phases. In the first, they would make coordinated attacks on German lines of supply and communication. Then, as the Red Army advanced into the region, the partisans were to channel the retreating German troops into regions where their further retreat could be blocked more easily. When the German anti-partisan operations died down, there was an immediate resurgence in attacks on isolated German positions with the deliberate intention of sapping morale and forcing the Wehrmacht to divert troops from the front line. Garrisons along the main supply lines suffered repeated hit-and-run attacks, with the partisan formations making good use of their better weaponry, better leadership, and better command and control. German reports observed all of these factors, but there was no realisation that in many respects these increasingly ambitious attacks were in preparation for sustained operations in the near future.

The artillery assets of Bagramian's 1st Belarusian Front increased their preparatory activity in the third week of June, but care was still taken to try to combine registration fire with random bombardments. In other battles, at least one gun in every battery was involved in such calibration work, but this was now greatly restricted to try to prevent the Germans from making an accurate assessment of the scale of preparations. From 18 June, sappers began to move into no-man's land at night to start clearance of landmines from specific corridors; by the time *Bagration* commenced, they had removed nearly 8,000 mines in 1st Baltic Front's sector alone.[20] By contrast, the gunners of 3rd Belarusian Front to the south carried out their main preparatory work a week earlier in a further attempt to confuse German assessments of precisely what was being prepared. Careful Soviet reconnaissance work continued and correctly spotted minor German redeployments in the middle of June, allowing these to be taken into account in the artillery fire plan. But the concentration of Eleventh Guards Army, which would mount the main thrust of 3rd Belarusian Front, was on such a scale that it couldn't be hidden and its presence was finally confirmed in German reports on the very eve of *Bagration*.

By the middle of June, the number of officers who shared the doubts repeatedly expressed by Jordan was slowly rising. They could see the scale of

Soviet preparations was far greater than that required for pinning attacks and were alarmed by the complacency of Busch and others. Finally, on 19 June, Busch seemed to awake to the reality of what was happening. A report from his headquarters to *OKH* suggested that the imminent Soviet attacks would be more powerful than previously thought and went on to consider various locations along the front line:

> The intention to mount a concentric attack on Vitebsk cannot be deduced from what is known of the enemy situation at the moment ... the main focus of the enemy is assumed to be in front of the southern wing of Third Panzer Army [i.e. to the southeast of Vitebsk] ... The attacks on Bobruisk, Mogilev, Orsha, and possibly south of Vitebsk, which are anticipated on the frontage of the army group, will be more than local in character. In their entirety, depending on the extent of the deployment of army and air force units, their aim is to collapse the protruding bulge of the army group at several points by tearing open the front. On the other hand, as far as it is known or can be calculated, the strength profile of the Red Army does not yet indicate a far-reaching objective such as Minsk. However, reference must be made to the mismatch of both air and ground forces and also in particular the great difficulties in reconnaissance in the current situation ... The weakness in aerial reconnaissance is well known. In recent times it has been restricted to railway surveillance and photography of field artillery positions, but major movements close to the front have not been detected.
>
> Likewise, the difficulties regarding other sources [of information, e.g. radio intercepts] need no repetition. Particularly heavy use of infiltration in Second Army's sector has yielded good results, but it is almost impossible to penetrate through the firmly fortified sectors of the Eastern Front, including the northeast sector from Vitebsk to Polotsk. Unfortunately the use of parachutist reconnaissance teams, presumably as a result of their betrayal by non-military personnel, failed to deliver the hoped-for results despite heavy casualties. The number of prisoners and deserters is small.[21]

The following night saw a huge increase in partisan activity. There was a concerted series of attacks on railway lines during the night; about 14,000 attempts were made to detonate explosives, of which about 9,600 were successful.[22] In many cases, these attacks did little more than create minimal damage that could be repaired relatively easily, but the sheer scale of the attacks was ominous in itself. There were also heavy attacks against garrisons and security detachments in the rear of the German front line, and the result was severe disruption to the railway lines running from Minsk to Orsha and from Mogilev to Vitebsk. The following night there were nearly 900 further attacks. Such an increase in the scale of activity was unprecedented and was itself a huge warning to the Germans; but it was now too late for any serious measures to be taken, even if Busch and others had been willing and able to do so.

The strength of the German divisions that would face the Red Army varied greatly. Many infantry divisions could field barely a quarter of their establishment strength. For example, the entire combat strength of the ten divisions in Fourth Army's front line amounted to just 30,800 men and Ninth Army had ten infantry divisions with 43,500 men between them.[23] The overall strength of Army Group Centre was estimated to be about 486,000 combatants with 118 tanks and 452 assault guns.[24] The Red Army enjoyed an advantage of 3.4:1 in terms of soldiers, 10.2:1 in terms of tanks and assault guns, 10.1:1 in terms of artillery, and 8.5:1 in terms of aircraft. If the true scale of Red Army preparations had been known, it is inconceivable that *OKH* would have persisted in its belief that the coming attacks would be purely local and it is a measure of the efficacy of Soviet *Maskirovka* at every level that the build-up was so badly underestimated. It is also testament to the growing expertise of the Red Army that it was able to conduct such huge preparations; despite the concerns of Front commanders, supplies as well as men and equipment arrived in sufficient quantities for the operation to proceed as planned.

One of the German units that would face the Red Army was Generalmajor Otto Schünemann's 337th Infantry Division. By 20 June, it was clear to Schünemann that regardless of the opinions of those above him in the chain of command, his men faced a powerful enemy which was poised to attack. Schünemann issued an order of the day:

> The preparations of the enemy before our front leads us to assume that the enemy will launch a major offensive very soon. The division will therefore find itself in the fight for the freedom of the German people in one of the most decisive sectors. The battle will be fierce. The enemy will risk everything to defeat us. Prevailing in this struggle is the duty of every soldier in the front line and the rear areas. It will require full combat readiness and the most strenuous exertions of everyone. Our slogan remains the same as always: 'Do not concede a single piece of ground, keep up the most stubborn resistance.'
>
> The division has plentiful artillery, an adequate quantity of anti-tank weapons, and substantial reserves, and occupies a well-constructed and favourable defensive line. Thus, we have all the prerequisites for a successful battle.

Soldiers, defeat the enemy wherever you encounter him. Show yourselves to be equal to the German soldiers on the Atlantic Wall. Always remember what each individual action means for the preservation of our homeland.

Long live the Führer! Long live Germany![25]

Even if Schünemann genuinely believed that his division was in good shape to face the Red Army, he would have known that it would need substantial help if it was to emerge victorious. The panzer divisions that would be essential if any major Soviet offensive was to be blunted were still deployed to the south, either in anticipation of an assault on Army Group North Ukraine or for Model's proposed pre-emptive attack. Like most German divisions, the panzer divisions were generally below their establishment strength, but they were also hamstrung by a further problem. The structure of panzer divisions altered several times as the war progressed and in the summer of 1943 this required them to have a panzer regiment made up of two battalions, one equipped with Pz.IV tanks and the other with Panther tanks. Many divisions received a mixture of vehicles including assault guns, and the development of the Panther tank was troubled by reliability issues. Moreover, the Panther was markedly different from its predecessors – the version of the Pz.IV that was most widespread weighed 25 tons, whereas the Panther was a much heavier vehicle of nearly 45 tons. Its gun was a longer barrelled weapon with greater penetrative power, and equipping panzer battalions with the new tank wasn't as simple as introducing a new variant of the older Pz.IV, which in any case was similar enough to the older Pz.III for crews to use it with little or no additional training. In order to become proficient with the Panther tank, panzer crewmen had to undergo a prolonged period of training. In many armies, it was customary for the entire division to be pulled out of the front line for retraining when new tanks were introduced, but the pressure upon the Wehrmacht was too great to permit this. As a consequence, from the summer of 1943 onwards many panzer divisions in the front line had to cope with one of their two panzer battalions returning to Germany to re-equip and retrain whilst the rest of the division continued to fight. By the summer of 1944, this process was still incomplete.

To the south of Army Group Centre, in the concentration area of LVI Panzer Corps – recently detached from Busch's forces and handed over to Model – there were two panzer divisions that would play a major part in the forthcoming fighting. Generalmajor Clemens Betzel had recently taken command of 4th Panzer Division, which had spent most of the war with the Soviet Union in the central sector. On the eve of *Bagration*, his division had 76 Pz.IV tanks, of which six were awaiting repairs. In addition, its Panther tank battalion had just returned to the front line after being absent in France since August 1943; its training and re-equipment had been badly disrupted by a British air raid in May 1944, but in mid-June it returned to 4th Panzer Division with 76 new Panther tanks. Betzel also had a temporary boost in the strength of his division due to the attachment of 5th SS-Panzer Regiment with a further 70 Panther tanks – this regiment was formally part of the *SS-Wiking* panzer division, which was undergoing replenishment.[26]

Hans Schäufler, a signals officer in 4th Panzer Division, wrote extensively about his wartime experiences. He described the return of the newly equipped battalion to the division:

> After 29 May we were once more at full strength. Our long absent II Battalion …
> returned to 4th Panzer Division. It was equipped with new Panther tanks and in
> view of its 'superiority' it was now assigned the title of I Battalion. Its commander
> was Hauptmann Schaeffer. Having had the title of I Battalion for a year, the other
> battalion somewhat grumpily took the title of II Battalion, and was commanded
> by Major Schultz …
>
> The reformed 35th Panzer Regiment would be led on the principles and in
> the spirit of its founder, Heinrich Eberbach, who now had the rank of general.
> That was the wish and intention of everyone … It was made known to everyone
> that henceforth the regiment would be known as the *Eberbachers*.[27]

Not far from 4th Panzer Division was Generalleutnant Karl Decker's 5th Panzer Division. It too had recently been reunited with its Panther-equipped battalion and fielded 70 Panther tanks and 55 Pz.IVs.[28] Like 4th Panzer Division, it had been part of Army Group Centre until the transfer of LVI Panzer Corps to Model's Army Group North Ukraine. Between them, the two divisions fielded a total of 347 tanks – nearly three times as many tanks as Army Group Centre possessed. Most of the tanks of the two divisions were the powerful Panthers, and the presence of these units behind the front line would have done a great deal to provide the powerful mobile resources that were vital if a major Soviet offensive was to be defeated. Instead, they remained in the south where *OKH* continued to insist the main Soviet effort would fall.

In his headquarters in a forest just outside Bobruisk, Jordan remained convinced that these assessments were incorrect and that his Ninth Army was about to bear the brunt of the Red Army's summer assault. He continued to send reports to Busch in Minsk about unmistakable signs of an imminent heavy attack and was increasingly exasperated by the lack of any meaningful response. On the eve of *Bagration*, he wrote in the diary of Ninth Army:

Ninth Army stands on the eve of another great battle, unpredictable in extent and duration. One thing is certain: in the last few weeks the enemy has completed an assembly on the very greatest scale opposite the army, and the army is convinced that this assembly overshadows the concentration of forces off the north flank of Army Group North Ukraine. Unfortunately, in addition to the great threat of an enemy offensive, the depleted Army Group Centre and Ninth Army are absolutely unable to sustain a strong front line or even to hold sufficient reserves ready to be able to guarantee a successful defence, because of the extensive transfer of our own forces that commenced in mid-March to the Kovel–Tarnopol sector where the enemy's main focus is still assumed to be due to the deliberations of *OKH*. The army has felt bound to point out repeatedly that it considers the signs of [enemy] strength on its front to constitute the preparation for this year's main Soviet offensive, which will have as its object the reconquest of Belarus.

The army believes that even under the present conditions, it would be possible to stop the enemy offensive, but not under the present directives which require an absolutely rigid defence. There can be no doubt that if a Soviet offensive breaks out, given the fundamentally changed ratio of forces the army will either have to go over to a mobile defence or see its front smashed. The army therefore hopes that orders will be changed immediately if an initial enemy assault is successful. The army considers the orders establishing the *feste Plätze* [fortresses] particularly dangerous.

The army therefore looks ahead to the coming battle with bitterness, knowing that it is bound by orders to tactical measures which it cannot in good conscience accept as correct and which in our own earlier victorious campaigns were the causes of the enemy defeats – one recalls the great breakthrough and encirclement battles in Poland and France, and the swift thrusts as our panzer divisions bypassed the enemy's fortresses. The army regrets that the army group leadership is not willing to use the conquered Russian territory as manoeuvring space against a superior enemy, something that is necessary and possible and according to timeless principles of tactical and operational warfare is the only option with any prospect of success.

The commanding general and chief of staff presented these thoughts to the army group in numerous conferences but there, apparently, the courage was lacking to carry them higher up, for no counterarguments other than references to *OKH* orders were given. And that is the fundamental source of the anxiety with which the army views the future.

Despite all of these concerns, the army is nonetheless proud of the defensive successes that the troops under its command have repeatedly been able to achieve in the three years of the eastern campaign, despite the most serious crises. This awareness and the conviction of the world-historical necessity of the German fight against the Bolshevik threat gives the army the inner strength to do everything in its power to master the enemy onslaught once more. The army has done everything it can to ensure the best possible defensive preparations.[29]

CHAPTER 5

A FATEFUL ANNIVERSARY: 22–24 JUNE

On 22 June 1941, the Wehrmacht rolled across the western frontier of the Soviet Union with a force of over 3,000 tanks and 3.8 million troops. Operation *Barbarossa*, which Hitler expected would be largely complete by the end of the year, had commenced. Three years later, the war that Hitler had intended to win in a few short months was still raging and it was now the Red Army that was poised to strike in strength. Soviet commanders had high expectations, but the intervening years had taught them to be cautious. There was little thought of bringing the war to a conclusion before the end of the year, but every prospect of inflicting a blow that would mortally wound Germany. If *Bagration* was successful, it would unquestionably bring a successful conclusion to the war much closer and make it an inevitability.

On the anniversary of the start of the war between Germany and the Soviet Union, several battalions in the northern half of the huge battlefield conducted reconnaissance in force. This was a far more organised business than had been the case in earlier years, intended to destroy German positions that might interfere with the main attack and to confirm approach routes. Bagramian was preparing to move into his forward headquarters on 21 June in anticipation of these probing attacks, and thought back to the events of that day in the summer of 1941:

> Nobody thought at that time that the enemy already had his finger on the trigger and only a few hours separated us from war. And today, did the Fascists know what awaited them in the morning? ... Before we released our main forces in their attack we had to assure ourselves and undertake reconnaissance measures of the first layer of enemy defences. We therefore dispatched a reinforced rifle battalion

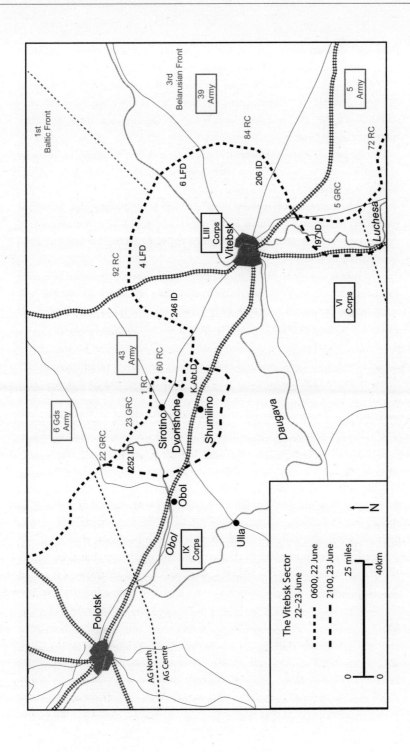

1st
Baltic Front

3rd
Belarusian Front

39
Army

5
Army

84 RC

72 RC

6 LFD

206 ID

5 GRC

197 ID

Luchesa

92 RC

4 LFD

LIII
Corps

Vitebsk

VI
Corps

246 ID

43
Army

60 RC

1 RC

23 GRC

K.Abt.D.

Shumilino

6 Gds
Army

22 GRC

252 ID

Sirotino

Dvorishche

Daugava

Obol

Obol

IX
Corps

Ulla

Polotsk

AG North
AG Centre

The Vitebsk Sector
22–23 June

······ 0600, 22 June
── ── 2100, 23 June

25 miles

40km

N

0

0

from each division in the first wave for a powerful reconnaissance at dawn on 22 June. I asked Vasilevsky for permission to conduct this at 0500.

At first light on 22 June I made my way with a group of officers to the B position to oversee the reconnaissance in force. It was misty and there was poor visibility. But then the sun broke through and the fog dispersed. By 0500 we had more or less good vision.

I went up to [Lieutenant General Ivan Mikhailovich] Chistiakov [commander of Sixth Guards Army], who was impatiently scanning the landscape, and said quietly, 'It's time.'

At 0500 precisely our artillery thundered. After 16 minutes the cannonade reached its crescendo. Chistiakov and [Lieutenant General Afanasy Pavlantevich] Beloborodov [commander of Forty-Third Army] reported that the battalions had commenced their assault.

The enemy was silent. Either we had taken him by surprise or he was preparing a surprise for us. But a little later, in the enemy's first line of defence, we ran in to machine-gun bursts and mortar shells howled down. The firing strengthened and we could see that the enemy's main forces were in their old positions.[1]

Attempts to conduct reconnaissance in force in earlier assaults on strong German positions, for example around the Rzhev salient in 1942, had yielded minimal results at a disproportionate cost, but the probes carried out by 1st Baltic Front on 22 June were more successful. Before the reconnaissance groups could move forward, sappers infiltrated towards the German lines shortly after midnight to start clearing obstacles. Repin, who had helped construct corduroy roads and prefabricated bridge components before the offensive, was in one such group:

By 0300 the sappers in our battalion had made the required number of lanes [through the minefields] in front of the villages of Volotovka and Byvalino. The men worked so skilfully and carefully that they didn't give themselves away with any unexpected noise. The enemy didn't notice anything and remained unaware of the attack that was being prepared until the powerful strike of our artillery and assault aircraft …

The advance of our tanks was blocked by deep anti-tank ditches. But that was why each tank had two sappers riding on it. Before the offensive, we spent a lot of time with the tankers working out how we would work together. If for example a tank became stuck in the swamps, of which there were many, the sappers could immediately get to work to help the fighting vehicle out of its difficulty and to help with this a log was strapped to the armour of each tank. If they encountered a ditch that was impossible to bypass, here too the sappers would try to help …

The tankers and machine-gunners covered our activity with their fire. Dima Levsha and I, like other sappers, carried heavy charges prepared in advance to destroy enemy obstacles … The Nazis tried to stop the advance of the sappers to the anti-tank ditch by all means possible [but] we quickly planted explosives in several places in the anti-tank ditch. Our charges worked perfectly: the walls of the ditch collapsed, leaving gentle slopes, and the T-34s rushed forward again, overcoming the ditch via these slopes and stubbornly gnawing through the enemy's defensive lines they proceeded to overcome his strongpoints.[2]

Several German strongpoints were destroyed and the first prisoners were brought back. Interpreters told Bagramian that the Germans had assumed the main Soviet offensive had commenced. Further reports began to arrive of intensifying fighting as local German reserves responded to the Red Army's probes.

Many of the soldiers in the Soviet units were getting their first experience of combat. Maria Dmitriyevna Katayeva was a sniper who had just been sent to the front line:

As a sniper, I needed to move forward early in the morning to the front line and take up a position in a tree. I then waited for the infantry to yell, 'Forward! Urrah! For the Party and Stalin!' I remember clearly that my first position was about 8m up in an oak tree. My first task was to kill the crew of a machine-gun, and then to follow the simple instructions to 'Kill the Fritzes', that is, shoot at any enemy who appeared from their trenches. We were usually on our own. Throughout the war I used the SVT-40. It had a ten-shot magazine and was very accurate.

I remember the first enemy I killed. He was a middle-aged man firing a machine-gun. When I pulled the trigger, I felt no emotion. But later I began to sob. I cried for a long time, smearing my dirty cheeks with tears. Do you know why? All I could think was, somewhere there are children suffering, waiting to see their dad again, and I killed him. We were given 40ml of vodka to restore our courage. I drank it in one gulp, my throat burning, and it cleared my head of such thoughts. I never cried again after killing an enemy. But I also never drank alcohol again.[3]

The divisions of Third Panzer Army had few reserves available, and these were committed in counterattacks in mid-morning. The Germans had identified Soviet concentrations to the southeast of the city, but had completely failed to detect Bagramian's preparations; Reinhardt, the army commander, had an excellent reputation as an efficient and skilful commander, but his relaxed attitude during the weeks of Soviet preparations stands out as an anomaly in his military career. But with the notable exception of Jordan, this attitude was widespread. The entry in Army Group Centre's war diary for 22 June reads: 'The major attack to the northwest of Vitebsk is a complete surprise for the German high command, since according to the previous intelligence picture of the enemy such a strong concentration (six to seven divisions) had not been detected here.'[4]

It is a measure of the complacency that prevailed in Army Group Centre that Busch was visiting *OKH* when news arrived of the aggressive Soviet attacks to the northwest of Vitebsk; he was waiting to speak to Hitler, who often didn't appear until mid-morning, and he hastily sent his apologies and immediately boarded a plane to fly back to Minsk. When he landed, he learned that fighting had steadily intensified. The German IX Corps, commanded by General Rolf Wuthmann, had few reserves available at a local level and these had already been committed to little avail.

Shortly after he reached his headquarters, Busch received a report from Reinhardt. The front line was completely ruptured and he requested permission to pull back to more secure positions. Busch immediately forbade any withdrawal with the words 'If we start retreating, we'll only end up in a mess.'[5] A regiment from 95th Infantry Division – held in reserve by Third Panzer Army – was inserted into the rapidly widening gap on the right flank of 252nd Infantry Division but made almost no impression. Responding to the alarming reports, *OKH* belatedly woke up to the threat to drive a wedge between Army Group Centre and Army Group North and ordered the latter group's Sixteenth Army to mount an attack towards Vitebsk from Polotsk using 24th Infantry Division and a brigade of assault guns. These units, which constituted almost all of Sixteenth Army's reserves, began a difficult journey along roads running south, harassed continually by Soviet air attacks.

After some initial successes, the Soviet reconnaissance in force to the northwest of Vitebsk fended off the German attempts to restore the front line and then continued its advance; by the end of the day, the foremost German positions on a frontage of nearly six miles had been seized by the Red Army, and penetrated to a depth of over four miles. In the sector held by 252nd Infantry Division, several artillery positions had been overrun and the guns lost. The soldiers of the Soviet 71st Guards Rifle Division, part of Chistiakov's Sixth Guards Army, enjoyed considerable success in their first attack and their corps commander immediately fed additional battalions into the advance. By the end of the day, the Soviet troops were already through the second German defensive line and had reached the Obol River, threatening the direct road between Vitebsk and Polotsk to the northwest. Reinhardt grimly issued orders that the enemy drive to the south of Sirotino was to be halted at all costs; he also ordered rear area units to construct new defensive positions as quickly as possible to defend Obol and Shumilino, anticipating that, regardless of Busch's orders, a retreat was almost inevitable. Although Reinhardt had failed to comprehend the scale of the Red Army's preparations in his sector, the exposed salient around Vitebsk had always seemed to him to be indefensible. The city had been declared a 'fortress' by Hitler, but Reinhardt had ordered the construction of a defensive line immediately to the southwest of Vitebsk as a precautionary step; however, these defences would only be of any value if the German units in the city were given permission to conduct a timely withdrawal.

In the headquarters of the Soviet Sixth Guards Army, Chistiakov was bullish about the successes of his first probes. He contacted Bagramian in the afternoon to discuss further developments:

> I asked him to approve … the further deployment of XXII Guards Rifle Corps, introducing the main force of the corps into the fighting and to continue active operations with assault detachments through the night of 22–23 June. The commander of the corps should exploit the gains of his right hand neighbour. Parts of 51st Guards Rifle Division should bypass the strongpoint of Sirotino and prevent the enemy from withdrawing to the southwest. At dawn on 23 June, in combination with XXIII Guards Rifle Corps, it could strike at the rear of the enemy node of resistance around Sirotino.[6]

The proposed line of march for the regiment that was to bypass Sirotino lay through a swamp, but a reconnaissance patrol reported that there were no German defenders covering the area and the Soviet troops and their artillery horses waded through the innumerable streams running through the soft ground, dragging their equipment into position for the dawn attack. Even if Reinhardt's subordinates were able to halt the Soviet probes between Sirotino and Vitebsk, Sirotino itself was vital as it lay on the northern shoulder of the Soviet penetration. If it fell to the Red Army, the situation would deteriorate rapidly.

To the south of Chistiakov's Sixth Guards Army was Beloborodov's Forty-Third Army. Earlier trench raids had identified the German unit facing it as *Korps Abteilung D*. This was one of several improvised units that had appeared on the Eastern Front in the preceding months, formed from the amalgamation of badly degraded infantry divisions that were deemed too weak to be brought back to full strength – in this case, 56th and 262nd Infantry Divisions. Its commander was Generalmajor Bernhard Pamberg – born Bernhard Pampel, he changed his surname in 1939 to restore an old familial name that had disappeared due to the lack of male heirs. The conglomeration of units in his command had been together since late 1943 but could not be expected to show the same degree of cohesion as a properly organised infantry division and the first attack by Beloborodov's troops overran much of the front line of *Korps Abteilung D*. The German defensive line ran through an area of swampy forest punctuated by villages that had been heavily fortified and these – Novoselki, Dvorishche, and Chisti – were fiercely defended. From these positions, the Germans were able to use machine-guns to cover the gaps between the villages, but nevertheless the Red Army reconnaissance in force captured favourable positions for the commencement of the main offensive. As 22 June drew to a close, Chistiakov and Beloborodov compared their gains and joked about which army would make the most progress the following day.[7]

The Red Army's probes to the northwest of Vitebsk were forceful, but used only a fraction of the resources available. Yet already, the position of Reinhardt's Third Panzer Army was deteriorating rapidly with its meagre reserves exhausted. Throughout the night, Bagramian continued to apply pressure to prevent any German withdrawal to stronger positions further to the southwest. It was a highly encouraging start for 1st Baltic Front, and the brief hours of darkness saw constant traffic in the immediate rear area behind the Red Army's front line as troops and ammunition columns moved forward.

Busch and his subordinates had identified the area to the southeast of Vitebsk as a likely point for a Soviet attack and here too there was aggressive reconnaissance in force by Thirty-Ninth Army to the immediate southwest of Vitebsk and Fifth Army on its southern flank. The first probe was actually made on 17 June when the German 197th Infantry Division came under attack shortly before dawn. The Soviet probe was led by a penal battalion, made up of officers and men who had been convicted of various minor or medium-level offences and had an opportunity to redeem themselves by success on the battlefield; those guilty of more serious crimes such as attempted desertion were usually handed over to the NKVD and might subsequently be executed before their comrades. The penal battalion moved forward after a 20-minute artillery bombardment and swiftly captured a fortified village in the German front line. Immediately, the Germans counterattacked and reduced the width of the Soviet penetration and fighting continued in the days that followed, prior to the more energetic attacks of 22 June. Reinhardt correctly interpreted the attack of 17 June as an attempt to secure a better start line for the coming assault, but the manner in which his men managed to restrict the Soviet penetration left him confident that this sector would be able to hold firm.

His illusions were rapidly dispelled when stronger reconnaissance thrusts took place on 22 June. The German LIII Corps in Vitebsk was able to report that it had repulsed all attacks on its line, but remained unaware that these were merely the Soviet reconnaissance in force rather than the main offensive. To the south was General Georg Pfeiffer's VI Corps and it was less successful in fending off Soviet attacks, which secured several penetrations of the first defensive line. Having committed a regiment from 95th Infantry Division in the north, Reinhardt now sent another regiment from the division to prepare for a counterattack to restore the situation.

The first priority for the Red Army in this sector was to secure crossings over the Luchesa River and this was accomplished with ease. As was the case with Bagramian's forces in the north, the troops of 3rd Belarusian Front moved into position for their main assault the following day. The weather throughout 22 June was cloudy, limiting the ability of Soviet aviation to support ground operations, but it also greatly hindered Luftwaffe reconnaissance flights. Somewhat ominously, Third Panzer Army reported to Busch's headquarters that the Soviet

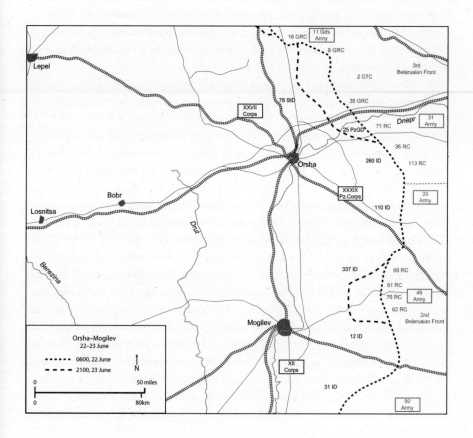

use of artillery throughout the day had been lighter than expected. Whilst the Germans could be grateful for this, it should have been interpreted as a sign that they were merely experiencing the first probes of the Red Army. The full weight of the storm was yet to break.

Further to the south too, there were reconnaissance probes by the Red Army as Galitsky – the commander of Eleventh Army – described:

> Four reinforced battalions carried out reconnaissance in force in the zone of the upcoming offensive. The aim was to clarify the enemy's system of fire and obstacles, and to capture prisoners. The battalions were detached from the divisions of the second echelon so as not to weaken the formations intended for the main assault. Each battalion was supported by a divisional artillery regiment.
>
> The attack began after a powerful 15-minute artillery strike on the front line and strongpoints of the enemy. The leading battalions broke into the first trench and took prisoners. In an effort to restore the situation, the Nazis launched several counterattacks supported by artillery and mortars. By the end of the day, we had detected 34 artillery and mortar batteries by muzzle flashes and sound systems …
>
> During the evening, the results of reconnaissance in the neighbouring sector were passed to us. On the right, in [Lieutenant] General [Nikolai Ivanovich] Krylov's Fifth Army, a great and somewhat unexpected success was achieved. The enemy's defences here were not strong and five forward battalions, with artillery support, managed to capture not just the first trenches but after repelling counterattacks they advanced to a depth of up to 4km and secured a substantial foothold …
>
> Things were different on the left, in [Lieutenant] General [Vasily Vasilyevich] Glagolev's Thirty-First Army. The enemy's defences here were solid and the advanced battalions failed to break into his trenches.[8]

Thirty-Third Army, on the southern flank of Galitsky's army, was on the northern flank of 2nd Belarusian Front. Its 70th Rifle Division also conducted energetic reconnaissance in force. Parts of the front-line trenches of the German positions were captured, triggering counterattacks supported by tanks and artillery. By the end of the day, the division reported that it had lost 60 killed and 148 wounded; it also claimed to have killed or wounded 120 Germans and to have knocked out five tanks and assault guns.[9] Compared to the attacks further to the north, it was far from successful and it triggered a critical report from Zakharov, the Front commander. He complained that reconnaissance in force was being conducted in a far too predictable and repetitive manner, with the raiding groups moving forward along easily predicted routes. Too often, the success of the raid was measured purely in terms of whether valuable prisoners had been captured for interrogation and any other benefits, e.g. identifying German positions, were discounted and even ignored, and it seems that Zakharov was eager to blame any perceived shortcomings on the preparations made by his predecessor. He had already irritated many of his subordinates with his constant criticism and bullying manner and his anger at the poor haul of prisoners can only have lowered morale amongst the troops nominated for these missions. Zakharov ordered that intelligence officers needed to remedy matters without delay. Reconnaissance in force was to be better organised and better planned in future.[10]

Despite the gains secured by the Soviet Fifth Army on his left flank, Tippelskirch reported from the headquarters of the German Fourth Army that almost all such attacks had been beaten off. Nonetheless, a number of dangerous situations were developing, in particular on the northern flank of the army and Tippelskirch requested reinforcements to cover any further developments. Busch's response was that the crisis developing in Third Panzer Army's sector required the deployment of whatever reserves were available; Fourth Army would have to deal with any further developments on its own. Ninth Army's sector remained largely quiet, but Jordan monitored reconnaissance reports with concern, particularly when Busch contacted him to ask if he could release any units that could be sent to help Third Panzer Army. Jordan insisted that he still expected a major attack on his lines in the next day or two and was adamant that the reserves in his sector – particularly 20th Panzer Division – should stay where they were. As it grew dark, Busch told him (and the other army commanders of Army Group Centre) 'Overall, I view the situation with optimism.'[11] The reactions of Jordan, who had been anticipating a crisis for several weeks, and other commanders are not known.

In the First World War, the artillery arm of the Russian Army was in many respects the only part of the army that functioned at a standard that was comparable to the armies of other Great Powers, but once the initial mobile phase of operations was replaced by trench warfare, there was growing dependence upon sheer weight of shelling to overcome trench lines and fortifications, as was the case with the armies of France, Britain, and Germany. When attacks failed, such as the Russian attack near Lake Naroch in 1916, the assumption was almost automatic that it might have succeeded if more guns, with more ammunition, had been available. The legacy of the artillery of the Imperial Russian Army continued after the Russian Revolution. Great importance was placed upon the use of guns to prepare the way for offensive operations throughout the years that followed and after the initial shock of *Barbarossa* had passed and the Red Army began to launch offensive operations of its own, the weight of artillery firepower steadily increased. As had been the case in the First World War, there was a tendency to assume that bombardments needed to be heavier if they were to suppress German defences effectively, but by early 1944 it was increasingly clear that this was not going to be sufficient. The volume of fire that could be delivered was now immense, but failure to identify German positions properly and to allocate appropriate weapons to engage those targets was a far greater factor than lack of gun barrels and ammunition. Hence the great importance placed upon reconnaissance in the last weeks of preparation for *Bagration*.

Bagramian's 1st Baltic Front had identified the precise locations of several important German headquarters before the battle began. The positions of the command elements of Sixteenth Army in the north at Ludza (part of the German Army Group North, immediately to the north of Army Group Centre), of Third Panzer Army (at Beshenkovichi), X Corps (in Rudnia), I Corps (in Borovukha), IX Corps (in Ulla), LIII Corps (in Vitebsk) and of the infantry divisions in the front line were all known to the Red Army. These were to be hit with a mixture of artillery fire and aerial attacks. Airfields too had been identified and would be attacked in order to try to destroy German aircraft on the ground and to cripple their support services – previous offensive operations against the Wehrmacht had seen the intervention of the Luftwaffe on the first day of the fighting, often operating from airfields close to the front line. Hundreds of artillery positions, bunkers, machine-gun positions, and supply dumps had also been identified. All of these targets were monitored carefully in the last two weeks of preparations to check if the Germans were taking any steps to pre-empt the Soviet offensive or if weapons were being relocated to alternative positions.[12] Similar steps were taken by the other Fronts.

As the aggressor, the Red Army had the huge advantage of being able to concentrate its resources. The frontage of the four Fronts from north to south was 99 miles, 87 miles, 99 miles, and 143 miles respectively, but they concentrated their resources on a fraction of this. The breakthrough sectors for the Fronts were 16 miles, 21 miles, seven miles, and 18 miles respectively. The artillery assets of the Fronts were then concentrated in these breakthrough sectors, with 76 per cent of 1st Baltic Front's guns in its key sector. The other three fronts achieved concentrations of 80 per cent, 54 per cent, and 71 per cent respectively. As a consequence, the number of artillery and mortar barrels per kilometre of front line was daunting – 151, 175, 181, and 204 for the Fronts from north to south.

By contrast, the Germans had to be prepared to deal with attacks at any point along the front line and therefore had much of their artillery assets positioned in sectors that would not face the initial Soviet assaults. In the key sectors, the Soviet gunners enjoyed a superiority of over 30:1.[13]

Many of the German soldiers caught up in the aggressive Soviet probes of 22 June might have believed that the long-expected offensive had commenced, but to date they had felt only a small fraction of the firepower assembled against them. In the northern sector, Bagramian was informed early on 23 June by his staff that there were reports of German troops abandoning their forward positions during the preceding night. In these circumstances, it seemed pointless to conduct the full artillery preparation that had been planned – many of these shells would fall on positions that were no longer being defended, and it was important to exploit any German withdrawals as quickly as possible. Accordingly, Bagramian issued instructions at 0400 that the bombardment was to be restricted to the areas where German defences were still intact. Two hours later, Chistiakov's troops attacked in strength, swiftly overwhelming the lines before them. Despite a mixture of fog and drizzle, Soviet aviation was active over the entire front line, and German units struggling along the few good roads in the region had to cope with constant strafing and bombing attacks.

Remarkably, some Red Army units had little idea that a major offensive was about to commence. Nikolai Kuzmich Stepanov was in a machine-gun platoon in the front line near Vitebsk:

> A bombardment began at night and our guns fired at the Germans for two hours without a break. We didn't know what was going on as nobody had told us that there were plans for an offensive. Then suddenly the roar of the cannonade stopped and it became quiet. Everyone was in good spirits, but anxious.
>
> The battalion commander gave the order: 'Quickly! Forward!' And then everyone rose up. Two crews, mine and that of Lesha Kursky, moved forward together, giving each other covering fire as we dashed forward. The crews were at full strength, five to seven people in each team with eight boxes of machine-gun belts – 2,000 rounds of ammunition. We reached the first trench, occasionally coming across German corpses, and everything was ploughed up by the shelling. But the Germans weren't fools and had set up their forward line in advance of their main positions, and as soon as we occupied the trench they shelled us with artillery. We had to move sideways and try to bypass the area through a forest.[14]

At the junction between the Soviet Sixth Guards Army and Forty-Third Army was the village of Shumilino, another fortified strongpoint and the last position at which the Germans could halt the Red Army before it reached the line of the Daugava River – hence Reinhardt's orders to prepare positions here just in case. The village was on a modest elevation, giving it good fields of fire, and the small German garrison from *Korps Abteilung D* was supported by powerful artillery formations. Between this strongpoint and the town of Obol to the northwest, the right flank of the German 252nd Infantry Division was driven back in disarray when the main offensive began on 23 June. Although Shumilino was technically an objective for Beloborodov's Forty-Third Army, Chistiakov ordered 71st Guards Rifle Division on his southern flank to bypass the German positions and then to work its way into the rear of the village.

Beloborodov's troops were also moving forward in strength:

At 0700 our artillery struck with great force. The German batteries attempted to answer but their fire grew weaker with every passing minute. On the basis of reports from the counter-battery gun group … we were certain that the enemy artillery was increasingly losing centralised coordination, even at lower levels. Attempts to concentrate the fire of three or four batteries were immediately suppressed by our artillery …

From the forward observation post, the entire 7km section of the breakthrough was clearly visible. A wall of fire and smoke stood over the enemy positions. Under a low canopy of morning clouds, nine attack aircraft flew overhead towards Shumilino. A salvo of rockets completed the artillery preparation. The smoke had not dissipated when the tanks and infantry of I Rifle Corps [on Beloborodov's northern flank] moved forward to attack.

'The enemy is running!' reported [Lieutenant] General [Nikolai Alekseyevich] Vasilyev [commander of I Rifle Corps].

And then came a signal from the commander of LX Rifle Corps, [Major] General [Anisim Stefanovich] Lyukhtikov [on Vasilyev's southern flank]: 'Fascist resistance is weak. Only the strongpoints at Novoselki, Dvorishche, and Chisti are still firing. We're going to use a smokescreen. Watch.'

I saw thick smoke creeping out of the trenches … near Belaya Dubrovka. It twisted and condensed and, driven by the northeast wind, crept over the swampy ground. A black wall of smoke 3km wide covered the slopes and the ruins of the houses in Dvorishche and Chisti and, spreading to the southwest, obscured the strongpoint in Novoselki.

The enemy was blinded. His firing towards our trenches became random. But now those trenches were empty, except for the chemical protection platoon of Lieutenant Frolov, which was creating the smokescreen … Lines of riflemen, hidden in the smoke, approached the outskirts of the village of Dvorishche. And on the right ... the leading elements of other battalions were making their way unobserved through the large swamp to Novoselki. By 1100, the enemy was completely isolated and an hour later the remnants of an infantry battalion, about 130 men, surrendered.[15]

Remarkably, Reinhardt was still unaware of the strength of the Soviet attack to the northwest of Vitebsk. As the day continued and *Korps Abteilung D* disintegrated, he issued a strong rebuke to its commander: 'It's scandalous to talk about the loss of any ability to resist after two days. The *Tigerstellung* [the defensive line to the west and southwest of Vitebsk] must definitely be held.'[16]

As the day progressed, the counterattack group from Sixteenth Army – 24th Infantry Division supported by part of an assault gun brigade – completed its concentration near Polotsk and in the late afternoon began to advance towards the southeast in an attempt to restore the front line, or at least to bring the Red Army's advance to a halt. Progress was modest but Army Group North received orders to release two more formations – 212th Infantry Division from Eighteenth Army and 290th Infantry Division from Sixteenth Army – as reinforcements for Reinhardt's rapidly collapsing Third Panzer Army. In the meantime, Bagramian's units pressed on towards the Daugava River. The strongpoint in Shumilino was cut off and fought on with little support, and a Soviet assault late on 23 June overran the position, killing or capturing the surviving German soldiers.

With his Front making good progress, Bagramian ordered I Tank Corps forward so that it could be unleashed as his exploitation force. The vehicles of Lieutenant General Vasily Vasilyevich Butkov's formations moved forward in three columns from their assembly area some ten miles to the rear of the original front line but the constant rain had softened the roads, which were further degraded by the passage of formations that had carried out the initial attacks on the German lines. At dusk, the leading elements of I Tank Corps struggled into Shumilino. Bagramian's intention to commit the tanks on the first proper day of the offensive was thus frustrated and instead he ordered Butkov to concentrate immediately behind the advancing infantry. Once they had forced their way through the German positions in front of the Daugava River – Reinhardt's *Tigerstellung* – Butkov would be unleashed. The left wing of Reinhardt's Third Panzer Army was already in serious difficulties; the advent of a powerful tank force would place it in even greater danger.

Although the front lines around Vitebsk were relatively quiet, Reinhardt secured permission from Busch for the troops of LIII Corps to pull back to the defensive lines around the 'fortress' itself. At this point, Gollwitzer's corps had 246th Infantry Division to the northwest of Vitebsk, 4th and 6th Luftwaffe Field Divisions in an arc to the north, northeast, and east, and 206th Infantry Division to the southeast. By pulling back to the city, Gollwitzer intended to release the two Luftwaffe field divisions so that they could take up positions to the southwest and keep open the lines of communication between Vitebsk and the rest of Third Panzer Army. Reinhardt still anticipated the main attack on his positions as coming from the southeast, and here the forces of 3rd Belarusian Front unleashed the full weight of their assembled artillery, though as was the case with Bagramian's Front the bombardment was modified to take account of the gains made by the reconnaissance in force of the preceding day. But before the shelling could commence, the waiting Soviet soldiers were surprised by a sudden burst of shelling by the Germans. Much of this bombardment accurately hit the preparation areas of Galitsky's Eleventh Guards Army. Hastily, Lieutenant General Petr Sergeyevich Semenov, the army chief of artillery, ordered long-range guns that had been assigned to counter-battery duties to retaliate. Shortly after, the massed guns of 3rd Belarusian Front began their preparatory bombardment. The first five minutes saw every available weapon bombarding the German positions before switching to more precise strikes against German fortifications and artillery emplacements for the next two hours. A further 40 minutes of suppressive fire on the forward edge of the German line and its immediate rear concluded the preparation – a far heavier bombardment than the brief shelling before the reconnaissance in force on 22 June. Arkady Grigoryevich Gurevich was an artilleryman in Eleventh Guards Army:

> During the night of 22–23 June, we heard our tanks taking up their starting positions for the offensive at low speed, to try to hide the noise of their engines. That same night, all the artillery including our battery took up their firing positions. Off-duty signallers helped the guncrews with their equipment. When dawn broke, we saw all the artillery lined up, one gun after another. The smaller calibre guns were closer to the front line. In front of us and behind, to the left and the right – everywhere, there were guns, deployed in clearly defined lines, stretching to the horizon … The *Katyushas* fired the first volley. That was the signal for the artillery preparation to begin. I'd never seen or heard such a thing before. The cannonade was so powerful that the smoke from my cigarette was blown away. To talk to the person next to you, you had to shout – otherwise, they wouldn't hear you. Because of the roar, I had great difficulty maintaining radio contact with the advanced artillery observation post.[17]

By first light on 23 June, Red Army sappers had already lifted thousands of mines from in front of the German positions and had started to dig approach trenches. As Soviet aircraft flew forward to strike at positions further to the rear, the ground forces moved forward at 0900; the northern wing of the attack consisted of Thirty-Ninth Army closest to Vitebsk, with Fifth Army in the centre and Eleventh Guards Army to the southeast.

Boiko, the senior political officer in Thirty-Ninth Army, later described his army's part in the assault on 23 June:

> Hundreds of guns and mortars, alternating powerful general bombardments with methodical targeted fire, destroyed the Nazi defences and degraded their manpower. At the beginning of the artillery preparation which, according to the fire plan, was supposed to last 110 minutes, I was in the forward command post of the Army with a group of intelligence officers. Suddenly I heard the alarmed voice of the commander. I went out to the trench where Lyudnikov was pointing towards the start line of V Guards Rifle Corps and shouting excitedly, 'Look! They're attacking already! What's going on over there?'
>
> I looked through the stereoscope and was alarmed: it seemed that our riflemen really were moving forward without waiting for the end of the artillery bombardment. And then the commander of V Corps, Major General [Ivan Semenovich] Bezuglyi, reported to the Army commander that in some areas his guardsmen were on the attack and had even overrun the enemy's first trench. The situation became difficult: our units might come under fire from our own artillery, or run into a counterattack from the enemy before he had been properly suppressed.
>
> General Lyudnikov turned to [Major] General [Nikolai Andreyevich] Deresh, who was the commander of Thirty-Ninth Army's artillery and was in the command post. 'Can the artillery switch immediately to support this attack?'
>
> 'Yes, maybe,' came the reply ...
>
> This incident was of course later the subject of an investigation. It transpired that in some areas in front of the waiting battalions of 17th and 19th Guards Rifle Divisions, the Nazis couldn't hold on under our artillery fire and began to pull back from the first trench line to the second. One of the first to spot this was the commander of a battalion from 19th Guards Rifle Divison, Major Fedorov. On his orders, his companies rushed forward and captured the enemy's first trench. The commander of a battalion from 17th Guards Rifle Division, Captain Kutenkov, made the same decision ...
>
> Powerfully supported by artillery and tanks, the units of V Guards Rifle Corps quickly broke through the enemy's first defensive line, crossed the Luchesa

without pausing, and before noon penetrated into the artillery positions of the Nazis, overrunning 23 guns. By 1300, after an advance of up to 8km, they cut the Vitebsk–Orsha railway line and captured the railway station at Zamostochye.[18]

The German defences in the sector to the south of Vitebsk were under the control of VI Corps and it was driven back along its entire front. At first, the line pulled back in a more or less cohesive manner, but at midday one of the central formations, 299th Infantry Division, began to give way when its northern flank was turned by a Soviet armoured attack. The northern flank of VI Corps, closest to Vitebsk, was formed by 197th Infantry Division and during the afternoon it was unable to hold a continuous front line. The Soviet V Guards Rifle Corps broke through at multiple points, reaching and crossing the railway line running south from the city. As the disintegrating units of 197th Infantry Division pulled back towards the north and northwest, a gap of 12 miles opened up between them and the rest of VI Corps to the south. In an attempt to simplify command arrangements, 197th Infantry Division was now transferred to the control of LIII Corps in Vitebsk but despite the damage inflicted to his northern flank and centre, General Pfeiffer informed his superiors that he remained confident that his VI Corps would be able to continue its defence on 24 June.

Lyudnikov, the commander of Thirty-Ninth Army, had every intention of preventing the Germans from catching their breath and he wasted no time in exploiting the success of his leading units. V Guards Rifle Corps had already advanced over eight miles as darkness fell and he ordered it to continue pushing west. He dispatched two rifle divisions to deploy on its flanks while LXXXIV Rifle Corps to the north was told to strike into Vitebsk from the east. Even if this attack failed to penetrate into the city, it would tie down German defenders while other Soviet formations enveloped the 'fortress' and then entered it from the west and southwest. After a brief discussion, Vasilevsky and Cherniakhovsky concluded that the gains made on 23 June were sufficient to trigger the deployment of the cavalry-mechanised group that was 3rd Belarusian Front's exploitation force. Its commander, Lieutenant General Nikolai Sergeyevich Oslikovsky, was ordered to move his units forward so that they would be able to enter the battle late on 24 June.

Beyond the southern flank of the German VI Corps was XXVII Corps with 78th Sturm Division on its northern flank. Originally 78th Infantry Division, Hitler awarded it its new name at the beginning of 1943 in recognition of its resolute defence in the fighting around the Rzhev salient. Like other infantry divisions, it had consisted of three infantry regiments supported by an artillery regiment and reconnaissance, anti-tank and sapper battalions. As a Sturm division – indeed, one of only two divisions in the Wehrmacht to receive this status – it had additional forces assigned to it: a mortar battalion with a mixture of heavy mortars and rocket launchers; an assault gun battalion; and an anti-aircraft battalion. Consequently, it was stronger than other infantry divisions in terms of its firepower and numbers.

Throughout 1943, 78th Sturm Division was involved in a series of battles that became known to its officers and men as the four *Rollbahnschlachten* ('main supply route battles'), as Army Group Centre was slowly driven back through Smolensk along the main road and rail axis that continued to Brest and Warsaw. The first weeks of 1944 passed with little action for the division, much to the relief of its exhausted men; they absorbed replacement drafts and strengthened their positions, watchfully guarding a desolate landscape of ruined villages, burned-out military vehicles and frozen corpses, but any hope that they would be left in peace before the spring thaw brought a temporary end to operations was broken by fresh Soviet attacks in early March. For several days, soldiers struggled in freezing water that was often waist-deep, but the front line barely moved. In the weeks that followed, the division once more became aware of increasing activity on the other side of the devastated strip of no-man's land. Whatever the views of Busch and other senior officers, the personnel of 78th Sturm Division had little doubt that they were about to come under attack and continued their labours to improve their positions. But their preparations were hindered by the fact that the weakness of Army Group Centre had necessitated 78th Sturm Division being assigned a broader front than in the past.

The reconnaissance in force carried out by the Red Army in this sector on 22 June took 78th Sturm Division by surprise in that the initial artillery bombardment was far shorter than the Germans expected for a major attack, and the leading Soviet troops took advantage of morning mist to make their attack. Nevertheless, the Soviet probes were driven off without difficulty. The following day, the Red Army's artillery opened fire once more, this time with far greater weight and duration of bombardment. The German division's headquarters was heavily bombarded by Soviet aircraft as the offensive began and its line felt the full weight of the assault by the Soviet Eleventh Guards Army, preceded by the three-hour artillery preparation. Rapidly, the focus of the Soviet assault was identified as being directed against the northern flank of the division. Despite being close to full strength, 78th Sturm Division was unable to hold its positions and contact with VI Corps was soon lost; by the end of 23 June, all divisional reserves had been committed. Red Army attacks had frequently targeted the seam between different formations in the expectation that if driven back, the German units might then withdraw on diverging axes, and in this case there was the further bonus that the seam between 78th Sturm Division and 256th Infantry Division to the north represented several boundaries – in addition to its being the junction of two divisions, it was also the seam between VI Corps (part of Reinhardt's Third Panzer Army) and XXVII Corps (part of Tippelskirch's Fourth Army). Perhaps due to its greater strength, 78th Sturm Division put up better resistance than most German infantry divisions on 23 June. It was driven back all along its frontage, but the maximum Soviet advance was about five miles and in places barely a mile.

To the south of the German XXVII Corps was XXXIX Panzer Corps, to the east of Mogilev. It came under powerful attack by the Soviet Forty-Ninth Army after a heavy artillery preparation that commenced at 0900, delayed by two hours due to persistent fog. When the Soviet ground troops moved forward two hours later, they were pleased to find that the German forward positions had been badly disrupted and at first they succeeded in advancing relatively easily. The first obstacle was the small Pronia River and sappers erected crossings even before the artillery bombardment was complete. As the tanks and infantry moved forward, they attempted to take full advantage of these early successes but in doing so they ran into the last moments of the preparatory barrage. Some of the Pronia crossings rapidly became unusable after they were damaged by the passage of tanks or by German artillery fire.

Although there were a few penetrations, particularly in the sector of 337th Infantry Division, most of the defences managed to hold firm, not least because so many Red Army tanks and assault guns were still struggling to cross the Pronia. Attempts by 2nd Belarusian Front to reinforce the advancing infantry with rifle divisions from the second echelon added to the congestion with little improvement in the advance, which now began to encounter local German counterattacks. These had mixed results and whilst they halted further Soviet advances, they did little to restore the old front line. Under considerable pressure, 337th Infantry Division lost nearly half its artillery. In response to the increasingly desperate requests from Schünemann, the division's commander, only two battalions could be sent as reinforcements, but to the rear of the embattled German division was the *Feldherrnhalle* panzergrenadier division. Although it was part of Busch's army group, he was not permitted to deploy it without Hitler's explicit consent and it took until 2145 on 23 June for this to be secured. But although Busch immediately assigned it to XXXIX Panzer Corps, the division was to be held in readiness behind the front line rather than be committed to an immediate counterattack. Tippelskirch's summary of the attacks on his Fourth Army, sent to Busch that evening, would have made gratifying reading for the senior Soviet commanders on the other side of the front line. The report highlighted several distinctive elements: the Soviet artillery fire had been heavier than in the past; control of that artillery had been far more effective, particularly in the highly successful use of counter-battery fire to silence German guns; the enemy had almost complete air superiority; Soviet infantry and tanks were cooperating together more skilfully than before; and the Red Army had been quick to exploit any local gains.[19]

Bagration was only one day into its fully active phase, but by mid-afternoon on 23 June Busch had to inform *OKH* that unless he received reinforcements, he would be unable to restore the situation in Third Panzer Army's sector. That evening, he added to the stream of bad news: the only way that a continuous front line could be restored was by a timely – in this context, immediate – withdrawal from Vitebsk. After a further exchange, Generalleutnant Adolf Heusinger, chief of the operations staff at *OKH*, concurred and suggested that both Third Panzer Army and Ninth Army should be given freedom to manoeuvre their limited forces in order to pull back and then fend off the Soviet attacks rather than attempting to stop them in their current fixed positions. Discussions continued into the night, expanding to involve the neighbouring army groups. To the north, Generaloberst Georg Lindemann, commander of Army Group North, was able to promise that two infantry divisions would be available for deployment in the Polotsk–Obol–Ulla sector, i.e. the northern flank of Third Panzer Army, by the end of 24 June.

The arrival of two infantry divisions was of course welcome, but even in the current situation it was a relatively modest addition to the strength of the Wehrmacht given its losses on 23 June; had the Germans been aware of the imminent commitment of I Tank Corps and other exploitation forces, they would have realised that it was a wholly inadequate response. And of course, far worse was yet to come: Rotmistrov's Fifth Guards Tank Army still lay in wait, completely undetected by the Germans. Nonetheless, Hitler's deep-seated unwillingness to concede ground had the inevitable effect. He declared that the reinforcements would be sufficient to restore the situation and that any discussion about pulling back to the west would have to await the deployment of the two divisions. A more forceful army group commander might have ordered the abandonment of Vitebsk in any case, perhaps using wording that the retreat was only permitted if all other options had been exhausted, but Busch was not of such a mindset and Reinhardt had survived in his post partly because he had observed the dire consequences of such disobedience in early 1942, when a whole swathe of senior commanders lost their posts. Busch and Reinhardt simply passed on Hitler's orders: there was to be no withdrawal from Vitebsk or on either flank of the threatened city.

The following day, 24 June, would see the battle expand to the entire breadth of Army Group Centre. In the north, the battered units of the German IX Corps had spent the night desperately trying to reorder their ranks, particularly those of *Korps Abteilung D*, and a new defensive line was hastily prepared between Usvitsa and Budilovo. A continuous front line was no longer possible given the losses of 22 and 23 June and Bagramian was determined to take full advantage. The tanks of I Tank Corps were now approaching the front line but wheeled elements of the force were still struggling to move forward, held up by congestion and roads that were rapidly deteriorating with the passage of so much traffic. The wide-ranging aircraft covering 1st Baltic Front spotted the approaching columns of the German infantry divisions sent from Army Group North and Bagramian decided that it was essential to secure a bridgehead over the Daugava River as quickly as possible; once this had been done, I Tank Corps could be committed over this bridgehead into the rear of the German positions.

Beloborodov and Chistiakov duly ordered their rifle divisions to press on to the Daugava. The first elements of Forty-Third Army reached and crossed the river in mid-morning, but neighbouring units failed to take advantage of this and instead they moved up towards the river line but made little attempt to cross it. Nonetheless, by the end of 24 June a substantial bridgehead had been seized. Chistiakov's Sixth Guards Army had about 12 miles to cover in order to reach the river; operating on the northern side of the thrust, his men had to deal with the increasing pressure from the northwest as German reinforcements from Army Group North were fed into the battle, but nonetheless his rifle divisions steadily advanced despite German resistance.

The speed of the Soviet advance was creating its own difficulties. The original plan had called for Sixth Guards Army to reach and cross the Daugava on the third day of the operation, i.e. 25 June, but Bagramian was pushing the pace of the advance and as a consequence Chistiakov was about a day ahead of schedule. This began to cause difficulties in moving forward sufficient supplies to the leading units, particularly given the growing German strength on the northern flank. To make matters worse, it began to rain during the afternoon of 24 June and the rapidly disintegrating roads deteriorated even faster. As a consequence, the bridging units that had been preparing to construct crossings over the Daugava joined the columns of I Tank Corps and supply formations in what seemed like insoluble traffic jams. Chistiakov moved forward to join his troops who had now reached the banks of the Daugava and watched as they improvised rafts from whatever material they could find. There were few German troops in their path and they were swiftly beaten off. Finally, as darkness fell the sapper

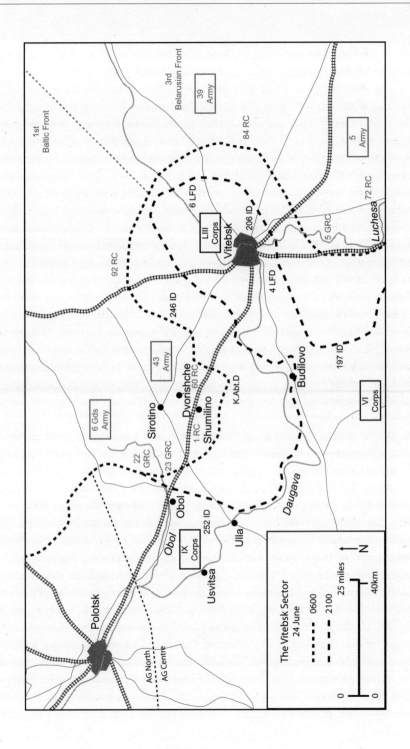

The Vitebsk Sector
24 June

.... 0600
- - - 2100

N

0 25 miles
0 40km

163

companies began to arrive. An improvised bridge was constructed and tanks and artillery began to cross during the brief hours of darkness.[20]

The position of the German LIII Corps in Vitebsk looked increasingly perilous as the day unfolded. Much of 197th Infantry Division was deployed in the 'neck' of the Vitebsk salient about three miles to the southwest of the city and by late morning it found itself fighting off increasingly powerful Soviet attacks from the east, southeast, and south as Lyudnikov's Thirty-Ninth Army exploited its gains of the previous day. The situation deteriorated with increasing speed and Gollwitzer, the corps commander, informed Reinhardt that his troops were effectively isolated in the city. By early afternoon, the telegraph cables connecting Gollwitzer with Third Panzer Army were cut and he spoke by radio demanding freedom to conduct a breakout. Perhaps in the awareness that speaking to Busch was pointless, Reinhardt then contacted *OKH* and spoke to Zeitzler. It is a measure of the self-deception that prevailed at the highest German levels that Zeitzler – who had been in Minsk visiting Busch's headquarters on the morning of 24 June and would have seen the steady stream of bad news that was arriving from all directions – asked if such a withdrawal was really necessary. Reinhardt gave a blunt and uncompromising response. If the troops in Vitebsk were to be saved – and importantly, if they were to continue adding to the fighting strength of Third Panzer Army – it was essential that they were extracted immediately. Reinhardt concluded by adding that he was fearful that as had been the case in the past, permission to withdraw would be given too late.[21]

Busch meanwhile continued to insist that LIII Corps restore the situation with the forces at its disposal. Specifically, it was to use the two Luftwaffe field divisions to counterattack towards the southwest in order to ensure lines of communication remained open while holding the city itself with its two remaining divisions. Even if four full-strength infantry divisions had been available, it would have been a difficult undertaking; to attempt it with the notoriously fragile Luftwaffe field divisions was an act of desperation. Reinhardt impatiently replied that the time for such half-measures was long past and in response, Busch promised to raise the matter with Hitler. After further discussions, orders arrived at the headquarters of LIII Corps by radio at 2025. Hitler had declared that the 'fortress' was to be held by Generalleutnant Alfons Hitter with his 206th Infantry Division. The rest of LIII Corps was given permission to fight its way to the southwest. If this order had been issued a few hours earlier, it would have represented a difficult task. The additional delay had made the difficulties an order of magnitude greater. Moreover, the insistence on maintaining the 'fortress' with 206th Infantry Division while the rest of LIII Corps attempted to break out was the worst of all worlds. The city defences had been intended for three divisions, and Hitter's formation was simply too weak to hold the perimeter; but its orders to stay in Vitebsk reduced the strength of the breakout force significantly.

To the south and southeast of Vitebsk, the troops of Cherniakhovsky's 3rd Belarusian Front spent the night of 23–24 June busily moving forward their supplies and reinforcements. Lyudnikov's Thirty-Ninth Army resumed its thrust before first light with V Guards Rifle Corps rapidly advancing to place itself astride the German lines of communication running southwest from Vitebsk. During preparatory training, Lyudnikov and his staff had impressed upon their troops – like all Red Army units, they included a large percentage of fresh, untried recruits – that the first three kilometres of an advance were the most difficult. If attacking units could cover this quickly, they would have penetrated the depth of the German front line and resistance would rapidly weaken; the alacrity with which they advanced must have been gratifying to their commanders.[22] At 2300, the leading units of Thirty-Ninth Army made contact with the advancing tanks and infantry of 1st Baltic Front's Forty-Third Army. The ring around Vitebsk was closed, though contact remained tenuous.

Further to the south, Galitsky's Eleventh Guards Army was having a much harder time. The terrain here was swampy and there were fewer 'corridors' of firm ground where tanks could operate. Recognising this, the soldiers of the German 78th Sturm Division had positioned their anti-tank assets with care to cover these routes, as Galitsky discovered when he visited the headquarters of 16th Guards Rifle Division:

I found [Major General Yefim Vasilyevich] Ryzhikov in his forward observation post. He reported that, supported by tanks and assault guns, his division had overcome the obstacles in front of the enemy lines and had swiftly occupied the first line of trenches. Then [two regiments] ... moved forward to take the second line. At the same time, the third regiment ... captured the strongpoint at Kirievo. 'The infantry and tanks cooperated well,' continued the division commander. 'They successfully crossed the minefield between the first two trench lines. But as they approached the third they ran into another minefield, which was very extensive. Several tanks were disabled. The tankers tried to bypass the minefield but came under flank fire from Nazi assault guns and lost several more vehicles. The sappers are now trying to make passages through the minefield but they're working under fire. The tanks supporting the infantry are having to manoeuvre in a very limited space.'

Everything that Ryzhikov told me was clearly confirmed by what I could see from his observation post. At that moment, dozens of artillery pieces were firing from previously undiscovered positions on our tanks. The enemy even engaged them with *Panzerfaust* rounds from nearby trenches. The tank and artillery regiments supporting the division continued to suffer losses but could make no further advances.

Immediately, I ordered the attack suspended while additional reconnaissance of targets, primarily the enemy batteries, was carried out, and sappers were moved forward. I sent a signal to the Army command centre to transfer two sapper companies from our reserves to 16th Guards Rifle Division. The offensive was only to be resumed after passages had been cleared through the minefield and a strong artillery bombardment had been carried out, and after tanks and infantry had regrouped so that they could work together more effectively. 'When will you be ready?' I asked.

'We will try to get everything done by 1400,' replied General Ryzhikov. 'I will need additional artillery and aviation support.'[23]

The fighting was often confused and despite the accounts written after the war by Soviet commanders of the lengthy training of soldiers prior to the attack, many were very inexperienced. Nikolai Mikhailovich Kubrak was a rifleman in 31st Guards Rifle Division, another of Galitsky's formations:

Our battalion, which consisted mainly of new recruits, lagged behind the other units because none of us had seen action before. After the powerful artillery preparation, we moved through passages in the minefields but the Germans cut us off from the other units and surrounded us. The few experienced soldiers retreated in time but we didn't know anything, there were no senior commanders nearby, just young boys. Only junior lieutenants were with us, and they had been sent to the front line after just six months of training. They were just as green as we were. We wandered through the forest and stumbled upon a dug-in German tank. We scattered hastily and came to some kind of single-track railway. About 25 of us gathered there and in the evening we took up all-round defensive positions. A sentry was posted, and we could hear fighting going on somewhere to one side ... Early in the morning, before it was light, we decided to press on, and suddenly we heard movement. There was a shout: 'Stop or we'll shoot!' We were so happy and shouted back, 'Boys, we've been looking for you everywhere!' It was our company commander. He led us to the battalion headquarters where we were given vodka. All the company commanders were there, none had been killed. They began to sort out the men ... Many recruits had been killed. The officers were terribly afraid that an investigation would take place. A report was sent to headquarters. I never saw those officers in the battalion again. They were moved elsewhere.[24]

Galitsky reinforced the western wing of his Eleventh Guards Army, which was enjoying greater success than other formations, but Vasilevsky monitored the slow progress of Eleventh Guards Army from Cherniakhovsky's headquarters with concern. The stubborn defence of 78th Sturm Division threatened to derail the planned entry of Fifth Guards Tank Army into the battle. With the southern flank of 3rd Belarusian Front making such slow progress, he now suggested to *Stavka* that Rotmistrov's army should be introduced through the ranks of Fifth Army a little to the north, where the German front line had melted away almost completely. At the same time, Oslikovsky's cavalry-mechanised group was to move its focus of attention slightly further north; this would have the benefit of allowing it to interact with the leading units of 1st Baltic Front once they had completed the encirclement of Vitebsk. At 2000, Stalin signalled Vasilevsky to approve this new arrangement.

The intervention of Galitsky to reorganise the attack of one of his divisions and of Vasilevsky to alter the deployment of exploitation forces both show how far the Red Army had evolved from earlier operations. In the bitter fighting around the Rzhev salient and in the attempts to break the siege ring around Leningrad, the Red Army had shown little flexibility, repeatedly attempting to bludgeon its way through German defences with increasingly costly and futile frontal attacks after the initial assaults had bogged down. The Red Army might remain a blunt instrument, but it was now being wielded with rather greater skill than before. But it is worth noting that this flexible approach was due to Vasilevsky, Cherniakhovsky, and Galitsky. All three were of a different character to the blunt, ruthless Zhukov who, right to the end of the war, would attempt to smash German positions with brutal force rather than using finesse to minimise casualties and to exploit enemy weak points.

Vasilevsky promptly passed the new instructions from *Stavka* to Fifth Guards Tank Army:

> I have to note that Rotmistrov was not exactly enthusiastic at the *Stavka* decision, both the transfer of his army [from *Stavka* reserve to 3rd Belarusian Front's control] and the change in direction of its introduction into the breach. Nor did this evade the attention of the Front commander Cherniakhovsky. I am not aware of the real reasons for this.[25]

Unfortunately, Rotmistrov was part-way through writing his memoirs when he died in 1982. His version of events is therefore unrecorded. His performance to date had been variable; although his army had consistently achieved its objectives, it was often at the price of heavy losses, as a consequence of which the ability of Fifth Guards Tank Army to continue operations into the depths of the German positions was often compromised. This had undoubtedly been discussed in the preparation phase of *Bagration* and he and his staff would have drawn up plans to try to remedy these past shortcomings. In anticipation of being committed in support of Eleventh Guards Army, Rotmistrov had moved his units into position immediately to the rear of Galitsky's forces and had gone to considerable lengths to determine which routes his troops would use when they moved forward. He clearly wished to leave his forces where they were but was overruled. In order to move to enter the battle through Fifth Army's sector, Rotmistrov's units would have to retrace their steps back to their original preparation area to the east before moving forward once more – there were no suitable routes for a lateral redeployment. This would result in a road journey of up to 54 miles.

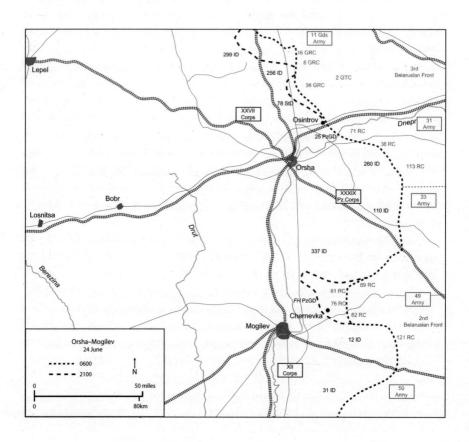

Despite the determined resistance of Generalleutnant Hans Traut's 78th Sturm Division, the northern half of the battlefield showed an increasingly bad situation for the Wehrmacht by the end of 24 June. The encirclement of LIII Corps in Vitebsk left a hole of at least 18 miles between the southern flank of IX Corps in the north and VI Corps in the south, and neither corps had any forces with which to try to remedy the situation. At army level too, there were no reserves available. The ability of Busch to respond to the growing crisis was also severely constrained. Besides, for the army group commander, there was further bad news from the southern half of his sector.

Tippelskirch's Fourth Army, to the south of Third Panzer Army, was under severe pressure throughout 24 June. In addition to the ongoing fighting in the north in 78th Sturm Division's sector, it had to deal with renewed Soviet attacks all along the front line that were preceded by further heavy shelling. On the southern flank, General Robert Martinek's XXXIX Panzer Corps found itself in an increasingly weak position. Soviet attacks continued through the night of 23–24 June and by mid-morning Martinek was receiving reports of T-34s entering Chernevka – the Red Army had advanced half the distance from its original positions to the Dnepr River. As the day progressed, Martinek's line simply disintegrated. Gaps of several miles opened up and Soviet forces demonstrated once more the degree to which they had improved their ability to exploit such gains. During the afternoon, 337th Infantry Division – under heavy pressure from the Soviet Forty-Ninth Army – reported that it had lost most of its artillery and could do little to halt the enemy, who swept through the gap to the north of the division to strike at the southern flank of 110th Infantry Division. The only armoured assets of the panzer corps – the panzergrenadier division *Feldherrnhalle* – was on the immediate southern flank of the remnants of 337th Infantry Division but could do nothing to help, having been forced to take up defensive positions.

Late in the morning, Tippelskirch contacted Busch's chief of staff. He reported that Fourth Army's units were still fighting as hard as they could but multiple gaps had appeared in the line and there was increasing danger of divisions being overwhelmed in isolation. In particular, the near-collapse of 337th Infantry Division created threats to the units on its northern and southern flanks. In the absence of sufficient reserves to counterattack and restore the continuous line, the only remedy was a wholesale withdrawal of Fourth Army back to the line of the Dnepr River. This would allow the army to occupy a shorter front line, thus freeing up sufficient troops to restore continuity. He added that although 337th Infantry Division and 78th Sturm Division were heavily engaged, many of his other divisions were still relatively unscathed and a redeployment would therefore enable them to be used decisively to remedy the situation. Krebs, the chief of staff in Minsk, was an experienced officer and would have recognised the correctness of this assessment, but his response was characteristic of the rigid attitudes that were increasingly causing paralysis throughout the Wehrmacht:

> The task [of the army group] remains very clear: to hold the current position and to support blocking lines [to stop further Red Army advances]. To achieve this, forces are to be withdrawn from divisions that have not come under attack (e.g. 260th Infantry Division).[26]

Such an order was absurd. Even if it had been possible to extract all of 260th Infantry Division, it wouldn't have represented sufficient forces to allow the current line to be restored. Shortly after came fresh orders. In order to try to restore contact with Reinhardt's Third Panzer Army to the north, Fourth Army was to pull back its northern flank to the *Tigerstellung* at the same time that Third Panzer Army attempted to do the same with what remained of its southern flank.

The only elements of Fourth Army that were putting up strong resistance were 78th Sturm Division and 25th Panzergrenadier Division on its southeast flank. But the collapse of the line to either side created the threat that these divisions might now find themselves isolated and Tippelskirch requested permission for an immediate withdrawal. It took several hours for Busch to agree, but only on condition that a modest withdrawal to the next defensive line was to be the only such retreat – permission for wider withdrawals, as Tippelskirch had urgently requested, was refused. In the meantime, the soldiers of 78th Sturm Division began to pull back to the *Tigerstellung* at the end of 24 June, noting with concern the light of burning villages on both sides; even if their division was still relatively intact, it seemed that there were threats on both flanks, regardless of Tippelskirch's assurances to Busch that most of his army was still not fully engaged.

After one day of forceful reconnaissance and two days of full-strength assault, the Red Army had reduced Third Panzer Army to a shambles and created a major crisis for Fourth Army. Dealing with this was far beyond the resources – both material and in terms of leadership – of Army Group Centre. But the scale of the crisis was growing rapidly. After a further heavy artillery bombardment of up to 90 minutes, Generalleutnant Friedrich Wiese's XXXV Corps, part of Jordan's Ninth Army and defending the approaches to Bobruisk, came under heavy attack. Once again, maximum pressure was applied to a seam in the German positions – the boundary between 134th Infantry Division in the south and 57th Infantry Division in the north was not only the line between XXXV Corps and XII Corps, but also the junction of Fourth Army to the north and Ninth Army to the south. By mid-morning, Soviet troops from the Soviet Third Army, on the right flank of Rokossovsky's 1st Belarusian Front, had torn another major hole in the German lines. This was the northern of the two Soviet attacks against Bobruisk. To the rear of the German lines were the weak units of 707th Infantry Division and these were immediately released for a counterattack to restore the link with Fourth Army to the north.

The German reserves were deployed in a wide area around Bobruisk and it would take precious time for them to assemble before they could be thrown at the advancing Soviet troops. In the meantime, Jordan spoke to Generalleutnant Mortimer von Kessel, commander of 20th Panzer Division. The two men agreed that the division should be committed in an immediate counterattack towards

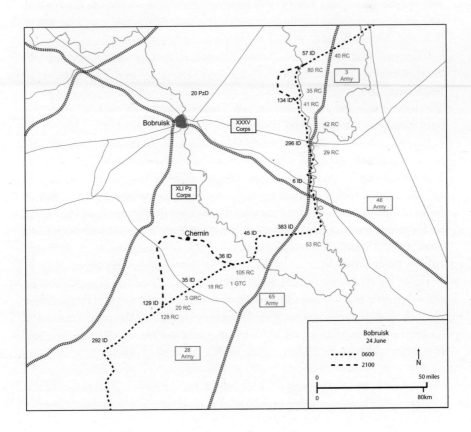

the north; Busch agreed, but bad news continued to arrive. The second thrust towards Bobruisk from the south struck XLI Panzer Corps; 35th and 129th Infantry Divisions were rapidly driven out of their positions. Generalleutnant Edmund Hoffmeister had taken command of XLI Panzer Corps on 19 June and was now dealing with a growing crisis. He informed Jordan that he might be able to halt the Soviet attacks in the depths of his defensive lines, but added that there were signs of further columns of Red Army units moving up from the rear. If these entered the battle before German reinforcements arrived, there was no prospect of prolonged defence.

It seems that Busch now changed his mind about where to counterattack with 20th Panzer Division. At first, Ninth Army received instructions that only parts of the division were being released to its control for deployment against the Soviet forces on Jordan's northern flank, and the division's operations officer was ordered to prepare for rapid deployment not to the northeast but to the south against the units battering their way through XLI Panzer Corps. Confusion continued to grow. Like most panzer divisions, Hoffmeister's units had organised themselves into several battlegroups, with the bulk of the tanks, self-propelled artillery, and half-track mounted panzergrenadiers forming an 'armoured battlegroup' while the wheeled units formed other groups. At midday, the division was ordered to dispatch its armoured battlegroup to the north with the intention of attacking while 707th Infantry Division completed its concentration. The order came with the warning that Jordan would have to hand back the battlegroup the following day.

The German units began to move into position; fortunately for them, the sky was overcast and Soviet air attacks were limited. The first regiment of 707th Infantry Division was thrown into a counterattack late in the afternoon, eliminating a Red Army penetration. After a morning of growing crisis, Wiese began to breathe more easily: it seemed that at least for the moment, the threat to his corps was reduced, particularly if 20th Panzer Division could restore contact with Fourth Army to the north.

By contrast, the situation to the south of Bobruisk was steadily moving in favour of the Red Army. Rokossovsky's attack in this sector had to contend with difficult terrain and although Forty-Eighth Army managed to grind through two German trench lines, it was then brought to a halt. Aleksandr Yefimovich Kashpur was a signaller in one of the assault units and he described the first day of fighting and how the terrain was as much a threat as the enemy:

I had seen a lot of artillery preparations but I didn't remember anything like this. There must have been a thousand barrels for every kilometre. And they blazed away for two hours. There was wild howling and hissing everywhere, literally tons of metal flying over our heads. We were driven half-mad in our trenches – what must it have been like for the Germans? The iron rain simply churned them into the earth.

And then after two hours: attack!

This was the first time I had encountered tanks operating in close support of the infantry. We were accompanied by a T-34. The radio set on my shoulders weighed 23kg and the second radio operator, Kabantsov, was running next to me carrying a rifle. My rifle was slung on his back. We crossed the Drut River by a marked ford. I had to hold my radio high over my head. The German forward positions simply didn't exist any more. Everything seemed to have been churned up by a terrible plough. We quickly scrambled through a few trenches. I followed Kabantsov, trying to step on raised ground sticking out of the swamp. In one place I slipped and fell into the mud with my radio. I began to sink into the mud. The thought that filled my head was this – I mustn't drop the radio in the water! Its batteries will get wet and I'll let everyone down! I could see Kabantsov's back as he walked on. He hadn't heard me fall. Was I going to drown? I strained and with a jerk I managed to push the radio onto a dry spot. That seemed the most important thing. Kabantsov would notice I wasn't with him and would run back and find the radio, all well and good. But what about me? Mud was slipping down on me. I felt like a fly in a spider's web. There was nothing solid under my feet. I tried to catch my breath. Oh God, how stupid! I felt my strength draining away.

A soldier from our battalion ran past and I shouted to him with joy, 'Mate, help me, help me out! Get the radio away from the water!' He stretched his rifle to me and I grabbed it with all my strength, and together we managed to get me out of the damned swamp. I poured mud from my boots and pressed on, trying to jump from one high area to the next.[27]

The neighbouring Sixty-Fifth Army fared rather better. Its commander, Batov, made good use of reconnaissance to identify marshy areas that the Germans were defending with only limited troops. Although the ground on the eastern flank of his sector was firmer, he decided to put the weight of his assault on the western flank. The first attack would have to be made by infantry, and as soon as they had secured sufficient ground the army's sappers would have to lay corduroy roads to permit tanks to move forward. To prevent the Germans from detecting preparations, Batov's engineers delayed construction of corduroy roads for tanks to move up to the front line until the preparatory artillery bombardment for the infantry attack had begun; thereafter, the roads were to be extended as quickly as possible so that Batov could commit I Guards Tank Corps at an early stage. Batov watched from a forward observation position as the attack began:

In the breakthrough zone, we deployed 207 guns and mortars per kilometre of front. The artillery preparation was to commence with a simultaneous salvo. Batteries of 152mm guns were stationed 200m from the command post. It was 0655. We could see the guns being loaded. The gunners took up the cords. One minute remained. Thirty seconds. Ten. The roar of volleys heralded the beginning of the battle to liberate Soviet Belarus.

For 90 minutes our guns, howitzers, mortars, and rocket battalions kept firing.

The rifle units of 69th Rifle Division were the first to cross the swamps. We had continuous contact with [Major General Pavel Vasilyevich] Shvydkoy [Batov's commander of engineers] from our post. He supervised the laying of the corduroy roads and the positioning of prefabricated sections. Twenty minutes after the commencement of the operation, he reported: 'The first 50m are laid. A further 350m remain.'

I hurried Shvydkoy. 'The pace of the attack depends on you.'

'We'll make it, Comrade Commander, don't worry.' After a while he reported further: 'We've completed another 50m. We'll complete it on schedule.' ...

The artillery bombardment had moved to the depths of the German position. Our infantry captured the first trench. And then came the good news: 'The corduroy road is complete! Infantry support tanks have moved up!'

Several units were waiting for the signal to advance. Anti-tank guns – special tractors capable of towing them at speed had been provided – moved through the swamp in just ten minutes. The infantry now had reliable support in the battle with firing points in the depths of the enemy's defences. A regiment of assault guns followed the anti-tank guns over the corduroy roads.[28]

Amongst the assault guns in Batov's army were two Guards regiments equipped with the formidable ISU-152. Aleksandr Fedorovich Pankin was a crewman in one of these vehicles, which were too heavy to use the corduroy roads:

We had to advance along hardened roads because our self-propelled guns weighed 46 tons and couldn't pass through the swamps. When our regiment appeared in the front line, the Germans tried to withdraw their heavy equipment if they spotted us because the firepower of the ISU-152 was devastating. And we were strongly armoured. We could demolish concrete pillboxes, we could penetrate anything. Our shells could break through 1.5m of reinforced concrete sometimes. I personally saw pillboxes blown apart by the detonation of our shells from direct hits. The gun aiming equipment in the assault guns was very good and allowed us to fire precisely. Even the machine-gun sights permitted accurate fire. Artillerymen in observation posts often corrected our fire.[29]

During the afternoon of 24 June, clearing skies permitted Soviet aircraft to operate more freely in support of Rokossovsky's Front. The attack through the swamps took the Germans by surprise and the full depth of the main defensive line was in Soviet hands by early afternoon. As the leading units of Batov's army approached the fortified villages of Chernin and Zahvatka, Batov ordered I Guards Tank Corps to enter the battle:

The three tank brigades motored forward over the log roads through the swamp. Everyone in the army headquarters and in the forward observation post waited anxiously. In the central sector, the crossing of the swamp proceeded smoothly. On the left flank, in 17th Tank Brigade's sector, things went less well. Some German gun batteries were still intact and opened fire. There was a volley, then a second and a third. Several shells struck the log road. One exploded near the leading tank, which began to sink slowly into the quagmire.[30]

Batov immediately ordered the struggling tank brigade to switch its line of march to the central route. Accompanied by the riflemen of CV Rifle Corps, the tanks now moved forward quickly to concentrate immediately behind the leading infantry units. The forces of I Tank Corps backed by the three rifle divisions of CV Rifle Corps were more than enough to swing the battle hugely in favour of the Red Army, and for Batov there was the additional satisfaction of knowing that Ivanov, the corps commander, was the man whom he had defended against Zhukov's demands for dismissal. But these units were in a literal sense the thin end of the wedge. Behind them, the cavalry-mechanised group commanded by Pliev also moved forward, eager to enter the contest.

The Soviet Twenty-Eighth Army, on the west flank of Batov's Sixty-Fifth Army, also enjoyed a largely successful day. Its commander, Lieutenant General Aleksandr Aleksandrovich Luchinsky, had only taken command in the last week of May and this was his first experience of commanding such a large force. Telegin, the political officer from 1st Belarusian Front's military council, spent much of 24 June with Luchinsky, still worried that Rokossovsky's two-pronged attack might prove to be a mistake:

> The observation post of the commander of Twenty-Eighty Army … was in some respects an unusual structure – it was a high wooden tower at the top of which, slightly higher than the tops of the majestic pines that surrounded it, a well-camouflaged observation deck had been constructed. From here, it was possible to oversee the enemy's defences in their complete depth …
>
> The enemy resisted fiercely. By midday, the weather improved and our aircraft launched the first massive strike against the enemy, with 224 bombers combining with round attack aircraft. By the end of the day, we were already able to appreciate the correctness of the decision of the Front commander. It was this left shock group that succeeded in seizing the initiative in the offensive … Sixty-Fifth Army as well as Twenty-Eighth Army advanced up to 10km by evening and increased the width of the breakthrough to 30km of front line.
>
> One can only imagine what the Front commander went through in those hours (though he hid his emotions from everyone standing nearby) …
>
> In the evening of that day, Zhukov called Rokossovsky and inquired about the course of the offensive of the left group. He listened to the end of the report and … congratulated Rokossovsky on the successful start of the operation. 'But it's not clear,' he admitted frankly at the end of the conversation, 'who will be stretching out a helping hand to whom from now onwards?'[31]

On the evening of 24 June, Zeitzler spoke to Busch and Jordan to try to sort out what was happening with 20th Panzer Division. The dangerous developments to the south of Bobruisk could not be ignored and the armoured battlegroup was ordered to disengage from its northward attack as quickly as possible. It was to leave a single company of tanks with 134th Infantry Division; the rest of the battlegroup would head south in order to counterattack against the southern threat to Bobruisk. Jordan was unhappy with this as it left a major threat unresolved at the junction of his army with that of Fourth Army to the north, but he accepted the reality that the developments in LVI Panzer Corps' area south of Bobruisk were an even greater danger. The lines of both 35th and 36th Infantry Division had been reduced to fragments and reports continued to arrive throughout the night of Soviet troops streaming through the gaps almost unchecked.

In Hitler's headquarters, one of the most striking issues was the complete lack of any reports of action in Army Group North Ukraine's sector. Busch too was aware of this; whilst the Red Army had repeatedly staggered the start dates of its offensives so that German reserves might be dispatched to deal with the earliest attacks before the main blow fell, there were no signs of imminent attacks against Model's armies. It was finally clear to Busch and his staff at least that their forces were facing the true summer offensive. At several points during 24 June, as the situation deteriorated at an alarming rate, Busch's chief of staff Krebs spoke to his opposite numbers on either flank – Generalleutnant Eberhard Kinzel at Army Group North and Generalleutnant Theodor Busse at Army Group North Ukraine. Busch and Krebs were agreed that the abandonment of Vitebsk – still forbidden by Hitler – would not be sufficient to salvage the situation. At least two fresh divisions, one of which would have to be a panzer division, were also needed. Zeitzler joined the discussions and agreed with this assessment. Everything would depend on a timely decision on the part of Hitler. When the response from the Führer came in mid-afternoon, it was greeted with mixed feelings. On the one hand, Army Group North was ordered to release two infantry divisions and Army Group North Ukraine was to transfer 5th Panzer Division to Army Group Centre. However, 'Fortress Vitebsk' was to be held with at least one division and land contact with the city was to be maintained.

Busch spoke to Hitler that evening and tried in vain to secure permission for the troops in Vitebsk – now cut off from the rest of Third Panzer Army – to attempt to fight their way to the southwest. Hitler replied with a lecture on the political importance of holding Vitebsk in order to prevent the Finns from losing heart and seeking a separate peace with the Soviet Union. It was a ludicrous line of argument; Hitler must have been aware that Finland was already exploring a way out of what was becoming an increasingly damaging war, and the fate of Vitebsk was not going to make any difference to what happened in the far north. A few hours later, after a further exchange between Busch and Hitler, there was only the most minimal concession: Fourth Army was given permission to fall back to the line of the Dnepr River, something that was already happening under huge pressure from the Red Army.

On the Soviet side of the front line, there was widespread satisfaction at how matters were unfolding. Bagramian was able to report that I Tank Corps was now in the front line and had reached the Daugava River, where its leading elements had captured a partly destroyed bridge. A small bridgehead had already been established, and further successes beckoned. Third Belarusian Front was pressing towards Vitebsk from the south and southwest and Oslikovsky's cavalry-mechanised group was moving into position between Thirty-Ninth and Fifth Armies. Eleventh Guards Army had endured tough fighting against 78th Sturm Division but nonetheless had created a hole in the German lines in swampy territory near Osintorf. Immediately, Galitsky had ordered II Guards Tank Corps to move into the gap; the tanks struggled forward, using the only viable road and a small railway line to cross the soft ground. They were unable to get into action, but there were no German forces in front of them and it seemed that the Germans had not spotted their presence. Further to the south, the armies of 1st and 2nd Belarusian Fronts were making good progress in places, though in others they were held up by tough German defences. But the imminent deployment of Rokossovsky's exploitation forces would, it was expected, rapidly swing the overall situation greatly in favour of the Red Army. Vasilevsky, Zhukov, and Shtemenko, together with the various Front and army commanders, could all look forward with optimism and enthusiasm.

As was repeatedly the case, Hitler's huge unwillingness to abandon territory left German units exposed in a dangerous position. It was by now inconceivable that Vitebsk could be held, and that a corridor to the city could be restored. In truth, even if Busch had been given permission to abandon the city, it was probably too late. The forces that were fighting his units were gaining the upper hand almost everywhere and it was increasingly unlikely that they could be halted without an influx of fresh forces far greater than had so far been promised. But even though Busch and Krebs in Minsk and Reinhardt, Tippelskirch, and Jordan in their headquarters looked to the future with foreboding, they had no idea that the situation was about to get far worse. The Soviet exploitation forces were moving forward and were about to enter the battle.

CHAPTER 6

THE FLOODGATES OPEN:
25-28 JUNE

In the northern sector of Army Group Centre, Reinhardt and Tippelskirch had placed great importance on the *Tigerstellung*, the defensive line to the west of Vitebsk where Third Panzer Army had always expected to conduct its defence in the event of a major Soviet attack against Third Panzer Army. But Reinhardt's plans had been drawn up on two assumptions. Firstly, he had anticipated the Soviet attack as falling to the south of Vitebsk. Instead, the assault to the northwest of the city – and in particular the completely undetected presence of Sixth Guards Army – had taken everyone on the German side completely by surprise. The second assumption had been that Third Panzer Army would be able to withdraw relatively intact to the *Tigerstellung*. Instead, a sizable part of the army was trapped in Vitebsk and the northern wing had disintegrated in the face of 1st Baltic Front's offensive. Reinforcements were hastening to the area, but the Red Army was also moving forward in strength. A great deal would depend on which side could build up its forces faster; Reinhardt was beginning to doubt that he could win this race.

As the skies lightened on 25 June after the short summer night, Bagramian monitored the performance of his armies with satisfaction and urged Chistiakov on:

I warmly congratulated General Chistiakov for his successful commencement to the operation and asked him to expedite his advance before the enemy could catch his breath. The army commander assured me that all appropriate measures were being taken. Boats had already been collected from the villages along the

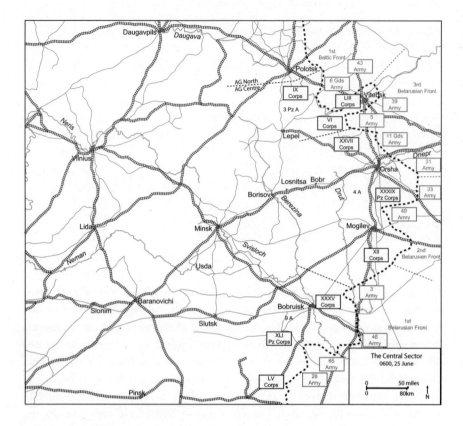

riverbank and rafts were being constructed from barrels and timber beams. The units of [Major] General [Arkhip Ivanovich] Ruchkin's XXII Guards Rifle Corps were making good progress towards Polotsk while [Major] General [Ivan Fedorovich] Fediunkin with the main force of CIII Rifle Corps was engaged in minor skirmishes with the retreating enemy in the swampy, forested area to the northeast of Ulla. The corps commander had been ordered not to get tied down in combat in the forests but to break through over the Daugava immediately and to build a bridgehead near Ulla. Chistiakov added that he would go to the sector where the crossing was being forced and would send his chief of staff, [Major] General Valentin Antonovich] Penkovsky, to CIII Corps to oversee its advance to the river …

And yet I couldn't dispel a sense of unease. There were serious grounds for this. The time had come when the outcome of the operation would be decided. If we did not succeed in crossing the Daugava quickly, the enemy could establish himself there and lengthy delays for 1st Baltic Front would be inevitable.[1]

Bagramian had another concern, which dominated his thinking throughout the summer of 1944. The city of Polotsk to the northwest of his Front's line of advance had good rail and road links to the north and west, and he was increasingly aware that as his units advanced, they ran the risk of converting the German-held bulge in the Eastern Front into a Soviet-held bulge projecting towards the west, with his armies forming its northern flank. This created the risk of a German counterattack into this flank, and in order to eliminate this he wanted to capture Polotsk as soon as possible and for units to his north to drive back the German Sixteenth Army, thus reducing the risk from the north. For the moment, though, attention remained on the successful unfolding of the operations around and to the west of Vitebsk and Beloborodov now turned his attention to his left flank. After a delay caused by Beloborodov's absence from his headquarters – which must have done nothing to help Bagramian's anxiety – the two men spoke. Beloborodov reported that his troops had crossed the Daugava and had made tenuous contact with the leading elements of Thirty-Ninth Army, which had advanced past the southern flank of the German positions in and around Vitebsk. Bagramian urged him to strengthen the encirclement as quickly as possible; aware that Forty-Third Army's artillery was struggling to move forward to support the advance, Bagramian assigned the bulk of his air assets to Beloborodov.

Bagramian needn't have worried about Chistiakov's advance to the west. The leading units of Sixth Guards Army were already across the Daugava River by dawn; one of the few units in their path was a German security regiment, equipped largely for anti-partisan operations. It took up positions in the small town of Svecha but had no artillery or anti-tank weaponry, and it was likely that it could do no more than briefly hinder the Red Army. In Beshankovichi, on the Daugava itself, the tattered remnants of *Korps Abteilung D* managed to set up a defensive perimeter. They could do nothing to stop Soviet units streaming past either flank and were soon surrounded. Chistiakov's account of his army's operations show a growing sense of exuberance at how the operation was unfolding:

> All night from 24 to 25 June, troops crossed over bridges [over the Daugava] and units went straight into combat from the line of march. Manoeuvring between small lakes and swamps, the army's units bypassed enemy strongpoints. We moved forward rapidly. The Belarusian partisans played a particularly important role in our breakthrough at this time. They led our formations along paths through forests and swamps to get behind the enemy …

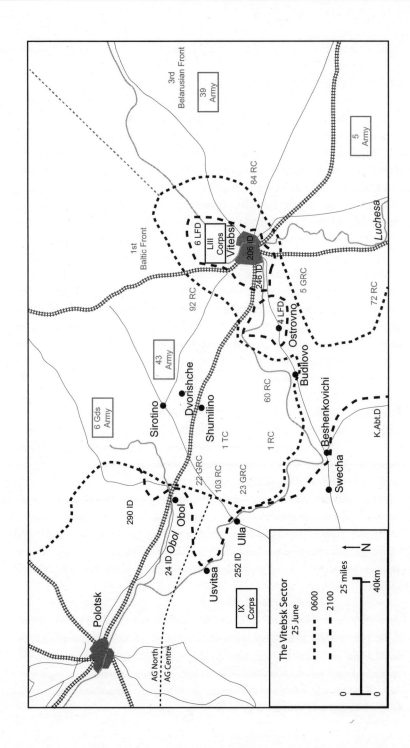

The Vitebsk Sector
25 June

0600
2100

N

0 25 miles
0 40km

On 25 June 1944, our army's troops continued to move forward vigorously on a broad front and to expand the bridgehead. The enemy had managed to bring up reserves during the night and with the help of tanks and aircraft he launched attack after attack, but could not stop our swift advance.[2]

Other Soviet units found themselves mixed up with the retreating Germans. Semen Moiseyevich Vinopol's mortar platoon found itself on the banks of the Daugava:

Nachart, the senior officer, began to give orders – 'Take up positions along the river bank.' He then called for volunteers to cross. While he was doing this, the commander of the artillery battery was the first to take off his tunic and boots and to swim to the enemy's bank. He returned and told us there were no enemy soldiers there. Then about 15 men swam across. I ordered my mortarmen to dig full-depth trenches on the shore and then to start making rafts from logs … The rifle battalions of our division began to mass in a big crowd. Nachart reported to the division commander that there were no Germans on the opposite side of the river and that we had seized a bridgehead. Without digging in, the rifle platoons began to prepare for the crossing. The battalions were massed in a huge huddle. And then the Germans began to bombard our shore with heavy artillery, literally mashing everything into the ground. Apparently they had been watching us all the time and their spotters were just waiting for the moment when there would be a lot of men on the riverbank.

It looked as if every square metre was shelled, and it hurt us a lot. We lost hundreds of soldiers and officers killed and wounded, but the mortarmen had no serious losses because my men had already dug in when the shelling commenced. We launched our first raft and I sent one of my platoons with mortars to the far bank. The raft returned and the Germans continued to fire at us. Then a regiment commander came up and wanted to take the raft, but I suggested to him that we should make a ferry crossing. My signalman Mandibura crossed with a cable and fixed it firmly, thus allowing us to organise a ferry point. The infantry began to make more rafts for themselves.[3]

With his northern flank torn to shreds, Reinhardt contacted Busch again shortly after midday on 25 June. The front line along the Daugava was almost non-existent and a Soviet advance towards Lepel would threaten to envelop all of Third Panzer Army from the north. In these circumstances, the Daugava line was no longer viable and a retreat to a line running through the cluster of small lakes further to the west was necessary. Despite Reinhardt warning that even this might be too late to implement, Busch – entirely characteristically – refused to go against Hitler's instructions. IX Corps was to extend its right flank along the Daugava to Ulla, and then along the Ulla River towards the south. All day, under intermittent air attack, the troops of IX Corps attempted to implement orders that bore little relation to the reality on the ground. The only crumb of comfort was that several retreating fragments of *Korps Abteilung D* succeeded in reaching German lines but by late afternoon Wuthmann reported that the best he could do was to occupy positions along parts of the Ulla and Daugava; even these had little contact with each other.

In Vitebsk, Gollwitzer's LIII Corps attempted to implement its equally unworkable instructions. While the fortress garrison – Hitter's 206th Infantry Division – took up its hopeless task, the rest of the corps tried to secure the corridor running southwest from the city in the afternoon of 25 June; in heavy fighting, 4th Luftwaffe Field Division had reached the village of Ostrovno when it ran into Soviet units advancing from the south. A report of the resultant action was later drawn up:

> The Russians approached Ostrovno from the southeast at about 1400 and began shelling the village with mortars and support guns and later with tanks. All-round defence was taken up. The only highway leading from the Vitebsk region to Ostrovno and Beshenkovichi was completely choked with vehicle convoys, civilians, and both motorised and horse-drawn units. Sensing the stubborn nature of the defence of Ostrovno, the Russians broke through to the north of the village via Buzany and reached and blocked this highway. Thus, Vitebsk and the units of the divisions conducting defensive operations in that area were isolated.[4]

During the afternoon, a group of Soviet SU-76 assault guns appeared and opened fire at short range on the traffic that was stranded on the highway. By the end of the day, 4th Luftwaffe Field Division had been almost completely destroyed and its remnants were left encircled in Ostrovno. Helpless to intervene in any material terms, Reinhardt sent a signal to LIII Corps shortly after midday on 25 June:

> *Heil und Sieg* to you and your troops in their attempt to force a breakthrough, the success of which is urgently required but in my opinion there remains a good chance of success. I also send my best wishes to General Hitter and his division, which must still carry out its mission and suffer if necessary for you all.[5]

With the Red Army pressing on all sides, the situation grew ever more serious. By mid-afternoon, Gollwitzer was reporting that 6th Luftwaffe Field Division and 246th Infantry Division were barely able to hold their positions. With no prospect of any help from outside the encirclement, he finally ran out of patience with the German chain of command and advised Reinhardt in a brief signal late on 25 June that LIII Corps had no option but to fight its way out towards the southwest at first light on 26 June; air support was requested for the attempt.

This triggered a frantic exchange of messages between Reinhardt at Third Panzer Army headquarters, Busch in his headquarters in Minsk, and *OKH*. Busch remained uncompromising and insisted that Hitler had ordered Vitebsk to be held for at least another week. Moreover, he told Reinhardt that the Führer demanded that Third Panzer Army send a senior staff officer to LIII Corps, if necessary by parachute, to ensure that the orders were followed. Reinhardt might have been reticent about the manner in which he responded to Hitler in the past, but showed greater mettle on this occasion. Heidkämper, his chief of staff, later described the response of Third Panzer Army's commander to Busch:

'Tell the Führer that I refuse to have a general staff officer or any other soldier parachuted into Vitebsk. It is because of the Führer's demand that I have now, most unwillingly, reminded Generalleutnant Hitter over the radio of the order to stand.' There was a silence on the line for a moment or two before Reinhardt continued: 'Herr Feldmarschall, please also inform the Führer that if he still insists on an officer being selected to parachute into Vitebsk, there is only one in Third Panzer Army who can be considered, and that is the commanding officer. I stand ready to carry out this mission.'[6]

An hour later, Busch called Reinhardt to tell him that the order to send a staff officer to Vitebsk had been cancelled.

Immediately to the south of the city, the Red Army continued to exert great pressure. One of the units of VI Corps, 299th Infantry Division, was effectively shattered and ceased to function as a coherent whole. This coincided with the arrival of the Soviet III Guards Cavalry Corps, part of Oslikovsky's cavalry-mechanised group. With VI Corps now out of contact with units to the north – by the end of 25 June the gap had grown to about 39 miles – Busch assigned it to Fourth Army instead of Third Panzer Army. It made little difference to the situation on the battlefield. On the southern flank of VI Corps, XXVII Corps had pulled back to the *Tigerstellung* but during 25 June it reported that the Red Army had already penetrated its positions at numerous points. There were similar pessimistic reports from XXXIX Panzer Corps and XXII Corps and the growing penetrations by the

Red Army were creating threats to the flanks of the few German units like 78th Sturm Division and 25th Panzergrenadier Division that were still putting up stubborn resistance. German command and control was now under growing strain as a result of telegraph wires being cut (through a mixture of artillery and aerial bombardment and the actions of partisans) and headquarters formations constantly changing location. In mid-afternoon, Busch ordered 12th and 31st Infantry Divisions, to the south of Mogilev, to fall back to the line of the Dnepr. The order didn't reach the embattled German divisions until early evening and in the growing confusion the divisions of XXVII Corps to the north, between Mogilev and Orsha, were not warned. They were now left in an increasingly vulnerable position. To make matters worse, *Feldherrnhalle*, immediately to the north of Mogilev, reported that its lines had given way late in the afternoon and that dozens of Soviet tanks had streamed past heading west.

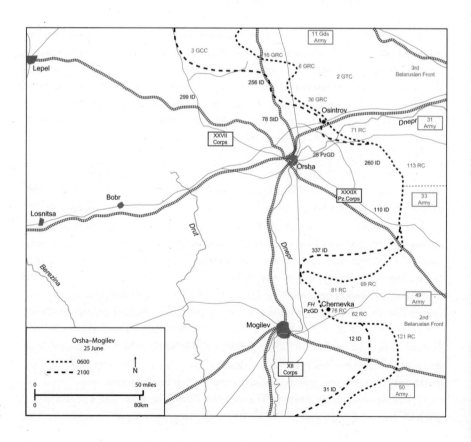

Just as Reinhardt and Gollwitzer found themselves in increasingly angry exchanges with Busch about the crisis in the north, Tippelskirch in the headquarters of Ninth Army was also engaged in what seemed endless arguments. Army Group Centre continued to insist that only those divisions already contacted had permission to pull back to the Dnepr and that XXVII Corps had to remain where it was. Moreover, Orsha was declared a fortress and 78th Sturm Division was nominated as its garrison. Tippelskirch stressed to Krebs that this was absurd and that the withdrawal of these divisions over the river was of pressing urgency. Busch joined the conversation and warned Tippelskirch that any such withdrawal would be regarded as deliberate disobedience and a failure to follow orders. Tippelskirch's protests that his front line was in tatters and that the only way to restore the situation was to pull back were dismissed. Angrily, he sent a brief signal to XXVII Corps and XXXIX Panzer Corps. They were to hold their positions unless driven back by superior enemy forces. It was the best that he could do to give his subordinates a little leeway. Such evasions were becoming increasingly normal in the Wehrmacht; the army might have prided itself on its long tradition of delegated decision-making, but the dead hand of Hitler's intransigence and of the men he had appointed to enforce his orders was now the norm.

The men in the headquarters of both corps interpreted Tippelskirch's orders exactly as he had intended. One of his staff officers wrote approvingly of the army commander's instructions in his diary, adding 'Be careful when talking to those above [in the chain of command].'[7] Shortly before midnight, further orders arrived from *OKH*, sent via Busch: Hitler had approved the withdrawal of the exposed divisions back to the Dnepr. As was so often the case, he had prevaricated until even he could see that further delay was pointless. In the meantime, soldiers had died on the battlefield and the benefit of the withdrawal was much reduced as the Red Army was continuing to control the initiative. An earlier withdrawal might have given the Germans some breathing space, but it was now purely a matter of survival. The frustration of Tippelskirch and his subordinates can only be imagined.

To the northeast of Mogilev, the Red Army was very much dictating the course of events. After being badly mauled in preceding days, the German 337th Infantry Division effectively collapsed and Soviet troops rapidly approached the Dnepr. A little to the north, 110th Infantry Division barely managed to prevent the entire front line being rolled up. Even if Tippelskirch's Fourth Army could pull back to the Dnepr, the line was already badly compromised.

Traut, the commander of 78th Sturm Division, travelled to Orsha on 25 June to assess the city's defences. There were few positions in existence and it was obvious to Traut and his staff that his men were being assigned a hopeless task. Even if the city could be held, there was little point in doing so if both flanks collapsed. Perhaps in awareness of this, Traut did little to expedite the movement of his division to Orsha. Even if he had wanted to take up positions as a doomed garrison, his men were too hard-pressed to disengage and reach the city in time.

The situation to the south was also deteriorating steadily for the Germans. Rokossovsky's southern attack on Bobruisk was still wrestling with the difficult terrain, and Pliev's cavalry-mechanised group struggled to move into position, as he described:

> At 1630, the formations of the cavalry-mechanised group finally moved through the combat units of the leading armies and immediately broke into the rear of the enemy's positions. The area where the group was entering into the breakthrough was mainly forested and swampy. There were very few roads and these were all in poor condition. Immediately before we could enter the breach there was the Tremlya River with swampy banks, and all bridges had been blown by the enemy. The roads to the river were clogged with troops of Twenty-Eighth Army. In addition, the commander of my I Mechanised Corps prematurely sent his reconnaissance groups and advance detachments forward, resulting in traffic jams on all routes. In general, the deployment of the group took rather more time and effort than was foreseen in our plans.[8]

Even with these delays, the Germans were unable to cope with the growing pressure. Pliev's force was to thrust towards the northwest while I Guards Tank Corps attacked north and this latter thrust was the reason why 20th Panzer Division had been ordered to intervene in this sector. The first elements of the panzer division's armoured battlegroup began to assemble shortly after dawn on 25 June and were ordered to strike south and destroy the Soviet forces in their path, while the other elements of the division made a similar attack a little further to the west; the intention was that the two groups would then converge. By mid-morning, there were reports that the German 35th Infantry Division immediately to the west was rapidly collapsing, but Kessel's armoured battlegroup resolutely set off towards the south in the early afternoon only to find that the planned start line for its attack had already been overrun by the Red Army. To make matters worse, Kessel now learned that 36th Infantry Division to his east was also being overrun. To the west, beyond the remnants of 35th Infantry Division, 129th Infantry Division had been reduced to a third of its combat strength. By the end of the day, 20th Panzer

Division claimed it had shot up 60 enemy tanks, but this made little difference to the overall situation.

Jordan, who had expressed great frustration at having to sit helplessly in his positions while the enemy dictated events, contacted Busch and advised him that withdrawals were urgently needed. The response was entirely predictable: no such retreats would be tolerated and all divisions had to hold their positions. Meanwhile, the Soviet attack towards Bobruisk from the east slowly ground forward and secured crossings over the Drut River, leaving LXI Panzer Corps in danger of being encircled. Jordan informed Busch that while 20th Panzer Division continued its increasingly futile attack towards the south, the enemy was streaming past its flanks, but if the panzer division was extracted to try to intervene on either flank, LXI Panzer Corps would be too weak to hold its positions, particularly given the presence of powerful Soviet units on both flanks. The only solution was greater flexibility and a

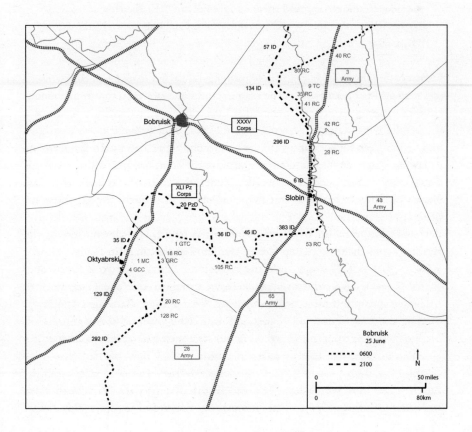

withdrawal to Bobruisk itself. Busch replied that the breaches in the German lines were too narrow for the Red Army to sustain and support major advances. Holding current positions and limiting the width of those breaches was therefore essential.

Jordan continued to feel that he was fighting a battle with his superiors tying his hands behind his back. That evening, he reported that 20th Panzer Division was reduced to about 40 tanks. By now, he was aware of one powerful Soviet tank force advancing north towards Bobruisk (this was I Guards Tank Corps) and a second force of tanks and cavalry concentrating a little to the west (Pliev's cavalry-mechanised group). If he was permitted to pull back his forces, Jordan believed that he could release 383rd Infantry Division to shore up the front line on one or other flank of Bobruisk. Busch's response was both predictable and disheartening:

> I anticipated this request. But the junction at Slobin is crucial. I can't approve your request this evening, as I need the approval of *OKH*. Therefore it is already too late to do this today. Withdraw two or three battalions from 383rd Infantry Division.[9]

Leaving aside the absurdity of Busch lecturing his subordinate on the importance of a road and rail junction – as the man in command of the sector, Jordan would have a far better awareness of this than his army group commander – it was a shamefully weak statement from a field marshal, that he could not act without permission from higher authorities. When Jordan replied that even if the two or three battalions made any difference against the southern penetration towards Bobruisk, the other penetration would still be a threat, Busch replied that he had made Zeitzler aware of this and that perhaps the Red Army would pause for breath in the morning.

Jordan wrote in his diary what amounted to a succinct summary of the manner in which Army Group Centre was handling the fighting:

> Having made a conscientious report, one has to accept the orders of one's superiors even when one is convinced of the opposite. What is worse is awareness that the completely inadequate orders from the army group are not the product of purposeful leadership striving to do its best, but merely an attempt to pass on orders that have long been overtaken by events.[10]

Busch spent most of 25 June engaged in discussions with his subordinates and with *OKH*, reduced to little more than passing on requests from below and orders from above. In fairness, he repeatedly made the case for the immediate abandonment of Vitebsk, but Hitler was adamant. Hitter's 206th Infantry Division was to hold the city until 12th Panzer Division – being sent south by Army Group North – was able to mount a relief operation. Even if this division had been more conveniently located rather than having to move from near Pskov, a distance of about 170 miles, it was absurd to expect a single division to make such an attack, especially as Third Panzer Army was in no position even to offer it a firm start line, let alone any support for the proposed advance to Vitebsk. Whilst this particular part of Hitler's instructions was clearly utopian, it should be borne in mind that the Germans were still unaware of the full scale of the crisis that was unfolding. They still had not detected Fifth Guards Tank Army and had not fully recognised the strength of the exploitation forces that were already entering the battle. In any event, nothing short of a precipitate withdrawal to a much shorter line would have sufficed, and in the absence of clear evidence that this was urgently needed, Hitler resorted to his favourite policy of prevaricating in the hope that some unexpected turn of events might obviate the need for decisions that he wished to avoid. By the time that sufficient information became available to make these decisions inevitable, it was too late for them to have whatever modest benefit might have accrued had they been made at an earlier point.

In any case, 12th Panzer Division was rapidly diverted to the southern sector of Army Group Centre, where other crises were developing. The division was far from full strength; on the eve of *Bagration*, it fielded just 13 Pz.IVs and nine Pz.IIIs in a single battalion and most of its anti-tank battalion and all of its armoured reconnaissance battalion were assigned to other units. Its commander, Generalleutnant Erpo Freiherr von Bodenhausen, was in Germany on leave; in his absence, the division was led by the highly experienced Oberst Gerhard Müller, a one-armed veteran of the North African campaigns. He and his men would need every bit of their experience and skill if they were to prevail.

In Vitebsk, conditions within the city were rapidly deteriorating by the end of 25 June. Gollwitzer had to dodge air attacks as he travelled from one area to another. When he reached Hitter's headquarters, he found Generalleutnant Rudolf Peschel, commander of 6th Luftwaffe Field Division, in a state of agitation and despair. An attempt by the field division to attack Soviet forces closing in on the escape route had ended with the near-complete destruction of one regiment. Since their inception in 1942, the field divisions had proved to be of little use, too weak to be used in attack and lacking resilience in defence. In an attempt to improve their performance, officers like Peschel – who had commanded a regular infantry division for most of 1943 – had been appointed to command them, but with limited results. Originally created using surplus personnel from the lavishly manned Luftwaffe, Göring and Hitler had blocked attempts to use these men to bring existing divisions up to strength – Göring in particular had argued successfully that the Luftwaffe was ideologically more committed to the Nazis than the army, and that this should not be diluted. But the only way that these divisions could have been turned into functional combat units would have been if their personnel were mixed with veteran soldiers. A few officers in command posts were not going to make a major difference.

Regardless of the orders he had received, Gollwitzer had no intention of leaving Hitter and his infantry division to die in Vitebsk – already, the perimeter was collapsing and there was little likelihood of the 'fortress' surviving another day, let alone the week that Hitler demanded. He told Hitter that Vitebsk was to be abandoned; he intended to extract as much of his corps as he could. The rest of Third Panzer Army was believed to be somewhere near the Ulla River, 27 miles to the southwest and Gollwitzer sent a terse message to his superiors. There was no longer any question of coherent divisions, he informed Reinhardt and Busch. Hitter's 206th Infantry Division had been reduced to just four combat-worthy battalions and was a completely inadequate force to hold Vitebsk for a week as ordered. In these circumstances, the only way that Hitler's 'fortress' order could be obeyed was if the entire corps remained in the city, and as its troops were urgently needed to help shore up the rest of the front line, he was breaking out with all his units. Busch replied that there was no leeway in Hitler's orders: the fortress had to be held by 206th Infantry Division.

During the night of 25–26 June, German soldiers in and around Vitebsk moved into position for the breakout attempt. The Daugava River flows into Vitebsk from the northwest and forms a bend as it runs first south, then west. In order to reach the roads that ran to the southwest, 246th Infantry Division would have to cross the river from the northern side of the perimeter, and the only viable route was via a railway bridge. Despite Gollwitzer's explicit orders that the bridge was not to be destroyed until the division had crossed the river safely, it was blown up just as part of the division's artillery was about to cross. Matters took a further turn for the worse shortly after. In accordance with Hitler's instructions regarding fortresses, there were stockpiles of food, fuel, and ammunition in Vitebsk sufficient to last for up to three weeks, together with substantial quantities of munitions at a Luftwaffe airfield. Gollwitzer had issued strict instructions that these stores were all to be abandoned so that the

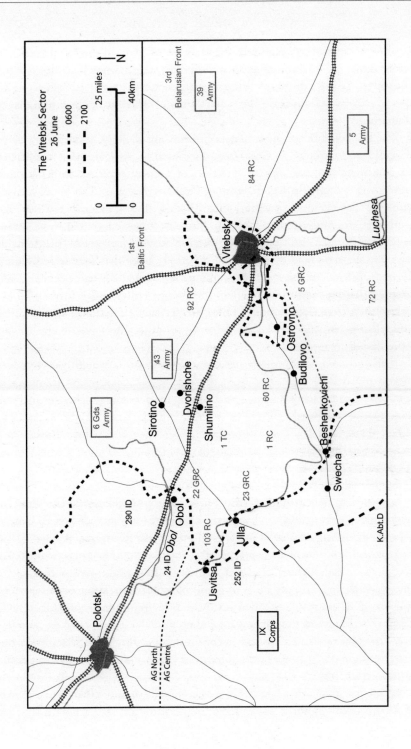

The Vitebsk Sector
26 June
.... 0600
- - - - 2100

N

25 miles
40km

3rd
Belarusian Front

39 Army

5 Army

84 RC

Luchesa

1st Baltic Front

Vitebsk

92 RC

5 GRC

72 RC

43 Army

Dvorishche

Ostrovno

Budilovo

60 RC

6 Gds Army

Sirotino

Shumilino

1 TC

1 RC

Beshenkovichi

290 ID

22 GRC

23 GRC

Swecha

Obol

Obol

24 ID

103 RC

Ulla

252 ID

K.Abt.D

Usvitsa

Polotsk

IX Corps

AG North
AG Centre

garrison could slip away quietly, but a series of huge blasts rocked Vitebsk before dawn on 26 June as explosive charges were triggered to destroy the stockpiles. As the explosions lit up the night, Gollwitzer remarked wryly to one of his staff officers, 'The encirclement breakout is beginning very dramatically!'[11]

Much of Vitebsk was now ablaze. Gunfire and shelling added to the chaos of smoke and darkness as Gollwitzer attempted to extricate what was left of his command – there was no question of even attempting to maintain a presence in the city. In heavy fighting, Gollwitzer managed to break contact with the Soviet units pressing into Vitebsk and struggled towards the southwest. In mid-afternoon on 26 June, he reported that he was under constant air attack and had no clear picture of what lay ahead – elements of the two Luftwaffe field divisions had reported earlier that they were holding isolated positions in his path, but all contact with them had been lost. He doubted that his exhausted men had the strength to go much further. To his rear, soldiers from Beloborodov's Forty-Third Army pressed into Vitebsk itself while Thirty-Ninth Army attacked from the south. Most of the city was in Soviet hands by nightfall.

If the breakout was to have any chance of success, it would need to cover ground much faster than had been the case so far. More elements of *Korps Abteilung D* had reached German lines during the preceding night, but this was scant comfort for Reinhardt; the defensive line to the northwest of Vitebsk was at best fragile and far from continuous. By midday on 26 June Bagramian's divisions had thrown back the southern flank of IX Corps beyond the small town of Lukoml, 52 miles to the southwest of Vitebsk.

Bagramian continued to worry about a possible threat to his Front – and by extension to the entire Red Army operation – from the north. On 26 June, he was given permission to change the axis of the advance of I Tank Corps. Instead of pushing southwest towards Minsk, it was to advance due west. The tanks of Butkov's corps were struggling to get across the Daugava and Ulla Rivers. The roads behind the Red Army's leading units were choked with reinforcements and supply units trying to move forward, and medical services attempting to evacuate wounded men; the bridging units assigned to I Tank Corps were caught in the congestion and only small elements had reached the river. The first tanks had crossed to the far bank of the Ulla River during the late afternoon of 25 June, but it took most of 26 June for Butkov to get his entire corps across.

At the same time that I Tank Corps laboured to cross the two rivers, Fourth Shock Army to the north was ordered to attack towards Polotsk with support from Chistiakov's Sixth Guards Army on its southern flank. Capture of the city would have numerous benefits. The configuration of railway lines and roads meant that it was a vital communication node: by seizing it, the Red Army would benefit from opening up a new line of supply for its advancing units, whilst simultaneously depriving the Wehrmacht of a location where it could concentrate newly arriving formations. The units that had already arrived and had been thrown into counterattacks had made little impression upon Bagramian's forces, and Reinhardt ordered a halt to all further counterattacks. Finally, he had become aware of the appearance of I Tank Corps and he wanted to preserve whatever little strength remained to deal with this formidable force. In the meantime, the southern flank of Third Panzer Army remained out of contact with Fourth Army.

To the south, Tippelskirch's army was in little better condition than that of Reinhardt. The northern flank was completely exposed with Soviet forces driving on towards the west; an attempt by VI Corps to protect this flank with a bicycle-mounted security regiment was crushed by a powerful group of Soviet tanks. After completing its hasty redeployment, Rotmistrov's Fifth Guards Tank Army was now moving into action, advancing through almost empty space towards Borisov and Minsk. This created a whole new problem for the Germans: Borisov was the designated forming up area for 5th Panzer Division, hastening to the region from Army Group North Ukraine. It was vital that the panzer division reached Borisov before the Red Army. In an attempt to protect the exposed flank of VI Corps, a battlegroup was improvised using part of a Tiger tank battalion and groups of stragglers.

The southeast flank of VI Corps was also in the air; there was a gap of about seven miles to the nearest elements of 78th Sturm Division, still resisting as best it could to the northwest of Orsha. To the east of this division, there was a further gap to 25th Panzergrenadier Division. Communications were now badly disrupted and General Paul Völckers, commander of XXVII Corps, took full advantage of this. He ordered elements of his units still facing east to be pulled out of line and sent to his northwest flank in an attempt to try to restore contact with VI Corps. Völckers had been given belated permission to start pulling back over the Dnepr and he intended to do so before any countermanding instructions could arrive. *Feldherrnhalle* continued to try to hold the line of the Dnepr near Mogilev but could do nothing to stop Soviet forces seizing two bridgeheads in the early afternoon. Attempts to mount counterattacks using troops from neighbouring units were sufficient to stop the Red Army from pushing on to Mogilev itself, but could do nothing to drive the Soviet troops back over the river.

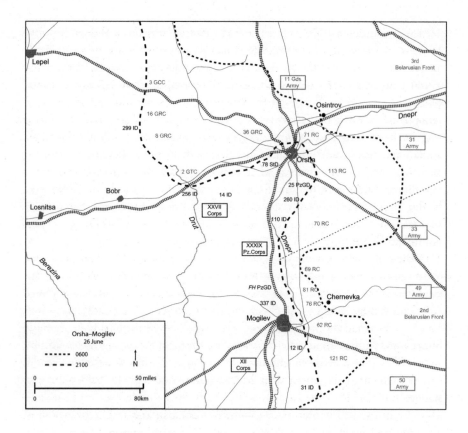

To the south, XXXIX Panzer Corps fell back over the Dnepr to Mogilev under huge pressure. Immediately to the west of Mogilev, 12th Infantry Division still held a few small bridgeheads across the Dnepr on the morning of 26 June and its positions came under heavy attack from the Soviet Forty-Ninth Army; with Mogilev now threatened, Tippelskirch ordered XII Corps to dispatch parts of 18th Panzergrenadier Division to the area south of the city. In little more than a day, the situation facing Fourth Army had deteriorated badly.

Matters were just as bad for Jordan's Ninth Army. At first light on 26 June, IX Tank Corps led the Red Army's charge towards Bobruisk from the northeast and the leading Soviet unit approaching Bobruisk from the south, I Guards Tank Corps, was about 12 miles from the city with only minimal German forces in its path. The embattled units of 20th Panzer Division were ordered to break off their action and pull back to the area to the southwest of Bobruisk in order to intercept the Soviet forces, but they were badly delayed when bridges over the Berezina were blown up as Red Army tanks approached from the southwest.

Jordan now ordered XXXV Corps and XLI Panzer Corps to withdraw from the increasingly congested salient they held that projected southeast from Bobruisk. In the meantime, he had to deal with a bad-tempered telephone call from Zeitzler at *OKH*; the chief of the general staff berated Jordan for using the panzer division in its abortive attack towards the south in unfavourable terrain, completely ignoring the fact that *OKH* had effectively dictated how the panzer division was to be used. Further unpleasant conversations took place between Jordan and Busch, with the latter insisting that bridgeheads to the east of the Berezina had to be maintained. Later that afternoon, Jordan received a peremptory summons: he was to travel immediately to Minsk, from where he would travel with Busch to see Hitler at his headquarters in Obersalzburg. General Helmuth Weidling, commander of XLI Panzer Corps, was to take command of Ninth Army in the interim.

When the plane carrying the two senior officers arrived in Bavaria, Jordan found himself facing accusations of mishandling the defence of Bobruisk. The deployment of 20th Panzer Division had in almost every detail been dictated to him either by Busch or by *OKH* and had he failed to execute those orders, he would have faced the wrath of every senior officer in the chain of command above him, but he was now held responsible for the disaster that was unfolding in Army Group South's southern sector. He was dismissed from command. His permanent replacement would be General Nikolaus von Vormann, who had been languishing in reserve since the end of the battles around Korsun in Ukraine in the late winter of 1943–44. It was harsh and unfair treatment of an army commander who had been one of the few to question the prevailing view that any attacks on Army Group Centre would be secondary, with the main Soviet effort being directed at Army Group North Ukraine. Towards the end of the war, he was dispatched to take up posts in Italy. He became a prisoner of the Western Allies at the end of the war and was released from captivity in 1947.

Late on 26 June, Busch sent a summary of the situation to *OKH*. He described how the Red Army had torn a huge hole in the German lines between Vitebsk and Orsha and was advancing towards Borisov; at the same time, converging attacks on Bobruisk to the south were creating insurmountable difficulties. He added that he assumed the two Soviet attacks were going to converge on Minsk but made little mention of the powerful attacks near Mogilev. Hitler approved a gradual withdrawal by Tippelskirch's Fourth Army to the line of the Drut River – in reality, this was already underway under constant Soviet pressure – but reiterated his orders that Orsha and Mogilev were designated as fortresses and had to be held.

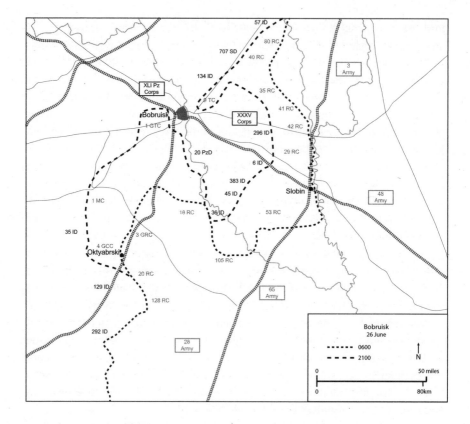

The soldiers of the Soviet Thirty-Ninth and Forty-Third Armies continued to move through the streets of Vitebsk through the night of 26–27 June, clashing from time to time with small pockets of Germans amidst the rubble and burning buildings. To the southwest of the city, Gollwitzer and the remnants of LIII Corps continued their desperate breakout attempt. As it grew light on 27 June, the leading elements were about six miles from the city and using the only surviving radio vehicle, Gollwitzer requested Reinhardt to organise air cover as constant Soviet air attacks were greatly impeding his men. A few hours later came a further message. The breakout group had managed to fight its way another two miles towards safety but was effectively at the end of its strength. Even as the signal was being sent, the radio truck slipped into a ditch and was hit by artillery fire.

There were no longer any coherent units left in LIII Corps – just groups of soldiers clustered around the more determined and energetic officers who gathered together whatever remnants they could. At midday, Gollwitzer encountered Hitter and the two men discussed the situation. In addition to fighting against the Red Army, the Germans were encountering strong partisan groups; emboldened by the clear signs of German collapse and spurred on by orders from above, the partisans took every opportunity to block the road to the west. Hitter told Gollwitzer that part of his division had attacked towards the southwest earlier but he had lost contact with it and had no idea whether it had made any progress or had melted away in the confusion. The main road towards Ostrovno, where Gollwitzer hoped to find the survivors of 4th Luftwaffe Field Division, was blocked by an improvised bunker manned by partisans and without artillery support it was impossible to capture it – Hitter had already made several costly attempts and ammunition was running low. The only practical solution that he could offer Gollwitzer was to wait until nightfall when it might be possible to slip past the bunker. This would necessitate abandoning most of the wounded.

Gollwitzer decided he needed a clearer picture of what was happening. Somewhere not far to the north, he could hear heavy gunfire where 246th Infantry Division was meant to be covering the flank of the breakout attempt, but he had little idea of where the rest of his men were. The first step was to try to ascertain what had happened to the group Hitter had already sent towards the southwest. Accompanied by a handful of officers, he and Hitter managed to bypass the bunker in dense woodland and succeeded in reaching the group from 206th Infantry Division; they had strayed off the intended path and were heading directly towards some T-34s that Gollwitzer and Hitter had spotted as they emerged from the woodland near the partisan bunker.

As they passed through the trees, Gollwitzer and his colleagues came across the corpses of several German soldiers. His account describes them as men who had been 'murdered' by partisans. This is a consistent characteristic of the memoirs of German soldiers on the Eastern Front, who almost always portrayed the partisans as brutal and cruel. Heidkämper, Reinhardt's chief of staff, left a typical description:

There are no words to describe the brutish and terrible ways in which the bandits fought … Over and over, small bandit groups would conceal themselves in marshland and would allow our troops to pass by. They would often lie there for several hours in the mud … They would then attack and murder our troops from behind in the cruellest manner. Such combat methods violated all international agreements. These bandits did not fight humanely.[12]

Such statements might be factually correct, but Heidkämper, Gollwitzer, and others had sufficient seniority to know that Hitler had explicitly declared that the war against the Soviet Union was different from any other conflict and that the normal rules of conduct in war did not apply to the German forces. To expect partisans – who it must be remembered were fighting to defend their homeland – to abide by such rules was at best hypocritical. The conduct of German forces in the Soviet Union could almost have been deliberately intended to stimulate the growth of the partisan movement, with widespread indiscriminate killings, forcible seizure of food and livestock, and deportation of civilians as forced labourers both locally and in the Reich.

It was now late afternoon and the group of officers took stock. They had no idea where the German lines were, or even if they had stabilised. Ammunition was almost exhausted and the men were approaching the end of their strength, having been in almost continuous combat since early on 23 June with no opportunity to rest or sleep. With no information about the two Luftwaffe field divisions and little sound of battle to the southwest, it was safe to assume that they had been wiped out. Gollwitzer ordered his officers to gather together what men they could. They would wait until dark and would then attempt to make their way north to establish contact with 246th Infantry Division.

Even if the rest of Third Panzer Army somehow stopped its retreat, the breakout attempt faced almost impossible difficulties. But the pressure upon IX Corps continued throughout 27 June as the battered remnants of 252nd Infantry Division and *Korps Abteilung D* attempted to hold a defensive line running through a series of lakes to the west of the Daugava and Ulla Rivers. A few reinforcements – parts of 201st Security Division and improvised battlegroups scraped together from rear area units – were appearing on the southern flank of Wuthmann's corps, but the gap to the north and the first elements of Sixteenth Army near Polotsk was wide open. Chistiakov's Sixth Guards Army continued its relentless attacks, levering the Germans out of one position after another and forcing through the line of lakes.

One of the formations promised as reinforcements from Army Group North – 212th Infantry Division – was detraining in the town of Lepel, on the southern flank of IX Corps, and Reinhardt and Busch hoped that it would be able to re-establish contact with Fourth Army, but even if this was achieved there were still no forces to close the gap towards Polotsk. In any case, it wasn't possible for IX Corps to hold its positions. During the afternoon, Wuthmann informed Reinhardt that he would have to pull back closer to Lepel. One of the disparate battlegroups on the southern flank of Third Panzer Army was under the command of Oberst Otto von Monteton, who had gathered together the personnel of the army's *Waffenschule* ('weapons school'); nearly every army on the Eastern Front had created such schools in attempts to augment the relatively

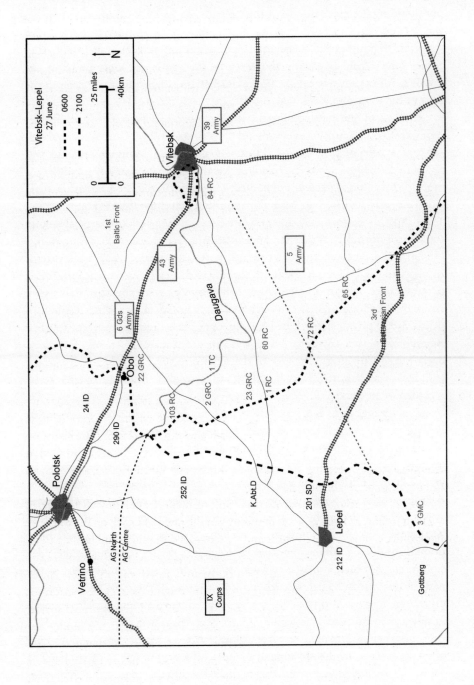

poor training of new drafts. With the strength of roughly a battalion, this group was far too weak to hold back the full weight of Beloborodov's Forty-Third Army; it fell back towards Lepel in increasing disarray and could do little to stop Soviet forces from bypassing the town to the south. At some point in the evening, Monteton was caught up in close-quarters fighting in a village to the west of the town and was killed.

Another of the battlegroups in the yawning gap between Third Panzer Army and Fourth Army was commanded by Brigadeführer Curt von Gottberg. He was a protégé of Heinrich Himmler and in the summer of 1942 was appointed *Höhere SS und Polizeiführer* ('Senior SS and Police Commander' or *HSSPF*) for *Weissruthenien*. He had earned a grim reputation in earlier years when he was involved in several paramilitary and *Freikorps* groups in the 1920s but his performance in the Nazi era had been lacklustre; he therefore took the opportunity of this new appointment to try to restore his reputation.[13] He devised a personal approach to anti-partisan warfare, using a mixture of troops from a police regiment of the SS and locally recruited anti-Soviet paramilitaries. His group carried out brutal sweeps across Belarus, destroying entire villages; one such sweep over four days in November 1942 resulted in nearly 3,000 people being killed for the loss of two dead and ten wounded in *Kampfgruppe von Gottberg*.[14] He was uncompromising in his approach, declaring shortly after: 'The task of the units under my command is to attack and destroy all bandits. Every bandit, Jew, Gypsy and criminal suspect is to be regarded as an enemy.'[15]

Kampfgruppe von Gottberg left a trail of destruction and death across Belarus in the months that followed. He openly acknowledged that many of his victims were innocent civilians, but justified this on the grounds that it instilled fear into the minds of surviving Belarusians. With a reputation to match that of Dirlewanger and the equally repugnant Bronislav Kaminski (a Belarusian who led a militia brigade in similar bloody sweeps), Gottberg was now ordered to deploy his men in the front line to bridge part of the gap that had opened up to the south of Third Panzer Army. Even if they had been properly trained soldiers, the men of *Kampfgruppe von Gottberg* lacked the equipment for such combat; to make matters even worse, they were in the path of Rotmistrov's Fifth Guards Tank Army, one of the most heavily armed units attacking the Wehrmacht. In just a few hours, Gottberg was driven back in disarray to Borisov.

Everywhere, German forces were disintegrating under the constant pounding of the Red Army. By the morning of 27 June, VI Corps on the northern flank of Tippelskirch's Fourth Army was able to do little other than report the progress of

Soviet columns towards the west. The next formation – XXVII Corps – had been broken into three separate fragments. The strongest remained 78th Sturm Division, fighting stubbornly near Orsha. Late on 26 June, tanks from the Soviet II Guards Tank Corps – part of Galitsky's Eleventh Guards Army – swept past the north of Orsha and then turned south, cutting the roads running to the west. During the morning of 27 June, Thirty-First Army on the southern flank of 3rd Belarusian Front cut the remaining escape route and linked up with II Guards Tank Corps. Traut's division was now surrounded near the city, and other units of Galitsky's Eleventh Army were continuing to move west, threatening to envelop all of Fourth Army.

As the morning progressed, the Soviet Eleventh Guards and Thirty-First Armies pressed into Orsha. Despite his orders to hold Orsha at all costs, Traut had no intention of sacrificing his men in such a futile stand and ordered them to break out to the southwest. It was a region the veterans knew well – as 78th Infantry Division, they had marched through the area on their way towards Moscow in the summer of 1941. Leaving behind much of their equipment and some of their wounded, the exhausted men of 78th Sturm Division abandoned the burning city. When he learned that Orsha had fallen, Busch issued a reiteration of his strident demands that the Führer's orders regarding fortresses remained in place and were to be followed to the letter, but events continued to unfold on the battlefield at a pace that made such declarations increasingly pointless.

Even as 78th Sturm Division faced encirclement in Orsha, to its south was a mixed group centred on 25th Panzergrenadier Division's surviving subunits, with both flanks in the air. Beyond this was another mixed group of men from 260th Infantry Division trying to pull back to the line of the Dnepr. Advancing Red Army columns were now intermingled with retreating German formations and there was widespread confusion as the entire mass headed for the river. A group of T-34s with accompanying infantry reached the river a little to the north of Mogilev and improvised a crossing, but on this occasion German artillery was able to intervene and the bridgehead was abandoned under heavy shellfire. Nonetheless, the seam between XXVII Corps in the north and XXXIX Panzer Corps to the south was ruptured, with 110th Infantry Division pulling back over the river in disarray while *Feldherrnhalle* to the south was pushed back towards Mogilev. The remnants of three German divisions – 78th Sturm Division, 25th Panzergrenadier Division, and 260th Infantry Division – were effectively in a 'wandering pocket', cut off from other German units. For the moment, they still had the ability to move, but already they faced a huge challenge if they were to retreat safely to the west.

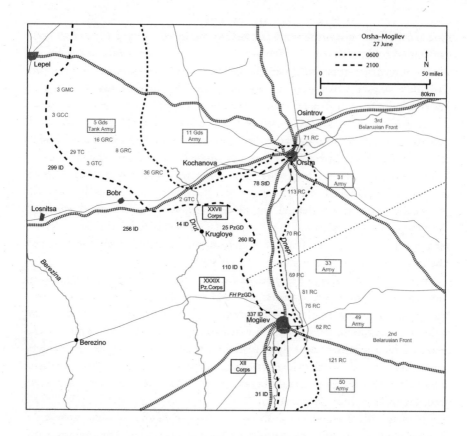

The city of Mogilev was no stranger to violence. It had seen terrible massacres of Jews in the 17th century and was razed by the army of Peter the Great a century later. During the First World War, it was the home of *Stavka*, and it fell to the Wehrmacht just four days after the commencement of the German invasion in June 1941. In the three years that followed, tens of thousands of Jews, prisoners of war, and Belarusian civilians died in prison camps in and around the city, particularly in the Lupalov camp in the southern part of Mogilev.[16] It was also another of Hitler's declared 'fortresses' and during the morning of 27 June Tippelskirch attempted to clarify the city's status. With increasing irritation, he repeatedly contacted Busch's headquarters in Minsk despite being told on each occasion that, like Orsha and Bobruisk, Mogilev was a fortress and was to be held at all costs. When he visited the headquarters of XXXIX Panzer Corps in the late morning, Tippelskirch learned that a second Soviet attempt to force a crossing over the Dnepr to the north of the city had been more successful and that the 'Dnepr

Line' was effectively breached even before the hard-pressed German units had pulled back to it.

The unit designated to defend Mogilev to the bitter end was 12th Infantry Division, commanded by Generalleutnant Rudolf Bamler; the city commandant was Generalmajor Gottfried von Erdmannsdorff. The city was soon under heavy attack by Forty-Ninth Army to the north and Fiftieth Army to the south. With Red Army units continuing to stream past his northern flank, Tippelskirch informed Busch that the Dnepr line was impossible to hold. Unless Fourth Army was permitted to fall back towards the west, it faced piecemeal encirclement and destruction. Indeed, XXVII Corps was already effectively encircled. Busch's predictable response was that all 'fortresses' were to be held, as was the line of the Dnepr. In the event of the river line being forced by the Red Army, Tippelskirch was to ensure that the Soviet units were halted on the Drut River a little to the west.

Bamler had arrived on the Eastern Front just three weeks before the commencement of *Bagration*, having previously held posts in Norway since May 1942. He was not popular with his men; Heinz-Georg Lemm, who was a major at the time in command of a battalion in 12th Infantry Division, had extracted his men with great difficulty from being trapped to the east of the Dnepr and found his division commander in a cellar in Mogilev, deeply downcast and repeatedly demanding that the city had to be held to the last man. Lemm asked for permission to break out with his battalion, but Bamler replied that he had unequivocal orders to hold the 'fortress'. Lemm protested that Hitler would surely not want to see a division that lacked the ammunition and resources for such a battle to be destroyed pointlessly. Bamler then summoned the division's legal officer to ask what would happen if he disobeyed Hitler's order. The legal officer replied that he would face court martial and execution. It is perhaps a measure of how much the famous discipline of the Wehrmacht had declined and how little faith Bamler's subordinates had in their commander that Lemm replied that surely it would be better to have one dead general than to lose a division that still possessed 8,000 men. Bamler told him to do whatever he wished.[17]

With constant reports of unopposed Red Army units motoring through the gaps in his army's lines, Tippelskirch attempted to rationalise his units with fresh orders during the afternoon. In the north, XXVII Corps was to take up positions from Kochanova, 16 miles west of Orsha, to Krugloye on the Drut, 35 miles northwest of Mogilev. At the same time, XXXIX Panzer Corps was to continue the line along the Drut with XII Corps to its south. There was no intention of holding the Dnepr line as Busch had ordered and even these orders would be difficult to fulfil, with retreating columns under almost constant aerial attack. In addition, partisans conducted hit-and-run attacks and damaged or destroyed bridges over the Drut; Tippelskirch had wanted all rear area units to pull back to the Berezina, but many were now trapped in a tangle of traffic at the Drut crossings, assailed by bombs and gunfire from Soviet aircraft.

In Mogilev, the German defenders were compressed into a small area around the city centre. Erdmannsdorff sent his last signal to Tippelskirch at 2200 on 27 June, a brief message that only a small part of the city remained in German hands. Shortly after, Bamler also made a brief transmission in which he requested a medal for one of his artillery officers. Fighting continued in Mogilev through the night and finally died down the following morning. It seems that Bamler was determined to obey his orders to the bitter end but some of his subordinates took it upon themselves to try to break out to the west.[18] Remarkably, at least one such group managed to slip through the encircling Soviet forces and over the next two days made its way to the west, linking up with other German forces.[19]

Both Bamler and Erdmannsdorff were among the 3,200 prisoners who laid down their weapons in Mogilev. Both officers became members of the anti-Nazi *Bund Deutscher Offiziere* ('League of German Officers' or *BDO*), a group founded by several senior German officers who had become prisoners after the surrender of Sixth Army in Stalingrad, but although this body and the related *Nationalkomittee Freies Deutschland* ('National Committee for a Free Germany' or *NKFD*) had been extensively promoted and encouraged by the Soviet Union, it was now seen as having less importance. Stalin had hoped to use these officers to contact their former colleagues in order to encourage them to lay down their weapons, but with the defeat of Germany now looking increasingly certain, the Soviet authorities felt there was far less need for these men. Despite turning against Nazi Germany, Bamler and Erdmannsdorff remained under suspicion because of the manner in which the defence of Mogilev had been conducted. In particular, there were repeated allegations that Erdmannsdorff had ordered the execution of civilians who refused to work on the construction of defences, and that he had organised the use of civilians as human shields; Bamler was not regarded as having instigated either of these actions, but of tacitly permitting the use of human shields. Nevertheless, Bamler made skilful use of his experience as a staff officer and of his earlier role in German military intelligence to ensure that he was regarded by his captors as a valuable asset. He helped draft several declarations calling on senior German officers to surrender and he provided the NKVD with information on his fellow prisoners and members of the *BDO*, resulting in some of them being charged with war crimes. His behaviour came as no surprise to many others; one fellow prisoner later observed that Bamler did whatever he was asked by the Soviets, actively seeking to ensure his early return to Germany and hoping for a senior post in whatever regime the Soviet Union established in its zone of occupation.[20]

In 1949, while still a prisoner, Bamler joined Friedrich Paulus, the former commander of Sixth Army in Stalingrad, in writing an appeal to Stalin stating that they and other senior officers would use all their strength to promote Soviet interests and to strengthen German–Soviet cooperation if they were permitted to return to Germany. He travelled back to the recently created DDR the following year. Here, he learned that his wife, who had been arrested by the Gestapo after he started cooperating with his Soviet captors, had died in the summer of 1945, probably as a consequence of the hardships of her imprisonment.[21] He held various posts in police organisations in the DDR but was dismissed in 1953 after allegedly failing to crack down on anti-Soviet demonstrations in Erfurt, where he was stationed. He gradually returned to favour and worked in a number of governmental roles and died in 1972.

Erdmannsdorff was not as fortunate as Bamler. His involvement in war crimes was far clearer and perhaps he also lacked the astute footwork needed to survive. He was put on trial in Minsk in 1946 and charged with involvement in the deportation of up to 10,000 civilians, the widespread destruction of buildings across Belarus, the execution of civilians who were physically unable to carry out manual work, the use of human shields, and involvement in the bloody anti-partisan sweeps. He was found guilty and was promptly hanged.

The dismissal of Jordan as commander of Ninth Army had no impact upon the rapidly deteriorating situation in the south. The army headquarters was heavily hit by a Soviet air raid early on 27 June resulting in numerous losses and disruption to the chain of command. Having moved all of its tanks forward through the difficult terrain in the original front line, Major General Mikhail Fedorovich Panov's I Guards Tank Corps was now advancing almost unopposed and during the morning reached and cut the main highway running northwest from Bobruisk to Minsk. A desperate counterattack by 20th Panzer Division towards the west, immediately south of Bobruisk, claimed the destruction of 20 Soviet tanks but failed to make a decisive impact; however, it bought a little time for the tangle of infantry divisions to the southeast of Bobruisk to fall back towards the city. The defensive line between Bobruisk and Mogilev effectively collapsed as the Soviet Third Army poured west, reaching the northern outskirts of Bobruisk late in the day. Struggling to restore communications and to salvage something from the wreckage, Weidling was hugely relieved when he learned that Vormann, currently on leave in Germany, was now hastening to take up his new appointment. In the meantime, what communications were possible with Busch's headquarters in Minsk took on an increasingly unreal character. During the morning, a courier arrived to tell Weidling he had to close the gap in the front line to the southwest of Bobruisk with 20th Panzer Division – it should be remembered that Jordan had been strongly criticised for deploying the panzer division in precisely this area. Aware that the division had failed to make significant headway in its morning attack, Weidling responded that he could only achieve significant success if he was permitted to extract the troops trapped to the east of Bobruisk and then use them to restore the front line; this would, however, require the abandonment of Bobruisk itself. Busch replied by radio that Weidling was permitted to use these troops to fight his way back towards the west and northwest, but 383rd Infantry Division was to remain in Bobruisk as the fortress garrison. Almost immediately after this, contradictory orders arrived. Whilst Weidling had permission to use troops additional to 20th Panzer Division to overcome the Soviet forces bypassing Bobruisk from the south, he was also to continue holding the line to the east.

In any event, Weidling's ability to pass instructions to his subordinate corps was almost non-existent. By the end of 27 July, 20th Panzer Division had lost most of its remaining armoured vehicles and commanders at all levels took it upon themselves to do what they could to save their men. Generalleutnant Kurt-Jürgen Freiherr von Lützow, commander of XXXV Corps, gathered together a mixed group that amounted to perhaps a division and attempted to fight his way past the northern outskirts of Bobruisk. During the evening there was heavy fighting near Osipovichi, 24 miles to the northwest of Bobruisk as an improvised battlegroup came under attack by Soviet infantry and tanks from Sixty-Fifth Army; even if the positions around Bobruisk continued to hold, they were badly outflanked. To the south of Osipovichi, Pliev's cavalry-mechanised group swept past whatever isolated German units were in its path, further widening the huge gap in the German lines. When he became aware of the attempts by the German forces to the east of Bobruisk to break out past the northern edge of the city, Rokossovsky ordered Colonel General Sergei Ignatevich Rudenko, commander of Sixteenth Air Army, to intervene. Throughout the evening, hundreds of Soviet aircraft bombed and strafed the

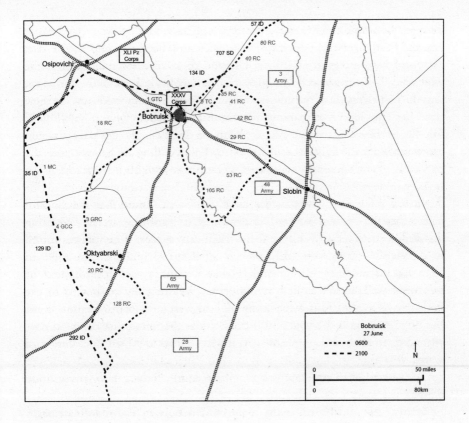

German columns, adding hugely to the chaos. Zhukov was not far away and watched the devastation:

> Hundreds of bombers ... struck repeatedly at the enemy group. The battlefield was ablaze and dozens of vehicles, tanks, and fuel and lubricant dumps went up in flames. The entire battlefield was illuminated by the devastating inferno. More and more waves of our bombers were drawn to it, dropping bombs of various sizes on the enemy. All of this terrible 'choir' was supplemented by artillery fire from Forty-Eighth Army.[22]

Despite the growing sense of disaster at the headquarters of Army Group Centre, there were a few tiny flashes of light in the darkness. Two of the formations detached from Army Group Centre in anticipation of the main Soviet effort falling on Army Group North Ukraine – 4th and 5th Panzer Divisions – had been ordered to move back to Busch's army group as quickly as possible. Both divisions had continuous, distinguished records of service on the Eastern Front and had been involved in dealing with several crises, but none on this scale. The armoured battlegroup of 4th Panzer Division began to board trains on 27 June while Betzel, the division commander, travelled to Minsk. Towards the end of the day, the first elements of the division began to arrive in Baranovichi. At the same time, the armoured reconnaissance battalion and combat engineer battalion of 5th Panzer Division reached Minsk. Without question, these divisions would greatly enhance the fighting ability of Army Group Centre, but nonetheless the prevailing gloom remained; many openly questioned whether it was a case of 'too little, too late'.

In just a few days, the situation of Army Group Centre had deteriorated almost beyond recognition and at an unprecedented rate. From occupying fortified positions, the Wehrmacht had been driven back at key points; forced to abandon the areas where the line had either not been attacked or had held firm, the German line had fragmented right across the breadth of the battle zone and the critical shortage of motorised reserves had been fully exposed. Now, the Red Army's exploitation forces took full advantage of the numerous gaps, pushing on towards the west and increasing the chaos and dislocation as they advanced. In their wake, groups of German soldiers were left floundering in search of safety.

To the west of Vitebsk, Gollwitzer, Hitter, and the others in the small group of survivors from LIII Corps gave up their attempts to reach 246th Infantry Division to the north during the night of 27–28 June. The sounds of heavy fighting had died down and as a new day dawned, it was clear that whatever battle had been fought was now over. When they reached the edge of the forest through which they had struggled all night, the Germans found that Soviet infantry units were deployed in their path; they could hear small bursts of gunfire, presumably as German stragglers were caught and overwhelmed, and everywhere there seemed to be Red Army motor vehicles heading west. Not long after, a group of Soviet soldiers from Lyudnikov's Thirty-Ninth Army that had been pursuing Gollwitzer's group caught up with them and took them prisoner, as Lyudnikov later described:

> Gollwitzer, a lean, energetic, middle-aged man, turned out to be very talkative, much to the anger of the ardent Nazi Oberst [Hans] Schmidt. During his interrogation, Gollwitzer told us amongst other things, 'We were mistaken about your plans and intentions. The Soviet tactics of breaking through our defences and their sudden manoeuvres took my headquarters by surprise. I lost control of my troops.' He paused and added, 'There was no time.'

After interrogation, I ordered the head of army intelligence, Lieutenant Colonel Voloshin, to deliver Gollwitzer and Schmidt to the Front headquarters. On his return, Voloshin told me some remarkable things. He had travelled with the prisoners in an open car. When they entered a clearing in the forest, Schmidt had turned and looked around but immediately stopped when he saw that the second car, full of soldiers, was close behind. Gollwitzer and Schmidt then had a furious quarrel. Perhaps to annoy Schmidt, the general asked Voloshin if he spoke French. Maksim Afanasyevich spoke excellent French. Unembarrassed by the presence of Schmidt, Gollwitzer spoke to him in French in a friendly manner.

After going through the forest, the car drove onto a small country road. Noticing a large group of soldiers in a field, Gollwitzer asked Voloshin to stop the car. As this was perhaps the last time he saw his soldiers, he was keen to wish them farewell and asked the Russian officer's indulgence. 'I give you permission,' said Voloshin, 'but on one condition: no political statements. A short word of farewell, and then we go on.'

'Thank you!' replied Gollwitzer. The car slowed. Beside the roadside, guarded by Soviet soldiers with submachine-guns, lay hundreds of [German] soldiers. Even those nearest the road didn't get up when they saw their former commander. Gollwitzer stood up and raised his hand. None of the prisoners moved. '*Meine Soldaten!*' There was a tragic note in Gollwitzer's voice. 'I stood with you on the battlefield and share the bitter fate of captivity with you. At this hour, soldiers, I appeal to you –' But some of the soldiers turned their backs on Gollwitzer and others got up and walked away. He broke off, flopped down on the seat, and whispered to Voloshin in French, 'Take me away from here. Yesterday this was still an army, today it's just a rabble.'[23]

Kharin, the anti-tank gunner who described the resentment of his fellow gunners to the disparaging nicknames given to their 45mm guns, was amongst the Soviet troops that entered Vitebsk and he described his surprise at encountering Russians who had been working for the Wehrmacht as *Hilfswillige*:

Not far from the city, a significant group of German troops was surrounded. The liquidation of this group continued all day.

Then for the first time I saw large masses of prisoners lined up in columns and being marched to our rear. There were even Russians in one of the columns. I asked myself, 'Why did these guys – our guys – join the German Army to fight against us? What do they believe in – Fascism?' One of them, aged just 17, told me, 'Your government mobilised you and the German government mobilised us. We fought here. And we didn't want to fight, so we surrendered.'[24]

Fighting continued for the rest of 28 June as other groups of Germans were rounded up. Estimates vary as to how many Germans were taken prisoner; nearly 30,000 men had been encircled in and near Vitebsk and between 10,000 and 20,000 were captured. Only a few handfuls of men managed to escape back to German lines. Hitter, who had been nominated as the commandant of 'Fortress Vitebsk', later became a member of the *NKFD* but like Gollwitzer he remained a prisoner until 1955. After the war, the former corps commander faced legal proceedings in 1969 about an incident in Poland in September 1939, when he had allegedly ordered the shooting of 18 Polish civilians. Gollwitzer didn't deny his actions but justified them on the grounds that his regiment had been attacked by Polish partisans shortly before and the prosecution was discontinued.

Some of the other division commanders of LIII Corps were less fortunate. Generalleutnant Robert Pistorius, commander of 4th Luftwaffe Field Division, was killed when the last elements of his division were overrun on 27 June; Generalleutnant Rudolf Peschel, commander of the sister formation, 6th Luftwaffe Field Division, wandered through the forests west of Vitebsk for several days before running into Soviet troops on 30 June and was killed in the subsequent firefight. Generalmajor Claus Müller-Bülow, commander of 246th Infantry Division, also remained at large for several days before he was captured on 7 June. He became a member of the *BDO* but he too remained a prisoner until 1955. Of the thousands of soldiers of LIII Corps who were captured, many were released in the years immediately after the war; some perished in captivity, and others remained in prison and labour camps until 1955.

From the point of view of the Soviet leadership, the destruction of Gollwitzer's LIII Corps was precisely how they had wanted the operation to unfold. The German lines were breached and the resultant gaps exploited without delay, resulting in the isolation of Vitebsk; the encircled German troops were then attacked so that they didn't have the opportunity to form a secure defensive perimeter; and the Red Army then overwhelmed the defenders in a commendably short period of time, thus ensuring that the fighting in Vitebsk didn't become a drag anchor on the advance towards the west. Some 15 months before, the Red Army had succeeded in cutting off two German corps in what became known in western accounts as the Cherkassy encirclement, even though the town of Cherkassy was outside the encirclement. On that occasion, the Germans were able to set up a proper defensive line for all-round defence and eventually broke out to link up with a relief column, albeit at high cost. Vasilevsky and Zhukov had been determined to prevent any such sequence of events in *Bagration*, and the manner in which the fighting around Vitebsk unfolded was testament to how well the lessons of the past had been learned.

Whilst LIII Corps was in its death throes, the rest of Reinhardt's Third Panzer Army continued to be driven back in near-rout. On the northern flank of VI Corps, 252nd Infantry Division was no longer a coherent combat unit and reported that it was in full retreat in the area between Polotsk and Lepel; Generalleutnant Walter Melzer, the division commander, reported to Reinhardt that he estimated he had no more than 300 combatants left under his command. The rest of the division was dead, prisoner, or scattered to the winds. To the south, *Korps Abteilung D* was in a similar state with its remaining battalions reduced to perhaps 50 men each. Busch's orders to Reinhardt for the day were to seal off and eliminate Soviet penetrations in the lines of Third Panzer Army; Reinhardt replied that it wasn't a question of penetrations, more of huge gaps. The best he could do was try to hold Lepel, but by mid-morning on 28 June there was already fighting in the western parts of the vital town. Beloborodov's Forty-Third Army had at its disposal 10th and 39th Guards Tank Brigades and the army commander threw these forward in support of I Rifle Corps. The combined force vastly outnumbered and outgunned the Germans in its path and rapidly overran Lepel. Even the bridge over the Essa River in the town was captured intact.[25]

As they took control of Lepel, the soldiers of Forty-Third Army made a grim discovery. Just outside the town was a prison camp, and several hundred civilian prisoners were still there when the Soviet I Rifle Corps took control of the area. The prisoners told the soldiers that hundreds – perhaps thousands – of civilians had perished there in the years of German occupation. The discoveries near Lepel did little to improve the prospects of any German soldiers who fell into the hands of the advancing Red Army.

Bagramian was generally satisfied with the performance of his Front, but his concerns about his northern flank remained. After further discussions with Vasilevsky, Bagramian managed to secure the promise of additional reinforcements and supplies so that Fourth Shock Army, which until now had barely moved, would drive towards Polotsk from the east while Chistiakov's Sixth Guards Army moved forces towards the city from the south.[26]

Between Third Panzer Army and Tippelskirch's Fourth Army there was a yawning gap, barely protected by any meaningful German forces; Oslikovsky's cavalry-mechanised group motored through this space, brushing aside whatever weak, improvised defenders there were. To make matters worse for the Germans, the two tank corps of Rotmistrov's Fifth Guards Tank Army were moving forward and adding their weight to the avalanche that was overwhelming Army Group Centre. By the end of 28 June, III Guards Mechanised Corps – part of Oslikovsky's group – had advanced past the southern flank of the battered German units pulling back from Lepel. Even if they could halt the Soviet units of Forty-Third Army that had captured the town, the Germans were in danger of being rolled up towards the north, thus widening the gap still further.

It had been the intention of the Germans to send the trains carrying 5th Panzer Division to Borisov, but constant Soviet air attacks on Borisov and the railway line to the west of the city made this impossible. Instead, various elements of the division detrained in Minsk throughout 28 June and the division's armoured reconnaissance battalion was ordered to probe into the area to the north of Borisov to determine the location of the advancing Red Army units – it was clear to Decker, the division commander, that the sparse information he had been given by Busch's headquarters was both inaccurate and out of date. The reconnaissance battalion moved forward against a tide of German rear area units and personnel from the various occupation authorities, all desperately attempting to retreat to the west; from time to time, there were exchanges of fire with small groups of T-34s that vanished as quickly as they appeared. During the afternoon, panzergrenadiers from 5th Panzer Division took up defensive positions a short distance to the north of Borisov but were startled by the sudden appearance of another group of Soviet tanks supported by truck-borne infantry. None of 5th Panzer Division's tanks or anti-tank units had arrived yet and the panzergrenadiers had little choice but to attempt to engage the Soviet tanks at close range with a mixture of demolition charges and light anti-tank weapons. During the night, the arrival of 5th Panzer Division's artillery and tanks gave the position a little more stability.[27]

In an attempt to control the disparate units strewn across the gap between Third Panzer Army and Fourth Army, a new formation was created. The various improvised battlegroups, including Gottberg's SS, together with 5th Panzer Division and a Tiger tank battalion, were placed under the command of Generalleutnant Dietrich von Saucken. Compared to many of his contemporaries, Saucken had a relatively small physique, but he undoubtedly had the ability to impose his authority. Photographs consistently show him in immaculate uniform regardless of the circumstances, often with a monocle in one eye; he was in many respects the epitome of the austere, professional Prussian officer. He was a highly experienced panzer commander, having led cavalry and infantry units before taking command of 4th Panzer Division in late 1941 and III Panzer Corps in May 1944. The Wehrmacht would need every ounce of his abilities in the coming days.

Orders issued by Busch on the evening of 27 June, for a general withdrawal towards the west whilst continuing to hold the 'fortresses' of Mogilev and Bobruisk, only reached Fourth Army the following morning. There was now a growing risk that the Soviet forces that had turned the northern flank of Tippelskirch's army west of Orsha would continue their thrust towards the southwest while the disintegration of Ninth Army to the south would allow the Red Army to push north and northwest, enveloping both German armies. Lines to the east of the Berezina River were designated for the various German units, but Tippelskirch and his staff had no illusions that these lines could be held; a retreat beyond the Berezina River was, they felt, inevitable. With both its flanks driven in, 25th Panzergrenadier Division pulled back from a position immediately south of Orsha, frequently having to beat off Soviet attacks from all sides. The exhausted troops of 78th Sturm Division were in no better state a little to the east, struggling to hold back the full weight of the Soviet Thirty-Third Army. Late on 27 July, Traut had sent a message to Tippelskirch outlining the situation. He informed the army commander that tight encirclement of his division and the neighbouring formations was only a matter of hours away and attempting to march west through the lines of the enemy formations in his path would be impossible without supplies of all kinds. Evacuation of the numerous wounded men with the division was effectively impossible and in order to attempt to retain any level of mobility, the division was going to have to abandon most of its vehicles as it lacked the fuel for them.[28]

Aware that the main penetrations of the German positions were to be carried out by the Fronts to his north and south, Zakharov was urging his armies forward to keep up pressure on the German troops in order to prevent an orderly withdrawal to the west. Like 78th Sturm Division, all German units still fighting were now running short of ammunition, fuel, and food. Tippelskirch had already requested the Luftwaffe to deliver supplies by air, and repeated the request with added urgency. During the afternoon, there were further alarming reports: Soviet tanks had entered Krugloye, threatening to outflank Fourth Army from the north. These were the leading elements of II Guards Tank Corps, advancing almost unopposed. The withdrawal ordered by Fourth Army was effectively already underway even before formal orders arrived as the troops clustered to the south of Orsha – in most respects, they could no longer be regarded as individual regiments and divisions, more just accumulations of survivors from different units with one or other formation dominating a particular group – began to pull back to the west.

Before they could reach the Berezina, the German units had to cross the Drut River, which runs from north to south between the Dnepr to the east and the

215

Berezina to the west. Inevitably, traffic jams appeared at the few crossings over the river, attracting the attention of Soviet air attacks. Many elements didn't cross until late on 28 June, leaving behind abandoned vehicles and equipment. Until now, 78th Sturm Division had succeeded in bringing most of its artillery with it; Traut now reiterated his order for all non-essential vehicles to be abandoned, adding that horse-drawn guns and equipment were to be destroyed. Amidst the chaos, command and control deteriorated further due to the relocation of Tippelskirch's headquarters to the town of Berezino. Roads were choked with abandoned and broken-down vehicles; many small bridges collapsed, adding to delays; and Soviet aircraft were everywhere, spoiled for choice by the profusion of targets and the almost complete absence of Luftwaffe fighters. During the afternoon, ground attack planes struck the headquarters group of XXXIX Panzer Corps; General Martinek was killed and command passed to Generalmajor Otto Schünemann, commander of 337th Infantry Division. A few hours later, General Pfeiffer, the commander of VI Corps, was mortally wounded; some accounts attributed this to an attack by a Soviet anti-tank gun, others to close-quarters fighting with hand grenades, and some to an air strike. Orders from Army Group Centre continued to arrive several hours after events had made them superfluous. In the evening, a message arrived that had been issued at midday for Mogilev to be abandoned; even when the order was issued, the city was already in Soviet hands. Tippelskirch decided that it was pointless to await orders that were going to arrive so late and instructed all his units to pull back to the Berezina River.

The congested roads behind the German front line were in many respects matched by the congestion behind the advancing Soviet armies as supply columns and reinforcements competed with artillery units that were attempting to keep up with the advance. Lieutenant General Vasily Dmitriyevich Kryuchenkin, commander of Thirty-Third Army, was under constant pressure from Zakharov at 2nd Belarusian Front headquarters to pursue the Germans as closely as possible and he issued orders to his front-line units that they were to form reconnaissance detachments to operate up to 12 miles ahead of the main force so that any German attempt to break contact would be spotted.[29]

The war diary of Ninth Army summed up the situation in the south in two brief sentences on 28 June: 'As a combat formation, Ninth Army has practically ceased to exist. The Army no longer has any units capable of mounting operations.'[30]

Bobruisk was now another place that was full of retreating German units, tangled together in inextricable traffic jams. A report from XLI Panzer Corps described the chaos: in addition to the headquarters of the panzer corps and that of the 'fortress' commandant, the commanders of five divisions were in the city;

the commander of 134th Infantry Division, Generalleutnant Ernst Philipp, had handed command of what remained of his formation to one of his regiment commanders and had then shot himself.

The Red Army was pressing in on all sides; Third Army was to the northeast, Forty-Eighth Army to the south, and Sixty-Fifth Army to the west. Hoffmeister, commander of XLI Panzer Corps, asked for permission to break out with all forces present and must have been surprised when a reply arrived at 0835 granting permission; but this was followed 90 minutes later by fresh instructions from Busch. Whilst permission was granted for a breakout, a division was to be left in the 'fortress'. Further orders followed, informing Hoffmeister that he could not expect any help from outside the city and would have to break out using just the units he had; the Luftwaffe would attempt to drop supplies on Bobruisk.

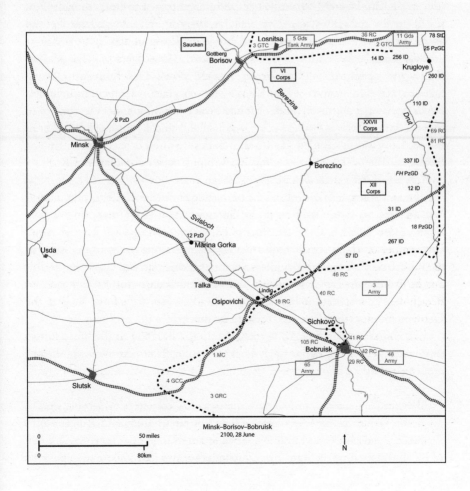

217

Hoffmeister held a brief conference during the afternoon with the other senior officers in the city. They concluded that the instructions regarding a fortress garrison were unworkable and orders were issued for a breakout attempt that would commence that evening, with no provision for a fortress garrison. At 2300, 20th Panzer Division's few remaining armoured vehicles set off at the head of the column, supported by the remnants of the various infantry divisions, while 383rd Infantry Division attempted to act as a rearguard. About 3,600 wounded had to be left behind. In almost constant fighting, the Germans slowly struggled to the forests to the north of Sichkovo, about six miles northwest of Bobruisk. To the west, the gap to the nearest German units – the first elements of 12th Panzer Division, arriving in Marina Gorka – was 47 miles. Accustomed to being dispatched to deal with crises, the officers of 12th Panzer Division had rapidly organised their units to make best use of the limited railway capacity available, creating an armoured battlegroup as the first element to be dispatched. As it deployed to the east of Marina Gorka, the officers tried in vain to get a clear idea of what was happening. When the operations officer finally tracked down Generalmajor Helmut Staedke, the chief of staff of Ninth Army, he was given a depressing summary. LV Corps on the southern flank of Ninth Army was now under the control of Second Army and was falling back towards Slutsk and Baranovichi; the rest of Ninth Army was fighting for its life after being engulfed in the fighting around Bobruisk. The only formation over which Ninth Army could exert any direct control was 12th Panzer Division.[31]

The increasing breakdown of communications on the German side made a bad situation far worse, and made the fantastical nature of Hitler's instructions all the more striking. Orders from the Führer stated categorically that Army Group Centre was to retreat no further than a line along the Berezina River in the north and centre; in the southern sector, the 'final' defensive line was to run about 50 miles to the southeast of Minsk. By the time these orders reached Busch's headquarters, they had already been overtaken by events. Even if the shattered German divisions could reach this line before the pursuing Red Army, they no longer had the strength to mount an organised defence. The instructions used language that was depressingly familiar to the officers and men who had to implement Hitler's orders:

> The enemy advance on Army Group Centre's sector must now be halted once and for all. To this end I have ordered reinforcements with panzer and infantry divisions and assault gun brigades from other Army Groups and from Germany … What I now expect of the Army Group is, however, that no yard of ground

shall be given up without fighting for it, and that every commander and man in the Army Group shall have instilled in him the iron will to hold firm …

I am confident that the Army Group will do everything in its power to accomplish the task set it. I expect my confidence to be justified.[32]

Ever since the Battle of Moscow, Hitler and those in his immediate circle had behaved as if 'iron will' and 'fanatical resistance' were satisfactory substitutes for adequate numbers and supplies. But no amount of determination was going to restore the wreckage that now constituted Army Group Centre. During the morning of 28 June, Busch briefed Zeitzler and told the chief of the general staff that Ninth Army had been crushed in the fighting around Bobruisk and Third Panzer Army was in little better shape, having lost a third of its strength in the disaster that had unfolded around Vitebsk. Only Fourth Army was still conducting a properly constituted defence, and it was running out of strength at an alarming rate; from the reports sent by Tippelskirch, Busch must have known that this was a considerable exaggeration and that Fourth Army was also close to collapse. Shortly after, a fresh message arrived from *OKH*. Busch was dismissed as commander of Army Group Centre, and was to be replaced by Model.

It was effectively the end of Busch's military career. He had served with distinction in the First World War, being awarded the *Pour le Mérite* or 'Blue Max' in 1918.[33] Like many people of his era, he was a firm believer in the concept of social Darwinism, writing in 1937 that he saw future wars as the means by which 'superior' nations would prevail over their weaker counterparts in ruthless combat. His command of Sixteenth Army, part of Army Group North, during the first months of the German invasion of the Soviet Union was stolid and unspectacular and he was sharply criticised for the encirclement of part of his army in Demyansk, but he retained his post largely because of his unequivocal loyalty to Hitler. Partly rehabilitated after the successful breaking of the Demyansk encirclement, he oversaw defensive fighting in the months that followed, with neither the opportunity nor the inclination to demonstrate any particular flair, but – again, largely due to his personal loyalty to the Führer – he was promoted to Generalfeldmarschall in early 1943 and awarded the Oak Leaves for the Knight's Cross a few months later. He was arguably out of his depth as an army commander, and was certainly not competent for higher command, but he was Hitler's choice as the new commander of Army Group Centre when Kluge was injured in a car crash in October 1943; again, this reflected his unquestioning obedience, a trait that Hitler valued highly at a time when the military situation was increasingly bad for Germany and the Führer believed that this was largely due to the unwillingness of senior officers to obey instructions and to instil the required levels of 'iron will' and 'fanatical resistance' in their troops. In the weeks that followed Busch's dismissal, he lived in Germany and was apparently deeply depressed by the manner in which events had unfolded. There were even rumours that he was suicidal. In March 1945, with final German defeat just a matter of weeks away, he was appointed commander of Army Group H, which was then renamed Army Group Northwest – in reality, it was merely a collection of broken and defeated units scattered across northwest Germany and parts of the Netherlands. He became a prisoner of war at the end of the conflict and was interned in England. Some of those imprisoned with him later said that he was a broken man, still heavily affected by the disaster that had overtaken Army Group Centre. In July 1945, he suffered a fatal heart attack.[34]

CHAPTER 7

EXPLOITATION: 29 JUNE–3 JULY

The mood in German circles by the end of 28 June was marked by foreboding, crisis, and disaster. On the other side of the front line, matters couldn't have been any more different. Zhukov described the atmosphere in senior military circles:

> When we observed and analysed the actions of the German troops and their high command during this operation, we were frankly surprised at their obviously erroneous actions, which doomed their soldiers to a catastrophic outcome. Instead of a swift retreat to a rearward line and moving strong groups to their flanks, which were threatened by Soviet exploitation groups, the Germans were drawn into protracted defensive frontal battles east, southeast and northeast of Minsk.[1]

In earlier operations in the war, *Stavka* had found it necessary to issue new instructions as the campaign unfolded largely because early objectives had not been achieved. By contrast, during *Bagration* the new directives – which were drawn up on 28 June – were needed because of the growing success of the operation. In seven days of reconnaissance in force and full-scale assaults, the Red Army had shattered two German armies and was in the process of destroying a third army. Bagramian was given permission to deal with Polotsk in order to secure his northern flank, and was then to drive on towards the west; in the centre, 2nd and 3rd Belarusian Fronts were to attack aggressively to capture Minsk and prevent the stabilisation of the retreating German forces along the Berezina; and in the south, 1st Belarusian Front was ordered to direct its main strength towards Slutsk and Baranovichi in the west, whilst also closing in on Minsk from the south and southeast. There was no longer any question of whether *Bagration* was a success: the only matter to be settled was just how great this success would be.

Even as Busch prepared to leave Army Group Centre, the headquarters staff were busy relocating from Minsk to Lida, 91 miles to the west. Zeitzler travelled to Lida to discuss matters with Busch and Model and offered reassurances to Busch that his dismissal was not a reflection of his recent requests to abandon the 'fortresses', more a matter of organising a better defence by having Army Groups North Ukraine and Centre under a single command. Busch clearly found this of little comfort. The staff of Army Group Centre knew of Model's reputation as an energetic and successful defensive commander, and such skills were manifestly needed if the army group was going to survive, but they were also aware from past experience that he was a difficult person to work for. When he arrived in Lida, Model made little attempt to follow the expected courtesies with regard to his predecessor and instead gave the impression – as he had done on previous occasions when taking up a new command – of being abrupt and rude. Oberst Hermann Teske, the staff officer with responsibility for transport matters in Army Group Centre, found Model's behaviour to be 'toxic and corrosive' and a few days later asked Krebs, the chief of staff in Lida, for a transfer to a different command. Krebs' reply was characteristic of many officers who had to deal with Model: 'What do you want me to do? Yesterday, he threatened me – his old chief of staff [from when Model commanded Ninth Army] – with court martial! But the man can achieve the impossible and at the moment he's our only hope here.'[2]

With Bagramian switching his attention towards Polotsk, Third Panzer Army enjoyed a relative respite and was able to pull back towards the west on 29 June. There was no contact with Sixteenth Army's I Corps to the north and with Soviet tanks reported to be approaching the Daugava crossings to the east of Polotsk, improvised units were hastily dispatched to try to create some sort of front line. In this area, Chistiakov's Sixth Guards Army was moving forward steadily, but the combination of losses suffered in achieving the breakthrough, lengthening supply lines, and growing German resistance all played a part in slowing the Soviet advance. Nonetheless, it was highly doubtful that Polotsk could be held for anything other than a short time.

Some of the advancing Soviet forces found themselves tangled up with the retreating Germans. Semen Vinopol and his mortarmen were in one such group:

One night we realised that we were surrounded on all sides, but the telephone connection with our headquarters was still usable and when we reported to the regiment commander that the mortars and all of the 3rd Battalion were in a trap, he replied, 'Let them move past you.' At night, a German infantry unit passed right through our positions. We hid – there was, as they say, the sort of darkness you get if you're blinded, and the Germans jumped over our trenches, not suspecting that we lay in them silently, holding our breath and ready to fight. As quietly as they could, my men grabbed three Germans by the legs and dragged them to the bottom of the trench, there wasn't even a squeak. The Germans moved on but the tension in those minutes was terrible. We decided it was time for us to return to our own lines and we walked through the dark to a clearing where there was a German tank. We thought it was abandoned. We came closer and one of the soldiers hit the tank with the butt of his gun and said, 'Look, Slavs, what good armour!' And at that moment the 'wrecked' tank came to life, turning on its headlights and starting its engine – we had woken up the German crew sleeping inside the tank. We rushed away from the tank as we had no anti-tank grenades. The tank fired a few shells at random, but we were long gone.[3]

To the south of Bagramian's thrust, there were some concerns in the upper echelons of the Red Army. Rotmistrov's Fifth Guards Tank Army was still moving towards the front line through the ranks of Eleventh Army and only some elements had entered action, seizing Tolochin on the main Minsk–Moscow highway. Thereafter, they advanced west to Bobr where they ran into the Tiger tanks of *Schwere Panzer Abteilung 505*, part of *Gruppe von Saucken*. There were heavy exchanges of fire and several tanks were lost on both sides, but Rotmistrov's advance towards Borisov and then to Minsk was brought to a halt. Stalin was growing increasingly exasperated at the delays, and Rotmistrov was heavily criticised for repeatedly assaulting German positions head-on instead of attempting to bypass them. It was important to push on to Minsk before the Germans had a chance to catch their breath; at the same time, the infantry units were ordered to make every effort to keep up with armoured formations so that the close cooperation between infantry and armour that had been a feature of *Bagration* was sustained.

In the path of Rotmistrov's army was *Gruppe von Saucken*, with most of 5th Panzer Division now deploying around Borisov. Saucken made little secret of his displeasure at having *Gruppe von Gottberg* assigned to him; he advised Fourth Army headquarters that he regarded its troops as inadequately equipped for front-line warfare and its leadership as having no experience of such intense combat. Nonetheless, Saucken received a plethora of instructions. He was to block the main highway that ran through Borisov to Minsk; he was to intercept and block Soviet attempts to cross the Berezina to the north of Borisov; and he was to protect the northern flank of Fourth Army. The mismatch between his resources and the tasks assigned to him was obvious, and in any event even if he could hold the positions around Borisov and the front line that ran broadly from north to south, there was then a gap beyond his southern flank of about 45 miles to the northern flank of the rest of Fourth Army, still trying to pull back from Mogilev. The armoured reconnaissance battalion of 5th Panzer Division, probing towards the northeast, ran into the southern flank of Oslikovsky's cavalry-mechanised group, was split in two, and driven back in disarray. It took an energetic attack by a small group of tanks and panzergrenadiers to extract the reconnaissance battalion.[4]

At the headquarters of Eleventh Guards Army, Galitsky had every reason to feel buoyant. His men had crushed strong German resistance and helped take Orsha, and were now advancing west; in addition, he had just been informed that he had been promoted to Colonel General. Cherniakhovsky telephoned him to offer his congratulations and added that the task for Eleventh Guards Army was to advance swiftly to and over the Berezina; written orders would follow shortly. The river was a potentially formidable obstacle, as Galitsky described:

> We knew that the Berezina, with its swampy flood plain that spread up to 2km on either bank, was a serious water barrier, especially for tanks and artillery. In addition, we were still some considerable distance from it – about 40km. Moreover, there were quite a few enemy units on the routes to the river, and although they were scattered and retreating under the blows of the army's troops they were still capable of putting up local resistance, mainly on the roads to the main crossings to which they were hurrying.
>
> We had to do the same if we were to achieve success. It was all about a rapid pursuit and the destruction of the retreating enemy formations, and crossing the river on their very heels. This concept was the basis of our thinking. Another important matter was the crossing of the river along the entire 50km front of the army, from Lake Palik to the village of Novoselki. We based our calculations on the fact that in such a relatively wide zone, the enemy couldn't organise a powerful, continuous defensive front and would be forced to concentrate his troops at bridges and fords and the surrounding bridgeheads. We intended to tie them down, striking simultaneously at the weakest areas, while forcing the river in places where the enemy couldn't put up serious interference ...
>
> [In XVI Guards Rifle Corps' sector] there was 1st and 31st Guards Rifle Divisions in the first echelon with 11th Guards Rifle Division in the second echelon. VIII Guards Rifle Corps had to cross the river in the Borisov–Novoselki sector, the breadth of which exceeded 20km. Therefore, it was ordered to have all three divisions in the first echelon ...

Each division in the first echelon was to have two regiments advancing along parallel routes. The third formed a local reserve and was intended to support the advance. The divisions were ordered to send forward special groups with experienced officers. Their task was to reconnoitre the river and the local crossings, and to determine places convenient for forcing a crossing. At the same time, strong detachments that included sappers were to be deployed to try to capture crossings and to clear mines from the approaches to the river …

We didn't have much time to prepare the operation. Therefore, the main requirement was to conduct it, not only without a pause but also constantly intensifying the pursuit of the enemy. The corps commanders were warned that there would be no pause even when the river was reached, and that the crossings should commence without delay.[5]

Soviet aircraft flew unopposed, striking wherever they saw German units, and the vital bridge over the Berezina in the town of Berezino was badly damaged by bombs. Traffic piled up to the east of the river, attracting further air attacks; the bridge was further damaged, but German sappers managed to carry out sufficient repairs for crossings to resume in mid-afternoon. Meanwhile, Saucken lacked the resources to send any units north along the Berezina and as a result, the Soviet cavalry-mechanised group swept on through Lepel and reached the upper Berezina unopposed. By midday, combat engineers had deployed a heavy-duty bridge and parts of III Guards Mechanised Corps began to cross to the west bank.

Further to the east, other elements of Fourth Army were still struggling to withdraw. Generalleutnant Vincenz Müller, commander of XII Corps, reported to Tippelskirch that his divisions had suffered heavy losses both from the constant fighting and from having to abandon much of their equipment. The line of the Drut River had already been pierced in several places and was clearly no longer tenable, but it was essential to hold the river until all German units had crossed to the west bank. It took most of 29 June for the most exposed units – 78th Sturm Division, 260th Infantry Division, and 25th Panzergrenadier Division – to pull back over the river. Communications were now badly disrupted. Late on 29 June Tippelskirch received a brief message from Völckers, commander of XXVII Corps: he was attempting to reach the Berezina River at Chernyevka, to the north of Berezino, but the Red Army had already reached the crossings. Instead, he was going to try to join the units gathered in Berezino and attempt to cross there. It was the last message that Tippelskirch received from XXVII Corps for nearly five days, and the message told only part of the story – most of 78th Sturm Division was still to the east of the Drut River.[6] Schünemann, who had taken command of XXXIX Panzer Corps after the death of Martinek, was in one of the columns of vehicles attempting to reach Berezino when he came under air attack and was killed. He had been in command for barely a day; his corps had effectively ceased to exist.

In the south, Vormann – who had replaced Jordan and was now in the headquarters of Ninth Army – attempted to make sense of what was happening on the battlefield. It seemed that the Red Army had a profusion of tempting options for further advances. A thrust towards the north along the valley of the Berezina would place Soviet troops in the rear of Fourth Army, but this was regarded as an unlikely option as the Red Army units already operating against Fourth Army needed little assistance; if anything, such a thrust would simply add to the congestion on the roads of the region. A thrust directly towards Minsk with the intention of linking up with the Soviet units advancing on the city from the northeast was a more likely threat, as was a renewed drive to the west, driving Second Army away to the south and tearing wider the gap on the southern flank of Ninth Army. Until it became clearer which posed the greater threat, Vormann decided to hold back the assembling units of 12th Panzer Division – it was his only means of exerting any influence on the course of events. The fact that 1st Belarusian Front had sufficient strength to pursue both a drive towards Minsk and an attack towards the west at the same time does not seem to have featured in German thinking.

Meanwhile, the remnants of the German divisions that had been cut off in Bobruisk attempted to break out to the northwest early on 29 June. A group that was formed largely of the surviving armoured vehicles of 20th Panzer Division reached Golynka, ten miles northwest of Bobruisk, and was spotted by Luftwaffe reconnaissance aircraft. There was general relief in the headquarters of Ninth Army, but this was replaced by consternation when a major Soviet column of about 100 tanks and trucks was spotted not far away. Without any radio contact to the retreating columns, Vormann could only wait for further reconnaissance reports. Air attacks on the Soviet column were ordered but few planes were available. In the early evening, the German armoured group, now reported to be reduced to six tanks and ten other vehicles, was reported as having reached the area to the northeast of Osipovichi. A substantial column of German infantry was close behind.

Another German column managed to reach Osipovichi, marching along the road from Bobruisk. The defences here consisted of the usual muddle of improvised battalions of rear area personnel and stragglers, gathered under the command of Generalleutnant Max Lindig, the senior artillery officer at the headquarters of Army Group Centre. But even though elements of 12th Panzer

Division had now arrived in Osipovichi and took control of the exhausted men retreating from Bobruisk, the town of Talka, 15 miles to the west, was reported to be encircled by Soviet troops. These were elements of Pliev's cavalry-mechanised group; other cavalry units were already in Slutsk, further to the southwest. Here, they encountered increasing resistance and, as was often the case with relatively lightly armed troops such as cavalry or paratroopers, the Soviet forces were brought to a halt. Pliev promptly dispatched a tank regiment to support the cavalry, but it would not arrive until the following morning. Meanwhile, Soviet troops that had kept up the pressure on the Bobruisk perimeter throughout the night now pressed into the city, securing the urban area by mid-morning.

At several times during 29 June, Model had conversations with Zeitzler and other senior figures. In a manner that was characteristic of his behaviour when he commanded first Army Group North, then Army Group North Ukraine, he strove to secure reinforcements for his command with energy that, whilst commendable, showed a degree of disregard for the needs of other sectors. Zeitzler promised him a number of small formations as well as 28th Jäger Division and 7th Panzer Division from Army Group North Ukraine. The status of Polotsk was also discussed at length. Both Army Group North and Army Group Centre wanted to abandon the city so that Army Group North could pull back to a shorter line and thus release forces with which the gap to Army Group Centre could be repaired; in the evening, Hitler agreed, but on the proviso that Polotsk was regarded as another fortress. This decision effectively ensured that the number of men who could be released by the withdrawal would be lower than would otherwise have been the case.

With the Germans in such disarray, *Stavka* urged the Red Army units on to take full advantage. Bagramian's 1st Baltic Front was to push hard through Polotsk and head west while the other three Fronts converged on Minsk. Despite tough resistance from the German I Corps on the southern flank of Army Group North's Sixteenth Army, the leading units of Fourth Shock Army advanced steadily and by the end of 30 June they were within ten miles of Polotsk. A little to the south, Chistiakov's Sixth Guards Army – which had penetrated some distance to the southwest of Polotsk – now turned north and reached a similar distance from the city. For General Carl Hilpert, the commander of the German I Corps, there was no question of an energetic attack towards the south to try to restore contact with Third Panzer Army; he had his hands full preventing his corps from being rolled up and driven towards the northwest. Bagramian's exploitation force, I Tank Corps, had reached Vetrino on 29 June but despite this impressive advance, it was running behind schedule; the plans drawn up by

Bagramian and *Stavka* had expected the tanks to reach this area two days earlier. Bagramian now ordered Butkov to continue his exploitation on two axes: the bulk of the corps was to continue pushing west to reach the town of Luzhki, while a single tank brigade was to strike northwest and reach Disna on the Daugava River before the German I Corps could extend its southern flank far enough to protect the town.[7] This required an advance of up to 36 miles but was largely into open space with few German units in the area. By the end of 30 June, the T-34s of 159th Tank Brigade had seized Disna and the bridge over the Daugava River. The southern flank of the German I Corps in Polotsk was now badly outflanked.

The westward push by I Tank Corps was less successful, with a combination of terrain difficulties and long supply lines across an area choked with traffic. What remained of the German IX Corps – the northern flank of Tippelskirch's Third Panzer Army – was withdrawing towards the west, and German accounts describe the Soviet pursuit as slow and cautious, far from what *Stavka* was demanding.[8] The German Sixteenth Army had been ordered to move 132nd Infantry Division into the gap between Army Group North and Army Group South and the division now found its units divided into two groups by the Soviet thrust to Disna. Nonetheless, this offered an opportunity for a counterattack: the southern half of the division, reinforced by a regiment of troops from a Latvian SS division, was ordered to try to attack towards the northeast, while the rest of the division attacked towards the southwest with support from an assault gun brigade. It would take at least a day for the forces to deploy, and in the meantime Soviet rifle battalions continued to hurry forward to reinforce the tanks in Disna.

On the southern flank of IX Corps, the Germans could do nothing to stop the Red Army from surging forward over the Berezina River. Beloborodov's Forty-Third Army reported slackening German resistance as the broken Wehrmacht units reeled back. Beloborodov recorded the advance with satisfaction:

> The commanders of our leading units reported that the enemy's morale had been severely undermined. 'It's noteworthy,' they reported, 'that the Fascists have a significant and ever-increasing fear of encirclement, which creates good conditions for bold manoeuvre by our troops right down to company level.' There were cases when, after an unsuccessful counterattack, enemy units simply scattered and their officers couldn't gather together their soldiers.
>
> The panicked mood of the Fascist infantry also infected the artillery that supported it. Captured gunners told us that their observation posts were not moving forward into the foremost infantry line, as required by their regulations,

but instead were located behind it, up to 300m back. As a consequence, observation [of artillery fire] worsened and direct contact with infantry commanders was lost. The effectiveness of artillery fire dropped sharply, which in turn had a negative effect on the resilience of the infantry.

In general, the combat activity of enemy artillery was undermined at all levels. The retreat, which often turned into a general rout, and the loss of vehicles and ammunition depots, also had an impact and in our zone the consumption of artillery ammunition by the German Third Panzer Army on many days was almost zero. The non-stop retreat and poor reconnaissance gave the enemy no opportunity for accurate mapping both of their combat formations and ours.[9]

It is a measure of how far the Red Army had come that commanders down to company level were able to use their initiative to take advantage of the growing disorder in German ranks. In earlier phases of the war, such opportunities had been squandered either by waiting for approval from higher commands or by wasting energy and men in costly frontal attacks. German defensive tactics made extensive use of artillery to break up enemy attacks, and the disruption of such fire support had a serious degrading effect on the ability of any improvised line to hold firm.

Saucken, commander of the ad hoc group that included 5th Panzer Division, had made no attempt to hide his disdain for Gottberg's group and its unsuitability for front-line combat; he also regarded the so-called anti-partisan activities of the SS formation as ineffective and counterproductive. Gottberg also showed little pleasure in being placed under Saucken's control and contacted higher authorities via the SS chain of command, refusing to be subordinated to Saucken. For the moment, his group was left as an independent unit, and whilst Saucken might have had doubts about the fighting ability of Gottberg and his men, this new arrangement nonetheless represented a weakening of *Gruppe von Saucken* and made supply issues more complex.

After the near-complete destruction of Schünemann's panzer corps near Mogilev, *Gruppe von Saucken* was now renamed XXXIX Panzer Corps. Saucken had no staff and for the moment had to borrow officers and radio equipment from 5th Panzer Division. The leading Soviet units were now pressing into Borisov, where a panzergrenadier regiment from 5th Panzer Division was holding a small bridgehead over the Berezina. The commander of the regiment described the intense fighting:

The enemy tried with all his resources to enter the town during the night [of 29–30 June]. Without regard for his losses, he stubbornly dispatched tanks to

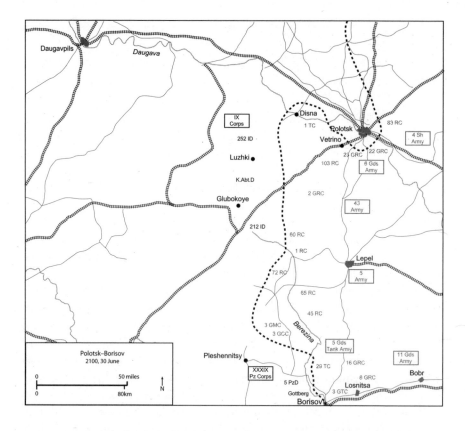

Polotsk–Borisov
2100, 30 June

0 — 50 miles
0 — 80km

N

roar into the city at a hellish pace along the main highway. There was an intense thunder of *Panzerfaust* rounds, *Panzerschreck* shots, and other defensive weapons. As a result the enemy tanks that had broken through were dealt with using close-quarters weapons either in or at the edge of the city. The fires blazing outside Borisov gave plenty of illumination for aiming at targets.[10]

The attacks were by the leading elements of Fifth Guards Tank Army. Increasingly under pressure to deliver results, Rotmistrov was throwing his armour forward in an attempt to make up for lost time but the troops of 5th Panzer Division were a far more formidable prospect than the broken German infantry units that were still streaming back from the east. In anticipation of its use in the expected Soviet attack on Army Group North Ukraine, Decker's panzer division was close to full strength and its panzergrenadiers were well equipped with *Panzerfaust* and *Panzerschreck* anti-tank weapons. These – a single-shot weapon and a German equivalent of the American bazooka respectively – were easily capable of dealing with tanks at close range, and attempts by Rotmistrov's tanks to penetrate into Borisov with inadequate infantry support were repeatedly beaten off. During 30 June, the attacks continued as more tanks and infantry were thrown at Borisov and with Soviet units beginning to move past the city to the north and south, Decker ordered his troops to pull back that evening. Even while the troops of 5th Panzer Division were heavily engaged, Gottberg's SS personnel were busy killing local civilians on the pretext that they had aided the enemy.

A clear indicator of the growing disintegration of German units still struggling to hold back the Red Army is the number of eponymous battlegroups that began to appear in Wehrmacht reports. Generalleutnant Hermann Flörke, commander of 14th Infantry Division, had managed to extract much of his command from the northern flank of the German attempts to hold the line of the Drut River and now led a mixture of his division's survivors, rear area personnel who had been gathered together in improvised battalions, and stragglers from other divisions. The force formed up on the southern flank of Saucken's group, on the Berezina River; the rest of 14th Infantry Division together with the survivors of 299th Infantry Division were gathered together a little further downstream, holding a small bridgehead across the river at Zhukovets in the hope of providing other retreating German units with an escape route. One of those formations was 110th Infantry Division, and by nightfall its rearguard was still holding back the pursuing Soviet forces at Somry, about 18 miles northeast of the Zhukovets bridgehead. Tippelskirch had no contact with the rest of XXVII Corps and could only hope that more groups would manage to fight their way west in the next day or two. What remained of the original XXXIX Panzer Corps – largely elements of *Feldherrnhalle* and 337th Infantry Division – was reported to be pulling back along the highway from Mogilev to Berezino, but was still 15 miles east of the town and was heavily assailed from north, east, and south.

By comparison with the formations to the north, XII Corps was in better shape, holding a more or less continuous line to the south of the Minsk–Berezino highway and falling back in good order. Nonetheless, the hard-pressed troops could do little to stop Soviet armoured forces from bypassing them and heading east. Late on 30 June, corps headquarters informed Tippelskirch that at least 50 Soviet tanks had slipped past the northern flank of the corps and were heading east towards the Berezina crossings. Other Soviet troops were already approaching Berezino from the south and a combination of artillery fire and air attacks repeatedly damaged the vital bridge in the town.

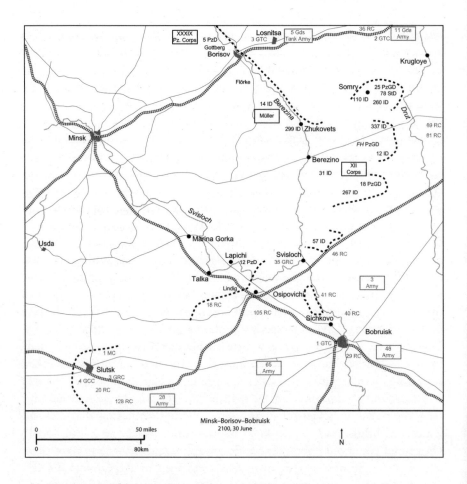

Minsk–Borisov–Bobruisk
2100, 30 June

A signal from Tippelskirch late on 30 June clearly illustrates the state of Fourth Army:

> The major decline in combat strength and the battles on two separate battlefields in the Army's sector make it necessary for all troops deployed south of Chernyavka [on the Berezina, about seven miles north of Berezino], inclusive of VI Corps, to be placed under a single command.
>
> Under the leadership of General Vincenz Müller, these units will therefore form *Gruppe General Müller*. This order is to be implemented immediately.
>
> General Müller will be responsible for ensuring that elements of XXXIX Panzer Corps that are extracted as a result of this reorganisation are pulled back by the fastest routes and sent to *Gruppe von Saucken* via Minsk.[11]

Finding a route by which the survivors of XXXIX Panzer Corps could be routed to Minsk and thence to Saucken's command was far from straightforward. The huge column of German formations waiting to cross the river at Berezino came under constant attack. Vehicles were abandoned due to lack of fuel, and overworked military police units were fully stretched trying to pull these obstructions from the highway. The difficult process of conducting a withdrawal under attack was greatly worsened by the failure of the Germans to organise an orderly withdrawal of non-combatant units in advance. When the Wehrmacht had advanced through this area in 1941, it had rapidly handed over control of conquered regions to the multiple German occupation authorities and had retained control of only a relatively narrow belt immediately behind the front line. As the Red Army slowly drove the Germans back to the west, there was huge reluctance by those occupation authorities to hand back control to the military, not least because Hitler's repeated insistence on obdurate defence meant that any precautionary evacuation might attract the Führer's wrath as a manifestation of defeatism. This was further reinforced by the quasi-Darwinian system of competition that Hitler had encouraged, with different agencies having overlapping and competing interests; to give up some of those interests ran the risk of losing status and power in the distorted world of Nazi Germany. But now, with the Red Army pouring west, it was long past time for all of these organisations to leave. Had they done so in a timely fashion, the Wehrmacht would have faced less difficulty in moving its forces; instead, military traffic competed with the numerous occupation units for precious road space and crossings. Soviet aircraft were constantly overhead, bombing and strafing with little or no interference from Luftwaffe fighters.

The German LIII Corps had been completely destroyed in Vitebsk and a similar fate seemed increasingly likely for Fourth Army's units to the west of Mogilev, as Tippelekirch's headquarters reported:

> Due to insufficient information about the situation of the neighbouring armies, the Army cannot judge whether there is a risk that the enemy will create another encirclement by pincer attacks meeting somewhere in the Minsk area. The large gap on the right wing to Third Panzer Army suggests that the advance of strong enemy forces on Minsk, especially from the north, cannot be prevented. The extraordinarily complete air superiority of enemy air forces, hitherto unimaginable for Eastern Front combatants, is resulting in particularly heavy losses, and the enemy's numerical strength in tanks and the constant threats to the flanks and rear of our troops as a result of contact with neighbouring armies being lost has led not only to a considerable reduction in combat capability but also to a sharp

drop in morale. Losses of heavy weapons are very high. The difficult terrain to the east of the Berezina, through which the units fighting their way westwards are penetrating, resulted in extremely heavy losses of motor vehicles and valuable materiel. The casualties among senior officers are appalling: XXXIX Panzer Corps has lost two commanders in 24 hours. Only a few formations are still under the firm control of their commanders.[12]

To the south of Tippelskirch's army, it was now clear to Vormann that his opponents were indeed pursuing both of the operational objectives that he had identified – a thrust towards Minsk while continuing to push towards the west. All he had available was 12th Panzer Division with several improvised groups supporting it; he had no contact on either flank with neighbouring armies and his weak forces were themselves often isolated from each other. Purely to buy some breathing space, 12th Panzer Division launched a limited counterattack towards the southeast along the Minsk–Bobruisk highway. For the moment, Soviet attacks towards Minsk were halted but Müller, the division commander, knew that his positions had completely open flanks and it was only a matter of time before he was forced to pull back unless further reinforcements arrived. For the moment, it was essential to try to hold out in the hope that the remnants of Ninth Army might be able to fight their way to safety and during the morning there was radio contact with Hoffmeister, commander of XLI Panzer Corps, whose forces were still intact and had concentrated at Svisloch, about 16 miles to the east of 12th Panzer Division. Hoffmeister reported that despite having little food, ammunition, or fuel, morale remained good. A later report gave a grimmer, more detailed picture. Since leaving Bobruisk, Hoffmeister's group had suffered over 12,000 casualties. Several senior officers, including Generalleutnant Adolf Hamann, who had been nominated as the commander of 'Fortress Bobruisk', were reported to be dead.

This last detail proved to be incorrect. Hamann had been commandant of Orel and then Bryansk before taking command of 383rd Infantry Division on the eve of *Bagration*. He was then designated as fortress commandant and led a group of soldiers who attempted to break out at the same time as Hoffmeister's group. Hamann's men were rapidly overwhelmed, but he was taken prisoner. He was then interrogated by his captors:

> Our general asked him: 'Why didn't you commit suicide, Herr Hamann? After all, in your own orders you described being a captive of the Soviet Union as a betrayal of your nation, your Fatherland. You argued that Bolshevik captivity resulted in inevitable and painful death. Why did you prefer captivity for yourself?' Hamann gave a wolfish look and remained silent.[13]

Hamann had been named by the Soviet Union in September 1943 as one of those responsible for mass killings of civilians in the various cities he had governed. He was put on trial after the end of the war and charged with involvement in the killings of 96,000 Soviet prisoners of war and 130,000 civilians, including by the use of mustard gas and by driving civilians across minefields to clear them. He was executed in Bryansk in December 1945.[14]

With up to 30,000 poorly supplied German soldiers attempting to escape from Svisloch, 12th Panzer Division was ordered to make an attack towards them regardless of the threats to the division's flanks. In tough fighting, Müller's troops had managed to reach Lapichi, and he replied to Vormann that he could make a further attempt with most of his division the following morning, but the urgency of the situation was such that Vormann told him to attack immediately. As a consequence, all that could be spared was a single battalion of half-track mounted panzergrenadiers under the command of Hauptmann Gustav-Adolf Blancbois supported by a company of Pz.IVs. They formed up overnight, rearming and refuelling in preparation.

Whilst rescuing the remnants of *Gruppe Hoffmeister* was an important task and took up most of his attention, Vormann continued to receive bad news. Soviet armour was detected massing to the south; these were elements of the Soviet Sixty-Fifth Army, but even more worrying developments were reported further to the southwest. Here, Pliev's cavalry-mechanised group had reached the city of Slutsk and attacked it from three directions early on 30 June. Pliev described how his men had to overcome German infantry supported by artillery and tanks, but at first the German defences consisted almost entirely of improvised and poorly equipped rear area units. By midday, the city was in Soviet hands. Even if the position held by 12th Panzer Division continued to hold, it was seriously outflanked. From Slutsk, Pliev had a variety of tempting options: he could turn north into the deep flank of the German Ninth Army; or he could continue towards the west and the city of Baranovichi, astride the major road and rail link from Minsk to Brest and Warsaw.[15]

Further German reinforcements were arriving. From Army Group North Ukraine, 4th Panzer Division had started the lengthy process of moving its forces to the central sector, where it would be placed directly in Pliev's path:

> The first elements reached the central sector on 28 June in order to be deployed against the great Russian offensive. It took four days for all the transportation to be completed because partisans repeatedly blew up segments of railway line.
>
> As soon as we detrained we were targeted by Russian ground attack aircraft.[16]

Throughout the region, partisan activity had increased. Even small attacks on railway lines proved to be very disruptive – the last trains bringing 12th Panzer Division to its new area of operations were delayed several times by damaged lines – and hit-and-run attacks on isolated German units added to delays in moving troops. Just a couple of weeks previously, the Germans had been congratulating themselves on the success of their latest anti-partisan sweeps; the escalation of attacks in the last week of June shows that despite causing considerable disruption, the German measures had little lasting impact on the ability of the partisans to conduct operations.

The infantry formations that were being transferred from other sectors were also beginning to arrive. Fourth Army was to receive 170th Infantry Division from Army Group North, while Ninth Army received 28th Jäger Division from Army Group North Ukraine. The latter was to be deployed to defend the gaping sector to the south of Minsk, and was ordered by Army Group South to detrain across a frontage of 21 miles to the southwest of the city, with the expectation that it would be able to intercept the Soviet forces attempting to close in on Minsk from the south, acting with support from 4th Panzer Division and a Hungarian cavalry division. In the meantime, Model made good use of the high esteem that Hitler had for him. He contacted *OKH* to discuss further plans, stressing that the defence of Minsk as a fortress would require at least two divisions and in the absence of such forces, there was no point in declaring the city a fortress. The arrival of fresh divisions would allow a defensive line to be created to the west of Minsk, but without these, the rapid Soviet advance made it highly unlikely that the city could be held in any event or that a defensive line could be established – even if the broken formations of Fourth and Ninth Armies succeeded in reaching safety, they would have little combat value without extensive re-equipment and replenishment.

Whilst German commanders shared their misgivings about the possibility of restoring the situation, their Soviet equivalents wrestled with the problems of success. The first week of *Bagration* had shattered the German front line and there was now an opportunity to drive the Wehrmacht far to the west. If the various German units that had been bypassed could be destroyed, it might be impossible for the Germans to create a solid front line, in which case *Bagration* would create a war-winning situation. The difficulties centred on ensuring that momentum was sustained: fuel and ammunition had to be brought forward, German stragglers had to be mopped up, and the exploitation forces had to continue their pressure. On 1 July, I Tank Corps in the north expanded its modest bridgehead over the Daugava River near Disna, but the main centre of attention was Polotsk. Bagramian had moved to the headquarters of Fourth Shock Army to oversee the assault on the city, which was made by XXII and XXIII Guards Rifle Corps in the early morning:

> The enemy made constant counterattacks. Every house had to be wrenched from his control by the guardsmen. In support of them we deployed a large number of ground attack aircraft. Under the massive blows against artillery and mortar positions, enemy fire slackened and the enemy had to pause his counterattacks. Bombers and ground attack aircraft struck at traffic on the railway line between Daugavpils and Polotsk and thus hindered the Fascists from bringing up more reinforcements.[17]

A closer examination of this account suggests that despite throwing four rifle divisions at Polotsk, Bagramian faced a tough task in overwhelming the German defenders; moreover, whilst his aircraft may have been disrupting rail and road movement to the west of the city, the Germans had already begun to withdraw from the area and the traffic that came under attack was unlikely to represent any reinforcements.

Third Panzer Army was effectively reduced to just IX Corps with 252nd Infantry Division on the northern flank, *Korps Abteilung D* in the centre, and 212th Infantry Division on the southern flank; it had no contact with Sixteenth Army to the north or Fourth Army to the south. Under heavy pressure on both flanks, Wuthmann managed to pull his exhausted troops back a short distance without any further major losses, but this was largely because he was no longer feeling the full weight of the Soviet attack. To his north, Chistiakov's Sixth Guards Army was moving forward through the gap between Third Panzer Army and Sixteenth Army towards Daugavpils, and to his south the Soviet Fifth Army crossed the upper Berezina River and advanced into the area to the north of Minsk. To make matters even more difficult for Wuthmann, he received reports that up to 12,000 partisans were now active in his rear area, greatly reducing the choice of roads that could be used for his men to pull back. The road junction at Glubokoye became the key point; it had to be held as long as possible.

During the night of 30 June–1 July, *Gruppe von Saucken* abandoned Borisov and pulled back a few miles to the southwest, repeatedly fending off sharp probes from Rotmistrov's Fifth Guards Tank Army. The northern flank of the position around Borisov had been badly outflanked and 5th Panzer Division was ordered to protect the railway line running northwest from Minsk. A group of Soviet tanks with infantry support was spotted moving towards the small town of Krasne and the division's *Feldersatzbataillon* ('field replacement battalion', a unit that received replacement drafts and prepared them for assignment to other parts of the division) was dispatched as a blocking force. Motorised transport was available for just one company, with the rest of the battalion moving on foot.

For the soldiers of Galitsky's Eleventh Guards Army, the capture of Borisov and crossing the Berezina was a significant moment:

> It should be noted that when crossing the Berezina, the army's engineers, led by Major General [Vitaly Ivanovich] Zverev, managed to construct temporary crossings and then bridges in difficult conditions and under enemy fire, ensuring the rapid transit of our troops. The army had reached the Berezina and crossed it in eight days rather than the ten envisaged in the operational plan …
>
> It was impossible not to recall the historical events of the Patriotic War of 1812, when Russian soldiers under the command of Kutuzov inflicted a final defeat on Napoleon's army on the Berezina! And now this river was once more an arena for the defeat of the invaders …
>
> The commander of the Front visited us. After listening to my brief report on the disposition of the army's troops he suggested that I accompany him to the Berezina crossings at Borisov. The route there from my command post led along the Minsk highway. I saw that on both sides of the road in the forests and copses there were numerous columns of camouflaged tanks, assault guns, fuel trucks, and other vehicles. It was Fifth Guards Tank Army. 'This is the second day they've spent like this,' said Ivan Danilovich [Cherniakhovsky], frowning. 'But the leading units of the tank army approached the Berezina on the evening of 29 June when the bridge in Borisov was still intact. Only one tank managed to penetrate into the city. The bridge was mined and the Germans promptly destroyed it …'
>
> In his words, I could sense the irritation of the inaction of 400 formidable tanks and assault guns, resting here near the Berezina.[18]

Further to the east, the disparate survivors of Fourth Army continued their attempts to escape. Under constant attack, 110th Infantry Division reached the bridgehead at Zhukovets in mid-morning and reported that the remnants of 25th Panzergrenadier Division were encircled in Shepelevichi, some 28 miles to the northeast. Müller's group was a little to the south of the panzergrenadier division, attempting to force its way along the main highway to Minsk from Mogilev, and reached the Berezina River during the afternoon. With fuel and ammunition almost exhausted, Müller sent a radio message that he hoped to gather his remaining men on the Berezina over the next day before crossing to the west bank; even after achieving this, he would still be several miles from safety. Tippelskirch made increasingly urgent requests for the Luftwaffe to deliver supplies by air and reported that even if these retreating formations were able to pull back, they were badly outflanked from the south where the Soviet Fiftieth Army was threatening to roll up the German line by pushing towards the northwest.

A Soviet thrust isolated the bulk of 78th Sturm Division from the rest of *Gruppe Müller* but Traut's soldiers were able to fight their way through to the Berezina late on 30 June, where they found that the bridge they were seeking had already been destroyed. Fortunately, a ford was located and the tired men of the leading group began to splash across and located another small wooden bridge close by, but most of the division remained a little to the east, seeking shelter in a small village. Here, it found itself involved in heavy fighting the following day, as the adjutant of one of the division's regiments later described:

In the early morning of 1 July the Russians probed forward. Then they attacked with powerful support from heavy weapons from the east against our thin lines. Heavy artillery strikes and air attacks accompanied the ground attack. The division had the difficult task as rearguard to hold its positions until 1000 in order to give the rest of the group time to slip away from woodland to the west, where they had been blocked by burning ammunition trucks and barely passable stretches of road. Our mission was carried out in heavy combat. Slowly the defensive line grew narrower …

After a forced march we succeeded in reaching the woodland near Zhukovets despite repeated Russian attacks and attempts to encircle us and constant airstrikes. Late in the evening it grew quiet and we were able to find the road to the crossing point. The congestion on the small tracks through the woodland was so great that men had to wait for hours just to move forward a few metres before coming to a halt again.

Most of the assault guns, Tigers and self-propelled guns had been blown up long ago due to fuel shortages. Next to the vehicles overloaded with countless wounded and those unable to walk, an endless column of horse-drawn carts of different divisions and other formations tried to push past, seemingly oblivious to what was happening. Now, on the Berezina crossing, all carts and slow-moving motor vehicles were stuck and were gathered together in assembly areas. This was the only way to keep the badly damaged, barely passable bridge free for troops and the combat vehicles that were still with us to cross.[19]

Despite the undoubted successes that had been achieved, the Red Army leadership continued to have concerns about some aspects of its performance. Vasilevsky later wrote:

> [I was concerned about] the continuing relatively slow pace of advance of Fifth Guards Tank Army. When it was fording the Berezina in the direction of Borisov the army was in line with or even behind both II Guards Tank Corps [part of Eleventh Guards Army] and a whole range of army formations. On 1 July, the Front commander [Cherniakhovsky] and I left for the Berezina in order to find out the situation on the spot. A quick glimpse of the terrain between the Bobr and Berezina Rivers testified to the fierce fighting which the tank army had had to engage in with the German 5th Panzer Division. Bridges at Borisov had been destroyed … Fifth Guards Tank Army, which had a large number of tanks on the west bank, reckoned on completing the crossing only at night on 2 July and reaching Ostroshitsky Gorodok some 18km to the northeast of Minsk by the end of that day. I assigned Rotmistrov the task of liberating Minsk by the end of 2 July.[20]

In the southern sector, another bypassed group of German soldiers continued to struggle towards the west, in this case from the disaster that had enveloped Ninth Army at Bobruisk. In an attempt to rescue *Gruppe Hoffmeister*, 12th Panzer Division commenced its attack long before dawn on 1 July towards Svisloch. At first, the thrust encountered no Soviet forces and reached the village of Malinovka, about a third of the distance to Svisloch, without incident; thereafter, it came up against increasing resistance. Nevertheless, it advanced to within a mile of Svisloch before it was driven back, but managed to make contact with some of the retreating remnants of Ninth Army. The report from Blancbois on his battalion's actions described how his men managed to link up with escaping German soldiers from Bobruisk:

> Whereas until now only small groups of stragglers had been sighted marching to the west in the area, the commander was now informed that an endless column of soldiers from Bobruisk had reached the retreat road at the junction at Malinovka. An officer was ordered to go to the junction to inform the stragglers of the overall situation. When he got there, he saw a poignant but also inspiring scene: in the dust and shimmering haze of the sweltering midday heat, the men from Bobruisk streamed past in a never-ending procession. The hardships and ordeals of the last week were deeply engraved upon their faces. For days they had received almost nothing to eat other than

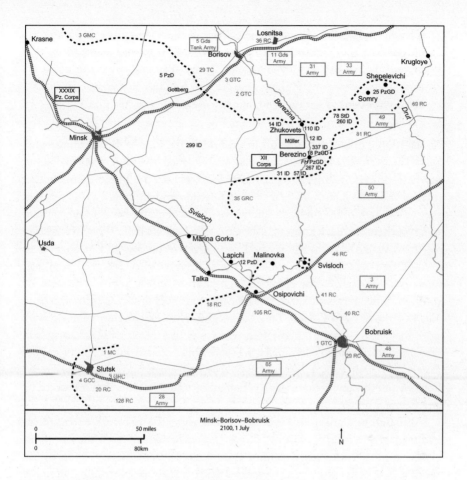

Minsk–Borisov–Bobruisk
2100, 1 July

some dry bread, which was often mouldy. They had to quench their burning thirst with muddy water from the swamps. Chased day and night by the Bolsheviks, they could not permit themselves any opportunity for rest. They had to stay alert no matter how tired they were to avoid being taken by surprise. Many had lost their boots when swimming across small rivers and now ran for many kilometres along stony, dusty roads with rags and straw wrapped around their feet.

The officer sent by the battalion called out to them, 'An armoured battlegroup from 12th Panzer Division is over there and will get you out. There's another 20km to the German main defensive line! If you've made it this far, you'll also make it over this last distance!' The words didn't fail to make an impression. Courage and the will to live appeared once more in their hard faces and with renewed strength they continued to move forward. The seriously wounded looked up gratefully with sunken, feverish eyes and supported by their comrades they dragged themselves past without a word. The battalion medic took care of the most serious cases, some of whom wore the same bandages on their wounds that had been put there a week ago and were now dirty and loose.[21]

About 15,000 exhausted survivors limped down the road to the west, protected by the panzergrenadier battalion that had rescued them. A group of seven surviving officers of 20th Panzer Division, led by Kessel, the division commander, reached the headquarters of 12th Panzer Division and requested a truck so that they could seek other surviving members of the division; Müller and his staff watched them drive back towards the east, wondering whether they would ever see them again. Most of the rescued men were weaponless and in no state to fight. Often effectively surrounded, the panzergrenadier battalion that had made possible their escape commenced a fighting retreat towards the west. At the same time, another panzergrenadier battalion was driven step by step from Talka by the Soviet I Guards Tank Corps and its accompanying infantry; both sides took heavy losses, but the Red Army was in a better position to sustain casualties. Soviet air attacks on Marina Gorka immediately in the rear of *Gruppe Lindig* and 12th Panzer Division added to the chaos and casualties. To the northeast of this town, there was a gap of at least 30 miles that wasn't covered by any German units.

Although one group of German soldiers from the Bobruisk encirclement had managed to escape, most of *Gruppe Hoffmeister* remained to the east; at its closest approach, the relief column from 12th Panzer Division came within about a mile of the exhausted German infantry. They were forced to surrender later that day. In total, about 24,000 Germans were captured in the fighting in Bobruisk and during the attempted breakout. When he was captured, Hoffmeister bitterly denounced the 'amateurs' who had led Germany to disaster, and the generals who meekly obeyed them. He became a member of the *Nationalkomitee Freies Deutschland* and made a broadcast a few weeks later, criticising his fellow generals who failed to recognise the stupidity of Hitler and those around him. Despite making himself useful to his Soviet captors, he remained a prisoner after the war and died in a prison camp in the Ural Mountains in 1951.[22] In addition to Hoffmeister, the Soviet forces captured two division commanders, Generalmajor Joachim Engel (45th Infantry Division) and Generalmajor Alexander Conrady (36th Infantry Division). Conrady also cooperated with the Soviet authorities, but was charged with war crimes and sentenced to 25 years' hard labour. He was released in 1955. Engel showed little willingness to join men like Hoffmeister and Conrady in their attacks on the Nazi regime, and he died in captivity in 1948.

Although Rokossovsky's 1st Belarusian Front was attempting to advance directly towards Minsk from the southeast and simultaneously thrusting west towards Slutsk and Baranovichi, the drawn-out ordeal of Hoffmeister's men had a disrupting effect. Eliminating the remnants of Ninth Army tied up large numbers of Soviet units and the roads to the northwest of Bobruisk were choked with wrecked and abandoned vehicles and the corpses of horses and men, and Rokossovsky now urged Sixty-Fifth Army to accelerate its advance. In the meantime, it was the push towards the west that caused most concern for Model and Vormann as it might give the Red Army the opportunity to outflank whatever defensive line they could cobble together. Soviet tanks and cavalry from Pliev's cavalry-mechanised group reached the outskirts of the town of Stolpce (now known as Stowbtsy), roughly midway between Minsk and Baranovichi, on 1 July. Vormann had raised the possibility of Soviet forces moving into this area the previous day but his suggestion of sending part of 12th Panzer Division to defend Stolpce had been overruled by Army Group Centre; he now sent a reproachful message to Model and during the evening of 1 July he ordered one of 12th Panzer Division's panzergrenadier battalions to move immediately to Stolpce, simply informing Model of his decision rather than seeking permission. The rest of the division, together with the neighbouring battlegroups, began to pull back towards Minsk and the west as darkness fell. The area was still teeming with men who had escaped from Bobruisk; tired and hungry, many lacked the strength to continue marching and attempted to enter buildings to find somewhere to sleep until they were driven out by energetic officers and military police.

As the first day of July came to a close, Model surveyed the wreckage of the army group that he had inherited. To the north, he had no contact with Sixteenth Army on the southern flank of Army Group North and Third Panzer Army was falling back towards Postavy and Lake Naroch. Between the southern flank of Reinhardt's army – essentially little more than IX Corps – there was a gap to *Gruppe von Saucken*, through which it was reported that the Soviet Fifth Army and accompanying cavalry-mechanised group were advancing steadily. Saucken's hotchpotch of improvised units, stiffened by the firepower of 5th Panzer Division, held a more or less continuous front line to the west of the Berezina, but there was a confused picture of the exact situation around Berezino where *Gruppe Müller* was believed to be attempting to escape to the west. Beyond this sector, there was a further gap to *Gruppe Lindig* and 12th Panzer Division, then yet another gap to the units of 4th Panzer Division and the

Hungarian cavalry units that were attempting to defend the Stolpce–Baranovichi sector. Model knew that 28th Jäger Division was being sent towards Stolpce and 170th Infantry Division was detraining to the northwest of Minsk; in addition, 7th Panzer Division was on the way and would shortly be joining it. In a telephone conversation with Lindemann, the commander of Army Group North, he learned that Hitler had refused a further request for the abandonment of Polotsk and had even ordered an attack towards the south from the city. Even if Army Group North could have released sufficient troops for such an attack, it would have faced superior enemy forces.

The stubborn resistance of the German forces in Polotsk continued overnight into 2 July. In many respects, this confirmed Bagramian's concerns about his northern flank and the importance of seizing this vital communications centre, in which the Germans could conceivably have attempted to concentrate sufficient forces to mount a major counterattack. Fighting in the city intensified after dawn, with the soldiers of XXIII Guards Rifle Corps clearing the urban centre south of the Daugava River. A wooden bridge across the river was only partially destroyed by the retreating Germans and the Soviet troops swiftly established a small bridgehead on the northern bank. But even if his northern flank was making heavy weather of storming Polotsk, Chistiakov could be more satisfied with the progress to the south where his Sixth Guards Army continued to advance into what was almost open space in the gap between the northern flank of Tippelskirch's Third Panzer Army and the southern flank of Sixteenth Army. While Beloborodov's Forty-Third Army continued to apply pressure on the German IX Corps' front, Chistiakov urged his units on towards the west. Satisfied that the capture of Polotsk would reduce the risk to his northern flank, Bagramian ordered Butkov's I Tank Corps to move through the gap being created by Sixth Guards Army and then to turn south into the rear of Third Panzer Army's paper-thin line. To all intents and purposes, 1st Baltic Front had achieved its objectives for *Bagration*. In cooperation with 3rd Belarusian Front, it had reduced the German Third Panzer Army to a weak corps, taken Vitebsk, and was about to take Polotsk.

Tippelskirch had hoped that IX Corps would be able to hold its positions at Glubokoye and that it might be possible for local counterattacks towards the north to go at least some way towards restoring contact with Army Group North, but the pressure from the east was unrelenting. The road junction at Glubokoye came under attack from powerful Soviet formations. To the south of IX Corps, the Germans had hoped that the swampy area to the east of Lake Naroch would prove to be a hindrance to the Red Army; instead, the Soviet Fifth Army moved

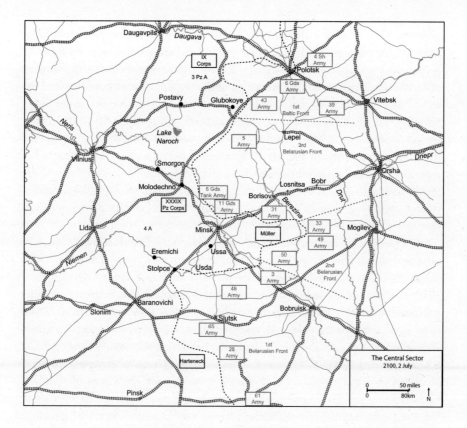

rapidly forward, aided by partisans who led the Soviet troops along the few firm routes through the area. Oslikovsky's cavalry-mechanised group carefully picked its way through the marshes and was close to Lake Naroch by the end of 2 July, operating perhaps 30 miles behind the southern flank of the German IX Corps. By early evening, the fighting around Glubokoye had reached the perimeter of the town. Generalleutnant Franz Sensfuss, commander of 212th Infantry Division, was ordered to detach some of his subunits and send them to the west to prevent Glubokoye from being completely surrounded. He sent a terse report to Tippelskirch that evening: 'My men are barefoot. I'm so stretched that I have to defend in a semi-circular perimeter. All sorts of fragmented units were sent to me by IX Corps, but they promptly fled.'[23]

Hurrying south from Estonia, the German 170th Infantry Division had originally been ordered to detrain in Minsk, but the threat to the city from the northeast was too great to be ignored. Generalleutnant Siegfried Hass was now ordered to take up positions in Molodechno instead with at least his leading regiment. Generalleutnant Hubert Lendle, formerly commander of 221st Security Division and currently awaiting a new assignment, was to form an eponymous battlegroup with the first of Hass' regiments together with elements of his old security division, an assault gun brigade, and a police battalion and use it to hold the line to the southeast of Molodechno. At the same time, Generalleutnant Eduard Metz, a senior artillery commander who had led 5th Panzer Division in 1943, was dispatched to Molodechno where he gathered together the remnants of 14th and 299th Infantry Divisions and another police regiment. It was a feeble force with which to oppose the northern flank of the Soviet Eleventh Guards Army, but Model promised to send him further reinforcements as quickly as he could organise them. Lendle's battlegroup was also subordinated to Metz's command.

Gruppe von Saucken was slowly fighting its way back from Borisov. Constantly criticised for his slow progress, Rotmistrov threw his tank corps at the lines of 5th Panzer Division with little effect; by the end of 2 July, the division's claimed 'kills' since its arrival on 27 June reached a total of 295 tanks. This is almost certainly a considerable over-estimate, in that many tanks that were seen to be hit might have been repaired quickly and returned to service, and on other occasions individual Soviet tanks were hit by several different German gunners, all of whom claimed a 'kill'. Nevertheless, 5th Panzer Division – supported by a battalion of Tiger tanks – was a tough opponent for the forces of Eleventh Guards Army and Fifth Guards Tank Army. In Krasne, on the northern flank of 5th Panzer Division, Major Wilhelm Drewes was in command of the division's field replacement battalion:

[Early on 2 July] in the distance we could already see a fire blazing before us and the smoke grew ever thicker. Gunfire could be heard in the distance. As we moved forward we saw trucks loaded with fuel and ammunition burning brightly on the road along a stretch of at least 300m. In order to get a good view of the situation we took up positions on the right of the road on a fairly steep slope. We quickly encountered two enemy scout cars to the northeast, shooting wildly. Three more Russian armoured cars pushed past the burning vehicles on the road towards us. A bold attack by my men and Hauptmann Voland's sappers put them out of action with close-range weapons. We were still taking fire from the two scout cars on the outskirts of the village.

As the fire died down at about 0800 we edged north towards the next village, Macole. I left two companies on the high ground south of the village and secured the northern outskirts with another company. In the absence of heavy weapons, I decided to unload two assault guns loaded on a railway flatcar. They were still able to fire but were no longer fully mobile. On this occasion, the congested railway lines were a benefit for us. Unfortunately, I couldn't move them forward …

At midday a gigantic cloud of dust at least 5km long appeared in the woodland before us. I knew that this augured a major Russian attack with tanks. I passed these observations immediately to the division's operations officer and requested armoured support … At 1500 Oberleutnant Nökel and his tank company rolled forward. We had barely moved into position when the spearhead of the Russian tanks moved out from the woodland along the road. They had to advance about 150m along the slightly elevated road to reach a small area of woodland …

Oberleutnant Nökel waved to the first four of our tanks and they took up positions. Meanwhile, the first two Russian tanks had disappeared into the woodland. The first salvo from our tanks was sufficient to set the following tanks ablaze. A major tank battle now developed in which our tanks had the advantage in the undulating terrain. During the afternoon, I was aware of 26 or 28 enemy tanks being shot up.[24]

For the moment, the German line running northwest from Minsk was holding, but 5th Panzer Division's reconnaissance battalion, scouting further to the northwest, reported that beyond Molodechno there were effectively no German defences and Soviet units were advancing freely. The Soviet thrust directly towards Minsk from the northeast was also moving closer. During the afternoon of 2 July, II Guards Tank Corps – originally part of Eleventh Guards Army but now reassigned to Thirty-First Army – reached and captured part of Smolevichi, just 22 miles from the centre of Minsk, but here it ran into a determined German rearguard that succeeded in destroying several tanks. Major General Aleksei Semenovich Burdeiny, the corps commander, angrily berated his subordinates for moving into the town without adequate reconnaissance, but the men were exhausted after fighting through the battles around Orsha, advancing to and over the Berezina, and now pushing on towards Minsk. Throughout this time, they had been involved in running battles with German groups attempting to pull back from Orsha and Mogilev as well as growing German resistance; supply lines were stretched, and most of the tank crews and their officers had been living and fighting in their vehicles without a pause since the beginning of *Bagration*. Nonetheless, Burdeiny ordered them on towards Minsk but although his reconnaissance battalion reported that there were only minimal German forces in the path of II Guards Tank Corps, there were further fierce exchanges of fire and a decision was made to wait until the following morning. In the meantime, supply columns struggled forward with vital fuel, ammunition, and food for the tank crews.[25]

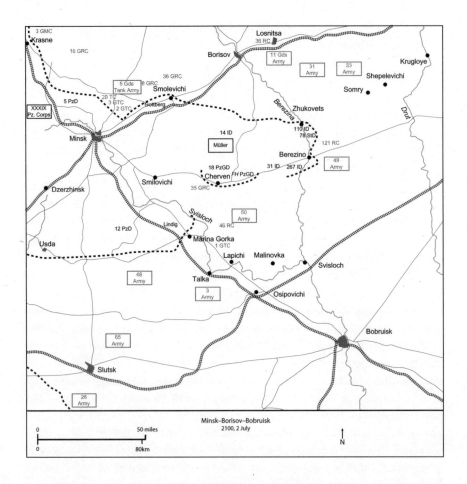

Minsk–Borisov–Bobruisk
2100, 2 July

0 _____ 50 miles

0 _____ 80km

N

Meanwhile, the long retreat of *Gruppe Müller* from Mogilev continued. The Soviet attack towards Minsk from the northeast had effectively turned the northern flank of Fourth Army and the best hope for the retreating units was to try to link up with German units before they pulled back into Minsk from the east, or to try to reach the area to the south of the city. By the evening of 2 July, some of Müller's survivors were reported to be perhaps six miles to the northeast of Minsk, but the rearguard, consisting of 78th Sturm Division, had only just crossed the Berezina River with the last soldiers reaching the west bank late on 2 July. The adjutant who had overseen the withdrawal of his regiment to the river noted that only 100 combatants of his unit remained with the division; gathering other stragglers, he organised two weak rifle companies, but the men had been without proper food for four days and had almost no ammunition.[26]

If they were to escape, it was essential that the German positions in Smolevichi continued to hold, but the growing pressure on *Gruppe von Saucken* to the northwest demanded urgent attention. If this line collapsed, the Red Army would be able to push on swiftly to and beyond the western frontiers of Belarus and even if the remnants of Fourth Army could be extracted via Minsk, they would face destruction in an even greater encirclement. Saucken discussed this with Model and Tippelskirch and the three men agreed: the protection of the line to the northwest was the greater priority. Those elements of 5th Panzer Division that were fighting in Smolevichi were ordered to withdraw and join the rest of the division to the northwest. *Gruppe von Gottberg*, the anti-partisan unit that had refused to be subordinated to Saucken, was left to hold the vital town for as long as possible. Sappers had already commenced the destruction of installations in Minsk during the previous night, and now stepped up their efforts.

Tippelskirch made one last attempt to get the remnants of his command to safety. He sent a signal to the units that had crossed the Berezina. A withdrawal was imminent and it was essential for them to reach Smolevichi as quickly as possible. The exhausted soldiers who had fought and marched back from Mogilev were near the end of both their physical and mental resources. Ammunition was almost completely expended; most hadn't eaten or slept properly for several days; and although morale and discipline were relatively good in the early phases of the retreat, both declined sharply after the soldiers reached the Berezina. They had expected to link up with strong German positions, but now found that they still faced a long march through an area where there were multiple Red Army units and large numbers of partisans. One of the few units that was still in relatively good shape, 110th Infantry Division, managed to cross the Berezina at Zhukovets during the early morning of 2 July; a little to the southwest, the remnants of XII Corps came under heavy attack in and around Pogost and the remnants of three divisions – *Feldherrnhalle*, 18th Panzergrenadier Division, and 337th Infantry Division – were forced into an almost circular defensive position on the main road that ran east to Smolevichi. An urgent signal was sent to Tippelskirch's headquarters: all remaining units would attempt to reach Smolevichi on 3 July, and it was essential to ensure that supplies were made available to them if they managed to reach their objective. Müller sent a further message that evening:

All … are confident and have the will to push through to Smolevichi. However, help from outside in terms of guiding our direction via constant radio messages about our and enemy positions in general is essential, as is contact by aerial reconnaissance and aerial supply.[27]

The Soviet thrust towards Minsk from the southeast – by Rokossovsky's 1st Belarusian Front – had been slowed by a combination of terrain difficulties and the need to overcome the German forces trapped in and around Bobruisk; moreover, the intervention of 12th Panzer Division had also checked progress. During 2 July, though, Gorbatov's Third Army steadily pushed *Gruppe Lindig* back towards Marina Gorka. Soviet tanks suddenly appeared at the town's railway station around midday, forcing a further German withdrawal. In any event, even if this position could be held, it was greatly outflanked to the south where Sixty-Fifth and Twenty-Eighth Armies, led by Pliev's cavalry-mechanised group, were streaming west almost unopposed. After taking Slutsk, Pliev was ordered to push on towards Baranovichi, a further 65 miles to the west. As they moved forward, the Soviet cavalry units came under increasing air attack – they were so far to the west that Soviet fighter formations struggled to provide them with adequate protection. In an attempt to reduce Luftwaffe interference, Pliev's officers ordered their men to light numerous campfires in the forest at night but then to move to new locations where fires were prohibited, in the hope that German bombers would hit the wrong locations.[28] During 2 July, the leading elements of the cavalry-mechanised group attacked the town of Stolpce, astride the main highway and railroad running from Minsk towards Brest and Warsaw.

Neither *Gruppe Lindig* nor 12th Panzer Division had good radio contact with Vormann at the headquarters of Ninth Army, and it wasn't until the evening of 2 July that a liaison officer reached Lindig with information about the overall situation. He confirmed the advance of Soviet units to the Minsk–Brest highway but also reported that 4th Panzer Division, 28th Jäger Division, and 1st Hungarian Cavalry Division would counterattack from the south towards the northeast. *Gruppe Lindig* was to take over the defence of the approaches to Minsk while 12th Panzer Division was dispatched to Stolpce. Both Army Group Centre and Ninth Army hoped that with panzer divisions making convergent attacks, the situation to the south and southwest of Minsk could yet be salvaged. But if his 4th Panzer Division was to attack in strength, Betzel needed fuel. Logistic support was completely disrupted and he had to beg for supplies from the Hungarian division. A small amount of gasoline was made available, sufficient only for half of Betzel's Panther tanks.[29]

Ultimately, sufficient supplies were secured to permit 4th Panzer Division to attack as planned. Peter Oberhuber was a driver in a reconnaissance platoon:

A company from 33rd Panzergrenadier Regiment attacked alongside our reconnaissance platoon. The regiment's two battalions were advancing on our right. In this manner we quickly reached the first village and the important

Baranovichi–Minsk railway line. We had to stop here for the time being to secure the regiment's flank while it moved further forward. We spread out along the edge of the village. It wasn't long before four Russian tanks approached over the bill beyond the railway line without seeing us.

We were well camouflaged and next to a house, and we allowed the Russians to come within 600m. We had loaded a round some time before. Ehebauer took aim calmly. In rapid succession, two shells left our gun – two hits! The T-34s were ablaze and their crews abandoned them. The third round was already loaded but I heard no shot. The gunner tried repeatedly because the other two T-34s were already moving off. We struggled hopelessly with the dud round. We opened the breech but the shell couldn't be ejected. We quickly pulled back behind the house. Loader, radio operator, and driver leapt from the tank, screwed together the cleaning rods and with all their might pushed the dud round from the barrel. With a new round loaded we edged back around the corner of the house. Just as the two T-34s were about to disappear behind the ridge, Ehebauer pulled the trigger. A cloud of black smoke immediately rose into the sky. We quickly drove forward and were able to knock out two anti-tank guns and rescue a handful of German comrades who had been taken prisoner by the Russians.

We were really proud that after our first operation we could paint three rings around our barrel, and that with just three shots – not counting the dud.[30]

The city of Minsk, capital of Belarus, was in chaos. Numerous installations had already been destroyed and fires were burning in various locations, largely out of control. About 15,000 German soldiers were in Minsk – rear area units and survivors of the disasters that had befallen Fourth and Ninth Armies – most of them without weapons and too disorganised to be used in combat. Model contacted Hitler to repeat his previous message that even if Army Group North was able to attack towards the southwest from Polotsk as the Führer had ordered, further reinforcements were urgently needed if a coherent defensive line was to be created. The crisis to the southwest of Minsk also demanded urgent attention and he intended to send 7th Panzer Division to Baranovichi. Late in the evening, Model spoke to *OKH* again, largely repeating points that he had already made: even if reinforcements arrived immediately, it would be impossible to hold Minsk, and there was now little hope of the remnants of Fourth Army reaching the dubious safety of the German positions near the city. He summarised the situation in terms that laid bare the extent of the disaster that had engulfed Army Group Centre: even if all the reinforcements that he had requested or had been promised were taken into account, he would have just 12 divisions with which to hold a front of about 360 miles. To the west lay Vilnius, Brest, Warsaw, and

East Prussia. There was a real threat of the Red Army pushing on and reaching German territory in the forthcoming weeks.

The response from Hitler arrived at midnight. Polotsk and Minsk were no longer to be regarded as 'fortresses' and were to be abandoned. Even as the message was received, there came news that Soviet tanks – the leading elements of II Guards Tank Corps – had entered Minsk from the northeast. There was also another item of news from Hitler's headquarters. Kurt Zeitzler, who had become chief of the general staff in 1942 after the departure of Franz Halder and had run *OKH* through the Stalingrad crisis, Kursk, the retreat of 1943 across Ukraine, and the first half of 1944, was declared to be too sick to continue. Zeitzler had been appointed largely because Hitler saw him as a pliant officer who would pass on orders from above, merely acting as someone who would add the necessary details to the instructions he received. Zeitzler had indeed functioned very much in this mode, but also saw himself as an intermediary between Hitler and field commanders and attempted to intercede on their behalf when they protested about the impossibility of carrying out those orders. He was now blamed for the German defeat in Crimea in 1944, despite this being largely a consequence of Hitler's insistence on holding onto territory that the Wehrmacht lacked the resources to defend. The relationship between the two men had never been comfortable; during the siege of Sixth Army in Stalingrad, Zeitzler placed himself on the same diet as that endured by the encircled Germans as an act of solidarity, losing about 26lb in two weeks, until an irritated Hitler ordered him to desist. As one of the few figures in the military who was in a position to see the overall situation of the German armed forces, he was aware by early 1944 that the war was unwinnable and that Hitler's determination to cling to every metre of ground would only result in the needless destruction of German units.

After another acrimonious and ill-tempered outburst from Hitler, Zeitzler left the Führer's headquarters on 1 July without first securing permission, telling his staff that it was impossible for him to continue as chief of the general staff. Hitler was furious about his departure; in early 1945, he ordered that Zeitzler was to be dismissed from the army with loss of all pension and other privileges. After the war, Zeitzler appeared as a witness at the Nuremberg tribunals. He was not charged with any crimes personally and worked with the US Army, in charge of a group of German officers who worked for the Historical Division. His replacement as chief of the general staff was Generalleutnant Adolf Heusinger.

The fighting in Polotsk continued through the night into 3 July without respite. The German defenders had been ordered to pull back to the east and did so in an organised manner, inflicting heavy losses on the Soviet attackers. In some respects, the battle represented a reversion by the Red Army to the bloody tactics that had resulted in such heavy loss of life in earlier engagements. With Soviet troops across the Daugava to the west of Polotsk, there was at least an opportunity for the city to be bypassed, but Bagramian threw the riflemen of Fourth Shock Army and Sixth Guards Army into costly urban warfare with little regard for casualties – his longstanding fears of Polotsk being used as the start point for a dangerous counterattack against his Front may have left him with a fixed view that the city had to be captured as soon as possible, regardless of the cost. By the end of 3 July, most of the urban area was in Soviet hands, though it would take a further day for all German resistance to be eliminated.

The soldiers of the German IX Corps were forced back from Glubokoye during 3 July. Despite heavy losses – one regiment of 212th Infantry Division reported that it had started the summer fighting badly understrength with just 400 men but now had barely 100 left – the withdrawal was largely carried out without abandonment of artillery or other heavy equipment. When he was ordered to conduct a further withdrawal to a shorter line so that he could extend his flanks in an attempt to create a continuous front line with Army Group North, Reinhardt replied with an honest assessment:

> I cannot fulfil any missions [to restore contact] between the two army groups with these remnants. What remains here is so little that it could be commanded by a Generalmajor [i.e. a division commander]. We can achieve nothing and are powerless.[31]

By the end of the day, the leading elements of the Soviet I Tank Corps had reached Postavy, north of Lake Naroch and close to the frontier with Lithuania. There was almost nothing available to be placed in their path.

Further south, Gottberg informed both Saucken and Tippelskirch at 0900 that it was impossible to stop the Red Army from advancing into Minsk. His troops were attempting to hold a line immediately to the northwest of the city but he doubted that he would be able to do so for long. Decker had assembled the armoured battlegroup of 5th Panzer Division to the north of Minsk with the intention of attacking towards the south, but like Betzel's division he was delayed by fuel shortages and news now arrived that Minsk was largely in Soviet hands. There were renewed attacks all along the line by Soviet armour and infantry as Rotmistrov's Fifth Guards Tank Army attempted to drive west; casualties mounted on both sides at an alarming rate, and Decker abandoned all intentions to attack towards the south. Even with the support of the Tiger tank battalion, he had his hands full just holding his positions.

Vasilevsky had ordered Rotmistrov to capture Minsk with Fifth Guards Tank Army, but the task was carried out by Burdeiny's II Guards Tank Corps. The Soviet tank crews and their accompanying infantry faced considerable difficulties in penetrating into Minsk. After the mauling his spearhead had received a little further to the east, Burdeiny was anxious to avoid a repetition, but was hindered by having few maps of the city. A tank crewman in one of the leading units and his company commissar were actually natives of Minsk and advised their superiors of the best routes into the city. The leading element of a reconnaissance battalion was the first to penetrate into the urban area; its soldiers had hoped to get guidance from local civilians, but their success in advancing was at least partly because they were using captured German vehicles. In any case, the locals simply stayed indoors. But the three-pronged advance of the Soviet armour into Minsk slowly gained momentum. Fighting became intense in the late morning before Gottberg finally pulled out to the northwest; by the end of the day, Burdeiny's tanks had moved through the Belarusian capital and were taking up positions to the west.[32]

Minsk had fallen to the rapidly advancing Wehrmacht on 28 June 1941, just six days after the commencement of *Barbarossa*. Less than a month later, a ghetto was created – one of the largest in occupied Europe – as well as a prison camp near Drozdy, just outside Stolpce. Tens of thousands of Jews were crammed into the ghetto and were taken away for execution on a regular basis – by the end of 1942, an estimated 90,000 had perished as a result of either killings or malnutrition and disease, and perhaps only 8,000 remained alive. Like other ghettos, the Minsk ghetto was 'liquidated' in 1943 with the remaining Jews being taken to the extermination camp at Majdanek. The Jews were not the only people to suffer during the occupation. There was an increasingly active partisan movement in and around the city and every attack by the partisans resulted in mass killings of hostages. Other residents were taken away as forced labourers, and few of them ever returned to the city. Of an estimated 250,000 residents before the arrival of the Germans, only about 37,000 were still living amongst the ruins when the Red Army took control of the city.[33] By this stage of the war, all Red Army personnel were aware of the widespread atrocities committed by the Germans during the years of occupation either through personal knowledge or from the constant lectures delivered by political commissars and circulated in official newspapers; seeing a great city reduced to ruins and its population so depleted can only have strengthened their desire for revenge.

Even as the Red Army was taking possession of Minsk, *Gruppe Müller* was continuing its painful retreat. By first light on 3 July, the German soldiers had marched about 12 miles west from the Berezina crossings. In three columns, with only intermittent radio contact with Fourth Army, Müller pushed on, but in the early afternoon he reported that progress was effectively blocked:

> [The] road to Smilovichi [Smolevichi] is blocked by powerful enemy forces. There are small groups of [Soviet] tanks to the north. [There are] difficult roads, traffic congestion, signs of disintegration amongst the large numbers of stragglers. Due to the impossibility of movement, it is not possible to provide the combat troops and artillery with ammunition for an organised attack. Therefore [I] conclude: [we will] breakthrough with as many soldiers with strong morale with personal weapons as possible out of the threatening encirclement towards the west.[34]

All the time, Soviet aircraft were overhead, bombing and machine-gunning with impunity. Two German soldiers appeared in the lines still held by 78th Sturm Division, former members of the division who had been captured by the Red Army in the preceding days; they brought documents exhorting their comrades to lay down their arms, promising them good treatment and a swift release from captivity at the end of hostilities. Both sides had made similar offers in the past, and this latest attempt was ignored, just as almost all previous attempts had been. About 20,000 men continued to struggle through the forests and swamps and along the few good roads. Partisans attacked them with increasing impunity and the units of the Soviet Thirty-Third and Forty-Ninth Armies clashed with them regularly. But the main focus of attention of the Red Army remained to push on to the west as quickly as possible, and this probably contributed to the manner in which Müller's command managed to continue its precarious existence. Nevertheless, time was running out. Ammunition was almost exhausted and the hungry, sleepless men were close to the end of their strength. The unnamed adjutant from 78th Sturm Division described the ongoing battles being fought by the rearguard:

> The new line ran past the edge of a village. It was a good defensive position. There was a 400m wide strip of marshland towards the enemy. The road for the retreat was 500m to the rear of the position. Russian infantry attacked on a broad front at about 1130 with strong supporting fire from heavy weapons. The point of main effort was the village. Our right flank had already been bypassed. The last men were committed. Heavy close-quarters fighting raged in the village. Soon the Russians had taken it and stood just 500m from the retreat road. Our remaining 100 men fought their way back. Once more, we succeeded in bringing the enemy to a halt. After a brief pause to reorganise, we launched a counterattack. At the crucial moment the remnants of 17th Grenadier Regiment [part of 31st Infantry

Division] closed up with us and stormed forward alongside. The enemy backed off and the village was retaken. It was possible to hold on until the arrival of 267th Infantry Division. A decisive part in our counterattack was played by the two self-propelled guns of our 178th Anti-Tank Battalion. We linked up with the rest of the division again at 2100. They had already written us off.[35]

Much as Tippelskirch's Fourth Army was effectively reduced to 5th Panzer Division and the other elements of Saucken's XXXIX Panzer Corps, Vormann's Ninth Army to the south was also badly weakened, to the extent that on the morning of 3 July Model gave it the temporary name of *Gruppe von Vormann* and subordinated it to Second Army; it would be restored to its previous status a week later. Although 12th Panzer Division remained a formidable formation, radio contact between Ninth Army headquarters and its subordinate formations was intermittent at best. After regrouping, 12th Panzer Division began to move towards Stolpce where it hoped to make contact with the panzergrenadier battalion that had already been sent there. There was constant pressure from the Soviet Third and Forty-Eighth Armies from the south and southeast respectively, but despite heavy losses the improvised formations deployed to protect the withdrawing panzer division managed to hold back the Soviet units long enough for the redeployment to proceed more or less as planned.

As they pulled back towards the west, the German units faced a major potential obstacle in the Niemen River, running broadly from the southeast towards the northwest and passing through Stolpce. If the German units and stragglers that had gathered close to Minsk were to continue an orderly withdrawal, they would need to cross the river in order to ensure contact with units to the south around Baranovichi. Somewhat to the surprise of Vormann and Model, Kessel – the commander of 20th Panzer Division, who had managed to reach 12th Panzer Division with a small group of officers – succeeded in finding other survivors of his division and stragglers of other units during the night of 2–3 July. Organising them into a small battlegroup, he took it upon himself to attack towards the river. In heavy fighting – against a mixture of troops from Pliev's cavalry-mechanised group and partisan formations – he managed to reach the Niemen at Eremichi, to the west of Stolpce, where he secured a bridge. Reinforcements were promptly dispatched to support him.

In addition to demanding reinforcements, Model also wanted Army Group North to strengthen its southern flank. He anticipated a Soviet attack towards Vilnius and advised *OKH* that troops should be sent to the city immediately in order to try to retain at least the possibility of repairing the breach between Army

Group North and Army Group Centre. The response from Heusinger was both disheartening and predictable. He told Model that he agreed with him, but that Hitler refused to hear any opinions that disagreed with his beliefs. Late on 3 July he contacted Model to inform him that – as was so often the case – Hitler had belatedly conceded and Army Group North had received appropriate instructions to strengthen its southern flank. Model repeated his earlier estimates of how few units he had for such a broad front and suggested that if reinforcements could not be made available immediately, he should be given freedom of action to conduct a mobile defence. From the headquarters of Army Group North, Lindemann added that permission to withdraw from Polotsk had arrived about three days too late to be of any value – the units that might have been freed for deployment elsewhere were now badly degraded by the intense streetfighting in the city.

After successfully withdrawing to the west through the area south of Minsk, 12th Panzer Division now attempted to re-open the road to Baranovichi. A second panzergrenadier battalion reached Stolpce and there was general relief when it signalled that it had made contact with the battalion sent earlier to the town, where fighting had continued over the preceding day. A junior NCO in 12th Panzer Division later described the events of 3 July:

> During the morning fighting flared up again. Russian ground-attack planes had located our vehicles and fired on us time and again. Fortunately, they didn't achieve much. We were lucky in that we had plenty of sparkling wine, which was very good at quenching our thirst. We had to travel some distance to get drinking water. We were supposed to be cut off. There was only a small exit from the encirclement to the northwest. In this direction there was a constant, unbroken stream of vehicles along the road. It was a picture of misery. It couldn't have been much worse in Napoleon's time. Vehicles from about a dozen divisions had gathered together in a chaotic mass. There were rarely several vehicles from a single unit or of the same type in one spot. There was everything from refugees and the *Panjewagen* [small horse-drawn carts] of the German infantry to heavy tanks and bridging equipment. Russian refugees clung to Wehrmacht vehicles, wounded German soldiers lay in the wagons. And there were many, many on foot. Some without shoes.
>
> Towards evening several units of our division arrived ... Wherever one looked there were loads of tanks, half-tracks, and self-propelled anti-tank guns and artillery. The sight gave us a sense of reassurance. Above all we felt that even though we were far behind the Russian spearheads, we were no longer so isolated and abandoned.[36]

The biggest problem for 12th Panzer Division was that it had little knowledge about the precise location and movements of Soviet troops and there were intermittent clashes. An attack by about 25 T-34s – later identified as being part of the Soviet Forty-Eighth Army – attempted to push north and cut the line of march of the German division; they were engaged by a group of about eight German tanks and in a brief battle, two German tanks were lost but about half the Soviet force was shot up and the rest withdrew. Panzergrenadiers armed with *Panzerschreck* anti-tank weapons took advantage of the woodland to engage other Red Army tank units at close range, but in another battle a column of ambulances from 12th Panzer Division was badly shot up.

The road running southwest from Minsk crossed a number of small and large waterways. One was the Usa stream, and the bridge in the village of Ussa became a choke point for combat formations, stragglers, and rear area units that were trying to escape from the advancing Soviet forces. In an attempt to create order from the chaos, Müller – the acting commander of 12th Panzer Division rather than the commander of the eponymous group stranded to the east of Minsk – dispatched his senior logistics officer, Hauptmann Alexander Brosien-Bueschler, to take command of all the stragglers. Over about an hour, he managed to round up several hundred men and two field guns and organised them into a defensive perimeter. Meanwhile, troops began to gather to continue the attack to try to link up with 4th Panzer Division, which was expected to advance in the opposite direction.

Model continued to outline aggressive thrusts with 4th, 5th, and 12th Panzer Divisions (and 7th Panzer Division too when it arrived), but it seems highly unlikely that he actually believed in any such operations – the forces available were too weak to achieve anything other than local successes and any thrust towards the east ran a great risk of being bypassed on either side by the unstoppable torrents of Soviet units, ultimately leading to the encirclement and destruction of the German assault forces. He may have been at least partly motivated by a need to articulate aggressive operations in order to placate Hitler and the hope that, having shown that such attacks could not succeed, he would then have more success in persuading the Führer to accept reality and authorise retreats. But despite the crippling compartmentalisation imposed upon the Wehrmacht by Hitler, officers like Heusinger, Lindemann, and Model must have known via informal, personal contacts in the west that Germany faced catastrophe. Thousands of German soldiers were dying every day, fighting for a cause that was unwinnable. Yet very few of those who were aware of this were prepared to take the steps necessary to bring the increasingly pointless slaughter to an end.

CHAPTER 8

THE SURGE TO THE FRONTIER: 4–8 JULY

After several days of costly streetfighting, the Red Army took control of Polotsk. Intermittent clashes would continue for another day, but the city was in Soviet hands and with Sixth Guards Army in control of the Daugava River to the west of the city, Bagramian could regard his northern flank as secure. Chistiakov's drive had slowed with the commitment of so many troops to the assault on Polotsk, but now that the city had fallen, it was hoped that the drive to and over the frontier with Lithuania could accelerate. Bagramian discussed future operations with his fellow officers and Vladimir Vasilyevich Kurasov, his chief of staff – newly promoted to Colonel General – stressed the importance of speed:

> We must take note that in Soviet Lithuania there are numerous forests, rivers, lakes, and swamps. There are over 4,000 lakes! The enemy will undoubtedly seek to use this terrain to construct defensive zones and blocking positions. The more time we give him, the stronger will he fortify the area. Until further reserves arrive, we must attack further on the left bank of the Daugava and after the capture of Polotsk on the right bank with Fourth Shock Army.[1]

Kurasov was correct in the potential use of the landscape of Lithuania for defensive purposes, but the use of the expression 'Soviet Lithuania' is significant. After the annexation of Lithuania in 1940, the Soviet authorities had deported tens of thousands of Lithuanians and they would have been aware that anti-Soviet sentiment remained strong across the entire Baltic region, despite the widespread atrocities committed by the German occupation authorities. Just as Stalin was anxious to penetrate into Poland as quickly as possible to ensure that he had troops on the ground in the event of a sudden collapse of German resistance, so he wanted to ensure that there was no possibility of the Baltic region resuming the independent status it had enjoyed between the wars. There were therefore several reasons for a speedy advance. Whether Kurasov actually used this expression, or whether Bagramian added it in his memoirs to conform with post-war Soviet orthodoxy, is open to question.

Despite recognising the need for a rapid thrust, Bagramian was forced by logistic difficulties to await the arrival of supplies and fresh drafts; Sixth Guards Army could be satisfied with its impressive advance of about 120 miles over 11 days, but it had been at considerable cost. While these reinforcements and supplies were brought forward, Beloborodov's Forty-Third Army on his southern flank remained heavily involved in the ongoing pressure upon the German Army Group Centre. Although the remnants of the German IX Corps continued to pull back in stages towards the west, the men on both sides were exhausted through lack of sleep and constant combat. Many Soviet rifle battalions had been reduced to barely more than a company in terms of numbers.

The capture of Minsk and Polotsk effectively marked the end of the main phase of Operation *Bagration*. It had been a huge success, but further gains were within reach. The remnants of *Gruppe Müller*, still trying to retreat to safety, were still to be eliminated, and huge gaps had opened up everywhere in the German lines. The battles that followed are often described as separate Red Army operations – the Vilnius and Kaunas operations, the Białystok and Osovets operations, etc. – but they were largely organised in short periods of time to take advantage of the disarray of the Wehrmacht, with little opportunity for the extensive planning and concentration of resources that preceded *Bagration*. For the soldiers who fought on both sides, these operations represented almost continuous fighting that had commenced with the first Red Army reconnaissance in force on 22 June.

The units of the German IX Corps were also greatly reduced in strength. Reports reaching Wuthmann's headquarters advised that further Soviet units – from 3rd Belarusian Front's Thirty-Ninth Army – were advancing past the southern flank of IX Corps, being led through the swamps south of Lake Naroch by local partisan groups. This attack was directly towards Vilnius, but with both its flanks in the air, IX Corps faced the risk of encirclement and destruction close to the frontier with Lithuania. The remnants of *Korps Abteilung D* were ordered to try to intercept this thrust, but despite receiving reinforcements this formation was too weak to make much headway. An attempt by a Soviet group to push north into the rear of the southern flank of IX Corps was blocked, but it was impossible to achieve more.

Although it was unable to function as a concentrated formation, 5th Panzer Division was able to stiffen the line held by Saucken's XXXIX Panzer Corps, especially as a few battalions of reorganised stragglers from the units that were still trickling back from the east were now becoming available. The panzer division was ordered to attack south into the flank of the Soviet units that were now moving out of Minsk towards the west, but the order was cancelled when it became clear that the tanks and panzergrenadiers had their hands full holding off the repeated attacks of Rotmistrov's tanks. Tippelskirch had placed Weidling in command of the remnants of VI Corps and assigned *Gruppe von Gottberg* to this unit, but Gottberg continued to be obstructive. He had refused to be subordinated to Saucken, even though he then repeatedly called on Saucken for logistic support and anti-tank reinforcements; he now informed Tippelskirch that his men were too badly weakened by their combat to continue in action. His units remained in the field, directly under the control of VI Corps; without securing the permission of the local Wehrmacht chain of command, he personally left for Lida, about 84 miles to the west, where he ordered several police battalions to gather.

It was an outrageous act of disobedience. Given the intense suspicion of the army amongst Hitler and his inner circle, such insubordination by an officer in the army would have resulted in immediate arrest. But the fragmented and often competing chains of command in Nazi Germany meant that nobody was particularly surprised that no action was taken against Gottberg and that he was protected by Himmler. Even as he departed, he was informed that he had been awarded the Knight's Cross and a few days later he was promoted to Obergruppenführer. A few weeks later, the survivors of *Gruppe von Gottberg* and the police units that he gathered together in Lida were formed into XII SS Corps under Gottberg's command. XII SS Corps was then transferred to the west with the intention of being used in anti-resistance operations behind the front line in France but the rapid advance of the Western Allies made this impossible. At the end of the war, Gottberg was still operating behind the front lines, rounding up German soldiers who were retreating from the wreckage of the various fronts and executing them. He became a British prisoner of war at the end of hostilities and committed suicide at the end of May 1945.[2] There were a few attempts to bring surviving members of *Gruppe von Gottberg* before courts to be prosecuted for war crimes, but almost none ever faced justice.

The fall of Minsk and the ongoing stubborn resistance of XXXIX Panzer Corps to the northwest of the city seemed to signify a momentary pause in the headlong movement of the front line towards the west. From behind the Soviet front line there were still signs of life as the Germans who had marched and fought their way back from Mogilev continued their struggle. A signal from the headquarters of XII Corps – in reality, no more than a radio truck with Müller and a few other officers – stated that artillery and other equipment was being destroyed. If they were to escape, they would have to continue their march past the southern outskirts of Minsk; but the men were utterly exhausted and reduced to scouring wrecked and abandoned vehicles for food and ammunition. If this was to succeed, Ninth Army in the form of *Gruppe von Vormann* would have to attack to link up with them, but even if this were possible with the troops available, it ran the risk of the German relief column being trapped in a further encirclement. In any case, restoring a meaningful front line with contact on either flank had to take priority, which meant implicitly that Müller's group would have to be abandoned to its fate. In late 1942, when the German attempt to reach and break the siege ring around Stalingrad failed, the Germans had relied on the continuing resistance of the starving soldiers of Sixth Army to tie down large numbers of Soviet troops while the rest of the Wehrmacht attempted to rebuild its lines; although few if any were prepared to state this explicitly, there was now a similar expectation about *Gruppe Müller*.

Having reached the headquarters of 78th Sturm Division, the regimental adjutant who had overseen the actions of the rearguard took part in a briefing delivered by Müller before dawn on 4 July. It was a depressing summary:

> The remnants of about 12 German divisions and corps-level units were now compressed into a small encirclement no more than 2–3km wide. We were about 10km northwest of Chervyen … Dense, hilly woodland and swamps lay on all sides. The retreat road that ran west was blocked by powerful enemy forces. Repeated attempts to break through failed with heavy casualties. The few soldiers still capable of combat held thinly manned lines around the encirclement. The great number of wounded and several vehicles and horses were gathered in the centre of the encirclement, protected from air attack. The corps and division staffs were also gathered there. There was deep gloom due to the hopelessness of the situation. The lack of food, constant physical demands, and recurring fighting had greatly reduced combat capability. The constant breaking out from one encirclement into another had a considerable impact on troop morale. The anxious question that hung over everyone was what would happen next. In no time at all, word got around that despite the greatest courage of the troops it was not possible to clear the line of retreat.[3]

Radio contact remained problematic for the Germans. During the morning of 4 July, 12th Panzer Division's signals battalion managed to receive messages from

Vormann's headquarters but was unable to reply. A flood of messages that had been sent the previous day were now received, and Müller realised that his division and the hundreds of stragglers it had gathered were effectively trapped in a loose encirclement. To the southwest, 28th Jäger Division and 4th Panzer Division were trying to re-open the road from Baranovichi, but attempts by 12th Panzer Division to attack towards them ended in failure. The bridges over the Niemen River at the southwest edge of Stolpce were either destroyed or in Soviet hands and Müller had no idea whether his transmissions were being received by Vormann's headquarters – there was no response to his urgent requests for information about the location of 4th Panzer Division.

The officers of 12th Panzer Division discussed their options. Should they make a further attempt to break through the Red Army positions to the southwest, or should they instead move towards the northwest where the small group from 20th Panzer Division had seized a bridge over the Niemen? At that point, further orders were received by radio. The attack directly towards Baranovichi was to be abandoned. Instead, the division was to link up with Kessel's improvised battlegroup at Eremichi. Even this order was received several hours after it was sent and Müller decided to act as quickly as possible before he was once more overtaken by developments about which he had no knowledge. A group of panzergrenadiers and tanks was ordered to take up positions to the north of Stolpce to cover the flank of the planned march against any Soviet troops advancing from Minsk. Almost immediately, this group clashed with elements of the Soviet Forty-Eighth Army but managed to secure the vital high ground from which it could protect the rest of the division.

One of the few bits of good news for Müller was the appearance from the east of several groups of German soldiers, still more or less intact as combat units. These included a battalion-strength group from 14th Infantry Division under the personal command of the division commander, Flörke, and a further battalion from 12th Infantry Division. Such good news was desperately needed. The line of march was along a single sandy road and in addition to Red Army units, the soldiers of 12th Panzer Division also had to deal with encounters with partisan groups. At that moment, a Leutnant appeared on a motorcycle. He had been sent by Kessel to make contact with 12th Panzer Division and to guide it to safety. He advised Müller to detour to the north to avoid forests where the partisans held strong positions. After a difficult march, in which they encountered and rounded up further groups of stragglers, the men of 12th Panzer Division reached Eremichi in the early evening and began to cross the Niemen.[4]

Nearer to Baranovichi, 4th Panzer Division had been ordered late on 3 July to attack and capture the bridges to the southwest of Stolpce at all costs, but Betzel and his fellow officers doubted that they stood any chance of success until the rest of the division had assembled. There was constant pressure from the east as Pliev's cavalry-mechanised group did all it could to envelop the German forces, resulting in confused fighting; for much of the time, parts of 30th Guards Cavalry Division, part of Pliev's group, were as isolated as the soldiers of 12th Panzer Division, and Pliev had to organise local attacks to rescue his men. As had been the case since the commencement of the Red Army's exploitation of its initial successes, there was considerable aid from partisans. They repeatedly guided Red Army units through the difficult terrain, reported the locations of German troops, and attacked German units attempting to escape towards the west.[5]

Hitler had repeatedly assured Reinhardt that the situation of his Third Panzer Army would be improved by an attack from the north, where Lindemann's Army Group North had been ordered to assemble sufficient forces for a powerful thrust. Just as repeatedly, this thrust failed to take place because Lindemann didn't have the troops to spare. At first, the commander of Army Group North prevaricated and informed *OKH* that the thrust was delayed due to transport difficulties; finally, on 4 July he informed Hitler that an attack was impossible unless much of the Baltic region was evacuated. He was immediately dismissed. Lindemann was not a popular man with his subordinates; when he commanded L Corps in the second half of 1941, he unfairly heaped blame on a division commander for a setback suffered by the corps, and he owed his elevation – first to command of Eighteenth Army and then to command of Army Group North – to his enthusiastic loyalty to Hitler. He was later appointed Wehrmacht commander in Denmark, where he ended the war. He was captured by American forces in 1945 and then passed to the Danish authorities, who finally released him in 1948.

Lindemann's replacement as commander of Army Group North was Generaloberst Johannes Friessner, who had commanded an improvised *Armee-Abteilung Narwa* ('Army Detachment Narva') for much of 1944. Almost immediately, he contacted *OKH*:

When I arrived here [at the headquarters of Army Group North] the northern flank of Army Group Centre, threatened by envelopment, had already pulled back 15km northwest of Glubokoye. In keeping with what seemed possible at the time, orders had been issued for a thrust into the flank of the enemy ... The requisite conditions are no longer met, not least because the necessary forces are not actually available.[6]

Changing senior personnel was not going to change the underlying reality of the situation. Friessner rapidly added that he would take energetic measures to try to close the gap to Army Group Centre, but it would take until at least 14 July before even modest forces could be gathered for the attempt.

The near-rout of Army Group Centre continued on 5 July. The remnants of Third Panzer Army fell back under constant pressure, and towards the end of the day Reinhardt learned that Vilnius had been declared a fortress and was under his jurisdiction. Its garrison was intended to be composed primarily of 170th Infantry Division, dispatched from the Estonian front, but to date only a single battalion had arrived. Together with perhaps a further battalion of mixed personnel and some anti-aircraft batteries, this battalion was already reporting clashes with partisans. It would be a complex battle involving the Wehrmacht, the advancing Red Army, pro-Polish (and anti-Soviet) partisans, and pro-Soviet (and anti-Polish) partisans. The Germans made some tentative approaches to try to make common cause against the Red Army with the Poles, but no agreement was reached; nonetheless, the Germans deliberately left substantial stockpiles of small arms and ammunitions in a few locations with minimal or no guard so that the Poles could arm themselves.

Nikolai Stepanov, the Red Army veteran who told an interviewer many decades after the war that he and his comrades knew nothing of the intention to mount a major offensive in June, was in a rifle division that was now moving closer to Vilnius. In his interview recorded decades after the war, he referred to several incidents that he described as occurring close to Vitebsk, but the recorded movements of the division suggest that he was mistaken and, recalling the events after such a long period of time, it is likely that he confused Vitebsk with Vilnius. He described an incident that he said he witnessed:

We had been walking for two nights, up to 60km, with five-minute halts every 5km. Our legs trembled with fatigue. Fortunately, we had two carts with us so we loaded the guns, our kit bags, and ammunition onto the carts, or we would have been completely worn out … We came to a village on the third day [26 June] where the division headquarters was already dug in. There was a slope before us, with low-lying land beyond and a field of onions, about 500m wide, then German trenches.

But the area was actually a dense minefield and when our sappers ventured in they were killed almost immediately. So they brought up a penal battalion, lined up in a chain, and charged up the slope through the minefield. This 'reconnaissance in force' swiftly swept past our trench and we watched a tragedy unfold with our own eyes, really just murder. One by one, the penal companies ran into mines, and the Germans soon swept the entire area with heavy artillery and mortar fire and we, with lumps in our throats, were unable to speak a word as we watched how the penal battalion died. And then our commander shouted loudly, his exact words: 'These are enemies of the people! They atone for their guilt with blood!' When it was all over, in the late afternoon, we were ordered to provide covering fire for the sappers with our machine-guns ... The Germans responded to our machine-gun fire with mortars. Fortunately for us, just before the shelling we managed to dig shelters for ourselves in the trench under our machine-gun. The third mortar shell was a direct hit on our machine-gun position. I was covered with earth and when I recovered and climbed out, I saw just a crater where the machine-gun had been, two gunners were missing, just some hands sticking out of the ground. But they were alive and I dug one out, blood streaming from his mouth and ears. Then I dug the second man out from under a collapsed trench wall and when he came to his senses we dragged the wounded man back to the forest edge.

Lieutenant Medvedev ran up to us. 'Where's your machine-gun? How can you prove it was destroyed and you didn't just abandon it? How can I draw up a report?' That night I crawled back to the wrecked firing point and found the breech-block of the gun on the ground. I returned and the platoon commander was able to write off the Maxim.[7]

There are numerous accounts of the manner in which penal battalions were used by the Red Army (and indeed by the Wehrmacht), sometimes suggesting that the men were deliberately sacrificed in pointless attacks on strong positions. Many Soviet soldiers in these battalions were permitted to return to their original units after successfully surviving an attack in the ranks of a penal battalion, and there were even cases of some men spending more than one spell in penal battalions as a result of repeated misdemeanours. As the war progressed, the use of penal battalions with no regard to the casualties they suffered was replaced by a somewhat more cautious approach; even the Soviet Union was finding it difficult to sustain its huge losses of manpower and most of the men in these battalions were trained and experienced soldiers. However, Aleksandr Vasilyevich Pyltsyn, who commanded a penal battalion during the war, described an attack by his battalion when it was part of Batov's Sixty-Fifth Army. Although Pyltsyn personally marked a clear lane through a minefield, the battalion suffered heavy losses and he later wrote that – probably due to intelligence failures and reporting errors – the mines had not in fact been cleared. He concluded that it was simpler for senior commanders to write off the personnel of a penal battalion rather than acknowledge their failures to pass on accurate information.[8] In the case of the attack witnessed by Stepanov, something similar may have occurred. There may have been a few clear lanes in the minefield, but it was routine for both sides to cover such areas with artillery and machine-guns, and many of the penal battalion's losses would have been from these weapons rather than from the mines themselves. Simply throwing a penal battalion across a minefield as a means of clearing the mines seems an unlikely reason for the attack.

To date, 5th Panzer Division had consistently outfought the units of Rotmistrov's Fifth Guards Tank Army, but the division couldn't be everywhere at once. Late on 4 July, Soviet forces from Fifth Army succeeded in taking Smorgon, threatening to turn the northern flank of Saucken's XXXIX Panzer Corps. Model had already issued orders for 5th Panzer Division to attack towards the northwest in order to try to establish contact with the southern flank of Third Panzer Army, but during the morning of 5 July the Soviet III Guards Mechanised Corps – part of Oslikovsky's cavalry-mechanised group – attacked from Smorgon towards the southwest. Fresh orders were issued: in conjunction with the units of 7th Panzer Division, which were beginning to concentrate to the northeast of Lida, 5th Panzer Division was to counterattack and destroy the Soviet forces attacking out of Smorgon.

With so much of 5th Panzer Division already committed to fighting against the Soviet forces advancing against XXXIX Panzer Corps from the east, little could be spared for the planned counterattack. Nevertheless, a modest battlegroup was assembled and dispatched to intercept III Guards Mechanised Corps. There were numerous clashes, with casualties on both sides; the hard-pressed soldiers of the panzer division watched with a mixture of envy and resentment as columns of American-supplied trucks brought forward supplies and reinforcements to their enemies. By the end of the day, together with the Tiger tank battalion, 5th Panzer Division could field just 65 operational tanks. More than half its armour had either been destroyed or was unfit for action, awaiting repairs. Many of these disabled vehicles would have to be abandoned if the division was forced to make a rapid withdrawal.[9]

The first elements of 7th Panzer Division had arrived in Lida overnight and were ordered to deploy immediately to the northeast, against the Soviet forces attempting to attack from Smorgon. In 1941, the division had moved swiftly through Vilnius and into this very area as part of the bewilderingly rapid advance of the Wehrmacht into the Soviet Union. The current situation was very different, as an officer from the division noted in his diary:

> There is great chaos along the front, and in some cases men are retreating after the complete dissolution of their formations. The command elements have no

knowledge about the situation at the 'front' and cannot give any information about the enemy, nor the units that have fought alongside them until now, [and] there is a complete absence of cohesion.[10]

Meanwhile, more in hope than expectation, the headquarters of Tippelskirch's Fourth Army continued to send situation reports to *Gruppe Müller* about Soviet troop locations and movements. During the early evening, there was a brief response: 'All attempts to force a breakthrough with the last resources have failed. The corps is defending its positions.'[11]

It was the last signal that would be received from the encircled men. Compressed into a small area east of the town of Chervyen to the southeast of Minsk, the exhausted soldiers lacked the ammunition or physical strength to continue their unequal struggle. Some divisions had managed to reach the area with considerable quantities of equipment – the remnants of 25th Panzergrenadier Division, for example, still fielded 32 assault guns and 25 self-propelled anti-tank guns – but without fuel and ammunition there was little more that could be achieved, despite repeated attempts to parachute supplies to them. Müller and Völckers – the commander of XXVII Corps – discussed the situation during the afternoon of 5 July. According to the latest information that they had received from Tippelskirch, the nearest German front line was about 60 miles to the west, an impossible distance to cover. Nonetheless, many senior officers were reluctant to give up. Generalmajor Adolf Trowitz, commander of 57th Infantry Division, had been trapped in the encirclement of much of the German Eleventh Army in the Cherkassy pocket in March 1944 and urged the others to continue fighting, but the situation was very different: the distance that the encircled forces had covered to escape that earlier encirclement was far smaller, and at the time more than half the panzer divisions on the Eastern Front were attempting to rescue them. Some, like 78th Sturm Division's commander Traut, felt that the best they could do was defend their positions as any breakout would necessitate abandoning several thousand wounded men, but a decision was made to divide the troops available into several groups and attempt one last breakout that evening.

After its narrow escape to the south of Minsk, 12th Panzer Division had no opportunity for rest. The rearguard abandoned the burning ruins of Stolpce and made its way to the river crossing at Eremichi, constantly assailed by both the Red Army and partisans. Casualties, particularly amongst the numerous stragglers accompanying 12th Panzer Division, were heavy, but most of the division assembled immediately south of the river near Eremichi. Here, during the afternoon, Luftwaffe planes and gliders delivered a substantial quantity of fuel;

some of it was dropped on the east bank, where partisans and Soviet soldiers seized it, and the fuel that landed on the German side of the river was grabbed by whichever troops were closest. There was little organised distribution and a glider pilot who had delivered supplies was given an urgent message to take back with him as he boarded a Storch liaison plane: the division needed accurate maps as well as supplies – some units were relying on maps cut from German newspaper articles – and reliable radio contact with higher commands remained problematic.[12]

Further south, 4th Panzer Division enjoyed a relatively successful day, making several counterattacks. Just like 5th Panzer Division, it was beginning to feel the strain of combat. It had been forced to parcel out small groups of tanks to support other formations and in combination with vehicles destroyed, disabled, or suffering mechanical failures, its fighting strength was greatly reduced. The two panzer battalions of its 35th Panzer Regiment could field just 20 and eight tanks respectively by the end of 5 July. The division's tank repair workshops were still in the original deployment area in Army Group North Ukraine's sector and there were urgent requests for their speedy transfer to Army Group Centre, particularly as the division had large numbers of Panther tanks unavailable due to mechanical problems.[13] Since its entry into service, the Panther was troubled by such issues and Panther units routinely reported more tanks disabled due to breakdowns than as a result of enemy action. It was a highly effective armoured vehicle in combat, but this efficacy was greatly compromised by poor reliability.

Vormann was beginning to believe that the worst of the crisis might be easing, even if only temporarily. The Red Army had to be at the end of its logistic leash and would surely have to make an operational pause while its formations were replenished and resupplied. German reinforcements were arriving; in addition to the panzer divisions that were in action, 28th Jäger Division was now fully deployed and had spent much of 5 July mounting a slow attack towards the north to establish contact with 12th Panzer Division – by nightfall, the gap was just three miles and there was every expectation that this could be closed the following day, but although orders to that effect were issued late on 5 July, communications difficulties continued and Vormann couldn't be sure that his divisions had received all his instructions. In any case, he knew that any stability that his units could achieve was likely to be temporary at best. It was only a matter of time before the Red Army resumed its pressure and attacked towards Baranovichi. Thereafter, the road would be open for a Soviet thrust to Brest and Białystok, and perhaps even on to Warsaw.

Model gave *OKH* a pessimistic though accurate summary of the situation of his army group. In the north, there was a serious threat to Vilnius. Soviet spearheads were not far from Lida, and he doubted that the situation in the south around Baranovichi would hold for long. Reinforcements were desperately needed and he urged the transfer of a further infantry division to Vilnius immediately. He was promised that 225th Infantry Division was already en route, but its first elements couldn't be expected until 7 July. In addition, other formations were also on their way, though again they would take several days to arrive. One of these, 18th SS-Panzergrenadier Division *Horst Wessel*, had been formed earlier in the year using ethnic Germans from Hungary and had been deployed to Hungary almost immediately as part of Operation *Margarethe*, a German-backed *coup d'état* to prevent Hungary from leaving the Axis. Its combat capability was limited; despite having a good level of equipment, including a panzer battalion and an assault gun battalion, the level of training of its personnel was modest. In any case, it wouldn't arrive before 10 July. Other units would also take time to reach Army Group Centre: 6th Panzer Division was expected on 13 July at the earliest; 19th Panzer on 16 July; and 19th Infantry Division on 17 July. Model would just have to cling on with the resources at hand until these units could arrive.

Shortly after midnight on 6 July, the two breakout groups near Chervyen commenced their final, hopeless bid to reach safety. Leaving a single doctor and a small medical group to care for the thousands of wounded men, 25th Panzergrenadier Division attacked with the last of its fuel and ammunition in an attempt to reach Dzerzhinsk, to the southwest of Minsk. Immediately, the Germans ran into Soviet forces from Fiftieth Army and came under heavy fire. Generalleutnant Paul Schürmann, the division commander, commenced the attack with perhaps 1,000 men; by dawn, 90 per cent were gone, either casualties or lost in the darkness. After a series of clashes with Soviet troops, this little group – eventually reduced to just 30 men – managed to reach German lines and was immediately dispatched to reinforce 5th Panzer Division.

The second breakout group was centred on 57th Infantry Division and *Feldherrnhalle*. It too came under heavy fire throughout the pre-dawn hours of 6 July and reached the Chervyen–Minsk highway, where there was almost constant Soviet traffic heading west. The surviving Germans hid in nearby forests for much of the day before attempting to cross the road late on 6 July. Almost all of *Feldherrnhalle* was scattered and destroyed over the following 24 hours, and although Trowitz, the commander of 57th Infantry Division, had gathered over 10,000 men for his attempt, he lacked the supplies for the group to act as a coherent whole. Instead, the Germans broke into small groups and attempted to infiltrate their way towards the west. Almost all were killed or captured in the following two days.

Traut's 78th Sturm Division, which had put up such stern resistance to the initial Soviet attacks, gathered its last strength for the breakout late on 5 July. A survivor later described what followed:

> The troops formed up for the assault at 2300. Individual units began to sing the *Deutschlandlied*. The survivors will never forget that night. Burning villages, howitzer and rifle fire, dull explosions mixing with the thunderous shouts and singing of the attacking units. Enemy units which tried to resist were overrun.
>
> By dawn of 6 July the enemy encircling positions had been left behind. However, the Russian units quickly regrouped. Enemy motorised forces arrived as reinforcements. The larger breakout groups were soon caught and surrounded again. The only chance was to break out in very small groups. It was the last hope. There was no clear information about the extent of the Russian advances. Finding a way through the territory that was strongly held by Russian troops came down to the abilities of individuals. Without maps or other means of orienting ourselves, most of the small groups infiltrated towards the west. It was a terrible scene. The roads were full of Russian units moving forward, the villages were all occupied by partisans or troops.
>
> We only had the short hours of the eastern summer evening to try to press on. Whoever dropped out due to wounds or sickness faced the grim fate of those left behind. Exhaustion or disability due to wounds led to the rapid decline of the speed of march. Swamps, streams, thick woodland, the burning sun all day long, hunger, and often a lack of water had severe effects. Some licked the dew from the grass in the mornings to ease their thirst.
>
> We were driven on by the unshakable will to reach the German front line which was already hundreds of kilometres to the west, and the hope to find better conditions beyond the border of Belarus, in Poland or Lithuania.[14]

Few of these small groups escaped. The remnants of 267th Infantry Division formed three columns. The southern column ran into Soviet armour and surrendered when it came under devastating fire; harassed by partisans and small groups of Soviet infantry, the second slowly disintegrated and was eliminated, though intermittent fighting continued for several days. The third column, led by Generalleutnant Otto Drescher, the division commander, also divided into small groups of about 100 men; few escaped.

A Soviet officer described the state of the Germans who were captured:

East of Minsk, I saw two columns of German prisoners of war, about 400–600 men, marching in the direction of Moscow. The majority of the prisoners were barefoot. In spite of the heat, they were allowed no water from the local streams during the march and therefore they drank muddy water. Whoever staggered was beaten, and if a prisoner collapsed he was shot. Once I saw a row of executed German prisoners lying in a roadside ditch. When they passed through a town, they would beg for bread, but the civilians didn't dare give them any. I saw a German senior lieutenant sitting on the edge of a trench. He wore a uniform shirt with shoulder insignia and bravery awards but he had no trousers and was barefoot. The guards removed the better clothing from the prisoners and traded it for liquor with the local population.[15]

Several senior German officers became prisoners. Müller was captured on 7 or 8 July when soldiers searching the area were met by a German officer carrying a white flag. He informed the Red Army troops that he had been sent by a German general who wished to discuss the surrender of his remaining men with a Soviet officer of equivalent rank. Müller then came forward and was driven to the headquarters of CXXI Rifle Corps, where he was met by Major General Dmitry Ivanovich Smirnov, the corps commander:

[He gave] the impression of a sullen, downcast man in dishevelled uniform with only one shoulder strap, and his boots were dirty. General Smirnov … asked him if he wanted to have a moment to clean himself up. He answered, 'Yes, thank you.' General Müller was taken to a separate house. After he had tidied himself a little, he emerged accompanied by his orderly.[16]

Müller agreed to draft a letter urging survivors of Fourth Army to lay down their weapons, and copies were dropped over the area. Several Germans emerged from the forests and swamps bearing these letters, which promised safety if they surrendered.[17] Like many other officers who were captured during the course of *Bagration*, he immediately joined the *NKFD* and *BDO* and showed great willingness to cooperate with his captors. Some of his contemporaries expressed surprise and disgust at the speed of his conversion to an anti-Hitler stance, but as early as 1939 he had been involved in an anti-Hitler conspiracy with Generals Erwin von Witzleben and Kurt von Hammerstein-Equord. He was released from captivity in 1948 and held various posts in East Germany. He had intermittent contacts with former colleagues in the west and died in 1961 after apparently committing suicide by jumping from a high window; immediately after, his son and daughter-in-law escaped to the west.[18]

Müller was just one of several senior officers to be captured as what became known as the Minsk–Chervyen pocket collapsed. Völckers, commander of XXVII Corps, surrendered a day after Müller. He too joined the *BDO* but died in captivity in 1946. Several division commanders were also captured. Generalmajor Günther Klamm (commander of 260th Infantry Division), Generalleutnant Eberhard von Kurowski (commander of 110th Infantry Division), Generalmajor Friedrich-Carl von Steinkeller (commander of *Feldherrnhalle*), Generalleutnant Hans Traut (78th Sturm Division), and Generalmajor Adolf Trowitz (commander of 57th Infantry Division) all remained in captivity until 1955. Thousands of lower-ranking officers, NCOs, and soldiers were also taken prisoner and many were then paraded through Red Square in Moscow a few weeks later. Most of the wounded men who were left behind by

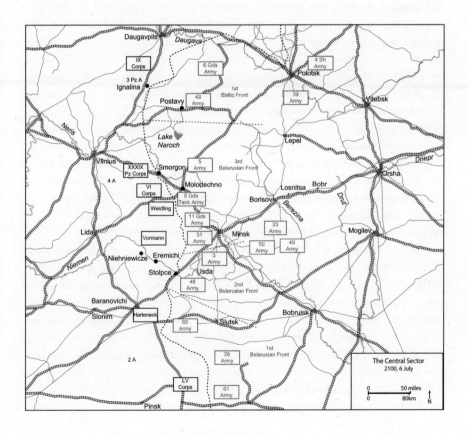

Müller during the breakout attempt either were killed immediately by the Red Army or succumbed to their injuries shortly after. The treatment of prisoners of war was harsh, with little attempt made to care for wounded soldiers – any help they received was usually from their comrades. But however badly the Wehrmacht prisoners were treated, it still fell short of the terrible suffering of Red Army prisoners in German hands, particularly in the first year of the conflict, when hundreds of thousands were allowed to starve to death.

Meanwhile, the Red Army continued to flood westward. Bagramian's 1st Baltic Front was now tasked with continuing the offensive towards the west and northwest to reach a line running from Daugavpils to Kaunas. The town of Lyntupy, close to the frontier with Lithuania, fell early on 6 July without a fight; a counterattack was immediately organised and retook the town, destroying or driving away the Soviet reconnaissance units that had appeared almost from nowhere. Attempts to extend the flank of Third Panzer Army to the south were too weak to have any impact and the gap to Vilnius remained open. With both his flanks still in the air, Reinhardt issued orders to Third Panzer Army for a withdrawal in the night of 6–7 July back to positions within Lithuania. His report that evening summed up the situation clearly:

> The Russians do as they please in the north as well as the south [of Third Panzer Army's sector]. Apparently they are weakening their forces in front of Sixteenth Army in order to thrust into the gap between Army Groups North and Centre with three armies and to thrust into the depths. III Guards Mechanised Corps is moving from Smorgon towards Vilnius. Third Panzer Army is being driven increasingly towards the northwest. The enemy has been able to replenish his ranks swiftly using partisans. He advances only through open space [i.e. bypassing German units] merely at the cost of fuel and other supplies, which he supplements from captured stocks.[19]

On the northern flank of the German Fourth Army and at the southern end of the gap that yawned invitingly to the east of Vilnius, the German 221st Security Division clashed with the southern flank of the Soviet Fifth Army in Smorgon. The security division was effectively surrounded in the town by mid-morning and on his own initiative Generalleutnant Bogislav von Schwerin, the division commander, ordered a breakout to the west. He succeeded in extracting most of his men but the division's limited heavy weaponry was largely lost. Saucken's XXXIX Panzer Corps was now in a horseshoe formation with both its flanks being driven back; a counterattack by 5th Panzer Division from the southwest made good initial progress but then had to be abandoned in the face of growing

Red Army tank strength. In any event, there were reports of Red Army penetrations in the sector held by 170th Infantry Division, at the easterly end of the 'horseshoe', and Decker had to dispatch tanks to deal with this. In an attempt to avoid being outflanked further, Saucken ordered his units to pull back broadly to the south of the remnants of Third Panzer Army, though the reports of small groups of Red Army tanks operating in the rear of the German positions made the safety of even this line questionable. The only crumb of comfort came from a radio intercept recorded by 5th Panzer Division's signals battalion: a Soviet commander told his subordinates, 'If you encounter 5th Panzer Division, go around it!'[20] But if the Red Army was unwilling to engage the tough panzer division head-on, there were plenty of gaps for the Germans to be bypassed.

Like Bagramian's 1st Baltic Front, Cherniakhovsky's 3rd Belarusian Front had also received new orders: it was to capture Vilnius. The new instructions for 2nd Belarusian Front called for a rapid advance to Grodno and Białystok, and further to the south Rokossovsky's 1st Belarusian Front had received new orders to continue the offensive towards the west with the aim of reaching and capturing Baranovichi no later than 12 July. Thereafter, Rokossovsky was to move on towards Brest and was to secure a bridgehead over the Western Bug River. As part of this operation, Pliev reinforced his leading elements and despite the efforts of 12th Panzer Division large parts of the southwest bank of the Usha were in Soviet hands by the end of the day; in places, Pliev's forces were up to 12 miles beyond the river.[21]

There seemed to be little that could be done to stop the Soviet forces. With only the briefest of pauses while supplies were brought forward, the Red Army resumed its relentless advances through the numerous holes in the German lines. One such gap was to the south, where a few scattered units – the remnants of *Gruppe von Gottberg* amongst them – covered a large area and could do little more than send reports of how fast the Soviet units were advancing. After completing its crossing of the Usha River at Eremichi, 12th Panzer Division made successful counterattacks against elements of Pliev's cavalry-mechanised group that had crossed the river and were attempting to advance towards the southwest.

With Rokossovsky's armies now advancing on Baranovichi from both the northeast and the east, the continuing resistance of 4th Panzer Division and supporting units to the east of the city was increasingly futile and carried the risk that the precious panzer division might find itself dangerously isolated. Accordingly, together with the neighbouring Hungarian cavalry and 28th Jäger Division, Betzel's panzers began to pull back towards Baranovichi, which Hitler had designated as a 'fortress' under the command of Generalmajor Albert Newiger. Vormann discussed the situation with Weiss, commander of Second Army, to whom *Gruppe Vormann* had been subordinated. He advised Weiss that despite being commander of a security division, Newiger effectively had no troops with which to garrison his 'fortress'. Weiss replied that Newiger would have to gather together what few stragglers he could until the 'fortress' order could be rescinded. Vormann protested that this was nonsensical; whilst Weiss agreed with him, he felt unable to act against Hitler's edict.

Both Weiss and Model were doing their best to improve matters within the limited freedom granted to them by Hitler. Model demanded the immediate transfer of 225th Infantry Division to Third Panzer Army and the withdrawal of the southern flank of Army Group North to what had become known as the *Lettland-Stellung* ('Latvia Position'), i.e. giving up all territory east of the old frontier between the Soviet Union and the Baltic States. Hitler agreed to the former, but refused to permit the latter on the grounds that he wished to avoid making a decision that he judged would have 'severe consequences' for a further week. These consequences were the arguments that Hitler frequently raised when his generals demanded permission to retreat: he would respond that a retreat was impossible either for political reasons (e.g. the effect that such a retreat might have on Germany's allies), or because of the need to secure vital resources such as fuel or minerals, or to protect the Baltic coastline in order to permit U-boat training to continue. Just how much difference a week would make was beyond the comprehension of the hard-pressed officers on the Eastern Front. With regard to Baranovichi, Hitler accepted Model's suggestion that no further troops should be sent there, but insisted that the city had to be held for as long as possible.

Looking back on the confusion and paralysis created by Hitler's constant grasping at any excuse to refuse permission for a timely retreat, it is difficult to understand why so many senior officers acquiesced to instructions that they knew placed their men in grave danger. The consequences of the utterly flawed 'fortress' policy had already been demonstrated at Vitebsk, Mogilev, and Bobruisk; none of these 'fortresses' had tied down Soviet forces for any meaningful length of time and they had merely resulted in the destruction of irreplaceable veteran Wehrmacht formations. To continue implementing such a policy was an excellent demonstration of the principle that the definition of madness is to repeat the same steps in the hope of a different outcome. Yet the sense of obedience to orders, instilled into German officers throughout their training, remained largely unshaken, at least for men like Model, Reinhardt, Tippelskirch, Vormann, and Weiss. Despite the evidence before them that Germany faced catastrophe – indeed, the catastrophe was already unfolding on the front line and in the bombed cities of the Reich – they continued to obey orders that they knew were senseless.

But others had long run out of confidence in the Führer, or had never believed in him in the first place. To date, they had made a few attempts to kill Hitler, but none had succeeded. The plotters approached several senior officers at various times and received a variety of excuses. Some hid behind their personal oath of loyalty to Hitler; others said that no action could be taken until there was greater acceptance across the army of the futility of continuing; and, aware of the insistence of the Allied Powers on Germany's unconditional surrender, some wanted to achieve a form of stalemate from which they might be able to negotiate a better way out. A few like Manstein wrote in later years that their only practical option would have been to tender their resignation, but they felt unable to do this as such an option was not available to their subordinates. And while the generals prevaricated, the plotters grew ever more fearful that their schemes would be discovered before they could be put into effect.

Hans Gisevius, who would be one of the few anti-Hitler plotters to survive the coming weeks, later wrote:

> I need merely glance through my appointment calendar for the last weeks of June and the beginning of July 1944 to confirm once again the condition of nervous tension which was mine throughout that period … When would the thunder and lightning break? Would the generals let pass this very last chance to act?
>
> The disaster on the Eastern Front could no longer be covered up. The Russians had ripped a huge hole through the army group in the centre and their victorious armies were advancing without pause into this gap. Dozens of generals, cut off from their communications, were surrendering their troops virtually without a fight. It seemed evident that the military collapse was so drastic precisely because it was also a moral breakdown.
>
> The situation in the west was no better. The invasion was still in its first stages; the decisive breakthrough had not yet taken place. But the very fact of the success of the invasion could not be explained away … It was evident that the dykes would soon give way and then there would remain no more insane excuses for those vacillating generals who insisted that the *Putsch* must wait until the invasion was beaten back or at least contained so that, coupling it with the Bolshevik threat from the east, they would have a basis for negotiations with the Anglo-Americans.[22]

The assertion that dozens of generals were surrendering without a fight is of course an exaggeration, but Gisevius wrote the original German version of his book in 1946 when information about the battles in Belarus was probably far more limited. Even as the front-line generals wrestled with the enormous burden of fighting against a superior enemy while their highest leadership continued to send out nonsensical orders, the plotters finally ran out of patience and made their final preparations. If anything was to be saved from imminent disaster, they could wait no longer for the army to face reality.

By first light on 7 July, the exhausted survivors of Third Panzer Army had completed their withdrawal across the border into Lithuania. The forces of 1st Baltic Front were close behind. The northern flank of Reinhardt's forces continued to have no contact with Army Group North and the leading Soviet units reached and captured Ignalina; the nearest units of the German Sixteenth Army were parts of 225th Infantry Division in Dukstas, about 13 miles further north. With constant pressure both on his front and on either flank, Reinhardt ordered a further withdrawal of about 15 miles. The only good news was that Army Group North was relieving 225th Infantry Division with other units so that it could be used to try to close the gap. Whilst granting permission to Reinhardt for this further withdrawal, Model also advised him that no future retreats would be tolerated. The units arriving from the north, together with the mechanised *Führer-Begleit* Battalion – a unit created from army personnel who had formed Hitler's personal escort – would have to be sufficient to halt the Red Army. The *Führer-Begleit* Battalion was at least a mechanised unit, and the only way that such a modest quantity of troops could make a difference was if they were used in mobile operations; Reinhardt repeatedly made this point and requested permission for the battalion to be deployed in such a role to the north of Vilnius. The response from Model was hardly a surprise: the battalion could only be deployed with Hitler's specific permission, and he had decreed that it was to be sent to Vilnius. Both Reinhardt and Model must have known that if this order was followed, the battalion faced almost certain destruction in the city when it came under attack.

After being in constant action for several weeks, many Red Army units were now badly degraded. Losses had been heavy, particularly in the opening days of the campaign, and even the days of rapid advance towards the west saw further casualties and a diminishing of strength due to stragglers and sickness. Gurevich, the artilleryman who had watched the shock waves from the initial artillery bombardment of 23 June dispersing his cigarette smoke, was still advancing, but his battery was in poor shape:

> In some guncrews, there were only three men left. It got to the point that the batteries began to use captured Germans to help dig in the guns, carry shells, and for other unskilled work, since there was no shortage of them during the offensive.

They took one or two prisoners for each guncrew, all illegal of course, without the permission of senior officers. It didn't last long. Once the deputy division commander Subbotin saw Germans riding along with the guncrews on the gun carriages, he gave everyone a big dressing-down ... Subbotin was very cruel towards the Germans. All of these prisoners were shot on his orders.[23]

Galitsky's Eleventh Guards Army put huge pressure upon both flanks of Saucken's XXXIX Panzer Corps, and even with the arrival of the first elements of 7th Panzer Division on the southern flank it was impossible to establish contact with German units further south. Once again, the entire corps was ordered to pull back towards the west to a line that was approximately due south of Vilnius – staying in its current positions would result in its envelopment. Since its arrival in Army Group Centre, 5th Panzer Division had repeatedly defeated Red Army units wherever it made contact with them, but had been forced to retreat about 100 miles. The effect of this on the morale of the division's exhausted personnel was considerable, and many must have wondered when the endless retreats would come to an end.

After redeployment overnight, 12th Panzer Division was finally able to establish good contact with 28th Jäger Division to the south. There was even tentative contact with *Gruppe Weidling*, the southern flank of Fourth Army, to the north, but only at the cost of stretching the division's four panzergrenadier battalions over an excessive frontage. When a brief report reached the division headquarters that 'Cossacks' had been spotted in the village of Niehniewicze, about 36 miles north of Baranovichi, a panzergrenadier battalion was dispatched to the area:

During the evening we moved to Niehniewicze to deal with the 'handful of Cossacks' there. But when we ran into the enemy we realised that there was no question of just a handful of Cossacks. In fact, Ivan had set up a sizable *Pakfront* in the most favourable position possible, supported by a few tanks, and our attack failed especially since he also interdicted our advance with ground attack planes and bombers. The night was so well lit up by his 'fir trees' [clusters of parachute flares tied together and dropped by aircraft] that one could easily read a newspaper. We were just about to move to a safe line a little distance back from a row of burning houses when a radio command was received, telling us to pull back to our original area. Here, we were finally able to get a night's sleep.[24]

The *Pakfront* – an organised line of anti-tank guns under unified command – was originally a German innovation, but had been developed further by the Red

Army with the use of combat engineers who laid mines to channel German vehicles onto the guns of the defensive position. The speed with which such barriers could be created was an impressive sign of the continuing improvement in the abilities of the Red Army, and the Wehrmacht failed to come up with an adequate response.

Often deployed as 'firefighters' to deal with crises as they developed along the front line, the soldiers of the panzer divisions had become adept at scavenging for supplies. The men of 4th Panzer Division enjoyed a surprise windfall, as Robert Poensgen, a war journalist attached to the division, discovered. The division's repair workshops had finally arrived and Poensgen was with a tank with an inoperative gun that had been sent to Slonim for repairs. Here, he and the tank crew witnessed a remarkable scene:

> First we saw a soldier trotting past with a pan full of eggs, then another and another. Two came past carrying a whole bathtub filled with eggs. Eggs, which we had just been dreaming of! Somewhere in the city there was a substantial source of eggs. But where? We stopped and asked, and were told that there was a huge store of eggs in the town centre that was being cleared. But we should hurry, they said, because there weren't many left.[25]

The tank crew found a large warehouse with a tank of cold water, in which eggs had been stored. Many had already been broken by soldiers attempting to harvest them, and Poensgen earned the accolades of his comrades by volunteering to be lowered into the water to get as many eggs as he could. He added that after a feast of scrambled eggs with canned meat and improvised eggnog, he delivered a rucksack full of eggs to the division command post, but it was many years before he could face a meal with eggs again after such over-indulgence. But such moments of good fortune and enjoyment were all too rare, with 4th Panzer Division repeatedly required to commit its units in local counterattacks to blunt the Soviet advance. The armoured battlegroup, led by the able and very popular Oberst Hans Christern, was in constant action:

> *Kampfgruppe Christern* – consisting of 35th Panzer Regiment, the armoured reconnaissance battalion, a half-track battalion, an artillery battalion and a company of combat engineers – was the mobile 'fire brigade'. Wherever things flared up, it was thrown into action. Cooperation within the battlegroup was excellent. The armoured assault troops smashed every enemy attack. The artillery went into position next to an ammunition dump and fired every round it could. They only paused their firing when their barrels were glowing with red heat.

At one point the Russians succeeded in reaching our route of march behind us. The combat vehicles were gathered together quickly and deployed on the road. They broke open the ring and the wheeled elements were able to move back. This wasn't possible without losses, but the enemy's attempt to cut us off failed.

The supply units had to do their utmost in these battles, ensuring that ammunition and fuel was always in position. The operational tanks fought now in the south, now in the north, always where the enemy sought a success ...

We managed to snatch some sleep now and then. We were even loaned to neighbouring divisions from time to time ...

In the meantime, our repair workshops were operational again. Suddenly an astonishing number of repaired tanks returned to the regiment.[26]

Throughout 7 July, the Soviet Forty-Eighth and Sixty-Fifth Armies were edging closer to Baranovichi. Army Group Centre continued to pass on Hitler's orders that the city was to be defended at all costs, but Vormann had no intention of allowing any more German units to be encircled; he told his chief of staff that the flanks of the position around Baranovichi were to be strengthened, even if this was at the cost of permitting Soviet penetrations into the urban area. Several key installations in Baranovichi were destroyed and when elements of 4th Panzer Division and the Hungarian cavalry operating in the southern part of the city reported that they were having to fall back, Vormann used this as justification for withdrawing towards the west.

The main attack on Baranovichi was made by Batov's Sixty-Fifth Army, and the army commander, who had been with the leading elements to ensure they kept up the highest possible tempo, later described an incident that highlights further the poor personal relationship between Batov and Zhukov, the deputy supreme commander of the Red Army:

I wished [Major General Dmitry Fedorovich] Alekseyev [commander of CV Rifle Corps] luck and together with [Major General Nikolai Antonovich] Radetsky [the political commissar of Sixty-Fifth Army] I made my way from Alekseyev's command post, just 3km from the city, to the small village of Velka to my army headquarters. All the army staff had gathered here already under the command of [Major General Mikhail Vladimirovich] Bobkov [Batov's chief of staff]. For the first time in several days we had an opportunity to do something about our appearance. But we had barely finished shaving and cleaning our boots when several trucks approached our huts. 'It's Zhukov,' said Radetsky after a quick look through the window. We hurried to the door intending to give the *Stavka* representative an optimistic report. But it turned out differently.

'That's all very well,' grumbled the marshal, 'You're shaving and perfuming yourselves, but Baranovichi still hasn't been taken.'

We urged Zhukov to go into the hut with us. But he still didn't calm down. Never in my long service did I ever encounter such humiliating behaviour. Radetsky's face was frozen. When I finally got a chance to speak and reported that our troops were making good progress, and that the city could be taken at any moment, the marshal started raging again.

'The army commander's report corresponds with the facts,' said Radetsky. But he was ignored. When Radetsky repeated himself, the marshal turned on him too. This undignified scene ended with Zhukov ordering Radetsky to go to Baranovichi and not to return until the city was in our hands. He then kicked aside his chair and left the room, slamming the door behind him.

There was an oppressive silence. 'Don't worry about it,' Radetsky assured me. 'We don't serve Zhukov, we serve the Soviet armed forces. Let's have our evening meal. It's all nonsense. But I'd like to know what got the marshal so agitated.' I didn't really care, but Radetsky continued. 'I think I can see what's going on. Vasilevsky's already outside Vilnius. Zhukov's wrestling with him for attention, to be the first to report a major success to *Stavka*. But I'll have to go. Orders are orders!'

So I was left alone. I didn't have to worry about my troops. The battle was proceeding as planned. Still, I couldn't find any solace. We army commanders were unaccustomed to being treated like this by our superiors. Late that night [7–8 July] Radetsky contacted me. 'Everything's going as planned.'

'Where are you calling from?'

'I'm in Baranovichi. I've driven around the whole city with Alekseyev. I'm in [Major General Kuzma Yevdokimovich] Grebennik's command post [15th Rifle Division] in the cemetery. Our troops are about 1.5km further west, advancing successfully.'

A senior officer was hunched over a briefcase in front of the hut where Zhukov was sleeping. I had the marshal awakened and informed him that Baranovichi had been taken.

'Are there any reports from Vilnius?' he asked. 'No? Then I'll sleep a little more.'[27]

By midnight, Baranovichi was in Soviet hands. Orders arrived shortly after in Vormann's headquarters from *OKH*: Hitler was still insisting that Vormann held his previously designated positions.

There was a little relief for Third Panzer Army on 8 July; the pace of the Red Army's pursuit seemed to be slowing. The substantial gap between Army Groups

North and Centre was still open, and Reinhardt and General Paul Laux, commander of Sixteenth Army, had little clear idea of how many Soviet units were moving through this area. Additional reinforcements were sent to the gap by Sixteenth Army but there were worrying signs for the Germans that Soviet troops were concentrating to the south of Ignalina making the success of any renewed German attack unlikely. Despite the comparative lack of pressure, Reinhardt made a request to Model to pull back once more in the coming night; Model refused, telling his subordinate to wait until all intended reinforcements had arrived.

Despite both its flanks being exposed, XXXIX Panzer Corps also had a slightly quieter day, though it too continued its withdrawal. Oberst Erich Dethleffsen, chief of staff at the headquarters of Tippelskirch's Fourth Army, recorded in the war diary, perhaps more in hope than anything else, that 'apparently the enemy is anxious about our courageous fight.'[28] Model, in a dinner conversation with visitors from Berlin, was rather more honest. When he was congratulated on bringing at least the beginnings of order to Army Group Centre, he replied that he had inherited a command that largely existed only on paper. If the Soviet advance was slowing, it wasn't down to his efforts, and had far more to do with the need for the Red Army to pause its high tempo of operations while supplies and reinforcements were brought forward and units were regrouped.[29]

In the southern sector, there was little sign of any such drop in the tempo of operations near Baranovichi. The Hungarian cavalry units deployed alongside 4th Panzer Division had looked quite splendid when they rode to the front line, but the panzer crewmen had immediately speculated how long this would last once they encountered tanks and modern weaponry. By 8 August, the cavalrymen were at risk of scattering in confusion. Orders from *OKH* arrived during the afternoon officially ending the status of Baranovichi as a 'fortress', over 12 hours after the city had fallen. The priority now was to try to bring order to the numerous bodies of stragglers and rear area units to the west of the city before the Red Army attacked again. In the day after the fall of the city, Soviet units probed about nine miles west; much of 28th Jäger Division was effectively surrounded to the north of Baranovichi.

In the headquarters of 12th Panzer Division, a relieved Müller, who had been acting as temporary commander, packed his bags and headed west; Bodenhausen was expected to return from leave at any moment. The division was now part of LV Corps rather than under the direct control of Vormann, with the immediate consequence that many of the communications problems that had hindered operations were eliminated as LV Corps headquarters was far closer to the front line. Still pulling back to the west, the panzer division was ordered to make a relieving attack to rescue 28th Jäger Division, but it proved impossible to concentrate forces for such an operation. During the afternoon of 8 July, Oberst Müller surprised everyone at the headquarters of 12th Panzer Division by returning. He told the division staff that as he was travelling towards the west, he had found about a battalion of Soviet troops in the village of Dvorets; hastily gathering together soldiers he found nearby – largely rear area personnel from 12th Panzer Division and a few tank crews whose vehicles had been destroyed or were awaiting repair – he had led a counterattack to drive the Soviet battalion out. He had no idea where the Red Army soldiers had gone, but the division's line of retreat was once more open.[30]

Other elements of 12th Panzer Division also had unexpected clashes with Soviet units, as a report from one of the division's panzergrenadier battalions described:

In the middle of a wooded area the battalion came under fire from about seven enemy tanks and assault guns that were covering the road. A company and the staff were attacked from the front and right by tanks supported by infantry. We immediately dismounted and engaged them. Only a small number of vehicles at the head of our column managed to break out quickly; they were able to reach the main road. In bitter fighting at close quarters and by making constant counterattacks, we were able to hold the Russians away from the road. Assault guns were put out of action using hand grenades. A large number of our vehicles were already burning brightly after being shot up by tanks. About three companies managed to pull back, hindered by bad roads and paths, and reached the main road by a different route. Contact with regimental headquarters was only by radio. The line of march was repeatedly altered by orders from the regiment as the Russians had already blocked it at several points. After several detours ... the battalion reached Novoyelniya, where it met up with the regiment commander. It was a black day with heavy losses of men, vehicles and equipment.[31]

Not far away, 4th Panzer Division was also enduring a difficult day. Through a mixture of losses in battle and vehicles awaiting repair, the tank strength of the division stood at 17 Pz.IVs, 35 Panthers, 22 assault guns, and 12 self-propelled anti-tank guns by first light on 8 July.[32] Even in the short time since they had arrived, the repair workshops had already returned several tanks to service, and without this the division would have been in far worse shape. Operating in the area to the west of Baranovichi, the division pulled back slowly towards Slonim, engaging Soviet spearheads several times to blunt their probes.

That evening, Zhukov was in Moscow, meeting Stalin, Molotov, Malenkov, and others. In his memoirs, he described how he had put the Soviet leader in a good mood with his reports from the southern part of the battlefield, and that a telephone call from Vasilevsky added to the general sense of optimism:

Discussing the possibilities of Germany continuing the armed struggle, we all agreed that German human and material resources were effectively exhausted, while the Soviet Union, benefiting from the liberation of Ukraine, Belarus, Lithuania, and other regions, would receive significant replenishment from partisan units and from the people who remained in these territories. And the second front would compel Germany to continue strengthening its forces in the west. The question arose: what could the Nazi leadership hope for in such a situation?

The supreme commander [Stalin] answered the question: 'The same thing that a gambler hopes for when he stakes his last coin. All the hope of the Nazis was on the British and Americans. In deciding to go to war with the Soviet Union, Hitler considered the imperialist circles of Great Britain and the USA to be his ideological adherents. And not without reason: they did everything to direct the military operations of the Wehrmacht against the Soviet Union.'

'Hitler will probably make an attempt at any cost to reach a separate agreement with the American and British governments,' added Molotov.

'That's right,' said Stalin, 'but Roosevelt and Churchill will not make a deal with Hitler. They will strive to secure their political interests in Germany, not by entering into an agreement with the Nazis, who have lost the confidence of their people, but by seeking the possibility of forming a government obedient to them in Germany.' Then he turned to me: 'Can our troops reach the Vistula without stopping and begin the liberation of Poland, and in what sector can the First Polish Army, which has now worked up to the required combat standard, be brought into action?'

'Our troops can not only reach the Vistula,' I said, 'but must also secure good bridgeheads over it to ensure a further offensive operation in the strategic direction of Berlin. As for First Polish Army, it must be directed at Warsaw.'[33]

Assuming this is an accurate account of the discussion, it gives insights into the attitude of the Soviet leadership towards the Western Powers. There was still great resentment at the long delay in establishing a second front, with suspicions that this had been a deliberate attempt to weaken the Soviet Union by having it shoulder the bulk of the burden of the land war against Germany. And in view of the declarations of the western leaders that they would not make a separate peace with Germany, Stalin – probably correctly – interpreted this as meaning that they wouldn't negotiate with Hitler. But if an opportunity arose for the Western Powers to establish a different regime in Berlin, Stalin fully expected them to take advantage of it; hence the need to push on to and over the Vistula.

CHAPTER 9

VILNIUS: 9–14 JULY

During the summer of 1944, Hitler declared many locations on the Eastern Front as fortresses, to be held to the last man. Almost none of these achieved their declared purpose of holding up the Red Army while a relief column was prepared; instead, the cities, towns, and in some cases patches of bare ground became graveyards for their garrisons and the Soviet soldiers who overran them. Vilnius, the ancient capital of Lithuania, was one of the largest cities to be designated as a fortress. Would the outcome of the fighting here be any different from what had taken place in Vitebsk, Bobruisk, and other fortresses?

As early as 1323, Vilnius was the capital city of the Grand Duchy of Lithuania, which grew rapidly after Grand Duke Gediminas invited Germans and Jews to move to his city from the towns of the Hanseatic League. It flourished further after the creation of the Polish–Lithuanian Commonwealth in 1569, but became part of the Russian Empire after the Third Partition of Poland in 1795. With such a complex history, it was unsurprising that it had a very mixed population. At the end of the First World War, the single biggest ethnic group in the city was Polish, followed by the Jews. Ethnic Lithuanians were only the third largest group, though they formed a larger proportion of the population in the rural areas around Vilnius. In the turmoil of the early 1920s, the entire region was annexed by Poland, only to be returned to Lithuania by Stalin in 1939. By 1944, the Jewish population of the city was hugely reduced to less than 3,000. The overall Jewish population of Lithuania had been at least 210,000, though in addition to this there were tens of thousands of Polish Jews who had fled the German invasion of Poland. Fewer than 9,000 Jews managed to flee into the interior of the Soviet Union after the commencement of *Barbarossa*, and in the years that followed between 196,000 and 250,000 were killed by the Germans. Most had been executed in mass shootings in the first months of the German occupation.[1]

The small number of surviving Jews – most in a small number of work camps, but a handful who were hiding within Vilnius – listened to the approaching sounds of fighting with a mixture of hope and trepidation. Even with regular air attacks on the railway station in attempts to disrupt the arrival of German forces and with Soviet ground forces reported to be approaching the outskirts, some German units in the city were busy with tasks other than preparing for the imminent battle. A battalion from 16th SS Police Regiment had been assigned to the city garrison, and many of its personnel – assisted by paramilitary troops from the Baltic States – carried out further executions of Jews.

Most of the partisan groups in the Vilnius region were part of the Polish *AK*, which was regarded by Stalin as just as much an enemy as the Germans. In the months preceding *Bagration*, pro-Soviet partisans had repeatedly attacked *AK* groups, and the Poles had little doubt that they would face further attacks when the Red Army arrived. But there was an additional factor at work. *Stavka* was aware of Polish plans to try to seize major cities immediately before the Red Army arrived in an attempt to prevent the Soviet forces from being able to portray themselves as liberators. As a result, there were occasions when it suited the Red Army to pause while the Germans and Poles fought each other, thus ultimately making the task of the Red Army a little easier. This policy was rapidly developing as Soviet units encountered the first signs of such Polish uprisings, and would reach a terrible climax later in the summer in Warsaw.

Vilnius had served as the destination for wounded soldiers in a previous war, when Napoleon's *Grande Armée* was retreating from Moscow in 1812. Once more, its hospitals – and many buildings hastily converted to such a role – were overflowing with casualties. If the city was to have any hope of functioning as a 'fortress', it required a garrison, but by 4 July just a single battalion of 170th Infantry Division, together with the SS and paramilitary units, had arrived. A soldier from 170th Infantry Division described the situation:

> We detrained some distance from the city. From it, there came a stream of refugees towards us, many women and children with handcarts, choking the roads. There were also numerous wounded soldiers ... Everyone was getting out of the city. Someone shouted at us, 'Guys, get out of here!' but we had to march on together. We were given a good meal in the city and then took up positions on the outskirts.[2]

Further troops from 170th Infantry Division and other units designated to form the fortress garrison arrived over the next two or three days. On 7 July, there were fierce clashes on the southern outskirts against pro-Polish partisans. It was the start of the local implementation of an operation codenamed *Burza* ('Storm'), the attempt by the Polish *AK* to take control of important locations before the arrival of the Red Army. There was no expectation that these Polish forces would be able to hold places like Vilnius after the arrival of the Red Army, but it was seen as an important political gesture. In Vilnius, the local operation was codenamed *Ostra Brama* ('Gates of Dawn'), named after a historical landmark in Vilnius. However, the city garrison – supported by an armoured train – was strong enough to defeat the attempts by the lightly armed *AK* units to penetrate into the heart of the city.

The Soviet units closing in on Vilnius were led by III Guards Mechanised Corps, part of Oslikovsky's cavalry-mechanised group; it was followed closely by the bulk of Fifth Guards Tank Army, with Rotmistrov smarting under constant criticism for the lack of urgency in his advance. But even if the tank army had yet to make its presence fully felt, the other Soviet formations in the area were creating more than enough difficulty for the Wehrmacht. Ion Lazarevich Degen was a junior tank officer, and his reminiscences shed light on the grim circumstances in which he experienced the war:

We were in the second battalion of a Guards tank brigade under the command of Lieutenant Colonel Yefim Yevseyevich Duchovny ...

The brigade had 65 tanks in three battalions, a motorised rifle battalion, a signals company, reconnaissance troops, a medical platoon, and assorted other subunits. We were used only for breakthrough operations and suffered enormous losses in every offensive.

Indeed, it was a brigade of damned warhorses, and the average tank driver was unlikely to survive more than two offensives. After I survived the summer offensive in Belarus and Lithuania, everyone in the battalion called me 'lucky guy' for my amazing survival. But newcomers to the brigade weren't told what sort of 'lucky' unit they had joined ...

Our rear area units were stuck far beyond the Berezina and there were shortages of fuel and ammunition. When the brigade was tasked with advancing on Vilnius, the remaining shells and fuel in the bled-out brigade were sufficient for just a platoon of three tanks to be sent forward ...

I was nominated for a 'probation assignment'. Lieutenant Varivoda, the political officer, offered to go with us as a liaison officer. Although he was a commissar he was a decent fellow, the complete opposite of the foolish and cowardly Smirnov [another political officer in the brigade]. We had covered more than 200km on unpaved roads and dirt tracks without pause, wearing out the rubber tyres of our vehicles ...

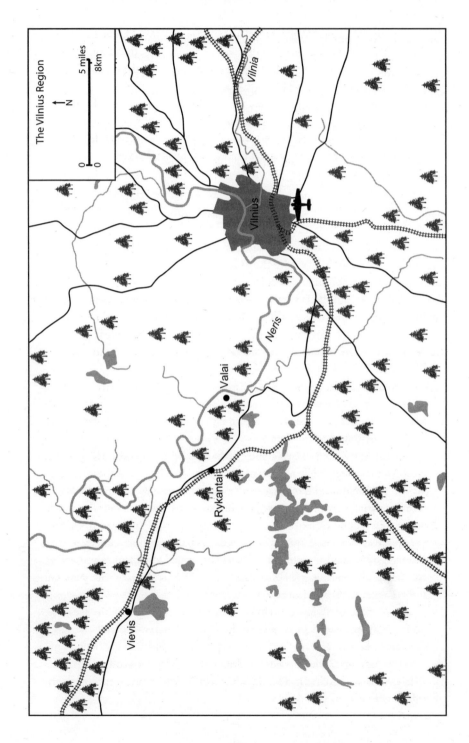

The Vilnius Region

N

5 miles
8km

Vilnia

Vilnius

Neris

Valai

Rykantai

Vievis

We stopped at the headquarters of a rifle corps in a grand Lithuanian house about 6km from Vilnius. The commissar and I went inside. As the senior, Varivoda reported to the corps commander, a lieutenant general, that the vanguard of the Guards tank brigade had arrived, three tanks strong.

The lieutenant general – I believe his name was Krylov [actually Lieutenant General Nikolai Ivanovich Krylov, commander of Fifth Army] – eyed me critically from top to bottom, thrust out his chin, and said, 'And this is the famed 2nd Guards Tank Brigade that's going to make sure I can take the city?'

We were silent. The general sat down with a smile. 'Well, so be it, I haven't any choice. Get some rest, boys. Get some sleep! Tomorrow is another day. You can go see a movie at my headquarters.'

All the time, we could hear the thunder of fighting from Vilnius [where the Germans were clashing with the *AK*]. Varivoda and I looked at each other in confusion, not understanding anything.[3]

Shortly after first light on 8 July, Degen and his three tanks were ordered to support a regiment of 144th Rifle Division as it attempted to penetrate into Vilnius. Regardless of whatever instructions he might have received about how to deal with the *AK*, he was happy to take whatever help he could find:

I was led to the regiment commander. This lieutenant colonel gave us assurances in the manner of a senior commander that the enemy had only a few hundred infantry, a couple of tanks, and one or two guns available in his defensive positions. It seemed a simple task for me to chase them with ease merely by putting in an appearance. So we three tanks split up and crawled through the streets without line of sight to each other. The two German guns the lieutenant colonel had mentioned had apparently multiplied themselves. Artillery began to shell us from every direction. We couldn't deal with them all. Our right track was shredded. The driver shifted into reverse and the tank turned sharply, leaving the broken track in front of us and crawling back into a yard where by sheer luck we found ourselves in a good position. A shell had shredded the sprockets and front idler. Since we couldn't repair such damage with what we had available, I ordered the crew to stay with the vehicle and wait for a repair crew. I went to look for the other tanks. One of my platoon's tanks had become stuck in an apparently abandoned tall building. The crew was still there and I climbed aboard.

I ordered the tank commander to drive over to my damaged tank, set up a perimeter defence, and waited for the maintenance crew to reach us. In addition to the Soviet troops, the Germans were under attack from the Poles, who wore red and white armbands on their sleeves. A group of Poles came up to the tank.

I climbed down and asked, 'Do you need any help?' Their commander – if I recall correctly, a colonel – was close to tears and shook my hand. He pointed to a school from which the German guns were putting up the most intense fire. It turned out they had been dealing with the Germans without any help since the previous day. This was why the lieutenant general had been so relaxed towards us. At that moment a lieutenant, whom I had seen earlier at the regiment's headquarters, ran up and gave me orders to support his battalion in the same direction as the Poles had indicated to me.

I found the battalion commander's observation post in a cellar. He explained the situation to me and assigned us our task. His battalion was reduced to 17 survivors. I smiled. 'Well, since my three tanks count as a tank brigade, why can't 17 men be a battalion?'[4]

The declining strength of both infantry and tank units in the Red Army's assault forces wasn't just down to casualties, though these were heavy enough; stragglers and broken-down vehicles were strewn across the roads to the east, where there was an almost insurmountable tangle of traffic. Degen was assigned support from a 76mm field gun, but it had only two armour-piercing rounds left and no high explosive ammunition. Within hours, Degen's tanks had no more ammunition left for their main weapons and could only use their machine-guns:

> The streetfighting was a nightmare. It was a sort of horror that is almost beyond human comprehension. Destroyed buildings, corpses on the pavements, the harrowing screams of the wounded, fragments of soldiers' words interspersed with constant swearing. Endless, unimaginable casualties.[5]

Despite being far below the expected strength for a 'fortress' of this size, the Vilnius garrison was clearly putting up tough resistance; as is so often the case, urban warfare proved to be a great leveller, with the numerically weaker German forces able to inflict heavy losses on the Red Army. The 17-man battalion that Degen was supporting ceased to exist within a day and the few rear area personnel – cooks, messengers, etc. – were thrown into the battle. Some of the motivation of the defenders came from widespread awareness that about 4,000 badly wounded men remained in the city with almost no prospect of being evacuated, but the sheer weight of Soviet troops pressing into the city – and the continuing attacks of the *AK*, with little or no cooperation between the two – drove the

Germans into an ever more precarious position. By the end of 8 July, Vilnius was almost completely encircled.

When Vilnius was declared a fortress, the remarkable Generalleutnant Reiner Stahel was appointed as *Kampfkommandant*. He served in the German Army in the First World War and then moved to Finland where he joined the Finnish Army, helping it defeat pro-Soviet forces in the Finnish Civil War. Returning to Germany in 1933, he was employed in the Air Ministry and returned to uniformed service, this time in the Luftwaffe. In the first half of 1942, with the rank of Oberstleutnant, he was commander of 99th Flak Regiment; in the German military, most anti-aircraft units were part of the Luftwaffe. He was then informed that he would be assigned to one of the new Luftwaffe field divisions but was caught up in the collapse of the Don front during the encirclement of Stalingrad. He found himself in command of one of the numerous improvised battlegroups created from rear area personnel, army stragglers, and whoever else could be scraped together. Stahel's group fought with considerable distinction before being overrun on 2 December 1942 and it was assumed that he and his men had perished, but two days later a group of survivors, led by Stahel, fought their way back to German lines. He was awarded the Oak Leaves to the Knight's Cross and promoted to Oberst a few weeks later and then to Generalmajor in early February 1943, when he led another battlegroup made up largely of Luftwaffe personnel from anti-aircraft regiments in the battles in Donbas.

After the crisis in Ukraine passed in the spring of 1943, Stahel was sent to Italy where he commanded anti-aircraft defences covering the Strait of Messina, and as the Western Allies invaded the Italian mainland and advanced on Rome he was appointed battle commander of the garrison of Rome. During his time in Italy, he received a delegation sent by Pope Pius XII protesting about the deportation of Jews from Rome, but refused to become involved, telling the delegates that this was entirely a matter for the SS.[6] When he was appointed commandant of the Vilnius garrison, Stahel had to be flown into the city aboard a Storch liaison plane. Before dawn on 9 July, Stahel sent two signals to Reinhardt's Third Panzer Army headquarters:

[There was] particularly heavy fighting in the evening with further ground lost. The northwest bank [of the Neris River] has been given up. Widespread panic; the state of the troops for the morning is very precarious. An attack from Ludvinovo [now Liudvinavas, in the southwest part of Vilnius] towards the east was brought to a halt in heavy fighting against strong enemy forces … 18 tanks were shot up.

The state of the troops is so questionable that dissolution during the morning is likely. [There is a] shortage of ammunition. If the remaining troops are to be saved, a breakout towards the west must be approved.[7]

On receipt of these signals, the operations officer at Third Panzer Army immediately contacted Model's Army Group Centre to request permission for a breakout. The reply was just as prompt: Hitler had refused permission for Vilnius to be abandoned.

The 16th Fallschirmjäger Regiment – paratrooper formations, like anti-aircraft units, were part of the Luftwaffe – had been designated as part of the Vilnius garrison and flew from Germany to Kaunas. From here, 50 Ju-52 transports flew a battalion to Vilnius but the main airfield to the southeast of the city – built by the use of Jewish slave labour from the ghetto in the city – was badly cratered. Two of the transport planes crashed trying to land, but nine managed to land and take off safely; in total, about 300 men disembarked. The rest of the regiment was meant to march overland from Kaunas but the road and rail link between the two cities had been cut by the Red Army.

The solitary, understrength battalion that reached the airfield immediately came under attack. With only relatively light weaponry and supported by a single 88mm gun, their ability to resist for long was highly questionable. Eugen Hinnen, one of the paratroopers, later recalled the fighting:

Opposite us, parallel to the road, was the railway line where the Russians were positioned. When an enemy machine-gun was set up on the embankment in remarkably clear view, about 250m away, two of our paratroopers moved to the edge of the road with a machine-gun. But before they could open fire, the Russians fired first.

I saw the dust kicked up from the ground. Both comrades had been hit and thrown back. I grabbed the foot of a machine-gunner and pulled him into cover. The other gunner had been hit in the head. When I turned the groaning comrade over, I saw he had been shot in the stomach or lung.

I stood up and took an aimed shot at the enemy machine-gun ... I had no time to judge the result but it stopped firing and while I pulled my comrade onto my back and ran back along the street there were no shots. It must have been a few hundred metres that I ran towards the village, and the comrade on my back lost consciousness. I caught up with the tractor of the 88mm flak gun ... We lifted the wounded man into this tractor. He was taken to the nearby field dressing station in the centre of the village.[8]

It was a bitter irony of war that the man Hinnen had carried to safety was later killed attempting to break out of Vilnius towards the west. The machine-gunner who had been hit in the head and left for dead, by contrast, turned out to be alive. He was pulled back to safety by his comrades and survived the war.

By this stage, elements of the Soviet LXXII Rifle Corps were advancing through the rubble of northwest Vilnius; to their south, Fifth Guards Tank Army had taken both the airfield and the railway station. The German soldiers in Vilnius learned about the orders forbidding retreat through a variety of sources. Some were informed by their superiors, as a radio operator wrote in his diary:

> Hauptmann Beneke brought us a message that we were not permitted to pull out [of Vilnius]. But yesterday we did have permission. So now we are condemned to stay here. At midday we withdrew to point 399 and after we had organised ourselves we had to move back further …
>
> We set up in the old fortress casemates, 20m underground. Who knows if we will get out of here? Alarms during the night, the Russians were on our hill and everyone left the bunker. Thousands of contradictory orders, then [I was told to] destroy everything. I did it. Our receiver was completely destroyed, the transmitter partially. Panic everywhere.[9]

At this stage, Vilnius was not completely encircled; there remained a tenuous escape route to the southwest, but if the garrison was to be extracted it faced the difficult task of conducting a fighting retreat whilst under pressure from superior Soviet forces. But despite repeated representations from Reinhardt and Model, Hitler remained adamant. The garrison was to continue to hold Vilnius until a relief column of four panzer divisions could be assembled. This was expected to be ready in the last week of July.

During 9 July, there were further communications from Vilnius. Stahel informed Reinhardt that supplies had successfully been dropped by the Luftwaffe, but there was a shortage of water. Stahel added that the troops were still willing to fight, but casualties were accumulating. Time was running out rapidly for the garrison. Reinhardt could offer little assurance to the fortress commandant; his army estimated that its total combat strength was at best just 4,000 men – less than half of what was required for just one infantry division.[10] All he could do was wait for the promised panzer divisions to arrive.

One of those was 6th Panzer Division. After being sent to the Eastern Front at the height of the Stalingrad crisis, its soldiers were in almost constant combat for over a year and were finally pulled back into the rear area of Army Group North Ukraine in April 1944 for some desperately needed rest and replenishment. Despite Model's wish to hold on to the division in his immediate rear area, it was ordered to move west in May – originally, it was to be sent to Denmark, but instead was directed to Lüneberg, to the southeast of Hamburg. This change of destination was apparently after the personal intervention of Oberst Klaus Schenk Graf von Stauffenberg, who was serving as a senior staff officer with the *Ersatzheer* ('Replacement Army'). Given the events of late July, when Stauffenberg and others attempted to carry out their plan to kill Hitler and seize control of Germany, there was speculation that he had moved the division to a strategically important location in case he needed to make use of it – he had served in 1st Light Division in Poland in 1939, before the division was transformed into 6th Panzer Division, and many of the officers with whom he had served were still part of the division. Indeed, as part of its replenishment and retraining, the division received orders from the *Ersatzheer* on 2 June to create a battlegroup so that 'in the event of an enemy attack in the northwest it can be ready for mobile operations at 12 hours' notice'.[11] For many of the soldiers of the division, it was the first time they had been on German soil for over a year and the widespread devastation of German cities – the division was recruited mainly from the Rhineland and Westphalia – was a shock, but the opportunity for some prolonged rest away from front-line service was gratefully accepted. The spell came to an end when orders arrived for the division to prepare to return to the Eastern Front. To date, it had not received any Panther tanks and merely had the older Pz.IVs, but the first detachments set off for East Prussia late on 9 July, from where they would be dispatched towards Vilnius.

The fighting in Vilnius continued on 10 July. The paratrooper Hinnen described his battalion's continuing travails:

> Late on 9 July, we were to march towards the city [from the airfield to the southeast of Vilnius]. We gathered for a roll call in some ruins outside the city. Despite searching as far as we could and repeated counts, 12 hours' fighting had really left us with just 60 out of 300 men. There were two officers, Hauptmann Swenson and the battalion adjutant.
>
> We marched without forming ranks to Vilnius, one after the other, constantly taking cover. At one point we were surprised by a Russian tank, and also by artillery fire. We gathered under a railway bridge. General Stahel had asked for our aid, so we had to continue. Just before Vilnius there was a bridge across the river. From here, we could see down to the station, where there were locomotives

under steam. After crossing the river we ran to the left into woodland. At the edge of the wood we suddenly ran into some of our comrades who had left us earlier to go to a supply dump. So they joined us and were added to our platoons and weapons were distributed. They hadn't suffered any losses, but were stunned by the casualties the rest of us had suffered. Here at the edge of the wood there were other comrades too, from anti-aircraft units …

Here we set up our machine-guns facing the far bank and the hill there. There were only a few houses nearby, apparently a fishermen's settlement, and the occupants gave us some milk and bread …

[The following morning, on the far bank] a vehicle with a water barrel drove up to the bank. I didn't have any binoculars so couldn't make out clearly if they were Russians. But in any case they looked like brown Russian uniforms.

One man wanted to get some water to fill the barrel. Although it was fairly light now, I fired at him with tracer rounds. I didn't realise that the bluish flashes would hang in the air for so long, travelling from our foxhole to their target. The man with the barrel crouched and ran back to the truck and he and the driver drove away.

In the stillness next to the river, I suddenly heard five rounds fired by mortars. I counted them and listened for a while longer. Then I heard them whistling and realised they were meant for me, so I crouched down in my foxhole.

I didn't think the rounds were particularly dangerous. I wanted to see the direction in which they were spread. Then came the first impact over on the other bank. The second shot was closer, landing in the water. The third round – even closer, in the middle of the river. The fourth was on our bank, coming straight towards me.

I hesitated – should I jump out and run off? But I stayed put, ducking even lower. I already expected a direct hit. The howling had stopped. Had I miscounted?

Then there was an unearthly explosion. The fifth mortar bomb landed 2m from me. The soil from the trench had saved me. I tried to rise up but the machine-gun was on top of me. A couple of comrades ran up, including Herbert Faulstich, from their position 50m upstream. 'Eugen,' he called, 'where are you wounded?' When the danger was over, I calmly replied, 'That's probably where it landed,' and pointed to a spot 2m away. 'I'm fine,' I added. Then I said to Faulstich, 'Help me dig out this foxhole again.' He replied, 'No, let's get out of here, they know where we are.'

Suddenly we heard loud voices from the fishermen's settlement and the noise of motor vehicles. Shortly after came an order to pack up everything. We were moving into the city. We were to carry what we could to the anti-aircraft positions above us. Here, I saw General Stahel for the first time. He had come with a few vehicles to get us out. It was a couple of kilometres to the new position. There the general let us get some rest. He shook hands with everyone and handed out some chocolate.[12]

Third Panzer Army had ordered the Vilnius garrison to fall back and hold the line of the Neris River that ran through the heart of the city, but this order was already meaningless. The Red Army had erected a temporary bridge at one point and had actually seized an intact footbridge; Soviet troops were therefore already crossing the river, making its use as a defensive line impossible. During the afternoon, Stahel sent a brief signal to Reinhardt:

> We are effectively fighting on all sides, ground will have to be given up in the east this coming night. Substantial casualties will force further withdrawals, so this will only be sustainable until noon on Wednesday [i.e. 12 July].
> Ongoing help from the outside is required.[13]

Probably to Stahel's surprise, such outside help did materialise almost immediately: a small group of Stuka dive-bombers struck the Soviet forces gathering at the eastern edge of Vilnius, forcing a brief pause in major attacks, but the siege perimeter continued to shrink slowly. The nearest German ground forces outside the city were now about nine miles to the west, another improvised force labelled *Kampfgruppe Tolsdorff*, with barely sufficient strength to prevent further Soviet advances and nowhere near enough firepower to attempt a relief operation. The nearest unit of any significant strength was 7th Panzer Division, some 36 miles to the southwest of Vilnius, and even this unit would be unable to help as Soviet forces from Fifth Guards Tank Army had advanced to the west and were approaching the outskirts of Alytus.

The Red Army was anxious to avoid committing too many troops to the fighting in Vilnius – this could only be at the expense of continuing the drive towards the west. Consequently, *Stavka* reiterated orders to Bagramian early on 11 July, previously sent two days before, to limit involvement in the Vilnius battle to just two divisions. The rest of the forces in the area were to continue the advance and III Guards Mechanised Corps was assigned to Fifth Army in order to provide it with more firepower and mobility. Fifth Guards Tank Army was ordered to extract its forces entirely from Vilnius and to prepare for an attack towards the northwest.

The city garrison's situation was rapidly deteriorating. Medical supplies had been exhausted, leading to terrible scenes in the numerous improvised hospitals around Vilnius. The paratrooper Eugen Hinnen had been wounded the previous day and was in one such hospital:

A medic was always doing his rounds. When I awoke I called him over, but he already wanted to give me some pain relief. There were moans and cries all around as everyone wanted some. I realised that he didn't have enough for everyone.

I got to my feet, limped back and forth leaning on my rifle, still carrying my shoes. Then I reached a spiral staircase that led to a tall tower above. It was probably the tallest building still standing in the area. Increasingly it was targeted by Russian planes that dropped small bombs on it but never hit it very hard.

Suddenly Oberfeldwebel Schmidt appeared and said that someone had to go up the tower as an observer. When he saw me sitting at the bottom of the stairs he said, 'Yes, you can go up straight away.' He didn't realise I was wounded. I tried to explain to him that I had been wounded in the fighting at the crossroads. He asked me, 'Where are you wounded then? Come on, bandages off. If it's not for real, I'll shoot you immediately.' There was no superior from my unit who could help me. Schmidt was from another company. I showed him my shrapnel wounds. He then said, 'It's just a trifle, you can still go up.' I then told him my heel bone was broken too. If low-flying planes attacked, I wouldn't be able to descend the stairs quickly. Schmidt replied indignantly, 'That's quite enough for me, you can do everything I need!'[14]

In Berlin, Goebbels wrote in his diary on the evening of 11 July:

The situation in Vilnius is not remotely pleasing; the defenders have been squeezed into a comparatively small area in the city centre and consequently supplying them is not a simple matter. It is doubtful if Vilnius can be held. As a consequence of the extreme heat that is usual from time to time in the east, there are already shortages of drinking water. In the meantime the enemy has bypassed Vilnius to the northwest and southwest.[15]

Finally, Hitler bowed to reality and issued orders that the garrison could attempt to break out towards the west. If such permission had been granted on 9 July, an orderly withdrawal with preservation of combat strength would have been accomplished with comparative ease; even on 10 July, it would have been a much tougher proposition but nonetheless achievable. With ammunition stocks depleted and heavy casualties suffered, it was now questionable whether a breakout could succeed at all. In the preceding two days, the garrison had admittedly inflicted heavy casualties on the attacking Soviet units, but already Bagramian's 1st Baltic Front had taken steps to reduce its losses by extracting troops and sending them west. The declared function of the 'fortress' – to hold down substantial enemy forces until a relief column could arrive – had not been achieved in any of the fortresses where the soldiers of Army Group Centre fought and died in the summer of 1944; nor had there ever been any prospect of a relief column reaching them. When he received the order authorising a breakout, Stahel swore his signals staff to secrecy lest the news should leak, leading to a precipitate attempt by his men to try to escape.

During the morning of 12 July, the first trains carrying elements of 6th Panzer Division from Germany arrived in Kaunas; there had been repeated delays en route with trains being redirected to avoid junctions damaged by air attacks in recent days. Generalleutnant Rudolf Freiherr von Waldenfels, the division commander, reported immediately to Reinhardt's headquarters, where he was informed that the armoured battlegroup – which, prudently, was the first part of the division to be dispatched from Lüneberg – was to be committed to the fighting the following day against the Soviet units edging towards the west from the Vilnius area. The division staff would have a busy day ensuring that adequate fuel and other supplies were prepared.

Ion Degen, the Soviet tank crewman who had been sent into action supporting a 17-man rifle battalion, was still heavily involved in the ongoing fighting:

We crushed an anti-aircraft gun that had managed to fire at us. Fortunately, the shell just glanced off the turret. We rushed to the next road intersection to avoid being hit by the fire of other anti-aircraft guns that had been deployed for direct fire and got lost in the labyrinth of streets. I didn't usually close the back of my sunroof [Red Army tank slang for the turret hatch] because to open it, I had to pull down a strap attached to two latches with one hand, while pushing up on a rather heavy latch with the other hand. But in the city, where they could fire on you from above, it was impossible to leave the hatch open. In order to avoid struggling with it, I pulled the latches off. The hatch was thus only lying closed, not latched. Through the roar of the diesel engine and the rumble of the tracks, I heard something scrabbling on the top of the turret. Two Germans clambered aft and tried to open the hatch. I grabbed the hanging belt from the latch and ordered Vasya to hold it. So I found myself in a situation that was very unpleasant for a tanker. I don't know how long we raced through the streets. Then I saw the church, our old landmark. We emerged near where our lone 76mm anti-tank gun was deployed with a few shells. Artillerymen began to aim at us with feverish speed. Just 40m from the gun, Boris – having stopped the vehicle and opened his hatch – shouted such an obscene tirade that, probably, all the streets of Vilnius blushed with embarrassment. The gunners immediately realised that the tank was one of their own side. The Germans on the rear deck were already dead. They had been shot by infantrymen from a nearby house.[16]

The paratrooper Eugen Hinnen was finally able to get some care for his wounds, over a day after being injured:

A truck drove up and all the wounded were loaded aboard. There wasn't a space for me. But I climbed onto a tank that led the way to another hospital on a hill. I was meant to hand over my gun but I kept hold of it, replying 'So long as I can shoot, I'm keeping my weapon.'

We drove through a few streets – the tank in front, the truck following – and came to a hospital, which was apparently the Hindenburg Hospital. It had been organised for all-round defence. Several soldiers of all arms were gathered here. Around the park and in the buildings there were slit trenches and positions. A large shelter had been dug in the park as protection against low-flying aircraft.

Now we were finally treated as normal wounded men. In an office, a medic took down our personal details. He even asked me if I had already received a wound badge. Judging by the question, there might still be a way out, to get 'home to the Reich', get some leave and to recuperate. Why else would he care about a wound badge?

While the medic poked around in my wound with a magnet, I glanced around. Next door they were carrying out surgery on a man shot in the abdomen. Then I heard low-flying aircraft, shells striking the roof above, our flak responding, then bombs falling, small explosions. The doctors just ducked their heads a little and continued working, and then came a cloud of smoke that spread quickly through the room. But surgery continued.

Then I was even given a bed in a normal room. There were about 15 men there. Supplies were still available. The nurses brought food to all the wounded in their beds. I had put my equipment under my bed so that I could leave on my own initiative if needed. The medic had put a thin bandage on my foot so I was able to slip it back into my shoe, which had been cut open. I didn't know how long it would be before I could run, but I hoped to be able to get back to my comrades soon. I never thought that I would be limping or hobbling with my injured foot for nearly half a year.

I stayed in the hospital until the night of the breakout. During this time I at least received food as normal and was able to sleep, talk to others and observe our comrades as they prepared fighting positions.[17]

Other soldiers were less fortunate. Matthias Korth had also been wounded and was in the Basilius Hospital:

Suddenly word went around among the wounded that everyone who was still able to walk should set out to leave the city. There were still three trucks available for evacuation to take those who wanted to try to break out to the edge of the city. I really wanted to get out, but the trucks were already full.

Several men clung to the outside, to the mudguards and rear lights so that they could be taken along too. We drove for a while. Ultimately, however, further movement was impossible as the bridge over the river had been blown and we couldn't cross.

In addition, there were fires all around and smoke everywhere. All of a sudden, we heard German marching music played loudly and clearly from the Russians' loudspeakers. And then it was suddenly quiet, there was no more shelling, and the German soldiers were asked to surrender: 'German soldiers, lay down your weapons, there are a thousand clean beds and a thousand pretty girls waiting for you.'

Everyone froze. Then all of a sudden the shelling started again and several people were killed – they had brought up ammunition during the pause. The attempted breakthrough turned out to be a total failure. I then wanted to get back into the city to a hospital. Finally I reached a large building. The door was open so I could look inside. There was blood everywhere. It looked like a slaughterhouse. Screams and moans from all directions. To one side there were four large wash-baskets filled with amputated arms, legs and hands. There was no time to empty the baskets. The wounded kept coming. With several others, I fled to a small forest near the city. But there, we came under such heavy mortar fire that I wanted to flee back to the city.[18]

Stahel and his staff made preparations throughout 12 July for the breakout attempt, which was to take place the following night. The Neris River flows into Vilnius from the northeast and in the centre of the city turns west, with the old city centre immediately to the south; it then forms a loop to the south before angling to the northwest. The area of Vilnius to the east of the river above the old city was already in Russian hands, but the garrison in the old centre would have to cross the river as it looped to the south. Once across the Neris, the soldiers would attempt to move along the north bank of the river in the hope of encountering German units further to the west. But part of the garrison was pinned against the river in the northeast of Vilnius, cut off from Stahel's main group; if these men were to escape, they would first have to break through to join their comrades.

It began to rain in the Vilnius region during the afternoon of 12 July and the downpour continued into the night. Even as Stahel and his men prepared for their breakout attempt, the news from Oberst Theodor Tolsdorff's battlegroup was not encouraging. The regiment was part of the battle-hardened and highly experienced 1st Infantry Division and had the nickname of *Graf-22* in the army because so many Prussian aristocrats had served in its ranks, but Tolsdorff now reported that Soviet units were outflanking his group and threatening to cut it off. If the Vilnius garrison was to reach safety, it had to link up with *Gruppe Tolsdorff* as quickly as possible so that a further withdrawal towards Kaunas could then be carried out. Wounded soldiers in the city who could walk were told to join the men preparing to leave; the despair of those left in the hospitals was seared into the memories of those who left. During the afternoon of 12 July, soldiers began to assemble for the attempt to cross the Neris. Eugen Hinnen was in a building where many wounded had gathered together with soldiers of all arms:

I stayed close to the radio set and the command group where the general [Stahel] was. At one point he shouted, 'Damnation, every officer is to gather a group – we're breaking out tonight at midnight!' Now I knew, I just wanted to go. It was about 2200.

I took up my bed pallet and dragged it across the room. When I reached the corridor, a reconnaissance tank raced towards the hospital with a roar. Then suddenly there was a huge crash as it was hit by one of our anti-tank weapons. Our men thought it was Russian, but it was one of ours. Through the window I could see directly into the burning and exploding tank. The crew cried out for help but all of them perished in the flames.

The badly wounded men in the rooms were shocked by these events and joined in their screams, it was terrible. Now I made my way to the cellar with my pallet and my equipment, constantly passing soldiers …

The cellar was also full of soldiers, weapons lying at their feet. I lay down in the middle – helmet and belt loosened, rifle in my arms. Then a comrade came past and shared out chocolate and cigarettes. I grabbed his foot and told him, 'When it starts, wake me up.' How naïve of me to have thought that a man would sneak past 3,000 soldiers in the dark, away from his platoon, just to wake me, to haul out a hobbling soldier who couldn't swim. But believing this, I slept peacefully. Either someone would wake me or I would wake myself.[19]

The last of the garrison's artillery ammunition was expended in a brief bombardment of Soviet positions to the southwest of Vilnius, in an attempt to mislead the Red Army about Stahel's intended direction of breaking out. The guns were then destroyed and the soldiers made their way to their assembly areas. Stahel had organised three distinct groups: about 1,800 men under Major Schubert, from the southern part of the siege perimeter; a force of 800 men mainly from 170th Infantry Division under Major Soth, who had been involved in the toughest of the fighting against the Red Army; and Stahel's personal group of about 600 men.[20] Together with less well-organised groups, these men gathered in the woodland of a park near the river where the river crossing was to be attempted.

It seems that for the first part of the rainy night, the Soviet units didn't detect the withdrawal of German troops from the perimeter. When they became aware that the Germans had gone, they correctly concluded that a breakout was underway and commenced heavy artillery bombardment of most of the areas they had yet to occupy, including the woods where about 3,000 German soldiers had gathered. Shells descending through the canopy of branches often exploded in the air, their blasts adding wooden fragments to the rain of shrapnel on the men below. Order rapidly broke down and men began to cross the river in small groups or individually. Many were swept away by the strong current, but some succeeded in reaching the far bank, as one survivor described:

> In this area the river was about 150–300m wide and so swift that even good swimmers only succeeded in reaching the far bank with difficulty, laden with weapons and clothing. Attempts to cross using ropes were also ineffective. These difficulties, the screams of drowning men, and constant shelling, discouraged many soldiers from attempting a crossing. Many considered retreating to the few houses nearby where they would defend themselves until the following evening when they could try again.
>
> Only when it began to grow light [on 13 July] was a ford discovered a little downstream through which, if several people stuck together, one could cross despite the current. A large number succeeded here, but the fate of those who didn't make it because of the constant shelling wasn't known to us.[21]

Only about 600 men succeeded in crossing the river in the first attempt; most were without weapons and many had lost their footwear. Behind them, the sky was lit up bright as day by the fires raging in Vilnius, a scene that haunted many of the soldiers for the rest of their lives. Stahel was with a group of paratroopers who readied themselves in the ruins of a small monastery:

> With General Stahel in the lead we were to move through the water quickly in a quick thrust and then clear a path on the other bank. We left the woodland and before us was the Neris, over 100m wide, but flowing nearly as fast as the Rhine. We felt our way along the wall of the monastery to the bank. A brief breath, a couple of quick strides, and we were in the water and commencing a march into the unknown. The water reached as high as my knee, then to my waist, finally as high as my chest.
>
> The current was very strong and we were in full kit. Holding our machine-pistols above our heads – our lives might depend upon them – we edged forwards. The water sometimes rose up to our chins, but was mainly chest-deep. It seemed to be going better than I had anticipated.
>
> When I was still 50m from the far bank, the first of my comrades were already scrambling ashore. They disappeared into the bushes. We stood still, listening. Everything remained quiet. While the tension eased, did I become a little careless and stop holding firmly to the man in front? I don't know now. Suddenly the current pulled me away, swept the ground from under my feet, and pulled me down by flooding into my smock. We were under strict instructions to stay silent whatever happened. I had to drop my machine-pistol, tear my helmet from my head, and my webbing with my pistol, pack, magazine case, my document case all disappeared, but finally I surfaced and grabbed a lungful of air …
>
> I reached the bank about 100m downstream from the planned crossing point. I looked around cautiously – there was nothing to see or hear, neither friend nor foe. So I sat down to catch my breath.
>
> Then there was a splashing near me and an infantry captain climbed up the bank, as glad as I was that he had made it. We discussed what to do. Neither of us was armed. But we moved off and found a group of infantrymen. I found a rifle, a tarpaulin, and a cap. We set off towards the heights in front of us in the darkness.[22]

Behind the men attempting the river crossing, a group of surviving soldiers from 170th Infantry Division found themselves pressed against the riverbank further to the east by elements of the Soviet III Guards Mechanised Corps. The Žaliasis Tiltas Bridge at this point of the river had been partially demolished, but some soldiers managed to cross to the far bank and then attempted to infiltrate their way to the west to link up with Stahel's group; others attempted to fight along the southern bank to reach the designated crossing point. Most of those who had crossed the damaged bridge were from an SS police regiment and were overwhelmed before they could reach safety. Only a few were taken prisoner. Fighting continued in the centre of Vilnius for the rest of 13 July.

The men who had succeeded in fording the river had to move west as quickly as they could before dawn on 13 July. Clashing intermittently with Red Army patrols and groups of Polish *AK* fighters, the Germans made their way through woodland towards the west until they once more encountered the Neris River after a march of about seven miles close to the mounds of a series of iron age forts. A senior NCO who had swum across the river described the next stage of the breakout attempt:

> After moving across the landscape for about a kilometre that we covered in dead ground we ran into another Vilnius unit. They apparently had found a better crossing point as almost all of them were still together. A Russian quad anti-aircraft gun on a truck brought the entire group under fire and in short there was chaos with dead and wounded and an outbreak of the panic that had been building for days. The noise of tanks could be heard – Ivan had alerted the entire area and was hunting us.
>
> Those of us who had crossed the river [to leave Vilnius] now made a last attempt to break through here. After crossing an artillery position, where a sentry patrolled between the guns with his rifle still slung over his shoulder, we reached the edge of a forest. But the sentry had spotted us and a couple of men pursued us riding horses bareback and opened fire. I'd finally had enough and we deployed our machine-gun, bringing a rapid end to the nonsense.
>
> We now climbed into the ridge running along the Neris, where the trees gave us good cover. After joining up with another group, which included Generals [Gerhard] Poehl [commandant of Vilnius before Stahel took over] and Stahel, we ran into a group of Polish freedom fighters. An officer spoke to us in perfect German, explaining that the woodland in front of us was held by the 'Free Poland' Legion and that we would be permitted to pass through if we handed over our weapons. We refused. Our guns were made ready and machine-guns brought forward. We numbered about 500 men and with a loud 'Hurrah!' we advanced towards where the defenders were apparently dug in.
>
> I led a platoon of *Gruppe Lindner* and sent a raiding party with a machine-gun forward. With the courage of desperation we ran along the heights. We succeeded, the Poles fleeing from us, and the Russians following us piled through too. Unfortunately, we took casualties. In the woods we ran into a well-constructed blockhouse and two bunkers which we had to clear with hand grenades.[23]

Stahel and the other German troops reached the Neris once more close to a series of ancient hill forts; they would have to cross it again to reach safety. There was no bridge available and at first the soldiers didn't realise that there was a small stretch of the river that could be forded, just to the south of the village of Valai. A quick search resulted in a single boat being found, and this was used to take wounded men across through a steadily increasing bombardment by mortars and through intermittent bursts of machine-gun fire. Some soldiers tried to make rafts out of various items but these were rapidly swept away by the strong current. Several men linked their rifle slings together and one man swam across so that others could then follow by holding onto the improvised 'rope'. Most men had no option but to discard their remaining equipment and boots and then to attempt to swim across. On the far bank, they found soldiers from *Gruppe Tolsdorff* waiting for them; the exhausted survivors walked a short distance to a road that ran parallel to the river, where they boarded trucks that took them to a nearby village. It was now late afternoon on 13 July and the men were grateful to be given some warm food and a chance to sleep in safety, and to try to dry their clothes, but their ordeal was far from over. In order to link up with the breakout attempt, *Gruppe Tolsdorff* had held its positions despite being badly outflanked and its line of retreat was tenuous at best.

Fortunately for the soldiers from Vilnius and those of *Gruppe Tolsdorff*, help was at hand. After detraining in Kaunas on 12 July, the armoured battlegroup of 6th Panzer Division was reinforced by elements of the *Grossdeutschland* panzergrenadier division and 500th SS-Fallschirmjäger Battalion; it was immediately ordered to take up blocking positions to protect Kaunas from the spearheads of the Red Army. Hitler continued to talk of creating a new 'panzer army' in the Kaunas area, speculating that the reinforcements being transferred from other sectors should instead be used to release battle-hardened divisions from Army Group North Ukraine that would then move to Kaunas; even if such plans had been realistic, they would have required substantial additional time, which was as precious a commodity as the reinforcements themselves. Heusinger, the acting chief of the general staff, sent a signal to Model even as 6th Panzer Division was arriving in Kaunas about Hitler's proposals for an armoured counterattack to restore the situation:

> General Heusinger asserted that in view of the changing situation he no longer regarded such a counterthrust as possible. Rather, one should strive to stabilise the situation in the area to the east of the East Prussian frontier through the use of these formations.[24]

By the end of 12 July, Waldenfels, the commander of 6th Panzer Division, had a substantial force gathered under his command: a battalion of half-track-mounted panzergrenadiers; a company of the division's armoured reconnaissance battalion; a battery of self-propelled artillery; about a battalion of tanks from *Grossdeutschland* under the command of Major Walter Pössl; and the soldiers of the SS paratrooper battalion. The bulk of this force was ordered to proceed immediately along the road towards Vilnius, under Pössl's command, in order to re-establish firm contact with *Gruppe Tolsdorff*, and as further elements of 6th Panzer Division arrived they would be sent along the same route to ensure that the first battlegroup didn't find itself cut off.

Pössl set off towards Vilnius at about the same time that the soldiers of the Vilnius garrison were moving away from the banks of the Neris in the western part of the city. The intention had been to set off at first light but there were delays assembling all of the forces; Reinhardt and Waldenfels joined the battlegroup in a half-track. Amongst the vehicles following the combat formations were several trucks carrying fuel, ammunition, and food to replenish both the Vilnius garrison and *Gruppe Tolsdorff*. About 15 miles to the east of Kaunas, there was the first clash with Soviet troops, but there was no serious opposition until the column reached Vievis, a further 15 miles to the west. Here, Pössl's leading elements ran into Soviet tanks, anti-tank guns, and infantry armed with anti-tank rifles; these might be obsolescent weapons in most circumstances, but if used at closer range and particularly from the upper floors of buildings, they were still highly effective. Pössl immediately deployed a panzer company and attacked in strength, sweeping aside the Soviet units, but the diary of 6th Panzer Division recorded that just a single Soviet tank – an American-made Sherman – was destroyed in the fighting, suggesting that this Soviet unit was not particularly strong.

After a brief pause, the advance continued. The Germans were now moving through a region of hilly woodland, giving their opponents ample opportunity for ambushes; progress slowed as panzergrenadiers had to be deployed to clear the trees closest to the road. Shortly after midday, contact was made with *Gruppe Tolsdorff* in the village of Rykantai, a further eight miles to the east. The exhausted men of the Vilnius garrison were once more put aboard trucks and evacuated to Kaunas, escorted by a small group of panzergrenadiers. Many were wounded and all of the men were screened by waiting medical personnel. In many cases, doctors recorded that the soldiers were suffering from 'genuine acute physical and psychological exhaustion'. The use of the word 'genuine' is of interest. Soldiers who had escaped from encirclements earlier in the war – for example, at Demyansk and Korsun – were often too drained by their ordeal to return to front-line service for a considerable period and many within the military had regarded these men with suspicion. The concept of what is now seen as post-traumatic stress was barely recognised in many armies, and the treatment of German troops who were psychologically damaged by their experiences was poor. Most were simply ordered back to the front, often under threat of execution if they refused. On this occasion, the German medics felt the need to emphasise their findings in order to protect the soldiers.[25]

The diary entry of a survivor of a signals company of 170th Infantry Division described the typical state of the survivors, whose transition from the fighting in the fortress and the exhausting escape attempt to the apparent calm of Kaunas must have been hugely disorienting:

> 14 July: One hour of sleep. The Russians are pursuing us. During the night, we're transported further to Kaunas. But this time we have 30 tanks acting as escorts. [We're in] Kaunas in the morning.
>
> I'm still completely exhausted. We're given food and can sleep. Items of kit are exchanged, accommodation assigned. Slowly, we gather our senses.
>
> But what a sad result. Of the 50 men in the signals section, there are only six here.
>
> 15 July: We're four signallers short. Roll call in the barracks in the morning. General Stahel reads a speech to the 'Vilnius fighters'. But what suffering did this breakout cost? It's only now that people can see what we had to endure. We're still not fully dressed.
>
> The survivors of the signals company are assigned to the artillery. We all want to return to our division. In the evening we get to bed early.
>
> 16 July: We spend the day being issued with new clothes. But we want to get away from here to avoid having to defend a 'fortress' again. The Russians continue to attack and it's not clear how they're going to be stopped. In the evening, Hannes and I go to the cinema.
>
> We still can't quite believe that we've been able to get out of that complete mess. Hannes is awarded the Iron Cross 2nd Class.[26]

Soldiers from the garrison continued to reach the banks of the Neris near Valai throughout 13 July. They approached the crossing point with the river to their south, running parallel to their line of march before it turned north across their path, and both banks to their south were in Soviet hands; to date, only modest numbers of Soviet troops had crossed to the northern bank but these men were able to direct artillery and mortar fire from further to the rear. Ultimately, of the soldiers of 170th Infantry Division who fought in Vilnius – a grenadier regiment of three battalions, an additional battalion, a bakery company, and an artillery battalion – just 469 soldiers survived.

Not all of the Vilnius garrison had succeeded in breaking out. In addition to the soldiers who continued to fight against Soviet and Polish attacks, there were about 3,000 men who were too badly wounded to be evacuated, together with several hundred medical personnel. Whilst some elements of the garrison fought to the last bullet, many were too exhausted or had run out of ammunition and simply surrendered. Although Soviet memoirs describe how the German wounded were given medical care, the reality was often very different. An artillery radioman described one incident:

> Suddenly, Polish Jews in uniforms came up to us and beat us with rifle butts, blaming us for the murder of 70 Polish Jews from Vilnius. These partisans told us they wanted to see our blood spilled and delayed our handover [to the Red Army].
>
> A Russian soldier who accompanied them explained that we were to be given into the custody of the partisans and would be shot. They took us and drove us through a gateway where we could see the words of the *Ave Maria* painted, to a backyard.
>
> We had to stand in a row and keep our hands raised while the Jewish officer issued orders in Polish. The partisans lowered their submachine-guns and stepped back when a Russian colonel came running through the gateway at the last moment and shouted incomprehensible curses at them.
>
> The Poles put down their guns and after a short discussion we learned that we were not going to be shot but would be held for other punishment.[27]

This incident shows a further element of the complex fighting in and around Vilnius. The partisans described here were not part of the Polish *AK* – there were few if any Jews serving in the ranks of the *AK*, which on occasion attacked Jewish groups as energetically as it engaged German units. In addition to the *AK*, there were small numbers of pro-Soviet partisans in the Vilnius area and also bands made up of Jews who had escaped from the Vilnius ghetto and elsewhere. The alignment of these Jewish groups varied between hard-line Zionists and equally hard-line Bolsheviks, with all shades in between. Regardless of their political ideologies, the Jews were united in their hatred for the Germans, with good reason. Vilnius had been home to one of the largest urban Jewish populations in Europe, and nearly all of them had been slaughtered during the German occupation of the city.

Many of the German prisoners, both wounded and unwounded, were shipped off to work camps within the Soviet Union. Some of those who were captured by the Polish partisans were made to run a gauntlet through an archway; they were beaten as they ran past, and those who were unable to reach the end of the passageway were then shot. Some Germans later ascribed their mistreatment as punishment for the crimes of the SS and other occupying authorities, but the reality was that every part of the German military and occupation forces had played roles in the massacres of Jews and others in the region. The individuals who were captured might personally have been innocent, but this was a distinction that was often ignored by their captors.

Eugen Hinnen had been unable to join the men breaking out of Vilnius and accompanied by a tank driver and a cook, was captured leaving the hospital:

We whispered to each other about what we could do. A tank driver, either a Lithuanian or a Latvian, said that we would be shot. A fat cook trembled and wept. He told the tank driver that we should stay here and shouldn't resist.

But the Russians snatched away the civilian coat he was carrying and threw it aside. I said to the cook, 'You damned dog, you didn't feed us properly in the hospital.' The Russian lieutenant shouted 'Shut up!' Our tank driver muttered, 'I'd rather be shot. Because if they find out I'm from the SS my punishment will be far worse.'

Several times, I glanced at the ditch where we would all probably be lying dead in a few minutes. I said to the tank driver, 'Come on, we'll rush the guards, no matter what happens a few of us might be able to get away.' He replied with great calmness, 'There's no point, they should just shoot us.' The fat cook didn't want to know anything about an escape attempt, he just trembled. I had known for a while how I was going to proceed and made up my mind to rush the guard on my own. I didn't want to just get shot. So I waited until the man in front was distracted so that I could jump him.

Actually, the six guards were standing just 3–4m apart. It should have been a simple matter to do something but my wounds hindered me too much. I knew I was going to be a dead man soon but I preferred to die fighting rather than just be gunned down. The lieutenant strode back through the entrance and issued instructions to the guards. If it were to be now, I thought, it was already too late for me. He had already drawn his pistol.

Unexpectedly, a captain suddenly marched through the entrance. I thought, either he's the executioner or we're saved. He asked, '*Chto takoye?*' ['What's going on here?'] But the lieutenant was clearly angry and gave the order for us to be killed. A heated argument developed between the two and they both reached for their pistols. The captain shouted, 'Lower your gun! I've got one too!' And after a long exchange, the captain said, 'Sit down by that tree trunk for now,' right by the ditch. 'Let's sit down, take a moment.'

Then finally the tank driver stepped forward and told the captain in Russian that none of us had wanted to go on fighting, and that we were just hiding here until the other men of the garrison had left. The captain patted him on the shoulder and said, '*Khorosho!*' ['Very good!']. But we were still in a perilous situation.

Everything depended on what the two officers decided. We waited nervously until they both came back. We still didn't know what they had decided. The captain walked up to us with a smile, saying '*Dawai*, go back to your comrade indoors. He'll take care of you.'[28]

In total, about 5,000 German soldiers – many of them wounded – were taken prisoner. It is estimated that up to 8,000 more were killed, either in the city or during the attempted breakout. Casualty figures for the Soviet forces involved in the fighting are difficult to estimate but were far higher. Compared to many of those taken prisoner, Hinnen was fortunate. Although he was born in Germany, he was a citizen of Switzerland and his captors released him shortly after the end of the war. He returned to Switzerland in November 1945. Many of the other men taken prisoner remained in Soviet captivity for several years. Some were sentenced to hard labour for war crimes, in many cases on flimsy charges, and thousands died in work camps across the Soviet Union. All of the remaining captives were finally released in 1955.

Many of the German prisoners captured in Vilnius were then marched east to Vitebsk; one of them was Matthias Korth, who was just 18 years old:

During the morning when I was taken prisoner [13 July] we were marched out of the burning city, passing many corpses. We had to march 30km every day along the highway ... the Russians took the shoes of the prisoners for themselves.

Right at the front were German officers. They too had to take off their good leather shoes and march barefoot. Everyone's feet were blistered. I constantly tried not to march along the verge where the guards were, but rather in the middle where they couldn't see me and thus take away my shoes. Russians constantly marched past us in the other direction. The thunder [of fighting] continued behind us.

Anyone who couldn't keep up was shot. In the evenings we made camp when possible wherever we found some water. We weren't given anything to eat for the first few days but because of the mental stress and fear we didn't really feel hungry at first. Occasionally I took a mouthful of bread from my pocket. I tried to scrape the green mould from it but the others were soon all over it. Everything was gone in no time. My blanket was also taken from me on the first night, but at least it meant I didn't have so much to carry …

[After boarding trains in Vitebsk] we were unloaded in Moscow. Here we had to take part in a propaganda parade as the Russians wanted to show the number of prisoners they had captured. We were driven through the city, watched by guards who prevented anyone from attacking us. The women cursed us while the children spat at us. We looked like dirty scum, as nobody had been able to wash or shave. Many were wearing shredded bandages.[29]

It is likely that the march that Korth described was merely a relatively small one from the station where they arrived; a far larger march had already taken place on 17 July, when about 57,000 German prisoners were paraded through Moscow, led by several of the senior officers who had been captured during the course of *Bagration*. It was degrading treatment, but nowhere near as bad as the manner in which Red Army prisoners were treated by the Germans. It is estimated that about two million Soviet soldiers starved to death in German captivity in the first eight months of the conflict.[30]

There remained the complex issue of the various partisan groups operating in and around Vilnius. The largest were affiliated to the Polish *AK* and were often openly hostile to the Red Army and in turn, the Red Army was under orders to treat the *AK* as a hostile force and to disarm its personnel and arrest its officers. The various Jewish groups were more willing to cooperate with the Red Army, as of course were the relatively few pro-Soviet partisans officially recognised by the Soviet Union, and there were even small numbers of Lithuanian nationalists, hostile to all those they regarded as foreign occupiers of Lithuanian territory. The leader of the local *AK* forces was General Aleksander Krzyżanowski, a former artillery officer in the Polish Army, and he spent many fruitless months in 1942 and 1943 attempting to establish contacts and cooperation with other anti-German groups. In the case of the *AK* partisans controlled by Krzyżanowski, their hostility towards the Red Army was a response to the official position of the Soviet Union towards the *AK*, but there were numerous occasions in the Vilnius area when *AK* units attacked Jewish resistance groups throughout the years of occupation.[31]

In the first weeks of 1944, Krzyżanowski was involved in negotiations with Seidler von Rosenfeld, an officer in the German *Sicherheitsdienst* ('Security Service' or *SD*) and Julian Christiansen, head of the local branch of the *Abwehr* (German military intelligence), though it isn't clear which side instigated these meetings. Christiansen was prepared to make detailed agreements under which the Wehrmacht would provide the *AK* with weapons up to and including light artillery in exchange for a ceasefire between the *AK* and the German occupation forces, and cooperation on economic matters. Krzyżanowski rejected these terms; despite his disappointment, Christiansen arranged for weapons and ammunition to be left in poorly guarded locations with the explicit intention of arming the *AK* in its fight against pro-Soviet partisans.[32] To his chagrin, one of the first uses of these weapons was in an attack against pro-German Lithuanian paramilitary troops under the command of Povilas Plechavičius.

With the Red Army moving swiftly towards Vilnius in July 1944, the Germans attempted once more to come to terms with the *AK*, this time approaching Colonel Lubosław Krzeszowski, one of Krzyżanowski's subordinates. The German officers proposed cooperation against the Red Army in return for civilian control of Vilnius being handed over to Polish leaders; additionally, several Polish prisoners would be released. Krzeszowski rejected the terms, as he and other officers were busy preparing their attempt to seize the city before the arrival of the Red Army. The sheer speed of the Soviet advance across Belarus played a part in the failure of the *AK* plans – the timetable for the seizure of Vilnius, codenamed *Ostra Brama* ('Gates of Dawn'), was brought forward, resulting in fewer *AK* troops being available than intended.

On 16 July, Krzyżanowski and other senior *AK* officers in the region were invited to a meeting with senior Soviet officers. A report produced by an officer of the NKVD described what happened:

> Yesterday [i.e. on 17 July] at 0800 hours, under the pretext of an inspection by the commandant of the Front, commandants of brigades and regiments [of the Home Army] were gathered around the village of Bogusze. Altogether, 26 officers, including nine commandants of brigades, 12 unit commanders, and five staff officers of the Polish Army were gathered.
>
> When directed by us to turn in their weapons, they refused, and only after the threat of force were they disarmed.
>
> ... Today, at dawn, we began combing operations through the forests, in which, according to our estimates, the Poles were present ... It was ascertained that during the night they marched away to the south. Because of the steps taken, we caught up with them, and disarmed them.
>
> According to the situational reports for 1600 hours, 3,500 men were disarmed, among them, 200 officers and NCOs.
>
> During the disarming, 3,000 guns, 300 machine-guns, 50 heavy machine-guns, 15 mortars, seven light artillery pieces, 12 vehicles, and a large number of grenades and ammunition were confiscated.[33]

Krzyżanowski was arrested and remained in prison until October 1947. A year after his release by the Soviet authorities, the Polish security service – run by the pro-Soviet government in Warsaw – arrested him, and he died of tuberculosis in 1951.[34]

Not all members of the *AK* were captured. An officer named Maciej Kalenkiewicz had succeeded in reaching France during the winter of 1939–40 from where he travelled to England. He was parachuted into Poland in late 1941 and was involved in several remarkable incidents – he and his group of fighters were captured by the Germans almost as soon as they arrived in Poland, but they managed to fight their way to freedom. Kalenkiewicz was one of the main architects of *Ostra Brama* but was injured in a clash with German forces in June 1944, as a result of which his hand was amputated. Consequently, he took no part in the battle in Vilnius and when he became aware that Soviet forces were arresting *AK* soldiers, he and a battalion of soldiers under his command managed to escape into dense woodland. Over a period of time, about 2,000 *AK* soldiers gathered there before dispersing in smaller groups to avoid detection. Kalenkiewicz sent a radio signal to the Polish government-in-exile in London, informing them that the *AK* was being systematically destroyed and was doomed unless the Western Powers intervened – he suggested that they might attempt to establish air bases in eastern Poland. On 19 August, he and his men were surrounded in a village near the frontier with Belarus and were overwhelmed by soldiers from the NKVD.

The demise of the *AK* was a clear example of how Stalin intended to proceed as the Red Army marched into Eastern Europe. In order to ensure that Soviet domination was undisputed, all potential opponents were to be eliminated. His intelligence service would almost certainly have been aware of the attempts by Kalenkiewicz to secure help from the Western Powers; such incidents merely reinforced his determination to ensure that his troops had firm control of as much territory as possible before the end of the war.

The German government attempted to portray the fighting in and around Vilnius in heroic terms. The official communiqué was read out on the radio as well as being printed in almost every newspaper:

> Vilnius was encircled, but not yet overrun. The garrison took up the almost hopeless battle. Generalleutnant Stahel ... flew to the encircled garrison of Vilnius and took command. The grenadiers and anti-aircraft gunners of Hauptmann Müller knew the importance of their resistance.
>
> The fallen Bolsheviks piled up in front of their positions, attacking tanks were left ablaze, and heavy weapons were silenced. But the powerful onslaught

continued without interruption. Enemy intelligence services prematurely reported the fall of Vilnius, the destruction of the garrison, and an attack on Kaunas. But the garrison held out. When the outer defensive line was broken, a new one was formed in the city centre.

The garrison continued their desperate struggle. Supplied only by air for some time and now cut off from their water supply, they continued to fight despite the seemingly hopeless situation even when the enemy drove them into the southwest quarter. Only the Luftwaffe, tirelessly engaging in ground attacks, showed them they were not alone.

The July sunshine burned through the heat of the burning houses, raising temperatures to unbearable levels. Meanwhile the Bolsheviks, advancing towards the northwest, were blocked by a German position halfway to Kaunas. The breakwater of Vilnius had sapped their momentum …

Fighting hard, *Gruppe Stahel* broke away from the enemy. On its way west it had to cross the Neris twice, fighting across the river with just personal weapons …

Throughout the fighting, the German fighting spirit had prevailed once again. A new and glorious page of the history of German soldiers was written in Vilnius.[35]

Compared to the 'fortresses' of Vitebsk, Orsha, Mogilev, and Bobruisk, Vilnius did appear to have a significant impact upon the Red Army's advance. Sufficient Soviet forces were drawn into the fighting to slow the thrust across Lithuania, giving the Wehrmacht invaluable time to rally its forces and to organise new defensive lines. This was achieved despite only a small part of the intended garrison reaching the city before it was encircled, and the success of Stahel's troops was largely because the Soviet forces approaching the city were degraded by constant combat; they were also operating at the end of long supply lines, and had consumed all of the stockpiles of fuel, food, and ammunition that had been assembled for the initial attack. It seems from Bagramian's memoirs that his concern was mainly about the slowness of the advance of 2nd Baltic Front to his north; he wanted to move the axis of his 1st Baltic Front slightly towards the north and instead of attacking towards Kaunas he suggested a thrust past the northern fringe of the city, aimed at Šiauliai and thereafter towards the Baltic coast.[36] With Vasilevsky's agreement, he ordered Chistiakov to shift the weight of his forces towards the north. This regrouping and redirection of resources had at least as much effect on the momentum of the Red Army's advance as Stahel's defence of Vilnius.

By reaching and capturing the Vilnius region, Bagramian's 1st Baltic Front had advanced more than half the distance from its start line to the Baltic coast in just three weeks. Although the German forces in front of him had been given a moment to catch their breath, they were still greatly outnumbered, and the overall balance of resources was still greatly in favour of the Red Army – even as the fighting in Vilnius was dying down, Vasilevsky authorised the release of 100 new T-34s to replenish the ranks of Rotmistrov's Fifth Guards Tank Army, at a time when German units regarded the delivery of just a dozen new vehicles as a welcome boost. Reinhardt's Third Panzer Army had been thrown back over 220 miles; it seemed that once the Red Army had gathered itself once more, there was every likelihood of Army Group North being cut off with its back to the Baltic Sea.

CHAPTER 10

FIRE BRIGADES: THE PANZER DIVISIONS AND THE RED ARMY, 9–19 JULY

Hitler's original expectation and requirement had been that Army Group Centre would defend its positions with its initial resources, falling back only when absolutely necessary. This strategy had rapidly collapsed and reinforcements had been trickled into the sector from neighbouring army groups, but this policy was also at an end; the reinforcing divisions were rapidly approaching the end of their strength and there seemed to be no end in sight to the pressure being applied by the Red Army. Since the beginning of the offensive, Soviet units had advanced up to 220 miles and even though this had been achieved at a heavy price, it seemed highly likely that further advances would take place in the coming days. All now depended on the intervention of the panzer divisions. After their early role in the war as the spearheads of the Wehrmacht's victorious advances, they were deployed increasingly as firefighters to deal with crises wherever they erupted, and the arrival of 4th, 5th, 6th, 7th, and 12th Panzer Divisions in the central sector – albeit in several stages – was almost the last chance for some semblance of a stable front line to be restored.

It was a tough demand. In defensive warfare, the panzer divisions were meant to operate immediately behind infantry divisions, dealing with any enemy forces that broke through the front line and energetically counterattacking so that the infantry could then reoccupy their former positions. But the only infantry available consisted of the shattered remnants of Army Group Centre's former armies, numerous improvised groups of rear area personnel, and a few relatively fresh units transferred from elsewhere – such was the intensity of the fighting that these new arrivals were soon as badly degraded as the units that had been driven back in disarray by the Red Army during *Bagration*.

Throughout the fighting in Vilnius, battles continued to rage all along the front line. To the south of Vilnius, 5th Panzer Division managed to hold onto its new positions, albeit under considerable pressure. The Red Army succeeded in capturing Lida and Voronov, two towns astride the road running from Saucken's XXXIX Panzer Corps north to Vilnius, during the night of 8–9 July, and both 5th and 7th Panzer Divisions were in constant action. Their panzer companies and anti-tank subunits continued to report impressive numbers of enemy tanks knocked out, but both German divisions were rapidly running out of tanks. On 27 June, 5th Panzer Division had fielded 55 Pz.IVs and 70 Panthers, but by the end of 9 July this had sunk to just six Pz.IVs and 12 Panthers ready for operations.[1] Provided that disabled tanks could be evacuated in a timely manner, there was every prospect of these numbers rising significantly, but only if these repaired vehicles outnumbered those put out of action; and if there was a requirement for a rapid retreat, many of the tanks awaiting repairs would have to be destroyed to prevent them falling into the hands of the Red Army. On the southern flank of Saucken's forces, the disparate units gathered together as *Gruppe Weidling* were reinforced by 50th Infantry Division and the group was now renamed VI Corps.

During the evening of 9 July, Model, Friessner (at the headquarters of Army Group North), and Hitler discussed what further options remained. From a purely military viewpoint, the best (or more accurately the least worst) option was to order Army Group North to commence a withdrawal from Estonia and perhaps Latvia too, allowing it to concentrate its forces on its southern flank from where it could intervene in the crisis in Lithuania. Indeed, this option was regarded by *Stavka* as the most logical and Stalin had ordered his armies in the north to be alert for any such signs of a German withdrawal. But Hitler rejected this option out of hand. He told his generals that Grand Admiral Karl Dönitz, the head of the U-boat forces, had informed him that retention of control of the Baltic coastline was essential for ongoing U-boat training. Once the Western Allies had been driven back into the sea, the new U-boat crews would be needed to resume the Battle of the Atlantic while German ground forces were transferred to the east to deal with the Soviet Union. Instead of a major withdrawal by Army Group North, Hitler gave permission for two infantry divisions to be transferred from Army Group North to Army Group Centre, together with the formations of 6th Panzer Division, currently undergoing replenishment in Germany, whose arrival in the Kaunas and Vilnius regions has already been described. Gottberg was to organise a new group consisting of four regiments in Grodno. Two further divisions were to be transferred from Army Group North at a later date – but crucially, Friessner was not given permission for any major withdrawals. In other words, he was to leave his front dangerously weakened.

Model returned to his headquarters where he issued a new order of the day:

> During a conference today the Führer expressed his particular satisfaction at the attitude of the troops of the army group who have been involved in hard fighting over the past few days. Reinforcements are on their way. With them, we must prevail in the tasks that have been assigned to us.[2]

Model was probably unaware of the details of events in the west that were hammering the final nail into the coffin of Hitler's strategy. The forces of the Western Allies had been struggling to break out of their Normandy beachhead for several weeks; the British were stuck outside the city of Caen, which they had been expected to capture on the first day of the operation, and had made several costly attempts to force their way through the German defences. On 8 July, the latest such operation – codenamed *Charnwood* – was preceded by a devastating air raid that reduced the historic city to rubble. When the ground forces moved forward, they gnawed their way into the German defensive belt, suffering heavy losses, and in two days succeeded in capturing most of Caen. The advance was halted at the Orne River, but Generalfeldmarschall Erwin Rommel – in command of the German Army Group B facing the Normandy beachhead – mentioned to Oberstleutnant Caesar von Hofacker, a Luftwaffe staff officer, that the losses being suffered in holding back the attempts by the Allies to break out of their beachheads could not be sustained for more than another three weeks and there seemed to be little or no prospect of being able to gather together sufficient forces for a counteroffensive sufficiently strong to destroy the enemy. Hofacker was a member of the anti-Hitler resistance and he reported these words to other conspirators, including his cousin Stauffenberg; the next plan to kill Hitler and take control of the German government, codenamed *Walküre* ('Valkyrie'), was brought forward.[3]

Charnwood wasn't the only battle that put pressure upon the German lines in the west. At the western end of the beachhead, US troops had commenced heavy bombardment of the town of Saint-Lô on 6 July and then launched an attack that would lead to the complete capture of the town over the following two weeks. In doing so, the American forces exhausted the last reserves of the German units opposing them and a breakout became inevitable.[4] But even before this breakout took place, it was clear to anyone who had access to the overall picture that Germany had no means, however remote, of winning the war. Therein lay the difficulty for men like Model, Friessner, and Rommel – they could see that the situation in their sectors and perhaps neighbouring sectors was desperate, but they were completely reliant upon Hitler for information about what was happening elsewhere. Some used personal contacts to learn the truth, but even those showed little inclination to act on the outcome of their investigations.

XXXIX Panzer Corps continued to beat off repeated Soviet attacks on 10 July, but both its flanks were still dangerously exposed. There was now the growing risk that just as so many German formations had been overwhelmed further to the east, Saucken's corps would be enveloped to the east of the Niemen River, and 5th Panzer Division was pulled out of line and ordered to concentrate on the

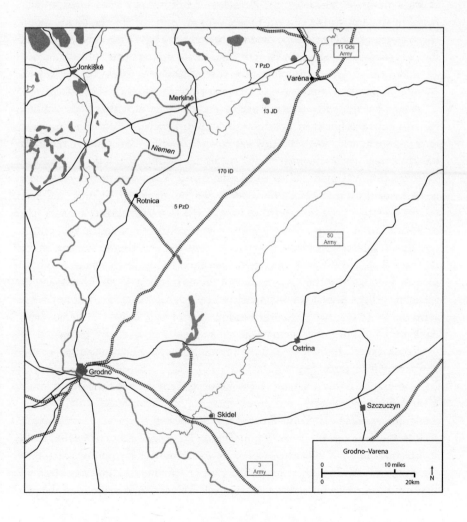

northern flank at Varena, from where it was to make a counterattack in order to establish firm contact with 7th Panzer Division to the north.[5]

Soviet units were also massing against the southern flank of XXXIX Panzer Corps and the neighbouring VI Corps. Thirty-First and Fiftieth Armies had enjoyed a comparatively quiet couple of days behind the front, replenishing immediately to the west of Minsk, and they now resumed their move towards the west; once they joined Eleventh Guards Army and Third Army respectively, the German lines would once more face overwhelming numbers.

By the morning of 11 July, 7th Panzer Division had gathered sufficient strength – and perhaps more importantly, sufficient fuel – to commence an attack towards the north against elements of Rotmistrov's Fifth Guards Tank Army in the area to the east of Alytus. Almost immediately, the attack group encountered a series of *Pakfronts* and was brought to a halt. Even as orders arrived for the group to withdraw to its start line, the opposing Soviet units launched attacks of their own. Even holding the current positions would be challenging enough – there was no prospect whatever of advancing to the aid of Vilnius.

After what must have seemed like an endless series of withdrawals, XXXIX Panzer Corps was finally in a position to catch its breath on 11 July and to make local counterattacks. With these, it was possible to bring some order to the front line, but huge gaps remained to the north and south. The various groups of survivors that had managed to escape the Minsk–Chervyen pocket were now being reorganised into battlegroups under the command of VI Corps, and here too the relentless pressure seemed to have eased. To a large extent, this was very deceptive. Soviet forces were regrouping and reorganising, and it was only a question of time before offensive operations resumed. Indeed, the pressure on the northern flank of LV Corps, next in line beyond VI Corps, was reported to have increased throughout the day, and any lifting of spirits at Model's headquarters would have been dispelled immediately when a signal was received from Oberst Johannes Hölz, chief of staff in the headquarters of LV Corps: 'On the northern flank of LV Corps, the enemy threat has increased markedly compared to preceding days … In three days, if the current level of fighting continues, we will have no infantry forces left.'[6]

Stabilisation of the northern sector was dependent upon the transfer of forces from Army Group North, and on an energetic attack from the north into the flank of Bagramian's 1st Baltic Front. Despite repeated assurances that he would shortly release troops for Army Group Centre, Friessner was in no position to do so. His front line was under heavy pressure and any attack he mounted would be too weak to make any difference. During the afternoon of 11 July, he contacted *OKH* and expressed concerns for the survival of his entire army group. If the two armies of Army Group North were to avoid being isolated from the rest of the front line by Red Army units reaching the Baltic Sea, it was essential for the northern flank to pull back from the Narva sector to the west, either withdrawing overland to the Latvian border or via a naval evacuation from Tallinn. At the same time, the rest of Army Group North would have to pull back to a line running roughly from Riga to Kaunas:

> I cannot reconcile with my conscience not having made every effort in this fateful hour to spare these loyal troops the worst that could befall them and not having found for them a role that would make it possible to hold the enemy away from the eastern border of our homeland … If the Führer is unwilling to grant me freedom of action, I ask to be relieved of my command.[7]

For the moment, Friessner was left in post, not least because he had only recently been appointed and a further change in leadership would simply create more chaos. Hitler assured his army group commander that a substantial number of panzer divisions would be gathered to the west of Kaunas from where they would be able to make energetic attacks to restore the situation. He had no answer to the protests from both Army Group North and the operations staff at *OKH* that this would take at least a week, during which the Red Army was likely to have changed the situation further to the detriment of the Wehrmacht; nor could he explain how such a powerful force could be gathered without fatally weakening the front line elsewhere.

The relative lull in the fighting on the front line of XXXIX Panzer Corps ended during the morning of 12 July, with 5th Panzer Division facing major attacks on both its flanks. The division was arrayed in a line facing southeast, to the north of Grodno; to its left were most of 170th Infantry Division and 13th Jäger Division, with 7th Panzer Division beyond them. For the moment, the line was able to hold and energetic counterattacks by 5th Panzer Division recovered most of the ground that had to be conceded during the morning.

The crises confronting the panzer divisions seemed endless. On 13 July, while dealing with several strong attacks along the frontage of XXXIX Panzer Corps, 5th Panzer Division received orders to dispatch its armoured reconnaissance battalion towards Grodno, which was threatened from the north by the Red Army. It was to be followed by further elements of the division as rapidly as they could be released, with the intention of concentrating all of 5th Panzer Division near Grodno before dawn on 14 July. Almost immediately, the order was overtaken by events as the Red Army seized the road running north from Grodno along which the German units had intended to march. This road ran to the east of the Niemen, and the operations officer of 5th Panzer Division suggested that instead of attempting to fight its way south along the road through dense forests, it would be better to cross the Niemen to the west bank and then proceed south, but the previous orders remained in force.

Overnight, the reconnaissance battalion reached Rotnica, about 24 miles north of Grodno, and reported that the Red Army had already occupied the village; moreover, additional Soviet forces were massing immediately to the east. A panzergrenadier battalion that was following close behind ran into Soviet troops a little further north, but before it could deploy to try to push aside the blocking position held by the Soviet troops it came under heavy attack from the east. Hauptmann Riemann, the battalion commander, hastily pulled his men back to the north to Merkinė, where the panzergrenadiers crossed the Niemen to the west bank, followed by the rest of 5th Panzer Division.

Regardless of the orders he had received, Decker – the commander of 5th Panzer Division – could see that there was no point in attempting to fight his way along the east bank of the Niemen to Grodno. He ordered the division to assemble instead immediately to the northwest of the city, but even as his columns began to move south they came under attack from Soviet forces that had already crossed the river. Local counterattacks drove some Red Army units back a short distance, but it was impossible to reach and secure the line of the Niemen. Ordered to hold an extended sector of front line facing the river, 5th Panzer Division was reduced to setting up a series of strongpoints, often separated by open ground. A few improvised groups of rear area personnel and police formations were rounded up and used in these gaps, but the line was porous at best.[8]

There was little respite for the panzer divisions of Army Group Centre on 14 July. After the failure to reach Grodno the previous day, 5th Panzer Division succeeded in holding most of its positions but was unable to secure the line of the Niemen as ordered. Things were little better on the northern flank of 5th Panzer Division, where Generalmajor Gerhard Schmidhuber's 7th Panzer Division found itself facing much of Galitsky's Eleventh Guards Army. Anxious to keep up the pace of his advance, Galitsky ordered his leading units to storm across the Niemen before the Germans could organise a coherent defensive line. Small units of soldiers crossed before dawn and provided cover for the main forces that followed; XVI Guards Rifle Corps had already established a bridgehead the previous day and after being reinforced early on 14 July, they marched on Alytus despite being low on ammunition. It was a risky move, but entirely justified in the circumstances and the Germans scrambled to respond. There were very few troops available to defend Alytus and 7th Panzer Division was ordered to dispatch its *Kampfgruppe Weitzel*, consisting of two panzergrenadier battalions with artillery support, to the city. Despite Weitzel's protests, the modest force was immediately dispersed to defend the city against attacks from the south, east, and north.[9]

After their successful escape from Vilnius, the troops of the garrison and of *Gruppe Tolsdorff* – which had endured almost complete encirclement in order to hold open the escape corridor – might have expected a few days of rest to gather their strength, but instead they were immediately ordered on 14 July to take up positions in the front line so that 6th Panzer Division could be extracted and held in reserve. The weather suddenly broke with heavy rain showers; men and machines struggled through the mud, fighting as much against the elements as against each other. For Bagramian in the headquarters of 1st Baltic Front, there was a considerable sense of frustration. He had been given control of III Guards Mechanised Corps – originally part of Oslikovsky's Cavalry-Mechanised Group – but it was badly weakened by its involvement in battles to the east and in Vilnius. It would take several days for it to be brought up to effective strength. Bagramian was now dealing with the problems of success:

> The slow tempo of our 1st Baltic Front was not merely due to insufficient forces and the breadth of frontage, but also due to acute shortages of ammunition and fuel. The troops were now about 300km from their railheads, and consequently the supply of ammunition and fuel had to be along roads that were more or less congested with traffic. To deal with this we had only a single truck brigade, which could deliver barely a third of the needs of the assault troops. The need to pause the attack for a few days was felt ever more forcefully. We would thus be able to regroup our forces, restore ammunition and fuel stocks, and after the arrival of fresh forces resume the offensive with new energy.
>
> But after we thoroughly assessed the situation and had held discussions with the representative of *Stavka* [i.e. Vasilevsky] we came to the conclusion that there should be no consideration of halting on this occasion. The enemy would be able to establish a stable defensive line during the pause. Breaking through it would then require huge consumption of munitions and unacceptable losses of personnel.
>
> With heavy hearts we decided that even if slowly, we would continue the advance. In keeping with what we agreed with Vasilevsky, we issued the necessary orders.[10]

According to Vasilevsky, these discussions took place on 12 July, while the battle for Vilnius was still raging:

> Having consulted Bagramian, I requested *Stavka* to release 1st Baltic Front from delivering the main attack with its left flank on Kaunas and to permit us to focus

our efforts on the right flank, opposite Daugavpils, directing Fifty-First and Second Guards Armies ... at Panevežys and Šiauliai. I expressed confidence that in subsequently developing this attack on Riga we should cleave the German defences there in two more quickly and with less risk, arrive at the Baltic coast, intercept the communications from the Baltic to East Prussia and cut off Army Group North from Germany. What is more, this would be bound to have an effect on the resistance of the German Sixteenth and Eighteenth Armies overall; it would then be easier for 2nd and 3rd Baltic Fronts to advance out of the Pskov region towards the Bay of Riga.[11]

In addition to giving Bagramian III Guards Mechanised Corps, Vasilevsky wanted to transfer Rotmistrov's Fifth Guards Tank Army to this new axis, on the grounds that given the ebbing strength of Soviet units, it would have a greater likelihood of reaching a clear objective – in this case, the Baltic coast – than if it continued to be used in attacks towards Poland and East Prussia. Stalin disagreed; there were some transfers of forces between Fronts, but for the moment the tank army remained under Cherniakhovsky's control.

Throughout 14 July, 5th Panzer Division was slowly driven back towards the southwest and was unable to retain contact with the Niemen River at any point. To add to the division's problems, there was little clear information about the precise positions of enemy forces; the armoured reconnaissance battalion, normally the eyes and ears of the division, was still somewhere beyond the Niemen, near Grodno. Orders for the division to conduct mobile operations to intercept and destroy Soviet units that had crossed the Niemen continued to arrive and were simply disregarded as utterly unachievable.

The German retreat continued on 15 and 16 July. The small garrison of Alytus abandoned the city under threat of encirclement and a little further south 5th Panzer Division gave up any pretence of mounting counterattacks as ordered. During the course of 15 July, the soldiers of the division marked a significant moment: they had retreated across the old frontier of East Prussia. The land war had reached German territory. But the following day, there was a more cheering development. The armoured reconnaissance battalion of 5th Panzer Division, separated from the rest of the formation during the attempt to reach Grodno, managed to make its way back to safety.

The relief felt by the men of 5th Panzer Division at the return of their armoured reconnaissance battalion was short-lived. Soviet pressure all along the line continued on 17 July; the wounded Hauptmann Karl Seckler, commander of one of the division's panzergrenadier battalions, had discharged himself from a military hospital prematurely to return to his men and was killed when leading the battalion in its fifth counterattack of the day.[12] Similar battles raged for the next two days with little gain for either side.

A little to the north, 7th Panzer Division was also in constant combat as the Red Army attempted to press on towards the west. One of its two panzergrenadier regiments reported that since arriving in this sector, it had lost 320 men dead, wounded, or missing in six days – this represented nearly 20 per cent of its establishment strength.[13] But the division received a welcome boost with the return of its second panzer battalion, which had been in France re-equipping with Panther tanks. The arrival of the battalion at full strength on 18 July greatly increased the fighting power of the division, but even as the trains carrying the tanks rattled towards the front, orders arrived by light aircraft. Instead of being deployed as a coherent whole, the battalion was broken into companies that were assigned to the infantry divisions fighting alongside 7th Panzer Division. However much the men of the panzer division resented this dispersal of their strength in this manner, it was almost unavoidable. Without tank support, the infantry divisions lacked the ability to defeat the Red Army formations arrayed against them, which were now almost always made up of a mixture of infantry and tanks with artillery support. The Soviet forces had learned a great deal in the three years of warfare.

On the same day that 7th Panzer Division's Panthers reached the front line, there was a change in German command. Kurt Tippelskirch, who had led Fourth Army since early June, was injured when a liaison plane in which he was travelling crash-landed. His injuries were not life threatening, but were severe enough to prevent him from continuing in his role. His replacement was General Friedrich Hossbach, a man with extensive experience of fighting on the Eastern Front. Despite his record as a combat leader, he would ultimately be better known for a memorandum that he drew up in November 1937 as an adjutant; he recorded a summary of a meeting in Berlin in which Hitler stated that he wished to avoid conflict with Britain and France if possible, but such a conflict might be unavoidable as it would be impossible for Germany to be self-sufficient in food supplies. The only means by which security of food supply – in this context, the ability to acquire sufficient food without being at the mercy of British naval blockade – was by German expansion into Eastern Europe: 'The one remedy, and the one which might appear to us as visionary, lay in the acquisition of greater *Lebensraum* ['living space'] – a quest which has at all times been the origin of the formation of states and the migration of peoples.'[14]

The memorandum would be used by the International Military Tribunal in Nuremberg after the war to demonstrate that Hitler had planned at length for a war of aggression and conquest.

Throughout this period, the panzer divisions further to the south were also under constant pressure. Desperately short of fuel, 12th Panzer Division contacted Vormann's headquarters on 9 July to advise that unless the situation improved immediately, many vehicles would have to be abandoned. Precious fuel was siphoned from the trucks and tractors that were to be left behind; the division's artillery regiment was forced to destroy seven of its guns as it no longer had the means to move them. Somewhat to the dismay of the division staff, a legal delegation arrived shortly after from Army Group Centre on Model's orders to investigate why the guns had been lost and whether any of 12th Panzer Division's officers should face court martial; when presented with the evidence, which showed that Army Group Centre had erroneously directed fuel supplies intended for 12th Panzer Division to Lida, where they had been destroyed by the advancing Red Army, the lawyers departed without taking any action.[15]

Nearby, 28th Jäger Division was also suffering. Broken into several fragments, it struggled back towards the west. Generalleutnant Gustav von Ziehlberg, the division commander, was unable to maintain contact with all of his subunits; he reached the headquarters of LV Corps shortly before midnight and informed General Friedrich Herrlein, the corps commander, that his men were utterly exhausted, and complained bitterly that he had not been supported or supplied in an adequate manner. Herrlein – who was wrestling with almost impossible demands on his resources – had little patience with this, sharply replying that Ziehlberg's place was with his troops, not at corps headquarters.[16] Ziehlberg's criticism was justified in that his troops had been fighting hard for several days without any meaningful supplies reaching them, but Herrlein was not personally to blame – the reality was that all of Army Group Centre was in a chaotic and broken state, making it impossible for even a semblance of normal supply lines to be maintained. At about the same time, Vormann's disparate forces were once more termed Ninth Army, in the expectation that this might improve command and control – and, importantly, logistic support.

Despite Model's order of the day on 9 July expressing the Führer's recognition of the great efforts of the soldiers on the Eastern Front, discussions between Army Group Centre and its subordinate units before dawn on 10 July were blunt, often acrimonious. Krebs, Model's chief of staff, informed Second Army in the south – which was responsible for most of the sector of Army Group Centre south of Slonim – that the current line had to be held, immediately to the

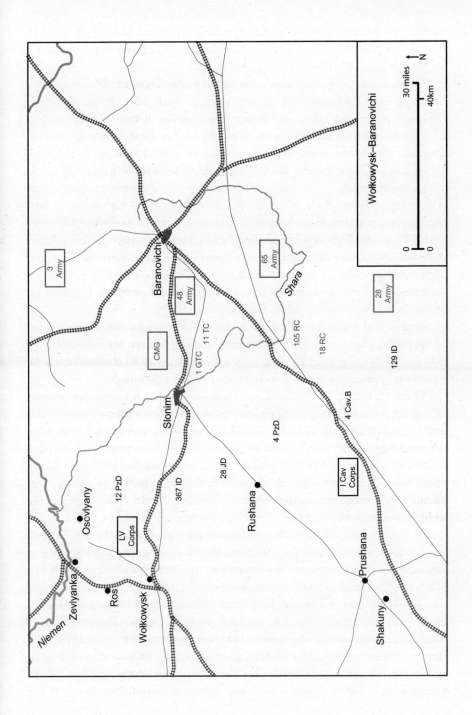

west of Slonim. The response from Generalmajor Henning von Tresckow, chief of staff at Second Army, was acerbic and indignant in equal measure:

> If the last intact army of the army group isn't also to be destroyed, [this defensive stand] can't be done. One can't lead with strong words, but with measures of proper leadership. Stubbornly holding a line achieves nothing and the task assigned to Second Army is unachievable. We must have freedom of action. It is certain that defence of the Shara sector is possible only for a limited time. The army commander [Walter Weiss] must have freedom to withdraw to the Zevlyanka sector.[17]

The response was equally uncompromising: the order was to be obeyed in every detail. Weiss then sent a personal signal to Krebs, informing him that Second Army was in a potentially disastrous situation with some elements – such as 28th Jäger Division, one of the reinforcement units that had rapidly been badly degraded – already knocked out of the front line, and found himself caught up in the increasingly surreal world that German officers were inhabiting. When Weiss reiterated that rigid defence of the current line would end in catastrophe, Krebs replied that the orders stated merely that the line was to be held if at all possible. Weiss asked if this meant he had been granted freedom to handle matters as appropriate; Krebs responded that this was not the case.

To a large extent, Krebs was merely doing what others had done before him in various posts: he was passing on instructions from Hitler, but trying to find small gaps in those orders which might allow the professional soldiers to do what was actually required. For an army that was facing destruction, it was an unwieldy and cumbersome method of operating. Tresckow was bitterly angry at the restrictions placed upon Second Army, but he had already been involved in attempts to remove the encumbrances imposed upon the Wehrmacht, in the most radical manner possible.

In March 1943, Hitler had visited Smolensk, where Army Group Centre's headquarters was based. At the time, Tresckow was the army group's operations officer and when Hitler's entourage prepared to return to Germany, he asked Oberst Heinz Brandt, a staff officer accompanying Hitler, if he would take a bottle of alcohol to Berlin as a present for Oberst Hellmuth Stieff, an acquaintance of Tresckow. It was payment for a lost bet, Tresckow explained. But the parcel actually contained a bomb and Tresckow and other conspirators waited anxiously for news that the Führer's plane had been lost en route for Berlin; they were dismayed when they received a signal that the flight had been completed without incident. When conspirators in Berlin managed to recover the parcel, they found that the timer fuse had malfunctioned because instead of being carried within the cabin of the aircraft, the bomb had been in the unpressurised and colder cargo bay.

By the summer of 1944, Tresckow was heavily involved in planning for *Walküre*. Some of his fellow conspirators doubted both the chances of success and the value of any such attempt as the military defeat of Germany was now inevitable, but Tresckow was one of those who felt that even if it failed, the attempt had to be made. As the avalanche of the Red Army continued to roll west, he and his fellow conspirators made their final preparations.

With his command once more designated as Fourth Army, Vormann visited several of his formations personally, reaching the headquarters of 12th Panzer Division during the night of 9–10 July. The following morning, fighting resumed, particularly in the city of Slonim where Pliev's cavalry-mechanised group was attacking with support from I Guards Tank Corps and a rifle corps; with just 90 miles separating his units from the old western frontiers of the Soviet Union, Rokossovsky urged his men to push on over the next obstacle, the Shara River. At the end of the day, 12th Panzer Division reported that it had just one operational tank left.[18] To the south, 4th Panzer Division was in rather better shape and even managed to mount a counterattack towards the north, but the continuing retreat of other parts of LV Corps made it impossible for the recaptured ground to be held. Regardless of the orders Krebs had passed down from Army Group Centre, soldiers and in many cases junior officers were often making their own decisions. Many could see no point in risking encirclement in the seemingly endless swamps and forests and unless they were supported with artillery and armour, infantrymen increasingly pulled back as soon as they came under any pressure from the Red Army.

As they pushed on towards the west, the Soviet soldiers had to cope with numerous minefields that had been laid hastily by the retreating Germans. Casualties from these were modest, and Batov – commander of Sixty-Fifth Army – noted that the mines had more of an impact upon the local wild elk, bison, and boar populations than on his men. The animals faced other threats too:

It should be mentioned that these animals were also threatened by the activities of passionate hunters of which there were many in our army. An order from Front headquarters threatened severe punishment for anyone involved in poaching and violating regulations to protect the wildlife. That dampened the hunting passion for many men. Nevertheless, an unfortunate incident occurred. Colonel Prokhorov, the commander of an artillery brigade, shot a bison. Rokossovsky ordered the colonel to appear before a military tribunal. I felt sorry for this brave and capable officer. In order to buy some time I asked the Front commander for permission to instigate a thorough investigation. When Prokhorov's artillery brigade distinguished itself in combat a few days later, I asked Rokossovsky to issue just a reprimand. At first he refused to revoke his decision. 'If a bison suddenly appeared in front of you in this forest, Comrade Commander,' I implored him, 'wouldn't you also be tempted by your passion for hunting?'

'It isn't fair of you to remind me of my weaknesses, Comrade Batov. I would have controlled myself. But I don't want to seem hard-hearted, and I accept your request. If you're this dedicated to protecting him, he must be a good officer.'[19]

This is a curious story, given the widespread looting carried out by Red Army soldiers after they crossed the frontier into the Reich, but it is quite possible that attempts were made to enforce a higher level of discipline while the soldiers were still on Soviet territory.

The energy-sapping heat of the previous few days was replaced by summer rainstorms across much of the region on 11 July. In the south, 4th Panzer Division came under repeated attack but succeeded in holding its positions all morning, despite increasingly crippling shortages of ammunition, particularly for anti-tank weapons. Supplies arrived in the evening, but like much of Army Group Centre, the division was functioning from day to day on what it received, unable to make any plans for the longer term.

Meanwhile, others continued to take steps to try to create circumstances in which ultimate disaster for Germany might be avoided. In the early afternoon of 11 July, Oberst von Stauffenberg arrived for the daily conference at the Berghof, Hitler's headquarters in Obersalzburg in Bavaria, carrying a faded yellow briefcase. He expected to find both Hitler and Himmler in the conference room, but the latter was not present. According to one account, the briefcase contained a bomb with which he had intended to kill the two men, but Stauffenberg aborted the assassination attempt due to Himmler's absence.[20] It is impossible to be certain what was happening amongst the conspirators, as so few of them survived the coming days; Hans Gisevius commented that some of the figures who had been active conspirators against Hitler since the 1930s complained that Stauffenberg was making decisions without reference to others.[21] Such secrecy was entirely to be expected, given the nature of what was being planned. But preparations continued for the plot, which involved far more than the assassination of Hitler. The *Ersatzheer* was to be used by the conspirators to ensure that their seizure of power in Germany was not opposed by the Nazi Party, the SS, or any other body.

Despite the clear evidence that Germany faced catastrophic defeat, most senior officers in the German military preferred to wait in silence, apart from the relatively small circle of active conspirators. Many senior figures had been approached and asked to join the conspiracy, but had refused, with most citing their oath of loyalty to Hitler. However, if he were to be killed, then they would no longer be bound automatically by their oath to any successor. It is noteworthy that whilst these officers felt honour-bound to refuse involvement in any plot to kill Hitler, none of those approached informed the authorities of these contacts. The wording of the oath stated:

I swear to God this holy oath
That I shall render unconditional obedience
To the leader of the German Reich and people,
Adolf Hitler, supreme commander of the armed forces,
And that as a brave soldier I shall at all times be prepared
To give my life for this oath.

The officers concerned would have argued that there was nothing in this oath that required them to betray the conspirators, but 'unconditional obedience' surely did not include remaining silent about a threat to the Führer's life. In any event, regardless of their oath, these officers had obligations to their soldiers and to Germany as a whole: the Wehrmacht was not the personal property of Hitler, and their refusal to act decisively against him was a betrayal of their greater responsibilities. But operating in what was now clearly a fight for survival against overwhelming external forces, it is perhaps understandable that so many officers chose to look the other way and avoid entanglement in the plot. Many would have known that their personal conduct would leave them open to prosecution for war crimes, even in the event of a negotiated peace – the sheer scale of the slaughter of Jews, Red Army prisoners of war, and others was hardly something that could be dismissed lightly.

Despite the widespread chaos and defeats on all fronts, it seems that ordinary German soldiers were still largely loyal to Hitler, and believed that – perhaps by the advent of new, wondrous weaponry – the Führer would be able to lead Germany to victory, or at least to a satisfactory conclusion to the war. Nevertheless, the apparently endless series of defeats and the loss of so many comrades must have had a hugely depressing effect on morale in Army Group Centre. By contrast, morale on the other side of the front line was predictably buoyant, as Pliev described:

I can still remember the radiant joy on the faces of the tired, dusty cavalrymen and tankers who had travelled such a long way from the Caucasus Mountains to the borders of the Soviet Union in the west. Columns of horsemen at times moved at a variable mixed pace of walk and trot. And when they slowed to a walk a song would break out, a dashing cavalry song, with whistles and warm enthusiasm. Residents of villages happily ran out onto the road, bringing bread and salt on embroidered towels as was the custom in our land from time immemorial, to meet the soldier-liberators. The mood in the regiments was excellent. We advanced victoriously towards the west operating in the rear of the German units. The initiative was now firmly in our hands and everyone in our ranks understood this very well.[22]

Like those of so many other senior Soviet figures, Pliev's memoirs comply with the official historiography that prevailed after the end of the war – that the victorious Red Army was greeted universally as a liberation force. This was certainly the case in many areas, but not all, particularly as Soviet troops began to enter the regions of western Belarus that had been annexed by Poland in the wake of the Polish–Soviet War of 1919–21. But even in these areas, the German occupation had been so brutal that even those who were opposed to Soviet rule welcomed the departure of the regime that had been responsible for so many atrocities since 1941. After taking into account the civilians who were forcibly taken to the Reich as labourers and who were worked to death, it is estimated that a minimum of 1.36 million Belarusians – equivalent to over 22 per cent of the population – died.[23] Other estimates put the number killed at closer to two million.

Meanwhile, 12th Panzer Division faced renewed attacks on 12 July. One of its panzergrenadier battalions was involved in bitter fighting just to the south of the Niemen River in the village of Osovlyany, and during the following evening the surviving German troops withdrew across the river towards the northwest. Briefly, the panzergrenadier battalion to the north of this sector established contact with elements of 50th Infantry Division – the southern formation of Fourth Army – but this link was lost during the afternoon as repeated Soviet attacks battered the Germans back to and across the Niemen. But if the situation on the northern flank of Vormann's Ninth Army was as good as could be expected, there was further deterioration to the south. Between 12th Panzer Division and 4th Panzer Division was 367th Infantry Division, and it came under heavy attack. By the end of the day it had lost contact with the panzer divisions on either flank; Vormann dispatched parts of 28th Jäger Division as reinforcements to prevent the Red Army from tearing up his fragile line once more, but the exhausted soldiers of Ziehlberg's division were in poor shape for such a role. It was, at best, a temporary measure.

After regrouping overnight, 4th Panzer Division was able to mount an energetic counterattack shortly before dawn on 12 July, recovering a small area of ground, but by midday it was clear that a withdrawal to the west would be needed to prevent the division being bypassed. However, Hitler had forbidden the movement of panzer divisions without his explicit consent and three hours passed before formal permission was granted; Betzel used the time to make sure that all of his units were ready to move so that they could then pull back as quickly and as efficiently as possible.

Arguments raged all day as officers at the various corps, army, and army group headquarters struggled to reconcile their orders with the weak forces they had available. Model insisted that the retreat to the west had to be slowed; Generalleutnant Gustav Harteneck, commander of I Cavalry Corps, consisting of 4th Panzer Division, the Hungarian 4th Cavalry Brigade, and 129th Infantry Division, replied that his infantry division was too weak to hold even a limited frontage of five miles. Tresckow, chief of staff at Second Army, added that LV Corps was in danger of giving way too and pleaded for a 'major resolution' – only a substantial retreat would save the German units from complete collapse. Model remained obdurate, insisting that with proper use of artillery, an effective defence was still possible. Krebs, his chief of staff, had further discussions with Tresckow and Second Army's operations officer, Oberst Ernst-August Lassen. Tresckow repeated that the orders for as rigid a defence as possible were unachievable and were constantly being overtaken by events. He added that the situation was almost exactly analogous to that of the summer of 1941, when it had been the German forces that were dictating the pace and course of events and the Red Army had been struggling to implement orders that were out of date even before they were issued. The rigid orders were either being ignored by the troops on the ground or were resulting in the loss of irreplaceable men. Such sacrifices were only justifiable if they bought sufficient time for fresh units to create a new defensive line further to the rear, but that was manifestly not the case: if Second Army was to bring the Soviet offensive to a standstill with the forces it had, it needed far more flexibility in how they were deployed.[24]

General Friedrich Herrlein, commander of LV Corps, added an uncompromising report on the situation of his forces:

The execution of orders for positions to be held rigidly is impossible due to the following factors:

1. The absolute massing of far superior heavy assault forces on a broad front with multiple points of concentration as well as the extensive mobility of

the enemy, which facilitates rapid follow-up and constant shifting of the point of main effort ...

2. The mobility of the enemy results in enemy attack forces being less fatigued, compared to the exhaustion of our own infantry that reduces it to a state of apathy. The uninterrupted pressure for several days has also had a detrimental effect on junior commanders.

3. The impression that the enemy's personnel and material superiority has barely weakened since the commencement of fighting has greatly impacted upon the confidence of troops in their own superiority, which previously still existed in defensive warfare. With these troops fighting in a thin line on a broad front with their last strength and without reserves, it is pointless to try to clear large enemy penetrations. The troops know from their experiences of the last days that the Russians will immediately carry out counterattacks in strength. Clearing penetrations is only possible in limited circumstances and even then only at the cost of comparatively heavy casualties that cannot be replaced.

4. The deployment of security and improvised battalions amongst the remaining intact units, which are under the threat of complete or near-complete encirclement, greatly reduces fighting power in defence, and even more so in counterattacks. The enemy effectively creates multiple points of effort against our thin front line with the result that it is no longer possible to move reinforcements sideways to seal off local penetrations at key locations.

5. The considerable losses of artillery and heavy infantry weapons as well as the loss of almost all tanks, self-propelled guns, and a large proportion of assault guns as well as the absence of supply columns of 367th Infantry Division (not yet arrived) and 28th Jäger Division (lost in action) further reduces the combat effectiveness of the troops.

6. The execution of the orders of the Field Marshal require:
   – one fresh, full-strength infantry division;
   – one assault gun brigade;
   – at least two army artillery battalions;
   – and replenishment of the panzer regiment of 12th Panzer Division.

Otherwise, the attempts to carry out these orders will result in a short time in the destruction of encirclement of the remaining formations.[25]

A report from 12th Panzer Division added that whilst it had only a single operational tank, it had sufficient crews for a further 56 tanks if they could be made available. But while these arguments continued, the fears of corps and army commanders were confirmed by further Soviet attacks early on 13 July. A panzergrenadier battalion from 12th Panzer Division was thrown back in disarray by a Soviet thrust southwards over the Niemen at Zevlyanka. By the end of the day, the entire line of the river had been forced and regardless of Model's instructions for obdurate defence, 12th Panzer Division was forced back to a line about six miles further west. The arrival of parts of the division that had been absent – its anti-aircraft battalion and most of its anti-tank battalion – was small comfort.

Although it remained under heavy pressure, 4th Panzer Division further south was in better shape and defeated Soviet attempts to force its positions. It too received reinforcements in the form of a trainload of factory-fresh Pz.IVs, but these would require time for gunsights to be aligned and radio batteries to be fitted before they could be brought into service. However, any satisfaction at the arrival of these welcome reinforcements was offset by news from further south.

In the preparations for *Bagration*, the Red Army had gone to considerable lengths to reinforce German expectations that the summer's main effort would fall on Army Group North Ukraine. With so many German units now being withdrawn from this sector to deal with the growing catastrophe in Army Group Centre, the Red Army attacked in strength to the east of Lviv with General Ivan Stepanovich Konev's 1st Ukrainian Front in what became known as the Lviv–Sandomierz Operation. Roads and bridges behind the front line had been repaired and improved, partly as the *Maskirovka* operation prior to *Bagration*, and once German attention switched to the huge offensive against Army Group Centre, Konev stepped up preparations for an attack. On the night of 12–13 July, his units carried out reconnaissance in force, and then went onto the offensive in full strength on 13 July.[26] This operation would inflict further severe damage upon the Wehrmacht, and would result in the Red Army securing a substantial bridgehead across the Vistula near Sandomierz; just as importantly, it ensured that there was no possibility of further reinforcements being sent to Army Group Centre from that region. Despite the compartmentalisation of command arrangements in the Wehrmacht, it must have been clear to Model and other senior commanders that the crisis facing Germany was now on all fronts. The Western Powers were about to break out from their Normandy beachheads; Army Group North was under too much pressure to be able to release sufficient forces to attack southwards in order to close the gap with Army Group Centre; and within days, Army Group North Ukraine was also in full retreat.

The exhausted formations of the German LV Corps also withdrew towards the west on 14 July. What remained of 28th Jäger Division, with 367th

Infantry Division on its northern flank, came under pressure near Wołkowysk from two rifle divisions of Colonel General Prokofy Logvinovich Romanenko's Forty-Eighth Army; a little to the rear of these Soviet troops, Luftwaffe reconnaissance flights reported the concentration of Soviet armour. These were the troops of IX Tank Corps and I Guards Tank Corps, refuelling and rearming in preparation for new assaults. It had been the intention of Herrlein, the corps commander, to use 367th Infantry Division to replace 12th Panzer Division in the front line so that the armoured formation could then be freed for mobile operations, but this proved to be impossible and the panzer division remained in almost constant combat. At one stage, most of one of its panzergrenadier battalions was cut off in the small town of Ros, managing to fight its way out to the west in heavy fighting. By the end of the day, there were no operational tanks left in the division. At the same time, the Germans were forced out of Wołkowysk. The small town had been a familiar spot for many soldiers in Army Group Centre: it was the location of a centre where soldiers returning to Germany on leave underwent delousing and were given clean uniforms. It was now in Soviet hands.

The withdrawal left I Cavalry Corps further south with little choice but to pull back in turn in order to avoid exposing its northern flank. Artillery ammunition was in short supply, and from the headquarters of 4th Panzer Division, Betzel asked Harteneck to ensure sufficient supplies were brought forward as quickly as possible – his panzergrenadiers were exhausted, and without the extensive use of artillery support they would not be able to continue holding their positions. The armoured battlegroup of 4th Panzer Division was in constant demand to deal with pressure upon 129th Infantry Division and the Hungarian cavalry brigade, but its strength was declining at an alarming rate. Even with the vehicles of an assault gun brigade and a Tiger tank battalion added to its strength, the division was reduced to just 14 Panthers, ten Tigers, nine assault guns, and 22 self-propelled anti-tank guns.[27]

Weiss – commander of Second Army – warned his corps commanders on 15 July that if the retreats of recent days continued at the same rate, the army would be driven back to the Narew River in another ten days; Herrlein replied that the combat strength of his units was so badly degraded that it was impossible to continue even at the current rate of withdrawal without LV Corps being annihilated. But despite having no tanks available, 12th Panzer Division was able to hold its current positions to the west of Ros, largely because the Red Army was having to pause its advance while supplies were brought forward. To the north of 12th Panzer Division, there was tentative contact with 50th Infantry Division, transferred from Army Group South

Ukraine, but the only way that this could be maintained was by shifting an increasing proportion of the panzer division to the north. The newly arrived companies of the division's anti-tank battalion were equipped with brand new Jagdpanzer IV vehicles; with a long-barrelled 75mm gun in a turretless mount on a Pz.IV chassis, it was a potent tank killer with good armour and a low profile, but the sheer length of the barrel often caused problems in confined spaces such as woodland and narrow streets. By the end of 16 July, the division could field a total of 12 of these tank destroyers together with three repaired Pz.III tanks.[28]

A large part of the reason why 12th Panzer Division had a better day was because the Red Army was switching its point of effort to the south. The two Soviet tank corps that had been identified by Luftwaffe reconnaissance flights – IX Tank Corps and I Guards Tank Corps – to the east of Wołkowysk attacked to the south of the town. Energetic counterattacks by 4th Panzer Division seemed to have overcome the crisis, but the front line continued to move inexorably to the west. The division's repair workshops worked tirelessly to return vehicles to the front line, permitting the division to maintain a near-constant combat strength, but fuel and ammunition supplies remained problematic. In one of the German counterattacks near the village of Shakuny, German anti-tank gunners opened fire on a group of Red Army vehicles on the morning of 16 July, destroying several of them. In one of the vehicles was Major General Boris Sergeyevich Bakharov, commander of IX Tank Corps. He was a popular officer, with a longstanding policy of being in the front line in difficult moments, and he was killed instantly in the explosion. He had commanded armoured forces with distinction throughout the war, leading 50th Tank Division in the Battle of Smolensk in 1941, then XVIII Tank Corps in the fighting in northeast Ukraine in 1942 and at Kursk in 1943; the battles at Prokhorovka, at the height of the Kursk fighting, saw him criticised for not driving home a sufficiently energetic counterattack, but it was the only minor blemish on his record.[29]

Despite having to mount these counterattacks, 4th Panzer Division – like 12th Panzer Division – had a chance to rest many of its men. It was badly needed. One of its officers wrote:

> Who measures the physical strain of the summer heat and the lack of sleep? The psychological strain of constant retreats with almost continuous contact with the enemy and the persistent danger of being bypassed? The breakdowns due to losses of officers and communications equipment? The bottlenecks in the supply of ammunition and fuel? The difficulties in food supplies?[30]

Robert Poensgen, the war journalist in 4th Panzer Division, gave a vivid account of a typical action:

In the evening, 3rd Company of 35th Panzer Regiment and the men of 12th Panzergrenadier Regiment drove into the village. During their withdrawal they had managed to get a head start on the pursuing enemy, overrunning them in a counterattack and creating a deep wedge. They secured the outskirts of the village during the night and the Russians didn't attempt to attack the strong group. They had run into what for them was an unpleasant block. Orders came by radio for the battlegroup to pull back. A new position was being set up further to the rear under their protection. They had accomplished their task.

The half-tracks rolled out. The road was still open. The Panthers covered the withdrawal of their comrades. They stayed in position around the village, holding the enemy in check with their long barrels. Then for them too came the command to withdraw.

The situation was very tense when Oberleutnant Goldhammer summoned the other officers. The heavy Panthers couldn't use the road that had been used by the panzergrenadiers, as they had to cross a bridge that was far too weak. There was only one possible route: they had to attempt to fight their way through the Russian attack group. That meant driving at full speed, avoiding getting caught up in fighting, and staying together through every twist and turn.

Sit up, start up, march! While the heavy tank engines roared and the fighting vehicles gathered in a row, the Russian artillery fired again and again into the village, which began to burn fiercely. Hatches were closed, weapons cleared for action …

Leutnant Göhrum's leading tank drove to the road exiting the village. Heavy fire was directed at him. Increase speed! Stay together! The drivers stepped on the gas pedals and changed gears. The speedometers climbed to 30, 40, 45km/h. From the right a Sherman fired. Leutnant Göhrum came to an abrupt halt. Two, three shots, and flames rose from the Russian tank. The drive continued. Russian infantry fired completely pointlessly from the woods with their rifles. Out of the village – onwards! Faster, faster! A wild race began. Earth-brown shapes scattered in panic along the road ahead, disappearing into the wheat fields on either side. But Russian anti-tank guns lurked there too, waiting for unwary victims. The tank engines roared. Long flames spat from the exhausts. Dust swirled up from the tracks in a cloud as high as a house. All turrets were directed to the right, at 3 o'clock, towards the muzzle flashes that blazed from the cornfield. Wherever the tank commanders and gun aimers looked, they saw anti-tank gun and artillery muzzles threatening them. They felt the hard blows of impacts and fired as fast as they could on the move. To halt now would be suicidal. Only good fortune could save us.

It was a drive through hell. There were anti-tank guns everywhere. It wasn't possible to avoid them. There were crashes and flashes all round. Shell strikes bounced off the sloping armour plates with bright flashes.

Nearby, the German panzergrenadiers in their trenches pricked up their ears. What was happening? In the part of the village occupied by Ivan there were suddenly relentless shell strikes. Anti-tank rounds flew over the German positions. Had the Russians suddenly lost their minds? They were now even setting their own buildings alight with their fire.

Suddenly the Germans saw how a tank emerged, shrouded in a great cloud of smoke from the village at breakneck speed, then a second, a third, an entire group – one after the other, all close together. 'Tanks approaching!' The alert was shouted from one foxhole to the next. Anti-tank weapons were prepared. Suddenly a Leutnant, who was observing the fighting through binoculars, roared, 'They're German tanks!'

He leaped up and waved his hat. The first tank turned directly towards him. It was an alarming moment for the Leutnant. What if it was Russians in the German tank? But a turret hatch was thrown open and a flare rose up, a black hat appeared. The tanks stopped a few metres from the grenadiers, one after the other. Hatches were opened. The tank crewmen blinked at the bright daylight. They clambered out and gasped in the fresh air after their mad drive.

While they smoked cigarettes, they counted the impacts on turrets, hulls, and rears. They looked back at the village, which was burning brightly, and were happy just to have survived. You could see it in their faces, even if they didn't say it.[31]

Poensgen was writing for the German newspapers of the day, but the piece contains details that say a great deal. The Panther tank was Germany's response to the T-34, and despite a long gestation it was an unreliable vehicle when it entered service in 1943; later models were rather better, but shortages of spare parts meant that Panther battalions often struggled to field all their tanks. Some components – particularly rubber seals – were of far lower quality than in the past, as German industry was forced to use synthetic rubber in the absence of natural rubber, resulting in crewmen complaining that the tanks often smelled strongly of gasoline. This sometimes led to a dangerous accumulation of fumes in the tank and the risk of it bursting into flames if hit. The T-34 that led to the German decision to build the Panther tank weighed 26 tons – the later T-34/85 with a bigger turret and 85mm gun weighed 31 tons – and when the T-34 appeared there were already projects underway to replace the Pz.III and Pz.IV with a new 20-ton tank, but this was increased to 30 tons after German forces encountered the T-34 and KV-1. The German *Waffenamt* ('Weaponry Office') advised against this increase in weight, on the grounds that the requirement was for a medium tank and that the increased weight would be a disadvantage, but was overruled.[32] At first, the tank was intended to have a diesel engine but ultimately it was decided to use the same gasoline engine as intended for the Tiger tank. The influence of the T-34 led to the adoption of heavily sloped frontal armour, making the Panther difficult to kill from the front – it was almost impossible for Soviet 76mm guns to penetrate, even at close range. The side armour was 60mm thick and was also sloped, but the steady upgrading of its protection before it entered service meant that it now weighed over 40 tons, placing it at a severe disadvantage in the Soviet Union where few bridges could cope with such a weight. This also put a greater strain on the engine and gearbox; although the Panther could reach speeds of 34 miles per hour, this pace was not sustainable without risking engine or transmission failure and it was routine for Panther drivers to restrict their speed to little more than half this value. A high-speed escape through enemy-held positions, as described by Poensgen, was a risky undertaking. There was a high likelihood of vehicles breaking down or becoming stuck on obstacles, and even if the armour of the Panthers was difficult to penetrate, the tracks of the tanks could be broken as easily as those of any tracked vehicle. Anti-tank gunners were of course aware of this, frequently trying to disable tanks by hitting their tracks and then directing the fire of heavy artillery onto the stationary vehicles.

Over 17 and 18 July, LV Corps managed to pull back to a new line where it hoped to be able to bring the Soviet advance to a halt, but pressure remained intense. The rapid collapse of German positions in the sector of Army Group North Ukraine, where Konev was attacking energetically towards Lviv, couldn't be ignored; Harteneck sent Betzel a warning order that 4th Panzer Division might have to be withdrawn so that it could be sent to prevent complete collapse further to the south. But how the division could be extracted from its current positions without precipitating a further collapse in Army Group Centre was not clear. Indeed, the near-impossibility of carrying out the orders passed down the chain of command continued to lead to bad-tempered exchanges. The chief of staff of Second Army wrote in the war diary on 17 July:

> The commander of Second Army [Weiss] has complained to the chief of staff of the army group about interference in the chain of command, even to the choice

of location for [Second Army's] command post. 'I'm not doing with that. It's not happening. I'm not a raw recruit. If you're not happy with my leadership, replace me.'

Chief of staff LV Corps to chief of staff Second Army: 'In 367th Infantry Division the rear area troops fell asleep [through exhaustion] and were surprised by the enemy. If we had fresh troops, we could give the Russians a punch on the nose.'[33]

The obvious frustration at almost every level of command only highlighted still further the near-impossible situation facing the Wehrmacht. Fresh troops were unavailable, yet without those fresh troops there seemed to be no prospect of restoring the situation. In the west, the US Army finally secured the ruins of Saint-Lô and began its preparations for Operation *Cobra*, the full-scale breakout from Normandy. A little to the west, British and Canadian forces continued to hammer at the German lines at Caen and constantly threatened to break through the German positions by sheer weight of firepower. With no prospect of the tide turning in the Wehrmacht's favour in the east or west, Germany desperately needed a way out of the war.

CHAPTER 11

INTERLUDE: 'MAKE PEACE, YOU FOOLS! WHAT ELSE CAN YOU DO?'

Gerd von Rundstedt was born in 1875, the son of a cavalry officer who had served with distinction in the Franco-Prussian War of 1870–71. Like many of the families that served in the armies of Prussia and Germany over the centuries, the Rundstedts were from a stratum of society known as the *Uradel*, who could trace their nobility to at least the 14th century; a common feature in these families was that they were not particularly wealthy. When he was aged 17, Rundstedt wanted to join a cavalry regiment but lacked the funding to do so, and instead became an officer cadet in an infantry regiment. His potential was swiftly recognised, resulting in him being sent to the *Kriegsakademie* in Berlin in 1903 for training as a staff officer.

In the First World War, he served as chief of staff in an infantry division during the invasion of Belgium and then in a similar role on the Eastern Front the following year. He ended the war with the rank of Major and as chief of staff of XV Corps. He stayed in the army and in 1920 was transferred to the cavalry; he steadily rose in rank and was one of several senior officers who met Hitler after the Nazis took power in 1933. Although Hitler assured the army that he would not interfere with its internal affairs, Rundstedt made no secret of his dislike of the Nazis and although he refused to join any anti-Hitler groups, he used his rank and influence to block the appointment of General Walther von Reichenau to the post of chief of the general staff on two occasions, on the grounds that Reichenau was too openly pro-Nazi. He retired from the army in 1938 with the rank of Generaloberst, but returned to service the following year and was appointed commander of Army Group South in the invasion of Poland. He protested about the indiscriminate killing of Poles both by the SS and by the army and banned *Einsatzgruppe VII* from the area under his control after the massacres of hundreds of Jews in Katowice and nearby towns, but although he remained on cordial terms with several men who would play prominent roles in the plots against Hitler, he refused to join them. The following year, he commanded Army Group A in the west, overseeing the triumphant thrust through the Ardennes, Belgium, and northern France to the English Channel.

When planning began for the invasion of the Soviet Union, Rundstedt was dubious about the likelihood of success, particularly with Britain remaining undefeated in the west. Nonetheless, he took command of Army Group South and his troops reached Rostov on 21 November. But seeing no prospect of victory, Rundstedt then advocated a major withdrawal to the line of the Dnepr River in order to shorten supply lines and authorised the abandonment of Rostov in the face of a Soviet counterattack. Hitler insisted that Rostov should be held at all costs and when Rundstedt asked Hitler to dismiss him if he no longer retained the Führer's confidence, Hitler promptly did so. To rub salt into the wounds, Hitler's choice of new commander for Army Group South was Reichenau.

From 1942, Rundstedt was *Oberbefehlshaber West* ('Supreme Commander West'), a post that he still held when the Western Powers carried out their landings in Normandy in 1944. He had repeatedly proposed a policy of mobile defence in depth, using panzer divisions and other mechanised forces to launch counterattacks to destroy any landings, but had been overruled by Hitler on the grounds that such a policy was unworkable given the air superiority of the British and American forces. Failure to reach a decisive conclusion in this proved to be disastrous; Hitler attempted to compromise by allocating half the available armour to forward defence, while the rest was held in reserve, though it couldn't be used without Hitler's explicit permission. When Rundstedt demanded the release of these reserves on 6 June, Hitler refused on the grounds that it wasn't clear whether the landings in Normandy constituted a genuine invasion attempt or were decoy operations before the real invasion occurred in the Pas-de-Calais.

As the fighting raged around the Normandy beachhead, Rundstedt authorised the withdrawal of armoured forces from the front line near Caen, where they were taking heavy losses due to naval gunfire. His order was promptly overruled by *OKW* on 1 July and he angrily telephoned Keitel, head of *OKW*, to demand the freedom to deploy his forces as he saw fit. The latest attempt to beat back the British with an attack by II SS-Panzer Corps had failed, he informed Keitel, and there was no point in leaving the two precious panzer divisions exposed to shelling from British and American warships. Keitel told him that it was impossible to change the Führer's mind. Even a man as closely associated to Hitler's regime as Keitel could see that such rigid adherence to wrong-minded orders was likely to end in disaster, and Keitel asked Rundstedt for advice on what he should do. According to General Günther Blumentritt, who was present in Rundstedt's headquarters, the elderly field marshal replied, 'Make peace, you fools! What else can you do?'[1] Two days later, he was dismissed and replaced by Kluge.

Rundstedt was perhaps the first senior figure in the military to articulate what must have been obvious to anyone in a sufficiently high post to have an overall view of the situation. Hitler's last strategy had been one of obdurate defence in the east while waiting for an invasion of France, and then crushing this invasion with the forces that had been assembled in preparation. With Hitler's failure to release armoured reserves on the first day of the Normandy Landings, the best opportunity for carrying out this policy was lost and by early July it was clear that the elimination of the Normandy beachhead was impossible. In the absence of any other strategic options, Rundstedt's blunt response to Keitel was absolutely correct. There was no longer any prospect of victory, and the pragmatic solution was to seek peace before the land war reached German territory. Rundstedt knew from his personal experiences in Poland and Ukraine that the Germans had been responsible for appalling crimes in the occupied regions, and that there was every likelihood of the Red Army seeking a terrible revenge. Others too had no doubts about the hopelessness of the situation, even if they were unwilling to put it into words. After the war, Rudolf von Gersdorff, who had the rank of Oberst at the time and was an active conspirator against Hitler, wrote:

> Despite a frank and lucid estimate of the situation by the High Command of the German forces in the west, Supreme Command [i.e. Hitler] did not alter its decisions, though the overall situation was so obvious that no realistically thinking person could entertain any doubts. However, Supreme Command deceived itself and the German people with its belief in Providence. The overall principle of command remained: 'We'll manage somehow.'[2]

Even if Keitel had been willing to listen to Rundstedt's advice, securing peace by negotiation with the Allied Powers seemed impossible. In the Casablanca Declaration of 1943, Roosevelt and Churchill had made clear that the Allied Powers would prosecute the war until they secured the unconditional surrender of Germany. Roosevelt then attempted to clarify this, stating that the intention was not to wage war upon the common people of the Axis powers, but 'to impose punishment and retribution upon their guilty, barbaric leaders.'[3] There was therefore no prospect of any negotiated end to the conflict if Hitler and those identified as being in his inner circle were still in power.

Whilst Keitel and others close to Hitler might have regarded this as meaning that there was no alternative but to fight on to the bitter end, others drew different conclusions. Plots against Hitler had existed almost since he came to power, resulting in an attempt to kill him with a bomb in a Munich beer hall in November 1939, when he addressed loyalists on the anniversary of the failed 'beer hall putsch' of 1923; Hitler left the meeting earlier than expected and thus wasn't present when the bomb detonated, killing eight of those present. The attempt by Tresckow to kill Hitler in 1943 has already been described, and a week after this failed there was another attempt when Gersdorff, who as a staff officer had overseen the exhumation of the mass burials at Katyn, planned a suicide bomb attack. He was to conduct a party that included Hitler, Göring, Himmler, Keitel, and Dönitz around an exhibition of captured Soviet weaponry and when the tour began he triggered two ten-minute timers wired to explosives concealed about his body; contrary to expectations, Hitler briskly walked around the exhibition in just two minutes and left, and Gersdorff dashed to a nearby toilet where he succeeded in disarming his bomb with moments to spare.[4]

This wasn't the only occasion that one of the conspirators considered sacrificing themselves to kill Hitler. In November 1943, Hauptmann Axel Freiherr von dem Bussche-Streithorst was meant to model new winter clothing before Hitler and his entourage; he improvised a bomb using a grenade fuse and explosives, but the train carrying the new uniforms was destroyed the night before the demonstration in an allied air raid. His intention to repeat the attempt in early 1944 was thwarted even as he prepared to travel from the Eastern Front to Berlin – he was badly wounded by artillery shelling, losing his leg. Rittmeister Eberhard von Breitenbuch, an aide to Busch, travelled to Bavaria with his commander in March 1944 intending to shoot the Führer, only to be denied entry to the meeting because the SS guards informed him that there had been a change to regulations and aides were no longer permitted into such meetings.[5]

After aborting his attempt to kill Hitler, Himmler, and Göring in the Berghof, Stauffenberg and several others decided that killing Hitler was the priority – if Himmler and others weren't present, the attempt should continue anyway. On 15 July, when Stauffenberg attended another meeting, he was pleased to discover that Hitler, Himmler, and Göring were all present, but Hitler was called away unexpectedly and the attempt was abandoned once more. Three days later, Stauffenberg was informed that the Gestapo was aware of the conspiracy and that arrests were imminent. There is no evidence to suggest that there were any actual plans for arrests, but in the climate of fear that prevailed, such rumours assumed huge importance.

The plotters now moved to implement their final attempt to decapitate the German leadership. The details of what happened in the eventful days of July 1944 are disputed, largely because so few of the conspirators survived, but they are nonetheless important for many reasons. Firstly, the plot – both to kill Hitler and to seize power – came close to success, which would have had almost incalculable consequences for the course of the war. Secondly, the motivations and expectations of the people involved are important in how they confirmed Stalin's deep suspicions that if the opportunity arose, the Western Powers would seek an accommodation with a new German government in order to limit the future power of the Soviet Union.

Hans Gisevius, who had been in Zurich as vice-consul for several months, returned to Berlin as the last preparations were made. He was staying with Wolf-Heinrich Graf von Helldorff, the head of Berlin's police, whose involvement in the conspiracy is one of the numerous elements that remains clouded. He was a close associate of Goebbels before the war and apparently advocated the creation of a Jewish ghetto in Berlin; he was also suspected of extorting money from Jews attempting to leave Germany. But others described incidents when Helldorff intervened on behalf of Jews to protect them, and the conspirators believed that as he was head of police in Berlin, he would be of great help in ensuring a smooth transition of power after Hitler's death. As he walked from the railway station to Helldorff's home, Gisevius saw at first hand the devastation being inflicted upon German cities by British and American bombers:

> Once this street had been a splendid boulevard lined with mansions. Now ruins gaped on either side. It was with difficulty that I found the house, which had recently received a direct hit. The police chief was now living in a hotel in the city; a few servants were still using the concrete shelter of his former home ...
>
> I had to take the subway, which was just as well because it gave me the opportunity to gather some impression of Berlin and the Berlin populace. Because of the continual night attacks, all the people were overtired; they fell asleep standing up. Accustomed to the normal, rested look on faces in Switzerland, I saw what human havoc had been wrought upon these people. And yet the shift from total war to total destruction had just started.

Alexanderplatz [location of the police headquarters] was a ghastly scene of wreckage. But the bombs seemed often to have spared the strongholds of the tyrants. In the midst of this smoke-blackened and razed area rose the remains of the police headquarters; what was left of the building still sufficed to shelter the most important offices.[6]

A few days later, Gisevius witnessed a daylight bombing raid on the city:

A year ago the nonchalance with which those great flights of bombers flew across all of Germany to Berlin would have been inconceivable. Now no one thought anything of it, or of the fact that fighter planes no longer rose to combat them and that the flak was pretty ineffectual. People accepted the inevitable apathetically and sighed with relief if the attack proved mild. A 'mild' attack meant, of course, that the quota of bombs rained down on some other quarter of the vast area of Berlin.

It was over in an hour. Although the attack had been directed against the centre of the city, I noticed on my way to Alexanderplatz that normal business activity continued in spite of fires and blockaded streets. When I asked the police officers in Helldorff's waiting room what had happened, they had to dig out their reports before they could give me a list of the larger fires and the more serious bomb damage. 'Nothing special,' I was told. They were so dulled to destruction that they took notice of it only when a serious traffic obstruction was created or when a government building was hit.[7]

The stoic attitude of the Berlin populace left Gisevius with mixed feelings. On the one hand, he was appalled by the destruction being visited upon the German capital and presumably on other large cities, and could see that the plotters needed to do whatever they could to bring the war to an end; but on the other hand, he observed the apathetic attitude of the police with concern, questioning whether they would be willing to take firm action either against the conspirators or against Nazi officials and the SS if they were ordered to do so. As a civilian, he had little information about what was happening in the front line and had to rely on information given to him by the soldiers in the conspiracy, such as Generaloberst Ludwig Beck, chief of the general staff until 1938. As the last days passed before 20 July, there were desultory discussions amongst those waiting in Berlin to put into effect their plans. The intention was to trigger Operation *Walküre*, a plan drawn up to deploy the *Ersatzheer* in order to prevent the breakdown of law and order in Germany, and the conspirators had added important modifications. General Friedrich Olbricht, head of the *Wehrersatzamt* ('Armed Forces

Replacements Office') had been key to this: when orders for *Walküre* were issued, they would include the arrest of Nazi officials and the disarming of any SS units that refused to accept immediate incorporation into the regular army.

On 20 July 1944, there was a conference in Hitler's headquarters in East Prussia, near the town of Rastenburg. In a somewhat puerile manner, the Führer had assigned a series of bombastic codenames to his various headquarters: the bunkers built in western Germany in preparation for the invasion of France were known as the *Felsennest* ('Rocky Eyrie'); the *Adlerhorst* ('Eagle's Nest') was another headquarters in the west, used extensively during the Ardennes offensive of late 1944; *Wolfsschlucht I* and *II* ('Wolf Canyon') were in Belgium and France; and the Rastenburg complex was known as the *Wolfsschanze* ('Wolf's Lair'). The conference was to take place just after midday, and there would be a total of 22 attendees. In addition to Hitler and Stauffenberg, these included Heusinger, chief of the general staff; Günther Korten, chief of the general staff of the Luftwaffe; Brandt, who had been asked by Tresckow to take the 'Cointreau bomb' with him from Smolensk to Berlin; Alfred Jodl, head of the Wehrmacht operations staff; and Wilhelm Keitel, head of *OKW*. It is noteworthy that despite previous attempts being derailed by their absence, both Göring and Himmler were not at the conference.

Stauffenberg's briefcase contained two bombs, each with a ten-minute fuse. Immediately before the meeting he went into a washroom, telling others that he needed to change his shirt, and activated one of the fuses. After being badly wounded in a British air attack in North Africa, he had lost his left eye, his right hand, and two fingers on his left hand; consequently, using pliers to activate the bomb fuses was awkward and he didn't have time to arm both bombs before having to return to the conference room. His aide, Oberleutnant Werner von Haeften, took the other bomb away. Stauffenberg placed the briefcase under the conference table close to Hitler shortly before a messenger entered the room, telling him that there was an urgent telephone call for him – pre-arranged with a fellow conspirator.

After Stauffenberg left the conference room, one of the officers – thought to be Brandt – knocked his leg against the briefcase and moved it out of the way, placing it beneath the conference table a little further away, behind one of the table legs. The bomb detonated a few minutes later.

On most previous occasions, the conference had been held in a concrete bunker; on 20 July, it was in a wooden building. The explosion would have been far more confined in the bunker conference room and would probably have killed everyone present. If both of the intended bombs had been in the briefcase, the resulting blast would of course have been greater, and even the single bomb would have killed the Führer if Brandt hadn't placed the briefcase behind the thick conference table leg. As it was, Hitler's trousers were left in shreds and he suffered a burst eardrum, as did most of those present. A stenographer was killed instantly and three of those present – including Brandt – were injured severely enough to die in the days that followed. But Hitler, who had escaped death on so many occasions in the past, once more survived, albeit badly shaken and injured.

Stauffenberg saw and heard the blast and assuming that the assassination attempt had been successful, he managed to bluff his way past no fewer than three checkpoints. As they drove swiftly to the nearby airfield, Haeften threw the unused bomb into some trees by the side of the road. Time was of the essence, and they managed to board a plane that had been prepared for them by General Eduard Wagner, the quartermaster-general of the Wehrmacht and a fellow conspirator. They were airborne and heading for Berlin before the alarm could be raised.

In Berlin, the other conspirators waited anxiously for news. The intention of the plotters was to implement their plans as soon as they had confirmation that Hitler was dead, and they had modified the signal that would trigger *Walküre*; the new signal would attempt to place blame for the killing on dissenting Nazi Party members and was issued in the name of Generalfeldmarschall Erwin von Witzleben, a longstanding critic of Hitler who had been involved in conspiracies against the Führer since before the war:

> The Führer Adolf Hitler is dead!
>
> An unscrupulous clique of Party leaders who are strangers to the front line has attempted to use this situation to betray the hard-pressed front and to seize power for their own selfish ends.
>
> In this hour of greatest danger, the Reich government has declared a state of military emergency to ensure the maintenance of law and order and at the same time has assigned to me full executive power and supreme command of the Wehrmacht.[8]

The order continued with instructions that the Waffen-SS was to be integrated immediately into the army and the *Sicherheitsdienst* ('Security Office', effectively the security and intelligence service of the SS) was to be disbanded and its personnel detained. A further order was sent to the German authorities in the *Generalgouvernement*, the administration that oversaw the remnants of Poland not incorporated into the Reich or under other control; this issued instructions for the arrest of senior party and police officials, including the heads of Gestapo offices, and the detention and disarmament of concentration camp guards. Any resistance by the SS or others was to be dealt with ruthlessly and any dissenters disarmed, by force if necessary.

Generaloberst Friedrich Fromm, who was head of the *Ersatzheer* and whose authority was required for the triggering of *Walküre*, knew of the plot but had refused to be involved; nor had he informed the Gestapo of the existence of the plot. According to Gisevius, he became aware of the momentous events in Rastenburg at about 1400, while Stauffenberg was still airborne, when Olbricht burst into his office and informed him that Hitler had been killed and suggested that *Walküre* be activated to prevent disorder. Fromm did what anyone would expect him to do in such circumstances: he telephoned Rastenburg. There had been plans to destroy the communications centre in the *Wolfsschanze*, but this had been beyond the resources of the conspirators, and Fromm spoke to Keitel. He was told that there had been an assassination attempt and that Hitler had been only slightly injured. He enquired if Fromm knew the whereabouts of Stauffenberg; Fromm replied that he had no idea. Ending the telephone call, he told Olbricht that there was no reason to initiate *Walküre*. The conspirators issued the order anyway without Fromm's permission, and in his name.

Stauffenberg arrived in Berlin shortly before 1600 and was horrified to discover that the conspirators had not initiated the seizure of power – even if Hitler wasn't dead, it would have been possible to gain sufficient control to remove him from office. Insisting that he could confirm Hitler's death, he confronted Fromm. There was a further tense exchange between Fromm, Stauffenberg, and Olbricht, which was reproduced by the Gestapo at a later date:

Fromm: It is impossible; Keitel assured me that it was not so.
Stauffenberg: Generalfeldmarschall Keitel is lying as usual. I myself saw Hitler being carried out dead.
Olbricht: In view of this situation we have issued the codeword for internal unrest to the commanding generals.
Fromm (springing to his feet and pounding his fist on the desk): That is sheer disobedience! What do you mean by 'we'? Who gave the order?
Olbricht: My chief of staff, Oberst Merz von Quirnheim [another of the conspirators].
Fromm: Send Oberst Merz in here at once.
(Merz von Quirnheim enters. He admits to having issued the codeword to the commanding generals without Fromm's permission.)
Fromm: You are under arrest. We shall see about further action.
Stauffenberg (standing and speaking icily): General Fromm, I myself detonated the bomb during the conference in Hitler's headquarters. There was

an explosion like that of a 150mm shell. No one who was in that room can still be living.

Fromm: Graf Stauffenberg, the assassination failed. You must shoot yourself at once.

Stauffenberg: I shall do nothing of the kind.

Olbricht: General Fromm, the moment for action has come. If we do not strike now, our country will be ruined forever.

Fromm: Does that mean that you too are taking part in the *coup d'état*, Olbricht?

Olbricht: Yes, sir. But I am not a member of the group that will take over the government of Germany.

Fromm: I hereby declare all three of you under arrest.

Olbricht: You cannot arrest us. You do not realise who holds the power. We arrest you![9]

Fromm found himself locked in an adjacent office. Elsewhere, other conspirators were already taking steps. Empowered by the *Walküre* telex, General Carl-Heinrich von Stülpnagel, military governor of France, placed most of the senior officers of the *Sicherheitsdienst* and many SS figures under arrest. He then proceeded to the headquarters of Kluge, who had replaced Rundstedt as *Oberbefehlshaber West*. During his time as commander of Army Group Centre on the Eastern Front, Kluge had vacillated repeatedly about involvement in the schemes of Tresckow and others, and Stülpnagel now urged him to contact the Western Allies urgently to seek a ceasefire. He was horrified when Kluge informed him that Hitler was still alive.

Elsewhere, too, steps were taken to remove the Nazis from power, in Vienna and other cites, but with every minute that passed, the opportunities to carry out the *coup d'état* diminished. General Joachim von Kortzfleisch, commander of *Wehrkreis III* ('Military District III', which covered the Berlin area) refused to implement martial law, insisting that Hitler was still alive and that he had to abide by his oath of loyalty to the Führer. The angry remonstrations of Beck and Generaloberst Erich Hoepner, who pointed out that such an oath was meaningless in the context of how often Hitler had broken solemn oaths to the constitution and the people of Germany, were in vain. Kortzfleich was dismissed from his post by the conspirators and permitted to return to his home.[10] His replacement as commander of *Wehrkreis III* was Generalleutnant Karl Freiherr von Thüngen, but he too refused to impose martial law.

A special guard battalion from the *Grossdeutschland* division, commanded by Major Otto Remer, had been ordered to secure the area immediately around Wilhelmstrasse where most government ministries were located and to arrest

Joseph Goebbels and other senior Nazi figures who, Stauffenberg told Remer, were part of the plot to kill Hitler. As afternoon turned into evening, Beck spoke to Kluge in France, urging him to remain resolute. As he had done on so many previous occasions, Kluge seemed to be wavering and insisted that he would have to discuss matters with his staff.

Meanwhile, Remer had been dispatched to Goebbels' residence to place the propaganda minister under arrest. By this stage, Hitler had recovered sufficiently to speak to various individuals by telephone and Goebbels knew that the Führer had survived. When the soldiers arrived to arrest him, he suggested that rather than take such a hasty step, they should telephone Rastenburg first so that Remer could hear for himself that Hitler was actually alive. Remer agreed and Goebbels was put through to Hitler. He handed the phone to Remer, who had met Hitler just a few weeks before when he was presented with a medal. In a shaky voice, Hitler spoke to the major:

> Can you hear me? I'm still alive! The assassination attempt failed. A small group of self-serving officers wanted to dispose of me. But now we have the saboteurs in front of us. We will deal with this plague decisively. I assign to you the task of immediate restoration of peace and security in the capital of the Reich, by force if necessary. You are personally subordinated to me until the *Reichsführer-SS* [Himmler] arrives in the capital.[11]

By this time, there had been numerous radio broadcasts declaring that Hitler had survived an assassination attempt. About an hour after he spoke to Hitler, Remer encircled the Wehrmacht headquarters with his troops but made no move to arrest those inside. Finally, as darkness fell, SS troops began to move towards the building. At midnight, Hitler spoke to the nation in a radio broadcast:

> If I speak to you today, I do so for two special reasons. In the first place, so that you may hear my voice and know that I myself am sound and uninjured; and in the second place, so that you may also hear the particulars about a crime that is without peer in German history.
>
> An extremely small clique of ambitious, conscienceless, and criminal and stupid officers forged a plot to eliminate me and, along with me, to exterminate the staff of officers in actual command of the Wehrmacht. The bomb, which was planted by Oberst Graf von Stauffenberg, burst two yards from my right hand side. It severely injured several of my colleagues; one of them has died. I myself am wholly unhurt ...

I am convinced that with the liquidation of these very small cliques of traitors and conspirators, we are at last creating at home in the rear the atmosphere that the fighters at the front need. For it is impossible that hundreds of thousands and millions of brave men give their best, while at home a very small group of ambitious, miserable creatures constantly tries to thwart this stance. This time they will be called to account in the way that we National Socialists are accustomed to ...

I also see it as a hint from Providence that I have to continue my work, and therefore I will continue it![12]

This was followed by declarations from Göring and Dönitz as heads of the Luftwaffe and navy respectively, urging their men to stay loyal.

Fromm was released from the room where he had been locked up by the conspirators. Perhaps acting out of a deep-seated sense of military honour, or perhaps seeking to demonstrate his personal loyalty to the regime whilst simultaneously disposing of any witnesses who might say otherwise, he declared that he was presiding over an impromptu court martial and condemned the military conspirators to death. Beck asked for permission to shoot himself, but aimed too high and the bullet merely wounded the top of his head. Several others were taken outside. Remer now entered the building and protested, insisting that he had personal orders from Hitler to arrest the conspirators, but Fromm refused to cooperate. Olbricht, Quirnheim, Stauffenberg, and Haeften were taken to a courtyard behind the building shortly after midnight and executed by firing squad, with a nearby truck's headlights providing illumination. Haeften was loyal to Stauffenberg to the last, deliberately stepping in front of his superior to shield him from the first salvo of shots. When the soldiers reloaded, Stauffenberg declared in a loud voice, '*Es lebe das heilige Deutschland!*' ('Long live our sacred Germany!'). Fromm ordered that all of those who had been executed should be interred immediately with full military honours; the badly wounded Beck was executed by a single shot to the back of the neck.

Shortly after, a group of SS personnel under the command of Obersturmbannführer Otto Skorzeny took control of the building and Fromm was ordered to desist from taking any further action. In Paris, over 1,200 SS and Gestapo personnel had been arrested, but they were now released. On 21 July, Himmler arrived in Berlin to take personal control and a widespread wave of arrests swept through Germany and the occupied territories in the days that followed. Many of those who had been involved in the conspiracy desperately tried to cover their tracks. In the west, Kluge was under suspicion because numerous members of the conspiracy had clearly been in contact with him and on 15 August, when he lost contact with his headquarters, Hitler feared that Kluge was attempting to negotiate a ceasefire with the Western Powers and demanded his recall to Berlin. In fact, Kluge had been forced to take shelter after his car was damaged in an air raid, but fearing arrest and execution, he committed suicide with a cyanide capsule on 19 August. He left a final statement that in many ways summed up his ambivalent loyalties; on the one hand, he declared his continuing loyalty to Hitler, but then added that Germany needed to end the war because 'the German people have undergone such untold suffering that it is time to put an end to this frightfulness.'[13] The men who were hastily executed on the night of the failed coup attempt were in many ways fortunate, as the Gestapo now demonstrated precisely what was meant by Hitler's declaration of an accounting of a kind to which National Socialists were accustomed. Most of those who were arrested, tried, and executed were first tortured extensively, and then many were hanged slowly with piano wire or thin straps from meat hooks, their suffering recorded on film and played for the benefit of Hitler and his inner circle. These victims included Berthold Schenk Graf von Stauffenberg, the elder brother of the bomber, who was repeatedly resuscitated and then hanged again for the benefit of the watching cameras.

Fromm, who had moved quickly to execute Stauffenberg, Beck, and others, went to see Goebbels immediately after the conspirators had been shot. He told the propaganda minister that his firm, decisive action had been key to suppressing the coup attempt, but Goebbels was unimpressed. He replied, 'You have been in a damned hurry to get your witnesses below ground.'[14] Fromm was placed under arrest the following day. Investigations failed to produce sufficient proof of his involvement in the conspiracy, but instead he was charged with cowardice in the face of the enemy and executed by firing squad in March 1945. Remer, the major who was sent to arrest Goebbels, ended the war with the rank of Generalmajor, commanding a division of the now expanded *Grossdeutschland* panzer corps. The Nazis made much of his role, proclaiming him as a loyal hero who had remained true to his oath, though in truth the plot was already unravelling by the time he reached Goebbels' residence. After the war, he was a prisoner of the Western Allies and became a right-wing politician in post-war West Germany and because of his continuing criticism of those involved in the plot, he was found guilty in a regional court in 1952 of defamation and denigration of the memory of the deceased. Although he was sentenced to three months' imprisonment, he fled the country, spending several years in Egypt. He continued his involvement with right-wing groups, even appearing in a meeting in 1990 in Munich where he spoke in support of a Holocaust denial group. He died in Spain in 1997.

Henning von Tresckow shot himself on 21 July when it became clear that the plot had ended in disaster. He left a last message for Fabian von Schlabrendorff, a fellow conspirator who had been involved in the 'Cointreau bomb' attempt of 1943:

> If God promised Abraham that he would not destroy Sodom if there were only ten righteous people in it, I hope for our sake that God will not destroy Germany ... The moral value of a person only begins to be significant when he is willing to give his life for his convictions.[15]

Generalfeldmarschall Erwin Rommel, the darling of Nazi propaganda for much of the war, was aware of the plot but although by the summer of 1944 he was an opponent of Hitler, it is highly unlikely that he was an active member of the conspiracy, and it seems that he was firmly opposed to assassinating the Führer. On 17 June, when he and Rundstedt met Hitler, Rommel tentatively raised the possibility of seeking a ceasefire in the west so that Germany could concentrate its efforts in the east; such suggestions were dismissed out of hand by Hitler, who knew that the Western Powers would never negotiate with him. On 29 June, in a meeting in Berchtesgaden, Rommel made the same suggestion to Himmler and Goebbels, who declined to comment. In the meeting with Hitler that followed, Rommel tried three times to raise the issue once more, only to be rejected by Hitler who repeatedly told Rommel to concentrate on purely military matters and finally ordered him to leave the room before he said anything that he might regret.[16]

In a final attempt to persuade Hitler to see reason, Rommel sent a telegram to the Führer on 15 July. He described how his Army Group B was rapidly running out of resources – his men might be preventing the Western Allies from breaking out of their beachhead, but the cost was enormous and unsustainable. Without large-scale reinforcements, there could only be one outcome; and given Rommel's personal contacts throughout the military, he would have been aware of the catastrophe that was unfolding in Belarus, making the appearance of such reinforcements impossible. Two days later, Rommel was badly wounded in an air attack on his car.

As various figures in the conspiracy were arrested and interrogated, the Gestapo began to draw links between many of the figures and Rommel. Kluge had been Rommel's immediate superior at the time of the bombing and his name was given to interrogators when Stülpnagel and Oberstleutnant Caesar von Hofacker, a Luftwaffe officer and cousin of Stauffenberg, were subjected to torture. Rommel had told many people, including his wife, that he regarded assassination of Hitler as unthinkable as it would result in chaos and civil war and the investigators failed to find any crucially implicating evidence against him. Nonetheless, the Gestapo concluded that given his attempts to persuade Hitler to bring the war in the west to a close and the circumstantial evidence that they had managed to find, he was a central figure in the plot and gave him the choice of committing suicide or facing disgrace and court martial, with severe consequences for his family. He chose the former, and he was declared to have died from wounds received in the air attack in France.[17]

Hoepner was one of those placed under arrest in Berlin. Like Beck, he was given an opportunity to commit suicide but instead insisted upon a trial. He was brought before the *Volksgerichtshof* ('People's Court'), and like all others who appeared there he was repeatedly humiliated in public. All of the prisoners were made to attend court wearing ill-fitting clothes and Hoepner was denied permission to use his dentures, forcing him to mumble for much of his appearance. Judge Roland Freisler became infamous for the manner in which he insulted and abused those appearing in the court; like so many others, Hoepner was sentenced to death and executed by being hanged from a piano wire noose attached to a meat hook. He left a final testament:

> First and foremost, every commander and above all every field officer must be a gentleman, a man of intellectual independence ... who can be tough and yet has a large, warm heart. He should be aware of his responsibility ...
>
> A military success is only of value if it is achieved with the fewest casualties possible, otherwise any fool can be placed in the position of military commander. Giving orders is often more difficult than obeying them. One should only issue orders for which one can answer in one's conscience.[18]

It was an interesting statement. At the onset of *Barbarossa* in 1941, Hoepner was commander of a panzer group (later renamed panzer army) and issued uncompromising orders to his subordinates shortly before the invasion of the Soviet Union began:

> The war against Russia is an essential part of the struggle for existence of the German people. It is the age-old struggle of Germans against Slavism, the defence of Europe against the Muscovite-Asiatic flood, the defence against Jewish Bolshevism. This struggle must aim for the destruction of present-day Russia and must therefore be conducted with unprecedented severity. Every combat action must be planned and executed with iron determination to destroy the enemy mercilessly and completely. In particular, there can be no mercy for the bearers of today's Russian-Bolshevik system.[19]

As was the case with so many of the conspirators, Hoepner's family was also punished, purely because of their association to Hoepner and not on the basis of any evidence showing their involvement in the plot. His son and his brother were placed under arrest, and his wife, daughter, and sister were sent to Ravensbrück concentration camp. His sister was released after a comparatively short time; the others were given additional punishment by being confined to the *Stafblock* ('punishment block') of the camp for a further month.[20] Hofacker's wife Ilse Lotte and her two eldest children were imprisoned first in Bavaria and then in a series of concentration camps, eventually being freed from the SS by a group of Wehrmacht soldiers in late April 1945. Her three younger children were held in an internment centre together with 46 other children of men and women arrested in connection with the plot.[21] Freisler, the brutal judge of the *Volksgerichtshof*, was killed in an air raid on Berlin in February 1945. Luise Jodl, wife of General Alfred Jodl, was working as a helper in a hospital in the city at the time. She later recalled that when his body was brought into the building, a fellow worker said, 'It is God's judgement.' She added that no one made any contradiction.[22] It was a timely death, at least for Schlabrendorff, who was yet to appear before Freisler. Had he done so, he would have been executed like the other conspirators; instead, he survived the war.

One of the first consequences felt by the armies, corps, and divisions attempting to hold the line was news that there was a new chief of the general staff. Heusinger had been standing next to Hitler when Stauffenberg's bomb exploded and was injured in the blast. He was then placed under arrest because of his repeated contacts with so many of the conspirators, but he was able to justify them as part of his duties. There is little evidence that he had any personal involvement in the plot, but he was clearly unable to continue as chief of the general staff. His replacement was Generaloberst Heinz Guderian.

Of all the names associated with *Blitzkrieg* and the innovative use of armour by the Wehrmacht, Guderian stands in the front rank. He was an early enthusiast for armoured warfare and pioneered several important developments; his experiments with a motor transport battalion in the 1930s were later lauded as being instrumental in the creation of panzer divisions and one of his most important contributions to the development of mechanised warfare was insistence on every tank having a radio set – the use of such radio sets ensured flexible and swift deployment of armoured formations in response to unexpected events. His importance as a pioneer of armoured warfare has perhaps been overstated, not least by Guderian himself in his memoirs. He was a prickly, argumentative officer, and clashed repeatedly with those he regarded as too conservative in their thinking.

As commander of XIX Corps, he led the German advance across West Prussia to establish a land link with East Prussia during the Polish campaign and was famously part of the great drive across Belgium and France in 1940. Like many in the German military, he drew conclusions from these campaigns that were overly optimistic and led to a widespread belief that not only could Germany defeat the Soviet Union, but it could do so with ease.

During *Barbarossa*, Guderian commanded Second Panzer Group (later renamed Second Panzer Army), advancing energetically on the southern flank of Army Group Centre. He was one of the advocates for an all-out drive to capture Moscow and vociferously opposed Hitler's plans to turn his group south to deal with the Soviet forces massed around Kiev; at the last moment, he changed his mind and declared his support for Hitler's demands, alienating many within the senior ranks of the Wehrmacht. After the successful encirclement of the Red Army's units in the Kiev area, Second Panzer Group returned to the central sector for what was intended to be the crowning victory of the campaign, an attack to reach and capture Moscow. Advancing towards the city from the southwest, Guderian's forces found themselves in an exposed salient and with his mood swinging from moments of optimism to deep despair, Guderian ignored Hitler's demands for all units to hold their positions and pulled back. Whilst this was the correct assessment for his panzer group, the unilateral decision left the formations on his flanks exposed and endangered. He was dismissed after a furious exchange with the Führer.

In September 1942, Rommel – recovering from illness in a hospital in Germany – suggested that Guderian might be a suitable replacement for him in North Africa; the proposal was brusquely rejected. But the following March, after the end of the disastrous Stalingrad campaign, Hitler created a new post of *Generalinspekteur der Panzertruppen* ('Inspector General of Armoured Troops') and selected Guderian to fill it. He played a substantial part in the recovery of strength of the panzer divisions, working closely with Albert Speer, the German armaments minister, and strongly opposed the planned summer offensive against the Kursk salient. In the wake of the failed assassination attempt, his first duty was to chair a so-called *Ehrenhof* ('honour court'), which discharged German officers suspected of involvement in the plot from the armed services. This then permitted their prosecution in the court presided over by Roland Freisler. Perhaps to demonstrate his personal loyalty to Hitler, he energetically implemented the thorough Nazification of the army, demanding that all officers should join the Nazi Party and that the Hitler salute should be adopted universally. Despite Guderian's later assertions that he found his duties in the *Ehrenhof* in particular 'repulsive', he showed considerable zeal in his behaviour from late July onwards

360

– whether this was purely out of self-preservation or genuine commitment to Hitler will never be known for certain.

Whilst Guderian had a reputation as a visionary, his appointment was not popular. He had alienated many in the upper ranks of the army in the past through his impatience, arrogance, and insubordination; similarly, he had been contemptuous of senior staff officers whom he regarded as lacking sufficient vision to grasp the possibilities of mechanised warfare. Moreover, he had no real experience for the role in which he now found himself. At first, he relied heavily on Oberst Johann von Kielmansegg, a senior staff officer in the operations department of *OKH*, but Kielmansegg was arrested (and later released without charge) by the Gestapo under suspicion of involvement in the plot. Thereafter, Guderian found himself surrounded by staff officers who were – like him – replacements for those who had been in these posts until late July. This lack of experience and expertise can have done nothing to alleviate the huge problems facing the armies in the east as the war ground on.

The plot came remarkably close to succeeding in killing Hitler. The change of venue for the conference; the failure to arm both bombs; the relocation of the briefcase behind a thick table leg – without these three factors, it is likely that Hitler would have been killed. Even without his death, the regime might have been toppled by more resolute and comprehensive action; for example, the failure to prevent radio and telephone communications from Rastenburg was an obvious oversight. Inevitably, this raises questions: what would have happened if Hitler had been killed?

A clue to the answer lies in the attitude of so many senior officers who had been approached by the conspirators. So many prominent figures – Manstein, Guderian, Rommel, Rundstedt, Kluge, even Model – had declined to take part in the conspiracy, with many declaring that their personal oath of loyalty to Hitler was paramount. But none of these men betrayed those who had approached them. This suggests that their interpretation of loyalty was selective and specific, and with Hitler dead, they would not be bound automatically to a replacement from within the Nazi regime. It seems likely that many – with varying degrees of enthusiasm – would have sided with the conspirators, and the traditions of loyalty and obeying orders were so strongly ingrained that other lower-ranking personnel would then have fallen into line. Even within the SS, there were those who had concluded that Germany faced disaster. The Gestapo investigators repeatedly tried to find evidence that would implicate Oberstgruppenführer Paul Hausser, who at the time was commander of Seventh Army in Normandy. Had a figure like Himmler seized power after Hitler's assassination, it is difficult on the one hand to imagine that many senior officers would have transferred their loyalty to a Nazi leader of Germany, but on the other hand the memories of civil strife in Germany in the months immediately after the First World War were strong and many might have concluded that order, even with a figure like Himmler in charge, was better than chaos. There would certainly have been the prospect of major armed clashes between supporters of the two sides, which would inevitably have accelerated the collapse of German resistance on the front lines. In the west in particular, this would have had major consequences. Most senior SS and Gestapo figures were already under arrest by the evening of 20 July and with Hitler's death confirmed, it seems highly likely that Kluge would have attempted to contact the Western Allies to seek a ceasefire.

This then raises the next major question: how would the Western Allies have reacted to such an overture? The Casablanca Declaration – stating that the enemies of the Axis powers would fight on until Germany and its allies surrendered unconditionally – was still in force, but since the declaration had been made, the British and Americans had endured heavy losses in the fighting in Normandy. The daily casualty rate was as high as most periods of the First World War; whilst Rommel had complained to Hitler that his losses were unsustainable, the same was ultimately true for his opponents, but they had the advantage of starting at a higher level and were thus able to continue fighting despite their losses. If the Western Allies had been offered a rapid end to the conflict, it seems likely that they would at least have considered it.

But a major problem in the path of this was the attitude of the conspirators. Although they have been commemorated in the years since the war, they were not committed to creating a democratic, free Germany. Rather, they intended to establish an authoritarian regime with little or no democratic freedoms, at least at first, and many had utterly unrealistic ambitions for establishing a post-war Germany with frontiers that resembled those of 1914, with large parts of Poland as well as the French provinces of Alsace and Lorraine being incorporated into the Reich. Moreover, many of the conspirators had problematic past records. Those who had served on the Eastern Front were certainly aware of the mass killings of Jews and others, and in some cases had been involved in providing logistic support for the murderous operations of the *Einsatzgruppen* and the numerous anti-partisan operations that resulted in indiscriminate slaughter. It is certainly arguable that their prime motivation in attempting to overthrow Hitler was to avoid the military defeat of Germany rather than to bring an end to the Nazi regime's continuing atrocities, and it is questionable whether they would have been regarded as an acceptable government to the British and Americans. In the case of the Soviet Union, there was absolutely no question of any such negotiated end to the war. Nothing short of complete surrender by Germany was acceptable to Stalin.

The attitude of Moscow was of course known to the conspirators. It was their intention to seek a ceasefire in the west so that Germany could continue fighting in the east until the Soviet Union could be worn down and forced to accept terms. Whilst there are some indications that Churchill was already thinking along similar lines, there is nothing to suggest that such an outcome would have been acceptable to the Americans. Roosevelt was still firmly committed to an equal relationship with Stalin and regardless of the casualties suffered by the US Army in Normandy, he and most of his administration would have been highly resistant to an outcome that left Stalin effectively in the cold. Indeed, he had insisted on aspects of the Casablanca Declaration as a means of ensuring that Stalin remained committed to the anti-Axis alliance. Nevertheless, if Kluge had offered even a temporary ceasefire in the west – and it would have taken time for the details of the unacceptable ultimate aims of the conspirators to emerge – the path of the war would have been very different.

If the conspirators had attempted to press on with the execution of the coup attempt even though Hitler was alive, there would probably have been little prospect of success. Far too many officers would have felt bound by their oath of loyalty to Hitler, and it seems unlikely that sufficient forces would have rallied to the side of the conspirators for the plot to succeed. Even if Kluge had shown more resolve and had opened negotiations for a ceasefire in the west, nothing short of its rapid acceptance by the Western Allies would have made any difference.

Reaction to the plot throughout Germany was generally hostile. Most ordinary soldiers and junior officers felt that it was a betrayal of their personal sacrifices and suffering in the front line. Despite all the disasters unfolding on every front line, many continued to have faith that the Führer would lead Germany to final victory. Hitler had an almost mystical belief in the new weapons that were being prepared – jet aircraft, new tanks, the V-weapon programme – and similar views prevailed amongst men at lower levels, where rumours of the new *Wunderwaffen* ('wonder weapons') persisted right to the end of the war. But if Hitler had died, all German officers would have been released from their oaths and would have had to decide whether they would obey the new regime or would side with whatever rival Nazi figure arose. Much would have depended upon how effectively the conspirators moved against people like Himmler, Goebbels, and the other senior figures in the regime.

The attitude of the general population is much harder to assess. There was huge war-weariness, and German citizens had grown accustomed to living in a surreal world in which they declared loyalty to Hitler in public and kept their personal views to themselves. Undoubtedly, many would have been horrified by Hitler's assassination, but others would have recognised it as a way to avoid disaster.

The reaction outside Germany was largely that the conspiracy was an indication of the rotten state of Nazi Germany. Churchill commented to parliament in early August that the coup attempt and resultant executions were little more than signs of internecine struggles in the Third Reich, no more than could be expected from a decaying, corrupt system approaching its last days, and the United States adopted a similar line. But Churchill was being a little disingenuous. The British had known of conspiracies against Hitler for many years, but had deliberately chosen not to act upon the information that they had gathered.

From at least late 1943, British intelligence officers had been aware of the existence of a group of officers in the Wehrmacht who were opposed to Hitler and who wished to overthrow the regime. Most of this information was gained from interrogation of prisoners captured in North Africa – it should be remembered that it was in this theatre that Stauffenberg was serving when he was badly wounded. Increasingly as the war progressed, British intelligence-gathering relied on the ability to decode German Enigma codes and thus to monitor radio transmissions, but this provided almost no information about the conspiracy because the plotters deliberately avoided using any form of radio transmission or even telephone conversations wherever possible. However, the information that had been gathered about disaffection in the Wehrmacht was covered by a policy that had been established in September 1941 in connection with any opposition groups within Germany. At that time, when the Soviet Union had just entered the war and the USA was still neutral, the British government was anxious to avoid anything that might endanger its new relationship with Stalin and Churchill sent a memorandum to Anthony Eden, the foreign secretary, insisting that there should be a policy of absolutely no contact with German dissenters:

> We should not depart from our policy of absolute silence. Nothing would be more disturbing to our friends in the United States or more dangerous with our new ally, Russia, than the suggestion that we are entertaining such ideas. I am absolutely opposed to the slightest contact.[23]

Churchill and those closest to him shared a negative opinion of what they saw as 'Prussian militarism' and the British prime minister had made many speeches stressing the need to dismantle the system that he blamed for inflicting two world wars on the world. In this context, he was completely unwilling to consider any new German government created by military figures as any more acceptable than Hitler's regime, and the manner in which the British intelligence service functioned both accentuated and exacerbated this mindset. The role of MI6 was to collect information and to pass it to the government; interpretation of the information was not part of its remit. The system worked on the basis of what might be termed 'pull-architecture' – the government tasked the service with providing information on a given subject, as opposed to 'push-architecture' in which the service would assess all intelligence gathered and would then submit those parts that it deemed relevant or important.[24] This system still exists today, and has been seen as having a risk of reinforcing existing beliefs by providing politicians with answers that they wish to hear. Given the hostility of Churchill, Eden, and others to the 'Prussian military class', the result was unwillingness on the part of MI6 to submit detailed information about the scale and activity of anti-Hitler groups in the German military. In January 1944, the Joint Intelligence Committee submitted a report entitled 'Signs of an Internal Collapse in Germany':

> There is at present no evidence that any faction exists within the army or within the Party or still less among the people as a whole which is likely to attempt to overthrow the present regime within the foreseeable future. We should, in any case, be unlikely to receive convincing evidence that such a conspiracy existed.[25]

The last sentence was the critical caveat that absence of evidence should not be regarded as evidence of absence, but such nuances were ignored. Less than a week before Stauffenberg's bomb detonated, a further report stated:

> The only effective alternative to the Nazi Party would be assumption of power by military leaders ... So far there is no sign of any move on the part of military leaders, and the promotion of Nazi supporters to some of the highest ranks in the Services and the vigilance of the Gestapo is likely to prevent any such move from being made, if it is made at all, until too late to be effective.[26]

Although these reports suggest almost complete ignorance of the plots to kill Hitler, other evidence shows that there was at least a degree of awareness. The deterioration in the relationship between Hitler and senior officers, particularly amongst the general staff, was clearly recognised. Although senior intelligence officers adopted the same point of view as Churchill, a group of more junior men submitted a report in late 1942 suggesting that it might be possible to bring the war to an end more quickly if senior German officers were given incentives to attempt a coup. The report was not circulated, largely through the intervention of the deputy head of Section V of MI6, who was none other than Kim Philby. Although Section V had responsibility for monitoring German intelligence operations in Spain and Portugal, Philby – who was working for the NKVD – used his influence within the service to quash a report that, had its recommendations been adopted, might have left the Soviet Union in the cold.[27]

Despite this setback, Hugh Trevor-Roper, who had overseen the preparation of this report, chose to bypass what he saw as unhelpful obstruction and passed a draft to Frederick Lindemann, 1st Viscount Cherwell, who was Churchill's scientific adviser. This resulted in Trevor-Roper being reprimanded for such a breach of procedure – this must mean that Cherwell passed the report to others, who then decided to take disciplinary action against its author. Nonetheless, the report was discussed at high levels, though no action was taken to exploit the rifts within the German regime that it identified.

Part of the reason for British refusal to get involved with anti-Hitler conspirators was what became known as the Venlo Incident. In late 1939, when the Netherlands and Belgium were still neutral nations, a man known as Fischer made contact with British intelligence officers in the city of Venlo, claiming to be a representative of a military group within Germany that wished to explore the conditions for a negotiated end to the war if they were able to remove Hitler from power. At the time, Neville Chamberlain, the British prime minister, had made clear in a speech that he regarded the war as being against Hitler and the Nazis, strongly hinting that the removal of Hitler might result in peace negotiations. After several meetings in Venlo, one of those attending – a certain Hauptmann Schämmel – offered to bring a German general to a subsequent meeting. Two British SIS officers, Major Richard Stevens and Captain Sigismund Best, arranged to meet Schämmel and the general the following day. But Schämmel was actually Sturmbannführer Walter Schellenberg, who would later rise to become head of the *Sicherheitsdienst*. When the British officers attended the meeting, they were kidnapped by the Germans and taken back across the border into Germany. Thereafter, the British were understandably very cautious of any entanglement with those claiming to be members of the anti-Hitler resistance, but some remained interested in the possibilities that might arise if Hitler were overthrown. From early 1942 onwards, the British intelligence officer Guy Liddell made several entries in his diaries about discussions within SIS, in which the possibility of a plot headed by Admiral Wilhelm Canaris, head of the *Abwehr*, was raised.

But given the hostility of Churchill and Eden to any such schemes, no practical steps were taken. In the words of the historian Paul Winter:

> Without the eyes and ears of SIS straining for any sight or sound of high-level disaffection within Hitler's regime, senior figures in Whitehall were left in the unenviable position of desiring a German collapse, preferably achieved from within, but without the means, ironically, to facilitate such an event.[28]

As a consequence, the Western Powers in general and Britain in particular failed even to recognise one of the biggest weaknesses in Nazi Germany: the fragile relationship between Hitler and the military class that formed most of the army's senior echelons. This relationship had always been problematic, but the cracks were papered over during the years of German success. As those were replaced by years of setback and catastrophe, the cracks began to open, but no attempt was made to exploit them.

After the war, Churchill would claim that he had been misled about the scale of resistance to Hitler.[29] This is simply untrue. Major Desmond Morton, who was Churchill's personal adviser on intelligence matters, knew of approaches made to British diplomats by Carl Goerdeler, the mayor of Leipzig who was involved in the conspiracy, and it is inconceivable that the diplomats would have failed to make Churchill aware of this. Even the names of some of the conspirators were known. A senior intelligence officer in the headquarters of Montgomery's Twenty-First Army Group later wrote that in the autumn of 1943, he was told by a German officer who had deserted and been captured that Witzleben was the most likely person to attempt to overthrow Hitler.[30] Stauffenberg's name was known to the British as a potential anti-Hitler conspirator at least as early as November 1943 as a result of the bugging of conversations between captured senior German officers.[31] For Churchill to claim that he was ignorant about this is therefore misleading at best. But throughout history, political figures have proved adept at hearing what they wish to hear and either ignoring or downplaying the importance of what contradicts their views.

The Americans were also aware of plots to remove Hitler, and their intelligence services seem to have avoided the political constraints that hindered SIS. Allen Dulles was the senior representative of the American Office of Strategic Services or OSS in Switzerland and oversaw a network of agents that included several in the *Abwehr* and the German foreign office. These included Fritz Kolbe, a diplomat who despite refusing to join the Nazi Party and being sidelined as a consequence, diligently worked to earn the trust of his immediate superiors. They were even prepared to overlook his brusque, outspoken comments – on one occasion, he referred to Mussolini as a pig and refused to retract the remark when challenged.[32] He rose to become deputy to Karl Ritter, who amongst other tasks was part of a foreign office liaison team dealing with senior officers in the Wehrmacht. Kolbe's duties included processing telegrams and telex messages from German delegations in neutral countries, and destroying secret signals that came to Ritter's office. In 1941, shortly before the entry of the USA into the war, he attempted unsuccessfully to make contact with US diplomats and in 1942 he became increasingly convinced of the need for Germany to find a way out of an increasingly disastrous war. Unlike several of the plotters who were at the heart of Stauffenberg's coup attempt, he was genuinely appalled by German atrocities across Europe. By the end of the year, he was regularly passing on information via an intermediary to the French Resistance, warning them of imminent arrests. He briefly made contact with the British, successfully warning them of a German spy in the British embassy in Stockholm, but was unable to interest the British in further work; instead, he succeeded in travelling to Switzerland in the summer of 1943 and made contact with an old associate, Ernest Kocherthaler.

Armed with the text of a deciphered telegram sent to Kolbe's office, Kocherthaler attempted to make contact with British diplomats, including the military attaché, Colonel Henry Cartwright, who acted on behalf of the British intelligence services with responsibility for interrogating refugees from Germany. Having been the victim of previous attempts by the *Abwehr* to plant a fake defector and aware of the very strict instructions from Churchill and Eden about avoiding contact with those purporting to be part of any anti-Hitler resistance movement, Cartwright refused to cooperate.[33] When he encountered Dulles at a meeting, Cartwright warned his American colleague about a possible approach from someone that he regarded as of dubious provenance, but when Kocherthaler met Gerald Mayer, an American who was linked to the OSS, he presented Mayer with three deciphered secret documents. When Mayer asked whether more such documents were available, Kocherthaler handed him 16 deciphered telegrams, saying that these were merely a gesture of goodwill and that his source was prepared to provide far more. Mayer took the documents to Dulles who was equally excited at the prospect of securing the services of such a highly placed source, though like his British counterparts he was acutely aware that the entire episode might be an *Abwehr* plot. The Americans met Kocherthaler and Kolbe that night; after discussions that lasted three hours, Dulles agreed to use Kolbe as an agent.[34]

Over the months that followed, Kolbe provided Dulles with over 1,600 documents; these included information about German assessments of possible areas for the planned invasion of Western Europe, the V-1 and V-2 weapons programmes, and data about the Messerschmitt Me-262 jet aircraft.[35] He was also able to provide information about the nature of the anti-Hitler movement, giving Dulles a far more accurate picture of what was happening than was possible for the British. Although Dulles passed much of the information he received from Kolbe and from other sources to his British counterparts, it seems that this information was treated very selectively. In particular, the British refusal to have anything to do with German resistance movements ensured that much of the intelligence provided by Dulles was routinely ignored.

Given the growing dependence in British circles on decoded radio intercepts, it is perhaps unsurprising that the first report of the attempted assassination came via an Enigma message that was decoded in Bletchley Park on the evening of 20 January. It was a brief signal from the headquarters of the Kriegsmarine to all subordinate stations, informing them that 'The Führer Adolf Hitler is dead. The new Führer is Generalfeldmarschall von Witzleben.'[36] Further signals were decrypted over the following days, but the process of converting coded messages into plain text was a time-consuming business, made worse by the sheer volume of traffic that was being gathered. Moreover, the deliberate refusal to look for evidence of disaffection in German military and political circles meant that these signals received a lower priority and attention than those regarded as more important. Finally, Churchill's frequent visits to the Normandy beachhead ensured that there were further delays before he received even summaries of what had been learned. When Churchill visited Montgomery's headquarters in Normandy a few days after the failed coup attempt, the commander of Twenty-First Army Group and his senior staff pressed him for details – to date, they had been limited almost completely to what they had read in newspaper reports. One of the staff officers later described how Churchill appeared to have no grasp of what had happened and invited Montgomery to see for himself, unlocking two despatch boxes. They were full of a muddle of documents relating to all manner of subjects. While the officers picked through the papers, Churchill began to compose a speech about the plot, and the gathered officers were shocked to realise that he had almost no knowledge of the true situation in Germany. This all contributed to the impression – deliberately encouraged by Churchill and others after the war – that the British political leadership had not been adequately briefed on the situation in the upper levels of the German regime. Of course, this was correct, but the official view failed to mention that this was because Churchill, Eden, and others had made clear that they were not interested in any contact with anti-Hitler groups. The consequences of this politically imposed straitjacket became clear when Churchill demanded a report on Stauffenberg a few days after the failed coup, and was told that there was 'no definite information about this man. The available information seems to be very scanty and it seems doubtful whether we shall learn much more.'[37] Embarrassed officials in Downing Street had to admit that even their knowledge of his rank and military appointments was largely based upon what they had learned from German radio news broadcasts since the coup attempt. But even if government officials knew little or nothing about Stauffenberg, officers in SIS certainly had far more information – they had been inhibited from passing this on.

It seems therefore that the relative ignorance in the west of what was about to happen in Germany in July 1944 was partly due to a deliberate decision not to become involved in such matters. But what of the Soviet Union – how much did Stalin and his associates know? Given the virulent anti-Bolshevik sentiment of almost all those involved in the plot, it seems unlikely that any would have passed information to the Soviet Union, or that pro-Soviet agents would have infiltrated the group. Moreover, it is impossible to gain access to documentation that would reveal just how much the Soviet leadership knew. However, the manner in which Philby attempted to suppress the report written by Trevor-Roper suggests that Stalin would probably have known much of what the Western Powers knew.

This raises a further important question. Could the British and Americans have adopted a different policy by actively building links with anti-Hitler groups? The simple answer must be that this would have been possible, but it would have required a different political mindset. Even before the war, Churchill was strongly opposed to what he saw as Prussian militarism, and this would shape his attitude to the partition of German territory at the end of the conflict, in particular to the effective elimination of East Prussia as a German entity. As the war progressed, Roosevelt developed a curious friendship with the Soviet leader, believing that if the American president's vision of a future world in which the United Nations organisation would be able to prevent wars was to be realised, this could only be done with Soviet cooperation. On numerous occasions, Roosevelt clashed with Churchill about the post-war future, in particular with regard to British imperial possessions, and had little time for Churchill's ongoing suspicions of ultimate Soviet intentions.[38] It is therefore highly unlikely that Roosevelt would have considered exploring a separate peace with a group of right-wing authoritarian German officers whose demands included the retention of large amounts of territory at the expense of France and Poland, and who intended to continue waging war against the Soviet Union while securing a ceasefire in the west.

But merely knowing more about what was about to happen would have permitted the Western Powers to position themselves far better to take advantage of the events of 20 July. On that day, Operation *Goodwood*, the latest attempt by Montgomery to break out beyond Caen, was grinding to a halt. Three days of heavy fighting resulted in only modest gains of territory, and the best that could be said of the operation was that it continued to tie down substantial German armoured resources. Further to the west, the Americans were yet to commence Operation *Cobra*, which would see a major breakout from the beachhead. But if the Western Powers had known of Stauffenberg's plans for 20 July, there was scope for altering the timing of attacks in Normandy, and for attempting to exploit them – radio and loudspeaker broadcasts, combined with leaflet drops, could have been used to inform German troops that Hitler had been killed, and this might conceivably have been sufficient to stiffen the resolve of wavering individuals like Kluge. At the very least, such a move would have added to the confusion and disruption in the German chain of command.[39]

However, even if the British and Americans had taken such steps without any intention of subsequently reaching any agreement with the new German government, the reaction of Stalin to such developments would almost certainly have been significant. If he had been warned by the British and Americans of such developments in advance, he might have insisted on the Allied Powers taking no action, as this was contrary to the agreed plan to prosecute the war until unconditional surrender was secured, particularly as he intended to ensure that the Red Army was in physical possession of as much territory as possible when the war did come to an end. And if the Western Powers had decided to take steps without officially informing Stalin, it is likely that he would have learned about such plans via agents like Philby, and his paranoia would have received strong confirmation that the Western Powers were about to betray him. Although the Germans had made some tentative approaches to discuss peace terms with the Soviet Union during the spring thaw of 1943, there was no real prospect of any accommodation between the two warring nations, and Stalin had little doubt that he would have to continue the war until Germany was utterly defeated; any failure of the Western Powers to show similar resolve would have placed severe strain upon the fragile alliance that bound the enemies of Germany together. There is an irony that although Hitler and other senior Germans had long predicted that the alliance of their foes would not last, it would have taken the assassination of Hitler to create the strains that might have ruptured the alliance.

There is a further fascinating issue about who knew what about the July Plot. As head of the SS, Himmler had control of much of the intelligence apparatus of the Third Reich. These agencies knew as early as February 1943 that there was a large anti-Hitler group within the *Abwehr*, operating with the knowledge of Admiral Canaris; the Gestapo also knew about a civilian circle of resistance around Carl Goerdeler, mayor of Leipzig. But no action was taken against either group. Even more strikingly, Johannes Popitz, a politician and member of

Goerdeler's group, spoke to Himmler in August 1943. During the conversation, Popitz advised Himmler that if he were to remove Hitler from power and then attempt to negotiate with the Western Allies, he would be assured of the support of those opposed to Hitler.[40] Popitz was also not arrested, and there were other indirect approaches to Himmler in the months that followed. It seems likely, therefore, that Himmler was certainly aware of the intentions of conspirators to try to remove Hitler from power, though this may have fallen short of knowledge about the details and timing of the bombing. Perhaps Himmler chose not to act in the belief that if the plot were to succeed, he would then be able to assume power and would then negotiate with the Western Powers. In this, he was mistaken on both counts. The military figures involved in the plot would not have accepted him as a new Führer; nor would any of the Allied Powers have been prepared to negotiate with him.

The consequences of the failure of the July Plot were numerous. The war would continue for nearly ten months, during which tens of thousands of soldiers and civilians would die. Huge damage would be inflicted upon the towns and cities of Europe. In addition to unleashing their vengeance on all real and imagined conspirators, the Nazis took steps to tighten their grip upon the army. The *Ersatzheer* came under Himmler's control, political officers analogous to Soviet commissars were appointed in all formations, and the military was ordered to adopt the 'Hitler salute'. In the absence of any possibility of following the pithy advice of Rundstedt to make peace, the soldiers of all sides had no choice but to continue what was an increasingly uneven struggle. The final outcome was not in doubt; all that remained to be determined was the precise form it would take, and the cost that would be paid.

CHAPTER 12

HIGH TIDE FOR THE RED ARMY

The news of the attempted assassination fell upon the German soldiers in the front line like a thunderclap. Many soldiers later wrote about their sense of shock and horror; for the men of 6th Panzer Division, there was additional turmoil when it was learned that Stauffenberg and Hoepner, who both had links with the division, were involved. But there was little time for the officers and men in the front line to reflect on events in Rastenburg and Berlin. This was replicated elsewhere along the front line. Accounts from both 12th Panzer Division and 4th Panzer Division to the south suggest that the soldiers of the two divisions – like the panzer divisions to the north – were too hard-pressed to spend much time thinking about the radio reports from Germany. For them, stopping the Red Army was the only priority. The frontiers of the Reich were now perilously close to the front line (and in the case of 5th Panzer Division had already been reached). Most soldiers would at least have been aware of the material and human damage inflicted upon the Soviet Union during the years of war; many of them would have taken part in some of the atrocities. For these soldiers, preventing a vengeful enemy from reaching their homeland was the only thing that mattered. German propaganda had made extensive use of the Casablanca Declaration to portray the Allies as being irrevocably committed to the complete destruction of Germany, and as a consequence many of the officers and soldiers in the front line could see little benefit in replacing one German leader with another. Moreover, the personal cult of Hitler remained strong. Many – perhaps most – soldiers continued to believe that only he had the strength and ability to extract Germany from its current situation. If they recognised the part that Hitler had played in creating that situation, they largely kept that to themselves.

In the northern sector, 6th Panzer Division continued to fend off repeated Soviet attacks, though the pressure was reducing. On 23 July, the constant assaults diminished significantly. There were several reasons for the drop in intensity of fighting. Having been given permission to direct his Front towards Riga and the Baltic coast, Bagramian had moved the main point of effort further to the north; the drive towards Kaunas would be the responsibility of Cherniakhovsky's 3rd Belarusian Front. It needed to regroup its units, and the long supply lines and the consequences of attrition were having their inevitable impact upon Red Army operations. But despite his logistic difficulties, Bagramian achieved considerable success to the north of 6th Panzer Division's sector, especially after Chistiakov's Sixth Guards Army resumed its offensive on 23 July; Chistiakov watched with satisfaction as his tanks and infantry worked in close cooperation, moving through the swampy terrain and overcoming the first line of German positions. He was especially pleased to find that when he visited the front line, he discovered that the artillery preparation prior to the assault had been particularly effective and there was little or no trace of German trenches in several areas.[1] Whether this was actually the efficacy of the artillery bombardment, the difficulty in constructing defensive positions in such terrain, or the absence of defences in the first place, is not clear.

The main problem for Bagramian was that he felt he lacked the resources to exploit the situation to the full:

> We really missed the tank army. With it we would have been able to raise the tempo significantly in this situation. But *Stavka* assigned it to Cherniakhovsky, apparently so that the operation towards Kaunas could be brought to a conclusion as quickly as possible. Also, we couldn't immediately deploy [Lieutenant] General [Viktor Timofeyevich] Obukhov's III Guards Mechanised Corps, as it had just taken control of replacement tanks and still needed a few days to prepare them for battle.[2]

To the south of Chistiakov, Beloborodov's Forty-Third Army fended off several German counterattacks but continued to advance, reaching and cutting the road between Daugavpils and Šiauliai; by doing so, Beloborodov was threatening to turn the southern flank of Army Group North and he confirmed this by directing LX Rifle Corps towards the town of Biržai. It fell to the Red Army on 27 July, and Beloborodov noted with satisfaction that his leading elements had now advanced 460km (276 miles) since the beginning of *Bagration* and his army had taken over 11,000 prisoners:

> Only about 80km remained between us and Riga. Our losses were not great, but the swift, uninterrupted advance, which on some days resembled forced marches, left the troops exhausted, especially the infantry. Equipment and vehicles needed

maintenance and repair, our rear area communications were overstretched, and we began to experience ammunition shortages.[3]

The main objective for Sixth Guards Army was Daugavpils, but as the Soviet forces edged closer to the city, German resistance stiffened. Friessner had finally moved substantial forces down from the north; at an earlier stage of the fighting, this had been anticipated as being necessary to mount a counterattack into the northern flank of the great Soviet offensive, but now the troops were desperately needed just to shore up the front line.

To the south, 5th Panzer Division also reported a slackening in the pressure it was facing. It was most timely, as a major in the division wrote:

> These battles had been the heaviest that we had experienced and could generally be described by our motto: let the enemy slash out, hit him on the head, disengage, attack ourselves, then vanish. This required both officers and the youngest grenadiers to labour with all their strength. Generally, there was no longer any thought of sleep. Words cannot describe the operations, ordeals, and heroism of these days. To give the names of individuals or combat units would be incorrect, as everyone gave everything they had.[4]

As fighting died down, there was finally an opportunity for a little sleep and rest, but for the workshop teams of the division there was no respite. They continued to work on damaged and broken-down vehicles, attempting to restore the division's fighting strength before a resumption of fighting. Everyone knew that such a resumption was purely a matter of time. The only question was how long the quiet spell would last.

The southern sector experienced a similar evolution of fighting. Fresh Soviet attacks on 20 July resulted in a deep penetration in the front line of 367th Infantry Division, opening a line of advance towards Białystok. At this stage, Tresckow was still alive and working as chief of staff at Second Army. He and the chief of staff of LV Corps discussed this new crisis, agreeing that the only option was to shift parts of 12th Panzer Division to deal with this new threat, regardless of the resultant risk in the sector currently defended by the panzer division. Model visited the headquarters of LV Corps during the day and made a good impression on the staff, but could offer nothing by way of material aid. He advised Herrlein, the corps commander, that Generalmajor Adolf Fischer, commander of 367th Infantry Division, was to be replaced by Generalleutnant Hermann Hähnele; nobody seriously considered that a different commanding officer would be able to produce a change in fortunes.

During the afternoon of 20 July, the situation deteriorated further with heavy pressure on 28th Jäger Division. These attacks were repulsed, but 367th Infantry Division's withdrawal following the collapse of its front required the entire line to pull back once more. Herrlein contacted Weiss at the headquarters of Second Army shortly before midnight and informed him that it was impossible to hold the current positions, not least because partisan groups were working closely with the advancing Red Army. If 367th Infantry Division was to be saved from complete destruction, it was necessary to pull back a substantial distance, for which Weiss' permission was required. Weiss rejected this suggestion on the grounds that Model had forbidden such a withdrawal unless the front line came under heavy attack. The only solution, he suggested, was to allow LV Corps to be driven back in combat, thus presenting Model with a *fait accompli*. Herrlein doubted that this would be a sustainable argument because although there were Soviet attacks all along the line, the main crisis was with 367th Infantry Division and higher commands would know that the rest of LV Corps wasn't under sufficiently heavy pressure to justify a major withdrawal. Eventually, it was agreed that the expedient option was to thin out the front line as much as could safely be accomplished, so that any attack on it would necessitate a withdrawal.[5] Such were the lengths to which staff officers had to go in order to create sufficient freedom of movement.

The Germans were not alone in worrying about the consequences of having almost no reserves. Batov's Sixty-Fifth Army was fully committed – he later wrote that he had only a single tank regiment that wasn't in the front line, and even this was purely because it had lost half its tanks in earlier fighting and was meant to be recuperating. Gaps were opening up between the various spearheads, and if the Germans became aware of these – and achieved sufficient freedom of movement to concentrate a suitable mobile force – the leading rifle divisions might find themselves badly exposed. To Batov's frustration, his reconnaissance reports and those provided by the increasingly active partisan groups indicated that behind the paper-thin front line that was being sustained by the German panzer divisions and their associated infantry divisions, a great opportunity beckoned:

> In the area between Brest and Wysockie [109 miles to the south] … there were the headquarters groups of 14 assorted formations that had been smashed with a large number of division-, corps- and army-level specialist units. It was a great opportunity! Unfortunately we lacked the forces to encircle the enemy completely. I therefore asked Rokossovsky by telephone to support us with reserves. In particular, we urgently needed tanks.

'I have barely any reserves,' replied the Front commander. 'Ivanov's corps [the leading rifle corps of Sixty-Fifth Army] is to stop its advance. The bridgehead over the Bug must be held. I will send you LXXX Rifle Corps from Front reserve. Its units and those of CV Rifle Corps are to combine with Pliev's cavalry in the area around Janów Podlaski [19 miles to the west of Brest-Litovsk] and then push on to Brest. Pliev will find it too tough on his own.'[6]

If Batov's army succeeded in carrying out this order, it would effectively form the southern pincer of an encirclement of Brest, at a time when Model was still insisting on holding a front line to the east of the city. In the meantime, the rapid advance of Pliev's cavalry-mechanised group past the northern outskirts of Brest-Litovsk had left it in an exposed position. To make matters more difficult for the Red Army, Batov couldn't establish radio contact with Pliev. Had he done so, the news from the cavalry-mechanised group would have been worrying: the leading division of Pliev's group had crossed the Bug River but had then come under repeated attack. Although the ad hoc German battlegroups often lacked the strength to stand toe-to-toe against Soviet rifle and tank units, they were quite capable of making life difficult for the more lightly armed cavalry divisions, and the spearhead of the cavalry-mechanised group found itself effectively surrounded. Hastily, Pliev improvised a group of artillery units and sent them to provide the cavalry with urgently needed fire support; supplied by air, the gunners succeeded in breaking up most of the German attacks on the cavalry division, but its situation remained precarious.

The German lines might have been fragile, but the anti-tank firepower of the panzer divisions continued to inflict heavy losses on Soviet units. Pankin, the ISU-152 crewman in one of Batov's regiments, might have felt safe in his armoured vehicle, but the accompanying troops were less fortunate:

Each ISU-152 was accompanied by five men with submachine-guns. These guys were youngsters mostly born in 1926 or 1927, yesterday's schoolkids conscripted from the newly liberated areas ... In one battle, a field commander decided to use us as a shield from shrapnel. He deployed his command post right behind our vehicle. Six of them settled in, digging foxholes. But the Germans deliberately aimed at self-propelled guns. All hell broke out. When it calmed down, I climbed out to look around. I was stunned. I would remember it for the rest of my life: shredded pieces of flesh scattered everywhere. Overcoats blowing in the wind. [The infantry command post had taken] a direct hit. They all died.[7]

Immediately to the west and northwest of Brest, the German LV Corps continued its struggle. In keeping with what had been discussed between corps and division commanders, the various formations continued a slow withdrawal towards the west whenever they came under pressure, and a steady stream of signals passed up the chain of command to Model's headquarters, justifying each withdrawal. The headquarters staff of 12th Panzer Division were expecting a visit from Tresckow, but received a radio signal during the afternoon of 21 July telling them that the chief of staff of Second Army had been killed whilst visiting 28th Jäger Division; he had in fact committed suicide. Gerd Niepold, at that time an officer with 12th Panzer Division, later recalled:

> I remember during a short stop whilst changing position, the division staff's command cell heard a radio broadcast by Robert Ley, head of the *Deutsche Arbeitsfront* ['German Labour Front' or *DAF*, the Nazi Party's organisation that replaced trade unions], in which he blamed the assassination attempt on Hitler on 'a few ambitious individuals' and 'blue-blooded swine'. There were serious doubts about this assertion, especially as I personally knew some of the would-be assassins to be excellent and honourable officers. General Bodenhausen was particularly deeply affected by Ley's insulting remarks. How many of his fellow noblemen were fighting for Germany, how many had already fallen in battle and would fall in future? Premonitions of a bleak future affected all of us. But the fighting didn't give us much time to think about matters like this, and swiftly demanded our full attention once more.[8]

Some German accounts implied that the many communications difficulties experienced by Second Army and LV Corps were deliberately created by Tresckow, but this seems unlikely.[9] Like all the conspirators, Tresckow was firmly committed to continuing the war in the east after securing a ceasefire in the west. In such circumstances, deliberate sabotage of operations against the Red Army would have been counterproductive.

The contribution of Rokossovsky's 1st Belarusian Front to *Bagration* had been by the armies of its right wing, i.e. those operating on the northern fringes of the Polesie region of swamps, forests, and rivers. In the first week of July, Rokossovsky's headquarters was ordered to submit plans for its left wing to attack with the intention of capturing Lublin and then advancing to secure bridgeheads across the Vistula River. It is an indication of the immense mismatch in terms of resources between the Red Army and the Wehrmacht that even with so many armies committed to the fighting in Belarus, Rokossovsky could still plan the deployment of no fewer than four armies in the first echelon of this new operation. These were Seventieth, Forty-Seventh, Eighth Guards and Sixty-Ninth Armies, and although some were relatively weak, they nonetheless greatly outnumbered their opponents. To make matters worse for the Germans, Rokossovsky could also count on an impressive array of forces for exploitation. The newly formed First Polish Army had been created around a Polish corps, raised originally from prisoners of war captured by the Soviet Union after its occupation of eastern Poland in 1939, but nearly 40 per cent of the army's officers were Soviet citizens, rising to 75 per cent in the higher echelons.[10] Its commander was Lieutenant General Zygmunt Berling, who had been part of the first wave of Polish forces organised by the Soviet Union after the onset of the war with Germany, but when the rest of the Poles were transferred to the west via Iran, he chose to stay in the east. It was intended that this army would exploit any initial success by Rokossovsky's left wing; the symbolism of Polish troops playing a leading role in the liberation of their homeland from the Nazis was of great importance. In addition to the Poles, Rokossovsky could also depend upon Second Tank Army and two cavalry corps. With the German Army Group Centre already in tatters and Army Group North Ukraine buckling under the pressure of Konev's offensive towards Lviv, this new assault began on 17 July with immediate success – commencing on 18 July, the first wave overcame the German defences in its path and reached the Western Bug River four days later. Rokossovsky ordered Colonel General Semen Ilyich Bogdanov's Second Tank Army forward to exploit this success as rapidly as possible.

Model visited 4th Panzer Division during 21 July, informing the division commander that there were welcome reinforcements on the way. A new SS panzer corps was being established and would control two panzer divisions – *SS-Wiking* and *SS-Totenkopf*. The first of these divisions was already in the front line and was to attack towards the north in order to link up with 4th Panzer Division and thus restore continuity in the front line; a security division would then be deployed in the new front line to allow the precious panzer formations to be extracted, but the poor resilience of such divisions meant that a swift release of armoured units would be unlikely. Nonetheless, the swift advance of Rokossovsky's left wing required urgent attention to prevent further catastrophes for the Wehrmacht.

Despite being in constant action, 4th Panzer Division still fielded 58 tanks and assault guns with a further 93 being repaired in its workshops, while *SS-Wiking* had a similar tank strength available. The SS division had endured a difficult year to date. It was one of the formations encircled in the Korsun pocket and escaped with heavy losses. Its commander, Obergruppenführer Herbert Gille, played a vital role both in the survival of the encircled troops and in leading the majority of them to safety, and whilst he may have lacked the tactical brilliance of some of his peers, his calm, unflappable manner proved to be perfect for the situation in which *SS-Wiking* found itself. He had been commander of the division's artillery regiment previously and was highly regarded by his men as an officer who cared deeply for his soldiers, who were used to seeing their balding, bespectacled commander visiting them regularly in the front line. When the breakout from the Korsun encirclement reached a small river, he rose to the occasion once more, establishing a chain of men across the freezing cold river so that others could then cross to safety. Unlike many officers in the SS, he seems to have owed his position to merit rather than patronage and was sometimes openly disdainful of Nazi figures, on one occasion telling one of his officers who was wearing a Nazi Party brown shirt that such dress was forbidden.[11] But he nonetheless remained a resolute follower of orders, believing like so many senior German officers that obedience to the chain of command was of paramount importance.

After its escape from the Korsun encirclement, *SS-Wiking* was moved a little to the north for recuperation and replenishment only to be caught in its second encirclement battle of 1944. When the Red Army isolated the city of Kovel, another of Hitler's 'fortresses', Gille was flown into the city to take command while a relief column was organised. He showed the same calm determination that he had demonstrated in the Korsun encirclement, taking firm action to prevent collapse of the pocket, including the execution of some army officers for cowardice. A mixed force made up of 4th and 5th Panzer Divisions and parts of *SS-Wiking* together with an infantry division finally managed to reach Kovel on 5 April, permitting the garrison to be relieved. Thereafter, the soldiers of *SS-Wiking* had a few weeks of sustained rest in Heidelager, now part of southeast Poland. But as the summer crisis developed, the division returned to front-line service; its personnel strength was much improved, reaching nearly 15,000 men by 1 July – twice the number who had been present at the end of the fighting around Kovel. This was still nearly 3,000 short of full strength, and the division also lacked about a third of its full quota of tanks. It was fortunate in that one of its panzergrenadier battalions and its Panther battalion had not been involved in the fighting around Kovel in March and early April.

Even as Gille moved his division into position to attack towards 4th Panzer Division, plans were being made for his reassignment. The new IV SS-Panzer Corps was originally to be commanded by Gruppenführer Matthias Kleinheisterkamp, but he was told on 19 July that he was to be transferred to take command of another new formation, XI SS-Corps. Instead, Gille would command IV SS-Panzer Corps. But for the moment, Gille was fully occupied with planning his new attack and the new appointment would have to wait.

In the meantime, the Red Army learned of the imminent intervention of the SS division via a radio intercept the same day in which Model informed Betzel of the planned operation, and there was considerable alarm in Batov's headquarters – much of his army lay between the two German divisions and was now in danger of being squeezed by powerful forces.

After becoming aware of the radio intercept, Batov contacted Rokossovsky once more, seeking urgent reinforcements, but the German counterattack was already underway. There was heavy fighting on 22 and 23 July before the two German divisions established contact in Kleszczele, about 37 miles south of Białystok. Immediately to the east of Białystok, 12th Panzer Division and the two infantry divisions fighting alongside it fell back towards the city as Weiss and Herrlein had intended, but the necessity to retreat only when under pressure resulted in steadily accumulating losses and the front line consisted of little more than small battlegroups with poor contact with each other. The Soviet advance towards Białystok was impeded more by its long supply lines and dissipation of forces during the advance than by German action. Both 28th Jäger Division and 367th Infantry Division had very little combat capability left; it was only through the repeated intervention of units of 12th Panzer Division, making sharp, limited counterattacks, that LV Corps managed to avoid the collapse of its entire front line. Bodenhausen would have preferred to use his division en masse, but it proved impossible to extract it from the front line – it was only on 24 July that he was able to free a panzergrenadier battalion mounted in half-tracks, reinforced by artillery and assault guns, thus giving him a modest intervention force.

Messages between senior officers attempting to hold the front line and those at higher levels continued to show the sense of frustration felt on both sides. Oberst Johannes Hölz, chief of staff of LV Corps, complained to the headquarters of Second Army that his corps had no contact with any formations to the north. When Oberst Ernst-August Lassen, the operations officer at Weiss' headquarters, replied that the orders from Army Group Centre remained uncompromising and demanded obdurate defence, Hölz retorted that it would be best if Krebs – Model's chief of staff – personally visited the front line so that he could appreciate the reality on the ground, rather than from a distant headquarters. With no tanks available for combat, 12th Panzer Division fended off Soviet attacks through the use of a small number of assault guns; a signal from Second Army informed Bodenhausen that a train carrying 34 tank destroyers was intended as replenishment, but there was no indication of when they would arrive.[12]

Bad news continued to arrive. Late on 24 July, it became clear that the new offensive by Konev's 1st Ukrainian Front further south had broken the German defensive lines to the northeast of Lviv and there were reports that the leading Soviet units had reached the Vistula at Puławy. The report was slightly premature: although the Red Army entered the city of Lublin on 23 July, it didn't reach the Vistula for another two days. Rokossovsky's southern wing moved through Lublin and Second Tank Army drove forward to carry the thrust to the Vistula. Bogdanov, the army commander, was wounded when a sniper's bullet struck him in the shoulder, shattering his upper humerus; he was replaced by Major General Aleksei Ivanovich Radzievsky who reached the Vistula at Deblin on 25 July. Huge opportunities beckoned: there were almost no German forces on the west bank of the river, nor were there any significant defences between Deblin and Warsaw to the north.

There was a further important development on 24 July. Almost immediately after Lublin fell to the Red Army, it became the temporary home of the new *Polski Komitet Wyzwolenia Narodowego* ('Polish Committee for National Liberation' or *PKWN*, often known in the west as the 'Lublin Committee'). This pro-Soviet body was part of Stalin's plans for the future of Poland, a direct challenge to the pro-western government-in-exile in London, but was deliberately portrayed as something far less threatening; although the committee supported land redistribution and nationalisation of industry, it carefully styled itself more as a political party than a new government, though it rejected the government-in-exile as quasi-Fascist and illegal. For the moment, the British and Americans were prepared to accept Soviet assurances that this was not a new puppet government; anything else would place their relationship with the Poles in London (and serving in the front line in Italy and elsewhere) under even further strain than was already the case.

Within days, attention switched from the political ramifications of the new body in Lublin to discoveries nearby. A concentration camp had been established immediately outside Lublin in October 1941, originally intended to hold about 25,000 Soviet prisoners of war, but this was steadily scaled up and the site became known as Majdanek. When Himmler instigated Operation *Reinhard*, the plan to use gas chambers in death camps to eliminate the Jewish population of Europe, Majdanek was initially used as a site for sorting and storing the property of Jews who had been taken to the death camps of Belzec, Sobibor, and Treblinka, but in March 1942 it was restructured so that it could function as a killing centre. By the time it was abandoned on 22 July 1944, the camp had seen the deaths of at least 60,000 Jews and 20,000 other victims. Other estimates give a far higher figure.[13] When the Red Army allowed foreign journalists and other representatives to visit the camp, it was the first time that the atrocities committed by Nazi Germany were confronted in shocking detail.

Grigory Sergeyevich Kornev, a crewman in a SU-76 assault gun, was moving out of Lublin towards Majdanek:

We were sent to the camp at Majdanek. There were rows of barracks there, I don't know how many. And the most striking thing was the heaps of shoes. Why did they need so many? Whole warehouses. A man who guided us was a servant or maybe a security guard. He showed us the ovens. There was a recess next to them and a German used to stand there with a club. When prisoners could no longer work [throwing corpses into the ovens for cremation], he hit them on the head as they passed him. They were then thrown into the ovens. He showed us barrels in which ashes had been collected for scattering on the fields.[14]

Another soldier in the same unit was left with memories that haunted him for the rest of his life:

Some of the furnaces were still warm and the ashes from human corpses were everywhere. There were three heaps of ashes in the yard, about 1.5m high. We went looking for rags to clean our vehicles' guns. We found a warehouse where it looked like victims had been undressed. What struck me was this: the clothes and shoes were all so clean, smoothed out and folded, children's shoes separated from women's shoes, everything laid out tidily. And there were lengths of women's hair bundled together. It was terrible. How could anyone do something like that?[15]

On the battlefield, events continued to unfold. The situation was confused to the north of LV Corps, with Pliev's cavalry division still encircled to the west of Brest-Litovsk and German units attempting to counterattack against Batov's army to the south of the city. At one stage, Batov and his headquarters staff found themselves in the midst of the fighting. The commander of Sixty-Fifth Army was attempting to give Rokossovsky a report by radio when Radetsky, who had commiserated with Batov earlier about Zhukov's brusque behaviour, shouted out that German troops were approaching:

Through the open door of our bus we saw the turret of a German tank appear behind a hummock in a field of rye, about 300m away. Its gun turned in our direction and there was a loud detonation. The first shell struck the poorly camouflaged truck that carried our generator.

'With me!' I shouted and jumped into the rye field ... Behind us there was the crash of another detonation. The bus was ablaze. Fortunately the radio operator had abandoned the vehicle and had followed us. At top speed we ran a few hundred metres under the noses of the German armoured troops across the rye field towards Hajnówka. The dense crop was our salvation.

I later learned that the Front commander, concerned by the sudden termination of our conversation, had tried to get in touch with me by radio. After several fruitless attempts he ordered a ground attack squadron to look for me. We saw the planes searching over the buildings of Kleszczele and Czeremcha, but they didn't spot us ...

Towards evening we reached our headquarters.[16]

Neither side had sufficient strength to make the most of the opportunities that presented themselves. The various Soviet units that had been isolated by German counterattacks were able to break free without too much difficulty – in the case of Pliev's cavalry division that had been encircled, Pliev described how it was ordered to make a feint towards the east, and then switched its weight to the west and penetrated even further into the rear areas of Army Group Centre. Despite this apparent success, Pliev's memoirs are conspicuously silent about the ultimate fate of this division. Valentin Nikolayevich Slavnov was a soldier in the division and he later described his experiences:

The Germans surrounded us on all sides and began to destroy our units. It was hard to fight back because we had no air support or reinforcements. We were hit very hard. Then we were ordered to break out of the encirclement and each regiment of 10th Cavalry Division was ordered to get out on its own. So 42nd Regiment, 36th Regiment, and our 40th all marched separately.

In general, the fighting was very fierce. We lost at least half of the platoon, maybe more, including the commander, and five or six out of the 12 men in my squad died. Basically, in the encirclement and the breakout, a lot of people died – soldiers, platoon commanders, regimental commanders, and division staff. Colonel Poprikailo, the division commander, died on 8 July, and the commander of our 40th Regiment was also killed in the encirclement. I was badly concussed but there were no hospitals, nothing, so I didn't get any treatment. I was riding my horse and a shell exploded nearby. A great blast! I was thrown off the horse by the pressure wave and fell and struck my head, losing consciousness ... If a soldier was very seriously injured, he was left with the local civilian population. If lightly wounded, if he could walk, he remained in the unit. To my great good fortune, we still had some motor transport. And I was taken out of the encirclement in the motorised column and finally got some rest ...

A lot of people in the corps were killed – in terms of numbers, roughly two divisions, somewhere around two thirds of our strength.[17]

Although many of 10th Cavalry Division's personnel managed to escape to the east, they had to abandon most of their equipment and the division effectively ceased to exist as a fighting formation. Not far away, Batov too lacked the strength to destroy the modest German units that were causing him such difficulties. Rokossovsky promised him reinforcements that were to be transferred from Romanenko's Forty-Eighth Army, including a tank corps that had been pulled out of the front line for replenishment, but none of these units were available immediately.

The shockwaves from the failed assassination attempt continued to have an impact. The operations officer of 367th Infantry Division had been arrested on suspicion of involvement in the plot but was permitted to return to his post late on 25 July; at the same time, orders came for the operations officer of 28th Jäger Division to be detained and sent to Berlin under escort. Herrlein, the commander of LV Corps, protested that the man was an outstanding officer but the order remained in force. When it was passed to 28th Jäger Division, Ziehlberg, the division commander, reported that the operations officer had been in the front line and had been wounded in combat; his whereabouts were unknown and it was assumed that he had been captured by the Red Army.[18] Shortly after, Model sent a declaration to all units in his army group:

> Today I had a conversation with the Führer. During this, the Führer expressed his satisfaction over the latest successful battles of Army Group Centre. In the near future these battles will reach their climax. The Führer therefore demands that all of us must continue to hold out with the utmost efforts until reinforcements of personnel and equipment arrive. As we veterans of the Eastern Front are accustomed, we wish to reaffirm our close bond with the Führer by our increased preparedness for action. *Heil dem Führer!*[19]

Most officers below the rank of division commander and all of their subordinates would have had no means of knowing that there wasn't the slightest possibility of significant reinforcements appearing. On 25 July, after a delay due to poor weather, the American First Army had commenced Operation *Cobra*. A heavy aerial assault devastated the German *Panzer-Lehr* Division with massive carpet-bombing and after a relatively slow start the US forces rapidly overcame the German defences. The German line collapsed completely on 28 July, beginning a retreat that would end with the encirclement of much of the Wehrmacht's units in and around Falaise. There was no theatre from which German reinforcements could be sent either to the east or to the west, with both front lines in tatters. It was a moment at which it should have been clear to German officers of sufficient seniority to have access to information from the various fronts that there was no longer even the slightest hope of a successful outcome to the war. But in the east, Model continued to urge his men to hold out. The Führer had promised reinforcements; the exhausted soldiers simply had to continue fending off the Red Army until these reinforcements arrived.

Model must have known how hollow his words sounded to his subordinates. Late on 27 July, Herrlein sent a report to Weiss from the headquarters of LV Corps:

> 28th Jäger Division is now just a thin screen. Its 83rd Jäger Regiment lost another 100 men and in one battalion all the company commanders were killed. Despite their best efforts, the infantry cannot halt the major attack that is expected in the morning … It is necessary to conduct an early withdrawal of the entire front to a line either side of Knyszyn [to the northwest of Białystok] as the front line of *Gruppe von Bodenhausen* [i.e. 12th Panzer Division and its subordinated elements] has been bypassed.[20]

Białystok itself was given up by the Wehrmacht on 27 July; as they fell back through the city, the retreating Germans systematically set fire to many of the buildings including the 18th century Branicki Palace. The city had already seen killing on a huge scale. After they occupied Białystok in June 1941, the Germans carried out a major attack on the Jewish population of the city, killing about 3,000 people on 27 June.[21] Thereafter, there were further mass executions and a ghetto was established, housing about 56,000 Jews. In August 1943, the Jews in the ghetto attempted an uprising against the Germans; in combination with a similar uprising in the Warsaw ghetto, this led to a decision by Himmler for all ghettos to be liquidated.

The local forces of the Polish *AK* had intended to try to take control of Białystok before the arrival of the Red Army but this proved impossible. Instead, Colonel Władysław Liniarski attempted to make contact with the headquarters of 2nd Belarusian Front; he would offer to raise troops for the creation of a Polish corps, in return for recognition of Białystok as part of Poland. The day after the Soviet Third Army took control of the city, the Poles met Lieutenant General Petr Petrovich Sobennikov, the deputy commander of Third Army, and other senior Soviet figures. They informed the Poles that in accordance with a vote that had been held in the region when it was under Soviet occupation in late 1939, Białystok was declared the capital of western Belarus. The following day, the Soviet authorities began to round up local workers as labourers to help repair the nearby airfield and other key installations in a manner that differed little from how the Wehrmacht had used civilian labourers. But despite Sobennikov's declaration, the city became part of post-war Poland.

Meanwhile, Hitler continued to demand that Brest was to be held at all costs. Model made repeated representations that this was impossible and would result in the loss of even more troops, making any restoration of the front line impossible. Finally, with the city almost surrounded, Hitler grudgingly accepted reality and gave permission for a withdrawal. Brest was abandoned almost without a fight late on 27 July even as the Soviet Twenty-Eighth and Seventieth Armies closed in on the city from north and south. The Red Army took possession of Brest the following day; in order to make good their escape, the German troops in the city were forced to abandon most of their heavy weapons and about a third were killed or captured as they clashed with Soviet forces to the west of the city. Like Białystok, most of the city was in ruins. It too had been the location of a major ghetto where thousands of Jews were forced to live in conditions of terrible overcrowding and when Himmler ordered its liquidation, almost all of those living there were killed; the liquidation was carried out mainly by local police units made up of Poles, Ukrainians, and Belarusians under German command.

The attack by *SS-Wiking* towards the north was effectively completed in just one day. By the end of 27 July it had made good progress, but the deteriorating situation to the south, with the Red Army streaming west and threatening to sweep over the Vistula, could not be ignored. Gille was ordered to turn his division around and attack towards the south. Until 8 August, he was in the unsatisfactory situation of leading his division in combat whilst also attempting to complete the creation of the headquarters of IV SS-Panzer Corps. One of his last gifts to his division was to ensure that Standartenführer Johannes-Rudolf Mühlenkamp, who had commanded an armoured battlegroup of *SS-Wiking*, was at least temporarily assigned as Gille's replacement as division commander. Himmler had wished to give the post to Standartenführer Eduard Deisenhofer, currently serving with one of the embattled SS divisions in Normandy, but Gille insisted that Mühlenkamp was more experienced. The panzer division *SS-Totenkopf*, which had been rushed to Army Group Centre to reinforce the front line near Grodno, was also withdrawn so that it could join Gille's corps.

Berling's First Polish Army reached the Vistula on 27 July. This effectively freed up Second Tank Army, which was ordered to move northwest towards Warsaw. Such an advance would place it in the rear of the German units falling back towards the Vistula from Brest-Litovsk and Białystok, and capture of the bridges over the Vistula at Praga – immediately to the east of central Warsaw – would be a huge blow to the Wehrmacht. Reconnaissance soon identified the

Soviet tank columns heading north, and Krebs discussed the situation during the afternoon of 28 June with Generalleutnant Walther Wenck, who was serving on Guderian's staff at *OKH*. The best overall option, the two men agreed, was as before. Army Group North should shift its centre of mass to the south in order to close the gap with Army Group Centre. This would potentially permit up to three armoured formations – from north to south, 7th, 6th, and 5th Panzer Divisions – to be extracted from the front line, and would allow Army Group Centre to use its limited resources more effectively to deal with the threat to the south. The price would be the inevitable abandonment of at least part of the Baltic region. Wenck took the proposal to Guderian, who in turn presented it to Hitler. That evening, he telephoned Krebs. The Führer's response was to order the three panzer divisions to form a united assault force that was to attack towards the north and thus restore firm contact with Army Group North. Far from agreeing to move the northern armies closer to the centre, he was demanding that the hard-stretched forces in the centre move north. The first step was the replacement of 6th Panzer Division in the front line by a mixture of improvised infantry battalions and a single security division.

There had been further command changes on the German side. Friessner, who had tried to balance assurances of his determination to carry out the increasingly unmanageable orders from Hitler with the realities of the situation, was transferred to take command of Army Group South Ukraine, swapping places with another of Hitler's favourites: Generaloberst Ferdinand Schörner. A physically imposing figure, Schörner had a grim reputation for rigid enforcement of orders, ordering the execution of stragglers and men who left the front line without permission. Some officers and soldiers regarded him with hatred and contempt, but others had a more favourable opinion. Like all armies throughout history, the front-line soldiers of the Wehrmacht had a generally low opinion of those in rear area formations, and therefore welcomed Schörner's orders for many of these men to be transferred to combat units. Earlier in 1944, he served briefly as chief of the *Nationalsozialistischen Führungsstabes des Heeres* ('National Socialist Leadership Staff'), in which role he was responsible for ensuring that all soldiers were sufficiently imbued with the principles of the Nazi Party, but resigned this post after just two weeks citing irreconcilable differences of opinion between him and Martin Bormann, Hitler's secretary. He seems to have been proud of his grim reputation; on one occasion, he remarked that soldiers should be 'more afraid of threats from behind than in front', and regularly tore medals and rank insignia from the uniforms of soldiers he encountered retreating from the front line.[22]

The situation to the north was growing increasingly serious. Despite being held up by terrain difficulties, the Soviet Sixth Guards Army succeeded in capturing Daugavpils on 27 July after intense fighting. It had been a tough battle for Chistiakov's troops, constantly having to defend against determined German counterattacks, as he recalled in later years:

> In no other operation of the Great Patriotic War did I have to report to the Front commander about the plight of the army as often as at Daugavpils. At times, our situation seemed quite critical and I knew that this meant that it was critical not just for Sixth Guards Army but for the entire 1st Baltic Front.
>
> I had no army-level reserves at all and the situation required us to parry the blows of the counterattacking enemy with urgency, especially when they were directed at gaps between my corps. In one of the numerous counterattacks, the enemy managed to bypass the flanks of a regiment of 46th Guards Rifle Division, which had advanced the furthest towards Daugavpils ... The regiment was surrounded for a short time ...
>
> By mounting active operations, the enemy tied down our troops. I couldn't take units from a less active sector and transfer them to the threatened area, as there were no longer any inactive sectors. We had only one division each in the second echelons of XXII Guards Rifle Corps and CIII Rifle Corps, but we didn't have sufficient time to move them to the sectors where the enemy was most active as they were at least 30km away ...
>
> After crossing the Daugava east of Daugavpils, 154th Rifle Division of CIII Rifle Corps from our army liberated the city on 27 July with the support of units from Fourth Shock Army [the southern flank of 2nd Baltic Front, to the north].
>
> More than three decades have passed since Daugavpils was liberated, but even now, when I look at the map and see the mass of lakes and swamps through which our soldiers advanced, often waist-deep, sometimes even chest-deep in water, under heavy bombardment and defensive fire, it seems an incredible achievement.[23]

On the same day, the Soviet III Guards Mechanised Corps reached and captured the town of Šiauliai, 124 miles further west. The breach between Army Group Centre and Army Group North was growing ever more critical, with every likelihood of the northern group being cut off, and Bagramian fully intended to take advantage of the opportunities before him. After discussions with Vasilevsky, he directed III Guards Mechanised Corps to turn north. The coast of the Gulf of Riga was just 72 miles away, and aerial reconnaissance reported that there were effectively no German forces in the area. A quick advance through Joniškis and Jelgava would be the crowning moment for 1st Baltic Front, with two German armies pinned to the coast of the Baltic Sea and cut off from the Reich.

The relative calm that had befallen the Kaunas sector ended abruptly on the morning of 29 July when the massed artillery of Cherniakhovsky's 3rd Belarusian Front subjected the German positions to a 40-minute bombardment. Although it was intense, the shelling failed to reach the level at the beginning of *Bagration* – despite the pause in operations, there had not been sufficient time to bring forward sufficient supplies. When it began, the Soviet advance had mixed success. There were several small bridgeheads held by the Red Army on the west bank of the Niemen to the southeast of Kaunas where two Soviet rifle corps faced the weak 52nd Security Division. The original 52nd Infantry Division had been disbanded after suffering catastrophic losses in the autumn of 1943 in heavy fighting near the city of Nevel, and the survivors were used to create 52nd *Feldausbildungs* Division ('Field Training Division'), one of three such training formations in Army Group Centre. In April 1944, it was renamed 52nd Security Division with three regiments but little or no artillery. It had already suffered heavily in combat against the Red Army since the beginning of *Bagration* and its presence in the front line was a further indication, if any was needed, of how desperate the Wehrmacht was for any troops that could fill the huge gaps that existed almost everywhere. With little difficulty, the Soviet rifle units brushed aside the weak line of trenches around their bridgeheads and advanced rapidly, pushing forward up to ten miles and threatening Kaunas from the south.

The direct advance towards Kaunas from the east by LXXII Rifle Corps was slower, grinding through German defensive lines and reaching a point about two miles from the outskirts of the city by nightfall; in this sector, 6th Panzer Division and elements of the *Grossdeutschland* division were present, able to put up strong resistance. To the north of Kaunas, 7th Panzer Division was able to fend off several Soviet attacks; but despite the resumption of Soviet offensive operations, the order for the transfer of at least the armoured battlegroup of 6th Panzer Division – the bulk of its tanks, half-track mounted infantry, and artillery – towards 7th Panzer Division remained in force. Nor was there any possibility of extracting 5th Panzer Division – it found itself dispersed in attempts to shore up the front lines of three infantry divisions. Hitler's solution to restoring the front line to the north was over even before it began.

On 30 July, the fragile German line near Kaunas disintegrated completely. The retreating formations managed to erect new defensive positions along the southern and eastern edges of Kaunas and Soviet units advanced further west, bursting through what remained of the German 52nd Security Division and cutting the main road running from Kaunas towards Marijampolė. It was now impossible to consider holding on to the city and orders were issued for its abandonment that evening. Reduced to just a handful of operational tanks and with its panzergrenadier battalions badly depleted, 6th Panzer Division was in no shape to do more than prevent its own sector from collapsing. The armoured battlegroup's orders to join 7th Panzer Division were cancelled and instead it found itself involved in running battles to the south of the city. Nikolai Petrovich Teplotanskikh was a tank driver who had taken part in the heavy fighting in and around Vilnius, and his tank was one of a group that encountered 6th Panzer Division's armoured battlegroup as the Soviet forces attempted to press on towards the west. His recollections of the fighting capture the terror and claustrophobia of being in an armoured vehicle in combat:

The tank commander said, 'We're moving forward,' and the infantry rose up from the fields around us. And then, there was a loud bang – they hit our tank from I don't know where. The tank caught fire, it was dark inside and the electrical system failed. I tried the starter motor but it didn't work. I was already beginning to choke. I tried to open my driver's hatch but it was stuck and wouldn't open. Then I tried to climb out over the ammunition rack to the turret hatch, but I just couldn't get out. A man was lying across the ammunition. It was the loader, Sasha Shestakov. As I looked around, a head appeared by the commander's hatch – it was the gunner/radio operator, Vanya Skachkov, who had just regained consciousness. He had an abdominal wound, his skin torn and intestines exposed. I told him, 'Help, Vanya!' I pushed with my foot and with Sacha I tumbled out onto the armoured deck. We dropped to the ground and for a moment I lost consciousness. As soon as we recovered our senses I grabbed my comrade and ran a few metres. We fell to the ground and suddenly there was a huge explosion. I lay on my back and watched my tank exploding. What should we do? The battle was raging but I had nothing more than a few grenades and my revolver. When we left the tank, we always had grenades and a dagger with us – in case of hand-to-hand combat.

Then I realised that the Germans were close by. I threw my lemons [Red Army slang for grenades] and lay down, and it became quiet. I could hear someone speaking close by. I tried to drag Sasha but I couldn't. Then I realised they were speaking in Russian, at first I had thought they were Germans. I crawled up to them and said, 'Guys, help Sasha.' His arm was hanging loose, held on just by a tendon. They wanted to cut it off right there and then. I don't know if they chopped his arm off or not, but in any case they pulled him along as best they could. I wanted to help, but for some reason my own hand wouldn't work properly. The guys asked me, 'Are you hurt?' I answered, 'No, guys, this is Sasha's blood.' When my sleeve was cut away, it turned out there was a wound from a fragmentation projectile. Apparently, when I was pulling Sasha out, the Germans fired on us with mortars and we were hit by shrapnel rounds. Who knows, maybe my wound was caused when our tank was hit. They bandaged my hand and we crawled on. There were others with me. Vanya Peretykin was also unconscious. They bandaged his abdominal wound. It was getting late and we saw someone running towards us. Someone warned it was a German and we lay down, but it turned out to be Senior Lieutenant Lyudmila, a medical officer in our tank battalion. She dropped down next to us and said, 'Don't go that way, the Germans are over there and the battle's still continuing. Keep away from there.'[24]

Despite some local successes, 6th Panzer Division could do nothing to stop the Soviet forces that continued their advance almost unchecked. New orders arrived for the division to pull back towards the west, a move that proved to be difficult, as the division's operations officer noted in his diary:

> Formal march orders can't be issued in the prevailing circumstances. But control of traffic by the military police is working fine. The march is affected by air attacks during daylight and mud on the road at night as a result of rain showers.[25]

It was a dispiriting retreat for the Wehrmacht. On 1 August, Soviet troops reached the East Prussian frontier – exactly 30 years, an officer noted glumly, since German soldiers had been mobilised for the First World War and had taken up positions along this sector.

The Soviet attack around Kaunas continued unabated. On 31 July, Red Army troops penetrated into the northern parts of the city. Kaunas was surrounded by a series of forts that had been built during the 19th century and although these were of limited value in the era of mechanised warfare, they still formed potent strongpoints for defensive fighting. Wherever possible, the Soviet units simply bypassed them. By the end of 31 July, the Soviet Fifth Army had captured most of the city. But despite the successful capture of the city, Cherniakhovsky struggled to make the most of the disintegration of the German defensive line. He had control of Rotmistrov's Fifth Guards Tank Army, but its two tank corps could field no more than 28 tanks. This greatly reduced force was ordered to push on towards Raseiniai to the northwest of Kaunas; however, the advance was coming to an end. Raseiniai was finally captured on 9 August, and Cherniakhovsky called a halt to the offensive operation. It had been a huge success. From its start line near Vitebsk, his Front had advanced over 300 miles and inflicted irreparable damage on the Wehrmacht.

The Soviet forces immediately to the north were also reaching the end of their operation. For Bagramian, the last remaining objective was to reach the Baltic

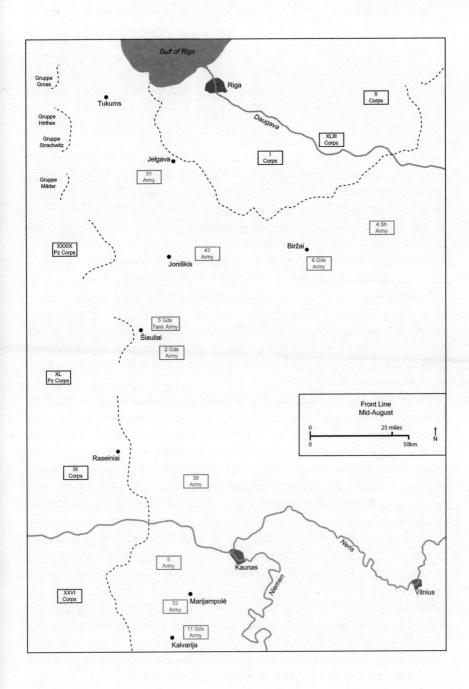

Gulf of Riga

Riga

Tukums

Gruppe
Gross

Gruppe
Hirthes

Gruppe
Strachwitz

Gruppe
Mäder

X
Corps

Daugava

XLIII
Corps

Jelgava

I
Corps

51
Army

4 Sh
Army

XXXIX
Pz Corps

43
Army

Biržai

6 Gds
Army

Joniškis

5 Gds
Tank Army

Šiauliai

2 Gds
Army

XL
Pz Corps

Front Line
Mid-August

0   25 miles

0   50km

N

Raseiniai

IX
Corps

39
Army

Neris

5
Army

Kaunas

Niemen

XXVI
Corps

33
Army

Marijampolė

Vilnius

11 Gds
Army

Kalvarija

coast and thus isolate the German Army Group North. After turning north on 27 July, III Guards Mechanised Corps reached and captured the town of Joniškis the following night, a third of the way to the coast. Bagramian awaited further news with a mixture of anticipation and anxiety – it seemed inconceivable to him that Schörner would permit Army Group North to be isolated without throwing everything he could in the path of the Soviet thrust. Schörner had indeed ordered an infantry division to move to Jelgava as quickly as possible and a race rapidly developed between the two armies. When the leading units of Lieutenant General Viktor Timofeevich Obukhov's III Guards Mechanised Corps attempted to attack the city with two mechanised brigades, it encountered determined resistance. Bagramian ordered Obukhov to wait for reinforcements in the shape of the rifle divisions of Fifty-First Army, which were hurrying forward.

The Baltic coast was almost within touching distance. The most powerful forces available to the Wehrmacht were too far away to intervene – the closest was 7th Panzer Division, about 39 miles south of Šiauliai. But for the moment, the Wehrmacht had won the race to reinforce its positions around Jelgava and Bagramian impatiently urged Lieutenant General Iakov Grigoryevich Kreizer to move his Fifty-First Army forward with greater alacrity. In the meantime, Obukhov was ordered to renew his assault; he reported back during the afternoon of 29 July that he had suffered heavy tank losses and that his men were reporting further columns of German reinforcements approaching from Riga. Further attacks on Jelgava were pointless until the infantry of Fifty-First Army arrived, and Bagramian told Obukhov to try sidestepping the German positions by sending a mechanised brigade past the western edge of the town towards Tukums.

The troops in and around Jelgava were under the command of General Curt Pflugbeil, a Luftwaffe officer in charge of *Luftflotte I*, which provided air support for Army Group North. Like so many of the German formations attempting to hold back the Red Army in the summer of 1944, his command was made up of disparate elements of various units and uniforms, but the presence of a large number of anti-aircraft guns permitted the Jelgava garrison to beat off the armoured attacks it had faced to date. Even creating this relatively weak force had resulted in a considerable thinning of the German front line further to the east, and Beloborodov's Forty-Third Army was now advancing steadily along the valley of the Daugava River, pushing forward up to 18 miles per day. In any case, Pflugbeil could do nothing to intercept the Soviet forces that bypassed Jelgava to the west. On 30 July, Colonel Semen Davidovich Kremer, commanding 24th Guards Mechanised Brigade, reported to Obukhov that he had reached and captured Tukums after a short but sharp action. From there, his leading battalion motored the last nine miles to the Baltic coast during the afternoon. Schörner's Army Group North was isolated with no land connection with the Reich.

For both sides, the corridor that Obukhov's mechanised corps had established from Šiauliai to the Baltic coast became the centre of attention: Vasilevsky urged Bagramian – as if any such urging was necessary – to widen the corridor as rapidly as he could, while the Germans rushed troops to the area to try to restore contact between Army Group North and Army Group Centre. On the last day of July, sufficient riflemen from Kreizer's Fifty-First Army had reached Jelgava for the assault to be resumed. Bagramian hurried forward to Kreizer's headquarters accompanied by Colonel General Nikolai Mikhailovich Khlebnikov, his Front artillery commander. When they were told that Kreizer was with his leading formations in Jelgava, they continued forward and came under mortar fire. In Kreizer's command post, the commander of Fifty-First Army told them in an embarrassed tone that although his men had captured Jelgava, a surprise German counterattack was now underway and it might be safer for Bagramian and Khlebnikov to return to the main army headquarters. But further Soviet reinforcements were arriving every moment, outflanking Jelgava to the east, and the moment of alarm passed.

Briefly, there was an opportunity for the Red Army to overrun much of the Courland Peninsula, to the west of the corridor that had reached the Gulf of Riga; the Germans had almost no troops covering that sector. But Bagramian had no troops for such an advance. Already, there was growing pressure on his southwest flank, and he correctly assessed that the Wehrmacht would soon make a major attempt to break through to Army Group North. The priority was to establish as strong a defensive line as possible.

Some of the Red Army soldiers who entered Kaunas and other Lithuanian cities and towns later described that they were greeted with enthusiasm by the locals, but most noted marked differences from their progress through Belarus. The Lithuanian towns and cities were generally less badly damaged than those to the east, as the Baltic region had been treated in a markedly different manner by the Germans. There hadn't been widespread anti-German partisan activity, particularly in the central and western parts of Lithuania, and therefore there had been no need for the devastating punitive sweeps that the Germans had conducted elsewhere. But the appearances were in some respects deceptive. There had been widespread slaughter across the region; Lithuania had had a large Jewish population before the German invasion, and it had been almost entirely destroyed. The ghetto in Kaunas had been converted into a concentration camp and the remaining inmates were moved elsewhere before the Red Army arrived; some were executed by their guards. Moreover, many Lithuanians had no desire for what they saw as one occupying force to be replaced by another, particularly as the Soviet occupation and annexation of Lithuania in 1940 had resulted in widespread arrests and deportations. Within days of Kaunas being occupied by Soviet troops, there were incidents of Red Army soldiers coming under attack with several being killed by hidden snipers. In the countryside too, there was considerable resistance to the Soviet forces, and the rise of an anti-Soviet partisan movement that would encompass much of the Baltic region. Known to friend and foe alike as the 'Forest Brothers', these fighters continued to oppose Soviet rule for many years. The Soviet Union characterised them as former Nazi collaborators and war criminals, and unquestionably many of them had been involved in atrocities against the Jews and others in the past, but many of the fighters were simply opposed to the return of Soviet control. The movement was largely crushed by Soviet anti-partisan operations in the mid-1950s, but isolated clashes continued into the 1960s. Inevitably, as tensions developed in the years after the end of the Second World War and former allies became opponents in the Cold War, British and American agencies attempted to take advantage of the 'Forest Brothers' movement and there were several attempts to land agents and supplies on the Baltic coast. All of these were intercepted and destroyed or captured; Kim Philby, who had taken careful steps to discourage any British links with anti-Hitler groups that might one day blossom into a tempting separate peace between Germany and the Western Allies, systematically provided Moscow with details of every such operation.

For the Red Army, one of the conspicuous aspects of what became known as the Kaunas Operation was the relative lack of impact of Fifth Guards Tank Army, which had been expected to be a decisive exploitation force. From the outset of *Bagration*, Rotmistrov's army was dogged with difficulties. It was required to redeploy to a new start line before entering combat and then became involved in heavy fighting as it advanced towards and beyond Minsk. Rotmistrov was widely criticised by other senior figures like Vasilevsky in their memoirs for the disappointing performance of the tank army, but the orders he received were often contradictory. Nonetheless, he was blamed for failing to keep adequate control of his forces and for allowing them to become embroiled in costly fighting, for example in the battles for Vilnius. As a result, Cherniakhovsky recommended that Rotmistrov should be replaced as commander. On 8 August, Rotmistrov received notification that he was being reassigned to a new, non-combat role as deputy commander-in-chief of Soviet tank and mechanised forces. In some respects, it was an appropriate post for a man who had repeatedly used his field experience to recommend modifications to both the equipment and organisation of Soviet forces, but to be removed from his prestigious command of Fifth Guards Tank Army, especially at the culmination of *Bagration*, must have been a serious personal blow. The losses suffered by his units during *Bagration* were in keeping with similar casualties in earlier operations in Ukraine, but despite this he held several senior posts after the war, and his contemporaries generally had favourable opinions of him. Shtemenko wrote after the war:

> Undoubtedly, Pavel Alekseyevich Rotmistrov also is ranked amongst the outstanding tank commanders. Based upon his rich practical experience gained on the battlefield and extensive theoretical knowledge, he also made a significant contribution to the post-war development of tank technology and the training of qualified command personnel.[26]

The Soviet armies on the northern flank of the great advance had finally come to a halt, but elsewhere the Red Army's tide was still running strongly. To the south of Kaunas, Soviet forces reached and captured Marijampolė on 31 July, where 5th Panzer Division was meant to be gathering its strength in preparation for taking part in Hitler's planned attack towards the north. Instead, the panzer division once more found itself in the thick of the action, attempting to shore up the broken units of 52nd Security Division that were streaming back from the Kaunas sector. Days of heavy fighting followed with the panzer division making repeated counterattacks to try to blunt the Soviet drive. A radio report on 3 August summarised the situation succinctly:

> Heavy fighting all day, massed enemy ground attack aircraft, front breadth together with the subordinated 52nd Security Division 48km. No more reserves available since midday, no ammunition for the heavy howitzers, shortages of tank ammunition. The result: an enemy penetration by a strong force of 800 infantry with eight tanks either side of the main road from Kalvarija to the west. [Enemy] spearhead near Akmenyai [five miles or 8km west of Kalvarija] at 2000, and 17 [Soviet] tanks at Eglebaliai ... Heavy losses suffered. Two battalions reduced to combat strength of 45 to 50 men. Serious crisis expected if there is a fresh major attack here. Reinforcements of grenadiers, tanks, and artillery urgently required.[27]

By the end of 3 August, 5th Panzer Division reported that it had five Pz.IVs and 11 Panthers in an operational state. Finally, fighting died down at the end of the first week of August. The performance of 5th Panzer Division since its arrival in the central sector had been impressive: it claimed the destruction of no fewer than 486 enemy tanks and 11 assault guns, but even if this figure was an exaggeration, the division had repeatedly fended off Soviet attacks and prevented the complete collapse of the German front line. Late on 10 August, the division was finally pulled out of the front line and replaced by 547th Grenadier Division.

A little to the north of 5th Panzer Division, 6th Panzer Division endured a similarly torrid few days. Several major Soviet attacks were fended off, but with the constant threat of being outflanked, the division had to pull back slowly towards the East Prussian frontier. On 5 August, the operations officer noted in his diary that the hitherto strong morale of the division's troops was showing signs of strain:

> The situation at the end of the day (the expected major enemy attack did not materialise) shows *Gruppe Quentin* holding a line consisting of small groups in disconnected strongpoints. The fact that this line could be held is only due to the constant counterattacks of the armoured battlegroup. It is particularly unfortunate that II Battalion, 4th Panzergrenadier Regiment showed little resilience today. Whilst this is partly due to low morale in the detachments overseeing this sector, the fact cannot be overlooked. The strict measures ordered from higher commands for the handling of stragglers and soldiers who are found to be weaponless must be implemented soon.[28]

The measures in question were the subject of an order issued by Model on 31 July, in which he stated that any signs of cowardice had to be dealt with in the severest possible manner, if necessary by summary execution of the offenders. In the days that followed, the pressure on 6th Panzer Division eased significantly. Cherniakhovsky's 3rd Belarusian Front, like 1st Baltic Front to the north, had achieved all that it could without a substantial pause. The achievements of the summer were considerable. The Red Army had marched across the breadth of Belarus and had seized a strip of land on the eastern edge of East Prussia.

In the southern sector, the German LV Corps continued to face difficult pressures. Despite repeated assurances, 12th Panzer Division had yet to receive its promised new tanks; on 28 July, it could field just two Pz.IVs and 15 assault guns. The pressure on the front line was far reduced from the massive blows of earlier weeks but was still too much for the weak German units to hold their positions. There was constant talk of extracting 4th and 12th Panzer Divisions in order to create a mobile reserve for counterattacks, but it was almost impossible to release any forces. On 30 July, orders were issued for the creation of two attack groups, with which the intention was to mount convergent attacks to bring the Red Army to a standstill: the northern group consisted of a reinforced battalion of panzergrenadiers centred on Czechowizna, about 17 miles northwest of Białystok; and the southern group, mainly 4th Panzer Division's reconnaissance battalion, would start from Makowo, 20 miles to the south. But even if this operation succeeded, it would do little to remedy matters further to the south. The troops retreating from Brest did so under constant pressure from the Red Army and it seemed that there was little that could stop them from advancing onwards to Warsaw.

Meanwhile, 4th Panzer Division continued to enjoy considerable local successes, but like the other panzer divisions it was constantly forced to concede ground to avoid being outflanked. Writing a summary at the end of July, Betzel could be proud of his division's achievements, but noted that his men were exhausted and faced overwhelming demands, and that it was unsurprising that their efficacy was noticeably reduced compared to the past. To an extent, this reflected the continuing improvements of the Red Army. There was also a worrying increase in what was described as 'deliberate exaggeration' – officers faced by Soviet attacks sometimes overstated the pressure on their units in order to justify further retreats, or to secure artillery and armoured support.[29] With the newly formed IV SS-Panzer Corps to the south, 4th Panzer Division continued to edge towards the southwest. The Bug River was crossed at Wyszków late on 1 August; only 30 miles separated the leading Soviet troops from Warsaw.

The capture of Brest by the Red Army was a considerable relief for Pliev's cavalry-mechanised group, as it restored firm contact between the far-flung exploitation force and the bulk of the Red Army, even though one cavalry division had effectively been knocked out. Writing about the achievements of his men after the war, Pliev drew comparisons with earlier battles:

> In July–August 1944, the enemy experienced what the troops of the Red Army experienced at the beginning of the war, in June–July 1941 … The flames of war that the Nazi Wehrmacht had kindled now incinerated the arsonist himself. It was clear to everyone that the day of complete catastrophe of the Fascist invaders and their Reich was not so far away.[30]

Pliev firmly expected that once his units had been replenished, they would lead the attack towards the Polish capital, but *Stavka* had other plans. The cavalry-mechanised group was to be withdrawn from the front line. In its place would be a Polish infantry division. In the Baltic region, the Red Army had ensured that Estonian, Latvian, and Lithuanian rifle divisions were used in its advance in an attempt to portray the arrival of the Red Army as liberation; the same policy would be followed here, but there was a major difference. Unlike in the Baltic States, there was a substantial armed group present that was highly unlikely to regard the Red Army as a force of liberation. Stalin was aware that the *AK* would

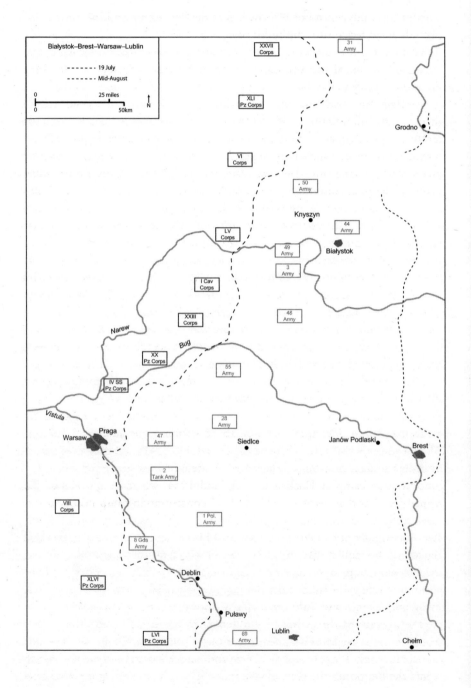

Białystok–Brest–Warsaw–Lublin

- - - - - 19 July
- - - - - Mid-August

0   25 miles
0   50km
N

attempt to secure control of Warsaw before the Red Army could reach the city. He fully intended to turn this to his advantage.

In an attempt to stop the Soviet Second Tank Army from reaching Praga, on the east bank of the Vistula from Warsaw, *OKH* assigned 73rd Infantry Division to Gille's IV SS-Panzer Corps. The division had suffered heavy losses in Sevastopol in April and May before its surviving troops – without any of their heavy equipment – were evacuated by sea to Romania, where they received replenishments of men and equipment, but the division was still not fully combat-ready when it was dispatched to Gille's corps. Hamstrung by incomplete preparations – the new headquarters of IV SS-Panzer Corps lacked many of the vital communications and logistic assets it required to function properly – Gille had to use some of the assets of the headquarters of *SS-Wiking* to try to take control of the situation. He was alarmed to learn that there was no contact with *SS-Totenkopf*, which was meant to form a major part of his corps; it wasn't until late on 28 July that one of his officers was able to make contact with the division. Its tracked vehicles were being moved by train from near Grodno to Warsaw, from where they would be transferred to the east; the wheeled vehicles were travelling down from the northeast by road. Both would take time to arrive. Moreover, the various scattered elements of *SS-Wiking* were being extracted from the old front line, a task complicated by so many signals and staff officers in the division having to assist with corps-level command and control.

The first elements of *SS-Totenkopf* to arrive in the new area of operations were the truck-mounted troops of its 6th SS-Panzergrenadier Regiment, named after the former commander of the division, Theodor Eicke, who had been killed near Kharkov the previous year. Whilst his men remembered him as a tough, aggressive front-line soldier, he would be regarded as infamous for his command of the concentration camp at Dachau in 1933 and 1934, where he introduced the striped pyjamas that became emblematic of concentration camp prisoners and replaced the previous regime of random brutality with one that was just as harsh but more rigidly organised. When some of his subordinates expressed concern about this, he replied that anyone in the SS who had such a soft heart should retire promptly to a monastery.[31] The regiment bearing his name took up positions to defend Siedlce from the rapidly advancing units of Second Tank Army, with elements of 73rd Infantry Division alongside.

The northward thrust by Second Tank Army was rapidly creating a new crisis. Unless it could be stopped, there was a risk that the Red Army would capture not only Praga, but also Zegrze and Serock immediately to the north. If this were to occur, the German Second and Ninth Armies would have their supply lines severed and would have no option but to withdraw towards the northwest if they were to escape encirclement and destruction. The Red Army would then be able to exploit across the Vistula towards the west without any German forces being able to stop it. The devastation inflicted upon the Wehrmacht during *Bagration* had been immense; this latest development threatened to turn a spectacular victory into one that could bring the war to a rapid conclusion.

CHAPTER 13

PRAGA AND WARSAW

Of all the crises that Model had overseen, the situation on the Eastern Front at the end of July 1944 was easily the worst, even if pressure in the northern sector had finally come to an end with Bagramian's troops reaching the Baltic coast. Army Group North was cut off, and Hitler was demanding that Army Group Centre use its northern assets to restore contact; there remained a gap between Second and Ninth Armies, with Soviet forces constantly threatening to slip through the spaces to disrupt attempts to establish a stable front line; and of course there was the growing threat from the south, with the Soviet Second Tank Army moving ever closer to Praga. In the wake of Radzievsky's armour, other units on Rokossovsky's left wing were forming up along the Vistula, threatening to burst into central Poland. The level of threat was greater than in any situation he had overseen before, and the resources available were far more restricted.

It was essential for Siedlce to be held as long as possible to allow *SS-Wiking* to concentrate to the west of the city alongside *SS-Totenkopf*. Fighting commenced to the south of Siedlce on 25 July and increased steadily in intensity in the week that followed. The first Soviet unit to threaten the German position was XI Tank Corps, rapidly reinforced by II Guards Cavalry Corps and three rifle divisions from Forty-Seventh Army. Since its inception, *SS-Totenkopf* had acquired a fearsome reputation. It was originally formed around a battlegroup of former concentration camp personnel under the command of Eicke and became a full division in October 1939.

During his time as commandant of Dachau, Eicke deliberately fostered an attitude of unconditional obedience and an attitude of treating the enemy with equally unconditional brutality. Rudolf Höss, who would be executed for war crimes committed when he was commandant of Auschwitz, later recalled his time as a subordinate of Eicke at Dachau:

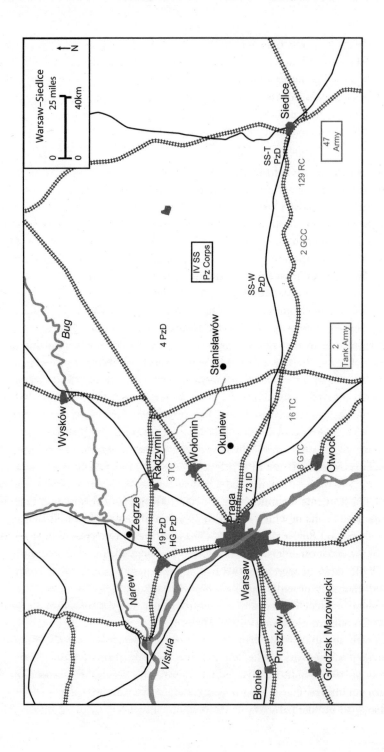

Eicke's instructions from first to last were: behind the wire lurks the enemy, watching everything you do so that he can use your weaknesses for his own advantage. Do not let yourselves be taken in, but show the enemy your teeth. Anyone who displays the slightest sympathy with these enemies of the state must vanish from our ranks. My SS men must be tough and ready for all eventualities and there is no room among us for weaklings.[1]

When the division was formed, many of its personnel had already been involved in indiscriminate massacres in Poland in 1939, and this behaviour continued when it was deployed in the west in 1940. Here, *SS-Totenkopf* encountered French Moroccan troops in Catillon-sur-Sambre; most of the French soldiers were killed either in the town or after capture, as the soldiers of the division showed no inclination to treat 'inferior' colonial troops as legitimate prisoners of war.[2] Shortly after, men from the division machine-gunned 97 British prisoners in the village of Le Paradis. There was a further massacre of French colonial soldiers, this time from Senegal, in Chasselay.

During *Barbarossa*, *SS-Totenkopf* was part of Army Group North and although it showed ferocious energy in combat, there were complaints from Wehrmacht officers that the division often diverted its personnel to carry out massacres of civilians instead of supporting neighbouring formations. The division was encircled near Demyansk in early 1942 where it lost over three-quarters of its personnel before it was extracted. Reformed as a panzergrenadier division, it returned to the Eastern Front a year later and was heavily involved first in the German counteroffensive that restored the front line along the Donets River, and subsequently in the Battle of Kursk. In October 1943 it was further upgraded to a panzer division and remained involved in heavy fighting in Ukraine and northeast Romania for much of early 1944. Throughout this period, there were constant incidents in which retreating German units were involved in massacres of civilians and Soviet prisoners; *SS-Totenkopf* was no exception and was often one of the worst offenders, and its soldiers were both feared and hated by the Red Army. The ethos of aggression that had been stamped upon the division by Eicke meant that it repeatedly suffered heavy losses. During his time as division commander, Eicke had tried to ensure that replacements were drawn from the ranks of concentration camp guards, believing that they were already sufficiently hardened to make excellent replacements, but this proved impossible. Nonetheless, the hard core of the division had been heavily indoctrinated and passed on its attitudes to new drafts. Eicke had ensured that men under his command inflicted harsh punishment on prisoners, rotating personnel so that all soldiers had to take part. Many of the senior SS officers involved in war crimes elsewhere – the Malmédy Massacre of December 1944, killings of civilians in Italy, and the brutal suppression of the Warsaw Ghetto Revolt of 1943 – had previously served in *SS-Totenkopf.*

On 29 July, there was a particularly heavy attack on the German lines to the south of Praga. The tanks of Second Tank Army struck at the thin line running west from Siedlce at the very moment that Generalleutnant Fritz Franek, commander of 73rd Infantry Division, was visiting the front line held by one of his regiments. He was cut off from his headquarters as the battle developed; his operations officer, Oberstleutnant Otto Becker, attempted to organise a counterattack but it was swept away by the Soviet forces. Many of the soldiers of the German infantry division were killed or captured and Franek, who had commanded the division for barely a month, was one of the prisoners. After breaking the German line, the Soviet armour raced towards Praga and the vital bridges over the Vistula and it was only through the hasty intervention of further recently arrived German reinforcements that the attack was blocked. Among these new arrivals in this sector was another manifestation of the constant rivalry and empire-building that bedevilled the German war effort: the *Fallschirm-Panzer-Division Hermann Göring.*

As already described, German paratroopers were part of the Luftwaffe rather than the army, and whilst this made some sense from an organisational point of view it nonetheless represented an unnecessary duplication of training establishments so that the paratroopers could receive sufficient basic infantry training. But the most serious consequence of assigning paratroopers to the Luftwaffe was that it established a precedent for troops intended for ground combat to be part of the Luftwaffe. In 1942, this resulted in the creation of 22 Luftwaffe field divisions using surplus manpower from the lavishly manned Luftwaffe; if these men had been assigned to regular infantry divisions, they would have been used to strengthen existing battalions and regiments and would have been mixed with seasoned veterans, but instead they were placed in formations where there were very few – if any – soldiers with ground combat experience. The result was disastrous, with the field divisions proving to be brittle and almost useless in action, particularly in the brutal conditions of the Eastern Front.

But with the practice of creating Luftwaffe ground combat units now established, Göring continued to develop further formations rather than relinquish personnel to the army. A *Division General Göring* was created in November 1942 around personnel who had originally been part of a brutal police regiment used by Göring during the 1930s. Its personnel had to have documentation proving their Aryan ancestry and were required to be confirmed supporters of the Nazi Party, but in the years that followed it became necessary to replace combat losses with other Luftwaffe personnel, diluting this ideological and racial 'purity'. From the outset, the division was intended to be the equivalent of a panzer division and tank crews were transferred from the army to form two panzer battalions, at a time when the army could ill afford such diversion of resources. After being rushed to Tunisia in late 1942, most of the division was effectively destroyed; its survivors were then used to create the bizarrely named *Fallschirm-Panzer-Division Hermann Göring* ('Parachute Panzer Division Hermann Göring'). After seeing action in Sicily – where it performed with considerable success as the rearguard during the German evacuation of the island – the division was heavily involved in fighting on the Italian mainland before being pulled out of the front line to be replenished.

Göring now ordered a further expansion of his ground forces; a new *Fallschirm-Panzerkorps Hermann Göring* was created, with a new *Fallschirm-Panzergrenadier-Division 2 Hermann Göring* being raised alongside the existing division, which was transferred to the Eastern Front in an attempt to shore up the front line after the disaster of *Bagration*. Although the growth of the Luftwaffe ground forces represented a wasteful diversion of resources from the army, the division was battle-hardened by the summer of 1944, and the rapid intervention of one of its battlegroups between Siedlce and Praga prevented the Soviet Second Tank Army from capturing the Vistula bridges in the last days of July. As the scattered survivors of 73rd Infantry Division were gathered together once more, they were reinforced by the arrival of the anti-tank battalion of *SS-Wiking* in an attempt to prevent repetition of their collapse of 29 July.

But although the soldiers of the *Hermann Göring* division prevented the capture of Praga, Radzievsky's tanks were not finished with their attack. Leaving forces to shield against any German counterattack from Praga, Radzievsky dispatched III Tank Corps towards the north, aiming to capture the bridges over the Narew and Bug Rivers. Further Soviet forces moved north on 30 July, creating a threatening salient between the *Hermann Göring* division in the west and the forces of Gille's IV SS-Panzer Corps in the east. The supply lines for all the German forces fighting against the last surge of the Red Army's forces were under threat. But the creation of any salient creates an opportunity for the opposing side to launch a counterattack against the flanks of the penetration, and the Wehrmacht had repeatedly demonstrated its ability to improvise such counterblows at both tactical and operational levels. After what had been an almost continuous period of setbacks and disasters for Army Group Centre, there was suddenly an opportunity to strike back; moreover, a successful counterattack would also go a long way to stabilising the overall situation.

When he took command of Army Group North in early 1944, Model attempted to implement what he termed *Schild und Schwert* ('shield and sword'). In many respects, this was little more than a restatement of standard German doctrine: forces would be used to create a shield against the enemy's advance, while other forces were concentrated to form the sword with which a counterthrust could be mounted. As the fighting between Leningrad and the Narva River then unfolded, it proved impossible for an effective shield to be created, and with only one panzer division available – and operating in terrain that made any rapid thrust almost impossible to execute, particularly in winter – the grand design failed to deliver. After Model took command of Army Group Centre following the dismissal of Busch, the remorseless pressure on the front line had prevented any such policy being followed, but although the dangerous thrust by Second Tank Army was a threat to the supply lines of the German forces, the advance of Radzievsky's tanks had left them in an exposed position. The corridor that they had created after turning north towards Praga was no more than 12 miles wide, and although Soviet losses hadn't been heavy to date – the tank army still had about 600 of its original 800 tanks and assault guns available – there were growing shortages of fuel, ammunition, and food. After continuous operations since 18 July, the officers and soldiers were tired; routine maintenance of vehicles, proper vigilance, and the quality of tactical decision-making were all beginning to suffer. Other Soviet units were moving up to support the tanks, but there was a window of opportunity, particularly as the German units concentrating against them – the *Hermann Göring* division, the two SS panzer divisions, and 4th Panzer Division – were all motorised units with considerable strike power. Model had been waiting for a moment when several factors combined: he required powerful mobile forces; he needed a target at which to direct them; and he needed the rest of the front line to be stable enough for the counterattack to be made. After weeks of catastrophe and retreat, these factors finally offered themselves.

The overall strategic situation for Germany was hopeless. At an operational level, there were disasters everywhere, and tactically the Germans had been at least matched both in Normandy and Belarus. But the quality of the officers of the Wehrmacht and the strengths of the German general staff system remained formidable. As soon as he became aware on 27 July of a potential opportunity to strike at Second Tank Army, Model issued orders to Vormann and Weiss at the headquarters of Ninth and Second Armies respectively to begin preparations. Even though there was little or no opportunity to brief division or even corps commanders of what was happening – particularly men like Gille, who was still struggling to organise a new corps headquarters with inadequate resources while keeping an eye on *SS-Wiking* – everyone in the German command chain implemented instructions smoothly and without fuss. Combat units readied their equipment and moved to their designated positions; supply officers at all levels laboured to ensure that fuel and ammunition would be made available in sufficient quantities; and staff officers worked tirelessly on the hundreds of details without which the operation would not be possible.

Model's plan was a mixture of making the best of where units were currently deployed and where they could be sent in time to strike. The first target of the counterattack was to be the Soviet III Tank Corps. As it was already some distance to the east, *SS-Wiking* was to attack from that side of the Soviet salient with 4th Panzer Division on its northern flank. The *Hermann Göring* division would concentrate to the west of the salient before advancing, with separate battlegroups from 19th Panzer Division on either flank. If all went according to plan, Betzel's 4th Panzer Division would be able to halt and pin down the Soviet armour while the other two thrusts pinched off the tip of the salient, thus encircling and destroying III Tank Corps. *SS-Totenkopf* would then be available to exploit the initial success, turning south to destroy the rest of Second Tank Army. Whilst these 'swords' were being wielded, the battered infantry divisions of Army Group Centre – still supported by 12th Panzer Division in the southern sector – would attempt to create an east-facing 'shield'. Their ability to maintain prolonged resistance was unquestionably weak, but the Red Army was running out of momentum and Model gave orders for a slow withdrawal towards the west; he could hope for a swift resolution to the fighting at Praga, after which the armoured formations could be switched back to the east if required.

The commander of III Tank Corps was Major General Nikolai Denisovich Vedeneyev, a man with long experience of mechanised forces. He had taken command of the corps in mid-July, having previously been deputy commander of VIII Guards Tank Corps, and his most pressing concern was to get adequate supplies to his men while he waited with growing anxiety for reinforcements to arrive. Just as the men of Second Tank Army were badly fatigued by their exertions, so too were the riflemen toiling in their wake along dusty roads under the burning sun; occasional sharp rain showers turned the sandy roads and tracks to mud, adding to the delays. Just as important as the infantry units were the anti-tank battalions that were essential for defence against German armour. In 1944, a Soviet tank corps consisted of three tank corps and a motorised rifle brigade, with motorised artillery, anti-tank and anti-aircraft battalions, but in many cases the anti-tank assets were held at army level and assigned to the subordinate tank corps as required. The rapid deployment of these anti-tank guns to create defensive lines that could engage German armour with coordinated fire – the *Pakfront* that hindered so many German operations – was an important factor in the declining ability of panzer divisions to assert themselves, but Vedeneyev had very limited resources at his disposal. Most of the vital anti-tank guns – and the accompanying sappers, who would rapidly deploy anti-tank mines in front of the *Pakfront* position to channel German armour into killing zones – were still struggling along the congested roads to the south. Nonetheless, the Soviet forces enjoyed a considerable numerical advantage. About half of Second Tank Army's tanks and assault guns were in the tip of the salient, compared with about 280 on the German side, and many of the latter would not arrive at their start lines in time for the planned commencement of the counterattack at first light on 1 August.[3]

On 31 July, III Tank Corps made its last attack and came within about a mile of the vital bridges over the Narew River near Zegrze; it was stopped by the hasty deployment of 19th Panzer Division. Weiss had hoped that 4th Panzer Division would at least have its armoured battlegroup deployed a little further to the east at Wysków by the end of 31 July, but shortly before midnight Betzel informed him that his troops were still engaged with the enemy. Although he intended to break contact imminently, his division would not be able to contribute significantly at the start of the counterattack until the afternoon of 1 August. To make matters more difficult, the weather changed to sustained rain and badly degraded roads rapidly disintegrated.

While the tanks, guns, and infantry of 4th Panzer Division struggled through the mud towards Wyszków, *SS-Wiking* undertook a reconnaissance in force towards Okuniew from the east. It encountered very little resistance as it moved forward about six miles; the mechanised rifle brigade of Second Tank Army, which would normally have been expected to deploy as flank protection, had suffered rather heavier losses than the tank brigades and in any case was strung out over an extended length. Eighth Guards Army and Forty-Seventh Army were meant to be taking over from them further to the south but had been badly delayed, and much of Forty-Seventh Army was tied down in combat with *SS-Totenkopf* around Siedlce.

On 1 August, *SS-Wiking* commenced its main attack with an armoured battlegroup – a battalion of panzergrenadiers, two panzer companies, and a battery of self-propelled artillery – moving towards Okuniew while other elements provided flank protection and scouted for other elements of Second Tank Army. Mühlenkamp, who had inherited operational command of *SS-Wiking* from Gille, was aware of the danger of his battlegroup becoming embroiled in combat with a numerically superior enemy and showed considerable caution; when he encountered Soviet tanks near Okuniew, he diverted the battlegroup past the northern edge of the town. A gunner in a Panther tank later described the moment when Mühlenkamp's group encountered the Soviet tanks:

> There was open ground in front of us. We were the leading tank as the spearhead emerged from the forest. Suddenly, there was a tremendous crash as we were hit … The other Panthers turned to the right and left and began to return fire. On the other side of the clear ground in front of us there were four Soviet tanks (Shermans and T-34s) with their sides exposed to us. It seemed that they had expected us to appear from another direction. There was a dreadful din as Russian tank shells flew through the woodland in all directions. As suddenly as the engagement began, it died down. Three Russian tanks had been shot up but the fourth was concealed by smoke and dust. We had taken a hit on the right side and our track was damaged, and we were unable to move. We had to wait for a repair team to reach us to help with repairs.[4]

The main difficulties experienced by *SS-Wiking* were caused by the poor state of the roads and the terrain, worsened by the overnight rain. Radio contact with higher commands was intermittent, resulting in anxious messages between Model, Weiss, and Gille about the precise location of Mühlenkamp. These exchanges were further hampered by the skeletal nature of Gille's corps headquarters – in order to try to create a functional organisation, Gille had been forced to borrow signallers and staff officers from *SS-Wiking*, leaving the division with reduced capacity for command, control, and communications. After finally determining the position of other German forces, Mühlenkamp made contact with the foremost elements of the battlegroup of 19th Panzer Division that was operating on the southern flank of the *Hermann Göring* division. In just a day, the first phase of the operation had succeeded. All the Soviet forces to the north of Okuniew were now cut off, but communications continued to be problematic. At one stage during the afternoon, there was a radio message from the *Hermann Göring* division claiming that it had reached a small town that was meant to have been captured by *SS-Wiking*; when the Luftwaffe division reached the town, it was still in Soviet hands. It is perhaps indicative of the complexities created by having a Luftwaffe division attempting to cooperate with a division of the Waffen-SS under the command of the army that the first Model heard of this was when Krebs, his chief of staff, brought it to his attention with the suggestion that there appeared to be organisational problems with IV SS-Panzer Corps. This was of course correct, but Krebs worded his comments in a manner that blamed Gille. Without any hesitation, Model dismissed the criticism. He was correct: the *Hermann Göring* division had reached a completely different town.[5]

The leading elements of 4th Panzer Division reached their new positions at about midday on 1 August, where they were relieved to find that fuel and ammunition had already been stockpiled. By the time that the bulk of the division's units had arrived, it was too late in the day for them to go into combat. To the west of the Soviet salient, the attack by the *Hermann Göring* division and the two battlegroups from 19th Panzer Division on either flank made only limited progress, but the most important objective – establishing contact with *SS-Wiking* – had been achieved. There was considerable satisfaction in the headquarters of Army Group Centre, Second and Ninth Armies, and IV SS-Panzer Corps, but the achievements of the day were overshadowed by a dramatic turn of events to the west. The Warsaw Uprising had begun.

Of all the various uprisings by the Polish *AK* in its attempts to seize key cities before the arrival of the Red Army, the Warsaw Uprising was the largest and most significant. From the German perspective, its importance was on several accounts. The city was the largest in what had been Poland before the war and remained one of the main population centres of the *Generalgouvernement*, the rump of Poland that had not been absorbed into Germany itself or other jurisdictions, and if the Vistula was to become the front line on the Eastern Front, it would be a vital point of defence. It was also a critical node of communications across the Vistula, and its loss would severely compromise German positions east of the river. For the Soviet Union, there was recognition that although the capture of Lublin had permitted the creation of a committee that could evolve into a pro-Soviet government, any Polish government would ultimately have to be based in the historic capital of Warsaw. If the city were to come under the control of the *AK*, this would create difficulties, potentially involving the Red Army in fighting against the *AK*. At the very least, this would cause considerable embarrassment, especially if it resulted in widespread destruction in the city. Whilst the ultimate outcome of any such battle was hardly in doubt, it might cost the Red Army substantial casualties and give the Germans some valuable breathing space.

For the *AK*, this element of Operation *Burza* was of obvious significance: Warsaw was the historical heart of Poland and if it could be liberated from the Germans by Polish forces, this would be of huge symbolic value. It was also at the limits of the reach of air power from the Western Allies, and the Poles hoped that they might be supported by British and US forces. Given the apparently imminent arrival of the Red Army in the city, the uprising represented perhaps the last opportunity for a pro-western Poland to be created before Stalin was in a position to impose his preferred solution on the map of Eastern Europe. From their initial high status as the 'First Ally', the Poles had diminished in importance for the Western Powers. Churchill remained strongly committed to supporting the government-in-exile, but for the Americans the question of the future of Eastern Europe was just one of many issues; if the Soviet Union showed restraint in its interest in areas such as the Middle East, the Americans were prepared to give Stalin a relatively free hand in Poland and elsewhere. Anthony Eden, the British foreign secretary, was inclined to accommodate Stalin's territorial ambitions in the Baltic region and Poland largely because he saw no alternative, and as they wrestled with the difficulties of honouring their obligations to the First Ally while not jeopardising the relationship with Stalin, the British produced a number of papers considering how territory might be redistributed to try to satisfy all sides. Whilst the 'Big Three' had largely settled the future of Poland at the Tehran Conference, this was a tightly guarded secret and had been done with no input from the Poles themselves. As a result the Poles continued to believe that there remained a possibility of altering the ultimate outcome by taking matters into their own hands.

The German occupation of Warsaw had been brutal. The Warsaw Ghetto, the largest such enclosure created for the Jews of Eastern Europe, was liquidated in May 1943 and thereafter the repression of non-Jewish Poles became increasingly severe as part of German plans to eliminate the undesirable Slav population in order to make space for German settlers, but the realities of the war situation began to be felt. Hans Frank, the governor-general of the *Generalgouvernement*, had long been critical of the policy of his superiors towards the region he controlled, describing it as 'attempting to slaughter the cow that they wanted to milk.'[6] He attempted to improve conditions for workers by increasing rations, but remained committed to the long-term elimination of the Slav population. His suggestion that Polish military units might be raised to support the Germans in their fight against the Soviet Union was bluntly rejected, and his tentative attempts to contact various Polish groups were also rebuffed. As the Red Army edged closer in the summer of 1944, tensions within the city rose steadily. Frank warned Berlin that he feared an uprising was imminent, and that there were insufficient troops in the city to counter it.

On 27 July, Ludwig Fischer, the governor of Warsaw, issued a proclamation:

Poles! In 1920, outside this city, you repelled the Bolsheviks and thus demonstrated your anti-Bolshevik feelings. Today Warsaw is once more the breakwater against the Red flood and in contribution to that struggle, 100,000 women should report for work to construct defences ... Those who refuse will be punished.[7]

Despite the clear threat – and there were regular public executions in Warsaw to underline the determination of the Germans to retain control – very few Poles came forward. Fischer decided not to take any action, but the Gestapo executed the political prisoners it was holding in the city's prisons.

During the preparations for Operation *Burza*, Polish officials in London had repeatedly attempted to secure the cooperation of the British, but with little success. It became clear to the Poles that the British regarded the entire region as falling within the Soviet sphere of influence. On 29 July, Brigadier General Stanisław Tatar – known more usually by his pseudonym 'Tabor' – had a meeting with the British Special Operations Executive or SOE. He informed the British that an uprising in Warsaw was imminent and made several specific requests. The Polish capital was within the range of British bombers and he wanted the Royal Air Force to attack German airfields around the city and to drop supplies to *AK* units in the area. He also asked for the transfer of Polish fighter squadrons currently forming part of the RAF to Poland as soon as airfields had been seized by the *AK*, along with at least part of the Polish Parachute Brigade, currently under British command. The *AK* was to be recognised as one of the official components of the alliance against Nazi Germany, and an Allied military mission should travel to Warsaw at the first opportunity.[8] The request was received favourably and Tabor departed with confidence that the British would aid the uprising, but almost immediately the British raised objections. There was no possibility of transferring Polish forces to Poland at the moment, and even bombing attacks and the delivery of supplies were impossible due to logistic constraints. In Warsaw itself, the local *AK* command met for final discussions on the last day of July. Bór-Komorowski, the commander of the *AK*, later wrote:

> That afternoon, a Wehrmacht High Command communiqué announced the Russians had commenced 'a general assault on Warsaw from the southeast'. It also said that the commander of 73rd Infantry Division, deployed across the river from Warsaw, had been taken prisoner … In my opinion, if we commenced our struggle at that moment, we would block the Germans from bringing reserves forward and would cut their supply lines … But if the Germans were forced back across the river under pressure from the Soviets, as could be expected at any moment, their troops would mass in the city in large numbers and would cripple any opportunity for action by us. The city would become a battlefield between the Germans and Russians and would be reduced to ruins. In my opinion, the right moment for commencing the uprising was at hand.[9]

Orders were issued: the uprising was to commence at 1700 on 1 August. But although the *AK* could call on up to 40,000 fighters in Warsaw, there were insufficient weapons for them all, not least because large stockpiles of guns and ammunition had been smuggled out of Warsaw into the surrounding countryside in preparation for uprisings in rural areas. The first attacks on German troops in the city actually took place several hours earlier than planned, in the early afternoon. Zdzisław Sierpiński, a young *AK* officer, was leading his group to their assembly point when they ran into a German patrol:

> For a moment we all stared at each other with utter concentration. The Germans were clearly calculating the potential gains and losses, whether to challenge us or to pretend that they hadn't seen this group of youngsters wearing poorly concealed uniforms with submachine-guns under their coats ... Then they decided to start a fight from which we emerged without losses. We threw our grenades into their truck, which exploded ... We managed to run across the street to take cover with the rest of our unit.[10]

With clashes breaking out at numerous points during the afternoon, Governor Fischer ordered the city garrison to be placed on alert shortly before the uprising was due to commence.[11] The garrison commander was none other than Reiner Stahel, who had led most of the Vilnius garrison to safety, and he ordered his modest forces – a mixed bag of about 11,000 men – to take up positions around key locations. These included the murderous bands commanded by Oskar Dirlewanger and Bronislav Kaminski.

At 1700, the fighting suddenly surged in intensity as the *AK* commenced its attacks. The tallest building in the city was the Prudential Building and the red and white Polish flag was flying proudly from its top floor by sunset; in addition, the *AK* captured a major German arsenal, the main post office, the power station, and the railway station in Praga. Stahel was isolated in the Saxon Palace in the city, and was unable to coordinate the units nominally under his command. But other key locations – the police headquarters and the large airfield outside Warsaw – remained in German hands. Perhaps the most important failure was that the bridges across the Vistula were not captured. Even if the Red Army succeeded in reaching the eastern bank opposite the city, there was a high likelihood that the bridges would be destroyed before Soviet units could cross and join the battle. The day's fighting cost the *AK* about 2,000 casualties. The Germans lost about 500 men.[12]

The tragic detailed course of the Warsaw Uprising is beyond the scope of this work. In brief, many of the areas that the *AK* managed to seize remained isolated, although most of the city was in Polish hands after the first few days of fighting. Himmler spoke to Hitler about the developments:

> My Führer, the timing is unfortunate, but from a historical perspective what the Poles are doing is a blessing. After five or six weeks we will leave the area. But by then Warsaw, the capital, the head, the centre of intelligence of this former state of 17 million Polish people will be extinguished, these people who have blocked our way to the east for seven hundred years and have stood in our way ever since the Battle of Tannenberg. After this, the Polish problem will no longer be a great historical problem for the children who come after us, nor indeed will it be for us.[13]

Provided that the Red Army didn't intervene, the Germans intended to concentrate sufficient forces to destroy the lightly armed *AK* and would then aim to destroy Warsaw entirely. The plans of the *AK* were based upon an assumption that the Soviet forces would arrive within days of the uprising, and if there were any substantial delays they would receive help from the west. The commencement of the uprising was triggered by the approach of the Soviet Second Tank Army to Praga; the *AK* assumed that this was the first element of a general Red Army advance to and across the Vistula. The Polish commanders had no way of knowing that the Germans were already moving into position to throw back the Soviet armoured units, but nonetheless the front line was sufficiently close to Warsaw that even if the Red Army didn't attack across the Vistula to try to seize Warsaw, it would be close enough to attack German forces with artillery and aircraft. All eyes were therefore on the response of the Allied Powers, to both the east and the west, to see how they would respond.

Stalin had already issued instructions that effectively doomed the Warsaw Uprising, even before he became aware that it was taking place. On 1 August, *Stavka* called a halt to further offensive operations. The gains since *Bagration* commenced had been immense and there was an urgent need for a prolonged operational pause while supplies and reinforcements were brought forward. This would permit the various armies to concentrate their resources in anticipation of further operations that would carry the Soviet advance across the Vistula and Narew Rivers. Before this could take place, hundreds of miles of roads and railway lines would have to be restored, telephone lines would have to be repaired, fuel and ammunition would have to be brought forward and stockpiled, and the assault forces would have to be brought up to strength once more. If an opportunity for a rapid advance presented itself, it would be taken, but costly attacks on a major city like Warsaw risked dragging the weakened Red Army units into a battle of attrition that would reduce their capability for future operations. For the moment, it would be sufficient to hold onto what had been gained. German counterattacks were inevitable – in addition to the attacks on Second Tank Army, there was already heavy fighting to the south where the Germans were attempting to reduce and destroy the Soviet bridgeheads across the Vistula, and the Germans were about to launch a major attack in the north codenamed *Doppelkopf* to try to restore contact with Army Group North. By taking up a defensive posture, the Red Army had an opportunity to inflict heavy losses on the German armoured units prior to a renewed drive towards the west.

As senior German officers took stock late on 1 August, they were unaware that Stalin had reined in his forces. The uprising in Warsaw was a major cause for concern – at the very least, it threatened to disrupt the already precarious supply lines of the German units still operating to the east of the Vistula. For the moment, Model had to assume that Stahel and other commanders would be able to crush the uprising in Warsaw; he had enough issues dealing with the Soviet forces opposing him. He ordered Gille to concentrate on preventing any Soviet relief column from reaching the tank corps that had been isolated by the day's successful attack. Gille responded by requesting air support: large columns of Soviet tanks and vehicles had been spotted heading north, and the pressure upon the lines of *SS-Totenkopf* around Siedlce was already heavy enough without having to contend with these additional forces.

Dawn on 2 August brought clouds and rain and fighting flared up after a quiet night. Gille was disappointed to receive only limited air support; several dive-bomber units were instead tasked to attack *AK* positions in Warsaw and low cloud further hampered Luftwaffe operations. Nonetheless, the two divisions of IV SS-Panzer Corps fended off several Soviet attacks from the south as Forty-Seventh Army tried to thrust northwards to reach the trapped men of III Tank Corps. The heaviest fighting was around this corps, which came under concentrated attack; from the west, the *Hermann Göring* division and the northern battlegroup of 19th Panzer Division recaptured the western parts of the town of Radzymin, while 4th Panzer Division attacked from the northeast. In order to improve coordination, these German units were now under the command of Saucken's XXXIX Panzer Corps, which moved to the area to take control of the operation. It was a welcome development for 4th Panzer Division – Saucken had formerly commanded the division and had an excellent relationship with the officers who had served under him. Leutnant Reinhard Peters, commander of one of the division's Panzer IV companies, was part of the force assembled for the counterattack:

> Our 35th Panzer Regiment was given the task of taking Radzymin from the east. The Panther battalion was meant to lead but it hadn't finished refuelling and rearming. So, as was so often the case, our II Battalion was the first to set off.
>
> It was early afternoon when the town was within our grasp. The only road from the east to our objective ran through a wide swampy area on a high embankment. We took up positions at a hedge that ran perpendicular to the road. Next to my Pz.IV, Generalfeldmarschall Model had gathered a whole row of generals. His discontent at the delays in troop movements was being vented in berating the generals. When it was the turn of our former division commander, General von Saucken let his monocle fall from his eye and said in the quiet tone that was so well known to us, 'You will not speak to me like that, Herr Feldmarschall.' Then he walked away. We grinned mightily.[14]

During the afternoon, a battlegroup from the division seized a bridge over the Rzadza River northeast of Radzymin; Betzel ordered the battlegroup to secure a modest bridgehead, but Model realised the opportunity that beckoned. He was visiting Betzel's division at the time and ordered Betzel to push forward with his entire division in order to encircle Radzymin from the east and southeast. Peters and his Pz.IV company was in the lead of the attack:

> What was before us now was little more than a textbook tank attack. We had to drive along this blasted embankment in column, a savoury treat for Russian anti-tank guns and tanks, which apparently had no more fuel. But we had our doubts. I sent Leutnant Graf Moltke forward with his platoon. We lay in wait with the rest of the vehicles to provide fire support. But nothing happened. The platoon reached the edge of the town without encountering enemy resistance. We followed it. I sent two tanks down each road radiating from the market square. We were now standing alone next to the church. Suddenly we heard the rattle of tank tracks right behind us. A T-34 rolled towards us. It had its turret turned to the rear. At first, my gun aimer was concentrating on an enemy tank that had already been knocked out, at the edge of the square. 'Further to the right,' I muttered to him. Finally, he could see it in his sights. The anti-tank round leapt from the barrel and brought the colossus to a halt just 10m from us. It was just in time, as it would have rammed us a few seconds later.[15]

It is likely that the Soviet tank was out of ammunition. Vedeneyev had made several urgent requests for supplies to be delivered to his unit, but it had been impossible for help to arrive from the south and to date, Soviet aircraft had been unable to deliver fuel or ammunition by air.

At the same time that 4th Panzer Division was moving into Radzymin, the Luftwaffe was able to switch its attention from Warsaw and provided close support as the German armoured units closed in on the town from all sides. One of the tank brigades of III Tank Corps was almost destroyed and pulled back to the south from the town. The rest of Vedeneyev's tank corps was now concentrated in and around Wołomin, about five miles to the south, and despite coming under heavy pressure from the *Hermann Göring* division it was largely able to hold its positions. Meanwhile, Radzievsky had ordered XVI Tank Corps to attack north to restore contact with the isolated units; as it attempted to do so, it ran into the defensive lines of 73rd Infantry Division. Despite the division's earlier disastrous performance and the loss of its commanding officer, it managed to perform rather better on this occasion, at least partly due to the timely support provided by the anti-tank battalion of *SS-Wiking*. But despite the numerous successes enjoyed by the German forces, the pressure from the south – where in addition to the other formations of Second Tank Army, the soldiers of II Guards Cavalry Corps and Forty-Seventh Army's CXXIX Rifle Corps made repeated attacks – resulted in the steady loss of men and tanks. Moreover, the communications problems that had caused concern on 1 August continued, with *SS-Wiking* experiencing difficulties in retaining contact with 19th Panzer Division. The operations officer of Gille's IV SS-Panzer Corps sent a report by radio to Second Army during the afternoon:

> We are taking heavy losses from powerful enemy artillery and mortar fire. Part of 19th Panzer Division appears to have withdrawn to the west from Okuniew without any attempt to inform us … The situation in Okuniew is now unclear. Our reconnaissance battalion needs to evacuate Stanisławów so we have ordered *SS-Totenkopf* to move sideways and take control of that town. The roads are poor, delaying our movements.[16]

Mühlenkamp was anxious to free up *SS-Wiking* so that it could strike towards Radzymin, but fresh orders from Second Army changed the emphasis. Instead of being the hammer that would destroy the trapped III Tank Corps, *SS-Wiking* would be the anvil; the destructive attack would be mounted from the north, by 4th Panzer Division. The role of the two SS divisions was to ensure that no relieving attacks by Red Army units to the south succeeded, and to prevent any breakout by III Tank Corps. The battle was becoming increasingly confused, with battalion-sized units from both sides fighting a series of encounter battles, often at close range, and Model stressed the importance of ensuring tight contact between *SS-Wiking* and 19th Panzer Division to the south of the encirclement. Matters were complicated by the need to transfer a substantial part of 19th Panzer Division back across the Vistula so that it could be deployed against Soviet bridgeheads further to the south. The diversion of Luftwaffe effort against the *AK* in Warsaw wasn't the only impact of the uprising on Model's counterattack: the anti-aircraft battalion of the *Hermann Göring* division was diverted to support German units attempting to recapture Warsaw, and several replacement drafts of SS personnel were sent to the city instead of to *SS-Wiking* and *SS-Totenkopf*.

On 3 August, the assembled German forces moved to destroy III Tank Corps with almost constant air support from Stuka dive-bombers. At the same time, Radzievsky stepped up his attempts to rescue his trapped unit and confused fighting raged all day. A great deal rested on the outcome of the fighting immediately to the south of the encirclement where Mühlenkamp and the soldiers of *SS-Wiking* were attempting to restore firm contact with German forces to the west. At first, the German operations went well and a thrust by the armoured battlegroup of *SS-Wiking* reached a forward position held by the *Hermann Göring* division, but almost immediately a Soviet counterattack drove the SS unit back towards the east. The commander of the Luftwaffe division was Generalmajor Wilhelm Schmalz, a former cavalryman who had competed for Germany in equestrian events in the Olympic Games; he had been in post since April and was in command when the division moved through northern Italy. Personnel from the division were involved in the massacre of at least 170 Italian civilians near Arezzo in revenge for partisan attacks on soldiers of the division. Schmalz had already caused consternation by submitting a report that had proved to be incorrect, and a similar incident now occurred when Saucken's headquarters contacted the *Hermann Göring* division for an update: on this occasion, Schmalz responded with a bland report from one of his formations that it had established firm contact with *SS-Wiking*, even though in reality there was a gap of over a mile between the two divisions. If sufficient fuel could reach the beleaguered survivors of III Tank Corps, they might escape to the south.

Throughout the day, the Polish fighters in Warsaw were cheered by the sound of heavy fighting to the east; they had no way of knowing that this did not represent signs of the Red Army moving closer to Warsaw, but marked the steadily progressing destruction of the nearest Soviet forces. Although much of Warsaw was in the hands of the *AK*, there could be little doubt about the outcome of any protracted fighting, given the lack of heavy weaponry on the Polish side.

On 30 July, Stanisław Mikołajczyk, the prime minister of the Polish government-in-exile, had arrived in Moscow in an attempt to try to improve relations with the Soviet Union. His round face, red cheeks, balding head, and generally diffident and unassuming appearance masked an underlying stubbornness and determination. He was aware that regardless of their fine words, the British and Americans had acknowledged the actuality of *Realpolitik*; some of his Polish colleagues might hold strongly anti-Bolshevik views, but the future of Poland required some kind of accommodation with the Soviet Union. There were several major issues for consideration, and Mikołajczyk was determined to seek whatever solutions he could.

The first issue related to the future frontier between Poland and the Soviet Union. When independence was restored to Poland at the end of the First World War, there was a level of agreement about the western and southern frontiers of the state, but far less certainty about the east. There was a plebiscite in the Masurian region of East Prussia, where there was a substantial Polish population and the Western Powers were confident that there would be a majority in favour of joining Poland, thus further weakening Germany, but to the surprise of the British and French, the region voted to remain part of Germany. In the east, there was even greater uncertainty. Lord Curzon, the British foreign secretary, proposed a frontier that bore his name in 1919; this was based upon the language spoken by the majority of the local population, but such data was incomplete and in a region with greatly mixed populations of Poles, Russians, Belarusians, Ukrainians, and Jews, the line left substantial minorities on both sides of the proposed divide. In any case, the war that then erupted between Poland and the Soviet state resulted in a frontier that was considerably further to the east; whilst this was seen by many in Poland as a benefit, others were concerned at the large numbers of non-Polish people in the region who had little sense of allegiance to the new Polish state. When Germany and the Soviet Union divided Poland between them in 1939, their demarcation line was close to the original Curzon Line, and Mikołajczyk knew that Stalin wished to regain much of the territory to the east of this line that had been seized by Poland in the Polish–Russian War.

The second major issue for Mikołajczyk was the precise status of the Lublin Committee. Would Stalin insist that it formed the future government of Poland, or was he willing to reach some accommodation with the pro-western government-in-exile? The developments in the eastern regions that had already been overrun by the Red Army were not encouraging, with *AK* units being forcibly disarmed and many of their officers and men then being placed under arrest. Mikołajczyk had no foreknowledge of the Warsaw Uprising's precise timing, though he knew that plans were in place, and he was anxious to try to determine Soviet intentions – ideally, before the uprising took place. His arrival in Moscow was inauspicious, with little by way of any official welcome.

On 31 July, the eve of the uprising, he met Molotov who suggested that it might be difficult to timetable a meeting with Stalin, and that Mikołajczyk should instead discuss matters with the Lublin Committee. Mikołajczyk declined to do so.

Mikołajczyk finally met Stalin on the afternoon of 3 August; to date, the only information that he had about events in Warsaw was what he had managed to learn from listening to news broadcasts. The first part of the discussion – which concerned the future eastern frontier of Poland – proved to be fruitless. Stalin claimed that he had to take into account differing points of view and that unless the Lublin Committee and the government-in-exile could agree a common position, he could make no decisions. This was hugely disingenuous, as the Lublin Committee would not have been permitted to exist if it was likely to express any opinion that was not in accordance with Stalin's views. The best that Mikołajczyk was able to achieve was an assurance from Stalin that – in accordance with what he had discussed with Churchill and Roosevelt in Tehran – Poland would receive territories from Germany in the west as compensation for the loss of any territory in the east.

The next topic of discussion was the Warsaw Uprising. Mikołajczyk asked Stalin to provide assistance to the *AK* units in the city; Stalin agreed to issue the necessary orders. When Mikołajczyk suggested that Stalin help him travel to the city, the Soviet leader pointed out that this would be impossible given that the *AK* didn't control all of Warsaw, and then seemed to retract his earlier commitment to supporting the uprising by adding that he was not prepared to allow any Soviet units to operate beyond the lines that they currently held. He referred Mikołajczyk to the Lublin Committee for further discussions. Believing that Stalin had actually agreed to provide military support to the *AK* in Warsaw, Mikołajczyk reluctantly agreed to meet the Lublin Committee over the next few days.[17]

The fighting to the east of Praga continued. Having isolated III Tank Corps, Model intended to complete its destruction as quickly as possible before striking against VIII Guards Tank Corps, the next unit of Radzievsky's Second Tank Army. Having contributed to the first phase of the German counterattack, 19th Panzer Division was ordered to pull back and return to the west bank of the Vistula, where it was urgently needed to mount attacks against the Red Army's bridgeheads across the river to the south of Warsaw. Preparations for operations on 4 August were badly disrupted when Soviet artillery fire cut the telephone cables between the headquarters of Gille's IV SS-Panzer Corps and Second Army; radio communications proved to be difficult and it was over an hour before contact was restored. Gille then informed Weiss that his units were not yet ready to commence their planned attack towards the south against

VIII Guards Tank Corps, but Weiss insisted that the agreed timetable had to be followed. When communications were disrupted once again, Model's headquarters became involved and – not for the first time – Krebs suggested that Gille was not showing sufficient willingness to fight. Like many senior officers in the army, Krebs seems to have had a dislike of the divisions of the Waffen-SS; they were lavishly equipped compared to their army equivalents and many of their senior personnel owed their positions more to the patronage of senior SS figures like Himmler than on any merit, but to apply such prejudices to Gille was unfair. He was an experienced and capable soldier, struggling to deal with a difficult situation with inadequate resources.

Finally, detailed information began to reach higher commands. *Kampfgruppe Mühlenkamp* had come under heavy attack by VIII Guards Tank Corps late on 3 August and had struggled to hold its positions, hence Gille's assertion that he would not be able to attack on time. Soviet pressure continued throughout the day and the planned strikes towards the south that had been intended to encircle much or all of VIII Guards Tank Corps became increasingly unlikely.

To the north, 4th Panzer Division continued to attack the remnants of III Tank Corps. At the end of 3 August, Betzel's units reported that they had destroyed a total of 53 enemy tanks; even allowing for inevitable exaggeration, this must have accounted for the bulk of the remaining assets of the trapped Soviet forces.[18] These successes were further augmented by the *Hermann Göring* division, which claimed a further 23 tank kills, but the growing threat from the Soviet bridgeheads to the south of Warsaw forced Model to order the withdrawal of the Luftwaffe division; it was to follow 19th Panzer Division across the river and head south. As a consequence, with *SS-Wiking* and *SS-Totenkopf* tied down in defensive fighting to prevent the attacks being made by the rest of Second Tank Army and Forty-Seventh Army, 4th Panzer Division was effectively the only offensive asset left in the counterattack. Throughout 4 August, Betzel's battlegroups moved forward steadily through Radzymin and Wołomin, and the following day they commenced attacks to take up positions between *SS-Wiking* and the Vistula. Despite some initial successes, the level of resistance increased steadily and at about midday 4th Panzer Division ran into a strong *Pakfront*. In a brief fight, the German division lost 11 tanks and the accompanying panzergrenadier battalion suffered 81 casualties. The German reports highlighted the limited artillery support that they received, without which it was impossible to overcome the *Pakfront*, but the counterattack was effectively over. The efficacy of the *Pakfront* was an increasingly common feature of fighting on the Eastern Front; if positioned properly, it proved almost impossible for the Wehrmacht to overcome and the Germans failed to come up with a satisfactory solution, particularly given steadily worsening problems with shortages of artillery ammunition.

Fighting continued to the east of Praga, but at decreasing intensity. By 9 August, 4th Panzer Division claimed to have accounted for the destruction of 111 Red Army tanks and assault guns. The result was the near-complete destruction of III Tank Corps and the mauling of VIII Guards Tank Corps. However, the elimination of the encircled tank corps was far from complete. Some of its men and vehicles managed to escape and it remained on the Soviet order of battle, albeit replenishing behind the front line after handing over its remaining 56 combat vehicles to VIII Guards Tank Corps; Vedeneyev, its commander, remained in post.[19] But many in Germany saw the end of the counteroffensive as another astonishing success for Model: he had restored order to the shattered ranks of Army Group Centre and had brought the Soviet offensive to a halt. There can be no doubt that his energetic use of his armoured formations, especially in the counterattack near Praga, was highly effective; but the reality was that the tide of the Red Army finally came to a halt more as a consequence of its greatly extended supply lines than due to German resistance. The new German front line might be fairly continuous, but it was made up of the remnants of old formations and other units – police battalions, security divisions, improvised battlegroups – that were of highly questionable resilience.

Attention now switched to fighting elsewhere. Betzel's 4th Panzer Division – together with 5th and 7th Panzer Divisions and the *Grossdeutschland* division – would take part in the attempt by the Wehrmacht to restore contact with Army Group North in the operation codenamed *Doppelkopf*. The attack was further augmented by the deployment of 14th and 16th Panzer Divisions, but ultimately failed to break through the Soviet defences to the west of Jelgava; however, contact with Army Group North was restored by a far smaller German group operating to the north of this assault.[20] This failed German operation – and the follow-on operation, *Cesar*, an attempt by the Wehrmacht once more to capture Jelgava – highlighted again the defensive prowess of the Red Army. In rolling countryside crisscrossed by small rivers, the avenues along which German combat formations could move were limited and it was comparatively straightforward for the Red Army to establish strong *Pakfronts* that proved almost impossible to overcome. The days when panzer divisions could seize the initiative with ease were long over.

In Warsaw, the insurgents of the *AK* had mixed success. Their losses were almost always higher than those of the Germans. Both sides showed little hesitation in executing prisoners who fell into their hands, and in addition the

Germans frequently killed large numbers of civilians whom they suspected of having aided the *AK*. On 4 August, with Stahel unable to coordinate the battle from the Saxon Palace, all German units involved in suppressing the uprising were placed under the command of Obergruppenführer Erich von dem Bach-Zelewski; increasingly supported by Luftwaffe units, his men began to drive back the *AK* from parts of the city. On 5 August, the SS units commanded by Gruppenführer Heinz Reinefarth operating in the Wola district of Warsaw, to the west of the old city centre, executed about 35,000 men, women, and children.[21] Reinefarth complained that he lacked the ammunition to kill more, but the death toll increased steadily. The Dirlewanger and Kaminski brigades were operating under Reinefarth's command and showed the same enthusiasm for mass murder that they had previously displayed in so-called anti-partisan operations in Belarus. In the Saxon Palace, Stahel ordered the execution of several Poles who had been captured and were believed to be *AK* members; he also authorised the use of civilians as human shields in the fighting around the palace.

The first outside support for the Warsaw Uprising came in the form of supplies dropped by air. A Polish squadron flying a mixture of Liberator and Halifax bombers parachuted munitions to the *AK* on 4 August after flying to Warsaw from Bari and Brindisi in southern Italy; its efforts were later augmented by aircraft flown by aircrews from South Africa and Britain. These flights continued for many weeks. The total tonnage of supplies delivered is disputed, with a lower estimate of 104 tons and a higher estimate of 240 tons.[22] The British contacted their Soviet counterparts as early as 5 August when the head of the British Military Mission in Moscow followed up on Mikołajczyk's meeting with Stalin to determine what assistance the Soviet Union would provide. Significantly, all Soviet responses described the *AK* as the 'illegal Polish Army in Warsaw', and there was clearly little enthusiasm for any concrete action.[23] Some of the flights carrying supplies to Warsaw from Italy strayed over territory held by the Red Army and even came under fire from Soviet anti-aircraft gunners, and on 22 August Stalin refused permission for aircraft to use Soviet-held airfields.

Under increasing pressure from the Polish government-in-exile, Churchill turned to the Americans for help and telephoned Roosevelt on 25 August. The British leader expressed growing frustration and concern for the outcome of the fighting, with the *AK* under increasing pressure from the German units arrayed against them; he suggested to Roosevelt that the British and Americans should simply mount a major airlift despite ongoing Soviet objections. Roosevelt refused to get involved. He was preoccupied with preparations for the next meeting with

Stalin, which would take place in Yalta, and he didn't want to take any steps that might antagonise the Soviet leader. It wasn't until mid-September that the USAAF joined the airlift after grudging permission had been granted by the Soviet Union for the aircraft to be refuelled at Soviet airfields. This cooperation came to an abrupt halt after the first such mission on 18 September, when the Soviet authorities complained that although about 100 tons of supplies were dropped by the Americans, only 4 per cent fell in areas controlled by the *AK* and that the Americans were therefore aiding the Germans. The true percentage that reached the Poles was rather higher at about 20 per cent, but permission for further operations with refuelling at Soviet airfields was not granted until 30 September. By this stage, the weather had deteriorated to the extent that further drops were impossible, and the situation on the ground had changed irrevocably in favour of the Germans. In the second half of September, Soviet aircraft also began to deliver supplies to Warsaw, but like the air drops carried out by British, American, Polish, and South African planes, most of the supplies fell in German-held areas.

The *AK* forces in Warsaw were hugely outgunned from the outset, but urban warfare is a difficult undertaking in any circumstances and the Germans struggled to assert their numerical and firepower superiority. Nonetheless, the areas held by the *AK* shrank steadily as the fighting raged in the city – one of the South African pilots flying supplies from southern Italy later recalled that the city could easily be seen over a hundred miles away due to the dense pall of smoke from the burning buildings. Realising that their earlier brutal tactics were counterproductive, the Germans began to treat captured *AK* fighters as prisoners of war in the second half of September in order to encourage others to lay down their arms. For the Poles, everything had depended upon the timely arrival of the Red Army – although the *AK* regarded the Soviet Union as at least a potentially hostile power, the reality was that without the help of Soviet forces, victory over the Germans was impossible. Throughout August, the Poles waited in vain for Soviet forces to reach the Warsaw suburbs to the east of the Vistula; perhaps anticipating a similar development, the Germans destroyed the bridges over the river in the city on 13 September, effectively giving up control of all territory to the east. Almost immediately, the First Polish Army – part of Rokossovsky's 1st Belarusian Front – occupied Praga.

Two days later, soldiers of the First Polish Army attempted to cross the Vistula immediately to the south of Warsaw. Two battalions were committed and suffered substantial losses in the face of German defensive fire and both artillery and air support for the attempted crossing was modest and relatively ineffective. A few of the troops succeeded in reaching the west bank where they managed to make contact with the *AK* forces, and established a small bridgehead in anticipation of further crossings. Several such attempts were made in the week that followed, with almost all of the troops being killed or wounded before they could reach the west bank. It seems that this attempt to reach Warsaw was made without the approval of *Stavka* and was largely on the initiative of Berling, commander of First Army; this would account for the lack of air support that his men received. Late on 19 September, the troops that had succeeded in crossing the Vistula were evacuated. At most, about 900 had succeeded in crossing to the west bank and few of them managed to escape.[24] Probably as a result of his unilateral attempt to reach Warsaw, Berling was dismissed from his post and transferred to the War Academy in Moscow.[25] It was the only meaningful attempt made by Soviet or Soviet-controlled ground forces to march to the aid of the *AK*.

For the *AK*, the situation was now hopeless. They had already held negotiations with the Germans in early September, which resulted in some 20,000 civilians being evacuated, but had then suspended talks when they learned of the arrival of the First Polish Army in Praga. Contact was resumed on 28 September with the Germans gaining ground almost everywhere, albeit at considerable cost. Prime Minister Mikołajczyk made a final desperate appeal to Stalin on 30 September:

> After sixty days of relentless fighting against the common enemy, the defenders of Warsaw have reached the limits of human endurance … At this extreme hour of need, I appeal to you, Marshal, to issue orders for immediate operations that would relieve the garrison of Warsaw and result in the liberation of the capital. General Bór-Komorowski has addressed the same appeal to Marshal Rokossovsky.[26]

Stalin made no response. In any case, it was far too late for any meaningful support. On 2 October, the negotiations between the *AK* and the Germans resulted in a surrender document being signed. In return for guarantees that the *AK* forces would be treated as prisoners of war, they laid down their arms. About 15,000 Polish fighters surrendered and were sent to prisoner-of-war camps; an estimated 5,000 slipped away with the intention of resuming their guerrilla war against the forces occupying their country, regardless of whether they were German or Soviet. The civilian population was expelled from the city by the Germans, and although the surrender document had included guarantees of humane treatment, about 90,000 were sent to labour camps across Germany and the occupied territories and up to 60,000 were sent to concentration camps; few of these survived.

With a deserted, devastated Warsaw now firmly in German hands, Himmler was in a position to carry out a longstanding plan: the complete destruction of the city. In mid-October, he addressed a conference of senior SS officers:

> The city must disappear from the surface of the earth and serve only as a transport station for the Wehrmacht. No stone can remain standing. Every building must be razed to its foundation.[27]

For several weeks, demolition squads moved through the shattered city streets, dynamiting buildings and setting ablaze many others. By the end of 1944, an estimated 85 per cent of all buildings had been demolished, including most of the historical monuments and churches. Large areas remained wastelands of rubble into the 1950s. Estimates of casualties in the fighting were vastly varied – western estimates calculated German losses at 2,000 dead, whereas those written on the eastern side of the Iron Curtain after the war put the figure at 17,000. The *AK* lost about 15,000, and the First Polish Army about 5,600. For the *AK*, it was the last attempt to create an impression that it could liberate major urban centres before the arrival of the Red Army. Henceforth, there would be no question of the supremacy of the Red Army in this role, and therefore in Stalin's ability to dictate events after the war.

CHAPTER 14

THE THIRD REICH ON THE BRINK

Shortly before dawn on 13 August, panzergrenadiers from 12th Panzer Division crossed the frontier into East Prussia near Osowiec. The division was being withdrawn to the town of Lyck for some desperately needed rest and replenishment. Since it had arrived in the midst of the crisis developing around Bobruisk, 12th Panzer Division had been in constant combat against numerically superior forces. The frontier post at Osowiec was about 250 miles in a straight line from where the leading battlegroup of the division had linked up with the retreating elements of Ninth Army near Svisloch; inevitably, the constant thrust and counterthrust of the intervening six weeks had resulted in far more miles being covered. The soldiers of the division must have had very mixed feelings. On the one hand, they had survived a long, difficult withdrawal and had prevented the Red Army from isolating and destroying neighbouring units on several occasions; on the other hand, it was still a huge retreat. They had also left large numbers of their comrades on the dozens of battlefields to the east – one panzergrenadier regiment alone recorded that it had lost over 1,300 men killed, wounded, or missing.[1]

In the space of a few months, the strategic picture in Europe had changed completely. At the beginning of 1944, the Germans were still in control of large sections of the Soviet Union and most of Western Europe; as the fighting in Warsaw came to an end, the front lines in the east had reached and crossed the old German frontiers in places and elsewhere the fighting was now in the states that with varying degrees of willingness had sided with Germany against the Soviet Union. In the west, France, Belgium, and parts of the Netherlands had been liberated. If there had been any doubts about the eventual outcome of the war in January, there could be no such uncertainty as the weather turned increasingly cold towards the end of the year. Hitler's last grand strategy had failed, though it would see one last desperate attempt to achieve victory in the west, when an offensive was launched to try to break through the Ardennes region in the winter. Even if what became known as the Battle of the Bulge had actually succeeded in reaching Antwerp, it would have made little difference to the ultimate end of the war.

When plans were drawn up for the summer campaign season, Stalin's priority – as stated at the Tehran Conference – was to launch a major attack that would coincide with the efforts of the Western Allies after they had established a beachhead on the European mainland. The logic was that simultaneous pressure from both east and west would severely limit the ability of Germany to shuffle forces from one front to the other, and would thus facilitate a major success on either or both front lines. Although Stalin and others in Moscow regularly made disparaging remarks about inaction in the west, the bitter fighting that followed D-Day resulted in heavy losses on both sides and ultimately resulted in the breakout that led to the liberation of France and Belgium. To date, there had been no occasion on which the Germans had attempted to transfer additional forces from the Eastern Front to the west – indeed, any troops that could be spared had already been sent to France and Belgium before D-Day. Thereafter, the feared attack on Army Group North Ukraine and the actual attack on Army Group Centre made further transfers impossible. Conversely, it was almost impossible to find troops to send as reinforcements to the east.

But *Bagration* was always intended to be far more than just an operation to pin down German resources. The painful lessons learned at such great cost in preceding operations were put into effect to produce an operation that, in terms of scale, ambition, and achievement, dwarfed anything that the Red Army had attempted before. The results were truly spectacular. At the beginning of the operation, Army Group Centre had a total of 28 divisions or equivalent-sized formations in the front line in Third Panzer Army, Fourth Army, and Ninth Army – 22 infantry divisions, two Luftwaffe field divisions, two panzergrenadier divisions, a reinforced infantry division (78th Sturm Division), and *Korps Abteilung D*. Of these, one panzergrenadier division, five infantry divisions, and *Korps Abteilung D* were still in existence at the end of the Soviet offensive. The rest had all been destroyed. In addition, a further five infantry divisions, a panzer division, a Jäger division, a panzergrenadier division, and three security divisions were badly degraded or completely destroyed after they arrived as reinforcements, and seven more panzer divisions and an infantry division took substantial casualties. No fewer than 22 officers with the rank of major general or higher surrendered during the course of the fighting. The scale of the losses was greater than those suffered by the Germans at Stalingrad. Just as that earlier disaster had been exacerbated by the destruction of German forces in North Africa a few weeks later, the blow dealt by the Red Army in *Bagration* coincided with the huge losses suffered in Normandy and the breakout that followed.

The German defeats in the summer of 1944 were at every level. Tactically, the Wehrmacht was outfought on both fronts; the past assumptions of tactical superiority were no longer as universally true as they might once have been, and in any case the losses of so many experienced personnel over the long years of the war had taken a heavy toll. Operationally, the Germans could achieve little, with their enemies largely dictating the course of events. The few moments of success, like Model's counterattack to the east of Moscow, were only possible in very specific circumstances where the Red Army was at the end of its logistic leash. And strategically, Hitler's last hope was gone. In the west, the intention to crush the landings on the beaches failed completely, and the intention to adopt an obdurate defence in the east also failed. Indeed, attempts to conduct such a stubborn defence added considerably to the scale of German losses.

Estimates of total numbers of dead, wounded, and prisoners in the fighting in the east vary considerably. The lowest figure for German casualties suffered in *Bagration* is 375,000; the highest is 540,000.[2] About 150,000 prisoners were taken. This represents between 44 and 64 per cent of German manpower committed to the sector. In the west, the Battle of Normandy ended with the Germans losing most of the equipment that had been carefully built up in preparation for repelling the invasion. Estimates of human losses vary, ranging from a minimum of about 290,000 to a maximum of 530,000.[3] With a total of 640,000 men committed by Germany, this amounts to losses of at least 45 per cent. During the summer, therefore, the Germans lost between 501,000 and 1.07 million men on the two fronts. Even the lower figure represented a mortal wound from which the German military machine could not recover. German military industrial production would peak in September 1944, but even if the equipment lost on the two fronts could be replaced and new manpower resources could be found, the loss of so many experienced infantry, gunners, tank crews, aircrews, etc. would result in a considerable reduction in overall capability. Thousands of men who had previously been excused military service on medical grounds were mobilised, often grouped together on the basis of their medical ailments. One such was 70th Infantry Division, known unofficially in the army as the *Magendivision* ('Stomach Division') or *Weissbrotdivision* ('White Bread Division') – the intention was that by having these men in a single formation, they could be provided with whatever specialist diets they needed. But even the most imaginative use of such measures could not compensate for the losses suffered in the summer of 1944. All prospect of victory was gone.

The Western Allies suffered heavy losses in the Battle of Normandy. About 226,000 men were killed, wounded, or missing, but this was dwarfed by the Soviet losses during *Bagration*. The Red Army started the operation with about 1.7 million men. At the end of the campaign, losses came to about 771,000 killed, wounded, sick, or missing.[4] This represents 45 per cent of the troops originally committed, but the true proportion is probably somewhat lower after the arrival of replacement drafts and reserve formations is taken into account. The bludgeoning approach that the Soviet Union had taken to the war might have evolved to a new level of efficacy, but it remained a costly way of waging war. By comparison, the losses suffered by the Western Allies in Normandy were about 11 per cent of all the manpower that was committed. The ratio of losses suffered to losses inflicted was also markedly different between east and west. For every casualty suffered by the Western Allies in Normandy, the Germans lost between 1.3 and 2.3 men. By contrast, for every Soviet casualty in *Bagration* and the follow-on operations, the Germans lost between 0.49 and 0.7 men. To put it another way: the Germans lost between 1.3 and 2.3 men for every man lost by the Western Allies and were defeated in France, but the Red Army lost between 1.4 and 2.1 men for every man lost by the Germans, but still triumphed. Clearly, total casualties are not a complete explanation for victory and defeat.

Comparison of the two front lines helps highlight the fundamental differences between the armies of the Western Allies and those of the Soviet Union, and to a large extent these differences also reflect the differences between the two societies. The Soviet Union was born out of the chaotic collapse of Tsarist Russia, with levels of illiteracy and poverty that were far worse than in any western nation. In many respects, the Soviet state made hugely impressive progress in the 1920s and 1930s, but this was matched by a rigid political system and a climate of fear and repression. At a time when the complexity of warfare was increasing rapidly, the ability of lower level commanders to make judgements and decisions without waiting for orders was vital if an army was to function efficiently. The fear of the Stalin purges effectively killed any such ability in the Red Army and indeed in Soviet society as a whole. Consequently, even when the tight control imposed by Stalin was progressively relaxed as the war continued, many of those in positions of command were ill-equipped to take advantage of the new circumstances.

In Normandy and during *Bagration*, the armies attacking the Germans had to learn how to unlock German defensive positions. In both cases, this proved to be a tough task and the Battle of Normandy was marked by a long attritional phase, during which American, British, and Canadian troops gnawed through the German lines and then ultimately broke out and advanced rapidly. By contrast, the breakthrough phase during *Bagration* was far shorter. The German lines were effectively breached in the first day or two of the operation and there were then two phases. In the first, the Red Army disrupted German attempts to rebuild the front line and in the process destroyed many of the divisions driven back from their initial fortified positions; in the second post-breakthrough phase, the Soviet forces pressed deep into enemy-held territory, making the most of the destruction they had already wreaked on the Wehrmacht. Such a rapid breakthrough was impossible in the west largely because huge quantities of men, equipment, and supplies had to be taken across the English Channel, whereas the Red Army started its operation with its resources already deployed right next to the German positions. But while this may explain the differing timescales for breaking through the German lines, it doesn't address the great discrepancy in casualties. This was more a reflection of very different attitudes to the expendability of manpower and the level of technical ability that was available – regardless of its numerical strength, Soviet military aviation failed to provide the level of air support that was seen over Normandy, for example.

The level of coordination between the various Fronts involved in *Bagration* was far higher than had been seen in previous operations. Clearly, lessons had been learned at every level, but the ability of senior officers – Zhukov and perhaps more effectively Vasilevsky and Shtemenko – to intervene and coordinate the Fronts was also markedly improved. The level of equipment and the provision of ammunition and other supplies in the Red Army in the summer of 1944 were also greatly improved. Many Soviet-era accounts place emphasis on improved training but this is an area where there may have been considerable progress but there remained considerable deficiencies in comparison with the Wehrmacht and the armies of the Western Allies. However much the Red Army had improved in its performance, it still fell short of the capabilities of other forces.

In order to make up for that deficiency, the Soviet forces had to resort to two traditional remedies. The first was sheer weight of numbers. Whilst the 'Russian steamroller' has become something of a historical cliché, there can be no doubt that without such a great numerical advantage, the Soviet Union's forces would not have been able to prevail if they had been forced to use tactics resulting in such appalling casualties. The second remedy was the use of artillery. The weight of firepower used in initial bombardments grew hugely in the course of the First World War and again in the Second World War, but it wasn't just the use of larger numbers of guns that led to the Red Army's successes in 1944 and 1945. The use of artillery became more sophisticated, with greater emphasis on reconnaissance to identify German positions as comprehensively as possible so that they could be destroyed, and improvements in the ability of artillery observers to correct the aim of the gunners. Compared to the Wehrmacht or the armies of the Western Allies, the Red Army still had limited ability for its artillery to provide swift support if an attacking force ran into unexpected defences, but the increased use of assault guns – particularly the heavyweight ISU-152 – compensated a great deal for this.

In previous battles, Army Group Centre was driven back steadily towards the west but avoided wholesale defeat. To a large extent, this was because the Soviet offensives of 1943 and early 1944 failed to break through the German defensive lines quickly; by the time the German lines were breached, the attacking forces had suffered such heavy losses that any formations intended for exploitation had already been committed to assist the breakthrough. By contrast, the initial assault during *Bagration* broke the German defensive line very rapidly without second echelon units having to be committed. Consequently, those units were then able to exploit the breakthrough with considerable success. Several factors contributed to this. Firstly, Army Group Centre had fought successful defensive battles in the past with far more reserves available, particularly panzer divisions. Secondly, the Luftwaffe was able to provide far more air support. Neither of these were available to assist the German ground forces in the summer of 1944 – both aerial and armoured assets had been diverted away to other sectors.

Writing in the 19th century, Helmuth von Moltke – the chief of the Prussian and then German general staff – wrote one of the most widely quoted dictums of warfare: 'No plan of operations extends with any certainty beyond the first encounter with the enemy's main forces.'[5] As *Bagration* unfolded, *Stavka* showed that it had learned from earlier failures when there had been a tendency to continue trying to impose an original set of plans in the face of unexpected difficulties. In particular, the adjustment of the axes of advance of the various Fronts to allow Bagramian's 1st Baltic Front to provide better protection against any threat from the north and the redeployment of Rotmistrov's Fifth Guards Tank Army showed far more flexibility than in the past. In the case of the tank army, this undoubtedly contributed to the disappointing performance of Rotmistrov's formations, but persisting with the original plan would have resulted in wasteful casualties for little benefit. By contrast, Busch was so heavily constrained by Hitler that he had no option but to persist in attempting to impose a plan of operations that he knew was unachievable.

The German plan of operations was doomed from the outset. The erroneous assumption about where the Red Army would attack – reinforced deliberately by Soviet *Maskirovka* – resulted in nearly all of the panzer divisions on the Eastern Front being deployed to the south of the Polesie region. Army Group Centre lacked the reserves to resist anything more than a modest local assault, and almost every decision made by Hitler before the battles of the summer compounded the problems. The failure to withdraw to a shorter line and the misplaced confidence in 'fortresses' to break up a Soviet offensive left the Wehrmacht holding exposed positions, practically inviting the Red Army to strike. Denied the ability to fight a manoeuvre battle, the Wehrmacht had to rely on static defence. Although the front-line fortifications were often formidable, the Red Army had learned how to unpick them.

At an operational level, therefore, the Soviet plans for *Bagration* were thorough and were implemented flexibly. German plans were inadequate and far too rigid. At a tactical level too, the Red Army demonstrated its considerable improvements. The encirclement of part of Third Panzer Army in Vitebsk was achieved largely by rifle divisions, though these now had integrated armoured assets to provide assistance to the infantrymen. Further south, the Bobruisk encirclement saw close and effective cooperation between Soviet rifle and tank formations. The former encirclement was in many respects far easier as Vitebsk lay in a dangerously exposed salient, whereas the latter encirclement required penetrations on either side of Bobruisk in order to create the preconditions necessary for encirclement. In all cases, Soviet units were able to destroy encircled German units rapidly, preventing the repetition of the problems seen in the Stalingrad and Cherkassy encirclements. This successful liquidation was achieved by rapid attacks to disrupt the isolated German units, which were harassed from the air and by ground units. Partisans too played an important role both in attacking retreating German formations and guiding Soviet units through difficult terrain.

At a strategic level, *Bagration* delivered all that Stalin could have expected. In November 1944, he described the achievements of the Red Army in a speech:

> The Red Army utterly defeated German forces at Vitebsk, Bobruisk, and Mogilev, and completed its blow by encircling 30 German divisions at Minsk. As a result of this blow, our forces completely liberated the Belarusian Soviet Republic; reached the Vistula and liberated a considerable part of our ally Poland; reached the Niemen and liberated a large part of the Lithuanian Soviet Republic; and forced the Niemen and approached Germany's borders.[6]

The reference to 30 divisions encircled at Minsk is of course a considerable exaggeration, but the scale of the military defeat inflicted upon Germany was clear for all to see. The political significance of the victory was also clear. Stalin may have been more than a little disingenuous in referring to Poland as an 'ally', particularly given how the Red Army treated members of the *AK*, but by describing Lithuania as a 'Soviet republic', he was making a clear statement that he had no intention of permitting a restoration of the 1939 frontiers. The Baltic States were to be part of the Soviet Union, regardless of the views of the Western

Allies, and Stalin's intention to ensure that the Red Army was in physical possession of the region had largely been fulfilled.

Nevertheless, there were areas where the performance of the Red Army fell short of what might have been expected or achieved. The lacklustre performance of Fifth Guards Tank Army has been described on several occasions, and the manner in which this large, powerful formation fought a series of grinding battles – at a time when the German lines were in shreds and there were gaps everywhere through which a more energetic commander might have pushed forward decisively – was disappointing. There was also at least one significant planning flaw. Bagramian's concerns about the importance of Polotsk proved to be accurate: the city became the point from which the German Army Group North was expected to mount its attacks towards the south. It is possible that Fourth Shock Army might have been used to attack the city at an earlier stage to tie down German forces, but the sheer scale of *Bagration* was such that this might have proved logistically impossible. The fact that these blemishes made little difference to the outcome of the campaign shows just what a great victory was achieved by the Red Army.

One of the controversies that arose after *Bagration* was the tragedy of the Warsaw Uprising. Many Poles who were opposed to the Soviet Union felt that the Red Army could and should have done more to assist the uprising; its success or failure ultimately depended upon external help. It is worth considering this question further. Could the Red Army have done more to help the Poles?

Zhukov and Rokossovsky travelled to Moscow for a meeting with Stalin on 1 August. According to Zhukov, Stalin was in an agitated state and repeatedly asked whether it was possible for the Red Army to advance further and to capture Warsaw. The two commanders demurred, saying that their troops were utterly exhausted, their ranks depleted. Beriya, Molotov, and Malenkov were all present; the former two pressured Rokossovsky and Zhukov to advance further but Malenkov sided with the professional soldiers. Zhukov later speculated on Stalin's motives for this exchange; he was unconvinced that Stalin genuinely wanted to risk further heavy casualties in order to come to the aid of the *AK*, but needed to be able to respond to any criticism from Churchill and Roosevelt by demonstrating that he had attempted to persuade his generals to push on to the Polish capital.[7] Clearly, it was in Stalin's interests for the Germans and the pro-western *AK* to inflict as much damage on each other as they possibly could. It seems unlikely that the Soviet leader, who had ordered the mass murder of Polish officers in the Katyn forest in order to eliminate those who might oppose the Soviet Union, had any genuine motivation to come to the aid of those that he had already declared to be enemies.

If the political will to intervene had existed, could the Red Army have done more? The casualties suffered by the various Fronts in their drive to the Vistula were shockingly high and several accounts describe the soldiers as being exhausted and short of supplies. Rokossovsky later wrote:

> Certain carping critics in the Western press did at one time charge 1st Belarusian Front and of course me as its commander with deliberately failing to support the Warsaw insurgents, thereby condemning them to death and destruction. But the Belarusian campaign had been without parallel in scope and depth. On the Front's right wing [i.e. north of the Polesie region] the advance had exceeded 600km. Fighting all the way, our forces had strained to the utmost to carry out the tasks set by *Stavka*. Warsaw, however, could have been liberated only in a new major offensive operation – which was launched later on. In August 1944 many important measures would have had to be taken to capture Warsaw, even if only as a large bridgehead.
>
> The fact of the matter is that those who had instigated the people of Warsaw to rise had no intention of joining forces with the approaching Soviet and Polish armies. On the contrary, they had feared this … For them the uprising had been a political move with the objective of assuming power in the Polish capital before the Soviet troops entered it. These had been their orders from the people in London …
>
> To be sure, Warsaw was close, but we were engaged in heavy fighting on the approaches to Praga. But every step cost a tremendous effort.[8]

Rokossovsky's description of the operational reality on the ground is correct. His troops were undoubtedly at the end of their strength and a major assault across a large river would have to wait until reinforcements and supplies had brought their formations back to strength. Nevertheless, the Soviet forces to the east of the Vistula could undoubtedly have done more to help the *AK*. Warsaw was within artillery range of the Red Army and Soviet aviation could have intervened at least to prevent the Luftwaffe from providing close air support to the suppression of the uprising. Had the insurgents been pro-Soviet partisans, surely these steps – and probably far more – would have been attempted.

The suppression of the uprising was brutal in the extreme and many of those involved were later brought to justice. Stahel survived his siege in the Saxon Palace and was sent to Bucharest in the last week of August, and he was ordered to seize control of the city before the Romanians could abandon its alliance with Germany. His troops were repulsed by the Romanians and in September he was captured by the Red Army. He was charged with war crimes, including the executions of unarmed civilians in Warsaw and their use as human shields; he died in Soviet captivity. Dirlewanger, whose murderous brigade was responsible for the slaughter of tens of thousands of Belarusian civilians as well as being involved in mass killings in Warsaw, attempted to slip back into civilian life at the end of the war but was arrested by the French near the town of Altshausen. He was living under a false name, but a Jewish former concentration camp prisoner recognised him. He died shortly after in the prison camp, officially as a result of heart disease, but other accounts suggest that the French handed him over to a group of Polish soldiers who beat him to death. Kaminski's SS brigade was also involved in widespread atrocities in Warsaw, and his command rapidly disintegrated as it concentrated almost exclusively on killing and looting. Himmler had him arrested and charged with stealing Reich property – he was meant to hand over all loot to Himmler. He was executed in late August 1944. Both Dirlewanger and Kaminski were operating as part of the group commanded by Reinefarth, who surrendered to British troops in north Germany at the end of the war. The Polish government later demanded his extradition and although he was arrested by German authorities, he was then released on the grounds that genocide had not been part of the German criminal code when he was involved in such crimes. He went on to become a prominent politician; although Poland repeatedly demanded his extradition, this was refused. He died in 1979 at the end of a life of considerable affluence.

Erich von dem Bach-Zelewski, who took command of the suppression of the Warsaw rising after Stahel was unable to continue controlling German forces, was arrested by US forces after the end of the war. Despite being involved in a large number of atrocities across the Soviet Union and Poland, he escaped being charged in return for cooperation with prosecutors at Nuremberg, but in 1951 he was convicted of involvement in the murder of political opponents of the Nazis in the 1930s. He was convicted of other similar offences in 1961 and died in prison in 1972 without ever facing prosecution for his war crimes.

As the weather deteriorated in the last months of 1944, the Red Army's depleted formations were brought back to strength in preparation for fresh operations. In some sectors, there was no pause – Soviet troops pressed into Hungary, reaching and besieging Budapest on 24 December. There was further fighting in the Baltic region, with the German Army Group North once more cut off from the Reich, this time by a successful thrust by Bagramian to the Baltic coast either side of the city of Klaipėda or Memel as it was known to the Germans. This was followed by repeated attacks against the isolated German forces in the Courland peninsula to the west of Riga. But the armies that had smashed the German Army Group Centre spent the winter resting and replenishing.

They had inflicted a huge defeat on the Germans, and were now in position for the final advances that would carry them first to the Oder River, and then to Berlin. At the same time, the armies of the Western Allies spent much of the winter securing the areas they had overrun before facing the last major offensive mounted by the Wehrmacht in the Battle of the Bulge. But despite this momentary scare, there could be no doubt that the double blow dealt to Germany in the summer – in the Battle of Normandy in the west and *Bagration* in the east – had brought Hitler's regime to its knees. Germany's industrial resources were close to exhaustion; fuel shortages, a constant problem for the military, were now catastrophic after the loss of the Romanian oilfields; Germany's cities were in ruins; and its armies were shadows of their former selves. There had perhaps been a brief moment in late July when the decapitation of the Nazi regime might have brought the war to a swift end, but that opportunity was gone almost before it appeared. The full horror and destruction of land warfare would now be visited upon the German heartland.

NOTES

INTRODUCTION: TEHRAN

1   W. Churchill, Radio broadcast on the Soviet-German War, 22 June 1941, available at https://www.jewishvirtuallibrary.org/churchill-broadcast-on-the-soviet-german-war-june-1941

2   For an account of British naval operations against Bolshevik Russia in the Baltic region, see G. Bennett, *Cowan's War* (Collins, London, 1964)

3   *Great Soviet Encyclopedia* (MacMillan, New York, 1980, 30 volumes), Vol. V, pp.220–21

4   *Sovetskaya Rossiya* (Moscow, 1941) 1/8/41, p.1

5   B. Haugen, *Joseph Stalin: Dictator of the Soviet Union* (Compass Point, Minneapolis MN, 2006), p.10

6   R. Edmonds, *The Big Three: Churchill, Roosevelt and Stalin in Peace and War* (Hamish Hamilton, London, 1992), p.242

7   S. Sebag Montefiore, *Stalin: The Court of the Red Tsar* (Weidenfeld & Nicholson, London, 2003), p.417

8   For an account of the winter fighting around Stalingrad, see P. Buttar, *On A Knife's Edge: The Ukraine, November 1942–March 1943* (Osprey, Oxford, 2018)

9   For a full discussion, see V. Mastny, 'Stalin and the Prospects of a Separate Peace in World War 2' in *American Historical Review* (University of Chicago Press, 1972), Vol. 77, pp.1365–88

10 Edmonds, *The Big Three*, p.321

11 M. Gilbert, *The Road to Victory: Winston S. Churchill, 1941–1945* (Heinemann, London, 1986), p.430

12 Ibid., p.431

13 L. Havas, *Hitler's Plot to Kill The Big Three* (Bantam, London, 1977)

14 P. Buttar, *Russia's Last Gasp: The Eastern Front 1916–17* (Osprey, Oxford, 2016), pp.82–117

15 E. Roosevelt, *As He Saw It* (Duell, Sloan and Pearce, New York, 1946), p.37; D. Reynolds, *In Command of History: Churchill Fighting and Writing the Second World War* (Penguin, Harmondsworth, 2005), p.54

CHAPTER 1: FRITZ AND IVAN: THE STATE OF THE ARMIES OF THE EASTERN FRONT

1   A. Beevor, *D-Day: The Battle for Normandy* (Viking, London, 2009), pp.76–99

2   B. Carruthers, *Hitler's Wartime Orders: The Complete Führer Directives 1939–1945* (Pen & Sword, Barnsley, 2018), pp.102–03

3   Ibid., p.144

4   P. Buttar, *The Reckoning: The Defeat of Army Group South, 1944* (Osprey, Oxford, 2020), pp.73–170

5   K.H. Frieser, K. Schmider, K. Schönherr, G. Schreiber, K. Ungváry, and B. Wegner, *Das Deutsche Reich und der Zweite Weltkrieg* (Deutsche Verlags-Anstalt, Munich, 1990–2017, 10 volumes), Vol. VIII *Der Krieg im Osten und an dem Nebenfronten*, p.154; G. Krivosheyev, *Soviet Casualties and Combat Losses in the Twentieth Century* (Greenhill, London, 1997), p.133

6   E. von Butlar (ed.), *Mirovaya Voina: Sbornik Statei* (Izdatelstvo Inostrannoy Literatury, Moscow, 1957), pp.216–17

7   E. Ziemke, *Stalingrad to Berlin: The German Defeat in the East* (Dorset, New York, 1986), p.312

8   Interview with V. Kharin, available at iremember.ru/memoirs/artilleristi/kharin-vasiliy-georgievich/

9   J. Dugan and C. Stewart, *Ploesti: The Great Ground-Air Battle of 1 August 1943* (Brassey's, London, 2002)

10 Pamphlet 248, *Rise and Fall of the German Air Force* (Air Ministry, London, 1948), p.349

11 I. Beer, *Adolf Hitler: A Biography* (Vij, New Delhi, 2016), p.35

12 H. Thöle, *Befehl des Gewissens: Charkow Winter 1943* (Munin, Osnabück, 1976), p.332

13 S. Shtemenko, *The Soviet General Staff At War 1941–1945* (Progress, Moscow, 1970), p.224

14 For more information on Belarusian nationalism, see G. Ioffe, 'Understanding Belarus: Belarusian Identity' in *Europe-Asia Studies* (University of Glasgow, 2003), Vol. 55 No. 8, pp.1241–72

15 P. Adair, *Hitler's Greatest Defeat: The Collapse of Army Group Centre, June 1944* (Cassell, London, 1994), p.62

16 K.-M. Mallmann and G. Paul (eds), *Karrieren der Gewalt. Nationalsozialistische Täterbiographien* (Wissenschaftliche Buchgesellschaft, Darmstadt, 2004), p.102

17 S. Lazarev, 'Repressii Protyv Komandnogo I Prepodavatelskogo Sostava v Voyennoy Akademii Mekhanizatsii I Motorizatsii vo Vtoroy Polovine 1930-kh Godov' in *Voyenno-Istoricheskiy Zhurnal* (Ministerstva Oborony SSSR, Moscow, 2017) No. 3, p.63

18 K. Rokossovsky, *A Soldier's Duty* (Spantech & Lancer, Godstone, 1992), p.5

CHAPTER 2: THE FRONT BEHIND THE FRONT: PARTISANS IN BELARUS

1   M. Bich and H. Pashkou (eds), *Encyklapiedyja Historyi Bielarusi* (Belaruska Entsyklapedyi Petrusi Brouki, Minsk, 1993–2003, 7 volumes), Vol. 5, p.413

2   V. Kvachkov, *Spetsnaz Rossii* (Russkaya Panorama, Moscow, 2007), p.206

3   V. Kovalchuk (ed.), *V Tylu Vraga Borba Partizan I Podpolshchivkov na Okkupirovannoy Territorii Oblasti* (Lenizdat, Leningrad, 1979), pp.27–28

4   A. Popov, *NKVD I Partizanskoye Dvizheniye* (Olma, Moscow, 2003), pp.47–53

5   A. Adamovich, *V Partisanach* (TD Algorithm, Moscow, 2018), p.102

6   Ibid., p.103

7   B. Shumilin (ed.), *Istoriya Partizanskogo Dvizeniya Rossiyskoy Federatsii v Gody Velikoy Otechestvennoiy Voiny 1941–1945* (Izdat Atlantida-XXI vek, Moscow, 2001), p.15

8   M. Cüppers, *Wegbereiter der Schoah. Die Waffen-SS, der Kommandostab Reichsführer-SS und die Judenvernichtung 1939–1945* (Wissentschaftliche Buchgesellschaft, Darmstadt, 2005), p.203

9   International Military Tribunal, *Nazi Conspiracy and Aggression* (United States Government Printing Office, Washington DC, 1946, 11 volumes), Vol. VIII, pp.961–63

10 B. Musiał, *Sowjetische Partisanen in Weissrussland: Innenansichten aus dem Gebiet Baranoviči 1941–1944: Eine Dokumentation* (Oldenbourg, Munich, 2013), p.13

11 Yad Vashem Archive, Jerusalem TR-10/823; C. Browning, *Ordinary Men: Reserve Police Battalion 101 and the Final Solution in Poland* (Harper Collins, London, 2017), p.12

12 Adamovich, *V Partisanach*, pp.40–44

13 B. Łojek, *Muzeum Katyńskie w Warszawie* (Polska Fundacja Katyńska, Warsaw, 2001), p.174

14 R. Overy, *Russia's War* (Penguin, Harmondsworth, 2010), p.53; Sebag Montefiore, *The Court of the Red Tsar*, p.341

15 R. Brackman, *The Secret File of Joseph Stalin: A Hidden Life* (Routledge, Milton, 2001), p.358

16 Musiał, *Sowjetische Partisanen in Weissrussland*, pp.84–86, 134

17 Ibid., p.225

18 *Nacionalnye Archiv Respubliki Belarus*, f. 1329, op. 1, d. 8, II., pp.1–15

19 M. Gnatowski, 'Dokumenty o Stosunku Radzieckiego Kierownictwa do Polskiej Konspiracji Niepodległościowej na północno-wschodnich Kresach Rzecypospolitej w Latach 1943–1944' in *Studia Podladskie* (Białystok University, 1995), Vol. V, p.243

20 B. Chiari (ed.), *Die Polnische Heimatarmee: Geschichte und Mythos der Armia Krajowa seit dem Zweiten Weltkrieg* (de Gruyter, Munich, 2003), p.571

21   Musiał, *Sowjetische Partisanen in Weissrussland*, pp.49–52

22   Ibid., pp.54–55

23   Y. Arad, *Oni Srazhalis za Rodinu: Evrei Sovetskogo Soyuza v elikoi Otechestvennoi Voine* (Mosty Kultury, Moscow, 2011), p.288

24   Ibid., p.301

25   Ibid., pp.302–03

26   *Bundesarchiv-Militärarchiv*, Freiburg, *Anlage 492 z.KTB 2, 12/08/1941* 16748/10, RH 26–221

27   P. Buttar, *Meat Grinder: The Battles for the Rzhev Salient, 1942–43* (Osprey, Oxford, 2022), pp.133–52

28   Ziemke, *Stalingrad to Berlin*, p.309

29   E. Howell, *The Soviet Partisan Movement 1941–1944* (Department of the Army, Washington DC, 1956), pp.198–200

30   Musiał, *Sowjetische Partisanen in Weissrussland*, pp.106–07

31   P. Longerich, *Heinrich Himmler: A Life* (Oxford University Press, Oxford, 2011), p.372

32   S. Kudriashov (ed.), *Partizanskoe Dvizhenie v gody Velikoi Otechestvennoi Voiny* (Izdatelstvo Istoricheskaia Literatura, Moscow, 2015), p.307

33   *Nacionalnye Archiv Respubliki Belarus*, f. 370, op. 1, d. 1880, II., pp.104–12

34   Musiał, *Sowjetische Partisanen in Weissrussland*, pp.113–14

35   Ibid., p.115

36   Ibid.

37   *Archiwum Akt Nowich*, Warsaw, MF 423, Bl.57

38   Musiał, *Sowjetische Partisanen in Weissrussland*, p.152

39   *Nacionalnye Archiv Respubliki Belarus*, f. 1329, op. 1, d. 35, II, pp.2–7

40   Musiał, *Sowjetische Partisanen in Weissrussland*, pp.156–57

41   Ibid., p.161

42   Ibid., pp.173–77

43   *Nacionalnye Archiv Respubliki Belarus*, f. 1329, op. 1, d. 28, I, p.117

44   M. Gilbert, *The Holocaust: A History of the Jews of Europe During the Second World War* (Holt, New York, 1987), p.297

45   H. Sakaida, *Heroines of the Soviet Union 1941–1945* (Bloomsbury, London, 2012), p.58

CHAPTER 3: PREPARING THE BLOW

1   D. Stahel, *Retreat from Moscow: A New History of Germany's Winter Campaign, 1941–1942* (Picador, New York, 2019), p.24

2   Interview with S. Vinopol, available at iremember.ru/memoirs/minometchiki/v inopol-semen-moiseevich/

3   Interview with N. Safonov, available at iremember.ru/memoirs/pekhonintsi/sa fonov-nikolay-ivanovich/

4   A. Solyankin, M. Pavlov and J. Zheltov, *Otechestvennyye Bronirovannyye Mashini XX Vek* (Eksprint, Moscow, 2005, 4 volumes), Vol. II, p.291

5   S. Zaloga and J. Ness, *Red Army Handbook* (Sutton, Stroud, 1998), pp.200–04

6   Ibid., p.181

7   A. Weeks, *Russia's Life Saver: Lend-Lease Aid to the USSR in World War II* (Lexington, Plymouth, 2010), p.142

8   Krivosheyev, *Soviet Casualties*, pp.85–97

9   K. Galitsky, *Gody Surovykh Ispytaniy 1941–1944* (Nauka, Moscow, 1973), p.430

10   Ibid., pp.430–31

11   Ibid., pp.448–52

12   V. Boiko, *S Dumoy o Rodine* (Voyenizdat, Moscow, 1982), pp.159–160

13   V. Repin, *Bez Prava na Oshibku* (Voyenizdat, Moscow, 1978), pp.79–80

14   Adair, *Hitler's Greatest Defeat*, p.56

15   Weeks, *Russia's Life Saver*, p.145

16   Adair, *Hitler's Greatest Defeat*, p.60

17   D. Glantz and H. Orenstein (eds and trans), *Belorussia 1944: The Soviet General Staff Study* (Frank Cass, London, 2001), pp.29–64

18   For details of the operational plans of the four Soviet Fronts, see Glantz and Orenstein, *Belorussia 1944*, pp.14–28

19   I. Bagramian, *So Schritten Wir zum Sieg* (Militärverlag der Deutschen Demokratischen Republik, Berlin, 1984), p.251

20   Shtemenko, *The Soviet General Staff At War*, p.242

21   Ibid., p.243

22   Ibid., pp.244–45

23   Rokossovsky, *A Soldier's Duty*, pp.237–38

24   K. Rokossovsky, 'Dva Glavnikh Udara' in *Voyenno-Istoricheskiy Zhurnal* (Ministerstva Oborony SSSR, Moscow, 1954), No. 6, p.14

25   Sebag Montefiore, *The Court of the Red Tsar*, pp.483–84; J. Erickson, *The Road to Berlin* (Yale University Press, New Haven CT, 1999), pp.199–231

26   See for example S. Bialer, *Stalin and his Generals* (Westview, Boulder CO, 1984), pp.460–61; K. Malanin (ed.), *Polki Idut na Zapad: Vospominanii Ocherki Ob Osvobozhdenii Belorussyii ot Fashistskich Okkupantor* (Voyenizdat, Moscow, 1964), pp.238–41

27   A. Isaev, *Operatsiya 'Bagration': Stalinskii Blitskrig v Belorussii* (Eksmo, Moscow, 2014), pp.166–75

28   K. Telegin, *Voyny Neschitannye Vorsty* (Voyenizdat, Moscow, 1988), pp.310–11

29   I. Pliev, *Pod Gvardeyskim Znamenem Ordzhonikidze* (IR, Ordzhonikidze, 1976), p.251

30   P. Belov, *Za Nami Moskva* (Voyenizdat, Moscow, 1963), p.182

31   P. Batov, *Von der Wolga zur Oder* (Deutscher Militärverlag, Berlin, 1965), pp.297–98

32   A. Vasilevsky, *A Lifelong Cause* (Progress, Moscow, 1973), p.356

33   Shtemenko, *The Soviet General Staff At War*, p.237

34   Frieser et al., *Das Deutsche Reich*, p.534

CHAPTER 4: WAITING FOR THE HAMMER TO FALL

1   For an overview of *Bodyguard* and *Fortitude*, see M. Barbier, *D-Day Deception: Operation Fortitude and the Normandy Invasion* (Greenwood, Westport CT, 2007); R. Hesketh, *Fortitude: The D-Day Deception Campaign* (Overlook, New York, 2000)

2   H. Höhne and H. Zolling, *The General Was a Spy: The Truth About General Gehlen and his Spy Ring* (Coward, McCann & Geoghegan, New York, 1972), p.13

3   H. Gackenholz, *Der Zusammenbruch der Heeresgruppe Mitte* (Bernard & Graefe, Frankfurt am Main, 1960), p.449

4   *Bundesarchiv-Militärarchiv*, Freiburg, *GenStdH 1428/44, Zusammenfassende Beurteilung der Feindlage vor der deutschen Ostfront im Grossen, 3//5/44*, RH-2 H.3/185

5   Ziemke, *Stalingrad to Berlin*, pp.265–66

6   G. Niepold, *Mittlere Ostfront Juni 1944* (Mittler & Sohn, Herford, 1985), pp.16–17

7   S. Platonov (ed.), *Operatsii Sovetskikh Vooruzhennykh sil v Velikoi Otechestvennoi Voine 1941–1945* (Voyenizdat, Moscow 1959, 4 volumes), Vol. III, p.285

8   O. Heidkämper, *Vitebsk: The Fight and Destruction of the Third Panzer Army* (Casemate, Oxford, 2017), pp.115–16

9   Adair, *Hitler's Greatest Defeat*, pp.91–92

10   A. Speer, *Inside the Third Reich* (Weidenfeld & Nicholson, London, 1995), pp.430–31

11   Niepold, *Mittlere Ostfront Juni 1944*, p.63

12   A. Price, *The Last Year of the Luftwaffe* (Pen & Sword, Barnsley, 2015), p.14

13   Niepold, *Mittlere Ostfront Juni 1944*, p.22

14 Adair, *Hitler's Greatest Defeat*, p.66

15 Niepold, *Mittlere Ostfront Juni 1944*, p.22

16 R. Hinze, *Bug, Moskwa, Beresina. Der Weg Eines Bespannten Artillerie-Regiments im 2. Weltkrieg bis zum Zusammenbruch der Heeresgruppe Mitte* (self-published, 1978), p.521

17 *Bundesarchiv-Militärarchiv*, Freiburg, *Heeresgruppe Mitte Ia Kriegstagebuch 14/6/44*, RH-19/II

18 Ziemke, *Stalingrad to Berlin*, p.315

19 Howell, *The Soviet Partisan Movement 1941–1944*, p.195

20 Isaev, *Operatsiya 'Bagration'*, p.179

21 Niepold, *Mittlere Ostfront Juni 1944*, pp.28–29

22 Howell, *The Soviet Partisan Movement 1941–1944*, p.202

23 Niepold, *Mittlere Ostfront Juni 1944*, pp.35–36

24 Frieser et al., *Das Deutsche Reich*, pp.531–34

25 A. Fisitov, *Geroicheskaya Istoria: 70 Strelkovoi Verkhneorovskoi Ordena Suvorova II Stepenyi Divizii (Vtorogo Formyrovnaya)* (Nauka, Moscow, 2013, 4 volumes), Vol. III, p.160

26 J. Neumann, *Die 4. Panzer-Division. Bericht und Betrachtung* (self-published, 1989, 2 volumes), Vol. II, pp.361–62

27 H. Schäufler, *So Lebten und so Starben Sie: Das Buch vom Panzerregiment-35* (Kameradscaft ehemaliger Panzer-Regiment 35 e.V, Bamberg, 1983), p.222

28 A.D. von Plato, *Die Geschichte der 5. Panzer-Division 1938 bis 1945* (Walhalla und Praetoria Verlag, Regensburg, 1978), p.338

29 G. Niepold, *Von Minsk bis Lyck: Die 12. Panzerdivision in den Rückzugsgefechten im Sommer 1944* (self-published, 1979), pp.4–6

CHAPTER 5: A FATEFUL ANNIVERSARY: 22–24 JUNE

1 Bagramian, *So Schritten Wir zum Sieg*, pp.267–68

2 Repin, *Bez Prava na Oshibku*, pp.85–86

3 Interview with M. Katayeva, available at iremember.ru/memoirs/snayperi/katae va-bondarenko-mariya-dmitrievna/

4 *Bundesarchiv-Militärarchiv*, Freiburg, *Heeresgruppe Mitte Ia Kriegstagebuch 22/6/44*, RH-19/II

5 Niepold, *Mittlere Ostfront Juni 1944*, p.68

6 I. Chistiakov, *Sluzhim Otchizne* (Voyenizdat, Moscow, 1985), p.203

7 A. Beloborodov, *Vsegda v Boyu* (Ekonomika, Moscow, 1984), p.250

8 Galitsky, *Gody Surovykh Ispytaniy 1941–1944*, pp.473–74

9 Fisitov, *Geroicheskaya Istoria*, Vol. III, p.164

10 Ibid., pp.164–65

11 Niepold, *Mittlere Ostfront Juni 1944*, p.70

12 Glantz and Orenstein, *Belorussia 1944*, p.30

13 Niepold, *Mittlere Ostfront Juni 1944*, p.58

14 Interview with N. Stepanov, available at iremember.ru/memoirs/pulemetchiki/s tepanov-nikolay-kuzmich/

15 Beloborodov, *Vsegda v Boyu*, pp.251–52

16 Niepold, *Mittlere Ostfront Juni 1944*, p.76

17 Interview with A. Gurevich, available at iremember.ru/memoirs/artilleristi/g urevich-arkadiy-grigorevich/

18 Boiko, *S Dumoy o Rodine*, pp.168–69

19 Niepold, *Mittlere Ostfront Juni 1944*, p.81

20 Chistiakov, *Sluzhim Otchizne*, pp.206–07

21 Niepold, *Mittlere Ostfront Juni 1944*, pp.85–86

22 I. Lyudnikov, *Doroga Dlinoyu v Zhizn* (Voyenizdat, Moscow, 1969), pp.115–16

23 Galitsky, *Gody Surovykh Ispytaniy 1941–1944*, pp.497–98

24 Interview with N. Kubrak, available at iremember.ru/memoirs/pekhotintsi/ku brak-nikolay-mikhaylovich/

25 Vasilevsky, *A Lifelong Cause*, p.377

26 Niepold, *Mittlere Ostfront Juni 1944*, p.88

27 Interview with A. Kashpur, available at iremember.ru/memoirs/svyazisti/kash pur-aleksandr-efimovich/

28 P. Batov, *V Pokhodakh I Boyakh* (Voyenizdat, Moscow, 1974), pp.405–06

29 Interview with A. Pankin, available at iremember.ru/memoirs/samkohodchiki/ pankin-aleksandr-fedorovich/

30 Batov, *V Pokhodakh I Boyakh*, p.407

31 Telegin, *Voyny Neschitannye Vorsty*, pp.311–12

CHAPTER 6: THE FLOODGATES OPEN: 25–28 JUNE

1 Bagramian, *So Schritten Wir zum Sieg*, pp.274–75

2 Chistiakov, *Sluzhim Otchizne*, p.209

3 Vinopol interview

4 National Archives and Records Administration, Washington DC, T78 R139 F6068444

5 *Bundesarchiv-Militärarchiv*, Freiburg, *Kriegstagebuch Ia, 3. Panzer-Armee 25/6/44*, RH 213

6 Heidkämper, *Vitebsk*, p.136

7 Niepold, *Mittlere Ostfront Juni 1944*, p.103

8 Pliev, *Pod Gvardeyskim Znamenem Ordzhonikidze*, p.258

9 *Bundesarchiv-Militärarchiv*, Freiburg, *Kriegstagebuch Führungsabteilung AOK-9*, Vol.10, 25/6/44, RH 20-9 59691/1

10 Ibid.

11 Adair, *Hitler's Greatest Defeat*, p.97

12 Heidkämper, *Vitebsk*, p.120

13 H. Heer, *Tote Zonen: Die Deutsche Wehrmacht an der Ostfront* (Hamburger, Hamburg, 1999), p.71

14 R.-D. Müller and H. Volkmann, *Die Wehrmacht: Mythos und Realität* (Oldenbourg, Munich, 2012), p.940

15 R. Hilberg, *Die Vernichtung der Europäischen Juden* (Fischer-Taschenbuch Verlag, Frankfurt am Main, 3 volumes), Vol. II, p.402

16 I. Shamyakin (ed.), *Mogilev: Entsiklopedicheskii Spravochnik* (Belorusskaya Entsiklopediya, Minsk, 1990), p.422

17 Adair, *Hitler's Greatest Defeat*, p.112

18 H. Ehlert and A. Wagner (eds), *Genosse General! Die Militärelite der DDR in Biografischen Skizzen* (Christoph Links, Berlin, 2003), p.38

19 O. Kappelt, *Braunbuch DDR. Nazis in der DDR* (Berlin-Historica, Berlin, 2009), p.260

20 S. Knapp, *Soldat: Reflections of a German Soldier 1936–1949* (Airlife, London, 1992), p.336

21 H. Müller-Enbergs and O. Reimann (eds), *Wer War Wer in der DDR?* (Links, Berlin, 2010, 2 volumes), Vol. I, p.102

22 G. Zhukov, *Vospomimaniya I Razmyshleniya* (Olma, Moscow, 2002, 2 volumes), Vol. II, p.229

23 Lyudnikov, *Doroga Dlinoyu v Zhizn*, pp.118–19

24 Kharin interview

25 Beloborodov, *Vsegda v Boyu*, p.262

26 Bagramian, *So Schritten Wir zum Sieg*, pp.281–82

27 Plato, *Die Geschichte der 5. Panzer-Division 1938 bis 1945*, pp.339–42

28 L. Merker, *Das Buch der 78. Sturmdivision* (Kameradenhilfswerk der 78. Sturmdivision, Tübingen, 1965), p.282

29 Fisitov, *Geroicheskaya Istoria*, p.193

30 *Bundesarchiv-Militärarchiv*, Freiburg, *Kriegstagebuch Führungsabteilung AOK-9*, Vol.10, 28/6/44, RH 20-9 59691/1

31 Niepold, *Von Minsk bis Lyck*, pp.14–15

32 Führer Operational Order No. 8, reproduced in Adair, *Hitler's Greatest Defeat*, pp.182–83

33   G. Ueberschar, *Hitlers Militärische Elite: 68 Lebenslaufe* (Wissenschaftliche
      Buchgesellschaft, Darmstadt, 2011), p.20

34   R. Brett-Smith, *Hitler's Generals* (Osprey, Oxford, 1976), p.197

CHAPTER 7: EXPLOITATION: 29 JUNE–3 JULY

1   Zhukov, *Vospomimaniya I Razmyshleniya*, Vol. II, p.230

2   W. Görlitz, *Strategie der Defensive: Model* (Limes, Wiesbaden, 1982), p.179

3   Vinopol interview

4   Plato, *Die Geschichte der 5. Panzer-Division 1938 bis 1945*, p.342

5   Galitsky, *Gody Surovykh Ispytaniy 1941–1944*, pp.480–81

6   Niepold, *Mittlere Ostfront Juni 1944*, p.149

7   Glantz and Orenstein, *Belorussia 1944*, pp.112–13

8   Niepold, *Mittlere Ostfront Juni 1944*, pp.154–55

9   Beloborodov, *Vsegda v Boyu*, pp.261–62

10   Plato, *Die Geschichte der 5. Panzer-Division 1938 bis 1945*, p.343

11   Niepold, *Mittlere Ostfront Juni 1944*, pp.157–58

12   *Bundesarchiv-Militärarchiv*, Freiburg, *Kriegstagebuch Führungsabteilung AOK-4*
      Vol.10 30/6/44, RH 20-4

13   P. Troyanovsky, *Na Vosmi Frontakh* (Voyenizdat, Moscow, 1982), p.175

14   G. Überschär and R. Blasius, *Der Nationalsozialismus vor Gericht: Die Allierten
      Prozesse gegen Kriegsverbrecher und Soldaten 1943–1952* (Fischer-Taschenbuch-
      Verlag, Frankfurt am Main, 2008), p.257

15   Pliev, *Pod Gvardeyskim Znamenem Ordzhonikidze*, p.264

16   Schäufler, *So Lebten und so Starben Sie*, p.222

17   Bagramian, *So Schritten Wir zum Sieg*, p.286

18   Galitsky, *Gody Surovykh Ispytaniy 1941–1944*, pp.498–99

19   Merker, *Das Buch der 78. Sturmdivision*, p.284

20   Vasilevsky, *A Lifelong Cause*, p.381

21   Niepold, *Von Minsk bis Lyck*, pp.31–32

22   *Tsentral'nyy Arkhiv Ministerstva Oborony*, Moscow, f.254, i.504, No. 9, pp.113–15

23   Niepold, *Mittlere Ostfront Juni 1944*, p.176

24   Plato, *Die Geschichte der 5. Panzer-Division 1938 bis 1945*, p.345

25   A. Burdeiny, *V Boykh Za Osvobozhdenye Velorussii* (Kavaler, Minsk, 2013),
      pp.80–82

26   Merker, *Das Buch der 78. Sturmdivision*, p.285

27   Niepold, *Mittlere Ostfront Juni 1944*, p.180

28   Pliev, *Pod Gvardeyskim Znamenem Ordzhonikidze*, pp.265–66

29   Neumann, *Die 4. Panzer-Division*, Vol. II, p.374

30   Schäufler, *So Lebten und so Starben Sie*, p.224

31   Niepold, *Mittlere Ostfront Juni 1944*, p.186

32   Burdeiny, *V Boykh Za Osvobozhdenye Velorussii*, pp.106–16

33   A. Chirigova, A. Murayova and I. Kurbatova, *Belarus u Vialikai Aichynnai Vaine 1941–1945: Bibliagrafichni Pakazalnik* (Natsianalnaya Bibliyateka Belarusi, Minsk, 1995), pp.360–62

34   Niepold, *Mittlere Ostfront Juni 1944*, p.188

35   Merker, *Das Buch der 78. Sturmdivision*, p.286

36   Niepold, *Von Minsk bis Lyck*, p.49

CHAPTER 8: THE SURGE TO THE FRONTIER: 4–8 JULY

1   Bagramian, *So Schritten Wir zum Sieg*, p.290

2   G. Paul and B. Schwenson (eds), *May '45. Kriegsende in Flensburg* (Gesellschaft für Flensburger Stadtgeschichte eV, Flensburg, 2015), p.22

3   Merker, *Das Buch der 78. Sturmdivision*, pp.286–87

4   Niepold, *Von Minsk bis Lyck*, pp.61–64

5   Pliev, *Pod Gvardeyskim Znamenem Ordzhonikidze*, pp.270–72

6   H. Friessner, *Verratene Schlachten: Die Tragödie der Deutschen Wehrmacht in Rumänien und Ungarn* (Holsten, Hamburg, 1956), p.18

7   Stepanov interview

8   A. Pyltsyn, *Shtrafnoy Udar, ili Kak Ofitserskiy Shtrafbat Doshel do Berlina* (Znayiye, St Petersburg, 2003), pp.262–64

9   Plato, *Die Geschichte der 5. Panzer-Division 1938 bis 1945*, p.348

10   H. von Manteuffel, *Die 7. Panzer-Division im Zweiten Weltkrieg 1939–1945* (Traditionsverband Ehemaliger 7. Panzer-Division-Kameradenhilfe EV, Krefeld, 1965), p.416

11   Niepold, *Mittlere Ostfront Juni 1944*, p.208

12   Ibid., pp.70–71

13   Neumann, *Die 4. Panzer-Division*, Vol. II, pp.381–82

14   Merker, *Das Buch der 78. Sturmdivision*, pp.287–88

15   Hinze, *Bug, Moskwa, Beresina*, p.250

16   A. Sidorenko, *Na Mogilevskom Napravlenii: Nastupelnaya Operatsya 49-y ARmii 2-Go Belorusskogo Fronta v Voine 1944r* (Voyenizdat, Moscow, 1959), p.119

17   P. Lapp, *General bei Hitler und Ulbricht. Vincenz Müller – Eine Deutsche Karriere* (Links Verlag, Berlin, 2003), p.139

18   Ibid., pp.241–43

19   *Bundesarchiv-Militärarchiv*, Freiburg, *Kriegstagebuch Führungsabteilung Panzer-AOK-3 Kriegstagebuch 6/7/44*, RH 21-3

20   Plato, *Die Geschichte der 5. Panzer-Division 1938 bis 1945*, p.348

21   Pliev, *Pod Gvardeyskim Znamenem Ordzhonikidze*, pp.273–74

22   H. Gisevius, *To the Bitter End: An Insider's Account of the Plot to Kill Hitler 1933–1944* (Da Capo, New York, 1998), pp.140–41

23   Gurevich interview

24   Niepold, *Von Minsk bis Lyck*, p.80

25   H. Schäufler, *Der Weg war Weit. Panzer Zwischen Weichsel und Wolga* (Vowinckel, Neckargemünd, 1973), pp.192–93

26   Schäufler, *So Lebten und so Starben Sie*, p.223

27   Batov, *Von der Wolga zur Oder*, pp.311–13

28   *Bundesarchiv-Militärarchiv*, Freiburg, *Kriegstagebuch Führungsabteilung AOK-4 Kriegstagebuch 8/7/44*, RH 20-4

29   Görlitz, *Strategie der Defensive: Model*, p.185

30   Niepold, *Von Minsk bis Lyck*, pp.84–85

31   Niepold, *Von Minsk bis Lyck*, p.85

32   Neumann, *Die 4. Panzer-Division*, Vol. II, p.387

33   Zhukov, *Vospomimaniya I Razmyshleniya*, Vol. II, pp.233–34

CHAPTER 9: VILNIUS: 9–14 JULY

1   P. Buttar, *Centuries Will Not Suffice: A History of the Lithuanian Holocaust* (Amberley Books, Stroud, 2023), p.313

2   J. Oevermann, *Vilnius-Wilno-Vilne-Wilna: Spurensuche 1944* (Createspace, North Charleston SC, 2015), p.108

3   Interview with I. Degen, available at iremember.ru/memoirs/tankisti/degen -ion-lazarevich/

4   Ibid.

5   Ibid.

6   S. Friedländer and M. Pfeiffer, *Das Dritte Reich und die Juden* (Beck, Munich, 2006, 2 volumes), Vol. II, p.869

7   *Bundesarchiv-Militärarchiv*, Freiburg, *Kriegstagebuch Führungsabteilung Panzer-AOK3 Kriegstagebuch 9/7/44*, RH 213

8   E. Hinnen, unpublished memoir

9   Oevermann, *Vilnius-Wilno-Vilne-Wilna*, p.177

10   Niepold, *Mittlere Ostfront Juni 1944*, p.240

11   W. Paul, *Brennpunkte: Die Geschichte der 6. Panzerdivision (1. Leichte) 1937– 1945* (Biblio, Osnabrück, 1993), p.380

12 Hinnen, unpublished memoir

13 *Bundesarchiv-Militärarchiv*, Freiburg, *Kriegstagebuch Führungsabteilung Panzer-AOK-3 Kriegstagebuch 10/7/44*, RH 21-3

14 Hinnen, unpublished memoir

15 J. Richter (ed.), *Die Tagebücher von Joseph Goebbels, Teil II Diktate 1941–1945* (Saur, Munich, 1993–96, 15 volumes), Vol. XIII, p.64

16 Degen interview

17 Hinnen, unpublished memoir

18 Oevermann, *Vilnius-Wilno-Vilne-Wilna*, pp.253–54

19 Hinnen, unpublished memoir

20 L. Kania, *Wilno 1944* (Bellona, Warsaw, 2013), pp.195–96

21 Oevermann, *Vilnius-Wilno-Vilne-Wilna*, p.274

22 Ibid., pp.285–86

23 Ibid., pp.298–99

24 *Bundesarchiv-Militärarchiv*, Freiburg, *Kriegstagebuch der Heeresgruppe Mitte 12/7/44*, RH 19-II/192

25 G. Berger, *Die Beratenden Psychiater des Deutschen Heeres 1939 bis 1945* (Peter Lang, Frankfurt am Main, 1998), p.221

26 Oevermann, *Vilnius-Wilno-Vilne-Wilna*, p.386

27 Ibid., p.331

28 Hinnen, unpublished memoir

29 Oevermann, *Vilnius-Wilno-Vilne-Wilna*, pp.392–93

30 C. Streit, *Keine Kameraden: Die Wehrmacht und die Sowjetischen Kriegsgefangenen* (Dietz, Bonn, 1997), p.128

31 T. Piotrowski, *Poland's Holocaust* (McFarland & Co, Jefferson NC, 1997), p.88

32 Ibid., pp.88–89

33 Report by L. Beria, to Stalin, Molotov, and Antonov, 18 July 1944 available at doomedsoldiers.com/armia-krajova-in-NKVD-NKGB-documents-pt-2.html

34 For a Polish account of Operation *Ostra Brama* and its aftermath, see J. Erdman, *Droga do Ostrej Bramy* (Niezależna Oficyna Wydawnicza, Warsaw, 1990)

35 *Bundesarchiv*, Berlin, DNB Meldung 1/7/44, BArch R-34, 4

36 Bagramian, *So Schritten Wir zum Sieg*, pp.303–05

CHAPTER 10: FIRE BRIGADES: THE PANZER DIVISIONS AND THE RED ARMY, 9–19 JULY

1 Plato, *Die Geschichte der 5. Panzer-Division 1938 bis 1945*, p.349

2 *Bundesarchiv-Militärarchiv*, Freiburg, *Kriegstagebuch der Heeresgruppe Mitte 9/7/44*, RH 19-II/192

3   S. Trew and S. Badsey, *Battle for Caen* (Sutton, Stroud, 2004), pp.47–48

4   For more information on the fighting at Saint-Lô and Caen, see L. Daugherty, *The Battle of the Hedgerows: Bradley's First Army in Normandy June–July 1944* (MBI, St Paul MN, 2001); D. Lodieu, *Mourir pour Saint-Lô: Juillet 1944, La Bataille des Haies* (Histoire & Collections, Paris, 2007)

5   Plato, *Die Geschichte der 5. Panzer-Division 1938 bis 1945*, pp.349–50

6   Niepold, *Von Minsk bis Lyck*, p.100

7   *Bundesarchiv-Militärarchiv*, Freiburg, *Meldung OB H Gr.Nord an der Führer 12/7/44*, RH 19-II

8   Plato, *Die Geschichte der 5. Panzer-Division 1938 bis 1945*, pp.350–52

9   Manteuffel, *Die 7. Panzer-Division im Zweiten Weltkrieg 1939–1945*, p.417

10 Bagramian, *So Schritten Wir zum Sieg*, p.309

11 Vasilevsky, *A Lifelong Cause*, p.388

12 Plato, *Die Geschichte der 5. Panzer-Division 1938 bis 1945*, p.353

13 Manteuffel, *Die 7. Panzer-Division im Zweiten Weltkrieg 1939–1945*, p.418

14 Hossbach Memorandum, available at http://avalon.law.yale.edu/imt/hossbach .asp

15 Niepold, *Von Minsk bis Lyck*, pp.89–90

16 Ibid., pp.92–93

17 Niepold, *Mittlere Ostfront Juni 1944*, p.244

18 Niepold, *Von Minsk bis Lyck*, p.94

19 Batov, *Von der Wolga zur Oder*, p.316

20 Paul, *Brennpunkte*, p.384

21 Gisevius, *To the Bitter End*, pp.496–98

22 Pliev, *Pod Gvardeyskim Znamenem Ordzhonikidze*, p.278

23 P. Polyan, *Zertvy Dvuch Diktatur: Zizn, Trud, Unizenie I Spert Sovetskich Voennoplennych I Ostarbajterov na Cuzbine i na Rodine* (Rosspen, Moscow, 2002), p.737

24 Niepold, *Von Minsk bis Lyck*, pp.104–06

25 *Bundesarchiv-Militärarchiv*, Freiburg, *Kriegstagebuch LV. Armeekorps 12/7/44*, RH 24-55

26 Buttar, *The Reckoning*, pp.389–427

27 Neumann, *Die 4. Panzer-Division*, Vol. II, pp.401–03

28 Niepold, *Von Minsk bis Lyck*, pp.122–23

29 L. Lopukhovskiy, *Prokhorovka Bez Grifa Sekretnosti* (Eksmo, Moscow, 2008), p.208

30 Neumann, *Die 4. Panzer-Division*, Vol. II, p.406

31 Schäufler, *So Lebten und so Starben Sie*, pp.227–29

32   T. Jentz, *Germany's Panther Tank: The Quest for Combat Supremacy* (Schiffer, Atglen PA, 1995), p.16

33   *Bundesarchiv-Militärarchiv*, Freiburg, *Kriegstagebuch der Armeeoberkommando 2 17/7/44*, RH 20-2

CHAPTER 11: INTERLUDE: 'MAKE PEACE, YOU FOOLS! WHAT ELSE CAN YOU DO?'

1   J. Fredrickson, *America's Military Adversaries: From Colonial Times to the Present* (ABC-CLIO, Santa Barbara CA, 2001), p.444; C. Messenger, *The Last Prussian: A Biography of Field Marshal Gerd von Rundstedt* (Pen & Sword, Barnsley, 2011), p.197

2   R. Gersdorff and P. Hausser, *Fighting the Breakout: The German Army in Normandy from 'Cobra' to the Falaise Gap* (Greenhill, London, 2004), p.19

3   S. Rosenman and W. Hassett (eds), *The Public Papers and Addresses of Franklin D. Roosevelt* (Random House, New York, 1938–49, 13 volumes), Vol. XII, p.71

4   R. Moorhouse, *Killing Hitler* (Jonathan Cape, London, 2006), pp.192–93

5   M. Thomsett, *The German Opposition to Hitler: The Resistance, The Underground, and Assassination Plots 1938–1945* (McFarland, Jefferson NC, 1997), p.102

6   Gisevius, *To the Bitter End*, p.496

7   Ibid., p.513

8   H.-A. Jacobsen, *Opposition Gegen Hitler und der Staatsstreich von 20. Juli 1944. Geheime Dokumente aus dem Ehemaligen Reichssicherheitsamt* (Seewald, Stuttgart, 1984, 2 volumes), Vol. I, p.24

9   Gisevius, *To the Bitter End*, pp.546–47

10   J. Fest, *Plotting Hitler's Death: The German Resistance to Hitler 1933–1945* (Weidenfeld & Nicolson, London, 1994), p.302

11   O. Remer, *20. Juli 1944* (Remer-Heipke, Bad Kissingen, 1990), p.12

12   *Deutsches Rundfunkarchiv*, Frankfurt, DRA 2623118

13   M. Hastings, *Overlord: D-Day and the Battle for Normandy* (Michael Joseph, London, 1984), pp.302–03

14   S. Mitcham, *Hitler's Commanders: Officers in the Wehrmacht, the Luftwaffe, the Kriegsmarine, and the Waffen-SS* (Rowman & Littlefield, Lanham MD, 2012), p.31

15   F. von Schlabrendorff, *Offiziere Gegen Hitler* (Europa, Zurich, 1951), p.195

16   P. Caddick-Adams, *Monty and Rommel: Parallel Lives* (Arrow, London, 2012), pp.417–18

17 For a further discussion of Rommel's involvement, see N. Jones, *Countdown to Valkyrie: The July Plot to Assassinate Hitler* (Casemate, Philadelphia, 2008), p.261; Caddick-Adams, *Monty and Rommel*, pp.426–27, 437–41

18 Paul, *Brennpunkte*, p.395

19 W. Wette (ed.), *Unternehmen Barbarossa. Der Deutsche Überfall auf die Sowjetunion 1941* (Schöningh, Paderborn, 1984), p.305

20 S. Helm, *Ravensbrück: Life and Death in Hitler's Concentration Camp for Women* (Anchor, New York, 2016), pp.396–97

21 V. Riedesel, *Geisterkinder. Fünf Geschwister in Himmlers Sippenhaft* (SCM Hänssler, Holzgerlingen, 2017), p.163

22 G. Knopp, *Hitler's Henchmen* (Sutton, Stroud, 2005), p.250

23 R. Lamb, *Churchill as War Leader: Right or Wrong?* (Bloomsbury, London, 1991), p.287

24 P. Davies, *MI6 and the Machinery of Spying* (Frank Cass, London, 2005), pp.13–18

25 *National Archives*, Kew, 'Signs of an Internal Collapse in Germany', CAB 81/120, JIC (44) 12 (0), p.2

26 *National Archives*, Kew, 'German Strategy and Capacity to Resist', CAB 81/124, JIC (44) 302 (0), p.6

27 H. Trevor-Roper, *The Philby Affair: Espionage, Treason, and Secret Services* (W. Kimber & Co, London, 1968), p.78

28 P. Winter, 'British Intelligence and the July Bomb Plot of 1944: A Reappraisal' in *War in History* (Sage, Thousand Oaks CA, 2006), Vol. 13 No. 4, pp.485–86

29 Von Schlabrendorff, *Offiziere Gegen Hitler*, p.98

30 R. Lamb, *Montgomery in Europe, 1943–1945: Success or Failure?* (Buchan & Enright, London, 1987), p.143

31 For a detailed account of the clandestine monitoring of conversations between captured German officers, see H. Fry, *The Walls Have Ears: The Greatest Intelligence Operation of World War II* (Yale University Press, 2020); S. Neitzel (ed.), *Tapping Hitler's Generals: Transcripts of Secret Conversations 1942–1945* (Pen & Sword, Barnsley, 2013)

32 J. Persico, *Piercing the Reich: The Penetration of Nazi Germany by American Secret Agents During World War II* (Barnes & Noble, New York, 2000), p.63

33 P. Knightley, *The Master Spy: The Story of Kim Philby* (Vintage, New York, 1990), p.106

34 For an overview of Kolbe's career and recruitment by Dulles, see G. Bradsher, 'A Time to Act: The Beginning of the Fritz Kolbe Story, 1900–1943' in *Prologue* (US National Archives and Records Administration, 2002), Vol. 34, No. 1, https://www.archives.gov/publications/prologue/2002/spring/fritz-kolbe-1

35 L. Delattre, *Betraying Hitler: The Story of Fritz Kolbe, The Most Important Spy of the Second World War* (Atlantic, London, 2005), pp.24, 298

36 M. Smith, *Bletchley Park: The Codebreakers of Station X* (Shire, Oxford, 2013), p.164

37 *National Archives*, Kew, 'Notes on the Attempted Assassination of Hitler', FO 954/10B

38 For a detailed analysis of the relationship between Roosevelt and Stalin, see S. Butler, *Roosevelt and Stalin: Portrait of a Partnership* (Alfred Knopf, New York, 2015)

39 C. D'Este, *Decision in Normandy* (Penguin, Harmondsworth, 2001), p.399; A. Tedder, *With Prejudice: The War Memoirs of Marshal of the Royal Air Force Lord Tedder* (Cassell, London, 1966), p.565

40 Fest, *Plotting Hitler's Death*, p.228; P. Padfield, *Himmler: Reichsführer-SS* (Cassell, London, 2001), pp.419–24

CHAPTER 12: HIGH TIDE FOR THE RED ARMY

1 Chistiakov, *Sluzhim Otchizne*, pp.213–214

2 Bagramian, *So Schritten Wir zum Sieg*, p.314

3 Beloborodov, *Vsegda v Boyu*, pp.263–64

4 Plato, *Die Geschichte der 5. Panzer-Division 1938 bis 1945*, p.353

5 Niepold, *Von Minsk bis Lyck*, pp.133–34

6 Batov, *Von der Wolga zur Oder*, p.317

7 Pankin interview

8 Niepold, *Von Minsk bis Lyck*, p.139

9 See for example E. Klapdor, *Viking Panzers: The German 5th SS Tank Regiment in the East in World War II* (Stackpole, Mechanicsburg PA, 2011), pp.299–305

10 C. Grzelak, H. Staczyk and S. Zwoliski, *Armia Berlinga I Ymierskiego: Wojsko Polski na Froncie Wschodnim 1943–1945* (Wydawn, Warsaw, 2009), pp.155–56

11 D. Nash, *From the Realm of the Dying Sun* (Casemate, Philadelphia PA, 2019, 3 volumes) Vol. I, p.70

12 Niepold, *Von Minsk bis Lyck*, pp.151–52

13 T. Kranz, *Ewidencja Zgonów I Śmiertelność Więźniów KL Lublin* (Zeszyty Majdanka, Lublin, 2005), pp.7–53

14 Interview with G. Kornev, available at iremember.ru/memoirs/samokhodchiki/kornev-grigoriy-sergeevich/

15 Interview with P. Pudov, available at iremember.ru/memoirs/samokhodchiki/pudov-petr-dmitrievich/

16 Batov, *Von der Wolga zur Oder*, pp.322–23

17   Interview with V. Slovanov, available at iremember.ru/memoirs/kavaleristi/sl avnov-valentin-nikolaevich/

18   Niepold, *Von Minsk bis Lyck*, pp.154–55

19   Görlitz, *Strategie der Defensive: Model*, p.203

20   Ibid., p.157

21   Browning, *Ordinary Men*, pp.11–15

22   K. Tofahrn, *Das Dritte Reich und der Holocaust* (Internationaler Verlag der Wissenschaften, Frankfurt am Main, 2008), p.268

23   Chistiakov, *Sluzhim Otchizne*, pp.216–17

24   Interview with N. Teplotanskikh, available at iremember.ru/memoirs/tankisti/ teplotanskikh-nikolay-petrovich/

25   Paul, *Brennpunkte*, pp.403–04

26   Shtemenko, *The Soviet General Staff At War*, p.505

27   Plato, *Die Geschichte der 5. Panzer-Division 1938 bis 1945*, p.354

28   Paul, *Brennpunkte*, p.407

29   Neumann, *Die 4. Panzer-Division*, Vol. II, pp.436–37

30   Pliev, *Pod Gvardeyskim Znamenem Ordzhonikidze*, pp.283–84

31   C. McNab, *The SS 1923–1945: The Essential Facts and Figures for Himmler's Stormtroopers* (Amber, London, 2009), p.137

CHAPTER 13: PRAGA AND WARSAW

1   R. Höss and J. Amann, *The Commandant* (Duckworth, London, 2011), p.266

2   C. McNab, *Hitler's Elite: The SS 1939–45* (Osprey, Oxford, 2013), p.170

3   Nash, *From the Realm of the Dying Sun*, p.115

4   P. Oosterling, H. Fischer and R. Erlings, *SS-Standartenführer Johannes Mühlenkamp und seine Männer* (De Krijger, Erpe, 2005, 2 volumes), Vol. II, p.339

5   Nash, *From the Realm of the Dying Sun*, pp.118–19

6   N. Rich, *Hitler's War Aims* (Andre Deutsch, London, 1974, 2 volumes), Vol. II, p.96

7   *Ośrodek KARTA*, Warsaw, *Tagebuch Heinrich Stechbarth 30/7/44*

8   N. Davies, *Rising 44: The Battle for Warsaw* (Macmillan, London, 2003), p.68

9   W. Bartoszewski, *Dni Walczącej Stolicy: Kronika Powstania Warszawskiego* (Świat Książgi, Warsaw, 2014), pp.11–12

10   Ibid., pp.13–14

11   A. Borowiec, *Warsaw Boy: A Memoir of a Wartime Childhood* (Penguin, Harmondsworth, 2014), p.204

12 Davies, *Rising 44*, p.245

13 A. Richie, *Warsaw 1944: Hitler, Himmler, and the Warsaw Uprising* (Farrar, Strauss & Giroux, New York, 2013), p.242

14 Schäufler, *So Lebten und so Starben Sie*, pp.229–30

15 Ibid., p.230

16 *Bundesarchiv-Militärarchiv*, Freiburg, *Kriegstagebuch Ia, Armeeoberkommando 2, 2/8/44*, RH 20-2

17 Davies, *Rising 44*, pp.274–75; A. Przygónski, *Stalin I Powstanie Warszawskie* (Wydawn Grażnya, Warsaw, 1994), p.101

18 Neumann, *Die 4. Panzer-Division*, Vol. II, p.442

19 I. Nebolsin (trans. S. Britton), *Stalin's Favorite: The Combat History of the 2nd Guards Tank Army From Kursk to Berlin* (Helion, Warwick, 2022, 2 volumes), Vol. II, p.99

20 P. Buttar, *Between Giants: The Battle for the Baltics in World War II* (Osprey, Oxford, 2013), pp.211–50

21 Davies, *Rising 44*, p.279

22 N. Orpen, *Airlift to Warsaw: The Rising of 1944* (University of Oklahoma Press, Norman OK, 1984), p.192

23 *Ośrodek KARTA*, Warsaw, *Dokumenty Brytyjskiej Misji Wojskowej w ZSRR Sierpień – Październik 1944*, M/II/18

24 W. Borodziej, *The Warsaw Uprising of 1944* (University of Wisconsin Press, Madison WS, 2006), p.120

25 A. Michta, *Red Eagle: The Army in Polish Politics, 1944–1988* (Hoover Press, Stanford CA, 1990), p.33

26 Davies, *Rising 44*, pp.409–11

27 K. Wituska, and I. Tomaszewski, *Inside a Gestapo Prison: The Letters of Krystyna Wituska 1942–1944* (Wayne State University Press, Detroit MI, 2006), p.22

CHAPTER 14: THE THIRD REICH ON THE BRINK

1 Niepold, *Von Minsk bis Lyck*, p.197

2 S. Zaloga, *Bagration 1944: The destruction of Army Group Centre* (Osprey, Oxford, 1996), p.71; D. Glantz and J. House, *When Titans Clashed: How the Red Army Stopped Hitler* (University of Kansas Press, Lawrence KS, 1995), p.176

3 M. Tamelander and N. Zetterling, *Avgörandets Ögonblick: Invasionen i Normandie* (Norstedts, Stockholm, 2003), p.341; D. Giangreco, K. Moore and N. Polmar, *Eyewitness D-Day: Firsthand Accounts from the Landing at Normandy to the Liberation of Paris* (Barnes & Noble, New York, 2004), p.252

4   Glantz and House, *When Titans Clashed*, p.298
5   H. von Moltke, *Militärische Werke* (Mittler, Berlin, 1890, 3 volumes), Vol. 2, p.291
6   Glantz and Orenstein, *Belorussia 1944*, p.193
7   A. Harriman and E. Abel, *Special Envoy to Churchill and Stalin 1941–1946* (Hutchinson, London, 1976), pp.314–39
8   Rokossovsky, *A Soldier's Duty*, pp.255–56

BIBLIOGRAPHY

Archiwum Akt Nowich, Warsaw
Bundesarchiv, Berlin
Bundesarchiv-Militärarchiv, Freiburg
Deutsches Rundfunkarchiv, Frankfurt
Nacionalnye Archiv Respubliki Belarus, Minsk
National Archives, Kew
Ośrodek KARTA, Warsaw
Tsentral'nyy Arkhiv Ministerstva Oborony, Moscow

Yad Vashem Archive, Jerusalem

American Historical Review (University of Chicago Press)
Europe-Asia Studies (University of Glasgow)
Prologue (US National Archives and Records Administration)
Sovetskaya Rossiya (Moscow)
Studia Podladskie (Białystok University)
Voyenno-Istoricheskii Zhurnal (Ministerstva Oborony SSSR)
War in History (Sage, Thousand Oaks CA)

http://avalon.law.yale.edu/imt/hossbach.asp
www.jewishvirtuallibrary.org

Adair, P., *Hitler's Greatest Defeat: The Collapse of Army Group Centre, June 1944* (Cassell, London, 1994)
Adamovich, A., *V Partisanach* (TD Algorithm, Moscow, 2018)
Arad, Y., *Oni Srazhalis za Rodinu: Evrei Sovetskogo Soyuza v elikoi Otechestvennoi Voine* (Mosty Kultury, Moscow, 2011)
Bagramian, I., *So Schritten Wir zum Sieg* (Militärverlag der Deutschen Demokratischen Republik, Berlin, 1984)
Barbier, M., *D-Day Deception: Operation Fortitude and the Normandy Invasion* (Greenwood, Westport CT, 2007)

Bartoszewski, W., *Dni Walczącej Stolicy: Kronika Powstania Warszawskiego* (Świat Ksiażgi, Warsaw, 2014)

Batov, P., *Von der Wolga zur Oder* (Deutscher Militärverlag, Berlin, 1965)

Batov, P., *V Pokhodakh I Boyakh* (Voyenizdat, Moscow, 1974)

Beer, I., *Adolf Hitler: A Biography* (Vij, New Delhi, 2016)

Beevor, A., *D-Day: The Battle for Normandy* (Viking, London, 2009)

Beloborodov, A., *Vsegda v Boyu* (Ekonomika, Moscow, 1984)

Belov, P., *Za Nami Moskva* (Voyenizdat, Moscow, 1963)

Bennett, G., *Cowan's War* (Collins, London, 1964)

Berger, G., *Die Beratenden Psychiater des Deutschen Heeres 1939 bis 1945* (Peter Lang, Frankfurt am Main, 1998)

Bialer, S., *Stalin and his Generals* (Westview, Boulder CO, 1984)

Bich, M. and Pashkou, H. (eds), *Encyklapiedyja Historyi Bielarusi* (Belaruska Entsyklapedyi Petrusi Brouki, Minsk, 1993–2003, 7 volumes)

Boiko, V., *S Dumoy o Rodine* (Voyenizdat, Moscow, 1982)

Borodziej, W., *The Warsaw Uprising of 1944* (University of Wisconsin Press, Madison WS, 2006)

Borowiec, A., *Warsaw Boy: A Memoir of a Wartime Childhood* (Penguin, Harmondsworth, 2014)

Brackman, R., *The Secret File of Joseph Stalin: A Hidden Life* (Routledge, Milton, 2001)

Brett-Smith, R., *Hitler's Generals* (Osprey, Oxford, 1976)

Browning, C., *Ordinary Men: Reserve Police Battalion 101 and the Final Solution in Poland* (Harper Collins, London, 2017)

Burdeiny, A., *V Boykh Za Osvobozhdenye Velorussii* (Kavaler, Minsk, 2013)

Butlar, E. von (ed.), *Mirovaya Voina: Sbornik Statei* (Izdatelstvo Inostrannoy Literatury, Moscow, 1957)

Butler, S., *Roosevelt and Stalin: Portrait of a Partnership* (Alfred Knopf, New York, 2015)

Buttar, P., *Between Giants: The Battle for the Baltics in World War II* (Osprey, Oxford, 2013)

Buttar, P., *Russia's Last Gasp: The Eastern Front 1916–17* (Osprey, Oxford 2016)

Buttar, P., *On A Knife's Edge: The Ukraine, November 1942–March 1943* (Osprey, Oxford, 2018)

Buttar, P., *The Reckoning: The Defeat of Army Group South, 1944* (Osprey, Oxford, 2020)

Buttar, P., *Meat Grinder: The Battles for the Rzhev Salient, 1942–43* (Osprey, Oxford, 2022)

Buttar, P., *Centuries Will Not Suffice: A History of the Lithuanian Holocaust* (Amberley Books, Stroud, 2023)

Caddick-Adams, P., *Monty and Rommel: Parallel Lives* (Arrow, London, 2012)

Carruthers, B., *Hitler's Wartime Orders: The Complete Führer Directives 1939–1945* (Pen & Sword, Barnsley, 2018)

Chiari, B. (ed.), *Die Polnische Heimatarmee: Geschichte und Mythos der Armia Krajowa seit dem Zweiten Weltkrieg* (de Gruyter, Munich, 2003)

Chirigova, A., Murayova, A. and Kurbatova, I., *Belarus u Vialikai Aichynnai Vaine 1941–1945: Bibliagrafichni Pakazalnik* (Natsianalnaya Bibliyateka Belarusi, Minsk, 1995)

Chistiakov, I., *Sluzhim Otchizne* (Voyenizdat, Moscow, 1985)

Cüppers, M., *Wegbereiter der Schoah. Die Waffen-SS, der Kommandostab Reichsführer-SS und die Judenvernichtung 1939–1945* (Wissentschaftliche Buchgesellschaft, Darmstadt, 2005)

Daugherty, L., *The Battle of the Hedgerows: Bradley's First Army in Normandy June–July 1944* (MBI, St Paul MN, 2001)

Davies, N., *Rising 44: The Battle for Warsaw* (Macmillan, London, 2003)

Davies, P., *MI6 and the Machinery of Spying* (Frank Cass, London, 2005)

Delattre, L., *Betraying Hitler: The Story of Fritz Kolbe, The Most Important Spy of the Second World War* (Atlantic, London, 2005)

D'Este, C., *Decision in Normandy* (Penguin, Harmondsworth, 2001)

Dugan, J. and Stewart, C., *Ploesti: The Great Ground-Air Battle of 1 August 1943* (Brassey's, London, 2002)

Edmonds, R., *The Big Three: Churchill, Roosevelt and Stalin in Peace and War* (Hamish Hamilton, London, 1992)

Ehlert, H. and Wagner, A. (eds), *Genosse General! Die Militärelite der DDR in Biografischen Skizzen* (Christoph Links, Berlin, 2003)

Erdman, J., *Droga do Ostrej Bramy* (Niezależna Oficyna Wydawnicza, Warsaw, 1990)

Erickson, J., *The Road to Berlin* (Yale University Press, New Haven CT, 1999)

Fest, J., *Plotting Hitler's Death: The German Resistance to Hitler 1933–1945* (Weidenfeld & Nicolson, London, 1994)

Fisitov, A., *Geroicheskaya Istoria: 70 Strelkovoi Verkhneorovskoi Ordena Suvorova II Stepenyi Divizii (Vtorogo Formyrovnaya)* (Nauka, Moscow, 2013, 4 volumes)

Fredrickson, J., *America's Military Adversaries: From Colonial Times to the Present* (ABC-CLIO, Santa Barbara CA, 2001)

Friedländer, S. and Pfeiffer, M., *Das Dritte Reich und die Juden* (Beck, Munich, 2006, 2 volumes)

Frieser, K.-H., Schmider, K., Schönherr, K., Schreiber, G., Ungváry, K. and Wegner, B., *Das Deutsche Reich und der Zweite Weltkrieg* (Deutsche Verlags-Anstalt, Munich, 1990–2017, 13 volumes)

Friessner, H., *Verratene Schlachten: Die Tragödie der Deutschen Wehrmacht in Rumänien und Ungarn* (Holsten, Hamburg, 1956)

Fry, H., *The Walls Have Ears: The Greatest Intelligence Operation of World War II* (Yale University Press, 2020)

Gackenholz, H., *Der Zusammenbruch der Heeresgruppe Mitte* (Bernard & Graefe, Frankfurt am Main, 1960)

Galitsky, K., *Gody Surovykh Ispytaniy 1941–1944* (Nauka, Moscow, 1973)

Gersdorff, R. and Hausser, P., *Fighting the Breakout: The German Army in Normandy from 'Cobra' to the Falaise Gap* (Greenhill, London, 2004)

Giangreco, D., Moore, K. and Polmar, N., *Eyewitness D-Day: Firsthand Accounts from the Landing at Normandy to the Liberation of Paris* (Barnes & Noble, New York, 2004)

Gilbert, M., *The Road to Victory: Winston S. Churchill, 1941–1945* (Heinemann, London, 1986)

Gilbert, M., *The Holocaust: A History of the Jews of Europe During the Second World War* (Holt, New York, 1987)

Gisevius, H., *To the Bitter End: An Insider's Account of the Plot to Kill Hitler 1933–1944* (Da Capo, New York, 1998)

Glantz, D. and House, J., *When Titans Clashed: How the Red Army Stopped Hitler* (University of Kansas Press, Lawrence KS, 1995)

Glantz, D. and Orenstein, H. (eds and trans), *Belorussia 1944: The Soviet General Staff Study* (Frank Cass, London, 2001)

Görlitz, W., *Strategie der Defensive: Model* (Limes, Wiesbaden, 1982)

Great Soviet Encyclopedia (MacMillan, New York, 1980, 30 volumes)

Grzelak, C., Staczyk, H. and Zwoliski, S., *Armia Berlinga I Ymierskiego: Wojsko Polski na Froncie Wschodnim 1943–1945* (Wydawn, Warsaw, 2009)

Harriman, A. and Abel, E., *Special Envoy to Churchill and Stalin 1941–1946* (Hutchinson, London, 1976)

Hastings, M., *Overlord: D-Day and the Battle for Normandy* (Michael Joseph, London, 1984)

Haugen, B., *Joseph Stalin: Dictator of the Soviet Union* (Compass Point, Minneapolis MN, 2006)

Havas, L., *Hitler's Plot to Kill The Big Three* (Bantam, London, 1977)

Heer, H., *Tote Zonen: Die Deutsche Wehrmacht an der Ostfront* (Hamburger, Hamburg, 1999)

Heidkämper, O., *Vitebsk: The Fight and Destruction of the Third Panzer Army* (Casemate, Oxford, 2017)

Helm, S., *Ravensbrück: Life and Death in Hitler's Concentration Camp for Women* (Anchor, New York, 2016)

Hesketh, R., *Fortitude: The D-Day Deception Campaign* (Overlook, New York, 2000)

Hilberg, R., *Die Vernichtung der Europäischen Juden* (Fischer-Taschenbuch Verlag, Frankfurt am Main, 2021–23, 3 volumes)

Hinze, R., *Bug, Moskwa, Beresina. Der Weg Eines Bespannten Artillerie-Regiments im 2. Weltkrieg bis zum Zusammenbruch der Heeresgruppe Mitte* (self-published, 1978)

Höhne, H. and Zolling, H., *The General Was a Spy: The Truth About General Gehlen and his Spy Ring* (Coward, McCann & Geoghegan, New York, 1972)

Höss, R. and Amann, J., *The Commandant* (Duckworth, London, 2011)

Howell, E., *The Soviet Partisan Movement 1941–1944* (Department of the Army, Washington DC, 1956)

International Military Tribunal, *Nazi Conspiracy and Aggression* (United States Government Printing Office, Washington DC, 1946, 11 volumes)

Isaev, A., *Operatsiya 'Bagration': Stalinskii Blitskrig v Belorussii* (Eksmo, Moscow, 2014)

Jacobsen, H.-A., *Opposition Gegen Hitler und der Staatsstreich von 20. Juli 1944. Geheime Dokumente aus dem Ehemaligen Reichssicherheitsamt* (Seewald, Stuttgart, 1984, 2 volumes)

Jentz, T., *Germany's Panther Tank: The Quest for Combat Supremacy* (Schiffer, Atglen PA, 1995)

Jones, N., *Countdown to Valkyrie: The July Plot to Assassinate Hitler* (Casemate, Philadelphia, 2008)

Kania, L., *Wilno 1944* (Bellona, Warsaw, 2013)

Kappelt, O., *Braunbuch DDR. Nazis in der DDR* (Berlin-Historica, Berlin, 2009)

Klapdor, E., *Viking Panzers: The German 5th SS Tank Regiment in the East in World War II* (Stackpole, Mechanicsburg PA, 2011)

Knapp, S., *Soldat: Reflections of a German Soldier 1936–1949* (Airlife, London, 1992)

Knightley, P., *The Master Spy: The Story of Kim Philby* (Vintage, New York, 1990)

Knopp, G., *Hitler's Henchmen* (Sutton, Stroud, 2005)

Kovalchuk, V. (ed.), *V Tylu Vraga Borba Partizan I Podpolshchivkov na Okkupirovannoy Territorii Oblasti* (Lenizdat, Leningrad, 1979)

Kranz, T., *Ewidencja Zgonów I Śmiertelność Więźniów KL Lublin* (Zeszyty Majdanka, Lublin, 2005)

Krivosheyev, G., *Soviet Casualties and Combat Losses in the Twentieth Century* (Greenhill, London, 1997)

Kudriashov, S. (ed.), *Partizanskoe Dvizhenie v gody Velikoi Otechestvennoi Voiny* (Izdatelstvo Istoricheskaia Literatura, Moscow, 2015)

Kvachkov, V., *Spetsnaz Rossii* (Russkaya Panorama, Moscow, 2007)

Lamb, R., *Montgomery in Europe, 1943–1945: Success or Failure?* (Buchan & Enright, London, 1987)

Lamb, R., *Churchill as War Leader: Right or Wrong?* (Bloomsbury, London, 1991)

Lapp, P., *General bei Hitler und Ulbricht. Vincenz Müller – Eine Deutsche Karriere* (Links Verlag, Berlin, 2003)

Lodieu, D., *Mourir pour Saint-Lô: Juillet 1944, La Bataille des Haies* (Histoire & Collections, Paris, 2007)

Łojek, B., *Muzeum Katyńskie w Warszawie* (Polska Fundacja Katyńska, Warsaw, 2001)

Longerich, P., *Heinrich Himmler: A Life* (Oxford University Press, Oxford, 2011)

Lopukhovskiy, L., *Prokhorovka Bez Grifa Sekretnosti* (Eksmo, Moscow, 2008)

Lyudnikov, I., *Doroga Dlinoyu v Zhizn* (Voyenizdat, Moscow, 1969)

Malanin, K. (ed.), *Polki Idut na Zapad: Vospominanii Ocherki Ob Osvobozhdenii Belorussyii ot Fashistskich Okkupantor* (Voyenizdat, Moscow, 1964)

Mallmann, K.-M. and Paul, G. (eds), *Karrieren der Gewalt. Nationalsozialistische Täterbiographien* (Wissenschaftliche Buchgesellschaft, Darmstadt, 2004)

Manteuffel, H. von, *Die 7. Panzer-Division im Zweiten Weltkrieg 1939–1945* (Traditionsverband Ehemaliger 7. Panzer-Division-Kameradenhilfe EV, Krefeld, 1965)

McNab, C., *The SS 1923–1945: The Essential Facts and Figures for Himmler's Stormtroopers* (Amber, London, 2009)

McNab, C., *Hitler's Elite: The SS 1939–45* (Osprey, Oxford, 2013)

Merker, L., *Das Buch der 78. Sturmdivision* (Kameradenhilfswerk der 78. Sturmdivision, Tübingen, 1965)

Messenger, C., *The Last Prussian: A Biography of Field Marshal Gerd von Rundstedt* (Pen & Sword, Barnsley, 2011)

Michta, A., *Red Eagle: The Army in Polish Politics, 1944–1988* (Hoover Press, Stanford CA, 1990)

Mitcham, S., *Hitler's Commanders: Officers in the Wehrmacht, the Luftwaffe, the Kriegsmarine, and the Waffen-SS* (Rowman & Littlefield, Lanham MD, 2012)

Moltke, H. von, *Militärische Werke* (Mittler, Berlin, 1890, 3 volumes)

Moorhouse, R., *Killing Hitler* (Jonathan Cape, London, 2006)

Müller, R.-D. and Volkmann, H., *Die Wehrmacht: Mythos und Realität* (Oldenbourg, Munich, 2012)

Müller-Enbergs, H. and Reimann, O. (eds), *Wer War Wer in der DDR?* (Links, Berlin, 2010, 2 volumes)

Musiał, B., *Sowjetische Partisanen in Weissrussland: Innenansichten aus dem Gebiet Baranoviči 1941–1944: Eine Dokumentation* (Oldenbourg, Munich, 2013)

Nash, D., *From the Realm of the Dying Sun* (Casemate, Philadelphia PA, 2019, 3 volumes)

Nebolsin, I. (trans. Britton, S.), *Stalin's Favorite: The Combat History of the 2nd Guards Tank Army From Kursk to Berlin* (Helion, Warwick, 2022, 2 volumes)

Neitzel, S. (ed.), *Tapping Hitler's Generals: Transcripts of Secret Conversations 1942–1945* (Pen & Sword, Barnsley, 2013)

Neumann, J., *Die 4. Panzer-Division. Bericht und Betrachtung* (self-published, 1989, 2 volumes)

Niepold, G., *Von Minsk bis Lyck: Die 12. Panzerdivision in den Rückzugsgefechten im Sommer 1944* (self-published, 1979)

Niepold, G., *Mittlere Ostfront Juni 1944* (Mittler & Sohn, Herford, 1985)

Oevermann, J., *Vilnius-Wilno-Vilne-Wilna: Spurensuche 1944* (Createspace, North Charleston SC, 2015)

Oosterling, P., Fischer, H. and Erlings, R., *SS-Standartenführer Johannes Mühlenkamp und seine Männer* (De Krijger, Erpe, 2005, 2 volumes)

Orpen, N., *Airlift to Warsaw: The Rising of 1944* (University of Oklahoma Press, Norman OK, 1984)

Otechestvennoiy Voiny 1941–1945 (Izdat Atlantida-XXI vek, Moscow, 2001)

Overy, R., *Russia's War* (Penguin, Harmondsworth, 2010)

Padfield, P., *Himmler: Reichsführer-SS* (Cassell, London, 2001)

Parfenov, D., *Rise and Fall of Belarusian National Identity* (MA Thesis, Dublin University, 2005, available at https://prfnv.keybase.pub/MA-Thesis-Rise-Fall-of -Belarusian-National-Identity-by-Denis-Parfenov.pdf

Paul, G. and Schwenson, B. (eds), *May '45. Kriegsende in Flensburg* (Gesellschaft für Flensburger Stadtgeschichte eV, Flensburg, 2015)

Paul, W., *Brennpunkte: Die Geschichte der 6. Panzerdivision (1. Leichte) 1937–1945* (Biblio, Osnabrück, 1993)

Persico, J., *Piercing the Reich: The Penetration of Nazi Germany by American Secret Agents During World War II* (Barnes & Noble, New York, 2000)

Piotrowski, T., *Poland's Holocaust* (McFarland & Co, Jefferson NC, 1997)

Plato, A.D. von, *Die Geschichte der 5. Panzer-Division 1938 bis 1945* (Walhalla und Praetoria Verlag, Regensburg, 1978)

Platonov, S. (ed.), *Operatsii Sovetskikh Vooruzhennykh sil v Velikoi Otechestvennoi Voine 1941–1945* (Voyenizdat, Moscow, 1959, 4 volumes)

Pliev, I., *Pod Gvardeyskim Znamenem Ordzhonikidze* (IR, Ordzhonikidze, 1976)

Polyan, P., *Zertvy Dvuch Diktatur: Zizn, Trud, Unizenie I Spert Sovetskich Voennoplennych I Ostarbajterov na Cuzbine i na Rodine* (Rosspen, Moscow, 2002)

Popov, A., *NKVD I Partizanskoye Dvizheniye* (Olma, Moscow, 2003)

Price, A., *The Last Year of the Luftwaffe* (Pen & Sword, Barnsley, 2015)

Przygónski, A., *Stalin I Powstanie Warszawskie* (Wydawn Grażnya, Warsaw, 1994)

Remer, O., *20. Juli 1944* (Remer-Heipke, Bad Kissingen, 1990)

Repin, V., *Bez Prava na Oshibku* (Voyenizdat, Moscow, 1978)

Reynolds, D., *In Command of History: Churchill Fighting and Writing the Second World War* (Penguin, Harmondsworth, 2005)

Rich, N., *Hitler's War Aims* (Andre Deutsch, London, 1974, 2 volumes)

Richie, A., *Warsaw 1944: Hitler, Himmler, and the Warsaw Uprising* (Farrar, Strauss & Giroux, New York, 2013)

Richter, J. (ed.), *Die Tagebücher von Joseph Goebbels, Teil II Diktate 1941–1945* (Saur, Munich, 1993–96, 15 volumes)

Riedesel, V., *Geisterkinder. Fünf Geschwister in Himmlers Sippenhaft* (SCM Hänssler, Holzgerlingen, 2017)

Rokossovsky, K., *A Soldier's Duty* (Spantech & Lancer, Godstone, 1992)

Roosevelt, E., *As He Saw It* (Duell, Sloan and Pearce, New York, 1946)

Rosenman, S. and Hassett, W. (eds), *The Public Papers and Addresses of Franklin D. Roosevelt* (Random House, New York, 1938–49, 13 volumes)

Sakaida, H., *Heroines of the Soviet Union 1941–1945* (Bloomsbury, London, 2012)

Schäufler, H., *Der Weg war Weit. Panzer Zwischen Weichsel und Wolga* (Vowinckel, Neckargemünd, 1973)

Schäufler, H., *So Lebten und so Starben Sie: Das Buch vom Panzerregiment-35* (Kameradscaft ehemaliger Panzer-Regiment 35 e.V, Bamberg, 1983)

Sebag Montefiore, S., *Stalin: The Court of the Red Tsar* (Weidenfeld & Nicholson, London, 2003)

Schlabrendorff, F. von, *Offiziere Gegen Hitler* (Europa, Zurich, 1951)

Shamyakin, I. (ed.), *Mogilev: Entsiklopedicheskii Spravochnik* (Belorusskaya Entsiklopediya, Minsk, 1990)

Shtemenko, S., *The Soviet General Staff At War 1941–1945* (Progress, Moscow, 1970)

Shumilin, B. (ed.), *Istoriya Partizanskogo Dvizeniya Rossiyskoy Federatsii v Gody Velikoy Otechestvennoiy Voiny 1941–1945* (Izdat Atlantida-XXI vek, Moscow, 2001)

Sidorenko, A., *Na Mogilevskom Napravlenii: Nastupelnaya Operatsya 49-y ARmii 2-Go Belorusskogo Fronta v Voine 1944r* (Voyenizdat, Moscow, 1959)

Smith, M., *Bletchley Park: The Codebreakers of Station X* (Shire, Oxford, 2013)

Solyankin, A., Pavlov, M. and Zheltov, I., *Otechestvennyye Bronirovannyye Mashini XX Vek* (Eksprint, Moscow, 2005, 4 volumes)

Speer, A., *Inside the Third Reich* (Weidenfeld & Nicholson, London, 1995)

Stahel, D., *Retreat from Moscow: A New History of Germany's Winter Campaign, 1941–1942* (Picador, New York, 2019)

Streit, C., *Keine Kameraden: Die Wehrmacht und die Sowjetischen Kriegsgefangenen* (Dietz, Bonn, 1997)

Tamelander, M. and Zetterling, N., *Avgörandets Ögonblick: Invasionen i Normandie* (Norstedts, Stockholm, 2003)

Tedder, A., *With Prejudice: The War Memoirs of Marshal of the Royal Air Force Lord Tedder* (Cassell, London, 1966)

Telegin, K., *Voyny Neschitannye Vorsty* (Voyenizdat, Moscow, 1988)

Thöle, H., *Befehl des Gewissens: Charkow Winter 1943* (Munin, Osnabück, 1976)

Thomsett, M., *The German Opposition to Hitler: The Resistance, The Underground, and Assassination Plots 1938–1945* (McFarland, Jefferson NC, 1997)

Tofahrn, K., *Das Dritte Reich und der Holocaust* (Internationaler Verlag der Wissenschaften, Frankfurt am Main, 2008)

Trevor-Roper, H., *The Philby Affair: Espionage, Treason, and Secret Services* (W. Kimber & Co, London, 1968)

Trew, S. and Badsey, S., *Battle for Caen* (Sutton, Stroud, 2004)

Troyanovsky, P., *Na Vosmi Frontakh* (Voyenizdat, Moscow, 1982)

Turonek, J., *Vaclau Ivanouski I Adrazenne Belarusi* (Medisont, Minsk, 2006)

Überschär, G. and Blasius, R., *Der Nationalsozialismus vor Gericht: Die Alliierten Prozesse gegen Kriegsverbrecher und Soldaten 1943–1952* (Fischer-Taschenbuch-Verlag, Frankfurt am Main, 2008)

Ueberschar, G., *Hitlers Militärische Elite: 68 Lebenslaufe* (Wissenschaftliche Buchgesellschaft, Darmstadt, 2011)

Vasilevsky, A., *A Lifelong Cause* (Progress, Moscow, 1973)

Weeks, A., *Russia's Life Saver: Lend-Lease Aid to the USSR in World War II* (Lexington, Plymouth, 2010)

Wette, W. (ed.), *Unternehmen Barbarossa. Der Deutsche Überfall auf die Sowjetunion 1941* (Schöningh, Paderborn, 1984)

Wituska, K. and Tomaszewski, I., *Inside a Gestapo Prison: The Letters of Krystyna Wituska 1942–1944* (Wayne State University Press, Detroit MI, 2006)

Zaloga, S., *Bagration 1944: The destruction of Army Group Centre* (Osprey, Oxford, 1996)

Zaloga, S. and Ness, J., *Red Army Handbook* (Sutton, Stroud, 1998)

Zhukov, G., *Vospomimaniya I Razmyshleniya* (Olma, Moscow, 2002, 2 volumes)

Ziemke, E., *Stalingrad to Berlin: The German Defeat in the East* (Dorset, New York, 1986)

INDEX

References to maps are in **bold**.